"Composed in the style of the great medieval *catenae*, this new anthology of patristic commentary on Holy Scripture, conveniently arranged by chapter and verse, will be a valuable resource for prayer, study and proclamation. By calling attention to the rich Christian heritage preceding the separations between East and West and between Protestant and Catholic, this series will perform a major service to the cause of ecumenism."

AVERY CARDINAL DULLES, S.J.
Laurence J. McGinley Professor of Religion and Society
Fordham University

"The initial cry of the Reformation was *ad fontes*—back to the sources! The Ancient Christian Commentary on Scripture is a marvelous tool for the recovery of biblical wisdom in today's church. Not just another scholarly project, the ACCS is a major resource for the renewal of preaching, theology and Christian devotion."

TIMOTHY GEORGE
Dean, Beeson Divinity School, Samford University

"Modern church members often do not realize that they are participants in the vast company of the communion of saints that reaches far back into the past and that will continue into the future, until the kingdom comes. This Commentary should help them begin to see themselves as participants in that redeemed community."

ELIZABETH ACHTEMEIER
Union Professor Emerita of Bible and Homiletics
Union Theological Seminary in Virginia

"Contemporary pastors do not stand alone. We are not the first generation of preachers to wrestle with the challenges of communicating the gospel. The Ancient Christian Commentary on Scripture puts us in conversation with our colleagues from the past, that great cloud of witnesses who preceded us in this vocation. This Commentary enables us to receive their deep spiritual insights, their encouragement and guidance for present-day interpretation and preaching of the Word. What a wonderful addition to any pastor's library!"

WILLIAM H. WILLIMON
Dean of the Chapel and Professor of Christian Ministry
Duke University

"Here is a nonpareil series which reclaims the Bible as the book of the church by making accessible to earnest readers of the twenty-first century the classrooms of Clement of Alexandria and Didymus the Blind, the study and lecture hall of Origen, the cathedrae of Chrysostom and Augustine, the scriptorium of Jerome in his Bethlehem monastery."

GEORGE LAWLESS
Augustinian Patristic Institute and Gregorian University, Rome

"We are pleased to witness publication of the
Ancient Christian Commentary on Scripture. It is most beneficial for us to learn
how the ancient Christians, especially the saints of the church
who proved through their lives their devotion to God and his Word, interpreted
Scripture. Let us heed the witness of those who have gone before us in the faith."

METROPOLITAN THEODOSIUS
Primate, Orthodox Church in America

"Across Christendom there has emerged a widespread interest
in early Christianity, both at the popular and scholarly level. . . .
Christians of all traditions stand to benefit from this project, especially clergy
and those who study the Bible. Moreover, it will allow us to see how our traditions are
both rooted in the scriptural interpretations of the church fathers while at
the same time seeing how we have developed new perspectives."

ALBERTO FERREIRO
Professor of History, Seattle Pacific University

"The Ancient Christian Commentary on Scripture fills a long overdue need for scholars and
students of the church fathers. . . . Such information will be of immeasurable
worth to those of us who have felt inundated by contemporary interpreters and novel theories
of the biblical text. We welcome some 'new' insight from the
ancient authors in the early centuries of the church."

H. WAYNE HOUSE
Professor of Theology and Law
Trinity University School of Law

"Chronological snobbery—the assumption that our ancestors working without benefit of
computers have nothing to teach us—is exposed as nonsense by this magnificent
new series. Surfeited with knowledge but starved of wisdom, many of us are
more than ready to sit at table with our ancestors and listen to their holy
conversations on Scripture. I know I am."

EUGENE H. PETERSON
Professor Emeritus of Spiritual Theology
Regent College

"Few publishing projects have encouraged me as much as the recently announced Ancient Christian Commentary on Scripture with Dr. Thomas Oden serving as general editor.... How is it that so many of us who are dedicated to serve the Lord received seminary educations which omitted familiarity with such incredible students of the Scriptures as St. John Chrysostom, St. Athanasius the Great and St. John of Damascus? I am greatly anticipating the publication of this Commentary."

FR. PETER E. GILLQUIST
Director, Department of Missions and Evangelism
Antiochian Orthodox Christian Archdiocese of North America

"The Scriptures have been read with love and attention for nearly two thousand years, and listening to the voice of believers from previous centuries opens us to unexpected insight and deepened faith. Those who studied Scripture in the centuries closest to its writing, the centuries during and following persecution and martyrdom, speak with particular authority. The Ancient Christian Commentary on Scripture will bring to life the truth that we are invisibly surrounded by a 'great cloud of witnesses.'"

FREDERICA MATHEWES-GREEN
Commentator, National Public Radio

"For those who think that church history began around 1941 when their pastor was born, this Commentary will be a great surprise. Christians throughout the centuries have read the biblical text, nursed their spirits with it and then applied it to their lives. These commentaries reflect that the witness of the Holy Spirit was present in his church throughout the centuries. As a result, we can profit by allowing the ancient Christians to speak to us today."

HADDON ROBINSON
Harold John Ockenga Distinguished Professor of Preaching
Gordon-Conwell Theological Seminary

"All who are interested in the interpretation of the Bible will welcome the forthcoming multivolume series Ancient Christian Commentary on Scripture. Here the insights of scores of early church fathers will be assembled and made readily available for significant passages throughout the Bible and the Apocrypha. It is hard to think of a more worthy ecumenical project to be undertaken by the publisher."

BRUCE M. METZGER
Professor of New Testament, Emeritus
Princeton Theological Seminary

ANCIENT CHRISTIAN
COMMENTARY ON SCRIPTURE

OLD TESTAMENT
IV

JOSHUA, JUDGES, RUTH, 1-2 SAMUEL

EDITED BY

JOHN R. FRANKE

GENERAL EDITOR
THOMAS C. ODEN

InterVarsity Press
Downers Grove, Illinois

InterVarsity Press
P.O. Box 1400, Downers Grove, IL 60515-1426
World Wide Web: www.ivpress.com
E-mail: mail@ivpress.com

InterVarsity Press* is the book-publishing division of InterVarsity Christian Fellowship/USA*, a student movement active on campus at hundreds of universities, colleges and schools of nursing in the United States of America, and a member movement of the International Fellowship of Evangelical Students. For information about local and regional activities, write Public Relations Dept., InterVarsity Christian Fellowship/USA, 6400 Schroeder Rd., P.O. Box 7895, Madison, WI 53707-7895, or visit the IVCF website at <www.intervarsity.org>.

Scripture quotations, unless otherwise noted, are from the Revised Standard Version of the Bible, copyright 1946, 1952, 1971 by the Division of Christian Education of the National Council of the Churches of Christ in the U.S.A., and are used by permission.

Selected excerpts from Fathers of the Church: A New Translation, ©1947-, and Origen: Spirit and Fire, edited by Hans Urs von Balthasar, ©1984. Used by permission of The Catholic University of America Press, Washington, D.C. Full bibliographic information on volumes of Fathers of the Church may be found in the Bibliography of Works in English Translation.

Selected excerpts from Gregory of Nyssa's Treatise on the Inscriptions of the Psalms, edited and translated by Ronald Heine, ©1995. Used by permission of Oxford University Press, London.

Selected excerpts from Cyril of Jerusalem and Nemesius, edited by William Telfer, Library of Christian Classics 4, ©1955, and Early Latin Theology, edited by S. L. Greenslade, Library of Christian Classics 5, ©1956. Used by permission of Westminster John Knox Press, Louisville, Ky., and SCM Press, London.

Selected excerpts from Bede: On the Tabernacle, translated by Arthur Holder, Translated Texts for Historians 18, ©1994. Used by permission of Liverpool University Press, Liverpool, U.K.

Selected excerpts from St. Augustine, Concerning the City of God Against the Pagans, translated by Henry Bettenson, ©1984. Used by permission of Penguin Press, London.

Selected excerpts from The Ascetical Homilies of Saint Isaac the Syrian, translated by Holy Transfiguration Monastery, ©1984. Used by permission of Holy Transfiguration Monastery, Brookline, Mass.

Selected excerpts from Chrysostom: Old Testament Homilies, translated by Robert Hill, ©2003. Used by permission of Holy Cross Orthodox Press, Brookline, Mass.

Selected excerpts from Faith Gives Fullness to Reasoning: The Five Theological Orations of Gregory Nazianzen, by F. W. Norris, ©1991. Used by permission of E. J. Brill, Leiden, The Netherlands.

Selected excerpts from Medieval Exegesis in Translation: Commentaries on the Book of Ruth, translated by Lesley Smith, ©1996. Used by permission of Medieval Institute Publications, Kalamazoo, Mich.

Selected excerpts from St. Gregory the Great: Pastoral Care, translated by Henry Davis, Ancient Christian Writers 11, ©1950; St. Paulinus of Nola: The Poems of St. Paulinus of Nola, translated by P. G. Walsh, Ancient Christian Writers 40, ©1975; St. Maximus of Turin: The Sermons of St. Maximus of Turin, translated by Boniface Ramsey, Ancient Christian Writers 50, ©1989; Cassiodorus: Explanation of the Psalms vol. 1, translated by P. G. Walsh, Ancient Christian Writers 51, ©1990; Cassiodorus: Explanation of the Psalms vol. 2, translated by P. G. Walsh, Ancient Christian Writers 52, ©1991; John Cassian: The Conferences, translated by Boniface Ramsey, Ancient Christian Writers 57, ©1997; Origen: An Exhortation to Martyrdom, Prayer, and Selected Works, translated by Rowan Greer, Classics of Western Spirituality, ©1979. Used by permission of Paulist Press, Mahwah, N.J.

Selected excerpts from Bede the Venerable, Homilies on the Gospels, translated by Lawrence T. Martin and David Hurst, Cistercian Studies 110 and 111, ©1991; Evagrius of Pontus, The Praktikos and Chapters on Prayer, translated by John Eudes Bamberger, Cistercian Studies 4, ©1981; Gregory the Great, Forty Gospel Homilies, translated by David Hurst, Cistercian Studies 123, ©1990; Pachomian Koinonia: Volumes Two and Three, translated by Armand Veilleux, Cistercian Studies 46 and 47, ©1981-1982. Used by permission of Cistercian Publications, Kalamazoo, Mich.

Selected excerpts from The Works of Saint Augustine: A Translation for the 21st Century, edited by John E. Rotelle, ©1990-. Used by permission of the Augustinian Heritage Institute.

Selected excerpts from Basil the Great, On the Holy Spirit, translated by David Anderson, ©1980; Ephrem the Syrian, Hymns on Paradise, translated by Sebastian Brock, ©1990; Isaac of Nineveh, On Ascetical Life, translated by Mary Hansbury, ©1989; John of Damascus, On the Divine Images: Three Apologies Against Those Who Attack the Divine Images, translated by David Anderson, ©1980. Used by permission of St. Vladimir's Seminary Press, Crestwood, N.Y.

Cover photograph: Scala/Art Resource, New York. View of the apse. S. Vitale, Ravenna, Italy.

Spine photograph: Byzantine Collection, Dumbarton Oaks, Washington D.C. Pendant cross (gold and enamel). Constantinople, late sixth century.

ISBN 0-8308-1474-4

Printed in the United States of America ∞

Library of Congress Cataloging-in-Publication Data

Joshua, Judges, Ruth, 1-2 Samuel/edited by John R. Franke; general
editor, Thomas C. Oden.
        p. cm.—(Ancient Christian commentary on Scripture. Old
        Testament; 4)
Includes bibliographical references and indexes.
ISBN 0-8308-1474-4 (hardcover: alk. paper)
1. Bible. O.T. Joshua—Commentaries. 2. Bible. O.T.
Judges—Commentaries. 3. Bible. O.T. Ruth—Commentaries. 4. Bible.
O.T. Samuel—Commentaries. I. Franke, John R. II. Oden, Thomas C.
III. Series.
BS1295.53.J67 2005
222'.077'09—dc22
                                                                            2005008618

P	27	26	25	24	23	22	21	20	19	18	17	16	15	14	13	12	11	10	9	8	7	6	5	4	3	2	1
Y	28	27	26	26	25	24	23	22	21	20	19	18	17	16	15	14	13	12	11	10	09	08	07	06	05		

Contents

GENERAL INTRODUCTION

The Ancient Christian Commentary on Scripture has as its goal the revitalization of Christian teaching based on classical Christian exegesis, the intensified study of Scripture by lay persons who wish to think with the early church about the canonical text, and the stimulation of Christian historical, biblical, theological and pastoral scholars toward further inquiry into scriptural interpretation by ancient Christian writers.

The time frame of these documents spans seven centuries of exegesis, from Clement of Rome to John of Damascus, from the end of the New Testament era to A.D. 750, including the Venerable Bede.

Lay readers are asking how they might study sacred texts under the instruction of the great minds of the ancient church. This commentary has been intentionally prepared for a general lay audience of nonprofessionals who study the Bible regularly and who earnestly wish to have classic Christian observation on the text readily available to them. The series is targeted to anyone who wants to reflect and meditate with the early church about the plain sense, theological wisdom and moral meaning of particular Scripture texts.

A commentary dedicated to allowing ancient Christian exegetes to speak for themselves will refrain from the temptation to fixate endlessly upon contemporary criticism. Rather, it will stand ready to provide textual resources from a distinguished history of exegesis that has remained massively inaccessible and shockingly disregarded during the last century. We seek to make available to our present-day audiences the multicultural, multilingual, transgenerational resources of the early ecumenical Christian tradition.

Preaching at the end of the first millennium focused primarily on the text of Scripture as understood by the earlier esteemed tradition of comment, largely converging on those writers that best reflected classic Christian consensual thinking. Preaching at the end of the second millennium has reversed that pattern. It has so forgotten most of these classic comments that they are vexing to find anywhere, and even when located they are often available only in archaic editions and inadequate translations. The preached word in our time has remained largely bereft of previously influential patristic inspiration. Recent scholarship has so focused attention upon post-Enlightenment historical and literary methods that it has left this longing largely unattended and unserviced.

This series provides the pastor, exegete, student and lay reader with convenient means to see what Athanasius or John Chrysostom or the desert fathers and mothers had to say about a particular text for preaching, for study and for meditation. There is an emerging awareness among Catholic, Protestant and Orthodox laity that vital biblical preaching and spiritual formation need deeper grounding beyond the scope of the historical-critical orientations that have governed biblical studies in our day.

Hence this work is directed toward a much broader audience than the highly technical and specialized scholarly field of patristic studies. The audience is not limited to the university scholar concentrating on the study of the history of the transmission of the text or to those with highly focused philological interests in textual morphology or historical-critical issues. Though these are crucial concerns for specialists, they are not the paramount interests of this series.

This work is a Christian Talmud. The Talmud is a Jewish collection of rabbinic arguments and comments on the Mishnah, which epitomized the laws of the Torah. The Talmud originated in approximately the same period that the patristic writers were commenting on texts of the Christian tradition. Christians from the late patristic age through the medieval period had documents analogous to the Jewish Talmud and Midrash (Jewish commentaries) available to them in the *glossa ordinaria* and catena traditions, two forms of compiling extracts of patristic exegesis. In Talmudic fashion the sacred text of Christian Scripture was thus clarified and interpreted by the classic commentators.

The Ancient Christian Commentary on Scripture has venerable antecedents in medieval exegesis of both eastern and western traditions, as well as in the Reformation tradition. It offers for the first time in this century the earliest Christian comments and reflections on the Old and New Testaments to a modern audience. Intrinsically an ecumenical project, this series is designed to serve Protestant, Catholic and Orthodox lay, pastoral and scholarly audiences.

In cases where Greek, Latin, Syriac and Coptic texts have remained untranslated into English, we provide new translations. Wherever current English translations are already well rendered, they will be utilized, but if necessary their language will be brought up to date. We seek to present fresh dynamic equivalency translations of long-neglected texts which historically have been regarded as authoritative models of biblical interpretation.

These foundational sources are finding their way into many public libraries and into the core book collections of many pastors and lay persons. It is our intent and the publisher's commitment to keep the whole series in print for many years to come.

Thomas C. Oden
General Editor

A Guide to Using This Commentary

Several features have been incorporated into the design of this commentary. The following comments are intended to assist readers in making full use of this volume.

Pericopes of Scripture

The scriptural text has been divided into pericopes, or passages, usually several verses in length. Each of these pericopes is given a heading, which appears at the beginning of the pericope. For example, the first pericope in the commentary on Joshua is "1:1 The Lord Commissions Joshua." This heading is followed by the Scripture passage quoted in the Revised Standard Version (RSV) across the full width of the page. The Scripture passage is provided for the convenience of readers, but it is also in keeping with medieval patristic commentaries, in which the citations of the Fathers were arranged around the text of Scripture.

Overviews

Following each pericope of text is an overview of the patristic comments on that pericope. The format of this overview varies within the volumes of this series, depending on the requirements of the specific book of Scripture. The function of the overview is to provide a brief summary of all the comments to follow. It tracks a reasonably cohesive thread of argument among patristic comments, even though they are derived from diverse sources and generations. Thus the summaries do not proceed chronologically or by verse sequence. Rather they seek to rehearse the overall course of the patristic comment on that pericope.

We do not assume that the commentators themselves anticipated or expressed a formally received cohesive argument but rather that the various arguments tend to flow in a plausible, recognizable pattern. Modern readers can thus glimpse aspects of continuity in the flow of diverse exegetical traditions representing various generations and geographical locations.

Topical Headings

An abundance of varied patristic comment is available for each pericope of these letters. For this reason we have broken the pericopes into two levels. First is the verse with its topical heading. The patristic comments are then focused on aspects of each verse, with topical headings summarizing the essence of the patristic comment by evoking a key phrase, metaphor or idea. This feature provides a bridge by which modern readers can enter into the heart of the patristic comment.

Identifying the Patristic Texts

Following the topical heading of each section of comment, the name of the patristic commentator is given. An English translation of the patristic comment is then provided. This is immediately followed by the title of the patristic work and the textual reference—either by book, section and subsection or by book-and-verse references.

The Footnotes

Readers who wish to pursue a deeper investigation of the patristic works cited in this commentary will find the footnotes especially valuable. A footnote number directs the reader to the notes at the bottom of the right-hand column, where in addition to other notations (clarifications or biblical cross references) one will find information on English translations (where available) and standard original-language editions of the work cited. An abbreviated citation (normally citing the book, volume and page number) of the work is provided. A key to the abbreviations is provided on page xv. Where there is any serious ambiguity or textual problem in the selection, we have tried to reflect the best available textual tradition.

Where original language texts have remained untranslated into English, we provide new translations. Wherever current English translations are already well rendered, they are utilized, but where necessary they are stylistically updated. A single asterisk (*) indicates that a previous English translation has been updated to modern English or amended for easier reading. The double asterisk (**) indicates either that a new translation has been provided or that some extant translation has been significantly amended. We have standardized spellings and made grammatical variables uniform so that our English references will not reflect the odd spelling variables of the older English translations. For ease of reading we have in some cases edited out superfluous conjunctions.

For the convenience of computer database users the digital database references are provided to either the Thesaurus Linguae Graecae (Greek texts) or to the Cetedoc (Latin texts) in the appendix found on pages 402-9.

Abbreviations

ACW	Ancient Christian Writers: The Works of the Fathers in Translation. Mahwah, N.J.: Paulist Press, 1946-.
AF	J. B. Lightfoot and J. R. Harmer, trans. *The Apostolic Fathers*. Edited by M. W. Holmes. 2nd ed. Grand Rapids, Mich.: Baker, 1989.
AHSIS	Holy Transfiguration Monastery, ed. *The Ascetical Homilies of Saint Isaac the Syrian*. Boston, Mass.: Holy Transfiguration Monastery, 1984.
ANCL	The Ante-Nicene Christian Library: Translations of the Writings of the Fathers down to A.D. 325. Alexander Roberts and James Donaldson, eds. Edinburgh: T. and T. Clark, 1867-1897.
ANF	A. Roberts and J. Donaldson, eds. Ante-Nicene Fathers. 10 vols. Buffalo, N.Y.: Christian Literature, 1885-1896. Reprint, Grand Rapids, Mich.: Eerdmans, 1951-1956; Reprint, Peabody, Mass.: Hendrickson, 1994.
CCL	Corpus Christianorum. Series Latina. Turnhout, Belgium: Brepols, 1953-.
CG	Augustine. *The City of God*. Translated by Henry S. Bettenson with an introduction by David Knowles. 1972. Reprint, with an introduction by John O'Meara. Harmondsworth, England: Penguin Books, 1984.
COTH	Chrysostom. *Old Testament Homilies*. 3 vols. Translated by Robert C. Hill. Brookline, Mass.: Holy Cross Orthodox Press, 2003.
CS	Cistercian Studies. Kalamazoo, Mich.: Cistercian Publications, 1973-.
CSEL	Corpus Scriptorum Ecclesiasticorum Latinorum. Vienna, 1866-.
CSCO	Corpus Scriptorum Christianorum Orientalium. Louvain, Belgium, 1903-.
EBT	Theophylact. *The Explanation by Blessed Theophylact of the Holy Gospel According to St. Matthew*. Introduction by Fr. Christopher Stade. House Springs, Mo.: Chrysostom Press, 1992.
ESH	Ephrem the Syrian. *Hymns*. Translated and introduced by Kathleen E. McVey. Preface by John Meyendorff. Classics in Western Spirituality. Mahwah, N.J.: Paulist, 1989.
ECTD	C. McCarthy, trans. and ed. *Saint Ephrem's Commentary on Tatian's Diatessaron: An English Translation of Chester Beatty Syriac MS 709. Journal of Semitic Studies* Supplement 2. Oxford: Oxford University Press for the University of Manchester, 1993.
FC	Fathers of the Church: A New Translation. Washington, D.C.: Catholic University of America Press, 1947-.
FGFR	F. W. Norris. *Faith Gives Fullness to Reasoning: The Five Theological Orations of Gregory Nazianzen*. Leiden and New York: E. J. Brill, 1991.
GCS	Die griechischen christlichen Schriftsteller der ersten Jahrhunderte. Berlin: Akademie-Verlag, 1897-.
GNTIP	Ronald E. Heine, trans. *Gregory of Nyssa's Treatise on the Inscriptions of the Psalms*. Oxford Early Christian Studies. Oxford: Clarendon Press, 1995.
HOP	Ephrem the Syrian. *Hymns on Paradise*. Translated by S. Brock. Crestwood, N.Y.: St. Vladimir's Seminary Press, 1990.

INAL   St. Isaac of Nineveh. *On Ascetical Life*. Translated by Mary Hansbury. Crestwood, N.Y.: St. Vladimir's Seminary Press, 1989.

LCC   J. Baillie et al., eds. The Library of Christian Classics. 26 vols. Philadelphia: Westminster, 1953-1966.

LF   A Library of Fathers of the Holy Catholic Church Anterior to the Division of the East and West. Translated by members of the English Church. 44 vols. Oxford: John Henry Parker, 1800-1881.

MEIT   *Medieval Exegesis in Translation: Commentaries on the Book of Ruth*. Translated by Lesley Smith. Kalamazoo, Mich.: Medieval Institute Publications, 1996.

NPNF   P. Schaff et al., eds. A Select Library of the Nicene and Post-Nicene Fathers of the Christian Church. 2 series (14 vols. each). Buffalo, N.Y.: Christian Literature, 1887-1894; Reprint, Grand Rapids, Mich.: Eerdmans, 1952-1956; Reprint, Peabody, Mass.: Hendrickson, 1994.

ODI   St. John of Damascus. *On the Divine Image*. Translated by David Anderson. Crestwood, N.Y.: St. Vladimir's Seminary Press, 1980.

OHS   Basil of Caesarea. *On the Holy Spirit*. Translated by D. Anderson, Crestwood, N.Y.: St. Vladimir's Press, 1980.

OSF   *Origen: Spirit and Fire*. Edited by Hans Urs von Balthasar. Washington, D.C.: Catholic University Press of America, 1984.

OSW   *Origen: An Exhortation to Martyrdom, Prayer and Selected Writings*. Translated by Rowan A. Greer with Preface by Hans Urs von Balthasar. The Classics of Western Spirituality. New York: Paulist Press, 1979.

PL   J.-P. Migne, ed. Patrologia cursus completus. Series Latina. 221 vols. Paris: Migne, 1844-1864.

PG   J.-P. Migne, ed. Patrologia cursus completus. Series Graeca. 166 vols. Paris: Migne, 1857-1886.

POG   Eusebius. *The Proof of the Gospel*. 2 vols. Translated by W. J. Ferrar. London: SPCK, 1920; Reprinted, Grand Rapids, Mich.: Baker, 1981.

PTS   Patristische Texte und Studien. New York: de Gruyter, 1964-.

SC   H. de Lubac, J. Daniélou et al., eds. Sources Chrétiennes. Paris: Editions du Cerf, 1941-.

SNTD   *Symeon the New Theologian: The Discourses*. Translated by C. J. de Catanzaro. Classics of Western Spirituality: A Library of the Great Spiritual Masters. New York: Paulist, 1980.

TTH   G. Clark, M. Gibson and M. Whitby, eds. Translated Texts for Historians. Liverpool: Liverpool University Press, 1985-.

WSA   J. E. Rotelle, ed. *Works of St. Augustine: A Translation for the Twenty-First Century*. Hyde Park, N.Y.: New City Press, 1995.

INTRODUCTION TO JOSHUA THROUGH 2 SAMUEL

To say that the interpretation of the Bible in the writings of the early church often strikes modern readers as strange would be something of an understatement. The hegemony of scientific and historical principles of interpretation that emphasize social and cultural backgrounds along with linguistic and philological concerns in pursuit of the precise meaning of the textual author can seem to condemn the theological and spiritual exegesis of the early church to the scrap heap of the past. While it may be interesting to scholars and historians attempting to chart the advances in biblical interpretation over the centuries, it has often appeared to be of little use in attempting to come to terms with the contemporary task of reading Scripture. This has been particularly true with respect to the narrative portions of the Christian canon and especially those of the Old Testament. This introduction will seek to orient readers to the interpretive rationale that guided the early Christian exegetes as they sought to understand and expound the meaning and significance of the Old Testament narratives for the ancient church as well as introduce some of the most significant early Christian interpreters.

One of the immediate challenges for the earliest Christians, who were converts from Judaism, concerned the interpretation of the Jewish Scriptures. On the one hand, they found in the Hebrew canon numerous passages that they readily understood as prophecies concerning Christ that confirmed to them that Jesus was the promised Messiah. On the other hand, these portions made up only a small fraction of the canon inherited from Judaism, and much of the rest seemed to be less germane to the Christian context, particularly the extensive material concerning ritual and ceremonial law and the historical narratives. How was this material to be interpreted and understood as the guidance and instruction of God for the new church? An additional aspect of this question was raised by Paul, who warned the early Christians about the dangers of falling back into Jewish teachings and practices. He asserted that while the law of God contained in the Jewish Scriptures was certainly good and important, it had been only a temporary measure in the economy of redemption. The law had been fulfilled in Christ whose life, death and resurrection marked the climax of the old covenant and the inauguration of a new covenant of grace that was not restricted to the parameters of national, ethnic Israel. Thus, while Paul continued to make extensive use of the Jewish Scriptures in his teaching and writing, his notion of the fulfillment and completion of the law in Christ and the corresponding emphasis on grace provided the conceptual context that allowed others to raise questions about the significance and relevance of the Hebrew Bible for the Christian faith, particularly as the demographic profile of the church shifted away from Jewish converts to those who came from pagan backgrounds.

These pagan converts did not bring with them an inbred commitment to the Jewish Scriptures. They affirmed faith in Christ and were then faced with the challenge of making sense of the culturally strange and foreign set of Hebrew texts that they had inherited as part and parcel of their allegiance to Christ and the church. In this context some, like Marcion, maintained that these texts contained a portrayal of God that was not consistent with the God of love found in the writings that would come to make up the New Testament canon. Hence, Marcion advocated that the Hebrew Bible, which came to be called the Old Testament, be removed from the church as an unfitting witness to the Christian faith. While the church did not accept Marcion's teaching and expelled him from the church as a heretic, it was faced with a crisis of interpretation. How should the Hebrew Bible be read in relation to the revelation of God in Jesus Christ?

Irenaeus of Lyons (d. 202) addressed the problem of relating the Old and New Testaments and maintained that all of human history could be comprehended and summarized in the figures of Adam and Christ, who taken together narrate and represent the story of humanity. The Old Testament tells of a beginning in Adam and the subsequent disobedience and fall from grace brought about by human rebellion against God and goes on to speak of the promise of God in the covenant with Abraham to bring about healing and reconciliation. The New Testament bears witness to the reality of a new beginning in the recapitulation and restoration of humanity brought about by the life and obedience of Jesus Christ. As the fulfillment of the covenant and the promises made in the Old Testament, Christ provided Christians with an interpretive key to understanding the full significance of the ancient Hebrew texts, a significance that extended beyond the literal meaning of the Scriptures.

While Irenaeus provided a model for relating the Testaments in the light of Christ, the challenge of providing detailed interpretation of the particular and peculiar texts of the Old Testament remained. In addressing this challenge, no figure from the early church is more significant than Origen of Alexandria (d. 254). He wrote extensively on the Old Testament in the form of commentaries and homilies on almost every book of the Jewish canon, thus ensuring its place in the Christian church and helping to establish the principles of Christian exegesis of the Old Testament. In light of the significance of Origen in the history of early Christian exegesis, let us briefly consider his approach to the interpretation of Scripture in the context of his intellectual setting.

Origen and Spiritual Exegesis

In spite of his prominence, few figures in the history of the church have stimulated the level of debate and controversy that surrounds Origen. While he was certainly one of the most influential and seminal thinkers in the history of the early church, he has also been frequently vilified and condemned over the course of Christian history by those who believe that his interest in spiritual exegesis and philosophical speculation led to the development of teachings that were in conflict with later standards of orthodoxy. In light of this, it is worth noting that Origen believed the Bible to be the Word of God, and as such it occupied a central place in his life and thought, serving as the touchstone for all of his teaching. Indeed, one of the major concerns of Origen's work was to assist Christians facing the intellectual challenges of the third century by providing answers to the questions posed by Hellenistic philosophy and culture that were in keeping with the teaching of Scripture. However, in spite of his intentions and clear commitment to the principle of biblical authority, many believe that Origen's use of Scripture significantly compromised that authority and provided fertile conditions for the germination and growth of heresy. In order to better understand the rationale that shaped Origen's approach to biblical exegesis, it is important to remember the intellectual and cultural context in which he was situated.

Origen was reared in a Christian home in which his father, a prosperous and influential man, provided his son with an education that was Hellenistic and Christian, centered on the study of the classic literary works of ancient Greece and the Bible. Hence, young Origen grew up as a learned Greek and a devoted Christian. This dual education undoubtedly caused something of an internal tension in Origen as he sought to reconcile his commitment to Christian faith and the Bible with the Hellenistic outlook he was taught. From the perspective of Hellenism, Christianity was little more than another barbarous superstition and the Bible constituted an inferior collection of texts that were not worth serious consideration from the standpoint of Greek aesthetic standards. Origen was not the first to grapple with this tension, and he was able to learn from previous Jewish and Christian engagements with Hellenism, particularly Platonic philosophy, in his attempt to affirm the teaching of the Bible in the context of the Greek intellectual milieu. In responding to the cultural and philosophical challenges of Hellenism, Origen was immensely productive, teaching, preaching, traveling and writing. His writings include numerous scholarly and intellectual works concerning theology, philosophy, apologetics and biblical interpretation. In fact, Origen was one of the most prolific writers of the ancient world. Unfortunately, the majority of his works have not survived while many others remain available only in Latin translations.

Among Origen's many works, two are of particular importance in the history of the early church and Christian thought. *On First Principles* is an ordered and systematic account of Origen's theological and philosophical positions concerning God, creation, Jesus Christ, the Logos of God and salvation. It is one of the great classics of Christian thought and constitutes both a philosophical discussion on the relation of God to the world and an attempt at developing a coherent set of theological teachings that may be derived from the logical elaboration of the basic doctrines of the Christian faith. As such, it may be construed as the first formal attempt at systematic theology in the history of the church. The second, *Against Celsus*, is a detailed defense of Christian faith against the critique of the Roman philosopher Celsus, in which Origen attempts to demonstrate the superiority of the teaching and wisdom of the Bible over against that of Greek philosophy. This thorough point-by-point response to Celsus made an important contribution to the growing cogency and respectability of Christian faith in the ancient world and stands as an apologetic milestone in the history of the church. These works effectively refuted the contention that Christianity was simply another superstitious folk religion and helped to establish the intellectual credentials of the faith in relation to Greek philosophy and Hellenistic culture.

While Origen appreciated a great deal of Plato and the Greek philosophical tradition, he argued that at its best it merely anticipated the fullness of truth that was to be found in divine revelation. Further, he maintained that for all the benefits of philosophy, it could not finally lead to a true and proper knowledge of God since it was contaminated with too much false and erroneous teaching that could not be separated from the good. In spite of his reservations concerning philosophy, Origen believed that Christian faith itself was a kind of divine philosophy which, while surpassing and superceding all other philosophies, could make use of them by leading persons to a true knowledge of God and to salvation. Thus, Christians can profitably study Greek philosophy or other pagan learning and borrow the truths found in these sources in order to explicate the gospel and the Christian faith. Origen used an analogy from the Hebrew Bible to make this point. In the same way that the Israelites took the property of the Egyptians with them in the exodus,[1] so the people of God are permitted to make use of the truths of pagan culture and philosophy, the "spoils of the Egyptians," in the work of theology and biblical interpretation.

This willingness to make use of Greek thought is perhaps nowhere more evident than in Origen's spiritual or allegorical approach to the interpretation of Scripture. He maintained that the Bible contained three levels of meaning corresponding to the tripartite conception of a human being, consisting of body, soul and spirit, derived from the writings of Paul and Platonic philosophy. The bodily level of Scripture is the bare letter of the text or its literal meaning, which is particularly useful in meeting the needs of the more simple-minded. The psychic level can be understood as the moral meaning of the text, providing guidance concerning right and proper conduct, although some ambiguity exists as to the exact ways in which Origen made use of this sense. In many cases he simply maintains that biblical narratives contain ethical and moral principles that may be derived from or hidden beneath the surface of the literal and historical meanings of the text. The third and most important level of meaning is the spiritual or allegorical, which concerns the deeper meaning of the text and points to Christ and the relationship of the Christian with God. Origen believed that this spiritual/mystical meaning, while often hidden, is always present in the text. The task of the Christian interpreter is to uncover this hidden meaning in order to glean the most profound and significant benefits of its teaching for the church. The spiritual approach to interpretation sought to yield this hidden, symbolic meaning, and Origen became the leading figure in its establishment as the dominant method of biblical interpretation in the history of the church until the sixteenth century.

Examples of this attempt to uncover the hidden spiritual significance of biblical texts abound in Origen's writings, particularly in his commentaries and homilies on the narrative portions of the Old Testament that address the history of Israel. For instance, in Origen's twenty-seventh homily on the book of Numbers, he provides a detailed exposition of growth in the spiritual life based on the forty-two stopping places of Israel in the wilderness listed in Numbers 33. Origen begins by asking why the Lord wanted Moses to write this passage down: "Was it so that this passage in Scripture about the stages the children of Israel made might benefit us in some way or that it should bring no benefit? Who would dare to say that what is written 'by the Word of God' is of no use and makes no contribution to salvation but is merely a narrative of what happened and was over and done a long time ago, but pertains in no way to us when it is told?"[2] For Origen, because the Bible is the inspired Word of God, it is never merely concerned with mundane matters of history and factual occurrences. Rather, it expounds the mysteries of God in Christ and gives direction to the spiritual life. Hence, the Christian interpreter must probe the text in various ways in order to uncover its true and deepest significance. According to Origen, the stopping places of the wandering Israelites are recorded in Numbers in order that we come to understand the long spiritual journey that we face as Christians; in light of this knowledge we must not "allow the time of our life to be ruined by sloth and

---

[1] See Ex 12:35-36
[2] OSW 248.

neglect."[3] Further, each stopping place has some particular spiritual significance until the sojourn ends on the banks of the Jordan. This makes us aware that the whole journey takes place and "the whole course is run for the purpose of arriving at the river of God, so that we may make neighbors of the flowing Wisdom and may be watered by the waves of divine knowledge, and so that purified by them all we may be made worthy to enter the promised land."[4]

This approach to interpretation often strikes contemporary readers as strange, unwarranted and potentially dangerous. Why did Origen adopt such a method? First, it must be pointed out that allegory is a legacy of Greek thought and would have been one of the staples of Origen's Hellenistic education. It was initially used to defend belief in the inspired character of the Homeric writings, the *Iliad* and the *Odyssey*, in the face of charges against such a claim because of the suspect morals they contained and the changing religious convictions of Greek culture. Homer's supporters maintained that the poems were symbolic and when read in their true, allegorical sense contained no moral or religious difficulties. Over time, allegorical interpretive methods became increasingly sophisticated with the development of the Platonist contention that myths and symbols were necessary components in the communication of truths that were otherwise inaccessible. This Platonist appreciation for the value of myths and symbols became an essential part of Origen's outlook in which allegory served as a powerful and important means of conveying religious and philosophical truth.

On top of this general philosophical appreciation for allegorical interpretation, Origen was exposed to a lengthy tradition of spiritual exegesis of the Bible that began with the Jewish community in Alexandria, which used the method to demonstrate that their Scriptures were compatible with Greek philosophy. The leading Jewish proponent of this movement was Philo, and although his work eventually fell out of favor with the Jews, it was accepted enthusiastically by Christians and was probably communicated to Origen through Clement of Alexandria. Hence, Origen inherited a strong belief in the appropriateness and effectiveness of allegory as a tool to communicate the deepest and most profound philosophical and theological truths, as well as the assumption that the Bible, the inspired Word of God, must be subject to such allegorical interpretation in order to grasp its spiritual significance.

In addition to his indebtedness to Hellenistic philosophy and culture, Origen found ample evidence in Scripture itself for the practice of spiritual exegesis beginning with the Christian conviction that the entire Old Testament is a prophecy concerning Christ, who is the interpretive key to understanding the Hebrew Bible. In 2 Corinthians 3, we read that the Jews who reject Christ have a veil before their faces and over their hearts that hides the true meaning of Scripture from their perception and limits them to the letter of the text that kills. Only through Christ can the veil be removed and the spiritual meaning of the text that gives life be revealed. For Origen, this led to the conclusion that spiritual exegesis was necessary in order to comprehend the true, christological meaning of the Old Testament.

Among the most significant New Testament passages that Origen cited as justifying his approach to spiritual interpretation is 1 Corinthians 10, in which the pillar of cloud, the crossing of the Red Sea, the

---

[3]*OSW* 254.
[4]*OS   2W* 268.

manna, the water from the rock and death in the wilderness represent baptism, the Eucharist and punishment for sin. Summing up these events is 1 Corinthians 10:11, which explains that each of these things happened to the Hebrews as a *typikos*, a figure or example, written down for those who live at the end of the age. For Origen, this implied that the Old Testament was written for future Christians who were under obligation to seek the spiritual interpretation that continues to apply since many of the ceremonies and legal precepts are no longer binding in the literal sense. In Galatians 4, another important passage, Sarah and Hagar symbolize the two covenants in which the Christians are prefigured by Isaac, the son of Sarah the free wife, and the Jews by Ishmael, the son of Hagar the slave. The significance of this passage arises from its explicit use of allegory. Other examples mentioned by Origen include Matthew 12:39-40, in which the three days Jonah spent in the great fish symbolize the three days Jesus will pass in the heart of the earth; Matthew 26:61 and John 2:19-21, in which the temple symbolizes the body of Christ; Galatians 3, in which the posterity of Abraham is portrayed in Christ, who will fulfill the promises made to the patriarchs; and Hebrews 8, in which the ceremonies of the old covenant are but shadows of heavenly realities. For Origen, it was abundantly clear that the numerous examples found in the apostolic writings that made up the New Testament authorized and validated the spiritual interpretation of the Old Testament and, by extension, all of Scripture.

Taken together, the cultural assumptions of the Hellenistic world, the Christian belief in the inspired nature of the Bible, the centrality of Christ and the teaching of the New Testament virtually demanded to Origen's mind the practice of spiritual interpretation. In this context we can summarize three additional apologetic or pragmatic impulses that would have sealed his commitment to allegory. First, in the context of Hellenistic Alexandria, the assertion that the Bible was divinely inspired would have required its allegorical interpretation. To assert that it could not or should not be interpreted in such a fashion would be tantamount to denying its inspired character. Affirming the Bible as the Word of God entailed the assumption that its form and teaching were consistent with the highest cultural standards. Second, Jewish critics of Christianity stressed Christ's failure to fulfill many of the prophecies concerning the Messiah. Origen believed that perceiving the deeper sense and meaning of Old Testament prophecies through spiritual interpretation would overcome these objections. Third, the Gnostic sects rejected the Old Testament on the grounds that it taught a different God than the one revealed in Christ. They believed that in contrast to the New Testament God of love, the deity of the Old Testament was vengeful, jealous, capricious and often directly responsible for sin and evil. Given his philosophical assumptions, Origen considered this conclusion unavoidable if the biblical texts were to be accepted as merely literal, and hence, he asserted that they must be understood allegorically. In fact, he argued that they are often intentionally obscure and incoherent in order to coax and compel the reader to seek their true, spiritual meaning. Finally, in response to those who might argue that the multiplicity of meanings generated by this approach would result in interpretive chaos, Origen insisted that the practice of Christian spiritual exegesis must always be conducted within the framework of the Rule of Faith, a brief summary of orthodox Christian teaching, such as the Apostles' Creed, that was allegedly taught by the apostles themselves and subsequently preserved in the church.

In assessing Origen's legacy, it is worth reminding ourselves that in his context many Christian theological beliefs were not well developed or respected. Origen's work was a decisive factor in changing this state of affairs, in terms of establishing the intellectual credibility of the faith in the Hellenistic setting and in exploring the internal coherence of Christian faith as well as its relationship to broader philosophical and cultural questions and aspirations. That he must sometimes be judged as mistaken in these explorations should hardly be surprising or cause for great concern. Origen was one of the first Christian thinkers to give sustained attention to many of the issues he addresses. And while he taught some positions deemed to be unorthodox by later standards, it is important to remember that he was a seminal thinker in a process of trial, error, revision and refinement from which an orthodox consensus emerged and that he was always faithful to the standards of orthodoxy that pertained to his time.

Major Christian Interpreters

While the importance of Origen in the history of early Christian exegesis provides the rationale for the extended discussion of the previous section, readers of this series will be well aware that he was by no means the only significant interpreter. Among the most prominent of these are the eight doctors of the church, four each from the Greek-speaking East and the Latin-speaking West: Athanasius, Gregory of Nazianzus, Basil the Great and John Chrysostom from the East; Ambrose, Jerome, Augustine and Gregory the Great from the West. Athanasius (d. 373) served as bishop of the church in Alexandria and was a staunch defender of the full divinity of Jesus Christ over against the position of Arius and his followers that the Son of God was a created being, an exalted creature to be sure, but nevertheless one who had a beginning and should not therefore be equated with God. Arius famously expressed this notion in the phrase "there was a time when the Son was not." Athanasius was convinced that such a position effectively undercut the Christian gospel, and he fiercely defended the incarnation, the belief that God the Son, who is true God with the Father and the Holy Spirit, had willingly joined his divine nature to human nature in an act of love and humility in order to bring about the reconciliation of rebellious human beings with their Creator. His most significant works, *On the Incarnation* and *Three Discourses Against the Arians,* defend these principles of orthodoxy and illustrate powerfully his interpretation and application of the Bible to the difficult and challenging theological questions of the early church. It is worth noting that although Athanasius vigorously opposed the teaching of Arius with respect to the person of Christ, a position that can be derived from the writings of Origen, it is nevertheless true that Athanasius also remained deeply indebted to Origen and the theological and interpretive traditions of Alexandria.

Gregory of Nazianzus (d. 389) and Basil the Great (d. 379) were great friends from the Roman province of Cappadocia who lived in the fourth century and together made up the core of the so-called Cappadocian fathers, the others being Gregory of Nyssa and Amphilochius of Iconium. Through the work of these figures the theological commitments of Athanasius were developed, extended and brought to fruition in the life and thought of the church. Gregory of Nazianzus was not a prolific writer and never produced a biblical commentary. However, as bishop of Constantinople he expounded and defended the orthodox faith of the church in a series of homilies that drew widespread attention and admiration. These came to be known as the *Theological Orations* and secured his reputation as one of the most able defenders of the faith as well as the distinctive title "the Theologian." They are the product of long, careful and intensive investigation of the meaning and implications of Christian orthodoxy for the life of the church and represent one of the most significant statements of trinitarian theology in the history of the ancient church. Basil the Great served as bishop of Caesarea and was an outstanding ecclesiastical administrator and statesman as well as a leading exponent of Christian teaching, often viewed as a second Athanasius for his defense of orthodoxy. He also engaged in the reformation of Christian liturgy and in the founding and development of Eastern monasticism. Perhaps his most important work is his treatise *On the Holy Spirit*, in which he considers the relationship of the Spirit with the Father and the Son and provides an important contribution to the development of trinitarian teaching. These works are saturated with exegesis.

Both Gregory and Basil possessed a great deal of respect and admiration for the work of Origen, and together they produced the *Philocalia*, a significant anthology of Origen's work that served to extend his influence on the church. Interestingly, in spite of his manifest appreciation for Origen, Basil is quite critical of allegorical exegesis in his interpretation of the creation account contained in the *Hexaemeron*, a collection of nine homilies he delivered on the opening chapters of Genesis. In the ninth of these homilies, he provides one of the most vigorous challenges to allegorical interpretation produced in the early church: "I know the laws of allegory, though less by myself than from the works of others. There are those truly, who do not admit the common sense of the Scriptures, for whom water is not water, but some other nature, who see in a plant, in a fish, what their fancy wishes. . . . For me grass is grass; plant, fish, wild beast, domestic animal, I take all in the literal senses."[5] It should be noted that Basil was particularly concerned with those individuals and groups, such as Gnostic sects like the Marcionites and Valentinians, who made use of allegorical or spiritual methods of interpretation in order to critique and escape the plain meaning of the biblical text for the purpose of promoting their own interpretive distortions at the expense of Christian orthodoxy.

John Chrysostom (d. 407) was the most famous preacher of his day and one of the most significant in the history of the church, accounting for his nickname, "golden mouth" (Chrysostom), which was first bestowed on him in the sixth century. None of the other Greek fathers left as significant and extensive a literary legacy in the form of numerous homilies on the various books of the Bible. In addition to his acclaim as a preacher, no other Eastern writer has enjoyed as widespread an admiration, such that he is among the most revered of the church fathers in the Western church as well as in the East. The full measure of his popularity is perhaps made most manifest by the fact that his extensive writings have been almost entirely preserved. As an interpreter of Scripture he is perhaps the leading representative of the Antiochean tradition of exegesis, an approach to reading the Bible that tended to focus on the literal or plain sense of the text and generally sought to avoid extensive allegorical explanations of the text that were favored by Origen and the Alexandrian tradition. Other leading representatives of this group are Diodore of Tarsus, Theodore of Mopsuestia and Theodoret of Cyr. While the Antiochean and Alexandrian schools of interpretation do manifest clear and distinct interpretive tendencies, it should also be pointed out that these labels, while helpful to a certain extent, can also be overly simplistic and misleading. So, for instance, while it is true that Origen, as we have seen, promoted an allegorical or spiritual approach to reading the Bible, he did not ignore the literal or plain sense of the text. Likewise, while John Chrysostom and other Antiocheans were particularly focused on the plain sense of the text, they also engaged in typological readings that were quite

---

[5]NPNF 2 7:101.

close to what Origen might have described as spiritual exegesis. Hence it is probably best to view the differences between the two approaches to exegesis in terms of particular interpretive tendencies and trajectories rather than as hard and fast, mutually exclusive positions.

In the Western church, Ambrose of Milan (d. 397) became one of the most influential figures in establishing the trajectory of interpretation among Latin writers. He was the son of the praetorian prefect of Gaul and received a traditional liberal arts education in preparation for a career as a lawyer and orator and was eventually appointed as a governor based in Milan. He became so well known in the region for the wisdom and impartiality of his administration that when the death of Auxentius, Arian bishop of Milan, triggered vigorous conflict between rival factions concerning the election of a new bishop, both sides demanded that Ambrose be appointed. In order to secure the peace, he reluctantly agreed, in spite of the fact that he had no theological training and had not yet even been baptized. Within one week he was both baptized and ordained bishop of Milan. In seeking to address his lack of theological knowledge, Ambrose read widely from the writings of earlier Christian thinkers and was particularly influenced by Origen and the Alexandrian tradition of biblical interpretation. He became one of the most significant preachers and teachers of his time, regularly employing allegorical interpretation in order to make sense of the biblical texts. Many of his sermons were eventually published and served as a major influence on the Western church in the direction of the spiritual exegesis of Origen and the Alexandrian tradition.

Jerome (d. 420) has generally been viewed as the finest scholar among the early church fathers and has also been called the greatest biblical scholar ever produced in the history of the Latin church. He received a rigorous education in Rome in which he studied classical literature, particularly Virgil and Cicero. He also learned Greek and Hebrew and was the only one of the eight major church fathers to learn Hebrew well. This background prepared him for the work of translation and allowed him to play a vital role in the transmission of biblical and patristic texts in the West. He produced numerous translations of the writings of the early Greek fathers as well as his well-known translation of extensive portions of the Bible, which later came to make up the Vulgate. Indeed, it is his work as a translator that accounts for his principal reputation in the history of the church. However, in addition to his work as a translator of Scripture and other early Christian exegetes, Jerome was also an outstanding interpreter of Scripture in his own right and produced a number of important commentaries and homilies. In addition to these works, he wrote a large number of letters that still survive and contain many interesting comments concerning matters of theology and biblical interpretation. While Jerome was very sympathetic toward Origen's theological positions and approach to exegesis in the early stages of his career, later he became quite critical, particularly as Origen came under increasing scrutiny. He was especially concerned that allegorical methods could easily fall prey to the danger of subjectivism and lead to distorted views of biblical teaching and Christian faith. The more Origen's particular theological positions came under scrutiny, the more questions were raised with regard to the hermeneutical approach he employed in order to substantiate those views.

The most prominent and prolific of the early Latin theologians was Augustine of Hippo (d. 430). He was also the most influential figure in the history of the Western church, leaving an indelible stamp on its theological and exegetical traditions and practices. He was born in Roman Africa and received a traditional Latin education before continuing his studies and teaching in Rome and Milan. For a time Augustine considered himself a Manichaean and later was also attracted to Neo-Platonist philosophy. As professor of rhetoric of Milan he came into contact with Ambrose and was converted to Christianity through his preaching. Of crucial significance in his conversion was the teaching of Ambrose regarding the spiritual interpretation of the Bible. Prior to Ambrose, many of the arguments of the Manichaeans against Christianity that Augustine had found most compelling were based on the assumption of an overly literal reading of the Bible, particularly the Old Testament. He found that it contained much that he believed to be unworthy of God, and he could not accept the notion that God had physical form, a presumption connected with a literal interpretation of the biblical teaching that human beings were made in the image and likeness of God. It was the spiritual, allegorical and figurative interpretation of Scripture that he discovered in the preaching and teaching of Ambrose that convinced Augustine of the Bible's intellectual credibility and vitality for philosophers and the illegitimacy of the Manichaean objections to the Christian faith. Where he had once thought Christianity to be defenseless in the face of the Manichaean critiques, he now found it to be more and more plausible, particularly as he listened to the teaching of Ambrose.

Shortly after his conversion, Augustine resigned his teaching position and was baptized by Ambrose before returning to North Africa, where he was ordained a priest and eventually elected bishop of Hippo, a post he retained until his death. While the *Confessions* and *The City of God* are his most well-known works, he also wrote a significant number of polemical works in defense of orthodoxy against groups such as the Manichaeans, the Donatists and the Pelagians, in which he displays his use of Scripture concerning a variety of theological, moral and practical questions. In addition, he produced numerous commentaries and homilies on the Bible.

Augustine's approach to exegesis is not easily classified. While he inherited a spiritual and typological approach to reading the Bible from Ambrose and most of the Christian tradition to that point, he also provided some of the most vigorous affirmations of the biblical text as history in the thought of the early church. In *The City of God* he sets forth an account of the entire history of humanity from the perspective of the history of salvation narrated in the Bible, thus providing a distinctively Christian historiography based on the belief that Scripture contains the record of God's guidance and actions in and through real people in concrete and particular historical situations for the purpose of revealing to them God's intentions and plan for all of creation. In addition to this blend of literal, historical and allegorical exegesis, Augustine contributed to the development of biblical interpretation through his emphasis on the centrality of love in the understanding and comprehension of Scripture and believed that the principle of love could be applied to all parts of the Bible and would open up the deepest mysteries of its teaching to the simple and the wise. In this way, he made the Bible accessible to the rank-and-file members of the church, even passages where its precise meaning and application could be difficult to determine.

This influence was developed and extended through the thought of the latest of the Western doctors, Gregory the Great (d. 604), who served as pope from 590 until his death. Gregory is an important transitional figure between the early church and the church of the Middle Ages, and he has been viewed by historians as both the last great figure of the patristic era and the first of the medieval period. He was a masterful administrator as well as a prolific author who tended to have a practical bent of mind as opposed to a speculative one. His most significant and influential work is the *Book of Pastoral Rule* (*Regula pastoralis*), in which he sets out directives and guidance concerning the pastoral life and calling of a bishop, who is to be seen as a shepherd of souls. This book became the standard textbook on the matter for medieval bishops and other church leaders and had a decisive impact on the shape of pastoral ministry in the history of the Western church. With respect to reading Scripture, Gregory, like Ambrose, delighted in employing the methods of allegory in order to discern its deeper, hidden mysteries. This approach to interpretation is amply displayed in his various commentaries and homilies on Scripture. These writings were also very significant in the establishment and development of exegetical practices in the medieval church and ensured the continuance of robust forms of allegorical and spiritual interpretation in the life of the Western church throughout this period.

In addition to these prominent figures, other significant interpreters in the early church include Ephrem the Syrian, the previously mentioned Gregory of Nyssa, Caesarius of Arles and the Bede the Venerable. Ephrem (d. 373) wrote voluminously and reflects a tradition of interpretation that is for the most part independent from the Greek churches of Alexandria and Antioch. He is regarded as the first great writer of the Syrian church. Gregory of Nyssa (d. 394) was the brother of Basil the Great and one of the aforementioned Cappadocian fathers who is well known for his formulations of trinitarian theology and his numerous philosophical, theological and moral treatises. Caesarius of Arles (d. 543) served as bishop for forty years and manifests a thorough awareness of the Latin interpretive tradition. His homilies, however, also reflect the influence of Origen, whose works he would have been able to access in the Latin translations of Rufinus and Jerome. Bede (d. 735) received a classical education in the monastic tradition and became one of the most learned and accomplished writers of his time. Although he is part of the early medieval period, his extensive knowledge of the ancient Christian exegetes and their interpretive traditions places his work in continuity with the thought of the early church.

Commentary on Joshua, Judges, Ruth and 1-2 Samuel

Running commentaries on the historical books of the Old Testament, or writings concerned specifically with detailed and extended consideration of these books, are uncommon in the writings of the early Fathers. Hence, most of the excerpts in this volume are drawn from occasional theological and pastoral treatises, sermons and letters in which comment is made concerning material from the first five of the historical books in the context of concerns other than those specifically related to the exposition and explanation of these books. This sort of passing or illustrative comment on various portions of Scripture is common in the work of the Fathers, such that nearly all of their writings contain some form of citation and comment on the texts of the Bible. Among the writings of the Fathers that deal specifically with scriptural texts are three literary forms or genres: homilies (or sermons), commentaries and questions. Of these, the first two, homilies and commentaries, are the most common, while the latter follows a question-and-answer format that would have been quite familiar to ancient philosophers and teachers as a well-established approach to pedagogy and as a commonly employed literary device. Each of these literary forms is represented among the few works dealing with Joshua, Judges, Ruth and 1-2 Samuel.

Of the works dealing specifically with these books, the most significant are the homilies of Origen. These are sermons on particular chapters or passages of Scripture that he delivered in various settings, particularly those connected with the teaching of the Christian faith to catechumens. By all accounts, Origen was a regular preacher over the course of his life. According to Pamphilus, his biographer, there were lengthy periods when he preached almost every day. Over the course of this activity, Origen left discourses and commentaries on nearly all the books of the Bible. Unfortunately, most of these have been lost. In fact, of the nearly six hundred that were produced, only twenty homilies on Jeremiah, one on 1 Samuel 28 and a few fragments are available in Greek. However, almost two hundred of these are available in various Latin translations, particularly from Rufinus and Jerome. Of particular relevance for this volume are the twenty-six homilies on Joshua that have been preserved in the Latin translation of Rufinus. These homilies constitute the only series of sermons on the book of Joshua and the only detailed exposition of it produced in the early church. In some cases, they provide the only available, extended discussions of the Fathers of some of the latter chapters. Hence, readers will notice a strong emphasis on these homilies in the extracts on Joshua, particularly in the latter portion of the book.

In addition to their significance as an extended commentary and treatment of the book of Joshua, these homilies also provide a significant demonstration of Origen's interpretive method. Of particular interest is the relationship that Origen draws between Joshua and Jesus. Since Joshua and Jesus are the same word in the Greek language, Origen assumes throughout his exposition that the name rendered *Jesu* by Rufinus refers not only to Joshua but also typologically to Jesus of Nazareth, allowing him to directly and explicitly connect the events concerning Israel and the conquest and division of the land narrated in the book with the Christian story of Jesus and the church. This sort of typological interpretation went on to become standard practice in the exegesis of the early church. In addition to the homilies on Joshua, Origen produced a series of homilies on Judges, of which we have nine in the translation of Rufinus, and 1 Samuel, of which we have only relatively small portions in Latin translation (with the notable exception of one on 1 Samuel 28, which is available in Greek). The only other series of homilies on the first five historical books of the Old Testament are eight from John Chrysostom dealing with figures and incidents from 1 Samuel, five on Hannah and three on David and Saul that were delivered in 387.

Procopius of Gaza offers a running commentary, more scattered at certain places, on the historical books in Greek, providing a number of textual and linguistic insights, as well as some insightful christological applications. There are also two full running commentaries on this material in Latin, both on 1 Samuel. The first, *Six Books on 1 Kings* (1-2 Samuel in the RSV are titled 1-2 Kings in the Septuagint, while 1-2 Kings are titled 3-4 Kings), is from Gregory the Great and provides an extensive and detailed exposition of the book in which he makes significant use of spiritual exegesis in order to demonstrate its relationship to the revelation of Christ and the Christian faith as well as to explain its significance for the situation of the contemporary church. The rich blend of theological, spiritual, pastoral and moral teaching provides an excellent example of Gregory's approach to exegesis. It also illustrates his significance as a biblical commentator who is one of the leading representatives of patristic interpretation and a seminal figure in the development of medieval exegesis in the Western church. The second, *Four Books on 1 Samuel* by Bede, is among his many works on biblical interpretation and, while less influential than the work of Gregory the Great, is nevertheless a fine and lucid example of biblical commentary in the Latin tradition of early Christian interpretation.

Other than these few examples of homilies and commentaries, the remaining works dealing with Joshua through 2 Samuel are from the question-and-answer genre. The first of these is from Augustine. In *Questions on the Heptateuch*,[6] he raises and attempts to solve various difficulties that he perceived in his reading of the text. Of the 651 questions he poses over the course of the work, 30 are related to Joshua and 55 to Judges and the majority of his comments on each of the questions consists of about one paragraph in length though sometimes they are a bit longer. He also wrote another work on the Heptateuch, *Seven Books of Expressions on the Heptateuch*, that contains a list of expressions and phrases that seemed problematic to him as well as a comparison of several Latin manuscripts of the Heptateuch. As with the volume of questions, he provides a brief explanation and resolution of the problems he identifies. Of the 735 he addresses, 31 are from Joshua and 64 are from Judges. Theodoret of Cyr (d. 466) and Bede produced similar works—*Questions on the Octateuch*[7] and *Thirty Questions on 1 Samuel* respectively—which contain discussions on various portions of Joshua through Samuel. In general, this material tends to be less interesting and helpful than other forms of commentary and has therefore been cited more sparingly than that from other works.

As can be seen, the number of works devoted to these books is quite small, and, apart from Origen's work, little is devoted to extended discussion and running detailed commentary. In addition to this situation regarding the paucity of specific works devoted to these books, the commentary of the Fathers on this portion of Scripture in other works tends to be uneven at best. While a significant amount of material can be found related to some of the more prominent and memorable portions of the biblical text, such as the story of Rahab and the confrontation of David and Goliath, comment concerning other more obscure events and passages is sparse or nonexistent. In other cases, one particular individual has provided extended commentary where others have been generally silent. The sporadic and uneven nature of the Fathers' comments on certain portions of Scripture has by necessity impinged on the shape of this volume. Hence, readers will find that at some points comment is abundant while at other places it is minimal or even absent, or that one particular individual dominates particular sections of the commentary. This should be viewed by readers as more reflective of the shape of patristic commentary rather than the preferences of the editor. Of course, the preferences and interests of the editor do play a part in the selection and presentation of material no matter the intention, but I hope that what is provided here is a representative sampling of the ways in which the Spirit of the living God has spoken to the ancient church through the witness of Holy Scripture to the gospel of Jesus Christ.

The Text of the Old Testament

Before concluding, we must comment briefly on the text of the Old Testament used by the early Christian interpreters as the basis for their commentary. The most influential version of the Old Testament was a Greek translation of the Hebrew Bible known as the Septuagint (LXX). The origins of this translation date to the third century B.C., when, according to an account contained in the *Letter of Aristeas* (second century B.C.) and to Jewish tradition, Ptolemy II (king of Egypt; d. 246 B.C.) wanted to have a translation of the Hebrew law for his library at Alexandria and engaged seventy-two Jewish translators from Jerusalem in order to complete the project. Eventually, this endeavor came to be associated with the entire Hebrew Bible. The prologue to the

---

[6]The Heptateuch is the first seven books of the Bible.
[7]The Octateuch is the first eight books of the Bible.

Greek version of Ecclesiasticus indicates that the whole canon was available in Greek by 132 B.C., but it is clear that the complete translation was produced over a considerable length of time.

This translation of the Hebrew Scriptures into Greek occasioned not only a new linguistic setting for the Bible but also its transference into a different world of thought in which concrete Hebrew expressions and ideas became abstract concepts in the Greek intellectual milieu. In addition to the establishment of new linguistic and intellectual contexts, the Septuagint differs from the Hebrew Bible in structural ways, such as in the order and division of the various books, in the order and inclusion of material within the books themselves, and in the addition of other books, known as the Apocrypha, which are not part of the Hebrew Bible.

The early Christian church inherited the Septuagint from the Jewish tradition as its own Bible. The writers of the New Testament commonly quoted the Old Testament from it, and the early Christian fathers generally regarded the Septuagint as the normative form of the Old Testament and rarely consulted the Hebrew text, believing that the Septuagint was inspired by God. The Christian adoption of the Septuagint, along with concerns that it was too free in its rendering of the Hebrew, led Jewish scholars to produce several other Greek translations that they regarded as more consonant with the Hebrew Bible. Thus, while the Septuagint was generally accepted as the standard form of the Old Testament, the Fathers were aware of these other versions and sometimes referred to them. Origen was particularly interested in the relationship of the Septuagint to the Hebrew text and the other Greek versions and produced the *Hexapla*, an important work of textual scholarship that set out in six columns the Hebrew text, a transliteration of it, three other Greek translations produced by Jewish scholars, and the Septuagint, along with an apparatus of signs and notations that served to identify the divergences of the Septuagint from the Hebrew text with respect to its additions and omissions.

Other versions of the Old Testament began to emerge later in the second century as Latin-speaking Christians began the task of translating the Septuagint into Latin. This occurred first in the provinces of southern Gaul and northern Africa, where the need for a vernacular translation was more acute than in Rome, where the use of Greek continued well into the third century. This need for translations of the Bible into Latin led to the production of several Old Latin versions that bore the distinct marks of their places of composition. These various Old Latin translations differed considerably from each other, and some of them provided evidence of a defective knowledge of Greek and sometimes even Latin. Until the fifth century, much of the commentary on Scripture in the Latin-speaking church is based on these differing Old Latin versions. The use of these translations created understandable problems in the Western church, and the desire to remedy the difficulties that arose from this situation led Jerome to produce a revision of the Latin Bible that became known as the Vulgate. Gradually, over a lengthy period of time from the late fourth century until the ninth, the Vulgate replaced the Old Latin versions and came to be viewed as the standard Bible in the Western church.

These developments help explain why the patristic commentary contained in this volume and throughout the Old Testament does not always follow the RSV text that is provided. The Fathers are commenting on the Septuagint, one of the Old Latin versions or the Vulgate. Contemporary translations such as the RSV are not based on any of these versions but rather on an iteration of the Hebrew text that was established and preserved by the Jewish Masoretes sometime between the fifth and ninth centuries. This version, know as the Masoretic text (MT), has come to be accepted as the definitive form of the Hebrew Bible. Throughout this volume, an attempt has been made to alert readers to the places where the patristic commentary included is based on texts that are accepted as Scripture by the church fathers but that differ from the Masoretic text and the corresponding translation of the RSV.

Acknowledgments and Dedication

In the compilation of this volume, I have had a great deal of help, apart from which the project would not have been completed. I would like to thank Joel Elowsky and the staff at the office for the Ancient Christian Commentary on Scripture Project. They engaged in digital and hardcopy searches, made photocopies of copious amounts of material, supplied important volumes related to the project and provided much appreciated support in the final preparation of the manuscript. All of this was done with a cheerful and generous spirit that was greatly appreciated in the midst of sorting out some of the editorial challenges associated with the project. I am particularly grateful for the assistance of Jeff Finch and James Kellerman, who provided Latin translations on short notice in the last stages of the project, and that of Chris Hall for his helpful editorial comments and observations on an initial draft of this manuscript. I would also like to express my thanks to Tom Oden for the invitation to edit this volume and for his unfailing support and encouragement since my days as one of his students at Drew University.

In addition, I would like to thank the board, administration and faculty of Biblical Theological Seminary in Hatfield, Pennsylvania, for their support of this project, particularly through the granting of a sabbatical from teaching responsibilities during the spring and summer of 2003.

All of the above have provided willing and generous assistance in the production of this volume and, indeed, have made it possible. However, pride of place in enabling the completion of this work goes to my former research assistant Linda Dietch, who is currently a doctoral candidate at Drew University. She did most of the data entry, organized material, tracked down references and checked the accuracy of entries and citations. Time and again her attention to detail saved the manuscript from inconsistencies and mistakes and has considerably strengthened the final product.

I would also like to express my appreciation to *Christian History* magazine for permission to include a portion of my article "Origen: Friend or Foe?" in this introduction. The full article appeared in issue 80 of the magazine.

Finally, I would like to thank Professor Elio Cuccaro, a teacher of the Christian faith at Nyack College, who first introduced me to the Fathers in a course during the spring semester of 1984 and instilled in me a strong desire to read and learn from them. For this, and for the gift of his friendship over the years, I gratefully dedicate this volume to him.

John R. Franke
Biblical Theological Seminary
Hatfield, Pennsylvania
July 2004

JOSHUA

1:1-9 THE LORD COMMISSIONS JOSHUA

¹After the death of Moses the servant of the LORD, the LORD said to Joshua the son of Nun, Moses' minister, ²"Moses my servant is dead; now therefore arise, go over this Jordan, you and all this people, into the land which I am giving to them, to the people of Israel. ³Every place that the sole of your foot will tread upon I have given to you, as I promised to Moses. ⁴From the wilderness and this Lebanon as far as the great river, the river Euphrates, all the land of the Hittites to the Great Sea toward the going down of the sun shall be your territory. ⁵No man shall be able to stand before you all the days of your life; as I was with Moses, so I will be with you; I will not fail you or forsake you. ⁶Be strong and of good courage; for you shall cause this people to inherit the land which I swore to their fathers to give them. ⁷Only be strong and very courageous, being careful to do according to all the law which Moses my servant commanded you; turn not from it to the right hand or to the left, that you may have good success wherever you go. ⁸This book of the law shall not depart out of your mouth, but you shall meditate on it day and night, that you may be careful to do according to all that is written in it; for then you shall make your way prosperous, and then you shall have good success. ⁹Have I not commanded you? Be strong and of good courage; be not frightened, neither be dismayed; for the LORD your God is with you wherever you go."

OVERVIEW: The Lord Jesus assumed power after the death of the law, which is prefigured by Joshua's succession of Moses (ORIGEN). Joshua's greatness resulted from his continual union with Moses (AMBROSE). Since Moses changed his name from Hoshea to "Jesus" (Joshua), he prefigured Christ by victoriously leading the Israelites into the promised land (LACTANTIUS, CHRYSOSTOM) and by ushering in the new law (LACTANTIUS).

Joshua was renowned, foremost, for his generalship in possessing and dividing the inheritance (GREGORY OF NAZIANZUS). Representing vices to be conquered, the land's pagan inhabitants must be removed in order to receive the fullness of the promised inheritance. By moving from the letter of the law to its spirit, which facilitates a mystical understanding of history, the journey to one's lofty inheritance is made (ORIGEN).

God's promise to never forsake or abandon should be relied upon—not money (AUGUSTINE). It also ensures that those who strive to draw near to God by subduing the passions will find the Lord's yoke easy (CLEMENT OF ALEXANDRIA). God's promise dispels the fear of just punishment for sins yet explains the presence of terrors and trials in this life (CHRYSOSTOM). God's presence offers protection from the enticements of the wicked (CASSIODORUS).

Being valiant brings deliverance (PACHOMIUS). Whether rich or poor, one should mind his own business and meditate on the oracles of God (APOSTOLIC CONSTITUTIONS). We must be zealous in learning sacred literature and in praying for it to be unveiled to us (ORIGEN). While the remembrance of God should be continual, limits are necessary for the discussion and discipline of theology (GREGORY OF NAZIANZUS).

1:1-2 The Lord Calls Joshua

THE DEATH OF THE LAW. ORIGEN: The book does not so much indicate to us the deeds of the son of Nun as it represents for us the mysteries of Jesus my Lord. For he himself is the one who assumes power after the death of Moses; he is the one who leads the army and fights against Amalek. What was foreshadowed there on the mountain by lifted hands[1] was the time when "he attaches [them] to his cross, triumphing over the principalities and powers on it."[2]

Thus Moses is dead; for the law has ceased, because "the law and the prophets extend only up to John."[3] Do you want me to bring forth proofs from the Scriptures that the law is called Moses? Hear what he says in the Gospel: "They have Moses and the prophets, let them listen to them."[4] Here, without any doubt, he calls the law Moses.

Therefore "Moses, the servant of God, is dead";[5] for the law is dead, and the legal precepts are now invalid. HOMILIES ON JOSHUA 1.3.[6]

MOSES' CONSTANT COMPANION. AMBROSE: Joshua the son of Nun became so great, because his union with Moses was the means not only of instructing him in a knowledge of the law but also of sanctifying him to receive grace. When in his tabernacle the majesty of the Lord was seen to shine forth in its divine Presence, Joshua alone was in the tabernacle. When Moses spoke with God, Joshua too was covered by the sacred cloud.[7] The priests and people stood below, and Joshua and Moses went up the mount to receive the law. All the people were within the camp; Joshua was without the camp in the tabernacle of witness. When the pillar of a cloud came down and God spoke with Moses, Joshua stood as a trusty servant beside him. He, a young man, did not go out of the tabernacle, though the old men who stood far off trembled at these divine wonders. DUTIES OF THE CLERGY 2.20.98.[8]

THE SUCCESSOR TO MOSES. LACTANTIUS: For the prophet does not speak this way: "And the Lord said to me," but to *Jesus* [Joshua],[9] in order to show that he was not speaking of himself but of Christ to whom God was then speaking. For that Jesus [Joshua] was a figure of Christ. Although he was first called Hoshea, Moses, foreseeing the future, ordered him to be called Joshua (or Jesus), so that, since he was selected leader of the soldiery against Amalek who was attacking the children of Israel, he might overcome the adversary through the figure of his name and lead the people into the land of promise.[10] And for this reason also he succeeded Moses, to show that the new law given through Jesus Christ would succeed the old law which was given through Moses. EPITOME OF THE DIVINE INSTITUTES 4.17.[11]

JOSHUA AS TYPE OF CHRIST. CHRYSOSTOM: The name of Jesus [Joshua] was a type. For this reason then, and because of the very name, the creation reverenced him. What then! Was no other person called Jesus [Joshua]? But this man was on this account so called as a type; for he used to be called Hoshea. Therefore the name was changed: for it was a prediction and a prophecy. He brought in the people into the promised land, as Jesus into heaven; not the law; since neither did Moses [enter the promised land] but remained outside. The law has not power to bring

---

[1]Ex 17:11. [2]Col 2:14-15. [3]Mt 11:13. [4]Lk 16:29. [5]Deut 34:5. [6]FC 105:29*. [7]Ex 24:12ff. [8]NPNF 2 10:58-59*. [9]Joshua and Jesus are the same word in the Greek language. Hence, the name Joshua is rendered "Jesus" in the LXX. Consequently, many Christian readers understood Joshua as a type of Christ. [10]Num 13:8, 16. [11]FC 49:289*.

in, but grace. Homilies on Hebrews 27.6.[12]

1:3-4 The Promise of Land

The Contribution of Joshua. Gregory of Nazianzus: What is the special excellence of Joshua? His generalship, and the distribution of the inheritance, and the taking possession of the Holy Land. On Basil the Great, Oration 43.72.[13]

On Conquering Vices. Origen: But let us consider what is promised to us in these words.

There are certain diabolical races of powerful adversaries against whom we wage a battle and against whom we struggle in this life. However many of these races we set under our feet, however many we conquer in battle, we shall seize their territories, their provinces and their realms, as Jesus our Lord apportions them to us. For they were once angels; they were glorified in the kingdom of God. Or do we not read that Isaiah says of one of them, "How did Lucifer fall, the one who rose in the morning?"[14] That Lucifer, without a doubt, had a throne in the heavens until he became a fugitive angel. If I should conquer him and set him under my feet, if I should deserve that the Lord Jesus "crush Satan under my feet,"[15] I shall be ready as a consequence to receive the place of Lucifer in heaven.

Thus we understand the promise to us from our Lord Jesus that "every place we set the soles of our feet"[16] will be ours. But let us not imagine that we may be able to enter into this inheritance yawning and drowsy, through ease and negligence. The wrath of his own race possesses the angel [Lucifer]. Unless you vanquish this [wrath] in yourself and cut off all violent impulses of anger and rage, you will not be able to claim as an inheritance the place that angel once had. For you will not expel him from the land of promise by your slothfulness. In like manner, some angels incite pride, jealousy, greed and lust and instigate these evil things. Unless you gain the mastery over their vices in yourself and exterminate them

from your land—which now through the grace of baptism has been sanctified—you will not receive the fullness of the promised inheritance. Homilies on Joshua 1.6.[17]

The Journey to Inheritance. Origen: What are the places we ascend with the soles of our feet? The letter of the law is placed on the ground and lies down below. On no occasion, then, does the one who follows the letter of the law ascend. But if you are able to rise from the letter to the spirit and also ascend from history to a higher understanding, then truly you have ascended the lofty and high place that you will receive from God as your inheritance. For if in these things that are written you perceive types and observe figures of heavenly things, and with reflection and intuitive feeling "you seek those things that are above, where Christ is sitting at the right hand of God,"[18] then you will receive this place as your inheritance. For our Lord and Savior says, "Where I am, there also will be my servant."[19]

If therefore you have arrived all the way to Christ, who sits at the right hand of God, by your faith, life, purity and virtue, and by those "soles of your feet"[20] that Jesus washed, you have approached that place. God will give it to you. Then not only "will you be made heirs of God" but also "co-heirs with Christ."[21] Homilies on Joshua 2.3.[22]

1:5 I Will Not Forsake You

God Will Provide. Augustine: Pay attention to what comes next: "Without love, a measure of money is sufficient for present needs,"[23] because he himself said, "'I will not forsake you, I will not desert you.'[24] You were afraid of I don't know what evils, for that reason you were saving up money; count me as your guarantor." That's

---

[12]NPNF 1 14:489*. [13]NPNF 2 7:420. [14]Is 14:12. [15]Rom 16:20. [16]Deut 11:24. [17]FC 105:33-34*. [18]Col 3:1. [19]Jn 12:26. [20]Jn 13:5. [21]Rom 8:17. [22]FC 105:39-40. [23]Cf. Heb 13:5. [24]Cf. Heb 13:5; Deut 31:6, 8.

what God says to you. It isn't a man, not your equal or you yourself, but God who says to you, "I will not forsake you, I will not desert you." If a man made such a promise, you would trust him; God makes it, and you hesitate? He made the promise, put it in writing, made out the bond; you needn't worry at all. Read what you've got in your hand, you're holding God's bond; as your debtor you hold the one whom you have asked to cancel your debts. SERMON 177.11.[25]

SELF-DISCIPLINE. CLEMENT OF ALEXANDRIA: We must join in disciplining ourselves to beware of all that is subject to the passions. We must, like true philosophers, escape from any foods that arouse sexual desire, from a dissolute relaxation in bed, from luxury and all the passions that make for luxury. We realize that others find this a grievous struggle. It is no longer so for us, since self-discipline is God's greatest gift. "He has said, 'I will never forsake you or abandon you,'" who has judged you worthy by a decision that is wholly genuine. In this way, as we carefully strive to go to him, the Lord's "easy yoke"[26] will receive us. STROMATEIS 2.20.126.[27]

FEAR NOT. CHRYSOSTOM: Nevertheless, I say, fear not. Paul comforts you saying, "God is faithful, who will not suffer you to be tempted above that which you are able, but will with the temptation also provide the way of escape, that you may be able to bear it."[28] He indeed himself has said, "I will never leave you or forsake you." For had he resolved to punish us in deed and in actual endurance, he would not have given us over to terror during so many days. For when he would not punish, he frightens; since if he were intending to punish, fear would be superfluous, and threatening superfluous. But now, we have sustained a life more grievous than countless deaths; fearing and trembling during so many days, and being suspicious of our very shadows; and paying the punishment of Cain;[29] and in the midst of our sleep, starting up, through constant agony of mind. So that if we have kindled God's wrath, we have

appeased him in the endurance of such a punishment. For if we have not paid the satisfaction due to our sins, yet it has been enough to satisfy the mercy of God. HOMILIES CONCERNING THE STATUES 6.3.[30]

GOD'S PRESENCE. CASSIODORUS: The fifth kindness follows, which is bestowed with true certainty on every really staunch Catholic. He means: "Even if I were to walk among heretics and schismatics" (they are rightly called the shadow of death since they have the form of death as they lead us to hell) "I will not fear their foul enticements, for you defend me with the protection of your presence." In the prophet's words: I will not leave you or forsake you; for in this world the church walks among the wicked, until he who separates the good from the evil shall come on judgment day. EXPOSITION OF THE PSALMS 22.4.[31]

1:6-9 Be Strong and Courageous

BE VALIANT. PACHOMIUS: Still, toss all pride far from your side, and be valiant. Look: when Joshua [son] of Nun was valiant, God delivered his enemies into his hands. If you are faint-hearted, you become a stranger to the law of God. Faintheartedness fills you with pretexts for laziness, mistrust and negligence, until you are destroyed. INSTRUCTIONS 21.[32]

CONTEMPLATE SCRIPTURE. APOSTOLIC CONSTITUTIONS: You should not be like a wanderer, rambling about the streets, without just cause, to spy out those who live wickedly. But by minding your own trade and employment, endeavor to do what is acceptable to God. And keeping in mind the oracles of Christ, meditate in the same continually. For so the Scripture says to you: "You shall meditate in his law day and night; when you walk in the field, and when you sit in your house,

---

[25]*WSA* 3 5:287-88. [26]Mt 11:30. [27]FC 85:239-40. [28]1 Cor 10:13. [29]Gen 4:11-12. [30]NPNF 1 9:382*. [31]ACW 51:237*. [32]CS 47:21.

and when you lie down, and when you rise up, that you may have understanding in all things."[33] No, although you are rich and so do not want a trade for your maintenance, don't be one that wonders and walks around at random; but either go to some that are believers, and of the same religion, and confer and discourse with them about the lively oracles of God. Or if you stay at home, read the books of the Law, of the Kings, with the Prophets; sing the hymns of David; and peruse diligently the gospel, which is the completion of the other. Constitutions of the Holy Apostles 1.2.4-5.[34]

Prayerful Meditation. Origen: I fear, however, lest by too much negligence and dullness of heart the divine volumes be not only veiled to us but also sealed, so that "if a book should be put into the hands of a man who cannot read, he would say, 'I cannot read'; if it should be put into the hands of a man who can read, he would say, 'It is sealed.'"[35] Whence it is shown that we must not only employ zeal to learn the sacred literature, but we must also pray to the Lord and entreat "day and night"[36] that the lamb "of the tribe of Judah" may come and himself taking "the sealed book" may deign to open it.[37] Homilies on Exodus 12.4.[38]

Limits for Theology. Gregory of Nazianzus: What aspects of theology should be investigated, and to what limit? Only aspects within our grasp, and only to the limit of the experience and capacity of our audience. Just as excess of sound or food injures the hearing or general health, or, if you prefer, as loads that are too heavy injure those who carry them, or as excessive rain harms the soil, we too must guard against the danger that the toughness, so to speak, of our discourses may so oppress and overtax our hearers as actually to impair the powers they had before.

Yet I am not maintaining that we ought not to be mindful of God at all times. My adversaries, ever ready and quick to attack, need not pounce on me again. It is more important that we should remember God than that we should breathe: indeed, if one may say so, we should do nothing else besides. I am one of those who approve the precept that commands us to "meditate day and night,"[39] to tell of the Lord "evening, and morning, and at noon,"[40] and to "bless the Lord at all times,"[41] or in the words of Moses, "when we lie down, when we rise up, when we walk by the way,"[42] or when we do anything else whatever, and by this mindfulness be molded to purity. So it is not continual remembrance of God I seek to discourage, but continual discussion of theology. I am not opposed either to theology, as if it were a breach of piety, but only to its untimely practice, nor to instruction in theology, except when this goes to excess. Fullness and surfeit even of honey, for all its goodness, produces vomiting;[43] and "to everything there is a season,"[44] as Solomon said I think, and "what's well is not well if the hour be ill." A flower is completely out of season in winter, a man's clothing is out of place on a woman, a woman's on a man. Immoderate laughter is unseemly during mourning, as are tears at a drinking party. Are we then to neglect "the due season" only in the discussion of theology, where observing the proper time is of such supreme importance? Theological Orations 1 (27).3-4.[45]

---

[33]Deut 6:7. [34]ANF 7:393*. [35]Is 29:11-12. [36]See Ps 1:2. [37]See Rev 5:5. [38]FC 71:372*. [39]Ps 1:2. [40]Ps 55:17 (54:17 LXX). [41]Ps 34:1 (33:1 LXX). [42]Deut 6:7. [43]See Prov 25:16. [44]Eccles 3:1. [45]FGFR 218-19*.

1:10-18 JOSHUA COMMANDS THE TRIBES

¹⁰Then Joshua commanded the officers of the people, ¹¹"Pass through the camp, and command the people, 'Prepare your provisions; for within three days you are to pass over this Jordan, to go in to take possession of the land which the LORD your God gives you to possess.'"

¹²And to the Reubenites, the Gadites, and the half-tribe of Manasseh Joshua said, ¹³"Remember the word which Moses the servant of the LORD commanded you, saying, 'The LORD your God is providing you a place of rest, and will give you this land.' ¹⁴Your wives, your little ones, and your cattle shall remain in the land which Moses gave you beyond the Jordan; but all the men of valor among you shall pass over armed before your brethren and shall help them, ¹⁵until the LORD gives rest to your brethren as well as to you, and they also take possession of the land which the LORD your God is giving them; then you shall return to the land of your possession, and shall possess it, the land which Moses the servant of the LORD gave you beyond the Jordan toward the sunrise."

OVERVIEW: As Joshua commands the people to prepare food for the three-day journey to enter the land they are to possess, the mystery of the Trinity and the sacrament of baptism are signified. To follow the Lord into the promised land, the food of good works is needed for the journey (CAESARIUS OF ARLES). The inheritances determined through Moses and Joshua represent two groups: those who are firstborn according to nature and those who receive the blessing through grace. Strong men, who signify defenders of the truth, go out into the battle, while the infants and women, who signify those who are silent and weak, offer us no aid in the fight (ORIGEN).

1:10-11 Joshua Commands the Officers

THE MYSTERY OF THE TRINITY. CAESARIUS OF ARLES: At the death of Moses, Joshua received the rule; and when the law ended, our true Lord Jesus obtained the rule of the whole world. Therefore, Joshua who typified the Lord said to the people when he came to the Jordan: "Prepare your provisions until the third day." The third day, dearly beloved, we recognize as the mystery of the Trinity. What food should we prepare so that we may come to the third day? It seems to me

that this food should be understood as faith; for Christians it is by faith that they believe in the Trinity and arrive at the sacrament of baptism. Therefore, what Joshua then told his people, the true Joshua or Jesus now tells the Christian people through his ministers. Indeed, what else does this mean: "Prepare your provisions until the third day," except to receive the mystery of the Trinity? After this the Jordan was crossed just as if the mystery of baptism were completed, and the people of Israel entered the promised land. It is true, brothers; unless a person crosses through the sacrament of baptism, he will not see the land of true promise, that is, eternal beatitude. SERMON 115.1.[1]

THE FOOD OF GOOD WORKS. CAESARIUS OF ARLES: For this reason Joshua said to the people, "Prepare your provisions for the journey." Today, if you willingly listen, Christ our Lord says to you, "If you will follow me, prepare food for the journey." This food is good works which accompany us like faithful food for the journey to future bliss. Therefore, consider, brothers, that if each one does not prepare food for himself, he cannot

[1]FC 47:167*.

follow Joshua when he enters the land of promise. Sermon 116.2.[2]

1:12-15 A Reminder of Moses' Words

Inheritance of the Firstborn. Origen: Let us look closely at what sign those two and a half tribes hold who receive the land of inheritance through Moses, and what sign the remainder of the nine and a half tribes hold who receive the promise of the holy land through Jesus [Joshua].

First of all, I think it is impossible for it to have happened accidentally that those who receive a portion through Moses were all firstborn. For Reuben was the firstborn of Leah;[3] Gad, the firstborn of Zilpah;[4] and Manasseh, the firstborn of Asenath the Egyptian whom Joseph married, the daughter of Potiphar the priest of Heliopolis.[5] For myself, I can never be persuaded that it was by chance that the firstborn were the only ones whose inheritance was determined through Moses. Rather, I believe that in these things the design of two groups of people was already foreshadowed at that time: One would seem to be the firstborn according to the order of nature; the other, the people who would receive the blessing of their inheritance through faith and grace. Homilies on Joshua 3.1.[6]

Assistance in the Battle. Origen: Rest is not given first to those who through Moses receive the inheritance—that is, those who pleased God through the law—unless they assist their brothers in the battles. Only women and infants receive rest through Moses. The others do not rest but go out to the aid of their brothers. . . .

Thus those who are strong men, their loins armed and girded with truth, go forth to our aid and fight with us. But "infants and women" do not go out to our battle. This is not an astonishing thing, for an infant is said to be one who does not speak. How is a person able to assist me who has spoken nothing, the one of whom I discover nothing that I may read, the one who does not instruct me by a word? But the apostle says that a woman is a "weak vessel."[7] Suitably, therefore, a weak vessel does not come to the conflict lest it be broken in pieces and destroyed. For concerning our Lord Jesus, it is also said in the Gospels that "he did not break a bruised reed."[8] Homilies on Joshua 3.1.[9]

---

[2]FC 47:172-73*. [3]Gen 29:32. [4]Gen 30:10-11. [5]Gen 41:50. [6]FC 105:41-42. [7]1 Pet 3:7. [8]Mt 12:20. [9]FC 105:42-43.

2:1-7 RAHAB HIDES THE SPIES

[1]*And Joshua the son of Nun sent two men secretly from Shittim as spies, saying, "Go, view the land, especially Jericho." And they went, and came into the house of a harlot whose name was Rahab, and lodged there.* [2]*And it was told the king of Jericho, "Behold, certain men of Israel have come here tonight to search out the land."* [3]*Then the king of Jericho sent to Rahab, saying, "Bring forth the men that have come to you, who entered your house; for they have come to search out all the land."* [4]*But the woman had taken the two men and hidden them; and she said, "True, men came to me, but I did not know where they came from;* [5]*and when the gate was to be closed, at*

dark, the men went out; where the men went I do not know; pursue them quickly, for you will overtake them." ⁶But she had brought them up to the roof, and hid them with the stalks of flax which she had laid in order on the roof. ⁷So the men pursued after them on the way to the Jordan as far as the fords; and as soon as the pursuers had gone out, the gate was shut.

OVERVIEW: The historical account of Joshua's sending of two spies was visibly fulfilled through John the Baptist, God's messenger, who preached repentance to prostitutes and publicans (ORIGEN). According to another interpretation, this event spiritually signifies Jesus' sending of two messengers, Peter and Paul, in order to lead his people into the gospel (JEROME). Still another interpretation maintains that the two spies symbolize two commands: to love God and neighbor (CAESARIUS OF ARLES). By receiving the spies, Rahab prefigures the church: the harlot was no longer a prostitute, as we are not in our own hearts when we cease to live according to the flesh (ORIGEN, GREGORY OF ELVIRA). As her name means "pride," Rahab typifies the church, which transforms the prideful into the humble (JEROME, CASSIODORUS). Rahab's lie, like all lies, is unjust. It is her benevolence and not her deception that is rewarded (AUGUSTINE). Scripture recalls Rahab's immorality. Yet it is for her lie that she is found deserving of eternal blessing (CASSIAN). Her repentance and faith, demonstrated by her lie that safeguarded the sacred, ensured her salvation. Even more so will ours (CHRYSOSTOM). She hid the spies on the roof, signifying the loftiness of her faith, and covered them with flax, in order that it would be purified (JEROME).

2:1-2 Joshua Sends Out Spies

MESSENGERS OF GOD. ORIGEN: Meanwhile, the spies are sent by Jesus [Joshua] to Jericho and are received by the prostitute Rahab. Those spies, who are sent before the face of Jesus [Joshua], can also be considered the messengers of God, just as it is written, "Behold, I send my messenger before your face who will prepare your paths."[1] This passage, fulfilled invisibly through others,

was fulfilled visibly through John, about whom this was also written. Because the scribes and Pharisees did not believe him, the Lord spoke concerning the baptism of John and said that the "prostitutes and publicans who believed"[2] were baptized. The same thing is fulfilled in the fact that the prostitute received the spies of Jesus [Joshua] and is snatched away and brought back from the destruction of every hostile nation. HOMILIES ON JOSHUA 3.3.[3]

THE TWO MESSENGERS. JEROME: We have been following so far the historical interpretation, and you perceive how from the history itself we are ascending upward gradually to a mystical understanding. Jesus [Joshua], the leader, who had led the people out of Egypt; Jesus [Joshua], whose name means Savior, after the death and burial of Moses in the land of Moab in the land of Arabia— that is, after the law was dead—Jesus desires to lead his people into the gospel and sends out two men on secret mission to Jericho. Two messengers he sends: one to the circumcised; the other to the Gentiles, Peter and Paul. Jericho seeks to kill them; the harlot takes them in, meaning, of course, the church gathered together from the Gentiles. HOMILIES ON THE PSALMS 18 (Ps 86).[4]

TWO COMMANDS. CAESARIUS OF ARLES: Moreover, Joshua sends two spies to the city of Jericho, and they are received by a harlot. Joshua sent two spies because the true Joshua was going to give two commands of love. In truth, what else do the men whom the true Joshua sends announce to us except that we should love God and our neighbor? SERMON 115.2.[5]

---

[1]Mt 11:10; Mk 1:2. [2]Mt 21:32. [3]FC 105:46-47. [4]FC 48:138.
[5]FC 47:167-68*.

NO LONGER A PROSTITUTE. ORIGEN: Nevertheless, our Jesus [Joshua] sends spies to the king of Jericho, and they are received hospitably by a prostitute. But the prostitute who received the spies sent by Jesus [Joshua] was no longer a prostitute since she received them. Indeed, everyone of us was a prostitute in his heart as long as he lived according to the desires and lusts of the flesh. HOMILIES ON JOSHUA 1.4.[6]

THE PROSTITUTE VIEWED FROM SALVATION HISTORY. GREGORY OF ELVIRA: "And Joshua the son of Nun," it says, "sent two spies from Shittim, saying to them 'Go up and survey the land and Jericho.' When they arrived in Jericho, the two young men entered the house of a prostitute by the name of Rahab and stayed there as guests." Pay attention to the structure of this mystery, most beloved brothers, and ask yourselves why men as great as these, for whom the Lord had performed such marvels and miracles, entered the house of a woman of ill repute, as if they were unable to lodge elsewhere. They did this not by chance, I believe, but intentionally by prophetic design. For I find this prostitute in many places, not only as a hostess of saints but also as their bride. The most holy prophet Hosea, for instance, was commanded by the Lord to accept a harlot as his wife: "For the Lord said to me, 'Take for your wife a prostitute and generate children of prostitution.'"[7] Even our Lord and Savior himself, when he had sat down by the well in Samaria, conversed with an immoral woman to whom no one had previously spoken there. After he said to her, "You have had five husbands and the one you have now is not your husband,"[8] she believed that he was the Messiah, that is, she confessed him to be the Christ. Then there was the harlot who washed the Savior's feet with her tears and wiped them with her hair and anointed them while kissing them.[9] Let us see, therefore, what our hostess represents. This Rahab, although she is called a prostitute, nevertheless is a sign of the virgin church, considered as a foreshadow of the coming realities at the end of the age, where she alone is preserved to life among all who are perishing. For even when it was said to the prophet Hosea, "Take for your wife a prostitute," surely then the image of the church as coming from the Gentiles was being prefigured, given that the people were to be gathered from the harlotry of the nations and from prostitution with idols, for, it says, "they prostituted themselves to strange gods."[10] Indeed, she is called "the church" because the Greek word *ecclesia* means "gathering of the people." And just as the apostle says, "An unfaithful wife is sanctified through her faithful husband,"[11] so also is the church, coming from the infidelity of the Gentiles and prostitution with idols, sanctified through the body of Christ, of which we are members, as we learn from the same apostolic author.[12] Because the church, as I have often said, gathered from the multitude of Gentiles, was then called a prostitute, therefore the church is found in the figure of Rahab, the hostess of saints. ORIGEN'S TRACTATES ON THE BOOKS OF HOLY SCRIPTURE 12.[13]

RAHAB'S NAME. JEROME: Rahab; what is the force of her name? We have been following the historical sense; let us now reflect upon the anagogic[14] significance of the name. Rahab thus admits of two interpretations: the name may imply either a "broad space" or, better, "pride." Consider, therefore, its impact. She who formerly walked the broad, spacious road to death,[15] she whose pride was driving her to destruction, was later converted unto humility. HOMILIES ON THE PSALMS 18 (Ps 86).[16]

RAHAB THE PROUD. CASSIODORUS: Rahab was a harlot who secretly admitted the spies of Joshua when they visited Jericho and let them out by another exit so that they should not be captured. Her name means "pride." She was converted by

---

[6]FC 105:31.　[7]Hos 1:2.　[8]Jn 4:18.　[9]See Lk 7:37-47.　[10]Deut 31:16.　[11]1 Cor 7:14.　[12]See Rom 12:5; 1 Cor 6:15; 1 Cor 12.　[13]CCL 69:91-92.　[14]"Leading upward" toward heaven and the age to come.　[15]Mt 7:13.　[16]FC 48:139.

God's generosity and deserved to obtain mercy. She is a type of the church, which takes in souls endangered by the vice of pride, and lets them out into life by another route, the way of humility and patience. Exposition of the Psalms 86.4.[17]

2:3-5 Rahab Lies to the King of Jericho

Her Mercy, Not Her Lying, Is Rewarded. Augustine: Therefore, no lie is just. Accordingly, when examples of lying are proposed to us from the sacred Scriptures, either they are not lies but are thought so for not being understood, or, if they are lies, they are not to be imitated because they cannot be just.

As for its being written that God dealt well with the Hebrew midwives[18] and with Rahab the harlot of Jericho, he did not deal well with them because they lied but because they were merciful to the men of God. And so, it was not their deception that was rewarded, but their benevolence; the benignity of their intention, not the iniquity of their invention. Against Lying 15.31-32.[19]

Through Deception Ironically Came Blessing. John Cassian: This was the case with Rahab. Scripture not only recalls nothing virtuous about her but even speaks of her immorality. Yet for her lie alone, whereby she chose to conceal the spies rather than betray them, she deserved to share an eternal blessing with the people of God. If she had chosen to speak the truth or to be concerned for the safety of her people, there is no doubt that she and her whole household would not have escaped the approaching destruction and that she would not have deserved to be included among those responsible for the Lord's birth, to be numbered on the roll of the patriarchs, and, through her offspring, to beget the Savior of all.[20] Conference 17.17.1-2.[21]

Rahab's Salvation Assures Ours. Chrysostom: "By faith Rahab the prostitute did not perish with those who were disobedient, having

received the spies, but she directed their departure by another road."[22] And pay attention to how much wisdom she blended with her prudence. When those sent by the king came and requested the spies, they ask her, "Did men enter in here and come near you?" She answers them, "Yes, they entered in." First she builds the truth, and then she applies the lie on top. For no lie like this becomes believable unless it first reveals the truth. For this reason all who tell lies probably to be believed, first speak of truths and reveal confessions and later add the lies and things which are questionable. "Spies entered in here and came near you?" "Yes," she says. If she had said "no" from the beginning, she would have challenged the messengers to investigate. However, "they entered in," she says, "and they came out and escaped by such and such a road. Pursue them and you will capture them." O this good lie! O this good fraud, which does not betray the divine but safeguards the sacred! When the mouths of saints preach the repentance that made Rahab worthy of such salvation, for example, Joshua the son of Nun, who shouts in the desert, "Let Rahab the prostitute live"; and Paul, who says, "By faith Rahab the prostitute did not perish with those who were disobedient,"[23] will we not receive salvation even more so when we offer to God our repentance? Homilies on Repentance and Almsgiving 7.5.17.[24]

2:6 Rahab Hides the Spies Under Flax Stalks

Flax Symbolizes Purity, Having Been Broken, Twisted and Washed. Jerome: "I will be mindful of Rahab," of Rahab, that harlot who lodged Jesus' [Joshua's] secret agents, who lived in Jericho where Jesus [Joshua] had come and had dispatched the two spies. Jericho, that collapsed in seven days, is a type of this world, and as such is determined to kill the secret agents. Because, therefore, Jericho is bent upon

---

[17]ACW 52:338-39. [18]See Ex 1:17-20. [19]FC 16:165. [20]Mt 1:5. [21]ACW 57:595. [22]Heb 11:31. [23]Heb 11:31. [24]FC 96:100-101.

killing the spies, Rahab, the harlot, alone received them, lodged them not on the ground floor but in the upper story of the roof—or, in other words, in the sublimity of her faith. She hid them under her stalks of flax. . . .

She believes in Jesus, and those whom Jericho is determined to destroy she protects in safety on her own roof. She harbors them on the roof—in the loftiness of her faith—and hides them under the stems of flax. Even though she is a harlot, she covers them with flax.

Flax with much labor and care becomes of dazzling whiteness. You yourselves know that flax grows from the soil and that when it has come

forth from the ground, it is black; it has no beauty; it has no use. First, it is pulled up from the ground, broken, then twisted, afterwards washed. Next, it is pounded; finally, combed, and after so much care and hard work, it finally becomes white. Here, then, is the meaning: this harlot took the messengers in and covered them with her flax so that these agents might turn her flax into dazzling whiteness. HOMILIES ON THE PSALMS 18 (Ps 86).[25]

---

[25]FC 48:138-39.

2:8-14 THE FAITH OF RAHAB

[8]*Before they lay down, she came up to them on the roof, [9]and said to the men, "I know that the LORD has given you the land, and that the fear of you has fallen upon us, and that all the inhabitants of the land melt away before you. [10]For we have heard how the LORD dried up the water of the Red Sea before you when you came out of Egypt, and what you did to the two kings of the Amorites that were beyond the Jordan, to Sihon and Og, whom you utterly destroyed. [11]And as soon as we heard it, our hearts melted, and there was no courage left in any man, because of you; for the LORD your God is he who is God in heaven above and on earth beneath. [12]Now then, swear to me by the LORD that as I have dealt kindly with you, you also will deal kindly with my father's house, and give me a sure sign, [13]and save alive my father and mother, my brothers and sisters, and all who belong to them, and deliver our lives from death." [14]And the men said to her, "Our life for yours! If you do not tell this business of ours, then we will deal kindly and faithfully with you when the LORD gives us the land."*

OVERVIEW: By abandoning her own beliefs and confessing God's work on Israel's behalf, Rahab demonstrates that God selected one race to call all others (THEODORET). She prefigures the church, which was once a harlot but later received Jesus' messengers, the apostles (CHRYSOSTOM). That she could be forgiven of her

fornication through repentance shows that salvation is not withheld from any who would repent (CYRIL OF JERUSALEM). Rahab's faith and prophecy are noted in her actions and words (CLEMENT OF ROME).

2:8-11 Rahab Confesses Fear of the Lord

All Races Called Through Israel. Theodoret of Cyr: For he selected this one nation to teach the knowledge of God to all the others. Just as he had selected one man—at one time Moses, at another Joshua, at another Samuel, at another some other of the prophets—to look after the welfare of this race, one man who benefited his fellows by practicing true wisdom, so through the one race, Israel, he called all the races of the earth that shared the same nature to share the same religion. Rahab, the harlot, testifies that this is so. Though she belonged to a different race and was a harlot, she relied solely on their reputation, accepted their religion, abandoned her own beliefs and entrusted herself to strangers. "We have heard," she said, "what things the Lord your God has done to the Egyptians, and fear of you fell on us." Accordingly, she made a pact with the spies and sealed it with an oath. On Divine Providence 10.49.[1]

Rahab Prefigures the Church. Chrysostom: Do you see how with faith she takes on her lips the word of the Lawgiver? "And I realize that your God is up in heaven and down on the earth, and that apart from him there is no God." Rahab is a prefiguration of the church, which was at one time mixed up in the prostitution of the demons and which now accepts the spies of Christ, not the ones sent by Joshua the son of Nun, but the apostles who were sent by Jesus the true Savior. "I learned," she says, "that your God is up in heaven and down on the earth, and that apart from him there is no God." The Jews received these things and did not safeguard them; the church heard these things and preserved them. Therefore, Rahab, the prefiguration of the church, is worthy of all praise. Homilies on Repentance and Almsgiving 7.5.16.[2]

Repentance Procures Salvation. Cyril of Jerusalem: Pass now, pray, to the others who were saved by repentance. Perhaps even among the women someone will say, "I have committed fornication and adultery. I have defiled my body

with every excess. Can there be salvation for me?" Fix your eyes, woman, upon Rahab, and look for salvation for yourself too. For if she who openly and publicly practiced fornication was saved through repentance, will not she whose fornication preceded the gift of grace be saved by repentance and fasting? For observe how she was saved. She said only this: "Since the Lord, your God, is God in heaven above and on earth below." "Your God," she said, for she did not dare call him her God, because of her wantonness. If you want scriptural testimony of her salvation, you have it recorded in the Psalms: "I will think of Rahab and Babylon among those who know me."[3] The salvation procured by repentance is open to men and women alike. Catechetical Lectures 2.9.[4]

2:12-14 Rahab Asks for a Pledge

Rahab's Faith and Prophecy. Clement of Rome: For her faith and hospitality Rahab the harlot was saved. For when the spies were sent forth into Jericho by Joshua the son of Nun, the king of the land perceived that they were coming to spy out his country, and [he] sent forth men to seize them, that being seized they might be put to death. So the hospitable Rahab received them and hid them in the upper chamber under the flax stalks. And when the messengers of the king came near and said, "The spies of our land entered into your house; bring them forth, for the king so orders," then she answered, "The men truly, whom you seek, came to me, but they departed immediately and are journeying on the way"; and she pointed out to them the opposite road. And she said to the men, "Without a doubt I perceive that the Lord your God will deliver this city to you; for the fear and the dread of you is fallen upon its inhabitants. When therefore it shall come to pass that you take it, save me and the house of my father." And they said to her, "It shall be even so as you have spoken to us. Therefore, when you per-

---

[1]ACW 49:150*. [2]FC 96:99-100. [3]Ps 87:4 (86:4 LXX). [4]FC 61:100-101.

ceive that we are coming, you shall gather all your folk beneath your roof, and they shall be saved; for as many as shall be found outside of the house shall perish." And moreover they gave her a sign, that she should hang out from her house a scarlet thread, thereby showing beforehand that through

the blood of the Lord there shall be redemption for all them that believe and hope on God. You see, dearly beloved, not only faith, but prophecy, is found in the woman. 1 CLEMENT 12.[5]

---

[5]AF 18*.

2:15-24 THE SPIES ESCAPE JERICHO

[15]*Then she let them down by a rope through the window, for her house was built into the city wall, so that she dwelt in the wall.* [16]*And she said to them, "Go into the hills, lest the pursuers meet you; and hide yourselves there three days, until the pursuers have returned; then afterward you may go your way."* [17]*The men said to her, "We will be guiltless with respect to this oath of yours which you have made us swear.* [18]*Behold, when we come into the land, you shall bind this scarlet cord in the window through which you let us down; and you shall gather into your house your father and mother, your brothers, and all your father's household.* [19]*If any one goes out of the doors of your house into the street, his blood shall be upon his head, and we shall be guiltless; but if a hand is laid upon any one who is with you in the house, his blood shall be on our head.* [20]*But if you tell this business of ours, then we shall be guiltless with respect to your oath which you have made us swear."* [21]*And she said, "According to your words, so be it." Then she sent them away, and they departed; and she bound the scarlet cord in the window.*

OVERVIEW: Rahab's words to the spies speak deeper truths of Christ and the rigor of the church's journey (JEROME). That all were to be gathered into one house for salvation is a figure for the church, outside of which no one is saved (ORIGEN, CYPRIAN). The scarlet cord she bound in the window was a sign of her faith (AMBROSE) that mystically represented the shedding of the Lord's blood (AMBROSE, JEROME, ORIGEN). The window, which illumines the house with adequate light, anticipates the incarnation, which allows us to behold, in part, the splendor of Christ's divinity (ORIGEN).

2:16 Hide Yourselves in the Hills

WAIT THREE DAYS. JEROME: She counsels them and says, "Wait here for three days." Not one day does she specify, nor two days, but definitely three days. Notice what she says: "Wait three days." She does not designate three nights but three days, for hers was an enlightened heart. Then she says, and after three days—but what does she say? "Do not go through the open plains," she warns, "but go up the mountain way." The faith of the church is not laid in the valleys but is established on the mountains. Later, indeed, Jericho is overthrown, but this harlot alone is preserved untouched; hence, the Lord says, "I will be mindful of Rahab"; that is, on the day of judgment, I will be mindful of her who welcomes my messengers. Homilies on the Psalms 18 (Ps 86).[1]

2:17-20 *The Oath of the Spies*

The House of Salvation. Origen: Also this commandment is given to the person who was once a prostitute: "All," it says, "who will be found in your house will be saved. But concerning those who go out from the house, we ourselves are free of them by your oath." Therefore, if anyone wants to be saved, let him come into the house of this one who was once a prostitute. Even if anyone from that people wants to be saved, let him come in order to be able to attain salvation. Let him come to this house in which the blood of Christ is the sign of redemption. For among those who said, "His blood be upon us and upon our children,"[2] the blood of Christ is for condemnation. For Jesus had been appointed "for the ruin and the resurrection of many."[3] Therefore, for those refuting his sign, his blood effects punishment; for those who believe, salvation.

Let no one persuade himself, let no one deceive himself. Outside this house, that is, outside the church, no one is saved. If anyone goes outside, he is responsible for his own death. This is the significance of the blood, for this is also the purification that is manifest through the blood. Homilies on Joshua 3.5.[4]

One House, the Church. Cyprian: Rahab, who also was a type of the church, expresses the same truth. The command given to her ran: "You shall gather to yourself into your house, your father, and your mother, and your brothers, and all your father's household; and whosoever shall go out of the doors of your house into the street, his blood shall be upon his head." This figure declares that all who are to live and escape the destruction of the world must be gathered into one house alone, the church, while if any of the gathered goes outside, that is, if anyone who once obtained grace in the church nevertheless abandons the church, his blood will be upon his head, that is, he will have himself to blame for his damnation. Letter 69.4.[5]

2:21 *She Bound the Scarlet Cord*

A Sign of Faith. Ambrose: A harlot saw this; and she who in the destruction of the city lost all hope of any means of safety, because her faith had conquered, bound a scarlet thread in her window, and thus uplifted a sign of her faith and the banner of the Lord's passion; so that the semblance of the mystic blood, which should redeem the world, might be in memory. So, from outside the city, the name of Joshua was a sign of victory to those who fought. From within, the semblance of the Lord's passion was a sign of salvation to those in danger. On the Christian Faith 5.10.127.[6]

A Scarlet Cord. Jerome: So, too, with a mystic reference to the shedding of blood, it was a scarlet cord which the harlot Rahab (a type of the church) hung in her window that she might be saved at the destruction of Jericho. Letter 52.3.[7]

The Sign of Blood. Origen: She herself puts the scarlet-colored sign in her house, through which she is bound to be saved from the destruction of the city. No other sign would have been accepted, except the scarlet-colored one that carried the sign of blood. For she knew there was no salvation for anyone except in the blood of Christ. Homilies on Joshua 3.5.[8]

The Window a Figure of the Incarnation. Origen: In that the sign hangs in a window I think this is indicated: A window is that which illumines the house and through which we receive light, not wholly but enough, enough to suffice for the eye and for our vision. Even the incarnation of the Savior did not give us pure

---

[1]FC 48:139. [2]Mt 27:25. [3]Lk 2:34. [4]FC 105:49-50. [5]LCC 5:152*. [6]NPNF 2 10:300*. [7]LCC 5:318. [8]FC 105:49.

wine and the whole aspect of divinity, but through his incarnation, just as through the window, he makes us behold the splendor of the divinity. For that reason, so it seems to me, the

sign of salvation was given through a window. HOMILIES ON JOSHUA 3.5.[9]

[9]FC 105:50.

3:1-6 ISRAEL PREPARES TO CROSS THE JORDAN

[1]*Early in the morning Joshua rose and set out from Shittim, with all the people of Israel; and they came to the Jordan, and lodged there before they passed over.* [2]*At the end of three days the officers went through the camp* [3]*and commanded the people, "When you see the ark of the covenant of the* LORD *your God being carried by the Levitical priests, then you shall set out from your place and follow it,* [4]*that you may know the way you shall go, for you have not passed this way before. Yet there shall be a space between you and it, a distance of about two thousand cubits; do not come near it."* [5]*And Joshua said to the people, "Sanctify yourselves; for tomorrow the* LORD *will do wonders among you."* [6]*And Joshua said to the priests, "Take up the ark of the covenant, and pass on before the people." And they took up the ark of the covenant, and went before the people.*

OVERVIEW: Joshua is recognized as a type of Christ in beginning his rule at the Jordan, appointing the twelve and collapsing the walls of Jericho (CYRIL OF JERUSALEM). As savior he led the people of Israel out of Egypt into the land of promise (JEROME). Although blessed to be very close to God, the priests and Levites do work that is tested by the fire of God's presence. True priests do not simply bear a religious title but are those who "carry the law of God" by doing what it says and living holy lives. Entrusted with bearing the ark, the priests lead the procession across the Jordan, thereby signifying their responsibility to enlighten the people concerning God's commands. The crossing of the Jordan bears baptismal significance. Joshua's sweet and fresh gospel proclamation succeeds Moses' briny and bitter dispensation through the law (ORIGEN).

3:1 Israel Comes to the Jordan

A TYPE OF CHRIST. CYRIL OF JERUSALEM: But Jesus [Joshua], son of Nave [Nun], was a type of him in many things; for when he began to rule the people, he began from the Jordan; thence also did Christ begin to preach the gospel after he was baptized.[1] The son of Nave [Nun] appoints the twelve to divide the inheritance;[2] and Jesus sends forth the twelve apostles, heralds of truth, into the whole world.[3] He who was the type saved Rahab, the harlot, who had believed;[4] the true Jesus . . . says, Behold: "the publicans and the harlots are entering the kingdom of God before you."[5] With but a shout, the walls of Jericho collapsed in the time of the type;[6] and because of these words of Jesus, "There will not be left here one stone upon another,"[7] the temple of the Jews just opposite us is fallen; not that this sentence

[1]Mt 3:13. [2]Josh 14:1. [3]Mt 10:5. [4]Josh 6:25; Heb 11:31. [5]Mt 21:31. [6]Josh 6:20. [7]Mt 24:2.

was the cause of its ruin, but rather the sin of the transgressors. Catechetical Lectures 10.11.[8]

Joshua the Savior. Jerome: I will pass to Joshua the son of Nun, who was previously called Ause, or better, as in the Hebrew, Hoshea, that is, Savior. For he, according to the epistle of Jude,[9] saved the people of Israel and led them forth out of Egypt and brought them into the land of promise. Against Jovinianus 1.21.[10]

3:2-4 The Officers Command the People

Near to God. Origen: Finally, see what is said: "Let the people be at a distance from the ark of the covenant," it says, "by two thousand cubits." The priests and the Levites, however, are very near, and near enough so that the ark of the Lord and the divine law are carried on their own shoulders. Blessed are those who deserve to be very close to God. But remember that it is written, "Those who draw near to me, draw near to fire."[11] If you are gold and silver and have drawn near to the fire, you will shine forth more splendid and glowing because of the fire. But if you are conscious of building "wood, hay and stubble"[12] upon the foundation of your faith, and you approach the fire with such building, you will be consumed. Blessed, therefore, are those who are very near, who are so very near that the fire illumines and does not burn them. Nevertheless, even Israel will be saved; but it will be saved from far away, and it makes its journey not by its own power but by the support and foresight of the priests. Homilies on Joshua 4.3.[13]

3:5-6 Joshua Charges the People and Priests

A Priestly Manner. Origen: It is the ark of the covenant of the Lord in which the tablets of the law written by the hand of God are preserved. And everyone who is "truly Israel"[14] proceeds around this ark of the covenant and is not far from it; but the Levites and the priests even carry it on their shoulders.

For indeed whoever lives by a priestly religion and by holiness are themselves truly the priests and Levites of the Lord. It is not just those who seem to sit in the priestly assembly, but even more those who behave in a priestly manner. Their portion is the Lord, and they do not possess any portion on the earth. They carry the law of God on their shoulders, namely, by doing and accomplishing through their work those things that are written in the law. Homilies on Joshua 9.5.[15]

The Priestly Role. Origen: It is the priestly and levitical order that stands by the ark of the covenant of the Lord in which the law of God is carried, doubtless, so that they may enlighten the people concerning the commandments of God. As the prophet says, "Your word is a lamp for my feet, Lord, and a light for my paths."[16] This light is kindled by the priests and Levites. Wherefore, if by chance anyone from this order "puts the kindled lamp under a bushel" and not "upon a lamp stand so that it may shine forth for all who are in the house,"[17] let him see what he must do when he begins to render an account of the light to the Lord for those who, receiving no illumination from the priests, walk in shadows and are blinded by the darkness of their sins. Homilies on Joshua 4.2.[18]

A Sweeter Baptism. Origen: In conformity with these words, let us also ask God to grant us the ability to understand spiritually the crossing of the Jordan through Jesus [Joshua]. We say that Paul would have said also of this crossing, "I do not wish you to be ignorant, brothers, that our fathers all passed through the Jordan and all were baptized into Jesus in the Spirit and in the river."

Jesus [Joshua], who succeeded Moses, was a type of Jesus the Christ who succeeded the dispensation through the law with the gospel procla-

---

[8]FC 61:202-3*. [9]Jude 5. [10]NPNF 2 6:361. [11]*Gospel of Thomas* 82. [12]1 Cor 3:12. [13]FC 105:55-56. [14]Jn 1:47. [15]FC 105:101. [16]Ps 119:105 (118:105 LXX). [17]Mt 5:15. [18]FC 105:55.

mation. This is why, although they are all baptized into Moses in the cloud and in the sea, their baptism has a bitter and briny element, for they still fear their enemies and cry out to the Lord and to Moses, saying, "Did you bring us out to die in the wilderness because there were no graves in Egypt? Why did you do this to us, having brought us out of Egypt?"[19]

But baptism into Jesus in the truly sweet and fresh river has many elements superior to that baptism, since the religion has by this time been clarified and received a proper order. The ark of the covenant of the Lord our God and the priests and Levites lead the way; the people follow the servants of God, which means that they follow those who are capable of understanding the commandment about purity. Jesus [Joshua] says to the people, "Purify yourselves tomorrow; the Lord will do wonders among us." COMMENTARY ON THE GOSPEL OF JOHN 6.228-30.[20]

---

[19]Ex 14:11. [20]FC 80:230-31*.

3:7-13 JOSHUA INSTRUCTS THE PEOPLE

[7]And the LORD said to Joshua, "This day I will begin to exalt you in the sight of all Israel, that they may know that, as I was with Moses, so I will be with you. [8]And you shall command the priests who bear the ark of the covenant, 'When you come to the brink of the waters of the Jordan, you shall stand still in the Jordan.'" [9]And Joshua said to the people of Israel, "Come hither, and hear the words of the LORD your God." [10]And Joshua said, "Hereby you shall know that the living God is among you, and that he will without fail drive out from before you the Canaanites, the Hittites, the Hivites, the Perizzites, the Girgashites, the Amorites, and the Jebusites."

OVERVIEW: The Jordan crossing manifests Joshua's exaltation by the Lord through representing the mystery of baptism, a dispensation that assures us of God's presence among us (ORIGEN).

3:7-10 The Lord Will Demonstrate His Presence

THE MYSTERY OF BAPTISM. ORIGEN: What great things were manifested before! The Red Sea was crossed on foot, manna was given from heaven, springs were burst open in the wilderness, the law was given through Moses. Many signs and marvels were performed in the wilderness, but nowhere is it said that Jesus [Joshua] was "exalted." But where the Jordan is crossed, there it is said to Jesus [Joshua], "In this day I am beginning to exalt you in the sight of the people." Indeed, Jesus is not exalted before the mystery of baptism. But his exaltation, even his exaltation in the sight of the people, assumes a beginning from then on. If "all who are baptized [into Christ Jesus] are baptized into his death,"[1] and the death of Jesus is made complete by the exaltation of the cross, deservedly then, Jesus is first exalted for each of the faithful when that person arrives at the mystery of baptism. Because thus it is written that "God exalted him and gave him a name that is above every name, that at the name of Jesus

---

[1]Rom 6:3.

17

every knee should bend, in heaven and on earth, and below the earth."[2] HOMILIES ON JOSHUA 4.2.[3]

BAPTIZED INTO JESUS. ORIGEN: And he commands the priests to go before the people with the ark of the covenant. It is then, too, that the mystery of the dispensation of the Father with the Son is manifested, since the Son is highly exalted by him who grants "that in the name of Jesus every knee should bow, of those that are in heaven, on earth, and under the earth; and that every tongue should confess that Jesus Christ is Lord, to the glory of God the Father."[4]

These matters are revealed through the follow-

ing words which have been recorded in the book of Joshua: "And the Lord said to Jesus [Joshua], 'In this day I will begin to exalt you before the sons of Israel.'" We must also hear our Lord Jesus saying to the sons of Israel, "Come here and hear the Word of the Lord our God. In this you shall know that the living God is among you." For by being baptized into Jesus we will know that the living God is among us. COMMENTARY ON THE GOSPEL OF JOHN 6.231-32.[5]

---

[2]Phil 2:9-10. [3]FC 105:53-54. [4]Phil 2:10-11. [5]FC 80:231*.

3:14-17 THE CROSSING OF THE JORDAN

[14]*So, when the people set out from their tents, to pass over the Jordan with the priests bearing the ark of the covenant before the people,* [15]*and when those who bore the ark had come to the Jordan, and the feet of the priests bearing the ark were dipped in the brink of the water (the Jordan overflows all its banks throughout the time of harvest),* [16]*the waters coming down from above stood and rose up in a heap far off, at Adam, the city that is beside Zarethan, and those flowing down toward the sea of the Arabah, the Salt Sea, were wholly cut off; and the people passed over opposite Jericho.* [17]*And while all Israel were passing over on dry ground, the priests who bore the ark of the covenant of the LORD stood on dry ground in the midst of the Jordan, until all the nation finished passing over the Jordan.*

OVERVIEW: Joshua caused the Jordan's flow to cease with the ark's presence (PAULINUS OF NOLA). This remains a unique and credible marvel (GREGORY OF NYSSA). The divided waters of the Jordan symbolize two varieties of the baptized: those who remain steadfast in God's grace and those who return to sinful living. The journey of those who followed Moses out of Egypt and Joshua into the promised land mystically signifies the progress of new converts (ORIGEN).

3:14-17 Israel Crosses the Jordan on Dry Land

THE DEEDS OF JOSHUA. PAULINUS OF NOLA: Then there are the deeds of Joshua, who was marked out with Christ's name; under his guidance the Jordan kept its stream stationary and its waters still as it recoiled from the countenance of the divine ark. A strange power divided the river. One section came to a halt, its stream flowing back, while another section hastened in its gliding course to the sea, leaving the river bed exposed. Where the current surged strongly from its source, it held back and piled high its waves, so that a threatening mountain of water hung poised in quivering formation and looked down to see human feet passing across the dry, deep bed, and grimy soles hastening over the congealed mud, dry-footed in mid-river. POEM 27.511.[1]

A UNIQUE EVENT. GREGORY OF NYSSA: Joshua son of Nun made the Jordan River stop, but only as long as the ark was in the water. As soon as the people had crossed to the other side and the ark had come through, he gave the river back its usual flow again. The bottom of the deep in the Red Sea was denuded of water when the sea was driven back to either side by the Spirit, but the duration of the marvel was the passage of the army through the deep on the dry strip. But after that the surface of the sea became one again, and the temporary gap was flooded over.[2] So this remains a unique event which occurred in such a way that the marvel did not lose credibility because of the passage of time, since it continues to be testified to by visible traces. THE LIFE OF GREGORY THE WONDERWORKER 7.55.[3]

BITTER AND SWEET WATERS. ORIGEN: Still I believe it was not without reference to a mystery that this was written, that part of the waters of the Jordan plunges into the sea and flows into bitterness, while the other part continues on in sweetness. For if all who are baptized maintained the sweetness of the heavenly grace they received and no one were changed into the bitterness of sins, it would never have been written that part of the river was plunged into the abyss of the salty sea. Therefore, it seems to me that the variety of those baptized is designated in these words, a variety we ourselves—I remember with grief—

often see occur. When some who receive holy baptism surrender themselves again to the affairs of the world and to the lures of pleasure, and when they drink the salty cup of avarice, they are symbolized by that part of the waters that flows into the sea and perishes in salty billows. But the part that continues steadfast and protects its own sweetness stands for those who unchangeably hold the gift of God they have received. HOMILIES ON JOSHUA 4.2.[4]

FROM EGYPT TO CANAAN. ORIGEN: And do not imagine that these deeds are only in former times and nothing so great as this is brought forth in you who are now the hearer of them. For all things are fulfilled in you according to a mystical reckoning. Indeed you who long to draw near to the hearing of the divine law have recently forsaken the darkness of idolatry and are now for the first time forsaking Egypt. When you are reckoned among the number of catechumens and have undertaken to submit to the precepts of the church, you have parted the Red Sea and, placed in the stations of the desert, you daily devote yourself to hearing the law of God and to looking upon the face of Moses, through which the glory of the Lord is revealed. But if, you also have entered the mystic font of baptism and in the presence of the priestly and levitical order have been instructed by those venerable and magnificent sacraments, which are known to those who are permitted to know those things, then, with the Jordan parted, you will enter the land of promise by the services of the priests. In this land, Jesus receives you after Moses and becomes for you the leader of a new way. HOMILIES ON JOSHUA 4.1.[5]

---

[1]ACW 40:289. [2]Ex 14:21-29. [3]FC 98:65*. [4]FC 105:54. [5]FC 105:52-53.

4:1-7 MEMORIAL STONES PRESCRIBED

[1]When all the nation had finished passing over the Jordan, the LORD said to Joshua, [2]"Take twelve men from the people, from each tribe a man, [3]and command them, 'Take twelve stones from here out of the midst of the Jordan, from the very place where the priests' feet stood, and carry them over with you, and lay them down in the place where you lodge tonight.'" [4]Then Joshua called the twelve men from the people of Israel, whom he had appointed, a man from each tribe; [5]and Joshua said to them, "Pass on before the ark of the LORD your God into the midst of the Jordan, and take up each of you a stone upon his shoulder, according to the number of the tribes of the people of Israel, [6]that this may be a sign among you, when your children ask in time to come, 'What do those stones mean to you?' [7]Then you shall tell them that the waters of the Jordan were cut off before the ark of the covenant of the LORD; when it passed over the Jordan, the waters of the Jordan were cut off. So these stones shall be to the people of Israel a memorial for ever."

OVERVIEW: With the twelve stones, Joshua anticipated the ministers of baptism (GREGORY OF NYSSA). These serve as types for Christ's twelve apostles (PRUDENTIUS). This typology is further identified in the number of the patriarchs destined to become tribes and the number of fountains in the desert (PETER CHRYSOLOGUS). As the stones served as visual reminders of God's salvation for later generations, so images should be used to record Christ's passion and miracles and remember the deeds of valiant exemplars (JOHN OF DAMASCUS).

4:3-4 Twelve Stones from the Jordan

JOSHUA GUIDES THE HEBREWS. GREGORY OF NYSSA: The people of the Hebrews, as we learn, after many sufferings, and after accomplishing their weary course in the desert, did not enter the land of promise until it had first been brought, with Joshua for its guide and the pilot of its life, to the passage of the Jordan. But it is clear that Joshua also, who set up the twelve stones in the stream, was anticipating the coming of the twelve disciples, the ministers of baptism. ON THE BAPTISM OF CHRIST.[1]

TWELVE STONES. PRUDENTIUS:
    Also, twelve stones from Jordan's bed,
    Left dry when waters backward flowed,
    He raised and firmly set in place,
    The type of Christ's apostles twelve.
HYMNS FOR EVERY DAY 177-180.[2]

TYPOLOGY OF TWELVE. PETER CHRYSOLOGUS: The twelve patriarchs destined to become twelve tribes[3] were arranged to be a type and pattern of the number of the apostles. So were the twelve fountains[4] in the desert and twelve stones taken from the bed of the Jordan. We leave it to the student of the law to find deeper proof of all this. SERMON 170.[5]

4:5-6 This May Be a Sign Among You

STONES RECORD SALVATION. JOHN OF DAMASCUS: God ordered twelve stones to be taken from the Jordan, and specified why, for he says, "When your children ask their fathers in time to come, what do these stones mean? Then you shall let your children know, Israel passed over this

---

[1]NPNF 2 5:522*. [2]FC 43:91*. [3]Gen 49:1-32. [4]Ex 15:27. [5]FC 17:279.

Jordan on dry ground, for the Lord your God dried up the waters of the Jordan for you until you passed over," and thus the ark was saved and all the people. Shall we not then record with images[6] the saving passion and miracles of Christ our God, so that when my son asks me, "What is this?" I may say that God the Word became man, and that through him not only Israel passed through the Jordan, but the whole human race regained its original happiness? Through him, human nature rose from the lowest depths to the most exalted heights, and in him sat on the Father's throne. ON DIVINE IMAGES 1.18.[7]

IMAGES GOD COMMANDED. JOHN OF DAMASCUS: Images are of two kinds: either they are words written in a book . . . or else they are material images such as the twelve stones which he

commanded to be taken from the Jordan for a second memorial (such a mystery, truly the greatest ever to befall the faithful people!) of the carrying of the ark and the parting of the waters. Therefore we now set up images in remembrance of valiant men, that we may zealously desire to follow their example. Either remove these images altogether, and reject the authority of him who commanded them to be made, or else accept them in the manner and with the esteem which they deserve. ON DIVINE IMAGES 3.23.[8]

---

[6]Within the Eastern Orthodox tradition, the use of icons as aids to worship or devotion became hotly contested and defended during the eighth century. John of Damascus had a key role as he provided theological justification for iconography by distinguishing between "worship," which was due God alone, and "veneration," which could be directed toward images as channels of the divine. [7]ODI 26. [8]ODI 77-78.

4:8-14 THE LORD EXALTS JOSHUA

[9]*And Joshua set up twelve stones in the midst of the Jordan, in the place where the feet of the priests bearing the ark of the covenant had stood; and they are there to this day.* [10]*For the priests who bore the ark stood in the midst of the Jordan, until everything was finished that the LORD commanded Joshua to tell the people, according to all that Moses had commanded Joshua.*

The people passed over in haste; [11]*and when all the people had finished passing over, the ark of the LORD and the priests passed over before the people.* [12]*The sons of Reuben and the sons of Gad and the half-tribe of Manasseh passed over armed before the people of Israel, as Moses had bidden them;* [13]*about forty thousand ready armed for war passed over before the LORD for battle, to the plains of Jericho.* [14]*On that day the LORD exalted Joshua in the sight of all Israel; and they stood in awe of him, as they had stood in awe of Moses, all the days of his life.*

OVERVIEW: The people's quick passage over the Jordan teaches us to be earnest and swift in our pursuit of godly virtues. Through Paul's teaching we learn that those girded for war against Jericho are those in Christ's army who are encircled with

the belt of truth. This sort of readiness for battle must be evident not only to human scrutiny but also to divine. As Joshua was exalted before those whom he ruled, so Jesus is exalted in our sight when we perceive his divinity. The change in reverence, from Moses to Joshua, corresponds with the shift in observance of the law to the gospel (ORIGEN, PROCOPIUS).

4:10-11 The People Passed in Haste

HASTEN TO CROSS. ORIGEN: It seems to me the words "the people hastened to cross" were not added idly by the Holy Spirit. For this reason, I also think that when we come to baptism for salvation and receive the sacraments of the Word of God, we should not do it idly or negligently, but we should hurriedly press on all the way until we cross over everything.

For to cross over everything is to accomplish all the things that are commanded. Therefore let us hasten to cross, that is, to fulfill at the beginning, what is written: "Blessed are the poor in spirit."[1] Then, when we have set aside all arrogance and taken up the humility of Christ, we may deserve to attain the blessed promise.

Yet even when we have accomplished this, we must not stand still or loiter but cross over the other things that follow, so that "we may hunger and thirst after righteousness."[2] We must also cross over that which follows so that in this world "we may mourn."[3] Then we must quickly cross the remaining things so that we may be made "meek" and remain "peaceable" and thus be able to hear as "sons of God."[4] Also we must hasten so that we may pass through the burden of persecution with the virtue of patience. Whenever we seek earnestly and swiftly—not slowly and languidly—those individual things that pertain to the glory of virtue, this, it seems to me, is "to cross over the Jordan with haste." HOMILIES ON JOSHUA 5.1.[5]

4:12-13 An Army Crosses to Jericho

GIRDED WITH TRUTH. ORIGEN: Let us learn from Paul, who explains who those "girded" ones are. Hear what he himself says: "Therefore, let your loins be girded with truth."[6] You see, therefore, that Paul knew the girded ones, those who were encircled by the belt of truth. So truth also ought to be our belt, if we have preserved the sacrament of this army and belt. For if truth is the belt by which we are girded for the army of Christ, then whenever we speak a falsehood and a lie proceeds from our mouth, we are ungirded from the army of Christ and loosened from the belt of truth. Therefore, if we are in the truth, we are girded; but if in the false, ungirded. Instead let us imitate those "forty thousand girded men proceeding to the war in the sight of the Lord," and let us always be girded with truth. HOMILIES ON JOSHUA 5.2.[7]

GIRDED IN THE LORD'S SIGHT. ORIGEN: To be sure, it is not enough for you in the sight of people to seem to preserve the truth. For certainly it is possible to deceive humans and to seem truthful. But in doing so you are not girded about "with truth," unless also "in the sight of the Lord" you have preserved truth, that is, not only the things people hear from your voice but also the things God examines in your heart. Let nothing false be on the tongue; let nothing counterfeit be in the heart, as the prophet says about such things, "Those who speak peace with their neighbor but have evil in their hearts."[8] Therefore the one who wishes to be "girded in the sight of the Lord" and to proceed to capture Jericho ought to be apart from all these things, because when we cross over the Jordan River, we cross over to battles and wars. HOMILIES ON JOSHUA 5.2.[9]

4:14 The Lord Exalted Joshua

EXALTED BY GOD. ORIGEN: Certainly, that exaltation of the son of Nun took place in order that the leader of those former people might be held eminent among those whom he ruled. But let us see how our Jesus my Lord, leader and ruler of this latter people, is "exalted" in the sight of all the descendants of the sons of Israel. I myself

---

[1]Mt 5:3. [2]Mt 5:6. [3]Mt 5:4. [4]Mt 5:5, 9. [5]FC 105:59-60. [6]Eph 6:14.
[7]FC 105:60-61. [8]Ps 28:3 (27:3 LXX). [9]FC 105:61*.

think that he was always exalted and elevated in the presence of the Father. But it is necessary that God exalt him in our sight. He is exalted in my sight when the sublimity and loftiness of his divinity is disclosed to me. When, therefore, is his lofty divinity revealed to me? At that time, assuredly, when I crossed over the Jordan and was equipped with the various defenses of the sacraments for the future battle. HOMILIES ON JOSHUA 5.3.[10]

CHANGED REVERENCE. ORIGEN: Everyone who is under the law reveres Moses. But when one crosses over to the gospel from the law, by the changed observance the reverence is also changed. It is just as the apostle says, "For I through the law have died to the law so that I may live for God; I was crucified with Christ, but now I live; not I, but Christ lives in me."[11] HOMILIES ON JOSHUA 5.4.[12]

AS JOSHUA IS EXALTED, WE SHOULD EXALT JESUS. PROCOPIUS OF GAZA: "In that day the Lord exalted Joshua." The Lord exalted Joshua, for as he increased in age his strength became obvious [for all to see]. They rightly feared the son of Nun with a lawful fear as is fitting for service. And we rightly revere our Jesus with holy fear who stands by us for all eternity. COMMENTARY ON JOSHUA 4.14.[13]

---

[10]FC 105:62. [11]Gal 2:19-20. [12]FC 105:63. [13]PG 87.1:1008-9.

4:15-24 THE TESTIMONY OF THE STONES

[18]*And when the priests bearing the ark of the covenant of the LORD came up from the midst of the Jordan, and the soles of the priests' feet were lifted up on dry ground, the waters of the Jordan returned to their place and overflowed all its banks, as before.*

[19]*The people came up out of the Jordan on the tenth day of the first month, and they encamped in Gilgal on the east border of Jericho.* [20]*And those twelve stones, which they took out of the Jordan, Joshua set up in Gilgal.*

OVERVIEW: The correspondence in the calendar date of the first Passover and the entry into the promised land bears spiritual significance for the believer (ORIGEN). Like the Jordan, the church increases to overflowing after the faithful have entered in (PROCOPIUS).

4:18 Crossing the Jordan

THE INCREASE OF THE MYSTICAL JORDAN. PROCOPIUS OF GAZA: After they had crossed over the Jordan, the waters returned to their place and overflowed all its banks as before. For the mystical Jordan also increases when the full number of the faithful enters in. Accordingly, we read, "Lift up your eyes and see that the fields are ripe for the harvest,"[1] and again, "The harvest is plentiful but the laborers are few."[2] But he does not simply say "harvest" but "wheat," according to what they have in the Septuagint.[3] For this is a symbol of

---

[1]Jn 4:35. [2]Mt 9:37. [3]Cf. the earlier reference in Jos 3:15.

nourishment. COMMENTARY ON JOSHUA 4:18.[4]

4:19 The People Camp at Gilgal

ONE DAY. ORIGEN: And when do they come to the crossing of the Jordan? For I have noted that this also has been indicated, so that even the time might be distinguished, and with good reason. "On the tenth," it says, "of the first month." That is also the day on which the mystery of the lamb was prefigured in Egypt.[5] On the tenth of the first month, these things were celebrated in Egypt; on the tenth of the first month, they go into the land of promise. This seems to me exceedingly fortunate, that on the very same day in which someone has escaped the errors of the world, that person may also be worthy to enter the land of promise, that is, on this day in which we live in this age. For all our present life is designated as one day. Therefore we are instructed through that mystery not to put off our acts and works of righteousness until tomorrow but rather "today"[6]—that is, while we are living, while we are lingering in this world—to make haste to accomplish all things that pertain to perfection, so that on the tenth day of the first month, we shall be able to enter the land of promise, that is, the blessedness of perfection. HOMILIES ON JOSHUA 4.4.[7]

---

[4]PG 87.1:1008-9. [5]See Ex 12:3. [6]See Heb 3:13. [7]FC 105:56-57.

5:1-9 THE CIRCUMCISION AT GILGAL

[2]At that time the LORD said to Joshua, "Make flint knives and circumcise the people of Israel again the second time." [3]So Joshua made flint knives, and circumcised the people of Israel at Gibeath-haaraloth.[a] [4]And this is the reason why Joshua circumcised them: all the males of the people who came out of Egypt, all the men of war, had died on the way in the wilderness after they had come out of Egypt. [5]Though all the people who came out had been circumcised, yet all the people that were born on the way in the wilderness after they had come out of Egypt had not been circumcised. [6]For the people of Israel walked forty years in the wilderness, till all the nation, the men of war that came forth out of Egypt, perished, because they did not hearken to the voice of the LORD; to them the LORD swore that he would not let them see the land which the LORD had sworn to their fathers to give us, a land flowing with milk and honey. [7]So it was their children, whom he raised up in their stead, that Joshua circumcised; for they were uncircumcised, because they had not been circumcised on the way.

[8]When the circumcising of all the nation was done, they remained in their places in the camp till they were healed. [9]And the LORD said to Joshua, "This day I have rolled away the reproach of Egypt from you." And so the name of that place is called Gilgal[b] to this day.

a That is the hill of the foreskins   b From Heb galal to roll

---

OVERVIEW: Joshua prefigures Jesus by ushering those lingering in the world into the promised land after their circumcision with stone knives, which are Christ's precepts (TERTULLIAN, JUSTIN

MARTYR). As the first circumcision came through Moses, signifying the law, the second comes through Jesus, the Rock, signifying the gospel (ORIGEN). This second circumcision is not of the flesh but signifies the circumcision of the heart and spirit (JUSTIN MARTYR, LACTANTIUS). It is a figure for baptism, by which we are circumcised of sin. Circumcision was to be a sign that set the Israelites apart from the Gentiles, as demonstrated by the lapse of practice while they sojourned in the desert (JOHN OF DAMASCUS). The physical ordeal of the cutting and healing symbolizes the process of Christ's work and ours in developing virtue. Jesus' circumcision purifies the believer by removing the reproach of sins. Continuing to sin after Christ's circumcision brings greater reproach than neglecting the law of Moses, as the former is equated with defilement of the temple of God, the body (ORIGEN).

5:2-3 Circumcise the People

JOSHUA PREFIGURES JESUS. TERTULLIAN: In the course of the appointing of a successor to Moses, Hoshea the son of Nun is certainly transferred from his pristine name and begins to be called Jesus [Joshua]. Certainly, you say. This we first assert to have been a figure of the future. For, because Jesus Christ was to introduce the second people (which is composed of us nations, lingering deserted in the world previously) into the land of promise, "flowing with milk and honey"[1] (that is, into the possession of eternal life, than which nothing is sweeter). This had to come about not through Moses (that is, not through the law's discipline) but through Joshua (that is, through the new law's grace), after our circumcision with "a knife of rock" (that is, with Christ's precepts, for Christ is in many ways and figures predicted as a rock[2]). Therefore the man who was being prepared to act as images of this sacrament was inaugurated under the figure of the Lord's name, even so as to be named Jesus [Joshua]. AN ANSWER TO THE JEWS 9.[3]

CIRCUMCISION BY THE STONE. JUSTIN MARTYR: Joshua is reputed to have circumcised the people a second time by means of stone knives (which was a sign of that circumcision by which Jesus Christ himself has cut us off from idols made of stone and other materials) and to have gathered together those who everywhere from the uncircumcision (that is, from worldly error) were circumcised with stone knives, namely, the words of our Lord Jesus. For I have already pointed out that the prophets used to call him figuratively a stone and rock. By the stone knives, therefore, we understand his words, by which so many who were in error have been circumcised from their uncircumcision with the circumcision of the heart. From that time God commanded through Jesus that they who had the circumcision which began with Abraham should be circumcised again with the circumcision of the heart, for he said that Joshua performed a second circumcision with stone knives upon those who entered into the Holy Land. DIALOGUE WITH TRYPHO 113.[4]

A SECOND TIME. ORIGEN: I may wish in this place to inquire of the Jews how anyone is able to be circumcised a second time with the circumcision of the flesh. For once anyone is circumcised, he does not have anything more to be removed a second time. But see how fittingly and consistently those things may be resolved by us, to whom it is said, "The law is spiritual."[5] For we say that that person who was skilled in the law and taught by Moses cast off the errors of idolatry and put aside the superstition and worship of images. This is the first circumcision through the law. But if he comes from the law and the prophets to the gospel faith, then he also receives the second circumcision through "the rock, who is Christ,"[6] and what the Lord said to Jesus [Joshua] is accomplished: "Today I have taken away the reproach of Egypt from the sons of Israel."

Just as the apostle said, "They drank from the

---

[1] Ex 3:8. [2] 1 Cor 10:4. [3] ANF 3:163*. [4] FC 6:323*. [5] Rom 7:14. [6] 1 Cor 10:4.

spiritual rock following them, but that rock was Christ,"[7] so also we are able to say aptly in this place that they were circumcised "from the spiritual rock following them, but the rock was Christ." For if anyone has not been cleansed through the gospel by a second circumcision, he is not able to put aside the reproach of Egypt, that is, the allurement of fleshly vices. HOMILIES ON JOSHUA 5.5.[8]

CIRCUMCISION OF THE HEART. LACTANTIUS: Also Moses himself: "In the last days the Lord God will circumcise your heart that you may love the Lord your God."[9] And in like manner in Jesus [Joshua], the son of Nun, the successor of Moses, we note: "And the Lord said to Jesus [Joshua]: Make for yourself knives of stone exceedingly sharp and sit and circumcise a second time the children of Israel." He said that this second circumcision would not be of the flesh as was the first, which the Jews still practice, but of the heart and spirit, which Christ, who was the true Jesus, gave. EPITOME OF THE DIVINE INSTITUTES 4.17.[10]

A FIGURE OF BAPTISM. JOHN OF DAMASCUS: Now, this was a figure of baptism, for, just as circumcision cuts off from the body a part which is not useful but a useless superfluity, so by holy baptism are we circumcised of sin. It is obvious that sin is a superfluity of concupiscence[11] and of no use. For it is impossible for anyone not to have any concupiscence at all or to be entirely without any taste for pleasure, but the useless part of pleasure, this is the sin which holy baptism circumcises. ORTHODOX FAITH 4.25.[12]

5:4-7 The Presence of the Uncircumcised Explained

A SIGN OF SEPARATION. JOHN OF DAMASCUS: The circumcision was given to Abraham before the law, after the blessings and after the promise, as a sign to set him and those born of him and those of his household apart from the Gentiles in whose midst he was living.[13] And this is obvious,

because, when Israel spent forty years alone by themselves in the desert without mixing with any other nation, all those who were born in the desert were not circumcised. However, when Joshua brought them across the Jordan, they were circumcised and a second law of circumcision was made. For, under Abraham a law of circumcision was given, and then it was inoperative for forty years in the desert. Then, after the crossing of the Jordan, God again gave the law for a second time, as is written in the book of Joshua, son of Nave [Nun]: "At that time the Lord said to Joshua: make knives of stone from the sharpest rock, and sitting down circumcise the second time the children of Israel"; and a little further on: "for during forty-two years Israel dwelt in the wilderness of Midbar, and for this reason very many were uncircumcised of the sons of the fighting men who had come out of Egypt, who had disobeyed the commandments of God and to whom he declared that they should not see the good land which he had sworn to give to their fathers, the land flowing with milk and honey. The children of these he made to succeed in their place whom Joshua circumcised because of their not having been circumcised in the way." Hence, circumcision was a sign by which Israel was set apart from the Gentiles among whom they lived. ORTHODOX FAITH 4.25.[14]

5:8 They Remained in Camp Until Healed

CLOSING THE SCAR. ORIGEN: For it is not enough for us to be circumcised, but [we must] also be healed after circumcision, that is, until a scar closes up the wound of circumcision itself. When, therefore, is the scar spread over the wound of our circumcision? I myself think that to be circumcised by our Jesus is this: to be free from faults, to put aside wicked habits and vile practices, to cut off filthy and rude customs and

---

[7] 1 Cor 10:4; cf. Ex 17:6. [8] FC 105:63-64. [9] Deut 30:6. [10] FC 49:289*. [11] Strong, ardent desire, especially sexual desire. [12] FC 37:398. [13] Gen 12; 13; 15; 17:10-14. [14] FC 37:397-98*.

whatever recoils at the rule of honesty and piety.

But, in the beginning, when we do this we are fettered in a certain measure by the difficulty of newness and, as if with a certain labor and anguish of spirit, we change the defects of the old habit for a new practice. On that account, as I said, there is a certain distress in the beginning, and with difficulty and grief are we able to remove the first things and to receive the second. Therefore, this seems to me to be the time when we are said to tarry, just as in the pain of our circumcision, until after the scar is closed and we are healed. And we close the scar when, without difficulty, we adopt new manners and there is within us a transformation to a practice that previously seemed difficult because we were not used to it. And at that time, we are truly said to be healed when, lacking vices, we instill a virtue in our nature by its new use. HOMILIES ON JOSHUA 6.1.[15]

5:9 The Lord Rolls Away the Reproach of Egypt

THE REPROACH OF SINS. ORIGEN: All persons, even if they come from the law, even if they have learned through Moses, still have the reproach of Egypt in them, the reproach of sins. Who will be like Paul even according to the observance of the law? Just hear him saying, "According to the righteousness based upon the law, I lived without blame."[16] Nevertheless, he himself publicly announces and says, "For we were even ourselves at some time foolish, unbelieving, wandering, enslaved to desires and various forms of pleasure, in malice and envy, hateful, hating one another."[17] Do these things not seem to you to be reproaches, even the reproaches of Egypt? But since Christ came and gave to us the second circumcision through "the baptism of regeneration"[18] and purified our souls, we have cast away all these things and in exchange for them we have received the affirming of a good conscience toward God. At that time, through the second circumcision, the reproaches of Egypt were taken away from us, and the blemishes of sins were purified. No one, therefore, fears the reproaches of past transgressions, if he has been wholly converted and has repented from the heart, and, by faith, has parted the waters of the Jordan and been purified through the second circumcision of the gospel. You hear that, "Today, I have taken the reproach of Egypt away from you." HOMILIES ON JOSHUA 5.6.[19]

THE CRIME OF SACRILEGE. ORIGEN: The Lord also signifies this in the gospel when he says, "Your sins are forgiven you,"[20] but "sin no longer, so nothing worse may happen to you."[21] For if, after the remission of sins you no longer sin, truly the reproach of Egypt has been taken away from you. But if you sin again, the old reproaches return again to you, and so much the more because it is a much greater charge "to tread underfoot the Son of God and to consider the blood of the covenant defiled"[22] than to neglect the law of Moses. For indeed, the person who commits fornication after the gospel merits a much greater reproach than the one still under the law, because that one, "taking away the members of Christ, makes them the members of a prostitute."[23] You see, therefore, that more serious and more abundant reproaches are returned to you if you have neglected them. Then, indeed, no one proves you responsible for defilement but condemns you for the crime of sacrilege, because it is said to you, "Do you not know that your body is the temple of God?"[24] "If anyone dishonors the temple of God, God will destroy that person."[25] HOMILIES ON JOSHUA 5.6.[26]

---

[15]FC 105:67-68. [16]Phil 3:6. [17]Tit 3:3. [18]Tit 3:5. [19]FC 105:64. [20]Mk 2:5; Lk 7:48. [21]Jn 5:14. [22]Heb 10:29. [23]1 Cor 6:15. [24]1 Cor 6:19. [25]1 Cor 3:17. [26]FC 105:64-65*.

5:10-12 THE MANNA CEASES

[10]While the people of Israel were encamped in Gilgal they kept the passover on the fourteenth day of the month at evening in the plains of Jericho. [11]And on the morrow after the passover, on that very day, they ate of the produce of the land, unleavened cakes and parched grain. [12]And the manna ceased on the morrow, when they ate of the produce of the land; and the people of Israel had manna no more, but ate of the fruit of the land of Canaan that year.

OVERVIEW: Once in the promised land, the Israelites celebrated the Passover with the produce of the land, food superior to the manna. Understanding the text spiritually is necessary to gain this greater and truer account of its meaning. Celebration follows circumcision because only those who have been cleansed may partake of the lamb. The three foods consumed during the Israelites' journey symbolize different, and progressively better, types of instruction (ORIGEN). Manna prefigured the sacrament of Eucharist (BEDE).

5:10-11 *The Passover Is Celebrated*

THE SECOND PASSOVER. ORIGEN: After they observed the Passover in Egypt, they began the exodus.[1] In the book of Joshua, however, after the crossing of the Jordan, on the tenth day of the first month they encamped in Gilgal....

Then the sons of Israel observed the Passover on the fourteenth day of the month much more cheerfully than the one in Egypt, seeing that they also "ate unleavened bread and fresh from the grain of the holy land," a food better than the manna.

For God does not feed them on lesser foods when they have received the land according to promise, nor do they obtain inferior bread through Jesus [Joshua] who is so great. This will be clear to the one who has perceived the true holy land and the Jerusalem above. COMMENTARY ON THE GOSPEL OF JOHN 6.233-35.[2]

A BETTER FOOD. ORIGEN: Now if the law is to

be understood only according to the letter, without doubt the sons of Israel will be found to have received poorer things from the promise since they had been partaking of better things—for they were receiving manna from heaven. When they had forsaken the prior food of Egypt, a better food by all means had followed, the manna from heaven. Now in what manner will it be reckoned that with a better food ceasing, a worse has followed, unless a greater and truer account is discovered in a spiritual understanding rather than in the literal text. HOMILIES ON JOSHUA 6.1.[3]

AFTER THE HEALING. ORIGEN: For not before circumcision were they able to celebrate a Passover; nor immediately after circumcision, before they were healed, were they able to eat the flesh of the lamb. But after they were healed it is said that "the sons of Israel celebrated the Passover on the fourteenth day of the month." You see, therefore, that no one unclean celebrates Passover, no one uncircumcised, but whoever has been cleansed and circumcised, just as the apostle also interprets, saying, "For indeed Christ our Passover has been sacrificed. Therefore, let us celebrate the feast day, not with the old leaven, nor with the leaven of malice and wickedness, but with the unleavened bread of sincerity and truth."[4] HOMILIES ON JOSHUA 6.1.[5]

5:12 *The Manna Ceased*

---

[1]Ex 12:31-37. [2]FC 80:232*. [3]FC 105:69-70. [4]1 Cor 5:7-8. [5]FC 105:68.

Three Kinds of Food. Origen: Indeed at that time, when the people went out of the land of Egypt, "they carried dough in their clothes."[6] And when the dough had run out and they had no bread, God rained manna on them.[7] But when they came to the holy land and "took the fruit of the province of the palms, the manna ceased for them," and then they began to eat of the fruit of the land.

In this manner, three kinds of food in general are described. The first one we certainly enjoy when going out of the land of Egypt, but this suffices for only a little time. Manna follows after this. But the third fruit we receive now from the holy land. By this diversity, as my insignificant perception comprehends, I think it is indicated that the first food that we carry with us when leaving Egypt is this little school learning (or even more advanced learning if, by chance, anyone has acquired it) that is able to help us only a little. But, placed in the desert, that is, in the condition of life in which we now are, we enjoy the manna only through what we learn by the instructions of the divine law. But the one who will deserve to enter the land of promise, that is, to obtain that which has been promised by the Savior, that one will eat fruits from the region of the palms.[8] For truly that person who arrives at these promises after having conquered the enemy will discover the fruit of the palm. For it is certain that however great those things are that we are now able to understand or to know in the law of God or in divine learning, those things that the holy ones will deserve to see "face to face" when the enigma is over, will be far more sublime and lofty.[9] For "what the eye has not seen or the ear heard, what has not ascended into a person's heart, these are the things God has prepared for those who love him."[10] Homilies on Joshua 6.1.[11]

Joshua's Manna Fulfilled by the Sacrament of Christ's Body and Blood. Bede: "And Jesus said to them: 'I have eagerly desired to eat this Passover with you before I suffer.'"[12] He desired first of all to eat the typical Passover with his disciples and thus to reveal the mystery of his passion to the world, so that the judge of the ancient and lawful Passover would emerge and forbid this to be displayed to have pertained to the type of its dispensation by further carnal teaching but would demonstrate instead through the passing shadow that the light of the true Passover has now come. The time and order of Joshua finishing the manna beautifully prefigures this, where it is written: "And they kept the Passover on the fourteenth day of the month at evening in the plains of Jericho, and they ate from the fruit of the earth on the next day, unleavened bread from the grain of the land of the same year. And the manna ceased after they ate of the fruit of the earth, nor did the children of Israel use that food any more." For, when Moses died, Joshua restored the people whom he had provided with manna for a time across the Jordan, by which food he himself was also restored, even though he knew and formerly tasted of the fruit of the promised land. Thereafter, he crossed the Jordan, circumcised with knives made of stone and did not take the customary manna for three and one half months, until the day of Passover. In fact, Joshua was ordained leader when Moses died because Christ was incarnated when the law had been corrupted by the traditions of the Pharisees. Joshua fed with and was fed by manna across the Jordan because, until the time of his baptism, the Lord observed the ceremonies of the law and wanted them to be observed by everyone else. After they had crossed the Jordan, Joshua circumcised the people with knives made from stone because the Savior celebrated the grace of baptism with thoughts that the law, in its severity, had been unable to cut off the attractions of faith. And for three and one half years [after his baptism], although provoking gradual movement

---

[6]Ex 12:34. [7]Ex 16:13; Ps 78:24 (77:24 LXX). [8]Jericho is referred to in Scripture as the "city of the palms," which Origen uses as a metaphor for the heavenly promised land. [9]1 Cor 13:12. [10]1 Cor 2:9. [11]FC 105:68-69. [12]See Lk 22:15.

toward the promised heaven, Christ does not cease to observe the sacraments of the law, as though to be nourished with the customary manna, until, while eating the desired Passover with his disciples at a foreordained time, as morning was breaking, he finally offers the most pure sacrament of his body and blood, conse-crated on the altar of the cross for imbuing the faithful, as though it were the unleavened bread of the promised land. EXPOSITION OF THE GOSPEL OF LUKE 6.22.[13]

[13]CCL 120:376-77.

5:13-15 THE COMMANDER OF THE LORD'S ARMY

[13]*When Joshua was by Jericho, he lifted up his eyes and looked, and behold, a man stood before him with his drawn sword in his hand; and Joshua went to him and said to him, "Are you for us, or for our adversaries?"* [14]*And he said, "No; but as commander of the army of the LORD I have now come." And Joshua fell on his face to the earth, and worshiped, and said to him, "What does my lord bid his servant?"* [15]*And the commander of the LORD's army said to Joshua, "Put off your shoes from your feet; for the place where you stand is holy." And Joshua did so.*

OVERVIEW: While outside Jericho, it is surely the Lord who appears to Joshua as the fellow soldier and combatant of his people (EUSEBIUS, ORIGEN). Through purification and constant meditation on God, those in need of great encouragement received the faculty to perceive God's presence (ISAAC OF NINEVEH). Joshua's bow before the angel of God demonstrated honor, not adoration for the angel. He paid homage to an image of God's servant, which brings worship and honor to the ministering spirit's sender (JOHN OF DAMASCUS). Maturity in spirituality is demonstrated by rightly discerning between visions (ORIGEN).

Though not a holy place, the ground of Jericho was sanctified by the Lord's presence (ORIGEN). Coverings are needed to protect the feet while in this world, but in the kingdom of heaven none will be needed as we will follow the Lamb (JEROME).

5:13-14 Joshua Sees an Armed Man

THE DIVINE WARRIOR. EUSEBIUS OF CAESARIA: And as Joshua, the successor of Moses, was about to fight against the former possessors of Palestine, his enemies, foreign and most ungodly races, he rightly appears to him with a sword drawn and pointed against the enemy, showing by the vision that he himself is about to attack the ungodly with an unseen sword and with divine power, the fellow soldier and the fellow combatant of his people. Wherefore he gives himself the name of Chief and Captain of the Lord to suit the occasion. PROOF OF THE GOSPEL 5.19.[1]

THE PRINCE OF THE LORD'S HOST. EUSEBIUS OF CAESARIA: Joshua, the successor of Moses, calls the leader of the heavenly angels and archangels and of the supernal powers and as if he were the power and wisdom of the Father,[2] entrusted

[1]POG 1:263*. [2]1 Cor 1:24.

with the second rank of sovereignty and rule over all, "prince of the host of the Lord," although he saw him only in the form and shape of a man. At any rate, it is written: "And it came to pass, when Joshua was in the field of the city of Jericho, he lifted up his eyes, and saw a man standing over against him, holding a drawn sword, and he went to him and said: 'Are you one of ours, or of our adversaries?' And he said to him, 'I am prince of the host of the Lord and I have now come.' And Joshua fell on his face to the ground and said to him, 'What does my Lord command to his servant?' And the prince of the Lord said to Joshua, 'Loose your shoe from off your feet, for the place on which you stand is a holy place.'" Here, too, you will perceive from the identity of words that this is no other than he who also spoke to Moses.[3] ECCLESIASTICAL HISTORY 1.2.[4]

THE CHIEF OF CHIEFS. ORIGEN: What is it that Jesus [Joshua] teaches us through this? That, doubtless, which the apostle says: "Do not believe every spirit, but test if it is from God."[5] Therefore, Jesus [Joshua] recognized not only something from God but that which is God; for certainly he would not have worshiped unless he had recognized God. For who else is chief of the army of the powers of God except our Lord Jesus Christ? For every heavenly army, whether angels or archangels, whether powers or "dominions or principalities or authorities,"[6] all these that were made through him, wage war under the chief himself, who is the chief of chiefs and who distributes sovereignty to the sovereigns. For he himself is the one who says in the gospel, "Have power over ten cities," and, to another, "Have power over five cities."[7] This is the one who has returned after accepting the kingdom.[8] HOMILIES ON JOSHUA 6.2.[9]

THE INVISIBLE MADE VISIBLE. ISAAC OF NINEVEH: Divine providence surrounds all persons at all times, but it is not visible except to those who have purified their souls of sin and think about God at all times. To these it is luminously re-vealed at that time; because when they have undergone great temptations for the sake of truth, then they receive the faculty to perceive sensibly as if with eyes of flesh also when necessary, even palpably, according to the kind and cause of the temptation, as if for greater encouragement.

So it was with Jacob and Joshua son of Nun, Hananiah and his companions, Peter and others to whom the form of a man appeared to encourage them and to console their faith.[10] ASCETICAL HOMILIES 5.31-32.[11]

ADORATION AND VENERATION DIFFER. JOHN OF DAMASCUS: Joshua, the son of Nun, and Daniel[12] bowed in veneration before an angel of God, but they did not adore him. For adoration is one thing, and that which is offered in order to honor something of great excellence is another. ON DIVINE IMAGES 1.8.[13]

HOMAGE PAID TO GOD. JOHN OF DAMASCUS: Joshua the son of Nun did not see the angel as he is by nature, but an image, for an angel by nature is not visible to bodily eyes, yet he fell down and worshiped, and Daniel[14] did likewise. Yet an angel is a creature, a servant and minister of God, but not God. And they fell down in worship before the angels, not as God, but as God's ministering spirits. Shall I not make images of friends? Shall I not honor them, not as gods but as the images of God's friends? Neither Joshua nor Daniel worshiped the angels they saw as gods. Neither do I worship an image as god, but through the images of Christ and of the holy Theotokos and of the saints, I bring worship and honor to God, because of the reverence with which I honor his friends. God did not unite himself with angelic nature but with human nature. God did not become an angel; he became a man by nature and in truth. ON DIVINE IMAGES 3.26.[15]

---

[3]Cf. Ex 3:5. [4]FC 19:41*. [5]1 Jn 4:1. [6]Col 1:16; cf. Col 2:10. [7]Lk 19:17-19. [8]Lk 19:15. [9]FC 105:70-71*. [10]Gen 32:24-29; Dan 3:23-25; Acts 12:6-11. [11]INAL 84-85*. [12]Dan 8:15-17. [13]ODI 19. [14]Dan 8:15-17. [15]ODI 80-81.

DISCERNING BETWEEN SPIRITS. ORIGEN: And so you must beware and exercise great care in order to discern with knowledge the kinds of visions, just as Joshua the son of Nun, when he saw a vision and knew there was temptation in it, immediately asked the one who appeared to him and said, "Are you for us, or for our adversaries?" So, then, the soul progresses when it comes to the place where it begins to distinguish between visions; and it is proved to be spiritual if it knows how to discern them all.[16] That is why, as well, one of the spiritual gifts, given by the Holy Spirit, is mentioned as "the ability to distinguish between spirits."[17] HOMILIES ON NUMBERS 27.11.[18]

5:15 Remove Your Shoes

HOLY GROUND. ORIGEN: And in what manner is Jericho holy ground since it is retained by the enemies? This indicates, and not by accident, that the chief of the army of the power of the Lord sanctifies every place to which he comes, for Jericho itself was not a holy place. But because the chief of the army of God came there, the place is said to be holy. I also dare something more and say that even the place where Moses stood was not holy through Moses himself but because the Lord stood with him. The presence of the Lord had sanctified the place; and on that account, it is said to him, "Loosen the latchet of your sandal; for the place on which you stand is holy ground."[19] HOMILIES ON JOSHUA 6.3.[20]

THE SIGNIFICANCE OF SANDALS. JEROME: Now, grasp the mystical meaning of Holy Writ. As long as we are walking through the wilderness, it is necessary that we wear sandals to cover and protect our feet, but when we shall have entered the Land of Promise, we shall hear with Jesus [Joshua], the son of Nave [Nun]: "Remove your sandals from your feet, for the place upon which you are standing is holy." When, therefore, we enter into the kingdom of heaven, we shall have no need of sandals or for protection against this world, but—to give you a new thought—we shall follow the Lamb that has been slain for us. HOMILY ON THE EXODUS 91.[21]

---

[16]1 Cor 2:15. [17]1 Cor 12:10. [18]OSW 261. [19]Ex 3:5. [20]FC 105:71. [21]FC 57:241-42*.

6:1-7 THE LORD'S BATTLE PLAN

[2]And the LORD said to Joshua, "See, I have given into your hand Jericho, with its king and mighty men of valor. [3]You shall march around the city, all the men of war going around the city once. Thus shall you do for six days. [4]And seven priests shall bear seven trumpets of rams' horns before the ark; and on the seventh day you shall march around the city seven times, the priests blowing the trumpets. [5]And when they make a long blast with the ram's horn, as soon as you hear the sound of the trumpet, then all the people shall shout with a great shout; and the wall of the city will fall down flat, and the people shall go up every man straight before him."

OVERVIEW: The command Joshua received from God to have the priests and people march for seven days around Jericho demonstrates that exemption from work on the sabbath was not an eternal precept (TERTULLIAN). God's strength and presence in battle are the surest weapons (PAULINUS OF NOLA). The invincible power of Joshua's priestly voice was perfected in the Word of Jesus, which is proclaimed in the church even today (MAXIMUS OF TURIN).

6:2-5 The Lord Gives Joshua Battle Orders

WORK ON THE SABBATH. TERTULLIAN: But the Jews are sure to say that ever since this precept was given through Moses, the observance has been binding. But it is clear according to the text that the precept was not eternal or spiritual but temporary, which would one day cease. In short, so true is it that it is not in the exemption from work of the sabbath—that is, of the seventh day—that the celebration of this solemnity is to consist, that Joshua the son of Nun, at the time that he was reducing the city Jericho by war, stated that he had received from God a precept to order the people that priests should carry the ark of the testament of God seven days, making the circuit of the city; and thus, when the seventh day's circuit had been performed, the walls of the city would spontaneously fall. This was done. When the space of the seventh day was finished, just as was predicted, down fell the walls of the city. [By this] it is manifestly shown that in the number of the seven days there intervened a Sabbath day. For seven days, whenever they may have commenced, must necessarily include within them a Sabbath day; on which day not only must the priests have worked, but the city must have been made a prey by the edge of the sword by all the people of Israel. AN ANSWER TO THE JEWS 4.[1]

UNSEEN ARMOR. PAULINUS OF NOLA: Though we appear unarmed in body, we nonetheless are bearing arms with which even in time of sunny peace we grapple in spirit against the unsubstantial foe. Now we need God to help us, and him only we must fear; without him our armor falls from us, but with him our armor gains strength. He will be your tower within the walls; he will be your wall where there are no walls.

Let us hereafter recall the deeds of our ancestors recorded in the consecrated books. Observe who had the better protection—those enclosed in a city girded by great walls but without God, or those defended by God's strength and friendly support but without city walls. I refer to the city destroyed by the eager Joshua, whose own name was changed to delineate his power. He did not subdue it in the usual military way, by conducting the regular long and weary blockade. No, through God's help his army in sacred symbolism performed a lustration, brandishing its weapons without using them. It withdrew its violence; its arms were silent. For seven days they made seven repeated circuits round the walls. By the strength of this powerful number and by the fearful din of the priests' trumpets, which aped the flashing thunder of divine wrath, they laid hold of the enemy trapped within. Then that people which trusted in its wealth and city perished, and their graves were mingled with their houses. POEM 26.99-114.[2]

THE PRIESTLY VOICE. MAXIMUS OF TURIN: The walls of Jericho fell down on account of the priestly trumpets because they contained within themselves a sinful people. A battering ram did not strike it, nor did a machine of war storm it, but—what is remarkable—the terror of the priestly sound brought it down. The walls that had stood impervious to iron collapsed at the sacred voice of the trumpets. Who would not be amazed that when the sound had been made, stones were broken to pieces, foundations were shattered by the noise, and everything collapsed in such a way that, although the conquerors did not injure their own forces, nonetheless among the enemy nothing remained standing? But although no one touched those walls, still they were taken from without at the sound of the righteous while sinners dwelled within. For this reason, then, they gave way, lest they offer resistance

---

[1]ANF 3:155*.　[2]ACW 40:258*.

to the ones or somehow protect the others. To the righteous they opened a path and to the faithless they denied protection. Therefore, brothers, if the sound of the priestly voice was so powerful at that time, such that its blast in the air announced a certain confusion, how much more do we believe that that priestly voice is living now, which shows forth something magnificent when it speaks Christ in words! . . . Or how could feeling creatures resist when even unfeeling ones were unable to endure the sacred dread? For we believe that hearts can more easily be softened than rocks at the words of the priests and that sins can be forgiven in a shorter time than those stones were split asunder. For the voice of the Spirit, when it comes, destroys the stain of sin more easily than it breaks apart a tangible fortification of rock. SERMON 93.2.[3]

---

[3]ACW 50:216.

6:8-14 MARCHING AROUND THE CITY

[8]*And as Joshua had commanded the people, the seven priests bearing the seven trumpets of rams' horns before the LORD went forward, blowing the trumpets, with the ark of the covenant of the LORD following them.*

OVERVIEW: The trumpet blasts symbolize the preaching of priests, which announce with dreadful sound the future doom for evildoers (MAXIMUS OF TURIN).

6:8 The Seven Priests Blow the Seven Trumpets

THE PREACHING OF PRIESTS. MAXIMUS OF TURIN: Last Sunday we said that the walls of Jericho were laid waste by the priestly trumpets and that, contrary to order and nature, an unfeeling thing gave way before the sacred sounds with a kind of dread of the threat, and everything so collapsed at the loud noise that the most solid fortifications fell to the ground and the sinful people remained without protection. The one occurred lest resistance be offered for any amount of time, the other so that they would be the more easily captured.

But we have said that all these things were done then in symbol, for we believe that the priestly trumpets of that age were nothing other than the preaching of the priests of this age, by which we do not cease to announce, with a dreadful sound, something harsh to sinners, to speak of what is dismal, and to strike the ears of evildoers with, as it were, a threatening roar, since no one can resist the sacred sounds and no one can gainsay them. For how could feeling creatures not tremble at the word of God when at that time even unfeeling ones were shaken? And how could human hardheartedness resist what a stone fortification could not withstand? For just as, when the stone walls were destroyed, the clash of the trumpets reached the people within, so also now, when evil thoughts have been destroyed, the preaching of the priests penetrates to the bare parts of the soul, for the soul is found bare before the Word of God when its every evil deed is destroyed. And that the soul is bare before God the holy apostle says, "But all things are bare and uncovered to his eyes."[1] In this regard, before the soul knows God and accepts the truth of the faith, it veils itself, so to speak, under superstitious works and surrounds itself with something like a wall of perversity, such that it might seem to be able to remain impregnable within the fortifications of its own evildoing. But when the sacred sound thunders, its rashness is overthrown, its thinking is destroyed, and all the defenses of its superstitions break asunder in such a way that, remaining unprotected, as it is written, the Word of God might penetrate even to the division of its spirit and its inmost parts. Just as the ring of the sacred sound destroyed, captured and took vengeance on a hardhearted people then, so also now the priestly preaching subjugates, captures and takes vengeance on a sinful people. SERMON 94.1.[2]

---

[1]Heb 4:13. [2]ACW 50:216-17.

6:15-21 THE WALLS OF JERICHO FALL

[15]*On the seventh day they rose early at the dawn of day, and marched around the city in the same manner seven times: it was only on that day that they marched around the city seven times.* [16]*And at the seventh time, when the priests had blown the trumpets, Joshua said to the people, "Shout; for the LORD has given you the city.* [17]*And the city and all that is within it shall be devoted to the LORD for destruction; only Rahab the harlot and all who are with her in her house shall live, because she hid the messengers that we sent.* [18]*But you, keep yourselves from the things devoted to destruction, lest when you have devoted them you take any of the devoted things and make the camp of Israel a thing for destruction, and bring trouble upon it.* [19]*But all silver and gold, and vessels of bronze and iron, are sacred to the LORD; they shall go into the treasury of the LORD."* [20]*So the people shouted, and the trumpets were blown. As soon as the people heard the sound of the trumpet, the people raised a great shout, and the wall fell down flat, so that the people went up into the city, every man straight before him, and they took the city.*

OVERVIEW: The world's existence, from its creation to its destruction, is symbolized in the elements of Jericho's fall (MAXIMUS OF TURIN). Its destruction prefigures the consummation of the age (MAXIMUS OF TURIN, ORIGEN).

Rahab the prostitute, granted clemency and life due to her words and disposition before God, is extolled for her piety and faith (CHRYSOSTOM).

True devotion to the Lord should be evidenced in the handling of those things God commanded to be devoted. They must not be taken for personal use (AUGUSTINE). The items declared anathema represent worldly matters and customs that should not be intermingled with the church's practice or teaching (ORIGEN).

Joshua's faith triumphed as Jericho's walls were felled by the blare of the trumpet and the badge of the priest (AMBROSE). Without the strength of God, all other means of defense are useless (PAULINUS OF NOLA). The fall of Jericho's walls after being repeatedly circled by the ark serves as a miraculous testimony to the law. This encircling symbolizes the destruction of the battlements of mortal life by the sevenfold gift of the Holy Spirit (AUGUSTINE). Under God's direction, the sounds of music have unleashed great forces (CASSIODORUS). The powerful priestly voice, which destroyed stone walls, lives on in the speaking of Christ's words. Like Jericho's fall, the consummation of the world will occur suddenly with the joyful shout of a heavenly army and the trumpet blast (ORIGEN).

6:15-16 The Seventh Day of Marching

THE WORLD SYMBOLIZED. MAXIMUS OF TURIN But what was done then to the city of Jericho, as we have said, was done in symbol, since now this very thing happens in reality. For we read that at that time the priests circled the aforementioned city continuously for seven days and that, although a band of armed men was unable to take it, it was overthrown by the sound of trumpets coming from all sides—of trumpets, I say, not played by a rough soldier but sounded by a consecrated priest. Who would not fear a person's trumpet if he did not fear his sword? After seven days, therefore, the walls that were circled fell at the priestly trumpets; we read that in seven days the works of this world were completed.[1] You see, then, that with this number seven it is not so much one city that is destroyed by the priests as the wickedness of the whole world that is destroyed. For just as in the naming of a single city the condition of the whole world is symbolized, so also the course of seven days indicates the space of seven thousand years during which the trumpets of priestly preaching announce destruction to the world and threaten judgment, as it is written: "For the world will also perish and all the things that are in the world, but the one who does the will of the Lord endures forever."[2] SERMON 94.2.[3]

6:17 Only Rahab Shall Live

RAHAB THE PIOUS. CHRYSOSTOM: Pay attention to me; how strange was the preaching of God's love toward humanity! He who says in the law, "You shall not commit adultery" and "You shall not commit prostitution," changes the commandment by clemency and proclaims through the blessed Joshua, "Let Rahab the prostitute live." Joshua the son of Nun, who says, "Let the prostitute live," prefigured the Lord Jesus, who says, "The prostitutes and tax collectors go into the kingdom of the heavens before you."[4] If she must live, how can she be a prostitute? If she is a prostitute, why should she live? "I speak about her previous condition," he says, "so you may marvel at her subsequent change." He asks, "What did Rahab, to whom he granted salvation, do?" She accepted the spies peacefully? Even an innkeeper does this. However, she reaped the fruits of salvation not only by speech but beforehand by faith and by her disposition before God.

And so you may learn the abundance of her faith, listen to the very Scripture that describes in full and bears witness to her achievements. She was in a brothel, like a pearl mixed up in mire, like gold thrown in mud, the rose of piety hidden in thorns, a pious soul enclosed in a place of impiety. Pay attention so you may understand well. She accepted the spies and the One whom Israel denied in the desert; Rahab preached this One in the brothel. HOMILIES ON REPENTANCE AND ALMSGIVING 7.5.15-16.[5]

6:18-19 Items Devoted to the Lord

DESTRUCTION AND DEVOTION. AUGUSTINE: And when temples, idols, groves, and other things of the sort are authorized to be torn down, although it is evident when we do this that we are not honoring but despising them, still we should not take away anything for private, or at least personal, use so that our purpose in tearing down must be manifest as devotion, not cupidity. However, when such things are turned over for public,

---

[1]Gen 2:2. [2]1 Jn 2:17. [3]ACW 50:218*. [4]Mt 21:31. [5]FC 96:98-99*.

not private or personal use, as when they are used to honor the true God, that same holds true for things as for people, when they turn from sacrilege and impiety to the true religion. God is understood to have taught this by those texts which you quoted, as when he ordered wood from the grove of foreign gods to be brought for a holocaust and ordered that all the gold, silver and brass vessels be carried into the treasury of the Lord. LETTER 47.[6]

DECLARED ANATHEMA. ORIGEN: This is what is indicated by these words: Take heed that you have nothing worldly in you, that you bring down with you to the church neither worldly customs nor faults nor equivocations of the age. But let all worldly ways be anathema to you. Do not mix mundane things with divine; do not introduce worldly matters into the mysteries of the church.

This is what John also sounds with the trumpet of his epistle, saying, "Do not love the world or the things that are in the world."[7] And likewise Paul: "Do not," he says, "be conformed to this world."[8] For those who do these things accept what is anathema. But also those introduce anathema into the churches who, for example, celebrate the solemnities of the nations even though they are Christians. Those who eagerly seek the lives and deeds of humans from the courses of the stars, who inquire of the flight of birds and other things of this type that were observed in the former age, carry what is anathema from Jericho into the church and pollute the camp of the Lord and cause the people of God to be overcome. But there are also many other sins through which anathema from Jericho is introduced into the church, through which the people of God are overcome and overthrown by enemies. Does not the apostle also teach these same things when he says, "A little leaven spoils the whole lump"?[9] HOMILIES ON JOSHUA 7.4.[10]

6:20 The Walls of Jericho Fall

NOT BY MIGHT. AMBROSE: And did Joshua, the son of Nun, err in recognizing the leader of the heavenly host? But after he believed, he forthwith conquered, being found worthy to triumph in the battle of faith. Again, he did not lead forth his armed ranks into the fight, nor did he overthrow the ramparts of the enemy's walls, with battering rams or other engines of war, but with the sound of the seven trumpets of the priests. Thus the blare of the trumpet and the badge of the priest brought a cruel war to an end. ON THE CHRISTIAN FAITH 5.10.126.[11]

THE STRENGTH OF GOD. PAULINUS OF NOLA: Human salvation is useless, and my strength lends me no strength if I lack the strength of God. What good was the boundless vigor of giants? Or the kings of Egypt? Or mighty Jericho? Their own inflated glory was the cause of death for all of them, and God's power broke them not by the strength of heroes but by that of the weak. The famed giant died like a dog, felled by a shepherd boy's sling.[12] The din of trumpets shook down the famous city. The renowned and haughty king lay dead on the sand of the shore, and the riches of the kingdom were equated with his naked corpse.[13] So wherever Christ is with us, a web is a wall; for the person without Christ, a wall will become a web. POEM 16.129.[14]

TESTIMONIES TO THE LAW. AUGUSTINE: Besides the signs just mentioned and the voices which could be heard in the neighborhood of the ark, other miraculous testimonies to the law were witnessed. For example, when the people were entering the promised land and the ark was crossing the Jordan, the river stood still above them and flowed on below them so that the ark and the people had a dry place for crossing. Again, when they came upon the first hostile city where the religion was pagan and polytheistic, the ark was

---

[6]FC 12:228. [7]1 Jn 2:15. [8]Rom 12:2. [9]1 Cor 5:6. [10]FC 105:78-79. [11]NPNF 2 10:300. [12]See 1 Sam 17. [13]Ex 14; Pharaoh was not personally present at the Israelites' crossing of the Red Sea; Paulinus here evokes Virgil's description of Priam's corpse (*Aenead* 2.557). [14]ACW 40:99-100*.

carried around it seven times and then, suddenly, the walls collapsed before a hand was raised or a battering ram was used. CITY OF GOD 10.17.[15]

THE SEVENFOLD GIFT OF THE HOLY SPIRIT. AUGUSTINE: So the walls of that city, called Jericho, which in the Hebrew tongue is said to mean moon, fell when they had been encircled seven times by the ark of the covenant. What, then, does the announcement of the kingdom of heaven portend—signified by the encircling of the ark—except that all the battlements of mortal life, that is, all the hope of this world, which is opposed to the hope of the world to come, will be destroyed by the sevenfold gift of the Holy Spirit, working through the free will? For, those walls fell of their own accord, not by any violent push of the ark in its circuit. There are other references in Scripture which suggest the church to us under the symbolism of the moon, as it makes its pilgrimage in this mortal life, amid toils and labors, far from that Jerusalem whose citizens are the holy angels. LETTER 55.[16]

THE POWER OF MUSIC. CASSIODORUS: The divine reading attests that the walls of Jericho at once collapsed at the din of trumpets. So there is no doubt that the sounds of music, at the Lord's command or with his permission, have unleashed great forces. EXPOSITION OF THE PSALMS 80.4.[17]

SOUNDING THE TRUMPET. ORIGEN: But when our Lord Jesus Christ comes, whose arrival that prior son of Nun designated, he sends priests, his apostles, bearing "trumpets hammered thin,"[18] the magnificent and heavenly instruction of proclamation. Matthew first sounded the priestly trumpet in his Gospel; Mark also; Luke and John each played their own priestly trumpets. Even Peter cries out with trumpets in two of his epistles; also James and Jude. In addition, John also sounds the trumpet through his epistles, and Luke, as he describes the Acts of the Apostles. And now that last one comes, the one who said, "I think God displays us apostles last,"[19] and in

fourteen of his epistles, thundering with trumpets, he casts down the walls of Jericho and all the devices of idolatry and dogmas of philosophers, all the way to the foundations. HOMILIES ON JOSHUA 7.1.[20]

THE JOYFUL SHOUT. ORIGEN: At the coming of Jesus [Joshua], the walls of Jericho were overthrown; at the coming of my Lord Jesus, the world is overcome. Yet I want to know more plainly how the world is overcome and to understand more clearly those things that are said. I myself, I who teach you, want to learn equally with you. Let us summon Paul as a teacher for all of us, for he is a fellow priest of Christ, so that he can disclose to us how Christ overcame the world. Therefore, hear him saying, "That which was opposed to us he took away from our midst and fixed to his own cross; and stripping principalities and authorities he exposed them openly, triumphing over them on the wood of the cross."[21] From these words, therefore, I understand that when the heavenly powers saw the fight of Jesus—the principalities and hostile authorities stripped of their authorities, "the strong one bound and his goods plundered"[22]— they thundered with their heavenly trumpets, because with the prince of this world bound, the world was overcome and the heavenly army gave the joyful shout at the triumph of Christ. Truly, therefore, blessed are the people of the nations, those who know this joyful shout of the heavenly army and who begin to recognize the mysteries and believe. HOMILIES ON JOSHUA 7.3.[23]

THE FALL OF JERICHO. ORIGEN: How, therefore, is Jericho captured? The sword is not drawn against it; the battering ram is not arranged, nor is the spear hurled. The priestly trumpets alone are employed, and by these the walls of Jericho are overthrown.

---

[15]FC 14:148. [16]FC 12:269*. [17]ACW 52:295*. [18]Num 10:2; Ps 98:6 (97:6 LXX); Sir 50:16. [19]1 Cor 4:9. [20]FC 105:74-75. [21]Col 2:14-15. [22]Mt 12:29; Mk 3:27. [23]FC 105:77-78.

We frequently find Jericho to be placed in Scripture as a figure of this world. . . . [24]

Consequently, this Jericho (that is, the world) is about to fall; for indeed the consummation of the age has already been made known a little while ago by the sacred books. In what way, therefore, will the consummation be given to it? By what instruments? By the sound, it says, of trumpets. Of what trumpets? Let Paul make known the mystery of this secret to you. Hear what he himself says: "The trumpet will sound," he says, "and the dead who are in Christ will rise incorruptible," [25] and, "The Lord himself with a command, with the voice of the archangel and with the trumpet of God, will descend from heaven." [26] At that time, therefore, Jesus our Lord conquers Jericho with trumpets and overthrows it, so that out of it, only the prostitute is saved and all her house. HOMILIES ON JOSHUA 6.4. [27]

THE CONSUMMATION OF THE AGE. ORIGEN: The consummation of the world will not happen in stages, but suddenly. With this ought to be compared, I think, what was written in Joshua, when by a single sound of a trumpet the crumbling city of Jericho suddenly perished; and like this example Babylon also in the consummation of the age will fall and suddenly be obliterated. HOMILIES ON JEREMIAH 28.11. [28]

---

[24]Cf. Lk 10:30; Mt 20:29-30. [25]1 Cor 15:52. [26]1 Thess 4:16. [27]FC 105:71-72. [28]FC 97:269-70.

6:22-27 THE DESTRUCTION OF JERICHO

[22]And Joshua said to the two men who had spied out the land, "Go into the harlot's house, and bring out from it the woman, and all who belong to her, as you swore to her." [23]So the young men who had been spies went in, and brought out Rahab, and her father and mother and brothers and all who belonged to her; and they brought all her kindred, and set them outside the camp of Israel. [24]And they burned the city with fire, and all within it; only the silver and gold, and the vessels of bronze and of iron, they put into the treasury of the house of the LORD. [25]But Rahab the harlot, and her father's household, and all who belonged to her, Joshua saved alive; and she dwelt in Israel to this day, because she hid the messengers whom Joshua sent to spy out Jericho.

[26]Joshua laid an oath upon them at that time, saying, "Cursed before the LORD be the man that rises up and rebuilds this city, Jericho.

At the cost of his first-born shall he lay its foundation,
and at the cost of his youngest son shall he set up its gates."

OVERVIEW: As Rahab's house alone was spared in the fall of Jericho, true communion and salvation is found in the one house of the church (JEROME). Rahab's union with the house of Israel endures, just as the union of any believer does who has been engrafted into the faith of Abraham. As Christ's bride, she is made a virgin through his sanctifying work (ORIGEN). Joshua's prophetic curse of the destroyed and rebuilt Jericho signifies condemnation of those who renounce Satan in baptism yet then return to their previous sins (BEDE).

6:22-25 Rahab the Prostitute Is Saved

COMMUNION IN THE ONE HOUSE. JEROME: Let us prepare ourselves for the sacrifice of the lamb. . . . Nor let us be under the impression that this yearling lamb can be eaten anywhere. The precept bids us to partake of it in one house only, lest we think that the lamb may be immolated outside the church. From this, it is evident that the Jews and heretics, and all assemblies of perverted doctrine, because they do not eat the lamb in the church, do not eat the flesh of the lamb but the flesh of the dragon, which, as the psalmist tells us, was given as food to the Ethiopians.[1] Just as in the flood no one was saved who was not in the ark of Noah, and in the fall of Jericho, only the house of the harlot Rahab—which signifies the faithful church of the Gentiles—was spared, so is it true that in the sacrifice of the lamb, the lamb is slain only when it is sacrificed in the one house. HOMILY ON THE EXODUS 91.[2]

TO THIS VERY DAY. ORIGEN: But the woman Rahab, how is she said to be joined to the house of Israel up to this very day? Is a succession of posterity on her mother's side ascribed so that she is considered to be preserved in a renewal of offspring? Or rather must it be understood that she has really been bound and united to Israel up to this very day? If you want to see more plainly how Rahab is bound to Israel, consider how "the branch of the wild olive tree is implanted in the root of a good olive tree."[3] Then you will understand how those who have been implanted in the faith of Abraham and Isaac and Jacob are rightly called attached and "joined to Israel up to this very day." For we have been attached up to this very day in the root of those former ones, we, the

branches of the wild olive taken up from the nations, who at one time were dealing with harlots and worshiping wood and stone instead of the true God.[4] HOMILIES ON JOSHUA 7.5.[5]

A PURE VIRGIN. ORIGEN: Therefore, our Lord Jesus will come, and he will come with the sound of trumpets. But just now let us pray that he may come and destroy "the world that lay in wickedness"[6] and all things that are in the world, because "everything that is in the world is the lust of the flesh and the lust of the eyes."[7] May he destroy that, may he dissolve it again and again, and save only this one who received his spies and who placed his apostles, received with faith and obedience, in the high places. And may he join and unite this prostitute with the house of Israel.

But now let us neither recall nor impute to her the old fault. Once she was a prostitute, but now "a pure virgin, to one man" she has been united, "to Christ." Hear the apostle speaking of her: "But I have determined this itself, to present you to Christ, a pure virgin to one husband."[8] It was also surely of her that someone said, "For once we ourselves were also foolish, unbelieving, wandering, serving desires and various forms of pleasures."[9] Do you still wish to learn more about how the prostitute is no longer a prostitute? Hear Paul saying in addition, "And this surely you have been; but you have been washed, you have been sanctified in the name of our Lord Jesus Christ, and in the Spirit of our God."[10] HOMILIES ON JOSHUA 6.4.[11]

6:26 Joshua Curses Whoever Rebuilds Jericho

JOSHUA'S CURSE FULFILLED. BEDE: It is said of the time when Ahab reigned, "In his days Hiel of Bethel built Jericho; he laid its foundations in Abiram, his firstborn; and he set up its gates in

---

[1]Ps 74:14 (73:14 LXX). The verse is quoted from the LXX. [2]FC 57:236-37*. [3]Rom 11:17. [4]Deut 28:36. [5]FC 105:79-80. [6]1 Jn 5:19. [7]1 Jn 2:16. [8]2 Cor 11:2. [9]Tit 3:3. [10]1 Cor 6:11. [11]FC 105:72-73.

Segub, his youngest son."[12] The apparent sense is that when the above-mentioned city's builder began to lay its foundations, his firstborn, named Abiram, died; and that after the city had been built, when he tried to fortify its gates, he lost his youngest son, named Segub. Joshua predicted that this would happen when, after Jericho's destruction he made it anathema by cursing it, saying, "Cursed be the man before the Lord that shall raise up and build the city of Jericho, and in his firstborn may he lay its foundation, and in the last of his children set up its gates." Because Hiel is translated as "living for God" and Bethel as "house of God," Hiel of Bethel restores Jericho's walls (which Joshua had destroyed and cursed) whenever any who have taken up the religious life in the church resume doing the evil deeds for which the Lord Jesus forgave them on the day of [their] baptism and whenever they who have renounced the devil's pomp return to it by wanton living or prefer false doctrines or Gentile fables to the church's truth in which they were instructed. THIRTY QUESTIONS ON THE BOOK OF KINGS 16.[13]

---

[12]1 Kings 16:34. [13]TTH 28:116*.

7:1-5 THE FAILURE OF ISRAEL

[1]*But the people of Israel broke faith in regard to the devoted things; for Achan the son of Carmi, son of Zabdi, son of Zerah, of the tribe of Judah, took some of the devoted things; and the anger of the LORD burned against the people of Israel.*

OVERVIEW: Christians in troubled times must heed the example of history, which testifies that calamity results from impiety (CHRYSOSTOM). The possessions of others should be treated as items devoted to God, the stealing of which exacts a severe penalty (GREGORY THAUMATURGUS). Those who imitate Achan's greed deserve the punishment he received (PRUDENTIUS). In the body of the church, the disgraceful actions of the few injure the whole (SALVIAN). The enormity of Achan's sin must be figuratively understood in that he defiled the church by cherishing perverse doctrines that were cleverly communicated (ORIGEN).

7:1 Achan the Son of Carmi

TRANSGRESSION BRINGS PUNISHMENT. CHRY-SOSTOM: Suppose any one should carefully examine all the communicants in the world, what kind of transgression is there which he would not detect? And what if he examined those in authority? Would he not find them eagerly bent upon gain? Making traffic of high places? Envious, malignant, vainglorious, gluttonous and slaves to money?

Where then there is such impiety as this going on, what dreadful calamity must we not expect? And to be assured how severe vengeance they incur who are guilty of such sins as these, consider the examples of old. One single man, a common soldier, stole the sacred property, and all were struck. You know, doubtless, the history I mean? I am speaking of Achan the son of Carmi, the man who stole the consecrated spoil....

On account of all these things, let us take heed

to ourselves. Do you not see these wars? Do you not hear of these disasters? Do you learn no lesson from these things? Nations and whole cities are swallowed up and destroyed, and myriads as many again are enslaved to the barbarians.

If hell does not bring us to our senses, yet let these things. What, are these too mere threats, are they not facts that have already taken place? Great is the punishment they have suffered, yet a greater still shall we suffer, who are not brought to our senses even by their fate. HOMILIES ON EPHESIANS 6.[1]

STEALING DEVOTED THINGS. GREGORY THAUMATURGUS: Look, did not Achan the son of Zerah dishonestly steal from the devoted things, and wrath came upon the whole people of Israel? And he alone sinned, but he was not the only one to die in his sin. Now to us, in the present circumstance every asset which does not belong to us but to someone else should be regarded as "the devoted things." For he, Achan, took as spoil, and these men now have taken "as spoil"; but he took what belonged to the enemy, while these now have taken what belonged to their brothers, making for themselves a deadly profit. CANONICAL EPISTLE 3.[2]

ACHAN'S FALL. PRUDENTIUS:
And Jericho had seen in her own ruin
   Our hand's control, when conquering Achan
   fell.
Renowned for bloodshed, proud of leveling
   walls,
He fell a victim to the enemy's gold
When from the dust he gleaned the stuff
   accursed
And snatched the mournful plunder from the
   ruins.
His tribe did not avail, nor his descent
From Judah, founder of the race of Christ
And patriarch blessed in his noble scion.
Let those who imitate his race accept
A similar form of death and punishment.
THE SPIRITUAL COMBAT 536-46.[3]

THE FEW BLOCK THE SPLENDOR OF THE WHOLE. SALVIAN THE PRESBYTER: You say these were the disgraceful acts of a few men and what was not done by all could not injure all. Indeed, I have said above quite often that the crime of one man was the destruction of many among the people of God, just as the people were ruined by Achan's theft, just as pestilence arose from Saul's jealousy,[4] just as death came from the counting of the people by the holy David.[5] The church of God is as the eye. As a speck of dirt, even though small, which falls into the eye blinds the sight completely, in the same way, if some, even though they are a few in the body of the church, commit filthy acts, they block almost all the light of the splendor of the church. THE GOVERNANCE OF GOD 7.19.[6]

A TONGUE OF GOLD. ORIGEN: But also we should not let it be passed over without comment that by one sinner wrath comes upon all the people. . . .

But let us also see what sort of sin this person did. He stole, it says, "a tongue of gold"[7] and placed it in his own tent.

I do not think so great a force of sin was in that theft of a little gold that it defiled the innumerable church of the Lord. But let us see if a deeper understanding does not reveal the enormity and severity of the sin. There is much elegance in words and much beauty in the discourses of philosophers and rhetoricians, who are all of the city of Jericho, that is, people of this world. If, therefore, you should find among the philosophers perverse doctrines beautified by the assertions of a splendid discourse, this is the "tongue of gold." But beware that the splendor of the performance does not beguile you, that the beauty of the golden discourse not seize you. Remember that Jesus [Joshua] commanded all the gold found in Jericho to be anathema. If you

---

[1]NPNF 1 13:79*. [2]FC 98:148-49. [3]FC 52:98*. [4]1 Sam 19. [5]2 Sam 24:2-15. [6]FC 3:213*. [7]That is, a bar of gold or a tongue-shaped ingot, Josh 7:21 LXX.

read a poet with properly measured verses, weaving gods and goddesses in a very bright tune, do not be seduced by the sweetness of eloquence, for it is the "tongue of gold." If you take it up and place it in your tent, if you introduce into your heart those things that are declared by the [poets and philosophers], then you will pollute the whole church of the Lord. HOMILIES ON JOSHUA 7.6-7.[8]

---

[8]FC 105:80, 82-83.

7:6-26 TRANSGRESSION OF THE COVENANT

[10]*The LORD said to Joshua, "Arise, why have you thus fallen upon your face?* [11]*Israel has sinned; they have transgressed my covenant which I commanded them; they have taken some of the devoted things; they have stolen, and lied, and put them among their own stuff.* [12]*Therefore the people of Israel cannot stand before their enemies; they turn their backs before their enemies, because they have become a thing for destruction. I will be with you no more, unless you destroy the devoted things from among you. . . ."*

[19]*Then Joshua said to Achan, "My son, give glory to the LORD God of Israel, and render praise to him; and tell me now what you have done; do not hide it from me."* [20]*And Achan answered Joshua, "Of a truth I have sinned against the LORD God of Israel, and this is what I did:* [21]*when I saw among the spoil a beautiful mantle from Shinar, and two hundred shekels of silver, and a bar of gold weighing fifty shekels, then I coveted them, and took them; and behold, they are hidden in the earth inside my tent, with the silver underneath." . . .*

[24]*And Joshua and all Israel with him took Achan the son of Zerah, and the silver and the mantle and the bar of gold, and his sons and daughters, and his oxen and asses and sheep, and his tent, and all that he had; and they brought them up to the Valley of Achor.* [25]*And Joshua said, "Why did you bring trouble on us? The LORD brings trouble on you today." And all Israel stoned him with stones; they burned them with fire, and stoned them with stones.*

OVERVIEW: God's will supersedes human will so that sin may be punished (AUGUSTINE). Achan's confession bears witness that the love of money has long held a place in the human heart (AMBROSE). God's supreme authority eliminates any basis for charges of divine injustice (JEROME). Scripture clearly teaches that even a single act of contumacy[1] toward God is severely punished (BASIL).

7:12 The People of Israel Cannot Stand

GOD RULES OVER THE HUMAN WILL. AUGUSTINE: For we find that some sins are also a punishment for other sins . . . as in the flight of the Israelites from the face of the enemy out of the city of Ai because fear was instilled into their hearts so that

---

[1]Stubborn resistance to authority.

they fled. And this was done to punish their sin and to punish it as it deserved to be punished, which is why the Lord said to Joshua, the son of Nun, "The children of Israel shall not be able to stand before their enemies." What is the meaning of "shall not be able to stand"? Why did they not use their free will to stand rather than take flight because their wills were thrown into confusion by fear? Was it not for the simple reason that God, as Master of people's wills, can in his anger instill fear into the hearts of whomsoever he pleases? Was it not of their own free choice that the enemies of the Israelites fought against God's own people when they had Joshua, son of Nun, as their leader? And yet the Scripture tells us that "it was by the will of the Lord that their hearts should be strengthened that they should fight against Israel . . . and should be destroyed."[2] ON GRACE AND FREE WILL 20.41.[3]

7:20-21 Coveting and Taking

THE ADMIRATION OF MONEY. AMBROSE: But human habits have so long applied themselves to this admiration of money that no one is thought worthy of honor unless he is rich. This is no new habit. No, this vice (and that makes the matter worse) grew long years ago in human hearts. When the city of Jericho fell at the sound of the priests' trumpets and Joshua the son of Nun gained the victory, he knew that the valor of the people was weakened through love of money and desire for gold. For when Achan had taken a garment of gold and two hundred shekels of silver and a golden ingot from the spoils of the ruined city, he was brought before the Lord and could not deny the theft but admitted it. DUTIES OF THE CLERGY 2.26.129.[4]

7:25 Israel Stoned and Burned Them

GOD'S IRRESISTIBLE WILL. JEROME: Achan sinned, and the entire nation transgressed. And the Lord said to Joshua, "The children of Israel will not be able to stand before their enemies but shall flee from their adversaries, because there is a curse in their midst. And I shall no more be with you, unless the anathema is destroyed out of you." And when they made search for the guilty person and the lot discovered him hiding, Achan, and his sons and daughters, and his asses and sheep are killed; his tent and all his possessions are destroyed by fire. Granted, that he himself committed a sin. What sin did his children commit, his oxen, his asses, his sheep? Reprehend God, why one man committed a sin and a number of people were put to death; why even he is stoned to death and all his possessions are destroyed by the avenging flame? Let us also quote the other testimony: "There was not a city," he says, "that the Lord did not deliver to the children of Israel, except the Hivites who dwell in Gibeon; they took all by fight, because it was the sentence of the Lord that their hearts should be hardened and they should fight against Israel and be killed, and that they should not deserve any clemency and should be destroyed, as the Lord commanded Moses."[5] If it was done by the will of God that they should neither make peace with Israel nor obtain peace from Israel, let us say with the apostle: "Why then does he find fault? For who can resist his will?"[6] DEFENSE AGAINST THE PELAGIANS 1.37.[7]

THE POTTER'S POWER. JEROME: What compulsion commands him [Paul] to do what he dislikes? And why must he not do what he wishes but what he dislikes and does not wish? He will answer you thus: "No, but, O man, who are you that replies against God? Shall the thing formed say to him that formed it, 'Why have you made me this way?' Has not the potter power over the clay, of the same lump to make one vessel to honor and another to dishonor?"[8] Bring a yet graver charge against God and ask him why, when Esau and Jacob were still in the womb, he said, "Jacob I have loved, but Esau I have hated."[9] Accuse him of injustice because, when Achan the

---

[2]Josh 11:20. [3]FC 59:298*. [4]NPNF 2 10:63*. [5]Josh 11:19-20. [6]Rom 9:19. [7]FC 53:287-88*. [8]Rom 9:20-21. [9]Rom 9:13.

son of Carmi stole part of the spoil of Jericho, he butchered so many thousands for the fault of one. LETTER 133.9.[10]

A SINGLE VIOLATION CONDEMNS. BASIL THE GREAT: Accordingly, I find, in taking up the Holy Scripture, that in the Old and New Testament contumacy toward God is clearly condemned, not in consideration of the number or heinousness of transgressions but in terms of a single violation of any precept whatsoever, and, further, that the judgment of God covers all forms of disobedience. In the Old Testament, I read of the frightful end of Achan and the account of the man who gathered wood on the sabbath day.[11] Neither of these men was guilty of any other offense against God, nor had they wronged a man in any way, small or great; but the one, merely for his first gathering of wood, paid the inescapable penalty and did not have an opportunity to make amends, for, by the command of God, he was forthwith stoned by all his people. The other, only because he had pilfered some part of the sacrificial offerings, even though these had not yet been brought into the synagogue nor had been received by those who perform this function, was the cause not only of his own destruction but of that also of his wife and children and of his house and personal possessions besides. Moreover, the evil consequences of his sin would presently have spread like fire over his nation—and this, too, although the people did not know what had occurred and had not excused the sinner—unless his people, sensing the anger of God from the destruction of the men who were slain, had promptly been struck with fear, and unless Joshua, son of Nun, sprinkling himself with dust, had prostrated himself together with the ancients, and unless the culprit, discovered thus by lot, had paid the penalty mentioned above.

Perhaps someone will raise the objection that these men might plausibly be suspected of other sins for which they were overtaken by these punishments, yet the Holy Scripture made mention of these sins alone as very serious and worthy of death. PREFACE ON THE JUDGMENT OF GOD.[12]

---

[10]NPNF 2 6:278*.   [11]Num 15:32-36.   [12]FC 9:43-44*.

8:1-17 THE SECOND ATTACK ON AI

[1]And the LORD said to Joshua, "Do not fear or be dismayed; take all the fighting men with you, and arise, go up to Ai; see, I have given into your hand the king of Ai, and his people, his city, and his land; [2]and you shall do to Ai and its king as you did to Jericho and its king; only its spoil and its cattle you shall take as booty for yourselves; lay an ambush against the city, behind it."

[3]So Joshua arose, and all the fighting men, to go up to Ai; and Joshua chose thirty thousand mighty men of valor, and sent them forth by night. [4]And he commanded them, "Behold, you shall lie in ambush against the city, behind it; do not go very far from the city, but hold yourselves all in readiness; [5]and I, and all the people who are with me, will approach the city. And when they come out against us, as before, we shall flee before them; [6]and they will come out after us, till we have drawn them away from the city; for they will say, 'They are fleeing from us, as before.' So we will

flee from them; [7]*then you shall rise up from the ambush, and seize the city; for the* LORD *your God will give it into your hand.* [8]*And when you have taken the city, you shall set the city on fire, doing as the* LORD *has bidden; see, I have commanded you."* . . .

[10]*And Joshua arose early in the morning and mustered the people, and went up, with the elders of Israel, before the people to Ai.* [11]*And all the fighting men who were with him went up, and drew near before the city, and encamped on the north side of Ai, with a ravine between them and Ai.* [12]*And he took about five thousand men, and set them in ambush between Bethel and Ai, to the west of the city.* [14]*And when the king of Ai saw this he and all his people, the men of the city, made haste and went out early to the descent*[d] *toward the Arabah to meet Israel in battle; but he did not know that there was an ambush against him behind the city.* [15]*And Joshua and all Israel made a pretense of being beaten before them, and fled in the direction of the wilderness.* [16]*So all the people who were in the city were called together to pursue them, and as they pursued Joshua they were drawn away from the city.* [17]*There was not a man left in Ai or Bethel, who did not go out after Israel; they left the city open, and pursued Israel.*

d Cn: Heb *appointed time*

OVERVIEW: The use of deception in war is permissible if the war was undertaken to remedy injustice (AUGUSTINE). In setting an ambush against Ai, which means chaos, the manner and order of the salvation of the Jews and the Gentiles is typified. Those who seem to flee the battle represent Christ's followers: they seem to be free of the law's regulations, yet they are bound to Jesus, the fulfillment of the law. As a type of Christ, Joshua's fleeing teaches his followers the virtuosity of fleeing from evil (ORIGEN).

8:1-8 Joshua Sets an Ambush at God's Command

ETHICS OF A JUST WAR. AUGUSTINE: Inasmuch as God ordered Joshua to plant an ambush in their rear, that is, to plant warriors in hiding to ambush the enemy, we can learn that such treachery is not unjustly carried out by those who wage a just war. Thus, a just man, if he wishes to undertake a just war, ought to think chiefly in these matters about nothing else than whether it is right for him to do so, for it is not lawful for everyone to wage war. However, once he has undertaken a just war, it makes no difference to the justice of the war whether he wins in open warfare or by treachery. However, those just wars ought to be defined as those which avenge injuries, if the tribe or state which is about to be sought in war, either neglected to punish a crime improperly committed by its own countrymen or neglected to repay what had been lost through those injuries. Moreover, without doubt that type of war is just which God commands, since there is no iniquity in him and he knows what ought to be done to each person. In this type of war the general of the army or the people themselves are not to be deemed so much the instigator of the war as much as its agent.

Joshua sent thirty thousand warriors to vanquish Ai. . . . We must consider whether every attempt at deception ought to be reckoned as a lie and, if so, whether a lie can be just, when someone who should be deceived is deceived. And if not even this kind of a lie is found to be just, we must still relate what transpired with the ambush to the truth with some other meaning. QUESTIONS ON JOSHUA 10-11.[1]

---

[1]CCL 33:318-19.

8:10-17 *The Ambush of Ai*

Jew, then Gentile. Origen: At first, we were overcome because of sins, and those who were living in Ai destroyed very many of us. Ai means chaos. But we know chaos to be the place or habitation of opposing powers, of which the devil is the king and chief. Against him, as Jesus [Joshua] comes, he divides the people into two parts; he stations some in the front and others in the rear, so they may come behind the enemies unexpectedly. Consider if the first part is not about the people of whom he says, "I came only to the lost sheep of the house of Israel,"[2] and of whom the apostle says, "But grace and peace to every person who does good, to the Jew first, then also to the Greek," that is, the later Gentile.[3] Those are the people, therefore, who are stationed in the front and seem to flee with Jesus. But the people in back are the ones who are gathered from the nations and who come unexpectedly. For who expected the nations to be saved? They strike more keenly behind the adversaries, and thus both people together overthrow and conquer the throng of demons confined in the middle. Homilies on Joshua 8.2.[4]

Following and Fleeing. Origen: But perhaps you say to me, "In what manner are the people in front placed as though fleeing?" In a most suitable manner. For truly, those who follow Jesus seem to flee from legal burdens and precepts, from the observation of the sabbath, from the circumcision of the flesh, and from cutting the throats of enemies. But on the other hand, the one who has followed Christ, the fulfillment and fullness of the law, does not flee. Homilies on Joshua 8.2.[5]

Virtue in Flight. Origen: But another thing occurs to me in this place as I consider Jesus [Joshua] fleeing before the face of the army of Ai. Why do you think it is that Jesus [Joshua] is described as fleeing? Let us consider whether perhaps there may be something that we may conquer by fleeing, and that there is some perfect virtue in flight. Paul the apostle teaches us saying, "Flee fornication."[6] You see therefore that there is a certain "spirit of fornication"[7] that we ought to flee, all who wish to remain chastely and piously and modestly in Christ. Thus this flight is that which holds salvation; this flight is of power; this flight confers blessedness. And not only must the spirit of fornication be fled, but in like manner, just as it is said, "Flee fornication," let us hear it said to us: "Flee wrath, flee avarice, flee greed and envy, flee detractions and slanders." Yet I do not know if anyone may flee these things; I do not know if anyone may escape them.

Such was that army of Ai that Jesus [Joshua] instructed his soldiers to flee, and perhaps concerning these things he charged his disciples, saying, "If they persecute you in this city, flee into another one; but if in that one also, flee into another."[8] For he wants us to flee from enemies of this kind; he wants us to be put out of reach of this kind of evil. If we are able in the meantime to escape the contagions of these evils by fleeing, then, seeing the devotion and intention of our heart, all those holy powers—those perhaps about which the apostle Paul says, "Are they not all ministering spirits sent into the ministry for the sake of those who will receive the inheritance of salvation?"[9]—who perhaps are holy angels who, seeing us exposed to pursuing demons, rise up against those who pursue us and, striking from behind, destroy them all. For Jesus is with those who are exposed to the ones pursuing, more than with those who follow after. And justly, because Jesus loves to be with those who flee fornication, those who flee pride, those who flee deceit, and those who flee falsehood. Homilies on Joshua 8.6.[10]

[2]Mt 15:24. [3]Rom 2:10. [4]FC 105:86-87*. [5]FC 105:87. [6]1 Cor 6:18. [7]See Hos 5:4. [8]Mt 10:23. [9]Heb 1:14. [10]FC 105:90-91.

8:18-29 THE DESTRUCTION OF AI

[21]*And when Joshua and all Israel saw that the ambush had taken the city, and that the smoke of the city went up, then they turned back and smote the men of Ai.* [22]*And the others came forth from the city against them; so they were in the midst of Israel, some on this side, and some on that side; and Israel smote them, until there was left none that survived or escaped. . . .*

[28]*So Joshua burned Ai, and made it for ever a heap of ruins, as it is to this day.*

OVERVIEW: That all of Israel's enemies were slain in battle symbolizes the believer's war against sin. The slaughter of Ai's inhabitants depicts the manner in which believers must rid themselves of evil actions and words. Rendering the city uninhabitable through burning signifies the cessation of sin's power and rule as the devil and his angels are consigned to eternal fire (ORIGEN).

8:22 None Survived the Battle

THE BATTLE AGAINST SIN. ORIGEN: You will read in the Holy Scriptures about the battles of the just ones, about the slaughter and carnage of murderers, and that the saints spare none of their deeply rooted enemies. If they do spare them, they are even charged with sin, just as Saul was charged because he had preserved the life of Agag king of Amalek.[1] You should understand the wars of the just by the method I set forth above, that these wars are waged by them against sin. But how will the just ones endure if they reserve even a little bit of sin? Therefore, this is said of them: "They did not leave behind even one who might be saved or might escape."

Do you perhaps not believe me that the battle is joined against our sin? Then believe Paul as he says, "Not yet to the shedding of blood have you resisted against sin."[2] Do you see that the fight proposed for you is against sin and that you must complete the battle even to the shedding of blood? Is it not evident that the divine Scripture indicates these things, even as it habitually says, "Sanctify war,"[3] and, "You will fight the battle of

the Lord"?[4] HOMILIES ON JOSHUA 8.7.[5]

SLAYING DEMONS. ORIGEN: When the Jews read these things, they become cruel and thirst after human blood, thinking that even holy persons so struck those who were living in Ai that not one of them was left "who might be saved or who might escape." They do not understand that mysteries are dimly shadowed in these words and that they more truly indicate to us that we ought not to leave any of those demons deeply within, whose dwelling place is chaos and who rule in the abyss, but to destroy them all. We slay demons, but we do not annihilate their essence. For their work and endeavor is to cause persons to sin. If we sin, they have life; but if we do not sin, they are destroyed. Therefore, all holy persons kill the inhabitants of Ai; they both annihilate and do not release any of them. These are doubtless those who guard their heart with all diligence so that evil thoughts do not proceed from it,[6] and those who heed their mouth, so that "no evil word"[7] proceeds from it. Not to leave any who flee means this: when no evil word escapes them. HOMILIES ON JOSHUA 8.7.[8]

8:28 Joshua Burns Ai

THE ETERNAL FIRE. ORIGEN: You see that these things that follow truly pertain more to the truth of a mystery than that of history. For it is not so

---

[1] 1 Sam 15:9-24.　[2] Heb 12:4.　[3] Joel 3:9.　[4] 1 Sam 18:17.　[5] FC 105:94.
[6] See Mk 7:21.　[7] Eph 4:29.　[8] FC 105:92.

much that a piece of land is forever uninhabitable, but that the place of demons will be uninhabitable when no one will sin and sin will not rule in anyone. Then the devil and his angels will be consigned to the eternal fire with our Lord Jesus Christ sitting as ruler and judge and saying to those who overcame before and afterwards, "Come, blessed of my Father, take possession of the kingdom that was created for you by my Father."[9] But to the others he will say, "Go into the eternal fire that God prepared for the devil and his angels,"[10] until he takes care of every soul with the remedies he himself knows and "all Israel may be saved."[11] HOMILIES ON JOSHUA 8.5.[12]

[9]Mt 25:34. [10]Mt 25:41. [11]Rom 11:26. [12]FC 105:90*.

8:30-35 ISRAEL WORSHIPS AT MOUNT EBAL

[30]Then Joshua built an altar on Mount Ebal to the LORD, the God of Israel, [31]as Moses the servant of the LORD had commanded the people of Israel, as it is written in the book of the law of Moses, "an altar of unhewn stones, upon which no man has lifted an iron tool"; and they offered on it burnt offerings to the LORD, and sacrificed peace offerings. [32]And there, in the presence of the people of Israel, he wrote upon the stones a copy of the law of Moses, which he had written. [33]And all Israel, sojourner as well as homeborn, with their elders and officers and their judges, stood on opposite sides of the ark before the Levitical priests who carried the ark of the covenant of the LORD, half of them in front of Mount Gerizim and half of them in front of Mount Ebal, as Moses the servant of the LORD had commanded at the first, that they should bless the people of Israel. [34]And afterward he read all the words of the law, the blessing and the curse, according to all that is written in the book of the law. [35]There was not a word of all that Moses commanded which Joshua did not read before all the assembly of Israel, and the women, and the little ones, and the sojourners who lived among them.

OVERVIEW: The unhewn stones Joshua used to build an altar represent those who bear Christ's humility and gentleness. The apostles qualify for such stones due to their unanimity and concord in prayer, as we may also if we show the same qualities. His writing upon the stones typifies Jesus' writing a new law upon human hearts. The apparent impossibility of writing so much in the presence of so many is resolved as this occurs at the moment one believes. The separation between the two mounts prefigures two classes of believers: those who eagerly seek blessing and those who are driven by the fear of punishment. Only Jesus is able to distinguish between the two. In Joshua's reading of the law we understand that the law of Moses is rightly grasped only when we possess a spiritual conception of its contents, which is given through Jesus. The diversity of people assembled for the reading of the law represents the differing degrees of maturity within the church (ORIGEN).

8:31 An Altar of Unhewn Stones

LIVING STONES. ORIGEN: Who do you think those whole stones are? The conscience of everyone knows who is whole, who is uncorrupted, unpolluted, unstained in flesh and in spirit. This is the one in whom iron has not been set, that is, who did not receive "the fiery darts of the evil one," the darts of lust, but by the shield of faith "quenched and repelled them";[1] or the one who never assumed the iron of battle, the iron of war, the iron of strife, but was always peaceable, always calm and gentle, formed out of the humility of Christ. Those, therefore, are "the living stones" out of which Jesus our Lord "constructed an altar from whole stones, in which iron had not been set," so that he might offer upon them "whole burnt offerings and the sacrifice of salvation." HOMILIES ON JOSHUA 9.2.[2]

OF ONE MIND. ORIGEN: I myself think that perhaps the holy apostles are able to be such whole and undefiled stones, making one altar all together on account of their unanimity and concord. For thus "praying unanimously"[3] and opening their mouths all together, they are reported to have said, "You, Lord, you who know the hearts of all."[4] Therefore, those of one mind who were able to pray with one voice and one spirit, they are perhaps the worthy ones who all together ought to build one altar, upon which Jesus may offer sacrifices to the Father. Yet may we also try to take care that "we all may speak the same thing"[5] with one accord, "perceiving one thing, doing nothing through contention or through vain glory"[6] but "remaining in one mind and in the same purpose,"[7] if perhaps we ourselves can also be made fit stones for the altar. HOMILIES ON JOSHUA 9.2.[8]

8:32 He Wrote on the Stones

TABLETS OF THE HEART. ORIGEN: He wrote, in the way the son of Nun was able at that time, to depict the law upon the stones of the altar; and, to the extent he was capable, he dimly sketched types. Let us see, however, how our Jesus wrote

Deuteronomy "on living" and "whole stones."

Deuteronomy is called, so to speak, a "second law." If therefore you wish to see how, after the first law was annulled, Jesus wrote the second law, hear him saying in the Gospel, "It was said in former times: You shall not kill. But I say to you that everyone who is angry with his brother is a murderer." [9] And again, "It was said in former times: You shall not commit adultery. But I say to you, if anyone has looked upon a woman to desire her, he has already committed adultery with her in his heart."[10] And, "It was said in former times: You shall not swear falsely. But I say to you, do not swear at all."[11] You see Deuteronomy, which Jesus wrote "on living" and "whole stones; not on stone tablets, but on the fleshly tablets of the heart; not with ink, but by the Spirit of the living God."[12] HOMILIES ON JOSHUA 9.3.[13]

THE SECOND LAW. ORIGEN: How was he able to depict so large a book to the sons of Israel—or even to those standing and remaining there—so that they did not disperse until the writing of so many verses was finished? Or even how were the stones of the altar able to bear the contents of such a large book? Such things let those Jewish defenders of the letter who are ignorant of the spirit of the law tell me. In what manner is the truth of the narrative demonstrated in this? Yet among those former ones "to this day, whenever Moses is read, a veil lies over their heart."[14] But for us, "who have turned to the Lord" Jesus, "the veil is taken away" because "where the Spirit of the Lord is, there is freedom of understanding."[15]

Therefore our Lord Jesus does not need much time in order to write Deuteronomy, in order to set up the "second law" in the hearts of believers and imprint the law of the Spirit in the minds of those who are worthy to be chosen for the construction of the altar. For immediately when anyone believes in Jesus Christ, the law of the gospel

---

[1]Eph 6:16. [2]FC 105:97. [3]Acts 1:14. [4]Acts 1:24. [5]1 Cor 1:10. [6]Phil 2:3. [7]1 Cor 1:10. [8]FC 105:97-98. [9]Mt 5:21-22. [10]Mt 5:27-28. [11]Mt 5:33-34. [12]2 Cor 3:3. [13]FC 105:98*. [14]2 Cor 3:15. [15]2 Cor 3:16-17.

is written down in that person's heart and written down "in the sight of the sons of Israel." HOMILIES ON JOSHUA 9.4.[16]

8:33 The Nation Divides Between the Mounts

SEEKING BLESSING IS DISTINGUISHABLE FROM FEARING PUNISHMENT. ORIGEN: But how shall we ourselves apply this narration of history to mystic discernment so that we may make known who they are who go near Mount Gerizim and who they are who go near Mount Ebal?

As I myself see, there are two species of those who through faith hasten and go quickly toward salvation. One of them are those who, kindled by the longing for the promise of heaven, press forward with the greatest zeal and diligence so that not even the least happiness may pass them by. They have the desire not only to lay hold of blessings and to be made "to have a share in the lot of the saints"[17] but also to station themselves in the sight of God and to be always with the Lord. There are others, however, who also reach toward salvation, but they are not inflamed so much by the love of blessings or by the desires for the promises. Instead their view is much more like this, as they say, "It is enough for me not to go into Gehenna, it is enough for me not to be sent into eternal fire, it is enough for me not to be expelled 'into outer darkness.' "[18]

Since there is such a variety of aims among individual ones of the faithful, it seems to me that what is designated in this place is this. The half who go near Mount Gerizim, those who have been chosen for blessings, indicate figuratively the ones who come to salvation not by fear of punishment but by desire of blessings and renewed promises. But the half who go near Mount Ebal, where curses were produced, indicate those others who, by fulfilling what was written in the law, attain salvation by fear of evil things and dread of torments. HOMILIES ON JOSHUA 9.7.[19]

JESUS ALONE. ORIGEN: Now it is for God alone to know who of all of us sons of Israel is kindled by desire of the good itself to do what is good, and who of us, out of fear of Gehenna and the terror of eternal fire, strives toward the good and is diligent and hastens to fulfill the things that have been written. It is certain that the nobler ones are those who do what is good by the desire of the good itself and by the love of blessings, rather than those who run after the good through the fear of evil. Therefore, Jesus alone is the one who is able to distinguish the minds and spirits of all such people, and to station some on Mount Gerizim for blessings and others on Mount Ebal for cursings. Not so that they may receive curses but that they may guard against incurring them by gazing at the curses prescribed and punishments set down for sinners. HOMILIES ON JOSHUA 9.7.[20]

8:34 The Reading of the Law

SECRET THINGS OF THE LAW ARE READ THROUGH JESUS. ORIGEN: I certainly think that whenever "Moses is read" to us and through the grace of the Lord "the veil of the letter is removed"[21] and we begin to understand that "the law is spiritual,"[22] then the Lord Jesus reads that law to us. . . . The law, which Paul names "spiritual,"[23] is thus understood and Jesus himself is the one who recites these things in the ears of all the people, admonishing us that we not follow "the letter that kills" but that we hold fast "the life-giving spirit."[24]

Therefore, Jesus reads the law to us when he reveals the secret things of the law. For we who are of the catholic church do not reject the law of Moses, but we accept it if Jesus reads it to us. For thus we shall be able to understand the law correctly, if Jesus reads it to us, so that when he reads we may grasp his mind and understanding. Therefore, should we not think that he had

---

[16]FC 105:99-100. [17]Col 1:12. [18]Mt 8:12. [19]FC 105:102. [20]FC 105:102-3. [21]2 Cor 3:15-16. [22]Rom 7:14. [23]Rom 7:14. [24]2 Cor 3:6.

understood this mind who said, "And we have the mind of Christ, so that we may know those things that have been given to us by God, those things that also we speak"?[25] Also, those who were saying, "Was not our heart burning within us, when he laid bare the Scriptures to us along the way?"[26] when "beginning from the law of Moses up to the prophets he read all things to us and revealed those things that were written concerning him"?[27] HOMILIES ON JOSHUA 9.8.[28]

8:35 Before All of Israel

LEVELS OF MATURITY. ORIGEN: But also even "women and infants and proselytes" are joined to the church of the Lord. If we understand women and infants and proselytes separately and consider each of them to be as though a certain follower of the church—because "in a great house there are not only gold and silver vessels, but also wood and earthen"[29]—we say that to strong men, indeed strong food is delivered. This is clearly to those of whom the apostle says, "Solid food is for the mature,"[30] out of whom he prepares for himself a church "not having spot or wrinkle or anything of these."[31] But those whom he sets apart by the name of "women or infants or proselytes,"[32] let us understand them to be persons who still "need milk" or as though "weak," since they are women, "they feed upon vegetables."[33] But if everyone together is accepted to be the church, the "men," indeed, are understood to be those who, perfect among all these, know to stand "armed against the wiles of the devil";[34] but the "women" are those who do not yet produce from themselves the things that are useful, but from imitating the men and following their example. They are even said to have their head from them: "For the head of a woman is man."[35] But the "infants" will be those who with the faith newly received are nourished by the gospel milk. "Proselytes" seem to be the catechumens, or those who now are eager to be associated with the faith. Even John, perceiving similar things about these separate groups, writes and determines in his epistle which deeds are peculiar to which individual ages.[36] . . .

For divine Scripture does not know how to make a separation of men and women according to sex. For indeed sex is no distinction in the presence of God, but a person is designated either a man or woman according to the diversity of spirit. HOMILIES ON JOSHUA 9.9.[37]

---

[25]1 Cor 2:12-13. [26]Lk 24:32. [27]Lk 24:27. [28]FC 105:103-4. [29]2 Tim 2:20. [30]Heb 5:14. [31]Eph 5:27. [32]Heb 5:12. [33]Rom 14:2. [34]Eph 6:11. [35]1 Cor 11:3. [36]See 1 Jn 2:12-14. [37]FC 105:105-6*.

9:1-15 THE GIBEONITE DECEPTION

[1]*When all the kings who were beyond the Jordan in the hill country and in the lowland all along the coast of the Great Sea toward Lebanon, the Hittites, the Amorites, the Canaanites, the Perizzites, the Hivites, and the Jebusites, heard of this,* [2]*they gathered together with one accord to fight Joshua and Israel.*

[3]*But when the inhabitants of Gibeon heard what Joshua had done to Jericho and to Ai,* [4]*they on their part acted with cunning, and went and made ready provisions, and took worn-out sacks upon*

their asses, and wineskins, worn-out and torn and mended, ⁵with worn-out, patched sandals on their feet, and worn-out clothes; and all their provisions were dry and moldy. ⁶And they went to Joshua in the camp at Gilgal, and said to him and to the men of Israel, "We have come from a far country; so now make a covenant with us." . . . ⁹They said to him, "From a very far country your servants have come, because of the name of the LORD your God, for we have heard a report of him. . . . ¹¹And our elders and all the inhabitants of our country said to us, 'Take provisions in your hand for the journey, and go to meet them, and say to them, "We are your servants; come now, make a covenant with us."' ¹²Here is our bread; it was still warm when we took it from our houses as our food for the journey, on the day we set forth to come to you, but now, behold, it is dry and moldy; ¹³these wineskins were new when we filled them, and behold, they are burst; and these garments and shoes of ours are worn out from the very long journey." ¹⁴So the men partook of their provisions, and did not ask direction from the LORD. ¹⁵And Joshua made peace with them, and made a covenant with them, to let them live; and the leaders of the congregation swore to them.

OVERVIEW: As the kings of old assembled against Joshua, rulers today attack Christians, precipitating the same outcome. The Gibeonites' salvation, secured through deception, is a figure for those who outwardly serve and minister to the church yet remain wrapped up in vices (ORIGEN). Joshua's deception by the Gibeonites exhibits his admirable innocence of evil (AMBROSE).

9:1-2 Amorite Kings Unite Against Israel

ASSEMBLED AGAINST JESUS. ORIGEN: The narrative of the exploits is clear, and what is plainly expressed does not need explanation. Nevertheless, out of these visible things that were done, let us consider the wars and triumphs that the Lord Jesus, our Savior, led, although we may also perceive these things to be visibly fulfilled in him. For the kings of the earth have assembled together, the senate and the people and the leaders of Rome, to blot out the name of Jesus and Israel at the same time. For they have decreed in their laws that there be no Christians. Every city, every class, attacks the name of Christians. But just as at that time all those kings assembling against Jesus [Joshua] were able to do nothing, so even now, whether princes or those opposing authorities, they have been able to do nothing to

prevent the race of Christians from being propagated more widely and profusely. For it is written, "The more greatly they abased them, the more they multiplied and they increased mightily."[1] HOMILIES ON JOSHUA 9.10.[2]

9:3-6 The Gibeonites Plan Deception

DIFFERENCES IN GLORY. ORIGEN: "In my father's house are many mansions,"[3] says the Word of God. Yet even the resurrection of the dead will not exhibit an equal glory of those rising again, for "there is one flesh of birds, another of cattle, and even another of fish. There are both heavenly bodies and earthly bodies; but the glory of heavenly things is one thing, that of the earthly, another. One glory of the sun, another glory of the moon, another glory of the stars. Star differs from star in glory; thus also, the resurrection of the dead."[4]

Therefore, many differences of those who come to salvation are depicted. Whence even now I think those Gibeonites, whose history has been recited, are a certain small portion of those who must be saved but in such a manner that they are not saved apart from the branding of some mark.

---

[1]Ex 1:12. [2]FC 105:107. [3]Jn 14:2. [4]1 Cor 15:39-42.

For you see how they are condemned to become "hewers of wood" or "bearers of water" for the service of the people and for the ministry of the altar of God,[5] because they indeed approached the sons of Israel with deceit and cunning, "clothed in old garments and shoes" and "carrying food of aged bread." Therefore, these persons come to Jesus [Joshua] with all their aged things and greatly beg of him that they may be saved.

Something such as this seems to me to be displayed in their figure. There are in the church certain ones who believe in God, have faith in God, and acquiesce in all the divine precepts. Furthermore, they are conscientious toward the servants of God and desire to serve them, for they also are fully ready and prepared for the furnishing of the church or for the ministry. But, in fact, they are completely disgusting in their actions and particular habit of life, wrapped up with vices and not wholly "putting away the old self with its actions."[6] Indeed they are enveloped in ancient vices and offensive faults, just as those persons were covered over with old garments and shoes. Apart from the fact that they believe in God and seem to be conscientious toward the servants of God or the worship of the church, they make no attempt to correct or alter their habits. For those, therefore, our Lord Jesus certainly permits salvation, but their salvation itself, in a certain measure, does not escape a note of infamy. HOMILIES ON JOSHUA 10.1.[7]

9:11-15 Make a Covenant with Us

INNOCENCE OF THE SAINTS. AMBROSE: Then the Gibeonites, fearing his strong hand, came with guile, pretending that they were from a land very far away, and by traveling so long had rent their shoes and worn out their clothing, of which they showed proofs that it was growing old. They said, too, that their reason for undergoing so much labor was their desire to obtain peace and to form friendship with the Hebrews, and [they] began to ask Joshua to form an alliance with them. And he, being as yet ignorant of localities and not knowing anything of the inhabitants, did not see through their deceit, nor did he enquire of God but readily believed them.

So sacred was one's promised word held in those days that no one would believe that others could try to deceive. Who could find fault with the saints in this, namely, that they should consider others to have the same feelings as themselves and suppose no one would lie because truth was their own companion? They do not know what deceit is, they gladly believe of others what they themselves are, while they cannot suspect others to be what they themselves are not. Hence Solomon says, "An innocent man believes every word."[8] We must not blame his readiness to believe but should rather praise his goodness. To know nothing of anything that may injure another, this is to be innocent. And although he is cheated by another, still he thinks well of all, for he thinks there is good faith in all. DUTIES OF THE CLERGY 3.10.67-68.[9]

---

[5]Josh 9:27. [6]Col 3:9. [7]FC 105:109-10. [8]Prov 14:15. [9]NPNF 2 10:78*.

9:16-27 THE GIBEONITES ARE PRESERVED

[16]*At the end of three days after they had made a covenant with them, they heard that they were their neighbors, and that they dwelt among them. . . .* [18]*But the people of Israel did not kill them, because the leaders of the congregation had sworn to them by the LORD, the God of Israel. Then all the congregation murmured against the leaders.* [19]*But all the leaders said to all the congregation, "We have sworn to them by the LORD, the God of Israel, and now we may not touch them.* [20]*This we will do to them, and let them live, lest wrath be upon us, because of the oath which we swore to them."* [21]*And the leaders said to them, "Let them live." So they became hewers of wood and drawers of water for all the congregation, as the leaders had said of them.*

[22]*Joshua summoned them, and he said to them, "Why did you deceive us, saying, 'We are very far from you,' when you dwell among us?* [23]*Now therefore you are cursed, and some of you shall always be slaves, hewers of wood and drawers of water for the house of my God."*

OVERVIEW: The word of God that one carries within and speaks in praise should be fresh like new loaves of bread, unlike the old ones carried by the Gibeonites. That these people were made servants is fitting: the condition for their salvation corresponds to the smallness of their faith (ORIGEN).

9:21-23 Hewers of Wood and Drawers of Water

FRESH LOAVES OF GOD'S WORD. ORIGEN: Thus, therefore, you also, if you have brought a word in praise of God, not new and fresh from the learning of the spirit, from the doctrine of God's grace, your mouth indeed offers "a sacrifice of praise," but your mind is accused on account of the sterility of yesterday's flesh. For the Lord did not delay and order the bread which he gave to the disciples to be reserved for the next day when he said to them, "Take and eat."[1] Perhaps there is something of this mystery in the fact that "he commands them not to carry bread on the way,"[2] that you always bring fresh loaves of the word of God which you carry within you. For this reason, the Gibeonites are condemned, and they become "cutters of wood and carriers of water" because

they had brought old bread to the Israelites whom the spiritual law ordered always to use fresh and new. HOMILIES ON LEVITICUS 5.8.[3]

A FITTING JUDGMENT. ORIGEN: Of course, it must be observed that the heretics reading this passage, those who do not accept the Old Testament,[4] are accustomed to make a malicious charge and say, "See how Jesus [Joshua] the son of Nun showed no human kindness, so that, although permitting salvation, he inflicted a mark of infamy and a yoke of servitude upon those men who had come to him in supplication." If the soul less instructed in the divine Scriptures hears these things, it can in consequence be enfeebled and endangered, so that it may shun the catholic faith; for they do not understand their deceptions. For Jesus [Joshua] passed a fitting judgment upon them according to the measure of their own faith.

Formerly Rahab the harlot, who believed with a sound faith with all her house and received the Israelite spies with fullest devotion,[5] was received

---

[1]Mt 26:26. [2]Lk 9:3. [3]FC 83:105-6. [4]For instance, Marcion, who did not consider the Old Testament authoritative for Christians. [5]Josh 2:12, 18.

fully into the community and society of the people; and it is written of her that "she was attached to the sons of Israel until today."[6] But those who did not so much love the community of the Israelite clan as they were terrified by fear of their destruction approached Jesus [Joshua] with cunning and fraud. How could they deserve the liberty of life and the community of the kingdom in their slavish deceits?

Finally, do you wish to know that the condition was dispensed toward them by Jesus [Joshua] because the inferiority of their disposition was fitting for them? They themselves say, "We have heard how many things the Lord did for you"[7] through the midst of the Red Sea and in the desert. And although they said these things and confessed that they had both heard and known of the divine miracles, yet they produced nothing worthy in faith, nothing in admiration of such great powers. And therefore Jesus, when he sees the narrowness and smallness displayed in their faith, preserves a very just moderation towards them, so that they might merit salvation. Although they had brought a little faith, nevertheless they did not receive the highest rank of the kingdom or of freedom because their faith was not ennobled by the increase of works, since the apostle James declares, "faith without works is dead."[8] HOMILIES ON JOSHUA 10.2.[9]

---

[6]Josh 6:25. [7]Josh 9:9. [8]Jas 2:17, 26. [9]FC 105:111-12.

10:1-11 AMORITE KINGS ATTACK GIBEON

[1]*When Adoni-zedek king of Jerusalem heard how Joshua had taken Ai, and had utterly destroyed it, doing to Ai and its king as he had done to Jericho and its king, and how the inhabitants of Gibeon had made peace with Israel and were among them, [2]he[x] feared greatly, because Gibeon was a great city, like one of the royal cities, and because it was greater than Ai, and all its men were mighty. [3]So Adoni-zedek king of Jerusalem sent to Hoham king of Hebron, to Piram king of Jarmuth, to Japhia king of Lachish, and to Debir king of Eglon, saying, [4]"Come up to me, and help me, and let us smite Gibeon; for it has made peace with Joshua and with the people of Israel." . . .*

[6]*And the men of Gibeon sent to Joshua at the camp in Gilgal, saying, "Do not relax your hand from your servants; come up to us quickly, and save us, and help us; for all the kings of the Amorites that dwell in the hill country are gathered against us." [7]So Joshua went up from Gilgal, he and all the people of war with him, and all the mighty men of valor.*

x Heb *they*

OVERVIEW: The attack on the Gibeonites demonstrates how friendship with Jesus brings hostility from other people and powers (ORIGEN).

10:1-7 *The Attack of Gibeon*

EXPECT RESISTANCE. ORIGEN: There is no

doubt that when a human soul associates itself with the Word of God, it is immediately going to have enemies, and that those it once considered friends will be changed into adversaries. The soul should not only expect to suffer this from humans, but it should also know that such will likewise be forthcoming from opposing powers and spiritual iniquities. Thus it happens that whoever longs for friendship with Jesus knows he must tolerate the hostilities of many. . . .

Even now, therefore, the Gibeonites, such as they are, are assaulted because of friendship with

Jesus [Joshua], even though they are "hewers of wood and carriers of water." That is, although you are the least worthy in the church, nevertheless, because you belong to Jesus, you will be assailed by five kings.

The Gibeonites, however, are not abandoned or scorned by Jesus [Joshua] or by the leaders and elders of the Israelites; instead they offer help for their weakness. HOMILIES ON JOSHUA 11.2.[1]

---

[1]FC 105:116.

10:12-21 THE SUN AND MOON STAND STILL

[12]*Then spoke Joshua to the* LORD *in the day when the* LORD *gave the Amorites over to the men of Israel; and he said in the sight of Israel,*

"Sun, stand thou still at Gibeon,
and thou Moon in the valley of Aijalon."

[13]*And the sun stood still, and the moon stayed,*
until the nation took vengeance on their enemies.

Is this not written in the Book of Jashar? The sun stayed in the midst of heaven, and did not hasten to go down for about a whole day. [14]*There has been no day like it before or since, when the* LORD *hearkened to the voice of a man; for the* LORD *fought for Israel.*

[15]*Then Joshua returned, and all Israel with him, to the camp at Gilgal.*

[16]*These five kings fled, and hid themselves in the cave at Makkedah.* [17]*And it was told Joshua, "The five kings have been found, hidden in the cave at Makkedah." . . .* [20]*When Joshua and the men of Israel had finished slaying them with a very great slaughter, until they were wiped out, and when the remnant which remained of them had entered into the fortified cities,* [21]*all the people returned safe to Joshua in the camp at Makkedah; not a man moved his tongue against any of the people of Israel.*

OVERVIEW: Great courage is exhibited in Joshua's engagement with the Amorite kings. As Moses' companion and successor, his worthiness and faith are extolled (AMBROSE). The passage of time is not bound to the movements of the heavenly bodies. Although contrary to human knowledge of nature, miracles such as the staying of the sun and moon exhibit God's power and favor (AUGUStine). Herein the value of righteousness is witnessed as Joshua, the friend of God, commanded his friend's creatures (Chrysostom). The staying of the sun's course is a figure for Christ's extension of the time for salvation to allow for the ingathering of the nations (Origen). By establishing and later circumventing the natural order, God proves that he is the creator for whom anything is possible (Nemesius of Emesa). The five kings represent the five senses, which hold dominion until Jesus conquers them (Jerome, Origen). Immature believers, immersed in earthly impulses, are assaulted through these. The one who fights as Jesus' soldier ought to be spared the injury of defilement and refrain from taking credit for the victory (Origen).

10:12-13 *Sun, Stand Still*

Joshua's Courage. Ambrose: But perhaps renown in war keeps some so bound to itself as to make them think that fortitude is to be found in battle alone and that therefore I had gone aside to speak of these things, because that was lacking in us.[1] But how brave was Joshua the son of Nun, who in one battle laid low five kings together with their people! Again, when he fought against the Gibeonites[2] and feared that night might stop him from gaining the victory, he called out with deep faith and high spirit: "Let the sun stand still"; and it stood still until the victory was complete. Duties of the Clergy 1.40.205.[3]

Joshua's Worthiness. Ambrose: Everywhere, therefore, he alone kept close to holy Moses amid all these wondrous works and dread secrets. In this way it happened that the one who had been Moses' companion in this intercourse with God succeeded to his power.[4] Worthy surely was he to stand forth as a man who might stay the course of the river,[5] and who might say, "Sun, stand still," and delay the night and lengthen the day, as though to witness his victory. Why?—a blessing denied to Moses—he alone was chosen to lead the people into the promised land. A man

he was, great in the wonders he wrought by faith, great in his triumphs. The works of Moses were of a higher type, his brought greater success. Either of these then aided by divine grace rose above all human standing. The one ruled the sea, the other heaven. Duties of the Clergy 2.20.99.[6]

Time Went On. Augustine: Let no one tell me, therefore, that the motions of the heavenly bodies constitute time. For when the sun stood still at the prayer of a certain man in order that he might gain his victory in battle, the sun stood still but time went on. For in as long a span of time as was sufficient the battle was fought and ended.

I see, then, that time is a certain kind of extension. Confessions 11.23.30.[7]

Miracles and Human Knowledge. Augustine: Actually, as we have recorded in our Scriptures, the sun itself stood still when the holy man, Joshua the son of Nun, asked that favor of God, and it remained where it was until a battle, already begun, ended in victory. . . . Such are the miracles which God grants as favors to his saints; although our adversaries would attribute them—if they believed them—to the arts of magic. . . .

In regard, then, to human knowledge of the natures of things, the unbelievers have no right to becloud the issue by their assumption that nothing, even by the power of God, can happen to a nature beyond what is known already by human experience. And remember, too, that there are qualities and powers in the natures of the commonest things that are nothing less than stupendous and would, in fact, be reckoned portents by anyone who examined them, except that humans have accustomed themselves to have no wonder to spare save for things that are unusual. City of God 21.8.[8]

---

[1]Ambrose wrote this treatise in order to reinforce the lessons he had taught the clergy in his diocese. [2]That is, at Gibeon. [3]NPNF 2 10:33. [4]Deut 34:9. [5]Josh 3:15ff. [6]NPNF 2 10:59*. [7]LCC 7:262*. [8]FC 24:360-61*.

THE VALUE OF RIGHTEOUSNESS. CHRYSOSTOM: Consider how great of value is the righteous man. Joshua the son of Nun said, "Let the sun stand still at Gibeon, the moon at the valley of Elom [Aijalon]," and it was so. Let then the whole world come, or rather two or three, or four, or ten, or twenty worlds, and let them say and do this; yet they shall not be able. But the friend of God commanded the creatures of his friend, or rather he besought his friend, and the servants yielded, and the one below gave command to those above. Do you see that these things are fulfilling their appointed course for service? ON THE EPISTLE TO THE HEBREWS 27.6.[9]

A LONGER DAY. ORIGEN: In this manner, therefore, Jesus [Joshua] with his chiefs and princes comes to those who are attacked for his name by opposing powers, and not only does he furnish assistance in war, but also he extends the length of the day and, prolonging the extent of light, dispels the approaching night.

Therefore, if we are able, we want to disclose how our Lord Jesus prolonged the light and made a longer day, both for the salvation of humans and for the destruction of opposing powers.

Immediately after the Savior appeared, it was already the end of the world. Even he himself said, "Repent, for the kingdom of heaven has drawn near."[10] But he restrained and checked the day of consummation and forbade it to come. For God the Father, seeing that the salvation of the nations can be established only through him, says to him, "Ask from me, and I shall give you the nations for your inheritance and the ends of the earth for your possession."[11]

Therefore, until the promise of the Father is fulfilled and the churches spring forth in the various nations and "the whole fullness of the nations" enter so that then "all Israel may be saved,"[12] the day is lengthened and the setting is deferred and the sun never sinks down but always rises as long as "the sun of righteousness"[13] pours the light of truth into the hearts of believers. But when the measure of believers is complete and

the already weaker and depraved age of the final generation arrives, when "the love of many persons will grow cold by increasing iniquity"[14] and very few persons remain in whom faith is found, then "the days will be shortened."[15]

In the same way, therefore, the Lord knows to extend the day when it is time for salvation and to shorten the day when it is time for tribulation and destruction. We, however, while we have the day and the extent of light is lengthened for us, "let us walk becomingly as in the day"[16] and let us perform the works of light. HOMILIES ON JOSHUA 11.2-3.[17]

10:14 No Other Day Like It

ALL THINGS ARE POSSIBLE FOR GOD. NEMESIUS OF EMESA: What we say is that God not only stands outside the power of all necessity; he is its Lord and Maker. For in that he is authority and the very source whence authority flows, he himself does nothing through any necessity of nature or at the bidding of any inviolable law. On the contrary, all things are possible to him, including those we call impossible. To prove this, he established once for all the courses of the sun and moon, which are borne on their way by inevitable laws, and forever and ever will be thus borne, and at the same time to prove that nothing is to him inevitable but that all things are possible that he may choose, just once he made a special "day" that Scripture sets forth as a "sign," solely that he might the more proclaim, and in no way invalidate, that divine ordinance with which, from the beginning, he fixed the undeviating orbits of the stars. ON THE NATURE OF MAN 38.55.[18]

10:16-17 The Five Kings Hide in the Cave at Makkedah

THE FIVE SENSES. JEROME: For if the armed host

---

[9]NPNF 1 14:489*. [10]Mt 4:17. [11]Ps 2:8. [12]Rom 11:25-26. [13]Mal 4:2 (3:20 LXX). [14]Mt 24:12. [15]Mt 24:22. [16]Rom 13:13. [17]FC 105:116-17. [18]LCC 4:408*.

of the Lord was represented by the trumpets of the priests, we may see in Jericho a type of the overthrow of the world by the preaching of the gospel. And to pass over endless details (for it is not my purpose now to unfold all the mysteries of the Old Testament),[19] five kings who previously reigned in the land of promise and opposed the gospel army were overcome in battle with Joshua. I think it is clearly to be understood that before the Lord led his people from Egypt and circumcised them, sight, smell, taste, hearing, and touch had the dominion, and that to these, as to five princes, everything was subject. And when they took refuge in the cave of the body and in a place of darkness, Jesus entered the body itself and killed them, that the source of their power might be the instrument of their death. AGAINST JOVINIANUS 1.21.[20]

ASSAULTED THROUGH THE SENSES. ORIGEN: But let us also see what it means when it says there were five kings and they fled into caves. We have often said the battle of Christians is twofold. Indeed, for those who are perfect, such as Paul and the Ephesians, it was not, as the apostle himself says, "a battle against flesh and blood but against principalities and authorities, against the rulers of darkness in this world and spiritual forces of iniquity in the heavens."[21] But for the weaker ones and those not yet mature, the battle is still waged against flesh and blood, for those are still assaulted by carnal faults and frailties.

I think this is indicated even in this passage; for we said that a war was declared by five kings against the Gibeonites, whose figure I maintained was of those who are immature. These, therefore, are assaulted by five kings. Now these five kings indicate the five corporeal senses: sight, hearing, taste, touch and smell; for it must be through one of these that each person falls away into sin. These five senses are compared to those five kings who fight the Gibeonites, that is, carnal persons.

That they are said to have fled into caves can

be indicated, perhaps, because a cave is a place buried in the depths of the earth. Therefore, those senses that we mentioned above are said to have fled into caves when, after being placed in the body, they immerse themselves in earthly impulses and do nothing for the work of God but all for the service of the body. HOMILIES ON JOSHUA 11.4.[22]

10:20-21 All Returned Safely

JESUS' SOLDIERS. ORIGEN: Whoever fights under the leadership of Jesus [Joshua] against opposing authorities ought to merit that which is written about those former warriors: "And the whole people," it says, "returned safely to Jesus [Joshua] and not one of the sons of Israel muttered with his tongue." You see, therefore, that the person who serves as a soldier under Jesus must come back safely from battle and ought not even receive a wound "from the fiery darts of the wicked one";[23] he ought to be neither polluted in heart nor defiled in thought, and [he] ought not allow any place for demonic wounds—not through wrath, lust, or any other occasion.

Moreover, what is added, "No one muttered with his tongue," seems to me to have been expressed because no one boasted about the victory, no one attributed it to his own power that he conquered. Indeed, knowing that it is Jesus who bestowed the victory, they do not mutter with their tongue. Understanding that well, the apostle said, "Not I, but the grace of God that is in me."[24] I think, in addition, that he has in mind that command of the Lord in which he said, "But when you have done all these things, say, 'We are unprofitable servants; we have only done what we should have done.'"[25] For in this similar manner he also seems to prohibit boasting about things well done. HOMILIES ON JOSHUA 12.2.[26]

---

[19]Josh 3. [20]NPNF 2 6:362. [21]Eph 6:12. [22]FC 105:117-18. [23]Eph 6:16. [24]1 Cor 15:10. [25]Lk 17:10. [26]FC 105:122-23*.

10:22-43 THE CONQUEST CONTINUES

²²*Then Joshua said, "Open the mouth of the cave, and bring those five kings out to me from the cave." . . . ²⁴And when they brought those kings out to Joshua, Joshua summoned all the men of Israel, and said to the chiefs of the men of war who had gone with him, "Come near, put your feet upon the necks of these kings." Then they came near, and put their feet on their necks. ²⁵And Joshua said to them, "Do not be afraid or dismayed; be strong and of good courage; for thus the LORD will do to all your enemies against whom you fight." ²⁶And afterward Joshua smote them and put them to death. . . .*

²⁸*And Joshua took Makkedah on that day, and smote it and its king with the edge of the sword; he utterly destroyed every person in it, he left none remaining; and he did to the king of Makkedah as he had done to the king of Jericho.*

²⁹*Then Joshua passed on from Makkedah, and all Israel with him, to Libnah, and fought against Libnah; ³⁰and the LORD gave it also and its king into the hand of Israel; and he smote it with the edge of the sword, and every person in it; he left none remaining in it; and he did to its king as he had done to the king of Jericho.*

³¹*And Joshua passed on from Libnah, and all Israel with him, to Lachish, and laid siege to it, and assaulted it: ³²and the LORD gave Lachish into the hand of Israel, and he took it on the second day, and smote it with the edge of the sword, and every person in it, as he had done to Libnah. . . .*

³⁶*Then Joshua went up with all Israel from Eglon to Hebron; and they assaulted it, ³⁷and took it, and smote it with the edge of the sword, and its king and its towns, and every person in it; he left none remaining, as he had done to Eglon, and utterly destroyed it with every person in it. . . .*

⁴⁰*So Joshua defeated the whole land, the hill country and the Negeb and the lowland and the slopes, and all their kings; he left none remaining, but utterly destroyed all that breathed, as the LORD God of Israel commanded. ⁴¹And Joshua defeated them from Kadesh-barnea to Gaza, and all the country of Goshen, as far as Gibeon. ⁴²And Joshua took all these kings and their land at one time, because the LORD God of Israel fought for Israel. ⁴³Then Joshua returned, and all Israel with him, to the camp at Gilgal.*

OVERVIEW: Kindness, not cruelty, is signified in the destruction of the Amorite kings since they represent the hostile powers that formerly reigned in us. We will be able to receive our inheritance after conquering our spiritual enemies through God's strengthening and deliverance. The meanings of the words Libnah, Lachish, and Hebron correspond with the twofold condition of each city. The obliteration of all the evil within us, signified in the devastation of the former inhabitants of the promised land, prepares us for our inheritance. Understanding the Israelite wars as figures for the destruction of evil from souls, rather than the souls themselves, portrays a more devout and merciful view of Jesus (ORIGEN).

10:24 Put Your Feet on the Necks of These Kings

THE REIGN OF SIN. ORIGEN: But meanwhile Jesus [Joshua] destroyed the enemies, not teaching cruelty through this, as the heretics think, but representing the future sacraments in these affairs, so that when Jesus destroys those kings who maintain a reign of sin in us, we can fulfill that which the apostle said, "Just as we presented our members to serve iniquity for iniquity, so now let us present our members to serve righteousness for sanctification."[1]

What is it then that is condemned by them in this place as cruelty? It is this, it says, that is written, "Set your feet upon their necks and slay them." But this is discovered to be humaneness and kindness, not cruelty, is it not?

Would that you might be the sort of person who can "set your feet upon serpents and scorpions and upon every hostile power"[2] and "tread underfoot the dragon and the lizard,"[3] the petty king who once reigned in you and maintained in you a kingdom of sin. Thus, with all those destroyed who used to rule in you by the work of sin, Christ Jesus our Lord alone will reign in you, "to whom is the glory and the dominion forever and ever. Amen!"[4] HOMILIES ON JOSHUA 11.6.[5]

10:25 Be Strong and of Good Courage

A SPIRITUAL BATTLE. ORIGEN: But Marcion and Valentinus and Basilides[6] and the other heretics with them, since they refuse to understand these things in a manner worthy of the Holy Spirit, "deviated from the faith and became devoted to many impieties,"[7] bringing forth another God of the law, both creator and judge of the world, who teaches a certain cruelty through these things that are written. For example, they are ordered to trample upon the necks of their enemies and to suspend from wood the kings of that land that they violently invade.

And yet, if only my Lord Jesus the Son of God would grant that to me and order me to crush the spirit of fornication with my feet and trample upon the necks of the spirit of wrath and rage, to trample on the demon of avarice, to trample down

boasting, to crush the spirit of arrogance with my feet, and, when I have done all these things, not to hang the most exalted of these exploits upon myself, but upon his cross. Thereby I imitate Paul, who says, "the world is crucified to me,"[8] and, that which we have already related above, "Not I, but the grace of God that is in me."[9]

But if I deserve to act thus, I shall be blessed, and what Jesus [Joshua] said to the ancients will also be said to me, "Go courageously and be strengthened; do not be afraid nor be awed by their appearance, because the Lord God has delivered all your enemies into your hands."[10] If we understand these things spiritually and manage wars of this type spiritually, and if we drive out all those spiritual iniquities from heaven, then we shall be able at last to receive from Jesus as a share of the inheritance even those places and kingdoms that are the kingdoms of heaven, bestowed by our Lord and Savior Jesus Christ, "to whom is the glory and the dominion forever and ever. Amen!"[11] HOMILIES ON JOSHUA 12.3.[12]

10:28-29 Joshua Conquers Libnah

TWO KINDS OF WHITE. ORIGEN: But if we examine the very meanings of the names more eagerly and more diligently, it will be discovered that the significance of the names can have an interpretation at one time of a wicked kingdom, and at another time, of a good kingdom. For example, I think Libnah means "whiteness." But whiteness is understood in different ways, for there is a whiteness of leprosy and a whiteness of light. Therefore, it is possible to indicate diversities in the meaning even of the name itself, and of either condition. Thus Libnah had a certain whiteness of leprosy under the wicked kings, and, after those are destroyed and overthrown, when Libnah comes into the Israelite kingdom, it receives the whiteness of light; because whiteness

---

[1]Rom 6:19. [2]Lk 10:19. [3]Ps 91:13 (90:13 LXX). [4]1 Pet 4:11. [5]FC 105:119. [6]Gnostic teachers. [7]1 Tim 6:10. [8]Gal 6:14. [9]1 Cor 15:10. [10]Josh 10:25. [11]1 Pet 4:11. [12]FC 105:123-24.

is mentioned in Scriptures as being both praise-worthy and blameworthy. Homilies on Joshua 13.2.[13]

10:31-32 Joshua Conquers Lachish

A Good Way and Bad. Origen: And again, Lachish is interpreted "way." But in the Scriptures, a way is both a laudable and a culpable thing. That is not difficult to demonstrate, as it says in the psalms, "And the way of the impious will perish";[14] and in another place, on the contrary, "Make straight the way for your feet."[15] Therefore it can also be understood here that the city of Lachish was at first the way of the impious, and afterwards, when it was destroyed and overthrown, it was won over to the right way with the Israelites reigning. Homilies on Joshua 13.2.[16]

10:36-37 Joshua Conquers Hebron

An Old and New Union. Origen: In like manner, there is also Hebron, which they say means "union" or "marriage." But the union of our soul was at first with a wicked man and a most evil husband, the devil. When that one was destroyed and abolished, the soul was "freed from the law"[17] of that former wicked man and united with a good and lawful one, him about whom the apostle Paul says, "I determined to present you a chaste virgin to one man, to Christ."[18] Thus even the understanding of the names themselves agrees with this twofold condition of every city. Homilies on Joshua 13.2.[19]

10:40-43 The Whole Land Is Defeated

Entitled to Inherit. Origen: Likewise, it is especially the work of the Word of God to pull down the diabolical structures that the devil has built in the human soul. For, in everyone of us, that one raised up towers of pride and walls of self-exaltation. The Word of God overthrows and undermines these, so that justly, according to the

apostle, we are made "the cultivation of God and the building of God,"[20] "set upon the foundation of the apostles and prophets with Christ Jesus himself the chief cornerstone, from whom the uniting of the edifice grows into a temple of God in the spirit."[21] And thus at last we may be entitled to be included in the inheritance of the holy land, in the Israelite portion. Then our enemies will be abolished and destroyed so "that none of them remains who may breathe in us," but only the spirit of Christ breathes in us, through works and words and spiritual understanding, according to the teaching of Christ Jesus our Lord, "to whom is the strength and the power forever and ever. Amen!"[22] Homilies on Joshua 13.4.[23]

Extinguishing Evil. Origen: I myself think it is better that the Israelite wars be understood in this way, and it is better that Jesus [Joshua] is thought to fight in this way and to destroy cities and overthrow kingdoms. For in this manner what is said will also appear more devout and more merciful, when he is said to have so subverted and devastated individual cities that "nothing that breathed was left in them, neither any who might be saved nor any who might escape."[24]

Would that the Lord might thus cast out and extinguish all former evils from the souls who believe in him—even those he claims for his kingdom—and from my own soul, its own evils; so that nothing of a malicious inclination may continue to breathe in me, nothing of wrath; so that no disposition of desire for any evil may be preserved in me, and no wicked word "may remain to escape" from my mouth. For thus, purged from all former evils and under the leadership of Jesus, I can be included among the cities of the sons of Israel, concerning which it is written, "The cities of Judah will be raised up and they will dwell in them."[25] Homilies on Joshua 13.3.[26]

---

[13]FC 105:126. [14]Ps 1:6. [15]Heb 12:13; Prov 4:26. [16]FC 105:126-27. [17]Rom 7:3. [18]2 Cor 11:2. [19]FC 105:127*. [20]1 Cor 3:9. [21]Eph 2:20-21. [22]See Rev 7:12. [23]FC 105:128-29. [24]Josh 8:22; cf. Josh 10:40. [25]Amos 9:14. [26]FC 105:127.

11:1-15 CANAANITE KINGS UNITE AGAINST ISRAEL

¹When Jabin king of Hazor heard of this, he sent to Jobab king of Madon, and to the king of Shimron, and to the king of Achshaph, ²and to the kings who were in the northern hill country, and in the Arabah south of Chinneroth, and in the lowland, and in Naphoth-dor on the west, ³to the Canaanites in the east and the west, the Amorites, the Hittites, the Perizzites, and the Jebusites in the hill country, and the Hivites under Hermon in the land of Mizpah. ⁴And they came out, with all their troops, a great host, in number like the sand that is upon the seashore, with very many horses and chariots. ⁵And all these kings joined their forces, and came and encamped together at the waters of Merom, to fight with Israel.

⁶And the LORD said to Joshua, "Do not be afraid of them, for tomorrow at this time I will give over all of them, slain, to Israel; you shall hamstring their horses, and burn their chariots with fire." ⁷So Joshua came suddenly upon them with all his people of war, by the waters of Merom, and fell upon them. ⁸And the LORD gave them into the hand of Israel, who smote them and chased them as far as Great Sidon and Misrephoth-maim, and eastward as far as the valley of Mizpeh; and they smote them, until they left none remaining. ⁹And Joshua did to them as the LORD bade him; he hamstrung their horses, and burned their chariots with fire. . . .

¹²And all the cities of those kings, and all their kings, Joshua took, and smote them with the edge of the sword, utterly destroying them, as Moses the servant of the LORD had commanded. . . . ¹⁴And all the spoil of these cities and the cattle, the people of Israel took for their booty; but every man they smote with the edge of the sword, until they had destroyed them, and they did not leave any that breathed. ¹⁵As the LORD had commanded Moses his servant, so Moses commanded Joshua, and so Joshua did; he left nothing undone of all that the LORD had commanded Moses.

OVERVIEW: The attack of the Canaanite kings, following the attack of the Amorite kings, instructs us that as the people of God increase in number, so do persecutors. The association between the kings' names, territories and actions yields figurative interpretations: Jabin is identified as the devil who rules the earth, and Jobab is an evil spirit who brings calamity upon mortals. The victory the Lord declares for Israel symbolizes the destruction of all that is evil at the consummation of this age. Representing demons, the horses and chariots are destroyed because they are a figure for those whom unbelievers invoke for help. The Lord's command to destroy these is obeyed when we subdue the body's passions through self-denial and possess a heart that burns for God's words (ORIGEN). God's works of judgment must be understood in conjunction with the sins that precipitate them (AUGUSTINE). Joshua's accomplishment of all he had been commanded through Moses symbolizes Jesus' complete fulfillment of the law (ORIGEN).

11:1-8 The Attack of the Canaanite Kings

THE MORE RIGHTEOUSNESS GROWS, THE MORE IT IS ATTACKED. ORIGEN: In prior readings, the king of Jerusalem had assembled four other kings with him against Jesus [Joshua] and against the sons of Israel.[1] But now no longer does someone assemble four or five; on the contrary, see how great a multitude one person assembles. . . .

You see how many swarms of opposing powers and of malicious demons may be stirred up against Jesus [Joshua] and the Israelite army. Before the coming of our Lord and Savior, all those demons, undisturbed and secure, were occupying human spirits and ruled in their minds and bodies. But when "grace appeared" in the world, the mercy "of God our Savior"[2] instructs us to live piously and purely in this world, separated from every contagion of sin, so that each soul may receive its liberty and the "image of God"[3] in which it was created from the beginning. Because of this, fights and battles spring forth from their iniquitous old possessors. If the first ones are overthrown, far more rise up afterwards, and they unite into one and conspire in evil, always remote from the good. And if they are conquered for a second time, again a third time other more wicked powers will rise up. So perhaps the more the people of God are increased, and the more they thrive and are multiplied, there are that many more who conspire to assault. HOMILIES ON JOSHUA 14.1.[4]

ON JABIN. ORIGEN: But let us attempt, as God grants, to investigate certain individual kings of the opposing army; and, through the meaning of the names of each one, let us consider also the work he performs in malice.

First of all, the one who is designated the author of this war, who collects the others and summons them to a conspiracy of wickedness, is named Jabin, who was king of Hazor. For he is the one who is said to have called the others together. But Jabin means "thought" or "prudence." What, then, is this "thought" or "prudence," if not that which the prophet Isaiah calls "proud thought"? For he says, "And moreover, I shall strike out the proud thought of the prince of the Assyrians, who said, 'I shall bring it to pass by

my power, and, by the wisdom of my perception, I shall remove the boundaries of the nations and plunder their power.' "[5]

Therefore, the one who is called "proud thought" in that place is this king of the Assyrians. But here, Jabin is "thought" or "prudence." For it is written that in paradise the serpent was "more prudent than all the beasts"[6] who were upon the earth. And even that "steward of iniquity" is said to have "done prudently"[7] that which he did. This Jabin, then, is king of Hazor. But Hazor means "court." Therefore, all the earth is the court of this king, the devil, who holds the supremacy of the whole earth as though of one court. But do you wish to verify that the court is itself the earth? In the Gospels it is written that the strong one sleeps unconcerned in his own court until a stronger one comes, who may both "bind" him and "carry away what he possesses."[8] The king of the court, therefore, is "the prince of this world."[9] HOMILIES ON JOSHUA 14.2.[10]

ON JOBAB. ORIGEN: This one sends word to Jobab; for he himself is the one who sends word to all nations and summons them to battle. He sends word to the king of Merom. Jobab means "hostilities," but Merom means "bitternesses." Therefore, the devil sends word to another hostile power, doubtless from among the fugitive angels, and this power is the king of bitternesses. All bitternesses and difficulties in this world that are inflicted on wretched mortals issue from this author and what he does. There are diverse kinds of sin. For nothing can be more bitter than sin, even if it seems somewhat delightful at first, as Solomon writes. "But in the end," he says, "you will find what seemed sweet in the beginning to be more bitter than gall and sharper than the edge of a sword."[11] But the nature of righteousness is the opposite: In the beginning, it seems more bitter, but in the end, when it produces

---

[1]Josh 10:1-17. [2]Tit 2:11-14. [3]Gen 1:27. [4]FC 105:130-32. [5]Is 10:12-13. [6]Gen 3:1, variously translated "subtle" or "crafty." [7]Lk 16:8. [8]Mt 12:29. [9]Jn 14:30; cf. Jn 16:11. [10]FC 105:132-33*. [11]Prov 5:4.

fruits of virtue, it is found to be sweeter than honey. Therefore, the devil sent word to the hostile Jobab, the king of bitterness. HOMILIES ON JOSHUA 14.2.[12]

VICTORY COMES TOMORROW. ORIGEN: Such is the list, therefore, of the entire army of invisible foes who are assembled by King Jabin in order to fight against us who follow Jesus, our leader and Savior. But what does the Lord declare? "Do not shrink back from their appearance," he says "because by tomorrow at this hour, I shall deliver them into your hands." I observe that today we are not able to overwhelm all those powers or to destroy them all, but they will be entirely taken away tomorrow, that is, after the consummation of this age.

For, at that time, every opposing power will be pulled down and the inmost part will be conquered when you see that those who are on the left are told, "Go into the eternal fire that God has prepared for the devil and his angels."[13] Then if, following Jesus the leader, we have conquered and have been able to take possession, even we shall occupy the kingdom that the Father has prepared for his saints and for these who "have fulfilled" his commandments and "righteousness"[14] through our Lord Jesus Christ himself, "to whom is the glory and the dominion forever and ever. Amen!"[15] HOMILIES ON JOSHUA 14.2.[16]

11:9 Joshua Destroys the Horses and Chariots

DEMONIC FIGURES. ORIGEN: The horses and the chariots that are removed seem to hold the figure of those who, although placed in the heavens, fell away through wantonness and pride, either when they set themselves aflame to desire the daughters of humankind or when they followed him who said, "I shall place my seat above the clouds and I shall be like the Most High."[17] Perhaps it is for that reason that the prophet also says, "False is the horse for salvation."[18] And again, concerning those who trust in demons, he says, "These call on chariots and those on horses,

but we shall call upon the name of our God."[19] Certainly Scripture would not apply chariots and horses to God, at least as far as invoking them. But, by all means, it shows that just as we ourselves call upon the true God, so the nations invoke "chariots and horses," that is, demons, those whom the nations who waged war against Israel invoked. Moreover, Scripture also mentions the horses of the Egyptians, even those very ones ordered to be destroyed at that time.[20] HOMILIES ON JOSHUA 15.3.[21]

HAMSTRUNG PASSIONS. ORIGEN: If we understand the horses that are commanded by the precept of God to be hamstrung, together with their chariots, as the passions of the body—that is, lust, petulance or pride, and fickleness, by whom the unhappy soul, just as a rider, is borne and carried to great dangers—this understanding will not be contrary to our reasoning. The horse, of course, is hamstrung when the body is humbled by fastings and vigils and by every pain of self-denial. And the chariots are consumed by fire when the word of the Lord is fulfilled in us, as he says, "I came to send fire on the earth, and how I wish that it be set ablaze!"[22] Those persons already revealed themselves to burn in that fire who said, "Was not our heart burning within us when he opened the Scripture for us?"[23] Also, therefore, the horse is called "false for salvation"[24] if we allow the impulses of the body to be endured unbridled and if we do not subdue the wanton and haughty necks of the flesh by the yoke of self-denial.

But now, if by chance anyone is stimulated and pricked by the words of God through what we say; if he who yesterday might have been carried into lust, flying headlong and impetuous as a horse, yet today, after hearing these things, repents and is converted; if this person even,

---

[12]FC 105:133*. [13]Mt 25:41. [14]Mt 3:15. [15]1 Pet 4:11. [16]FC 105:136-37*. [17]Is 14:14. [18]Ps 33:17 (32:17 LXX). [19]Ps 20:7 (19:7 LXX). [20]Ex 14:9, 26-28. [21]FC 105:141-42. [22]Lk 12:49. [23]Lk 24:32. [24]Ps 33:17 (32:17 LXX).

according to the prophet, "is subdued by the fear of God,"[25] bridles himself, withdraws from sin and henceforth loves the chaste and continent life, then indeed we shall seem "to have hamstrung horses" by drawing the sword of the word of God.[26] For the precept of God is more fittingly accomplished by this than by someone who hamstrings equine animals captured from the spoils of enemies. HOMILIES ON JOSHUA 15.3.[27]

11:14 They Did Not Leave Any Alive

JUDGING THE WORKS OF GOD. AUGUSTINE: One should not at all think it a horrible cruelty that Joshua did not leave anyone alive in those cities that fell to him, for God himself had ordered this. However, whoever for this reason thinks that God himself must be cruel and does not wish to believe then that the true God was the author of the Old Testament judges as perversely about the works of God as he does about the sins of human beings. Such people do not know what each person ought to suffer. Consequently, they think it a great evil when that which is about to fall is thrown down and when mortals die. QUESTIONS ON JOSHUA 16.[28]

11:15 Joshua Did As the Lord Commanded

THE FULFILLMENT OF THE LAW. ORIGEN: The verse says, "Just as Moses, the servant of the Lord, ordered him." Here, the word of the law itself is called Moses, the servant of the Lord, just as it says in the Gospel, "They have Moses and the prophets, let them listen to them."[29] Therefore, the law commanded us to destroy all of sin's kings, who incite us to sin. "Jesus [Joshua] accomplished this, and he did not transgress anything from all that Moses established for him." Indeed, according to the first stage of explanation, we said that whatever the law of God—which here is called Moses—ordered, Jesus fulfills in us and is himself the one who destroys vices in us and overthrows the most vile kingdoms of sin. Nevertheless, it can also be said about our Lord and Savior himself, that everything Moses commanded in the law, Jesus accomplished, and he did not transgress anything, since the apostle indeed says, "When the fullness of time had come, God sent his own Son, made from a woman, made under the law."[30] If, therefore, he was made under the law, since he was under the law, everything that the law commanded, he fulfilled, so that he might redeem us from the curse of the law. He also says concerning himself, "I came not to abolish but to fulfill the law."[31] HOMILIES ON JOSHUA 15.4.[32]

---

[25]Ps 119:120 (118:120 LXX). [26]Eph 6:17. [27]FC 105:142-43. [28]CCL 33:322. [29]Lk 16:29. [30]Gal 4:4. [31]Mt 5:17. [32]FC 105:145-46*.

11:16-23 THE CONQUEST ENDS

[16]So Joshua took all that land, the hill country and all the Negeb and all the land of Goshen and the lowland and the Arabah and the hill country of Israel and its lowland [17]from Mount Halak, that rises toward Seir, as far as Baal-gad in the valley of Lebanon below Mount Hermon. And he took all their kings, and smote them, and put them to death. . . . [20]For it was the LORD's doing to

harden their hearts that they should come against Israel in battle, in order that they should be utterly destroyed, and should receive no mercy but be exterminated, as the LORD commanded Moses. . . .

23So Joshua took the whole land, according to all that the LORD had spoken to Moses; and Joshua gave it for an inheritance to Israel according to their tribal allotments. And the land had rest from war.

OVERVIEW: Augustine suggests that the extent of Joshua's conquest was limited to those cities he battled against within the region described in the text. God's provocation of the Canaanites, which prompted attacks on Israel in order that they be destroyed, illustrates how the Lord permits hostile powers to assail us in order to rouse us to battle against sin (ORIGEN). However, the power of God is invincible (JEROME). Divine providence ensured that the Canaanites would attack the Israelites in order that God's judgment against them would be achieved (AUGUSTINE). In conquering the whole land, Joshua prefigures Christ, who captured and destroyed every sin and who calls a multitude of believers from all over the earth (ORIGEN).

11:16-17 So Joshua Conquered the Land

THE EXTENT OF JOSHUA'S SUCCESS. AUGUSTINE: It is asked how this can be true, since the Hebrews were not altogether able to capture all the cities of those seven nations either in the times after the judges or in the times of the kings. But one must understand it to mean that Joshua never approached any city with hostile intent that he did not capture. Or it may mean that no city remained uncaptured except for those which were in the regions mentioned above. For those regions were enumerated in which there were cities concerning which the conclusion was made: "and he captured all of them in war." QUESTIONS ON JOSHUA 17.[1]

11:20 The Lord Hardened Their Hearts

A PROVOKED FIGHT. ORIGEN: For as long as the

hostile powers that work sin in us do not come and incite us to sin or provoke us to fight, they cannot be killed or exterminated. For that reason, therefore, God is said in like manner to permit, even to excite, opposing powers to go out into battle against us so that we may seize the victory and they may pursue destruction. HOMILIES ON JOSHUA 15.5.[2]

THE IRRESISTIBLE WILL OF GOD. JEROME: "There was no city which the Lord did not deliver to the children of Israel, except perhaps those who lived in Gibeon. Israel violently overthrew all of them because the Lord hardened their hearts that they would fight Israel and be killed and not be shown mercy and die, just as the Lord had commanded Moses." If it happened by the will of the Lord that Israel not receive or accept peace, then let us say with the apostle, "Why, therefore, does he object? For who can resist the will of the Lord?"[3] DEFENSE AGAINST THE PELAGIANS 1.38.[4]

A DIVINE AND LOFTY JUDGMENT. AUGUSTINE: It is said that "their heart was strengthened through the Lord," that is, that their heart was hardened, just as in the case of Pharaoh. There can be no doubt that this is justly done by a divine and lofty judgment, when God abandons someone and the enemy takes possession of him; the same applies in this case as in Pharaoh's. But here something else sets in motion, as it is said that their hearts were emboldened to arise against Israel in war and therefore the Israelites would not show any mercy to them. The Israelites may very well

---

[1]CCL 33:322. [2]FC 105:146. [3]Rom 9:19. [4]CCL 80:48-49.

have showed them mercy, if the Canaanites had not gone to war, since God had ordered that none of the Canaanites were to be spared and yet the Israelites had spared the Gibeonites because they had represented themselves as having come from a far-off country and had made a treaty with them. But because the Israelites showed mercy to some, albeit against the command of God, it must be understood that it was said with this intention that the Canaanites waged war in such a manner so that the Israelites would not spare them, nor would the Canaanites be able to convince the Israelites to show mercy and neglect God's command. I cannot believe that this could have happened in any other way, even though Joshua was their leader and diligently obeyed all of God's commands. Nonetheless, not even Joshua would have annihilated them so quickly had they not gone against him in such a dastardly fashion. Thus it could have happened that Joshua, taking care to fulfill God's commandments, would have defeated them in a rather minimal way and they would have remained until the time when the Israelites could spare them after Joshua's death, when the Israelites did not do God's commandments with such care. For even while he was still alive the Israelites spared some Canaanites, although they subjugated them to their authority; some Canaanites, in fact, they never could conquer. But these things were not done while he was their leader but when as an old man he had retired from warfare and merely divided up the territories for the Israelites. He divided it with the intention that the Israelites would take possession of those lands that were emptied of the enemy and capture the rest by fighting, although he himself would no longer wage war. And the fact that they were able to conquer some of the Canaanites in a rather minimal way was owing to divine providence, as is clear in certain places in the Scriptures. Questions on Joshua 18.[5]

11:23 Joshua Took the Whole Land

Every Kind of Sin. Origen: It did not say that by war Jesus [Joshua] took some and did not take others but that he took all into his possession, that is, he captured and destroyed all. And, indeed, the Lord Jesus has purged every kind of sin and destroyed all. For we all "were irrational, unbelieving, errant, serving various desires, acting in malice and envy, hateful, and hating one another,"[6] and [we possessed] every type of sin that is found in persons before they believe. Therefore, it is well said that Jesus kills all who have gone to war. For Jesus—who is the Word and the "wisdom of God"—is greater than any kind of sin, no matter how terrible.[7] For he overcomes and conquers all sins. Or do we not believe this, that every kind of sin is carried away when we come to the saving bath?[8] For the apostle Paul also alludes to this, who, when he had enumerated the whole class of sins, adds something after them all and says, "And indeed you were these; but you were washed, you were sanctified, you were justified in the name of our Lord, Jesus Christ."[9] Therefore, in this way, Jesus [Joshua] is said to have seized all in battle and to have destroyed all. It happened that, through the work of the Lord, their heart predominated and they hastened into battle against Israel and were exterminated. Homilies on Joshua 15.5.[10]

Possession and Peace. Origen: I do not see that Jesus [Joshua] the son of Nun took possession of all the earth. For how much of the earth does one take who seizes only Judea? But our Lord Jesus truly took possession of all the earth, because a multitude of believers from all over the earth and out of all the nations flock to him. After these things, after "Jesus [Joshua] took possession of all the earth," it is also added, "And the earth rested from wars." How will this phrase—that "the earth rested from wars"—seem to have been uttered truthfully concerning the son of Nun, when the earth never entirely rested from wars in his time? This is fulfilled in

---

[5]CCL 33:322-23. [6]Tit 3:3. [7]Jn 1:14; cf. 1 Cor 1:24. [8]Baptism. [9]1 Cor 6:11. [10]FC 105:146.

my Lord Jesus Christ alone. Consider yourself—you have come to Jesus and through the grace of baptism have attained the remission of sins; and now in you "the flesh" does not "fight against the spirit and the spirit against the flesh."[11] Your land has ceased from wars if you still "carry around the

death of Jesus Christ in your body"[12] so that, after all battles have ceased in you, you may be made "peaceable" and you may be called "a child of God."[13] HOMILIES ON JOSHUA 15.7.[14]

---

[11]See Gal 5:17. [12]2 Cor 4:10. [13]Mt 5:9. [14]FC 105:150.

12:1-24 THE CONQUERED KINGS

[1]Now these are the kings of the land, whom the people of Israel defeated, and took possession of their land beyond the Jordan toward the sunrising, from the valley of the Arnon to Mount Hermon, with all the Arabah eastward: [2]Sihon king of the Amorites, . . . [4]and Og[e] king of Bashan. . . . [6]Moses, the servant of the LORD, and the people of Israel defeated them; and Moses the servant of the LORD gave their land for a possession to the Reubenites and the Gadites and the half-tribe of Manasseh.

[7]And these are the kings of the land whom Joshua and the people of Israel defeated on the west side of the Jordan . . . : [9]the king of Jericho, one; the king of Ai, which is beside Bethel, one; [10]the king of Jerusalem, one; the king of Hebron, one; [11]the king of Jarmuth, one; the king of Lachish, one; . . . [24]the king of Tirzah, one: in all, thirty-one kings.

e Gk: Heb the boundary of Og

OVERVIEW: Moses and Joshua were aware of and understood the anagogical sense[1] of their accomplishments (ORIGEN). As Joshua, unlike his master Moses, was able to enter and subdue the promised land, so apostles were able to perform more miracles than Jesus himself (EPHREM).

12:1-24 Thirty-one Kings

SHADOWS OF CERTAIN REALITIES. ORIGEN: And if "a wise man shall understand the words from his own mouth and shall hear knowledge on his lips,"[2] we must either declare rashly that the prophets were not wise, if they have not understood "the words from their own mouth," or admit that the prophets were wise, because they

have received what is correct and true and have understood "the words from their own mouth" and borne knowledge on their lips. It is clear that Moses saw in his mind the truth of the law and the allegorical meanings related to the anagogical sense of the stories he recorded, and that Joshua understood the true distribution of land which took place after the overthrow of the twenty-nine kings,[3] since he could see better than us that the things accomplished through himself were shadows of certain realities. COMMENTARY ON THE GOSPEL OF JOHN 6.21-22.[4]

---

[1]"Leading upward" toward heaven and the age to come. [2]Prov 16:23. [3]Josh 12:7-24. [4]FC 80:174.

MASTER AND HIS DISCIPLES. EPHREM THE
SYRIAN: Whoever believes in me will also do the
works which I do, and will do even greater ones.[5]
And where is this word which he said, "The disciple is not greater than his master" [illustrated]?[6]
For example, Moses killed only three kings, but
Joshua killed thirty.[7] [Moses] persevered in
prayer, made supplication, but did not enter [the
promised land]. It was Joshua rather who entered

and shared out the inheritance.[8] Likewise, Samuel was greater than Eli, and Elisha received a
double portion of his master's spirit after his
ascension,[9] like the Lord our Savior, for his disciples effected twice through their signs. COMMEN-
TARY ON TATIAN'S DIATESSARON 19.8.[10]

---

[5]Jn 14:12. [6]Mt 10:24. [7]Cf. Josh 12:1-24. [8]Deut 34:4-5; Josh 14:1-
19:51. [9]See 2 Kings 2:9-12. [10]ECTD 286.

13:1-14 THE DIVISION OF THE LAND

[1]Now Joshua was old and advanced in years; and the LORD said to him, "You are old and
advanced in years, and there remains yet very much land to be possessed. [2]This is the land that yet
remains: all the regions of the Philistines, and all those of the Geshurites, . . . [3] and those of the
Avvim, [4]in the south, all the land of the Canaanites, and Mearah which belongs to the Sidonians,
to Aphek, to the boundary of the Amorites, [5]and the land of the Gebalites, and all Lebanon,
toward the sunrising, from Baal-gad below Mount Hermon to the entrance of Hamath, [6]all the
inhabitants of the hill country from Lebanon to Misrephoth-maim, even all the Sidonians. I will
myself drive them out from before the people of Israel; only allot the land to Israel for an inheritance, as I have commanded you. [7]Now therefore divide this land for an inheritance to the nine
tribes and half the tribe of Manasseh."

[8]With the other half of the tribe of Manasseh[g] the Reubenites and the Gadites received their
inheritance, which Moses gave them, beyond the Jordan eastward, as Moses the servant of the
LORD gave them. . . .

[14]To the tribe of Levi alone Moses gave no inheritance; the offerings by fire to the LORD God of
Israel are their inheritance, as he said to him.

g Cn: Heb *With it*

OVERVIEW: Rather than an observation of his
physical age, Scripture's description of Joshua as
an elder "full of days" is a title of honor given for
his maturity and dignity. Since he prefigures
Jesus, this title is especially fitting as Jesus is the
beginning and "head" of all.

The territory that remained after the conquest

represents those whom Jesus will take possession
of at his second coming. The Sidonites are specifically mentioned among those who will be exterminated because they symbolize opposing powers
that seek to entrap souls in sin. The Levites,
whose inheritance is the Lord God, represent
those rare believers who pursue purity and wis-

dom and illumine the way of salvation to others (ORIGEN).

13:1 Joshua Was Advanced in Years

FULL OF DAYS. ORIGEN: Certain attentive persons even before us have observed in the Scriptures that presbyters or elders are not so called because they have lived to a great age, but they are honored by this title for their maturity of thought and venerable dignity of life, especially when there is added to presbyter this phrase that follows: "full of days."[1] For if any "presbyter" or "elder" seemed so named because of his great age, who would have been even more fitting to designate by this name than Adam, or surely Methuselah or Noah, who clearly are declared to have lived far more years in this world than the rest? Yet, we see that indeed not one of these is called "presbyter" or "elder" by Scripture. But Abraham, who lived a much shorter life, is the first to be called "presbyter" or "elder" in holy Scriptures.[2] Also it is said by the Lord to Moses, "Choose presbyters for yourself from all the people, those whom you yourself know to be presbyters."[3] But see, O hearer, whether anywhere in all Scripture you are able to find the title "an elder, full of days" attributed to any sinner. HOMILIES ON JOSHUA 16.1.[4]

HEAD OF ALL. ORIGEN: But since we have determined that the things that are said about Jesus [Joshua] also refer to our Lord and Savior, whom do we understand to be as much "the presbyter and elder, advanced of days" as the one who is "the beginning, the firstborn of every creature"?[5] And for that reason, perhaps, he alone, before whom there is no one, is truly and properly called presbyter. Therefore, although there are those in the Scriptures who are called presbyters or elders or high priests, nevertheless, among the presbyters or elders the Lord Jesus must be reckoned chief of presbyters, and among bishops, chief of bishops, just as among high priests he is "chief of high priests,"[6] and as among shepherds he is

"chief of shepherds."[7] The Savior must be held first and chief in this and in every honorable title, because he is the "head" of all.[8] HOMILIES ON JOSHUA 16.2.[9]

13:2 The Land That Remains

THE SECOND COMING. ORIGEN: But follow me, O hearer, through delicate threads of expression, and I shall disclose to you how for a second time he takes possession of this earth, very much of which is now said to Jesus to be left behind. Listen to what Paul says concerning this: "For he must reign until he makes all his enemies his footstool."[10] This, therefore, is the "land," much of which is now said to be left behind, until all are placed entirely under his feet and until he takes possession of all persons for his inheritance. "This," it says, "is the land that was left behind: all the regions of the Philistines," and, indeed, very many other lands that follow. Much still "remains," as far as this pertains to our times, which we see has not yet been "placed beneath the feet of Jesus," who is certainly to possess all. . . .

From this it is evident that in the second coming Jesus will obtain this extensive land that still remains. But blessed are those who were taken over at his first coming; for those will be truly dear who receive the inheritance of the land of promise in spite of the resistance of many adversaries and the attacks of many enemies by war and by weapons. HOMILIES ON JOSHUA 16.3.[11]

13:6 The Lord Will Drive Out the People

EVIL HUNTERS. ORIGEN: After these things, when he had enumerated very many nations, of the Sidonites alone he said, "And I shall exterminate all the Sidonites from the face of the sons of Israel." The Canaanites were also named, and those who were opposite Egypt were mentioned,

---

[1]Gen 35:29. [2]Gen 18:11-12. [3]Num 11:16. [4]FC 105:151. [5]Col. 1:15, 18. [6]Heb 4:14. [7]1 Pet 5:4. [8]See Eph 4:15. [9]FC 105:153. [10]1 Cor 15:25; Ps 110:1 (109:1 LXX). [11]FC 105:153-54.

and those who were from the region of Ekron and from the left portions of the river, and very many other nations; but concerning the Sidonites alone, the Lord says that he will destroy them. Just as we have said previously, however, the Sidonites are called "hunters." Who, therefore, do we understand as those evil hunters that the Lord exterminates if not those opposing powers of whom the prophet says, "They have prepared snares for my feet,"[12] [snares] by which they pursue and ensnare souls for sin? So then, the Lord exterminates them. For when such hunters as these have perished, when at last there will be no one who "stretches out snares" and nets in order to entrap souls in sin, then "each person will rest under his own vine and under his own fig tree."[13] HOMILIES ON JOSHUA 16.4.[14]

13:14 No Inheritance of Land for Levi

A DIVINE INHERITANCE. ORIGEN: Neither Moses nor Jesus [Joshua], however, gave an inheritance to the Levites, because "the Lord God himself is their inheritance."[15] What else can we understand by this, except that in the church of the Lord there are certain persons who precede all the rest by the strength of their spirit and on account of their merits? The Lord himself is said to be their inheritance. And if it is proper to venture into such things and unveil a profound secret, let us see what the figure of priests or Levites secretly discloses, in case there is something. For among every people—I speak of those who are saved—the great majority are no doubt those who please the Lord through good works, honest ways and acceptable deeds because they simply believe in and fear God. But there are a few persons, exceedingly rare, who give attention to wisdom and to knowledge, keep their mind clean and pure, and cultivate noble virtues for their souls. Through the influence of teaching, they can then illuminate the way for the other more simple ones to walk to and arrive at salvation. These persons are probably designated here under the name of Levites and priests, whose heritage is said to be the Lord himself, who is wisdom, which they dearly loved above all other things. HOMILIES ON JOSHUA 17.2.[16]

---

[12]Ps 57:6 (56:6 LXX). [13]Mic 4:4. [14]FC 105:154-55. [15]The LXX denotes the Lord as the inheritance, rather than the offerings by fire, in consonance with Numbers 18:20. [16]FC 105:159-60.

[13:15-23 THE INHERITANCE OF REUBEN]

[13:24-33 INHERITANCES BEYOND THE JORDAN]

14:1-5 THE ALLOTMENT OF CANAAN

¹*And these are the inheritances which the people of Israel received in the land of Canaan, which Eleazar the priest, and Joshua the son of Nun, and the heads of the fathers' houses of the tribes of the people of Israel distributed to them.* ²*Their inheritance was by lot, as the LORD had commanded Moses for the nine and one-half tribes.* ³*For Moses had given an inheritance to the two and one-half tribes beyond the Jordan; but to the Levites he gave no inheritance among them.* ⁴*For the people of Joseph were two tribes, Manasseh and Ephraim; and no portion was given to the Levites in the land, but only cities to dwell in, with their pasture lands for their cattle and their substance.* ⁵*The people of Israel did as the LORD commanded Moses; they allotted the land.*

OVERVIEW: Just as the law is a shadow of the true law, the division of Judea imitates a heavenly division. The distributions of the inheritance, first through Moses and later through Joshua, illustrate Judeo-Christian soteriology (ORIGEN). The historical division of the land is typical of the uneven gradations within heaven (JEROME).

14:1-5 The Distribution of Inheritances

A SHADOW AND COPY. ORIGEN: Just as those who submit to the law, which is the "shadow" of that true law, diligently serve a "shadow and copy" of "heavenly things,"¹ so those who divide the inheritance of the land in Judea imitate the "copy and shadow" of a heavenly division. Thus truth was in heaven, "but a shadow and copy" of truth was on earth. And as long as this shadow remained on earth, there was an earthly Jerusalem; there was a temple, an altar and a visible worship; there were priests and high priests; and there existed regions and towns of Judea and all these things that are described in this book and are now recited. HOMILIES ON JOSHUA 17.1.²

TWO DISTRIBUTIONS. ORIGEN: A first and a second distribution of the inheritance is reported. The first is indeed through Moses, but the second, and the more powerful, is depicted as accomplished through Jesus [Joshua]. Across the Jordan, Moses decrees property to the tribe of Reuben and the tribe of Gad and to half the tribe of Manasseh, but all the rest receive their inheritance through Jesus [Joshua]. We have already spoken first about how those who had pleased God through the law do not yet reach those things that have been perfected. They precede in time those who attain to the promises through faith in Jesus but must wait for those coming afterwards who will please God in a different time but by one faith, just as the apostle says, "They might not attain perfection without us."³ HOMILIES ON JOSHUA 17.2.⁴

A TYPE OF THE HEAVENLY CHURCH. JEROME: The whole account of the land of Judah and of the tribes is typical of the church in heaven. Let us read Joshua, the son of Nun, or the concluding portions of Ezekiel, and we shall see that the historical division of the land as related by the one finds a counterpart in the spiritual and heavenly promises of the other. What is the meaning of the seven and eight steps in the description of the temple?⁵ Or again, what significance attaches to the fact that in the Psalter, after being taught the mystic alphabet by the one hundred and eighteenth psalm⁶ we arrive by fifteen steps at the

---

¹Heb 8:5. ²FC 105:157. ³Heb 11:40. ⁴FC 105:159. ⁵Ezek 40:20-37. ⁶Ps 119 in many English translations.

point where we can sing: "Behold, now bless the Lord, all you servants of the Lord: you who stand in the house of the Lord, in the courts of the house of our God."[7] Why did two tribes and a half dwell on the other side of Jordan, a district abounding in cattle, while the remaining nine tribes and a half either drove out the old inhabitants from their possessions or dwelled with them? Why did the tribe of Levi receive no portion in the land but have the Lord for its portion?[8] And how is it that of the priests and Levites, themselves, the high priest alone entered the Holy of Holies where were the cherubim and the mercy seat?[9] Why did the other priests wear linen raiment only,[10] and not have their clothing of wrought gold, blue, scarlet, purple and fine cloth? The priests and Levites of the lower order took care of the oxen and carts; those of the higher order carried the ark of the Lord on their shoulders. If you do away with the gradations of the tabernacle, the temple, the church, if, to use a common military phrase, all upon the right hand are to be "up to the same standard," bishops are to no purpose, priests in vain, deacons useless. Why do virgins persevere? Widows toil? Why do married women practice continence? Let us all sin, and when once we have repented, we shall be on the same footing as the apostles. AGAINST JOVINIANUS 2.34.[11]

---

[7]Ps 134:1 (133:1 LXX). [8]Num 18:20. [9]Lev 16:2; Heb 9:7. [10]Ex 28, etc. [11]NPNF 2 6:413-14*.

14:6-12 MOSES' PROMISE REMEMBERED

[6]*Then the people of Judah came to Joshua at Gilgal; and Caleb the son of Jephunneh the Kenizzite said to him, "You know what the LORD said to Moses the man of God in Kadesh-barnea concerning you and me. [7]I was forty years old when Moses the servant of the LORD sent me from Kadesh-barnea to spy out the land; and I brought him word again as it was in my heart. [8]But my brethren who went up with me made the heart of the people melt; yet I wholly followed the LORD my God. [9]And Moses swore on that day, saying, 'Surely the land on which your foot has trodden shall be an inheritance for you and your children for ever, because you have wholly followed the LORD my God.'"*

OVERVIEW: God rewards those who prefer the virtue of obedience over the safety of inaction (AMBROSE).

14:6-9 Caleb Recalls Moses' Promise

PREFERRING VIRTUE TO SAFETY. AMBROSE: However, he [the Lord] said[1] they should not come to that land which they had refused, as a penalty for their unbelief; but their children and wives, who had not murmured, and who, owing to their sex and age, were guiltless, should receive the promised inheritance of that land. So the bodies of those of twenty years old and upwards fell in the desert. The punishment of the rest was put aside. But they who had gone up with Joshua, and had thought fit to dissuade the people, died without delay of a great plague.[2] Joshua and

---

[1]Num 14:29. [2]Num 14:37.

Caleb entered the land of promise together with those who were innocent by reason of age or sex. The better part, therefore, preferred glory to safety; the worse part safety to virtue. But the divine judgment approved those who thought virtue was above what is useful, while it condemned those who preferred what seemed more in accordance with safety than with what is virtuous. Duties of the Clergy 3.8.55-56.[3]

---

[3]NPNF 2 10:76*.

14:13-15 THE INHERITANCE OF CALEB

[13]*Then Joshua blessed him; and he gave Hebron to Caleb the son of Jephunneh for an inheritance.* [14]*So Hebron became the inheritance of Caleb the son of Jephunneh the Kenizzite to this day, because he wholly followed the Lord, the God of Israel.*

Overview: Understanding the meaning of his name, Caleb represents those who exercise and are devoted to divine wisdom. Symbolizing the zealous and wise believer, Caleb desires to refute deception and is therefore blessed by Joshua for the task. He deserved to receive Hebron, the land where the remains of the fathers lie, because he understood the true nature of the marriage union (Origen).

14:13-14 Joshua Gives Hebron to Caleb

Caleb, Son of Jephunneh. Origen: And so, let us see who it is who first receives the inheritance from Jesus [Joshua]: "Caleb," it says, "the son of Jephunneh." For he requests first with certain fixed reasons and words that are described, words that are also able to instruct us for salvation.

First of all, Caleb is interpreted "as a heart." Who, therefore, is "as a heart" if not the one who in all things has devoted effort to discernment, who is not said to be just any member of the body of the church but that one that is the more admirable in us, the heart? That is, he is the one who bears all things with reason and prudence and so arranges all things as if being none other than the heart.

But also Jephunneh, his father, is interpreted "conversion." Therefore, this Caleb is the son of conversion. Why, unless he were converted to God, could Jephunneh produce from himself such fruit that he begat a heart as a son? Thus Caleb is everyone who is devoted to divine understandings and who conducts all things wisely and reasonably. Homilies on Joshua 18.2.[1]

Ardor for Truth. Origen: Thus, therefore, even now this very wise Caleb stands before Jesus [Joshua] and promises to be mighty for war and ready for battle. On that account he earnestly demands to be granted the faculty of disputation that he may contend with the dialecticians[2] of the age who hold deceits for truth, to refute them and to subdue and to overthrow all the things that they have established with their false assertions. Moreover, finally, seeing his ardor, "Jesus [Joshua] blesses him," it says; doubtless because

---

[1]FC 105:163-64. [2]Those who attempt to determine what is true through the exchange of logical arguments.

he demands and dares such things. But you too, if you are willing to give attention to studies and wisely to contemplate the law of God and to be made a "heart" in the law of God, you can overthrow these great and fortified towns, that is, the assertions of falsehood. Then you also may deserve to be blessed by Jesus and to receive Hebron from him. HOMILIES ON JOSHUA 18.3.[3]

CALEB'S INHERITANCE. ORIGEN: But Hebron means "union" or "marriage." Perhaps this can be expressed by Hebron because the double cave[4] purchased by the patriarch Abraham is there, and the remains of the fathers and their wives lie there: Abraham with Sarah, Isaac with Rebecca, and Jacob with Leah. Thus Caleb deserved to receive the remains of the fathers for an inheritance, because no doubt through the wisdom that

was in him and by which he flourished both under Moses and under Jesus [Joshua], he had understood the nature of the union itself. He had perceived the reason why only Sarah lay there with Abraham and that neither Hagar nor Keturah deserved to be joined with him; or the reason why only Leah seems to lie with Jacob, and that neither Rachel, who had been loved more, nor any of the concubines was united with him in the tomb. Therefore, prudent and wise Caleb takes the inheritance with the monuments of the fathers. Jesus [Joshua] granted to him Hebron, a mother city of the Anakim nation, and it becomes "a share" for him "up to the present day." HOMILIES ON JOSHUA 18.3.[5]

---

[3]FC 105:166. [4]Gen 23:9, 19. Machpelah is translated "the double cave" in the LXX. [5]FC 105:166-67.

15:1-12 THE INHERITANCE OF JUDAH

[1]The lot for the tribe of the people of Judah according to their families reached southward to the boundary of Edom, to the wilderness of Zin at the farthest south. [2]And their south boundary ran from the end of the Salt Sea, from the bay that faces southward; [3]it goes out southward of the ascent of Akrabbim, passes along to Zin, and goes up south of Kadesh-barnea, along by Hezron, up to Addar, turns about to Karka, [4]passes along to Azmon, goes out by the Brook of Egypt, and comes to its end at the sea. This shall be your south boundary. [5]And the east boundary is the Salt Sea, to the mouth of the Jordan. And the boundary on the north side runs from the bay of the sea at the mouth of the Jordan; [6]and the boundary goes up to Beth-hoglah, and passes along north of Beth-arabah; and the boundary goes up to the stone of Bohan the son of Reuben; [7]and the boundary goes up to Debir from the Valley of Achor, and so northward, turning toward Gilgal, which is opposite the ascent of Adummim, which is on the south side of the valley; and the boundary passes along to the waters of En-shemesh, and ends at En-rogel; [8]then the boundary goes up by the valley of the son of Hinnom at the southern shoulder of the Jebusite (that is, Jerusalem); and the boundary goes up to the top of the mountain that lies over against the valley of Hinnom, on the west, at the northern end of the valley of Rephaim; [9]then the boundary extends from the top of the mountain to the

*spring of the Waters of Nephtoah, and from there to the cities of Mount Ephron; then the bound-
ary bends round to Baalah (that is, Kiriath-jearim);* [10]*and the boundary circles west of Baalah to
Mount Seir, passes along to the northern shoulder of Mount Jearim (that is, Chesalon), and goes
down to Beth-shemesh, and passes along by Timnah;* [11]*the boundary goes out to the shoulder of the
hill north of Ekron, then the boundary bends round to Shikkeron, and passes along to Mount
Baalah, and goes out to Jabneel; then the boundary comes to an end at the sea.* [12]*And the west
boundary was the Great Sea with its coastline. This is the boundary round about the people of
Judah according to their families.*

OVERVIEW: The division of the promised land is
understood typologically. Judah's inheritance,
which is past Edom and the wilderness of Zin,
may be reached after dealing with earthly things
and passing through the desert of temptations.
On this path to heavenly reward, the hills of
Akrabbim must be ascended, signifying the treading down of scorpions. Kadesh, or sanctification,
borders the region. The waves of the salt sea, or
the hazards of life, must be first surmounted in
order to reach the fountain of the sun, or the living water (ORIGEN).

15:1 Judah's Lot

EARTHLY THINGS. ORIGEN: "The boundaries of
Judah," it says, "were made according to their
people from the borders of Edom and from the
wilderness of Zin to the west." Therefore, the
borders of Judah are next to the borders of Edom.
But Edom, as we have already often said, means
"earthly things." Therefore, the regions of Judah
come just after earthly things. But it also says,
"from the wilderness of Zin." Zin means "temptations." Therefore, the regions of the inheritance
of Judah come after temptations. HOMILIES ON
JOSHUA 19.2.[1]

DESERT OF TEMPTATIONS. ORIGEN: Moreover, "from the boundaries of Edom" is the wilderness of Zin. We said a little before that the
wilderness of Zin signified "temptations," and
therefore it was necessary for us to pass through
the desert of temptations to attain to the inherit-

ance of the sons of Judah. HOMILIES ON JOSHUA
19.3.[2]

15:2-4 The South Boundary

TREAD DOWN SCORPIONS. ORIGEN: But also
we must go up the ascent of the hills of Akrabbim, which means "scorpions." Thus it is necessary for us to pass over and even tread down
scorpions, about which the Savior says, "Behold,
I have given you the authority to tread over serpents and scorpions."[3] Whoever therefore wishes
and longs to enter into the inheritance of the
tribe of Judah must go up these ascents and tread
down and escape from scorpions that stand in the
way. For this reason, I think that the Lord said to
the prophet Ezekiel making this journey, "Son of
man, you dwell in the midst of scorpions."[4] HOM-
ILIES ON JOSHUA 19.3.[5]

TOWARD SANCTIFICATION. ORIGEN: "And the
borders," it says, "are all the way to Kadesh."
Kadesh means "holy" or "sanctification." Therefore, the borders of Judah reach all the way to
sanctification. HOMILIES ON JOSHUA 19.3.[6]

15:5-10 The East and North Boundaries

ENTERING JUDAH'S PORTION. ORIGEN: Everyone, therefore, who wants to enter into the portion of the children of Judah must first pass

---

[1]FC 105:169. [2]FC 105:169. [3]Lk 10:19. [4]Ezek 2:6. [5]FC 105:170.
[6]FC 105:170.

through the Salt Sea. That is to say, he must surmount the waves and billows of this life and escape from all things in this world that, by virtue of their own uncertainty and hazardousness, are compared with the waves of the sea. Then he may be able to reach the land of Judah and to approach the fountain of the sun.[7] But what is the fountain of the sun, or of which sun? Of that sun, of course, about which it is written, "But for the ones fearing my name, the sun of righteousness will arise."[8] Therefore you will find the fountain

of this sun in the land of Judah, if you move away from the Salt Sea. Which fountain? That one of which Jesus said, "The water that I give will become a fountain of water leaping up into eternal life within the person who drinks from it."[9] Therefore, when you have found the kind of fountain of this sun that we have described, you will also find its city. HOMILIES ON JOSHUA 19.4.[10]

---

[7]Following the LXX translation of En-shemesh. [8]Mal 4:2 (3:20 LXX). [9]Jn 4:14. [10]FC 105:170-71*.

15:13-19 CALEB POSSESSES HIS LAND

[13]*According to the commandment of the LORD to Joshua, he gave to Caleb the son of Jephunneh a portion among the people of Judah, Kiriath-arba, that is, Hebron (Arba was the father of Anak).* [14]*And Caleb drove out from there the three sons of Anak, Sheshai and Ahiman and Talmai, the descendants of Anak.* [15]*And he went up from there against the inhabitants of Debir; now the name of Debir formerly was Kiriath-sepher.* [16]*And Caleb said, "Whoever smites Kiriath-sepher, and takes it, to him will I give Achsah my daughter as wife."* [17]*And Othni-el the son of Kenaz, the brother of Caleb, took it; and he gave him Achsah his daughter as wife.* [18]*When she came to him, she urged him to ask her father for a field; and she alighted from her ass, and Caleb said to her, "What do you wish?"* [19]*She said to him, "Give me a present; since you have set me in the land of the Negeb, give me also springs of water." And Caleb gave her the upper springs and the lower springs.*

Overview: Understood typologically, Caleb's possession of his inheritance represents the destruction of vain humility and the eradication of the unholy, unwise and unstable. Othniel's conquering of the City of Letters represents the receipt of divine revelation (ORIGEN).

15:13-14 Caleb Drives Out the Sons of Anak

THE CAPITAL CITY. ORIGEN: First, therefore, let us investigate why Caleb received the capital

city, the capital of Anak, the one first called a capital among all the rest in the land of promise. Anak means "vain humility" or "vain reply." Therefore, Caleb received the capital of "vain humility." It is certain that there are two humilities. One is laudable, about which the Savior said, "Learn from me because I am meek and humble in heart; and you will find rest for your souls."[1] And about this humility it is said, "Everyone who

---

[1]Mt 11:29.

humbles himself will be exalted,"[2] and else-where, "Therefore, be humbled under the almighty hand of God."[3] But there is also another humility, guilty of sins, just as that which Scripture speaks of concerning illicit sexual union: "He humbled her."[4] This is written concerning Ammon, that he "humbled" Tamar his sister. For it is vain humility that sinks down on account of sin. Therefore, Caleb seized or destroyed the capital city of vain humility and destroyed the three sons of Anak, who were sons of vain humility, and, after he had destroyed them, he occupied the city and did the things that are written later. HOMILIES ON JOSHUA 20.5.[5]

SONS OF VAIN HUMILITY. ORIGEN: But who are those sons of vain humility whom Caleb drove out? First Sheshai, which is interpreted "outside me," that is, "outside the holy," because the son of vain humility is outside the holy, and indeed outside God. And another is Ahiman, which means "my brother outside counsel" just as if we said, "brother without counsel." For it is certain all brothers who are born from vain humility are outside counsel. Third is Talmai, which means "precipice" or "suspension." This indicates that there is nothing stable in him, but

all things are unsettled and rushing headlong into great danger. HOMILIES ON JOSHUA 20.5.[6]

15:16-17 Achsah Is Promised to the Victor

THE REPLY OF GOD. ORIGEN: But now Caleb went up against that City of Letters[7] and said, "I shall give Achsah my daughter for a wife to who-ever demolishes the City of Letters and gains pos-session of it. And Othniel the son of Kenaz seized it." Moreover, Othniel, who received the City of Letters, is interpreted "the reply of God." But "the reply of God" can be said "he to whom God replies," that is, he to whom God reveals secrets and discloses hidden things. That one, therefore, is the younger brother of Caleb, the one who is able to take the City of Letters of the old covenant, and to demolish the "killing letter."[8] HOMILIES ON JOSHUA 20.6.[9]

15:18-19 Achsah Requests Springs of Water[10]

---

[2]Lk 14:11. [3]1 Pet 5:6. [4]2 Sam 13:14. [5]FC 105:180. [6]FC 105:180-81. [7]Following the LXX translation of Kiriath-sepher. [8]2 Cor 3:6. [9]FC 105:182*. [10]See comment for Judg 1:15.

15:20-63 THE BOUNDARIES OF JUDAH

[63]*But the Jebusites, the inhabitants of Jerusalem, the people of Judah could not drive out; so the Jebusites dwell with the people of Judah at Jerusalem to this day.*

OVERVIEW: The commingling of the Jebusites with the Judahites represents the mixture of the ungodly and the holy within the church. In our zeal to remain firm in our faith in Christ, we must diligently rid ourselves of evil thoughts (ORIGEN).

15:63 The Jebusites Dwell with the People of Judah

WEEDS AND WHEAT. ORIGEN: But let us under-stand these verses spiritually, claiming the parable of the Gospel, which says concerning the weeds,

"Let them grow up together, lest perhaps when you wish to pluck up the weeds, you also pluck up the wheat with them."[1] Therefore, as the weeds are permitted in the Gospel to grow up together with the wheat, in the same manner even here in Jerusalem—that is, in the church—there are certain Jebusites who lead an ignoble and degenerate life, and who are perverse not only in their faith but in their actions and in every manner of living. For while the church is on earth, it is not possible to cleanse it to such purity that neither an ungodly person nor any sinner seems to reside in it, where everyone is holy and blessed and no blot of sin is found in them. But just as it is said concerning the weeds, "lest perhaps plucking up the weeds, at the same time you may also pluck up the wheat with them," so it can also be said of those in whom there are either doubtful or secret sins. For we are not saying that those who are clearly and plainly sinful should not be expelled from the church. HOMILIES ON JOSHUA 21.1.[2]

FIXED AND FIRM. ORIGEN: Concerning Jerusalem, we have frequently said that it means "a vision of peace." If, therefore, Jerusalem has been built in our heart—that is, if the vision of peace has been established in our heart and we always contemplate and retain in our heart Christ, who is "our peace"[3]—if indeed we are so fixed and firm in this vision of peace that absolutely no evil thought or consideration of some sin ever rises up into our heart, if this could be so done, we would be able to say that we are in Jerusalem and no one else dwells with us except those who are holy. But now, even though we make great progress and improve ourselves with the utmost zeal, nevertheless I do not think anyone turns out to be so pure of heart that he is never defiled by the contamination of a contrary thought. Therefore, it is still certain that Jebusites dwell with the sons of Judah in Jerusalem. Yet we do not say these things so that we may neglect to cast them out as far as it may be done. On the contrary, we must be amply concerned and must attempt daily to cast them from Jerusalem; but, just as it is written, we cannot cast all out at the same time. HOMILIES ON JOSHUA 21.2.[4]

---

[1]Mt 13:29-30. [2]FC 105:184-85*. [3]Eph 2:14. [4]FC 105:187.

16:1—17:13 THE INHERITANCE OF EPHRAIM AND MANASSEH

[10]However they did not drive out the Canaanites that dwelt in Gezer: so the Canaanites have dwelt in the midst of Ephraim to this day but have become slaves to do forced labor. . . .

17 [5]Thus there fell to Manasseh ten portions, besides the land of Gilead and Bashan, which is on the other side of the Jordan; [6]because the daughters of Manasseh received an inheritance along with his sons. The land of Gilead was allotted to the rest of the Manassites. . . .

[12]Yet the sons of Manasseh could not take possession of those cities; but the Canaanites persisted in dwelling in that land. [13]But when the people of Israel grew strong, they put the Canaanites to forced labor, and did not utterly drive them out.

OVERVIEW: Canaanites in the land represent impurities of the soul (PROCOPIUS). The exile from Egypt to the promised land prefigures the forty-two generations from Abraham to Christ (ORIGEN). Noah's curse on Ham's son Canaan is fulfilled when the Israelites inhabit the promised land (EPHREM).

16:10 Canaanites in the Land

THE CANAANITES STILL WITH US. PROCOPIUS OF GAZA: "And the Canaanites have lived in the midst of Ephraim to this very day." But Ephraim is interpreted as "fruitful." Therefore, although it is fruitful, it is not able to eject the Canaanite (who is of a different and cursed seed) from its territory until this day. But we can also say this concerning the church. Taken another way, there is no soul who is able to remain pure in this present life seeking peace alone without sinning until he sees Christ, the peace of God and the one who [dwells] throughout all those who bear fruit. For no one is clean from sordidness, from strange or alien thinking [on his own]. And so, just as the Jebusites and Canaanites are always found in Jerusalem, it is also necessary to suffer for the casting out of these, but only those who call upon God are able to do so. COMMENTARY ON JOSHUA 16:10.[1]

17:6 The Land of Gilead

FORTY-TWO STAGES TO THE FULFILLMENT OF THE PROMISE. ORIGEN: If one examines as carefully as possible, he will find in the Scriptures that there are forty-two stages in the departure of the children of Israel from Egypt; and, further, the coming of our Lord and Savior into this world is traced through forty-two generations. This is what Matthew the Evangelist points out when he says, "from Abraham to David the king, fourteen generations. And from David to the Babylonian exile, fourteen generations. And from the Babylonian exile to Christ, fourteen generations."[2] Therefore, in descending to the Egypt of this world Christ passed those forty-two generations as stages; and those who ascend from Egypt pass by the same number, forty-two stages. . . . Therefore, the children of Israel by forty-two stages attained the beginning of taking their inheritance. And the beginning of taking their inheritance was when Reuben, Gad and the half tribe of Manasseh received the land of Gilead. And so the number is fixed for Christ's descent, when he came down to us through forty-two ancestors according to the flesh as through forty-two stages. And the ascent of the children of Israel to the beginning of the promised inheritance was through the same number of stages. HOMILIES ON NUMBERS 27.3.[3]

17:13 The Canaanites Put to Forced Labor

CANAAN ENSLAVED. EPHREM THE SYRIAN: After Ham had been cursed through his one son, [Noah] blessed Shem and Japheth and said, "May God increase Japheth and may he dwell in the tent of Shem, and let Canaan be their slave."[4] Japheth increased and became powerful in his inheritance in the north and in the west. And God dwelt in the tent of Abraham, the descendent of Shem, and Canaan became their slave when in the days of Joshua son of Nun, the Israelites destroyed the dwelling-places of [Canaan] and pressed their leaders into bondage. ON GENESIS 7.4.[5]

---

[1]PG 87.1:1033. [2]Mt 1:17. [3]OSW 249-50*. [4]Gen 9:27. [5]FC 91:146*.

17:14-18 THE TRIBE OF JOSEPH COMPLAINS

[14]And the tribe of Joseph spoke to Joshua, saying, "Why have you given me but one lot and one portion as an inheritance, although I am a numerous people, since hitherto the LORD has blessed me?" [15]And Joshua said to them, "If you are a numerous people, go up to the forest, and there clear ground for yourselves in the land of the Perizzites and the Rephaim, since the hill country of Ephraim is too narrow for you." [16]The tribe of Joseph said, "The hill country is not enough for us; yet all the Canaanites who dwell in the plain have chariots of iron, both those in Beth-shean and its villages and those in the Valley of Jezreel." [17]Then Joshua said to the house of Joseph, to Ephraim and Manasseh, "You are a numerous people, and have great power; you shall not have one lot only, [18]but the hill country shall be yours, for though it is a forest, you shall clear it and possess it to its farthest borders; for you shall drive out the Canaanites, though they have chariots of iron, and though they are strong."

OVERVIEW: Joshua's command to drive out the Perizzites illustrates the need to expel the fruit of sin and unrighteousness. The purging of the Rephaites symbolizes the purification of our souls of the filth produced by weak and unsound thoughts. Exterminating the Canaanites prefigures the pursuit of perfection achieved through crucifying the flesh. Clearing the woodland symbolizes the removal of those things that hinder our fruitfulness for the gospel (ORIGEN).

17:14-15 Joseph's Tribe Needs More Land

THE FRUIT OF SIN. ORIGEN: Thus if we too are a numerous people and the Lord blesses us, we hear from Jesus, "You are a numerous people; go up into the forest, and clear and prepare a place for yourself in the land. Purge the Perizzites and Rephaites." Therefore, we must cast out the Perizzites. Moreover, we find the Perizzites to mean "fructification." But just as we have already often said concerning other names, the meaning in this one is also twofold, for there is a good fructification and a bad one, as it is pointed out in the Gospels, "A good tree produces good fruit, and a bad tree produces bad fruit."[1] Therefore, it is fitting for us to expel everything that does not bear fruit

properly and to cut away the fruit of sin and to purge the fruit of unrighteousness. HOMILIES ON JOSHUA 22.4.[2]

PURGING IMPURITY. ORIGEN: It also says drive away, or rather, "purge the Rephaites from you." We find Rephaites to be interpreted "slack mothers." According to that which is said in a mystery concerning the soul as though concerning a woman, there is a certain power in our soul that brings forth perceptions and is, so to speak, the mother of those perceptions or understandings that proceed from us; "and she will be saved through the begetting of children, if they have persevered in the faith and in truth."[3] Therefore, those mothers, that is, that power of the soul, begets sound and powerful perceptions among those in whom it is strong, sound and robust. These cannot be overcome by someone contradicting them. In others, that power indicated by perceptions is indeed slack and languid when certain weak and absurd points possessing no strength are put forth. Therefore, this is indicated under the name Rephaites, so that we may purge ourselves of these languid mothers, who bear

---

[1]Mt 7:17.　[2]FC 105:191-92.　[3]1 Tim 2:14-15.

weak and useless thoughts. And this name adequately preserves the peculiar nature of the spiritual understanding, for it did not say that the Rephaites must be destroyed but purged. For we are not enjoined to demolish and to destroy the natural impulses of the soul, but to purge, that is, to purify and to drive away the filth and uncleanness that reached them from our negligence. Then the natural vigor of its own innate strength may shine forth. HOMILIES ON JOSHUA 22.4.[4]

17:16-18 You Shall Drive Out the Caananites

ATTAINING PERFECTION. ORIGEN: For if at last we come to perfection, then the Canaanite is said to have been exterminated by us and handed over to death. But as to how this is accomplished in our flesh, hear the apostle saying, "Mortify your members that are upon the earth: fornication, impurity,"[5] and the other things that follow. And again it says, "For those who belong to Christ have crucified their flesh with its vices and lusts."[6] Thus, therefore, in the third stage, that is, when we come to perfection and mortify our members

and carry around the death of Christ in our body, the Canaanite is said to be exterminated by us. HOMILIES ON JOSHUA 22.2.[7]

CLEARING THE WOODLAND. ORIGEN: You see what is being said to us in the spiritual interpretation, to clear the woodland that is in us and, cutting useless and unfruitful trees out of us, to make fallow lands there that we would always renew and from which we would reap fruit "thirtyfold and sixtyfold and a hundredfold."[8] Does not the word of the Gospel also proclaim the same things to us, saying, "Behold the axe has already been placed at the root of the trees; therefore, every tree that does not bear fruit will be cut down and cast into the fire"[9]? These are the things Jesus [Joshua] the son of Nun commanded to our ancestors concerning cutting down unfruitful trees; these are the mandates the Lord Jesus describes in the Gospel. So how is it not true that a shadow has preceded and truth has followed after? HOMILIES ON JOSHUA 22.5.[10]

---

[4]FC 105:192. [5]Col 3:5. [6]Gal 5:24. [7]FC 105:190-91. [8]Mt 13:8, 23. [9]Mt 3:10. [10]FC 105:193*.

18:1-10 THE SURVEY OF REMAINING LAND

[1]*Then the whole congregation of the people of Israel assembled at Shiloh, and set up the tent of meeting there; the land lay subdued before them.*

OVERVIEW: The tabernacle, with the sea to its west, symbolizes the relationship between the saints and the reprobate (BEDE).

18:1 The Tent of Meeting at Shiloh

THE TABERNACLE AND THE SEA. BEDE: For

surely the waves of the deep, brackish and turbulent sea can signify both the sins among which the reprobate are lost in this life when they delight in evil and also the pit of the future perdition, when at the last judgment they will be sent with the devil into eternal fire.

We should not forget that when the tabernacle

was built on Mount Sinai it had the Red Sea to its west, and when it was brought into the land of promise and set up at Shiloh by Joshua it had the Great Sea in the same direction. Mystically, therefore, we can understand by this that the saints who serve the Lord in this life and make a tabernacle for him in their hearts despise the proud boasting of the impious, confidently mindful that it is soon to pass away: when they are established with the Lord in the future homeland, they shall look at the perpetual punishment of the impious without any interruption of their own felicity. Consequently, the elders give thanks to the Lord because they also contemplate the evil things from which he has delivered them. ON THE TABERNACLE 2.6.66.[1]

---

[1]TTH 18:73-74.

18:11-28 THE INHERITANCE OF BENJAMIN

[21]*Now the cities of the tribe of Benjamin according to their families were Jericho, Beth-hoglah, Emek-keziz,* [22]*Beth-arabah, Zemaraim, Bethel,* [23]*Avvim, Parah, Ophrah,* [24]*Chepharammoni, Ophni, Geba—twelve cities with their villages.* [25]*Gibeon, Ramah, Be-eroth,* [26]*Mizpeh, Chephirah, Mozah,* [27]*Rekem, Irpeel, Taralah,* [28]*Zela, Ha-eleph, Jebus*[m] *(that is, Jerusalem), Gibe-ah*[n] *and Kiriath-jearim*[o]*—fourteen cities with their villages. This is the inheritance of the tribe of Benjamin according to its families.*

m Gk Syr Vg: Heb *the Jebusite* n Heb *Gibeath* o Gk: Heb *Kiriath*

OVERVIEW: The building of Jerusalem upon the former city of Jebus serves as a metaphor for conversion (AUGUSTINE, ORIGEN). Likewise, the cities of Babylon and Jerusalem depict the age-old intermingling of confusion and the vision of peace to be severed at the end of the world (AUGUSTINE). Apostasy is deemed worse than Jerusalem's treatment of Jesus. A model of the future inheritance in heaven is perceived in the bequeathing of Jerusalem to Benjamin (ORIGEN).

18:28 Jebus, That Is, Jerusalem

A CITY REBUILT. AUGUSTINE: But when Jerusalem was being built, it was not built in a place where there was not a city, but there was a city at first which was called Jebus, whence the Jebusites. This having been captured, overcome, made subject, there was built a new city, as though the old were thrown down; and it was called Jerusalem, vision of peace, City of God. Each one therefore that is born of Adam does not yet belong to Jerusalem: for he bears with him the offshoot of iniquity, and the punishment of sin, having been consigned to death, and he belongs in a manner to a sort of old city. But if he is to be in the people of God, his old self will be thrown down, and he will be built up new. EXPLANATIONS OF THE PSALMS 62.4.[1]

THE VISION OF PEACE. AUGUSTINE: And see the names of those two cities, Babylon and Jeru-

---

[1]NPNF 1 8:252-53*.

salem. Babylon is interpreted confusion, Jerusalem vision of peace. Observe now the city of confusion, in order that you may perceive the vision of peace; that you may endure the one and long for the other. By what can those two cities be distinguished? Can we in any way now separate them from each other? They are mingled, and from the very beginning of humankind mingled they run on until the end of the world. Jerusalem began through Abel, Babylon through Cain: for the buildings of the cities were erected afterwards. That Jerusalem in the land of the Jebusites was built: for at first it used to be called Jebus, from which the nation of the Jebusites was expelled, when the people of God was delivered from Egypt and led into the land of promise. But Babylon was built in the most interior regions of Persia, which for a long time raised its head above the rest of nations. These two cities then at particular times were built, so that there might be shown a figure of two cities begun of old, and to remain even until the end in this world, but at the end to be severed. EXPLANATIONS OF THE PSALMS 65.2.[2]

JEBUS TO JERUSALEM. ORIGEN: I pass from the letter—since even it has taken a way which the Word has given—to each soul already made worthy to see peace. For after divine studies, you have become Jerusalem, the prior place being Jebus. History says that the name of that place had been Jebus, but afterwards the name changed and became Jerusalem. The children of the Hebrews say that Jebus is interpreted as "what has been trampled." Jebus then is the soul which is trampled by hostile powers, has been changed and has become Jerusalem, vision of peace. If then you have sinned, when you have changed from Jebus

to become Jerusalem, and you have trampled upon the Son of God and held as profane the blood of the new covenant[3] as she had, and you have ended up in grievous sins, it will also be said concerning you, who will spare you, Jerusalem? And who will feel sorry for you if you become someone who betrays Jesus? When each of us sins, and especially if he sins grievously, he sins against Jesus. But if he is also an apostate, he does spiritually even more to Jesus the things that Jerusalem did to him bodily. HOMILIES ON JEREMIAH 13.2.[4]

A MODEL OF THE FUTURE. ORIGEN: Therefore we must believe that also here, in imitation of these things, Scripture relates that lots are drawn by Jesus [Joshua], and the inheritance for each of the tribes is determined by divine dispensation; and that in this casting of lots, through the ineffable providence and foreknowledge of God, a model of the future inheritance in heaven is dimly sketched. Since indeed, "the law is said to hold a shadow of good things to come,"[5] and there is some city in heaven that is called Jerusalem and Mount Zion—just as the apostle says concerning those who would come to the Lord Jesus Christ, "You have drawn near to Mount Zion and are come to the city of the living God, heavenly Jerusalem"[6]—certainly it is not without a reason that Benjamin receives Jerusalem and Mount Zion in his lot. Doubtless, it is because the nature of that heavenly Jerusalem established it that the earthly Jerusalem, which preserved a figure and form of the heavenly one, ought to be given to none other than Benjamin. HOMILIES ON JOSHUA 23.4.[7]

---

[2]NPNF 1 8:268*. [3]Heb 10:29. [4]FC 97:132*. [5]Heb 10:1. [6]Heb 12:22. [7]FC 105:200.

[19:1-39 THE INHERITANCES OF SIMEON, ZEBULUN, ISSACHAR, ASHER AND NAPHTALI]

19:40-51 THE INHERITANCE OF DAN

[49]When they had finished distributing the several territories of the land as inheritances, the people of Israel gave an inheritance among them to Joshua the son of Nun. [50]By command of the LORD they gave him the city which he asked, Timnath-serah in the hill country of Ephraim; and he rebuilt the city, and settled in it.

OVERVIEW: Joshua's inheritance of land in Ephraim represents the Lord's inhabiting the souls of those who produce the fruit of the Spirit (ORIGEN).

19:49-50 Joshua Receives an Inheritance

FRUIT OF THE SPIRIT. ORIGEN: And indeed we said above that even our Lord Jesus Christ asks us for a place he may build and in which he may live and that we ought to become so clean of heart, and so sincere of mind, so holy in body and spirit, that he may both deign to accept this place in our soul and to build it and dwell in it. And who do you think among all the people are so acceptable to God that they are worthy to be chosen for this? Or perhaps no individuals can be capable of this, but can the whole people and all the church together barely be capable of receiving the Lord Jesus in themselves so that he may dwell in them?

Let us see, therefore, what is this place in which Jesus is bound to dwell. "In Mount Ephraim," it says, that is, in the fruit-bearing mountain. Who do you think among us are fruit-bearing mountains, in whom Jesus may dwell? Surely those in whom exist "the fruit of the Spirit: joy, peace, patience, love,"[1] and the rest. Those, therefore, are the fruit-bearing mountains who produce the fruit of the Spirit and who are always lofty in mind and expectation. And although few are able to be like this, nevertheless, even if they are few, the Lord Jesus, who is the "true light"[2] dwelling in them, will send forth the beams of his light also upon all the rest, those whom he has not yet, in this first round, judged worthy of his habitation. HOMILIES ON JOSHUA 26.1.[3]

---

[1]Gal 5:22. [2]Jn 1:9. [3]FC 105:215-16.

20:1-9 CITIES OF REFUGE

¹*Then the LORD said to Joshua,* ²*"Say to the people of Israel, 'Appoint the cities of refuge, of which I spoke to you through Moses,* ³*that the manslayer who kills any person without intent or unwittingly may flee there; they shall be for you a refuge from the avenger of blood. . . .* ⁶*And he shall remain in that city until he has stood before the congregation for judgment, until the death of him who is high priest at the time: then the slayer may go again to his own town and his own home, to the town from which he fled.'"*

OVERVIEW: The difficulty of a literal interpretation prompts the spiritual understanding of Jesus as the high priest in a city of refuge (AMBROSE, JEROME). Scripture's prescription for cities of refuge demonstrate that accidental slayings are sins that may be redeemed by the Savior's blood (JEROME).

20:6 *Until the Death of the High Priest*

A SPIRITUAL MEANING PROPOSED. AMBROSE: There remains . . . what Scripture says concerning the death of the chief priest, "that the homicide shall be in the city of refuge even to that time, until the high priest dies." In this passage the literal interpretation causes difficulty. First, the period of flight is limited by chance rather than by any consideration of fairness; further, in like cases the result is unlike. For it could happen that the high priest might die on the day after the homicide took refuge. However, what is the meaning beneath the uncertainty? And so, because the letter causes difficulty, let us search for spiritual meanings.[1] Who is that high priest but the Son of God, the Word of God? We enjoy his advocacy in our behalf before the Father,[2] for he is free from every offense, both willed and unintentional, and in him subsist all things which are on earth and which are in heaven. For all things have been bound by the bond of the Word and are held together by his power and subsist in him, because in him they have been created and

in him all God's fullness dwells. And so all things endure, because he does not allow what things he has bound to be loosened, since they subsist in his will. Indeed, so long as he wills, he keeps all things in check by his command and rules them and binds them by a harmony of nature.[3] Therefore the Word of God lives, and he lives most of all in the souls of the holy, and the fullness of the Godhead never dies. For God's everlasting divinity and eternal power never die. To be sure, he dies to us if he is separated from our soul, not that our spirit is destroyed by death, but that it is loosened and stripped from union with him. Yes, true death is the separation of the Word from the soul. Thereupon, the soul begins at once to be open to sins of volition. FLIGHT FROM THE WORLD 2.13.[4]

REDEEMED BY THE BLOOD. JEROME: For the very words of Scripture indicate that even ignorance is a sin. [Thus], also, Job offers burnt offerings for his sons, [in the event] they may have sinned unwittingly in thought.[5] And, if a man is killed by the iron of an axe that flies off the handle when a man is hewing wood, the wood hewer is ordered to flee to a city of refuge[6] and remain in that place until the death of the high priest, that is to say, until he is redeemed by the blood of the Savior, either in the house of baptism or by repen-

---

[1]2 Cor 3:6. [2]1 Jn 2:1-2. [3]Col 1:16-20. [4]FC 65:289-90. [5]Job 1:5. [6]Deut 19:4-5.

tance, which supplies the efficacy of the grace of baptism through the ineffable mercy of the Savior who does not wish anybody to perish. Nor does he find his delight in the death of sinners, but rather that they be converted from their way and live. DEFENSE AGAINST THE PELAGIANS 1.33.[7]

[7]FC 53:279.

21:1-8 THE LEVITES REQUEST CITIES

[1]*Then the heads of the fathers' houses of the Levites came to Eleazar the priest and to Joshua the son of Nun and to the heads of the fathers' houses of the tribes of the people of Israel;* [2]*and they said to them at Shiloh in the land of Canaan, "The LORD commanded through Moses that we be given cities to dwell in, along with their pasture lands for our cattle."* [3]*So by command of the LORD the people of Israel gave to the Levites the following cities and pasture lands out of their inheritance.*

[4]*The lot came out for the families of the Kohathites. So those Levites who were descendants of Aaron the priest received by lot from the tribes of Judah, Simeon, and Benjamin, thirteen cities.*

[5]*And the rest of the Kohathites received by lot from the families of the tribe of Ephraim, from the tribe of Dan and the half-tribe of Manasseh, ten cities.*

[6]*The Gershonites received by lot from the families of the tribe of Issachar, from the tribe of Asher, from the tribe of Naphtali, and from the half-tribe of Manasseh in Bashan, thirteen cities.*

[7]*The Merarites according to their families received from the tribe of Reuben, the tribe of Gad, and the tribe of Zebulun, twelve cities.*

[8]*These cities and their pasture lands the people of Israel gave by lot to the Levites, as the LORD had commanded through Moses.*

OVERVIEW: In order that the distribution of towns for the Levites would not seem accidental, lots were drawn. This demonstrated reason and priority in order that will be preserved in the resurrection. The first lot rightly fell to the descendents of Aaron, the first high priest (ORIGEN).

21:1-8 The Levites Receive Cities by Lot

A DRAWING OF LOTS. ORIGEN: It was fitting that there be a drawing of lots even regarding the suburbs and cities so that perhaps the renowned division among the Levites might not seem perhaps indiscriminate and accidental. Therefore, the distribution by lot that took place among the sons of Israel was characterized by reason, by which someone was considered worthy of the first lot, and someone else the second, as we have already previously examined to the extent we were able. This was true in regard to both those who receive through Moses beyond the Jordan and those who receive from Jesus [Joshua] in the land of promise, where the first lot fell to Benjamin[1] and afterwards to the rest, among whom Dan was the last.[2] Even so it is necessary that there be some reason also in the order of

[1]Josh 18:11. [2]Josh 19:40.

priestly and levitical lots. Thus the first is drawn for someone, the second for someone else, and the third for another, through which these or those places are determined for each one. HOMILIES ON JOSHUA 25.1.[3]

RESURRECTION ORDER. ORIGEN: Who will explain the diverse sites of the encampments, how this distribution must be retained in the resurrection for each priestly or levitical order of the saints, so that, just as the apostle says, nothing is done haphazardly in the resurrection, but everyone comes "in his own order, Christ first, then those who belong to Christ who have believed in his coming, when he will hand the kingdom over to our God and Father, when he will subject to him every principality and power"?[4]

On that occasion, without doubt, there will be some such observances of encampments and priestly distributions and ranks and signals of trumpets. HOMILIES ON JOSHUA 25.4.[5]

FIRST PLACE. ORIGEN: "First," it says, "the lot fell out for Kohath, and it came to pass for the sons of Aaron, the priests, who were among the Levites." Whose lot was it suitable to be the first to fall out? To whom was it fitting to be given first place, if not to Aaron, the first high priest, first in life, in merits, first in honors and power? Is it resolved among you now at least that this casting of lots is not accidental but that a heavenly power is present, governing it according to the judgment of divine providence? Where, therefore, does this just lot determine the first dwelling places for the sons of Aaron? "Thirteen cities by lot," it says, "in the tribe of Judah, in the tribe of Simeon, and in the tribe of Benjamin." You see how the dwelling places are dispensed to select persons in select tribes. HOMILIES ON JOSHUA 25.2.[6]

---

[3]FC 105:208-9. [4]1 Cor 15:23-24. [5]FC 105:213. [6]FC 105:210.

[21:9-26 THE CITIES OF THE LEVITES]

[21:27-45 THE LORD'S PROMISES FULFILLED]

22:1-20 AN ALTAR BY THE JORDAN

[1]*Then Joshua summoned the Reubenites, and the Gadites, and the half-tribe of Manasseh,* [2]*and said to them, "You have kept all that Moses the servant of the LORD commanded you, and have obeyed my voice in all that I have commanded you;* [3]*you have not forsaken your brethren these many days, down to this day, but have been careful to keep the charge of the LORD your God.* [4]*And now the LORD your God has given rest to your brethren, as he promised them; therefore turn and go to*

your home in the land where your possession lies, which Moses the servant of the LORD gave you on the other side of the Jordan. [5]*Take good care to observe the commandment and the law which Moses the servant of the LORD commanded you, to love the LORD your God, and to walk in all his ways, and to keep his commandments, and to cleave to him, and to serve him with all your heart and with all your soul."* [6]*So Joshua blessed them, and sent them away; and they went to their homes. . . .*

[10]*And when they came to the region about the Jordan, that lies in the land of Canaan, the Reubenites and the Gadites and the half-tribe of Manasseh built there an altar by the Jordan, an altar of great size.* [11]*And the people of Israel heard say, "Behold, the Reubenites and the Gadites and the half-tribe of Manasseh have built an altar at the frontier of the land of Canaan, in the region about the Jordan, on the side that belongs to the people of Israel."* [12]*And when the people of Israel heard of it, the whole assembly of the people of Israel gathered at Shiloh, to make war against them.*

OVERVIEW: Joshua's blessing and dismissal of the two and a half tribes indicates the mystery of the ingathering of the nations: those who aided and awaited the day receive their reward and rest. These people foreshadowed the faithful who lived before Christ's coming yet who lacked the entire knowledge of the Trinity (ORIGEN).

22:1-9 The Two and a Half Tribes Return Home

THE FULLNESS OF THE NATIONS. ORIGEN: After these things Jesus [Joshua] assembles the sons of Reuben and the sons of Gad and the half-tribe of Manasseh, who had served as soldiers with him to overcome the foes of the Israelites, and he dismisses them to go to their inheritance with certain gifts given to them, as it is written. Whereby this seems to indicate the mystery that "when the fullness of the nations will come in,"[1] they receive from the Lord Jesus what was promised to them, those who had been taught and instructed by Moses and who by prayers and entreaties brought aid to us who are placed in the contest. They have not yet "attained the promises,"[2] waiting so that our calling might also be fulfilled, as the apostle says.[3] But now at last with the gifts they receive from Jesus they may attain the perfection that had been deferred for them so that each one may dwell in peace with every war and every battle ceasing. HOMILIES ON JOSHUA 26.2.[4]

22:10-12 An Altar Is Built

THAT PRIOR PEOPLE. ORIGEN: Do you still wish that I prove more clearly to you that all things among that prior people, whom Moses foreshadowed in the two and a half tribes, were neither complete nor perfect? Even the history written in this little book itself, Jesus [Joshua], son of Nun, also declares it when it says that the true altar was in the land that Jesus [Joshua] was distributing.[5] But those who were across the Jordan, that is, Reuben and Gad and half the tribe of Manasseh, made an altar for themselves, but it was not a true altar. It merely contained a type and sign of the true altar that was with Jesus [Joshua]. Thus you have no cause to wonder whether or not those people had received the entire knowledge of the Trinity, since they had built neither an entire nor a true altar. HOMILIES ON JOSHUA 3.2.[6]

---

[1]Rom 11:25. [2]Heb 11:39. [3]2 Thess 1:11. [4]FC 105:217-18. [5]Josh 8:30-31. [6]FC 105:46.

22:21-34 THE ALTAR OF WITNESS

²¹*Then the Reubenites, the Gadites, and the half-tribe of Manasseh said in answer to the heads of the families of Israel,* ²²*"The Mighty One, God, the Lord! The Mighty One, God, the Lord! He knows; and let Israel itself know! If it was in rebellion or in breach of faith toward the Lord, spare us not today* ²³*for building an altar to turn away from following the Lord; or if we did so to offer burnt offerings or cereal offerings or peace offerings on it, may the Lord himself take vengeance.* ²⁴*Nay, but we did it from fear that in time to come your children might say to our children, 'What have you to do with the Lord, the God of Israel?* ²⁵*For the Lord has made the Jordan a boundary between us and you, you Reubenites and Gadites; you have no portion in the Lord.' So your children might make our children cease to worship the Lord.* ²⁶*Therefore we said, 'Let us now build an altar, not for burnt offering, nor for sacrifice,* ²⁷*but to be a witness between us and you, and between the generations after us, that we do perform the service of the Lord in his presence with our burnt offerings and sacrifices and peace offerings; lest your children say to our children in time to come, "You have no portion in the Lord."'* ²⁸*And we thought, If this should be said to us or to our descendants in time to come, we should say, 'Behold the copy of the altar of the Lord, which our fathers made, not for burnt offerings, nor for sacrifice, but to be a witness between us and you.'* ²⁹*Far be it from us that we should rebel against the Lord, and turn away this day from following the Lord by building an altar for burnt offering, cereal offering, or sacrifice, other than the altar of the Lord our God that stands before his tabernacle!"*

Overview: We may recognize those who were righteous before Christ's coming as our brothers because they perceived that the altar of witness was merely a figure of the true altar that existed where Jesus was (Origen).

22:21-29 *The Altar's Presence Explained*

The True Altar. Origen: But let us see what sacrament lies within this deed. The former people of the circumcision are represented in Reuben,[1] who was the firstborn; but also in Gad, who also is the firstborn out of Zilpah;[2] and Manasseh, no less a firstborn.[3] But insofar as I say "firstborn," I speak chronologically. Therefore, these things are said not that it might be evident some division and separation is between us and those who were righteous before the coming of Christ, but that they might reveal themselves to still be our brothers even if they existed before the coming of Christ. For although they possessed an altar then before the coming of the Savior, nevertheless, they knew and perceived that it was not that true altar but that it was a form and figure of what would be the true altar.[4] Those persons knew this because the true victims and those who were able to take away sins were not offered on that altar that the firstborn people possessed but on this one where Jesus was. Here the heavenly victims, here the true sacrifices are consumed. Therefore, they are made "one flock and one shepherd,"[5] those former righteous ones and those who are now Christians. Homilies on Joshua 26.3.[6]

---

[1]Gen 29:32. [2]Gen 30:10. [3]Gen 41:51. [4]Heb 10:11-12. [5]Jn 10:16. [6]FC 105:218-19*.

23:1-16 JOSHUA URGES COVENANT OBEDIENCE

²Joshua summoned all Israel, their elders and heads, their judges and officers, and said to them, "I am now old and well advanced in years; . . . ⁴Behold, I have allotted to you as an inheritance for your tribes those nations that remain, along with all the nations that I have already cut off, from the Jordan to the Great Sea in the west. ⁵The LORD your God will push them back before you, and drive them out of your sight; and you shall possess their land, as the LORD your God promised you. ⁶Therefore be very steadfast to keep and do all that is written in the book of the law of Moses, turning aside from it neither to the right hand nor to the left, ⁷that you may not be mixed with these nations left here among you, or make mention of the names of their gods, or swear by them, or serve them, or bow down yourselves to them, ⁸but cleave to the LORD your God as you have done to this day. ⁹For the LORD has driven out before you great and strong nations; and as for you, no man has been able to withstand you to this day. ¹⁰One man of you puts to flight a thousand, since it is the LORD your God who fights for you, as he promised you.

OVERVIEW: While learning pagan classical literature is permissible to Christians, teaching it is not, because the one who teaches unwittingly affirms it (TERTULLIAN). The invocation of the names of gods is tantamount to idolatry (CLEMENT OF ALEXANDRIA). It is because of Joshua's righteousness and obedience that God granted him victories (GREGORY OF NYSSA).

23:6-8 Avoid Mixing with the Remaining Nations and Their Gods

CHRISTIANS AND PAGAN LITERATURE. TERTULLIAN: Learning literature is allowable for believers, rather than teaching; for the principle of learning and of teaching is different. If a believer teaches literature, while he is teaching doubtless he commends, while he delivers he affirms, while he recalls he bears testimony to, the praises of idols interspersed therein. He seals the gods themselves with this name [of gods]; whereas the Law, as we have said, prohibits "the names of gods to be pronounced,"[1] and this name [of God] to be conferred on vanity.[2] Hence the devil gets men's early faith built up from the beginnings of their erudition. Inquire whether he

who teaches about idols commits idolatry. But when a believer learns these things, if he is already capable of understanding what idolatry is, he neither receives nor allows them; much more if he is not yet capable. Or, when he begins to understand, it behooves him first to understand what he has previously learned, that is, touching God and the faith. Therefore he will reject those things and will not receive them, and will be as safe as one who from one who knows it not knowingly accepts poison but does not drink it. ON IDOLATRY 10.[3]

THE NAMES OF GODS. PSEUDO-CLEMENT OF ROME: Therefore Moses, when he saw that the people were advancing, by degrees initiated them in the understanding of the monarchy and the faith of one God, as he says in the following words: "You shall not make negation of the names of other gods,"[4] doubtless remembering with what penalty the serpent was visited, which had first named gods.[5] For it is condemned to feed upon dust and is judged worthy of such food, for this cause, that it first of all introduced the

---

[1]Ex 23:13; Hos 2:17. [2]Idol. [3]ANF 3:66-67. [4]Josh 23:7 LXX. [5]Gen 3.

name of gods into the world. But if you also wish to introduce many gods, see that you share not the serpent's doom. RECOGNITIONS 2.44.[6]

23:10 *The Lord Your God Fights for You*

VICTORY IS DUE TO RIGHTEOUSNESS. GREGORY OF NYSSA: For faithful is he who has promised that "a thousand shall be chased by one," and that "ten thousand shall be put to flight by two,"[7] victory in battle being due not to numbers but to righteousness. ANSWER TO EUNOMIUS'S SECOND BOOK.[8]

---

[6]ANF 8:109*. [7]Deut 32:30. [8]NPNF 2 5:250.

24:1-15 THE LORD'S FAITHFULNESS RECOUNTED

[2]*And Joshua said to all the people, "Thus says the LORD, the God of Israel, 'Your fathers lived of old beyond the Euphrates, Terah, the father of Abraham and of Nahor; and they served other gods.* [3]*Then I took your father Abraham from beyond the River and led him through all the land of Canaan, and made his offspring many. . . .* [6]*Then I brought your fathers out of Egypt, and you came to the sea; and the Egyptians pursued your fathers with chariots and horsemen to the Red Sea. . . .* [11]*And you went over the Jordan and came to Jericho, and the men of Jericho fought against you, and also the Amorites, the Perizzites, the Canaanites, the Hittites, the Girgashites, the Hivites, and the Jebusites; and I gave them into your hand.* [12]*And I sent the hornet before you, which drove them out before you, the two kings of the Amorites; it was not by your sword or by your bow.* [13]*I gave you a land on which you had not labored, and cities which you had not built, and you dwell therein; you eat the fruit of vineyards and oliveyards which you did not plant.'*

[14]*"Now therefore fear the LORD, and serve him in sincerity and in faithfulness; put away the gods which your fathers served beyond the River, and in Egypt, and serve the LORD.* [15]*And if you be unwilling to serve the LORD, choose this day whom you will serve, whether the gods your fathers served in the region beyond the River, or the gods of the Amorites in whose land you dwell; but as for me and my house, we will serve the LORD."*

OVERVIEW: Augustine offers possible explanations of what might seem to be inconsistencies in Scripture: he considers the prophetic implications of the Septuagint's substitution of "the whole earth" for "land of Canaan"; the manner in which closing the city gates and failing to ask for terms of peace is rightly equated with waging war; and the literal or metaphorical referent for the word *wasps.* The dialogue between Joshua and the people of Israel is appropriated for converts to Christianity. Denying one's pledge to serve the Lord nullifies the agreement with ruinous consequences (ORIGEN).

24:3 *Your Father Abraham*

THE WHOLE EARTH. AUGUSTINE: The Septuagint has translated "And I took your father Abraham from across the river and led him into all the earth." A literal reading of the Hebrew would be "And I led him into the land of Canaan." It is astonishing, therefore, that the translators of the Septuagint would have wished to insert "the whole earth" instead of "land of Canaan," unless they were considering the prophecy so much that they accepted as already done what was still at the time a promise from God. For it was announced beforehand in very clear terms what would take place concerning Christ and the church and that the true seed of Abraham would not be among the children of the flesh but among the children of the promise. QUESTIONS ON JOSHUA 25.[1]

24:11 You Came to Jericho

A SIGN OF WARFARE. AUGUSTINE: "And those who inhabited Jericho waged war against you." One might well ask how this statement could be true, when they were merely protecting themselves by hiding behind the walls and closing the city gates. But this is spoken correctly, since the closing of gates to an enemy is a sign of warfare. For the inhabitants of Jericho did not send ambassadors to ask for terms of peace. . . . For a war does not always have one battle after another. Some wars have frequent battles, some a few, still others none. A war, however, is when there is a disagreement involving arms in some way. QUESTIONS ON JOSHUA 26.[2]

24:12 I Sent the Hornet Before You

THE REFERENT OF "WASPS." AUGUSTINE: What does it mean when Joshua, the son of Nun, says among other things which he recalls that the Lord had done for the Israelites: "He sent wasps before you and drove out the Canaanites from your face"? One also finds that statement in the book of Wisdom, but nonetheless one cannot find any account of such a thing taking place. But perhaps "wasps" ought to be understood in a meta-

phorical sense to mean the sharp stings of fear, by which they were stung in a way as rumors flew about, so that they fled. Or wasps may refer to the invisible spirits of the air, as it says in the psalm, "through wicked angels."[3] Perhaps someone will say that not everything which took place has been written down and that the incident with the wasps also took place in a visible manner, so that this passage should be understood to refer to real wasps. QUESTIONS ON JOSHUA 27.[4]

24:14-15 Choose This Day

SIN NOT AGAINST THE LORD. ORIGEN: Therefore, what Joshua said to the people when he settled them in the holy land, the Scripture might also say now to us. The text reads as follows, "Now fear the Lord and worship him in sincerity and righteousness." And it will tell us, if we are being misled to worship idols, what follows, "Destroy the foreign gods which your fathers worshiped beyond the River and in Egypt, and worship the Lord."

Then in the beginning when you were going to be instructed, it would have been rightly said to you, "And if you be unwilling to worship the Lord, choose this day whom you will worship, whether the gods your fathers worshiped in the region beyond the River, or the gods of the Amorites among whom you dwell on the land." And the catechist might have said to you, "But as for me and my house, we will worship the Lord because he is holy."[5] He does not have any reason to say this to you now; for then you said, "Far be it from us that we should forsake the Lord, to serve other gods. For the Lord our God, he is God, who brought us and our fathers out of Egypt . . . and preserved us in all the way that we went." Moreover, in the agreements about religion long ago you gave your catechist this answer, "We also will worship the Lord, for he is our God."[6] If, therefore, the one who breaks agreements with men is

---

[1]CCL 33:330. [2]CCL 33:330. [3]Ps 78:49 (77:49 LXX). [4]CCL 33:330. [5]The LXX adds "because he is holy." [6]Josh 24:18.

outside any truce and alien to safety, what must be said of those who by denying make null and void the agreements they made with God, and who run back to Satan, whom they renounced when they were baptized? Such a person must be told the words spoken by Eli to his sons, "If a man sins against a man, then they will pray for him; but if he sins against the Lord, who will pray for him?"[7] EXHORTATION TO MARTYRDOM 17.[8]

---

[7]1 Sam 2:25. [8]OSW 52-53.

24:16-28 ISRAEL WILL SERVE THE LORD

[22]*Then Joshua said to the people, "You are witnesses against yourselves that you have chosen the* LORD, *to serve him." And they said, "We are witnesses."* [23]*He said, "Then put away the foreign gods which are among you, and incline your heart to the* LORD, *the God of Israel." . . .* [26]*And Joshua wrote these words in the book of the law of God; and he took a great stone, and set it up there under the oak in the sanctuary of the* LORD. [27]*And Joshua said to all the people, "Behold, this stone shall be a witness against us; for it has heard all the words of the* LORD *which he spoke to us; therefore it shall be a witness against you, lest you deal falsely with your God."*

OVERVIEW: Perfection comes through preserving the soul, which is God's creation, in its natural state of virtue (ATHANASIUS). As Joshua established a stone of witness, overseers of souls likewise provide witnesses for future testimony (BASIL); that stone signifies Christ (CYPRIAN).

24:23 Incline Your Heart to the Lord

PERFECTION COMES FROM WITHIN. ATHANASIUS: We need only to will perfection, since it is within our power and is developed by us, for, when the soul keeps the understanding in its natural state, perfection is confirmed. The soul is in its natural state when it remains as it was created, and it was created beautifully and exceedingly upright. For this reason, Joshua, the son of Nave [Nun], commanded the people: "Incline your hearts to the Lord the God of Israel," and John: "Make straight his paths."[1] Rectitude of soul, then, consists in preserving the intellect in its natural state, as it was created. On the other hand, when the intellect turns aside and deviates from its natural state, the soul is said to be evil. Thus, the matter is not difficult; if we remain as we were made, we are in a state of virtue; but, if we think evil thoughts, we are accounted evil. If, then, perfection were a thing to be acquired from without, it would indeed be difficult; but, since it is within us, let us guard against evil thoughts and let us constantly keep our soul for the Lord, as a trust received from him, so that he may recognize his work as being the same as when he made it. LIFE OF ST. ANTHONY 20.[2]

24:27 This Stone Shall Be a Witness

THE PROVISION OF WITNESSES. BASIL THE GREAT: Joshua, the son of Nun, even calls a stone to give testimony (a heap of stones had

---

[1]Mt 3:3. [2]FC 15:154*.

already been called to testify between Jacob and Laban)[3] when he said, "Behold, this stone shall be a witness against us; for it has heard all the words of the Lord which he spoke to us; therefore it shall be a witness against you, lest you deal falsely with your God." Perhaps he believed that the power of God would enable the stones to cry out in testimony against the transgressors or at least that everyone's conscience would be wounded by the force of the reminder. So those who have been entrusted with the care of souls provide various kinds of witnesses to testify at a future date. But the Spirit is organically united with God, not because of the needs of each moment but through communion in the divine nature. He is joined to the Lord; he is not

brought in by our efforts. On the Spirit 13.30.[4]

The Stone Is Christ. Cyprian: That Christ is called a stone. . . . Also in Joshua: "And he took a great stone, and placed it there before the Lord; and Joshua said unto the people, Behold, this stone shall be a testimony to you, because it has heard all the things which were spoken by the Lord, which he has spoken to you today; and it shall be for a testimony to you in the last of the days, when you shall have departed from your God." To Quirinius: Testimonies Against the Jews 2.16.[5]

---

[3]Gen 31:46ff. [4]OHS 52. [5]ANF 5:522*.

24:29-33 THE DEATH OF JOSHUA

[29]*After these things Joshua the son of Nun, the servant of the* Lord, *died, being a hundred and ten years old.* [30]*And they buried him in his own inheritance at Timnath-serah, which is in the hill country of Ephraim, north of the mountain of Gaash.*

Overview: Joshua's death and burial are a celebration of the victory of eternal life over death and of virtue over vice. It is not an occasion for mourning yet rather for joy (Jerome).

24:29 Joshua Died

Joshua's Death a Witness to His Chaste Life. Jerome: But it is now time for us to raise the standard of Joshua's chastity. It is written that Moses had a wife.[1] . . . We read that Moses, that is, the law, had a wife; show me then in the same way that Joshua the son of Nun had either wife or children, and if you can do so, I will confess that I am beaten. He certainly received the

fairest spot in the division of the land of Judah and died, not in the twenties, which are ever unlucky in Scripture—by them are reckoned the years of Jacob's service,[2] the price of Joseph,[3] and sundry presents which Esau who was fond of them received[4]—but in the tens, whose praises we have often sung. And he was buried in Thamnath Sore, which means "most perfect sovereignty," or "among those of a new covering," to signify the crowds of virgins, covered by the Savior's aid on Mount Ephraim, that is, the fruitful mountain; on the north of the Mountain

---

[1]Jerome here quotes as evidence Lk 16:29 and Rom 5:14. [2]See Gen 31:41. [3]See Gen 37:28. [4]See Gen 32:14.

of Gaash, which is interpreted "disturbance," for "Mount Zion is on the sides of the north, the city of the Great King,"[5] is ever exposed to hatred, and in every trial says "But my feet had nearly slipped."[6] The book which bears the name of Joshua ends with his burial. Again in the book of Judges we read of him as though he had risen and come to life again, and by way of summary his works are extolled. We read too: "So Joshua sent the people away, every man to his inheritance, that they might possess the land."[7] And "Israel served the Lord all the days of Joshua," and so on. There immediately follows: "And Joshua the son of Nun, the servant of the Lord, died, being a hundred and ten years old." Moses, moreover, only saw the land of promise; he could not enter, and "he died in the land of Moab, and the Lord buried him in the valley in the land of Moab over against Beth-peor: but no man knows of his sepulcher to this day."[8] Let us compare the burial of the two. Moses died in the land of Moab, Joshua in the land of Judea. The former was buried in a valley over against the house of Phogor,[9] the translation of which is "reproach," for the Hebrew *Phogor* corresponds to *Priapus;*[10] the latter was buried in Mount Ephraim on the north of Mount Gaash. And in the simple expressions of the sacred Scriptures there is always a more subtle meaning. The Jews gloried in children and childbearing; and the barren woman, who had no offspring in Israel, was accursed; but blessed was he whose seed was in Zion, and his family in Jerusalem. And part of the highest blessing was, "Your wife shall be as a fruitful vine in the innermost parts of your house, your children like olive plants round about thy table."[11] Therefore his grave is described as placed in a valley over against the house of an idol which was in a special sense consecrated to lust. But we who fight under Joshua our leader, even to the present day, know not where Moses was buried. For we despise Phogor and all his shame, knowing that they who are in the flesh cannot please God. And the Lord before the flood had said, "My spirit shall not abide in man forever, because he is flesh."[12] For this reason, when Moses died, the people of Israel mourned for him, but Joshua, like one on his way to victory, was not mourned. For marriage ends at death; virginity thereafter begins to wear the crown. AGAINST JOVINIANUS 1.22.[13]

24:30 Buried in His Own Inheritance

GRIEVE NOT FOR THE DEAD. JEROME: I cannot adequately extol the mysteries of Scripture or sufficiently admire the spiritual meaning conveyed in its most simple words. We are told, for instance, that lamentation was made for Moses; yet when the funeral of Joshua is described no mention at all is made of weeping. The reason, of course, is that under Moses—that is, under the old law—all people were bound by the sentence passed on Adam's sin, and when they descended into hell were rightly accompanied with tears. For, as the apostle says, "death reigned from Adam to Moses, even over them that had not sinned."[14] But under Jesus, that is, under the gospel of Christ, who has unlocked for us the gate of paradise, death is accompanied not with sorrow but with joy. The Jews go on weeping to this day; they make bare their feet, they crouch in sackcloth, they roll in ashes. And to make their superstition complete, they follow a foolish custom of the Pharisees and eat lentils, to show, it would seem, for what poor fare they have lost their birthright.[15] Of course they are right to weep, for as they do not believe in the Lord's resurrection they are being made ready for the advent of antichrist. But we who have put on Christ[16] and according to the apostle are a royal and priestly race,[17] we ought not to grieve for the dead. LETTER 39.4.[18]

---

[5]Ps 48:2 (47:2 LXX). [6]Ps 73:2 (72:2 LXX). [7]Josh 24:28. [8]Deut 34:6. [9]*Phogor* appears in the LXX as the translation for *Peor.* [10]The name of a pagan fertility god. [11]Ps 128:3 (127:3 LXX). [12]Gen 6:3. [13]NPNF 6:362-63*. [14]Rom 5:14. [15]Gen 25:34. [16]Gal 3:27. [17]1 Pet 2:9. [18]NPNF 2 6:52.

JUDGES

1:1-10 JUDAH ATTACKS THE CANAANITES

[1]*After the death of Joshua the people of Israel inquired of the LORD, "Who shall go up first for us against the Canaanites, to fight against them?"* [2]*The LORD said, "Judah shall go up; behold, I have given the land into his hand."* . . . [4]*Then Judah went up and the LORD gave the Canaanites and the Perizzites into their hand; and they defeated ten thousand of them at Bezek.*

OVERVIEW: Judah's prominence is ordained with the tribe's selection as the first to attack the Canaanites (EUSEBIUS).

1:1-2 *Judah Shall Fight the Canaanites*

THE HEADSHIP OF JUDAH. EUSEBIUS OF CAE-SARIA: And in the book of Joshua, son of Nave [Nun], when the land of promise was divided by lot among the other tribes, the tribe of Judah took its own portion of the land without casting lots, and first of all. And, moreover, "After the death of Joshua the children of Israel inquired of the Lord, saying, who shall go up for us against the Canaanite, leading our fighting against him? And the Lord said, Judah shall go up. Behold, I have given the land into his hands." These words, then, make it clear that God ordained the tribe of Judah to be the head of all Israel, and the account goes on... And in the book of Judges, when different persons at different times were at the head of the people, though individually the judges were of different tribes, yet speaking generally the tribe of Judah was head of the whole people; and much more so in the times of David and his successors, who belonged to the tribe of Judah and continued to rule until the Babylonian captivity, after which the leader of those who returned from Babylon to their own land was Zerubbabel, the son of Salathiel, of the tribe of Judah, who also built the temple.[1] Hence, too, the book of Chronicles, when giving the genealogies of the twelve tribes of Israel, begins with Judah.[2] And you will see it follows from this that in the days that succeeded, the same tribe had the headship, although different individuals had temporary leadership, whose tribes it is impossible to decide with accuracy, because there is no sacred book handed down to give the history of the period from then to the time of our Savior. THE PROOF OF THE GOSPEL 8.1.[3]

---

[1]Ezra 2:1-2; 3:8. [2]1 Chron 2:3. [3]POG 2:101-2*.

1:11-21 THE FAILURE OF BENJAMIN

[11]*From there they went against the inhabitants of Debir. The name of Debir was formerly Kiriath-sepher.* [12]*And Caleb said, "He who attacks Kiriath-sepher and takes it, I will give him Achsah my daughter as wife."* [13]*And Othni-el the son of Kenaz, Caleb's younger brother, took it; and he gave him Achsah his daughter as wife.* [14]*When she came to him, she urged him to ask her father for a field; and she alighted from her ass, and Caleb said to her, "What do you wish?"* [15]*She said to him, "Give me a present; since you have set me in the land of the Negeb, give me also springs of water." And Caleb gave her the upper springs and the lower springs.*

OVERVIEW: Achsah's request for springs typifies the compunctions of fear and love experienced by the penitent (GREGORY THE GREAT).

1:12 Achsah Is Promised to the Victor[1]

1:15 Achsah Requests Springs of Water

THE GRACE OF TEARS. GREGORY THE GREAT: There are two main types of compunction, however. The penitent thirsting for God feels the compunction of fear at first; later on, he experiences the compunction of love. When he considers his sins, he is overcome with weeping because he fears eternal punishment. Then when this fear subsides through prolonged sorrow and penance, a feeling of security emerges from an assurance of forgiveness, and the soul begins to burn with a love for heavenly joys. Now the same person, who wept out of fear of punishment, sheds abundant tears because his entrance to the kingdom of heaven is being delayed. Once we envision the choirs of angels and fix our gaze on the company of the saints and the majesty of an endless vision of God, the thought of having no part in these joys makes us weep more bitterly than the fear of hell and the prospect of eternal misery did before. Thus the compunction of fear, when perfect, leads the soul to the compunction of love.

This is beautifully symbolized in one of the historical books of the Bible. There we read that

Achsah, the daughter of Caleb, sighed as she sat upon her beast of burden.[2] "And Caleb asked her. 'What is troubling you?' She answered, 'Give me an additional gift! Since you have assigned to me land in the Negeb, give me also pools of water.' So he gave her the upper and the lower pools."

We say that Achsah sat on an ass because her soul presided over the irrational movements of her flesh. Just as she begged her father with a sigh for pools of water, so must we with deep groans obtain from our Creator the grace of tears. There are some who have received the gift of speaking out openly for justice, of defending the oppressed, of sharing their possessions with the needy, of professing their faith ardently, who still do not have the grace of tears. These we may say received "land in the Negeb," that is, "southern and dry land," but are completely lacking in "pools of water." It is of utmost importance, however, that those who are zealous for good works and devote much time to performing them should also weep over their past sins, either through fear of eternal punishment or through longing for God's kingdom.

Caleb gave Achsah the upper and lower pools. These correspond to the two kinds of compunction. The soul receives the upper pools when it weeps because of its longing for heaven; it receives the lower pools when the fear of hell

---

[1]See comment for Josh 15:16-17. [2]Judg 1:14 LXX.

causes it to break forth in tears. Actually, the lower pools are given first; then, only, the upper. Yet, since the compunction of love is greater in dignity, the upper pools were necessarily mentioned first and then the lower. DIALOGUE 3.34.[3]

---

[3]FC 39:173-75.

1:22-36 THE FAILURE OF THE NORTHERN TRIBES

[29]*And Ephraim did not drive out the Canaanites who dwelt in Gezer; but the Canaanites dwelt in Gezer among them. . . .*

[34]*The Amorites pressed the Danites back into the hill country, for they did not allow them to come down to the plain;* [35]*the Amorites persisted in dwelling in Har-heres, in Aijalon, and in Shaalbim, but the hand of the house of Joseph rested heavily upon them, and they became subject to forced labor.*

OVERVIEW: Taxation of the Canaanites signifies the imperfection of our life which, under scrutiny of self-examination, leads to humility (GREGORY THE GREAT). It is only by persistent practice of virtue that we are able to win the struggles of spiritual life (BEDE).

1:29 The Canaanites Lived in the Midst of Ephraim

TAXING FAULTS. GREGORY THE GREAT: For "the stars of this night" are "overshadowed with darkness,"[1] when even they that already shine with great virtues still bear something of the dimness of sin, while they struggle against it, so that they even shine with great luster of life and yet still draw along unwillingly some remains of the night. Which as we have said is done with this view, that the mind in advancing to the eminence of its righteousness, may through weakness be better strengthened and may in a more genuine manner shine in goodness by the same cause by which, to its humbling, little defects overcloud it even against its will. Hence, when the land of promise now won was to be divided to the people of Israel, the Gentile people of Canaan are not said to be slain but to be made subject to the tribe of Ephraim, as it is written: "The Canaanites dwelt in the midst of Ephraim under taxation." For what does the Canaanite, a Gentile people, denote, if not a fault? And oftentimes we enter the land of promise with great virtues because we are strengthened by the inward hope of eternity. But while, amid sublime deeds, we retain certain small faults, we as it were permit the Canaanite to dwell in our land. Yet he is taxed in that this same fault, which we cannot make subject, we force back by humility to our own well-being, so that the mind may think poorly of itself even in its highest virtues, as it fails to master by its own strength even the small things to which it aspires. MORALS ON THE BOOK OF JOB 4.24.[2]

1:34 The Amorites Pressed the Danites

BITTER STRUGGLES. BEDE: "The waters

---

[1]See Job 3:9. [2]LF 18:211.

increased and elevated the ark high above the earth. And the waters drenched the earth, filling it and covering everything."[3] The increased waters of baptism and faith also elevated the church throughout the world from an appetite for earthly things to the hope and desire for heavenly life. Hence, tossing the church about with great tribulations, the more vigorously these waters fill the earth, the higher they push it toward seeking the joys of the other life. This is well illustrated in sacred history when it is said, "The Amorites held the children of Dan to the mountains, nor did they permit them to descend to the plains." Amorite, of course, means "bitter," whereas Dan is translated as "judge" or "judgment." Who do the children of Dan designate, therefore, if not those who act with diligence that they may be upright, study the book of truth and vow and resolve to observe the revelation of God's justice,

walking by the lamp of his Word? On the other hand, who is indicated by the Amorites if not those who attempt to disturb or even to destroy the sweetness of the life of the saints with the bitterness of tribulations? The Amorites hold the children of Dan to the mountains, nor permit them to descend to the plains, when so great a storm afflicts the elect with persecutions that there is no time for them to indulge in timid thoughts, but they must work hard continuously with prayers, fastings, and meditations on the divine Scriptures, while living in the highest continence, since they will be able to overcome the struggles of great trials only by the exercise of greater virtue. ON GENESIS 2.7.[4]

---

[3]See Gen 7:17-19. [4]CCL 118A:118-19.

2:1-5 THE LORD'S JUDGMENT PRONOUNCED

[1]Now the angel of the LORD went up from Gilgal to Bochim. And he said, "I brought you up from Egypt, and brought you into the land which I swore to give to your fathers. I said, 'I will never break my covenant with you, [2]and you shall make no covenant with the inhabitants of this land; you shall break down their altars.' But you have not obeyed my command. What is this you have done? [3]So now I say, I will not drive them out before you; but they shall become adversaries[a] to you, and their gods shall be a snare to you." [4]When the angel of the LORD spoke these words to all the people of Israel, the people lifted up their voices and wept. [5]And they called the name of that place Bochim;[b] and they sacrificed there to the LORD.

a Vg Old Latin Compare Gk: Heb *sides*   b That is *Weepers*

OVERVIEW: The valley of tears (Bochim) is understood allegorically as this world, which is a place of repentance, weeping and labor for one's heavenly crown (JEROME).

2:4-5 The Israelites Weep at the Angel's Words

THE VALLEY OF TEARS. JEROME: Let us consider

where he has set his ascent: "In the valley of tears, in the place that he has appointed."[1] We have read in the book of Judges that when the angel came and preached repentance to the people, saying, "You have abandoned the Lord, and the Lord shall abandon you," the Israelites wept aloud when they heard the threat; and that place was called the valley of tears. We have called attention to ancient history in order to avoid heresy. The valley of tears, moreover, we may understand allegorically as this world, for we are not on the mountain, that is, in the kingdom of heaven, but in the valley, in the darknesses of this world; through a fault, we have been cast out of Paradise with Adam into a lowly vale of tears where there is repentance and weep-

ing. "In the valley of tears, in the place that he has appointed." What did the prophet mean? God made this world an arena that here we may strive against the devil, against sin, in order to receive our crown in heaven. Why did he ordain a contest? Could not he save us without the struggle? He gave us, as it were, a master of contests; he gave us a stadium in which to carry on our wrestling against vices, so that afterwards he may crown us meritoriously, not as those who sleep but as those who labor. HOMILIES ON THE PSALMS, ALTERNATE SERIES 63 (Ps 83).[2]

---

[1]Ps 83:6 LXX. [2]FC 57:47-48*.

2:6-15 ISRAEL FORSAKES THE LORD

[6]*When Joshua dismissed the people, the people of Israel went each to his inheritance to take possession of the land.* [7]*And the people served the LORD all the days of Joshua, and all the days of the elders who outlived Joshua, who had seen all the great work which the LORD had done for Israel.* [8]*And Joshua the son of Nun, the servant of the LORD, died at the age of one hundred and ten years. . . .* [10]*And all that generation also were gathered to their fathers; and there arose another generation after them, who did not know the LORD or the work which he had done for Israel.*

[11]*And the people of Israel did what was evil in the sight of the LORD and served the Baals;* [12]*and they forsook the LORD, the God of their fathers, who had brought them out of the land of Egypt; they went after other gods, from among the gods of the peoples who were round about them, and bowed down to them; and they provoked the LORD to anger.* [13]*They forsook the LORD, and served the Baals and the Ashtaroth.* [14]*So the anger of the LORD was kindled against Israel, and he gave them over to plunderers, who plundered them; and he sold them into the power of their enemies round about, so that they could no longer withstand their enemies.* [15]*Whenever they marched out, the hand of the LORD was against them for evil, as the LORD had warned, and as the LORD had sworn to them; and they were in sore straits.*

OVERVIEW: The apostles, who are the "light of the world," are typified by those elders who came after Joshua. Those who know God's work are

those who do it. The death of Joshua, who is a type of Christ, is recorded in order to indicate that Jesus may be either alive or dead in other persons. Those who worshiped Baal in former times represent those in the present who, bound by their sins, "bend their knees" to the devil. Abandoning the Lord by serving one's fleshly desires will result in being separated from the body of Christ (ORIGEN). With Joshua's death emerges a pattern of Israel's idolatry being met with God's wrath, meted out by the hand of its enemies (TERTULLIAN).

2:7 People Who Had Seen the Lord's Great Work

APOSTOLIC LIGHTS. ORIGEN: Who are these elders who either came with Joshua/Jesus or after him, if not the very apostles who illumined our hearts by their writings and precepts, even bringing a certain kind of "day" among us from that "true light" in which they were partakers?[1] Whoever, therefore, is enlightened and instructed from the precepts of the apostles and is ordained according to the apostolic rules for the service of the Lord is the very person who is said to serve the Lord in the days of the elders who came after Jesus. Do you wish to see that the apostles also were the "light of the world," just as the Savior "was the true light which illumines every person coming into the world"[2]? The Lord himself said to them, as it is written in the Gospel, "You are the light of the world."[3] But if the apostles are also the light of the world, then the "days" in which "we serve the Lord" undoubtedly illuminate us through their precepts and commandments. HOMILIES ON JUDGES 1.2.[4]

KNOWING AND DOING. ORIGEN: It mentions "the days of the elders who knew all the works of the Lord." Who is the person who "knows all the works of the Lord," except the one who does them himself? For just as it was said that the sons of Eli were "sons of pestilence, having no knowledge of the Lord,"[5] yet not meaning that these men who taught others were ignorant of the Lord, but rather that they behaved like those who did not know the Lord, so also in like manner is

this statement to be understood that the elders "knew all the works of the Lord." Moreover, it does not merely say that "they knew the works of the Lord" but specifies that "they knew every work of the Lord," that is, that they knew the Lord's work of justice and work of sanctification and patience and kindness and piety, for everything that comes from the commandments of God is called a "work of the Lord." . . . Therefore, they are said to "know" the work of God who do his work. But that its customary use of "to know" and "not to know" may shine still more clearly from the authority of the Scriptures, observe how it is written elsewhere that "he who keeps the commandment," it says, "will not know an evil word." Can, therefore, one who keeps the commandments become one who does not know evil? He knows, of course, but "not know" is said of him because he is careful to avoid the evil. It is even said of the Lord and Savior himself that "he did not know sin," certainly indicating in this case that to be ignorant of sin is equivalent to refraining from every sinful act. In this way, therefore, he is said to "know the works of the Lord" who performs "the works of the Lord," whereas he who does not do the work of God is ignorant of the work of God. HOMILIES ON JUDGES 1.4.[6]

2:8 Joshua Dies

JESUS ALIVE AND DEAD. ORIGEN: Joshua's death is also recounted for us. But it is nothing unusual that he who was the "son of Nun" died, for everything that is owed to nature gets paid. Yet, because we have established that what is read here about the son of Nun must be seen as referring to our Lord Jesus Christ, we need to ask how is it befitting to say that "Jesus died." It is my opinion, though speaking according to the authority of Scripture, that Jesus lives in certain persons and is dead in other persons. Jesus lives in Paul and in Peter and in all those who can

---

[1]See 1 Jn 2:8; Eph 5:14; Phil 2:14. [2]Jn 1:9. [3]Mt 5:14. [4]GCS 30:467.
[5]1 Sam 2:12. [6]GCS 30:470-71.

rightly say, "It is no longer I who live, but Christ lives in me"[7] and, again, "But for me to live is Christ and to die is profit."[8] In persons such as those, therefore, Jesus is rightly said to live. But in whom is Jesus dead? He is dead in those persons, undoubtedly, who are said to insult the death of Jesus by frequently repenting and then failing again, persons whom the apostle describes in his letter to the Hebrews as "crucifying the Son of God again for their own sake and holding him out for show."[9] You can see why, therefore, Jesus is not only said to be "dead" in those sinners but is also asserted to be "crucified" and "mocked" by them. But examine yourself as well and ask, when you have avaricious thoughts and desire to despoil others, if you are ever able to say that "Christ lives in me." If you have thoughts of defilement, if you are harassed by fury, if you are inflamed with envy and aroused with jealousy, if you revel in drunkenness, if you are exalted with pride, or if you act with cruelty, will you be able to say in all of these things that "Christ lives in me"? Christ is dead in sinners, therefore, because no justice, no patience, no truth, nor anything else that Christ is operates within them. But for saints, on the other hand, Christ is said to be the one who enacts whatever they do, as the apostle declares: "I can do all things in him who strengthens me, Christ."[10] HOMILIES ON JUDGES 2.1.[11]

2:11 Israel Serves the Baals

IDOLATRY THEN AND NOW. ORIGEN: It was the ancients who did this, of course, but because what was written is said to be "written for our sake, to whom the end of the ages has arrived,"[12] not on their account, we should watch lest these sayings are seen to be true of more of us than of them. Do you want to see that such things are applied to us through the apostle, rather than through me? Listen for yourself to what he said: "What does Scripture say about how Elijah interceded with God against Israel? 'Lord, they killed your prophets, they destroyed your altars, and I

am left alone and they seek my soul.' But what was the divine response? 'I preserved for myself seven thousand men who did not bend the knee to Baal,'" then the apostle adds "'thus, in this time also a remnant chosen by grace is saved.'"[13] You can see, therefore, that those who "bent the knee to Baal" and those who "did not bend the knee" are understood by the apostle as the multitude of unbelievers and the remnant of believers, respectively. This demonstrates, then, that those who lived in unbelief and impiety at the time of the Savior also "bent the knee to Baal" and worshiped idols, whereas those who believed and fulfilled the works of faith "did not bend the knee to Baal." It is never mentioned in the historical books or in the Gospels or in any other book of Scripture that some at the time of the Savior did in fact bend the knee to idols, but such an act is indeed attributed to those persons who were bound by their sins, as though held by fetters. Whenever we sin and "are taken captive to the law of sin,"[14] therefore, we "bend our knees to Baal." But we are not called to this, nor do we believe in this, such that we would again become servants of sin and again "bend the knee" to the devil. Instead, our calling and the purpose of our faith is both to bend the knee at the name of Jesus, for "at the name of Jesus, every knee bends in heaven and on earth and in hell,"[15] and to bend the knee to "the Father of our Lord Jesus Christ, from whom every family in heaven and on earth is named."[16] HOMILIES ON JUDGES 2.3.[17]

2:12-15 Israel Forsakes the Lord After Joshua's Death

ABANDONMENT BEGETS ABANDONMENT. ORIGEN: As long as a people serves God, they are not "delivered into the hands of plunderers." But when they "abandon the Lord" and begin to serve their own passions, then it is said of them that

---

[7]Gal 2:20. [8]Phil 1:21. [9]Heb 6:6. [10]Phil 4:13. [11]GCS 30:472-73. [12]1 Cor 10:11. [13]Rom 11:2. [14]See Rom 7:23. [15]Phil 2:10. [16]Eph 3:15. [17]GCS 30:474-75.

"God gave them over to shameful passions"[18] and, again, "He gave them over to a reprobate mind, that they would do unsuitable things."[19] Why? Because, he says, "they were filled with every iniquity, wickedness, fornication, greed" and all other evils.[20] It was because "they served and worshiped Baal and Ashtaroth" that "God delivered them into the hands of plunderers and handed them over to their enemies." This, as I have often said before, the Jews read as though it were merely a record of past events. We, however, "for whose sake this was written,"[21] it is said, ought to know that if we sin against the Lord and against our own souls by indulging the desires of the flesh as though we were worshiping our God, we also betray ourselves and concede our apostolic authority into the hands of Zebulun. Listen, then, to [Paul] speaking about one who sins: "I delivered this man to Satan for the destruction of the flesh, that his spirit might be saved."[22] You can see, therefore, that it was not only through his apostles that God "delivered" sinners "over to their enemies," but even now, through those who govern the church and have the power not only of releasing but also of binding,[23] sinners "are delivered for the destruction of the flesh" when they are separated from the body of Christ for their crimes. HOMILIES ON JUDGES 2.5.[24]

IDOLATRY IS MET WITH WRATH. TERTULLIAN: After the death of Joshua the son of Nave [Nun]

they forsook the God of their fathers and served idols, Baalim and Ashtaroth; and the Lord in anger delivered them up to the hands of plunderers, and they continued to be plundered by them and to be sold to their adversaries, and [they] could not at all stand before their enemies. Wherever they went forth, his hand was upon them for evil, and they were greatly distressed. And after this God sets judges, the same as our censors, over them.[25] But not even these did they continue steadfastly to obey. So soon as one of the judges died, they proceeded to transgress more than their fathers had done by going after the gods of others and serving and worshiping them. Therefore the Lord was angry. "Since, indeed," he says, "this nation has transgressed my covenant which I established with their fathers and has not hearkened to my voice, I will not remove from them any of the nations which Joshua left at his death."[26] And thus, throughout almost all the annals of the judges and of the kings who succeeded them, while the strength of the surrounding nations was preserved, he meted wrath out to Israel by war and captivity and a foreign yoke, as often as they turned aside from him, especially to idolatry. SCORPIACE 3.[27]

---

[18]Rom 1:26. [19]Rom 1:28. [20]Rom 1:29. [21]1 Cor 10:11. [22]1 Cor 5:5. [23]See Mt 16:19, 18:18; Jn 20:23. [24]GCS 30:478. [25]A censor was an official responsible for supervising public behavior and morality in ancient Rome. [26]Judg 2:20-21. [27]ANF 3:636*.

2:16-23 THE LORD RAISES UP JUDGES

[16]*Then the* LORD *raised up judges, who saved them out of the power of those who plundered them.* [17]*And yet they did not listen to their judges; for they played the harlot after other gods and bowed down to them; they soon turned aside from the way in which their fathers had walked, who had obeyed the commandments of the* LORD, *and they did not do so. . . .* [20]*So the anger of the*

LORD was kindled against Israel; and he said, "Because this people have transgressed my covenant which I commanded their fathers, and have not obeyed my voice, ²¹I will not henceforth drive out before them any of the nations that Joshua left when he died, ²²that by them I may test Israel, whether they will take care to walk in the way of the LORD as their fathers did, or not." ²³So the LORD left those nations, not driving them out at once, and he did not give them into the power of Joshua.

OVERVIEW: Do not deny the possibility of human sinlessness simply because there are no sinless persons (AUGUSTINE). The worth of the preserved Gentiles is fully recognized in Christian conversion (CAESARIUS OF ARLES). The tests of the nations exemplify the working of divine grace, which teaches humility and dependence upon God (CASSIAN). Humility and perfection are developed through the experience of such trials (ISAAC OF NINEVEH).

2:20-23 Surrounding Nations Are Left to Test Israel[1]

ON HUMAN SINLESSNESS. AUGUSTINE: Scripture tells you that the nations could have been cut off all at once from the land given to the children of Israel; yet God willed that it should only be little by little. We can think of any number of other things which we admit might have happened or may happen, though we can allege no instance of their occurrence. We should not then deny the possibility of human sinlessness, simply because there is no [sinless] person, save him who is not only man but very God, in whom we can show this perfection actually achieved. ON THE SPIRIT AND THE LETTER I.[2]

THE ALTAR IS PLACED AMONG THE GENTILES. CAESARIUS OF ARLES: Although all the nations in the surrounding country were subject to king David, still God did not allow the Jebusites to be destroyed entirely, as he himself says elsewhere: "I for my part will not clear away for them any more of the nations. Through them the Israelites were to be made to prove whether they would fear me." For this reason the prophet said to David, "Go up, and build an altar to the Lord in the threshing floor of Araunah the Jebusite."[3] That pagan king represented the people of the Gentiles. Notice, brothers, that no place in the land of the Jews was found worthy for the altar of the Lord to be built; but in the land of the Gentiles a place is chosen where the angel is seen and the altar of the Lord is built, and thus the wrath of the almighty Lord is appeased. Then already was prefigured the fact that in the hearts of the Jews no worthy place could be found to offer spiritual victims; the land of the Gentiles, that is, the conscience of Christians, is chosen as the place for the Lord's temple. SERMON 122.1.[4]

DIDACTIC GRACE WORKS THROUGH THE WILL. JOHN CASSIAN: Divine grace ever stirs up the will of human beings, not so as to protect and defend it in all things in such a way as to cause it not to fight by its own efforts against its spiritual adversaries, the victor over whom may set it down to God's grace, and the vanquished to his own weakness, and thus learn that his hope is always not in his own courage but in the divine assistance and that he must ever fly to his Protector. And to prove this not by our own conjecture but by still clearer passages of holy Scripture let us consider what we read in Joshua the son of Nun: "The Lord," it says, "left these nations and would not destroy them, that by them he might test Israel, whether they would keep the commandments of the Lord their God, and that they might learn to fight with their enemies."[5] And if

---

[1]For similar commentary, see Judg 3:1-4. [2]LCC 8:196*. [3]2 Sam 24:18. [4]FC 47:204*. [5]This appears to be a conflation of Judg 3:1, 2, and 4, which alludes to Josh 23:12-13.

we may illustrate the incomparable mercy of our Creator from something earthly, not as being equal in kindness but as an illustration of mercy: if a tender and anxious nurse carries an infant in her bosom for a long time in order sometime to teach it to walk, and first allows it to crawl, then supports it that by the aid of her right hand it may lean on its alternate steps, presently leaves it for a little and if she sees it tottering at all, catches hold of it and grabs at it when falling, when down picks it up, and either shields it from a fall or allows it to fall lightly, and sets it up again after a tumble, but when she has brought it up to boyhood or the strength of youth or early manhood, lays upon it some burdens or labors by which it may be not overwhelmed but exercised, and allows it to vie with those of its own age; how much more does the heavenly Father of all know whom to carry in the bosom of his grace, whom to train to virtue in his sight by the exercise of free will, and yet he helps him in his efforts, hears him when he calls, leaves him not when he seeks him, and sometimes snatches him from peril even without his knowing it. CONFERENCE 13.14.[6]

TRIALS DEVELOP HUMILITY. ISAAC OF NINEVEH: Some of his [humanity's] petitions God grants him promptly (I mean those without which no one can be saved), but some he withholds from him. And on certain occasions he restrains and dispels from him the scorching assault of the enemy, while on others, he permits him to be tempted, that this trial may become to him a cause for drawing near to God (as I said before), and also that he may be instructed and have the experience of temptations. And such is the word of Scripture: "The Lord left many nations, without driving them out; neither did he deliver them into the hands of Jesus [Joshua], the son of Nun, to chastise the sons of Israel by them, and that the tribes of the sons of Israel might be taught, and learn war." For the righteous person who has no consciousness of his own weakness walks on a razor's edge and is never far from falling, nor from the ravening lion—I mean the demon of pride. And again, one who does not know his own weakness falls short of humility; and he who falls short of this also falls short of perfection; and he who falls short of perfection is forever held by dread, because his city is not founded on pillars of iron, neither upon lintels of brass, that is, humility. ASCETICAL HOMILIES 8.[7]

---

[6]NPNF 2 11:432. [7]AHSIS 69*.

3:1-6 THE TESTING OF ISRAEL

[1]*Now these are the nations which the LORD left, to test Israel by them, that is, all in Israel who had no experience of any war in Canaan;* [2]*it was only that the generations of the people of Israel might know war, that he might teach war to such at least as had not known it before.* [3]*These are the nations: the five lords of the Philistines, and all the Canaanites, and the Sidonians, and the Hivites who dwelt on Mount Lebanon, from Mount Baal-hermon as far as the entrance of Hamath.* [4]*They were for the testing of Israel, to know whether Israel would obey the commandments of the LORD, which he commanded their fathers by Moses.*

OVERVIEW: Conflict, which confronts apathy and self-sufficiency, benefits human beings by fostering dependence upon God (CASSIAN). God allows small faults and failings to remain in those who possess great virtues to safeguard humility (GREGORY THE GREAT).

3:1-4 The Nations Are Left to Test Israel[1]

THE BENEFIT OF TESTING. JOHN CASSIAN: As useful as it is to me that you [the Lord] should leave me for a little while in order to test the steadfastness of my desire, so it is harmful if you let me be abandoned for too long because of my deserts and my sins. For no human strength will be able to endure by its own steadfastness if it is too long abandoned by your help in time of trial. Nor will it be able to give way instantly before the power and wherewithal of the adversary if you yourself, who are aware of human strengths and are the arbiter of our struggles, "do not permit us to be tried beyond our capacity, but with the trial also provide a way out, so that we may be able to endure."[2]

We read something like this as it appears in mystical fashion in the book of Judges with respect to the extermination of the spiritual nations that are opposed to Israel: "These are the nations that the Lord forsook, so that by them he might instruct Israel, so that they might grow accustomed to fighting with their enemies." And again, a little further on: "The Lord left them so that he might test Israel with them, whether or not they would hear the commandments of the Lord that he had laid down for their forefathers by the hand of Moses." God did not begrudge Israel their peace or look with malice upon them, but he planned this conflict in the knowledge that it would be beneficial. Thus, constantly oppressed by the onslaught of the nations, they would never feel that they did not need the Lord's help. Hence they would always meditate on him and cry out to him, and they would neither lapse into sluggish inactivity nor lose their ability to fight and their training in virtue. For frequently security and prosperity have brought low those whom adversities cannot overcome. CONFERENCE 4.6.3-4.[3]

SAFEGUARDS FOR HUMILITY. GREGORY THE GREAT: Almighty God shows wonderful providence in distributing his blessings. Frequently, by denying lesser gifts to those whom he has favored with great virtues, he offers their souls an opportunity for self-reproach. When they find themselves unable to reach the perfection they aspire to and see themselves struggling in vain for a mastery of virtues not granted them, they are not likely to pride themselves on the gifts they have received. For, when they see that of their own power they are incapable of overcoming small faults and slight imperfections, they begin to realize that their great virtues were not self-acquired. For a similar reason the Lord destroyed the powerful enemies who beset his chosen people on their way to the promised land, but [he] allowed the Philistines and Canaanites to survive, so that, as it is written, "he might try Israel by them." Sometimes, as I have said, those who have received exceptional graces are the very ones God allows to retain small imperfections so that they may always have obstacles with which to contend. As a result they do not foster pride in their hearts even though they are victorious over powerful enemies, for they realize that the weakest of adversaries still causes them great weariness. It is quite remarkable how one and the same person can be vigorous in virtue and weak with infirmity, and while strongly fortified on one side see himself laid waste on the other. The good, therefore, for which he is striving without success, makes him cherish humbly the gifts God has given him.

Why should we be surprised that this is true of people? Heaven itself witnessed the same occurrence, for some of its citizens were lost and some stood firm. Seeing one part fall through pride, the other, the chosen angels, kept their

---

[1]For similar commentary, see Judg 2:20-23. [2]1 Cor 10:13. [3]ACW 57:158*.

stand more humbly and therefore also more firmly. This loss, then, was beneficial for those citizens of heaven whom it helped to establish more firmly in their eternal condition. The same is true of us individually. A slight loss that safe-guards humility can at times be of immense profit to a soul. DIALOGUE 3.14.[4]

[4]FC 39:134-35*.

3:7-11 OTHNIEL JUDGES ISRAEL

[7]*And the people of Israel did what was evil in the sight of the* LORD, *forgetting the* LORD *their God, and serving the Baals and the Asheroth.* [8]*Therefore the anger of the* LORD *was kindled against Israel, and he sold them into the hand of Cushan-rishathaim king of Mesopotamia; and the people of Israel served Cushan-rishathaim eight years.* [9]*But when the people of Israel cried to the* LORD, *the* LORD *raised up a deliverer for the people of Israel, who delivered them, Othni-el the son of Kenaz, Caleb's younger brother.* . . . . [11]*So the land had rest forty years. Then Othni-el the son of Kenaz died.*

OVERVIEW: Othniel is understood to represent a member of the heavenly host who aids those who possess the inheritance of salvation. In the present, as he did in the past, God delivers the proud over to humiliation to heal them of their vice (ORIGEN). History illustrates that lesser or greater impulses for conversion do not ensure steadfastness (CASSIAN).

3:7-8 Israel Handed Over to Mesopotamia

HUMILIATION AND HUMILITY. ORIGEN: Now Chusarsaton's[1] name is translated as "humilia-tion." They were delivered, then, to the hands of one who would humiliate them. And it was because they acted wickedly on the heights of the mountains against the Most High that he sent them to their humiliation. But I don't want you to think that it is only in relation to the ancients that divine providence delivers those who were exalted in wickedness for the purpose of humili-ating them and that they may be healed by such a wholesome remedy. Presently as well, almighty God's healing providence is [not] lacking in rela-tion to his church. Even now, there is a "Chusar-saton king of Mesopotamia" to whom souls are handed over for humiliation and affliction, souls who had moved themselves from despised Chris-tian humility into pride and arrogance. The vice of pride is utterly hateful in the sight of God, for, as Scripture says, "pride is the beginning of departure from God"[2] and, again, "God resists the proud, but gives grace to the humble."[3] HOM-ILIES ON JUDGES 3.1.[4]

3:9 Israel Cried to the Lord

OTHNIEL THE ANGEL. ORIGEN: It calls the sav-ior "Othniel,"[5] which means "the time of God for me." Through this first Othniel, then, the people

[1]"Chusarsaton" follows the LXX rendering of "Cushan-rishathaim." [2]Sir 10:13-14 LXX. [3]Jas 4:6; 1 Pet 5:5; Prov 3:34. [4]GCS 30:480. [5]The LXX reads "Gothoniel."

were delivered from their humiliating servility and were restored to peace rather than having their longstanding pride and various deeds removed. But because we already said that a certain spiritual identity can be found in King Chusarsaton as one of the adversaries and a prince of the "powers of the air,"[6] it seems to me fitting to say that Othniel likewise, who was raised up to deliver the people, is a member of the "host of heaven"[7] and of the throng of archangels who "are sent to support those who receive the inheritance of salvation."[8] These angels are saviors, moreover, designated under the form of Othniel or Ehud, for, as we have often shown, we do not fight alone against the powers of the enemy, but good forces and powers are also sent to our aid by the Lord. HOMILIES ON JUDGES 3.3.[9]

BEGINNINGS DO NOT PREDICT PROGRESS.
JOHN CASSIAN: We frequently find this calling from need in Scripture as well, when we read that on account of their sins, the children of Israel were delivered over by the Lord to their enemies and that, having changed their course because of their domination and savage cruelty, they cried out to the Lord. "And the Lord sent them," it says, "a deliverer named Ehud, the son of Gera, the son of Jemini, who used either hand as if it were his right hand."[10] And again it says, "They cried out to the Lord, who raised up a deliverer for them, Othniel, the son of Kenaz, the younger brother of Caleb, and he freed them." And it said

of them in a psalm: "When he killed them, then they sought him, and they turned and at dawn they came to God, and they remembered that God was their helper."[11] And again: "They cried out to the Lord when they were troubled, and he freed them from their distress."[12]

Of these three kinds [of calling from need], then, although the first two seem to be supported by better beginnings, nonetheless we find that even on the third level [recorded by the psalmist], which seems inferior and lukewarm, there have been people who are perfect and very fervent in spirit, similar to those who have made an excellent beginning in the Lord's service and have passed the rest of their lives in praiseworthy intensity of spirit. Likewise there are many who have become tepid and have fallen from a higher level and very frequently ended up in tragedy. [Thus], just as it was no drawback to the former that they seem to have been converted not by their own will but by force of necessity, inasmuch as the Lord's kindness furnished the occasion whereby they might feel compunction, likewise their having been converted in some sublime fashion profited the latter nothing whatsoever, because they did not strive to live out the rest of their days accordingly. CONFERENCE 3.4.5-3.5.1.[13]

---

[6]Eph 2:2. [7]See Deut 17:3ff; Lk 2:13; Acts 7:42. [8]Heb 1:14. [9]GCS 30:482-83. [10]Judg 3:15 LXX. [11]Ps 78:34-35 (77:34-35 LXX). [12]Ps 107:6, 13, 19, 28 (106:6, 13, 19, 28 LXX). [13]ACW 57:122*.

3:12-31 EHUD DELIVERS ISRAEL

[15]But when the people of Israel cried to the LORD, the LORD raised up for them a deliverer, Ehud, the son of Gera, the Benjaminite, a left-handed man. The people of Israel sent tribute by him to Eglon the king of Moab. [16]And Ehud made for himself a sword with two edges, a cubit in length; and he girded it on his right thigh under his clothes. [17]And he presented the tribute to Eglon

king of Moab. Now Eglon was a very fat man. ¹⁸*And when Ehud had finished presenting the tribute, he sent away the people that carried the tribute.* ¹⁹*But he himself turned back at the sculptured stones near Gilgal, and said, "I have a secret message for you, O king." And he commanded, "Silence." And all his attendants went out from his presence.* ²⁰*And Ehud came to him, as he was sitting alone in his cool roof chamber. And Ehud said, "I have a message from God for you." And he arose from his seat.* ²¹*And Ehud reached with his left hand, took the sword from his right thigh, and thrust it into his belly;* ²²*and the hilt also went in after the blade, and the fat closed over the blade, for he did not draw the sword out of his belly; and the dirt came out. . . .*

³⁰*So Moab was subdued that day under the hand of Israel. And the land had rest for eighty years.*

OVERVIEW: Sparked by the Septuagint's translation of Ehud's handedness, favorable connotations for the right hand promote anagogical interpretations. Spiritual ambidexterity may be attained by receiving both fortunate (right-handed) and unfortunate (left-handed) things as beneficial (CASSIAN). The just possess two right hands and cheeks in order to defend against attackers (JEROME). Ehud's slaying of Eglon symbolizes how the sword of the gospel destroys hedonistic philosophy (ORIGEN). Israel experienced affliction by foreign foes before the monarchy, but also lengthy periods of peace (AUGUSTINE).

3:15-21 Ehud Kills Eglon, King of Moab

THE ARMS OF RIGHTEOUSNESS. JOHN CASSIAN: These are the persons, then, who are referred to in holy Scripture as *amphoterodexioi*[1] —that is, as ambidextrous. Ehud, "who used either hand as if it were his right hand," is described as such in the book of Judges. We shall also be able to possess this quality in a spiritual way if by a good and correct use we put the things which are considered fortunate and right-handed and the things which are called unfortunate and left-handed on the right side, that whatever befalls may become for us, in the words of the apostle, "the arms of righteousness." For we see that our inner man consists in two parts or, as I might say, two hands. No holy person can be

without what we call the left hand, but perfect virtue is discerned in the fact that by proper use he turns both into a right hand. CONFERENCE 6.10.1.[2]

TWO RIGHT HANDS. JEROME: What did you mean by saying, two thousand fall at the side? Naturally, when the right hand is designated and the left is not, the side is named in place of the left hand. It would not be right, certainly, for the just man to have a left hand: "If someone strikes you on the right cheek," counsels the Lord, "turn to him the other also."[3] Notice that he did not say, "the left also," for it is not the left cheek that is offered, but another right cheek. I shall express this very plainly, therefore, by saying that the just man has two right cheeks. The man, Ehud, for example, who is written of in the book of Judges, is said to have two right hands because he was a just man and killed that fat stupid king. "Though two thousand fall at your side, ten thousand at your right hand."[4] There are very many who lie in wait at our right hand, not so many who plot against our left; [thus], a thousand fall at our side and ten thousand at our right hand. Where there is greater combat, there is, of course, greater victory. Few lie in ambush at our side, but many at our right hand. HOMILIES ON THE PSALMS 20 (Ps 90).[5]

---

[1]Following the LXX. The Hebrew reads "hindered in his right hand." [2]ACW 57:224*. [3]Mt 5:39. [4]See Ps 91:7 (90:7 LXX). [5]FC 48:161*.

THE SWORD OF THE WORD. ORIGEN: Let's observe how Ehud, whose name means "praise," discharged his leadership. History teaches us, in its writings about King Eglon, how this most wise Ehud with particular skill and, if I may say, cunning but praiseworthy deception, would kill the tyrant Eglon, whose name means "round" or "circular." It was necessary, then, to have the quality of judges of our people as was this Ehud, whose name means "praise," so to cut through all his rolling motion and circuit of evil ways and to destroy the king of the Moabites. But Moabite is translated as "flow" or "effusion." Who can the ruler or leader of this flowing and dissolute people be seen or understood to be, therefore, other than the word of that philosophy which adjudges pleasure to be the highest good, a philosophy which the word of the gospel, which has been compared to a sword,[6] killed and destroyed? And this prophetic word would become enclosed within their belly and lowest stomach by means of the "ambidextrous" judge's arguments, to extinguish the Moabites by assertion of the truth, enclosing also every sense of perverse doctrine and dull understanding "which extols itself and rises against the spiritual knowledge of Christ,"[7] so that by acting thus and by doing battle with the word of God, each judge of the church may also become a praising Ehud, about whom the Lord would say, "Well done, good and faithful servant; you have been faithful over a few, so I will set you over many."[8] HOMILIES ON JUDGES 4.1.[9]

3:30 The Land Had Rest for Eighty Years

PERIODS OF WAR AND PEACE. AUGUSTINE: Now, judges were established over them from the time they took over the promised land and before the monarchy began. And even during this era, the children of iniquity, that is, foreign foes, afflicted them, for we read they had now peace, now war. Even so, you can find periods of peace in the age of the judges longer than that of Solomon, who reigned forty years. Specifically, under the judge named Ehud, there were eighty years of peace. CITY OF GOD 17.13.[10]

---

[6]Eph 6:17; Heb 4:12. [7]See 2 Cor 10:5. [8]See Mt 25:21ff. [9]GCS 30:487-88. [10]FC 24:60*.

4:1-10 DEBORAH AND BARAK

[4]Now Deborah, a prophetess, the wife of Lappidoth, was judging Israel at that time. [5]She used to sit under the palm of Deborah between Ramah and Bethel in the hill country of Ephraim; and the people of Israel came up to her for judgment. [6]She sent and summoned Barak the son of Abinoam from Kedesh in Naphtali, and said to him, "The LORD, the God of Israel, commands you, 'Go, gather your men at Mount Tabor, taking ten thousand from the tribe of Naphtali and the tribe of Zebulun. [7]And I will draw out Sisera, the general of Jabin's army, to meet you by the river Kishon with his chariots and his troops; and I will give him into your hand.'" [8]Barak said to her, "If you will go with me, I will go; but if you will not go with me, I will not go." [9]And she said, "I will surely go with you; nevertheless, the road on which you are going will not lead to your glory, for the LORD will sell Sisera into the hand of a woman." Then Deborah arose, and went with Barak to Kedesh.

OVERVIEW: Prudent and good women, having the power to shape events and their husbands for good, ought to be imitated (CHRYSOSTOM). The perishing of Midian, Sisera and Jabin are understood allegorically based upon the meaning of their names (JEROME). Deborah's success as a leader, judge, and prophetess demonstrates that it is valor, and not sex, that makes one strong (AMBROSE).

4:4-9 Deborah Summons Barak to Battle

THE POTENCY OF PRUDENT WOMEN. CHRYSOSTOM: Indeed, nothing—nothing, I repeat—is more potent than a good and prudent woman in molding a man and shaping his soul in whatever way she desires. For he will not bear with friends, or teachers, or magistrates in the same way as with his wife, when she admonishes and advises him. Her admonition, in fact, carries with it a kind of pleasure, because of his very great love of the one who is admonishing him. Moreover, I could mention many men, formerly harsh and stubborn, who have become more tractable by this means. She shares with him his table and couch, the procreating of his children, his spoken words and secret thoughts, his comings and goings, and a great many other things as well. She is devoted to him in all things and as closely bound to him as the body is fastened to the head. If she chances to be prudent and diligent, she will surpass and excel all in her solicitude for her husband.

Therefore, I beseech women to carry this out in practice and to give their husbands only the proper advice. For, just as a woman has great power for good, so also she has it for evil. A woman destroyed Absalom; a woman destroyed Amnon; a woman would have destroyed Job; a woman saved Nabal from being murdered; a woman saved an entire nation.[1] Furthermore, Deborah and Judith and innumerable other women directed the success of men who were generals.[2] And that is why Paul said, "For how do you know, woman, whether you will

save your husband?"[3] In his day, too, we see Persis and Mary and Priscilla sharing in the apostle's difficult trials.[4] You also ought to imitate these women and mold the character of your husbands, not only by your words but also by your example. HOMILIES ON THE GOSPEL OF JOHN 61.[5]

JUDGMENT ON SISERA AND JABIN. JEROME: Because these nations have come as enemies against your people, let us hear what judgment the psalmist calls down upon them. "Deal with them as with Midian; as with Sisera."[6] You have read the book of Judges; this is that Midian whom Gideon defeated.[7] "As with Sisera and Jabin." Jabin and Sisera are the foes whom Deborah and Barak conquered. "At the torrent Kishon, who perished at Endor."[8] Deborah and Barak destroyed Sisera, the general of the army. So much for what Scripture says; learn now what it means. Lord, because they are so arrogant, because they have come with a mighty army, because their prince is Nebuchadnezzar[9] the king of the Assyrians, because they are the forces of the sons of Lot,[10] because they follow the example of the fallen angels, because in their pride they have claimed equality with you; for all these reasons, I beg of you to overpower them, not by a man but to their shame by a woman.

"They became dung on the ground."[11] Who? Midian, Sisera and Jabin, these three became putrid on the ground like dung. The name Midian means "one who is negligent of judgment." The warriors against your people are heedless of the judgment that is to come. Sisera is understood as "the vision of a horse." Your people's enemies are not of your flock or of your herd but are stallions that rage with madness over the fillies. Stallions are always ready for battle. "And Jabin."

---

[1] 2 Sam 13; Job 2:9-10; 1 Sam 25; Esther 7—8. [2] Jdt 14—15. [3] 1 Cor 7:16. [4] Rom 16; 1 Cor 16:19. [5] FC 41:161-62*. [6] Ps 83:9 (82:9 LXX). [7] Judg 7—8. [8] Ps 83:10 (82:10 LXX). [9] As Israel's historical enemies, Nebuchadnezzar, who signifies the devil, and the Moabites and Ammonites, who signify the fallen angels, represent those who work against the church of Christ. [10] See Gen 19:37-38. [11] Ps 83:10 (82:10 LXX).

Jabin means "discernment." They who trust in their own wisdom and not in the glory of God rot on the ground like dung. They who were glorying in their army, whose king was the Assyrian, and who used to boast "I will scale the heavens,"[12] not only fell down to earth but on the ground became dung. HOMILIES ON THE PSALMS 15 (Ps 82).[13]

VALOR, NOT SEX, MAKES STRONG. AMBROSE: And in order that it may not seem as if only one widow had fulfilled this inimitable work, it seems in no way doubtful that there were many others of equal or almost equal virtue, for good seed corn usually bears many ears filled with grains. Do not doubt, then, that that ancient seedtime was fruitful in the characters of many women. But as it would be tedious to include all, consider some, and especially Deborah, whose virtue Scripture records for us.

For she showed not only that widows have no need of the help of a man, inasmuch as she, not at all restrained by the weakness of her sex, undertook to perform the duties of a man, and did even more than she had undertaken. And, at last, when the Jews were being ruled under the leadership of the judges, because they could not govern them with manly justice or defend them with manly strength, and so wars broke out on all sides, they chose Deborah, by whose judgment they might be ruled. And so one widow both ruled many thousands of men in peace and defended them from the enemy. There were many judges in Israel, but no woman before was a judge, as after Joshua there were many judges but none was a prophet. And I think that her judgeship has been narrated and her deeds described, that women should not be restrained from deeds of valor by the weakness of their sex. A widow, she governs the people; a widow, she leads armies; a widow, she chooses generals; a widow, she

determines wars and orders triumphs. So, then, it is not nature which is answerable for the fault or which is liable to weakness. It is not sex but valor which makes strong.

And in time of peace there is no complaint, and no fault is found in this woman, whereas most of the judges were causes of no small sins to the people. But when the Canaanites, a people fierce in battle and rich in troops, successively joined them, showed a horrible disposition against the people of the Jews, this widow, before all others, made all the preparations for war. And to show that the needs of the household were not dependent on the public resources but rather that public duties were guided by the discipline of home life, she brings forth from her home her son[14] as a leader of the army, that we may acknowledge that a widow can train a warrior; whom, as a mother, she taught, and, as judge, placed in command, as, being herself brave, she trained him, and, as a prophetess, sent to certain victory.

And lastly, her son Barak shows the chief part of the victory was in the hands of a woman when he said, "If you will not go with me I will not go, because I do not know on what day the Lord will send his angel with me."[15] How great, then, was the might of that woman to whom the leader of the army says, "If you will not go I will not go." How great, I say, the fortitude of the widow who does not protect her son from dangers through motherly affection but rather with the zeal of a mother exhorts her son to go forth to victory, while saying that the decisive point of that victory is in the hand of a woman! CONCERNING WIDOWS 8.43-46.[16]

---

[12]Is 14:13. [13]FC 48:114-15*. [14]That Deborah was Barak's mother is inferred by Ambrose, perhaps, in part, from their close association and to her ascription as "a mother in Israel" (Judg 2:7). [15]Judg 4:8 LXX. [16]NPNF 2 10:398-99*.

4:11-24 THE BATTLE AGAINST SISERA

[15]*And the* LORD *routed Sisera and all his chariots and all his army before Barak at the edge of the sword; and Sisera alighted from his chariot and fled away on foot. . . .*

[18]*And Jael came out to meet Sisera, and said to him, "Turn aside, my lord, turn aside to me; have no fear." So he turned aside to her into the tent, and she covered him with a rug.* [19]*And he said to her, "Pray, give me a little water to drink; for I am thirsty." So she opened a skin of milk and gave him a drink and covered him.* [20]*And he said to her, "Stand at the door of the tent, and if any man comes and asks you, 'Is any one here?' say, No."* [21]*But Jael the wife of Heber took a tent peg, and took a hammer in her hand, and went softly to him and drove the peg into his temple, till it went down into the ground, as he was lying fast asleep from weariness. So he died.* [22]*And behold, as Barak pursued Sisera, Jael went out to meet him, and said to him, "Come, and I will show you the man whom you are seeking." So he went in to her tent; and there lay Sisera dead, with the tent peg in his temple.*

OVERVIEW: The triumph of Deborah and Jael over Sisera prefigures the battle of faith and the victory of the church (AMBROSE). Jael is understood to prefigure the Christian church due to the meaning of her name, her status as a foreigner and her role in achieving victory over Israel's enemy (ORIGEN). To ensure that God receives credit for great deeds, God uses the lowliest to accomplish them (SALVIAN).

4:21-22 Jael Kills Sisera in His Sleep

THE RISE AND VICTORY OF THE CHURCH.
AMBROSE: So, then, Deborah foretold the event of the battle. Barak, as he was bidden, led forth the army; Jael carried off the triumph, for the prophecy of Deborah fought for her, who in a mystery revealed to us the rising of the church from among the Gentiles, for whom should be found a triumph over Sisera, that is, over the powers opposed to her. For us, then, the oracles of the prophets fought, for us those judgments and arms of the prophets won the victory. And for this reason it was not the people of the Jews but Jael who gained the victory over the enemy. Unhappy, then, was that people which could not follow up by the virtue of faith the enemy, whom it had put to flight. And so by their fault salvation came to the Gentiles; by Jewish sluggishness the victory was reserved for us.

Jael then destroyed Sisera, whom however the band of Jewish veterans had put to flight under their brilliant leader, for this is the interpretation of the name of Barak; for often, as we read, the sayings and merits of the prophets procured heavenly aid for the fathers. But even at that time was victory being prepared over spiritual wickedness for those to whom it is said in the Gospel: "Come, you who are blessed of my Father, take possession of the kingdom prepared for you from the foundation of the world."[1] So the commencement of the victory was from the fathers,[2] its conclusion is in the church.

But the church does not overcome the powers of the enemy with weapons of this world but with spiritual arms, "which are mighty through God to the destruction of strongholds and the high places of spiritual wickedness."[3] And Sisera's thirst was quenched with a bowl of milk, because he was overcome by wisdom, for what is healthful

---

[1]Mt 25:34. [2]The patriarchs. [3]2 Cor 10:4.

for us as food is deadly and weakening to the power of the enemy. The weapons of the church are faith, the weapons of the church are prayer, which overcomes the enemy.

And so according to this history a woman, that the minds of women might be stirred up, became a judge, a woman set all in order, a woman prophesied, a woman triumphed, and joining in the battle array taught men to war under a woman's lead. But in a mystery it is the battle of faith and the victory of the church. CONCERNING WIDOWS 8.47-50.[4]

JAEL PREFIGURES THE CHURCH. ORIGEN: What, therefore, does the web of all this mystical history show us? The woman Jael, that foreigner about whom Deborah's prophecy said that victory would be had "through the hand of a woman,"[5] symbolizes the church, which was assembled from foreign nations. But Jael's name means "ascent," for truly there is no route whereby one may ascend into heaven except "through the church of the manifold wisdom of God."[6] She, therefore, while ascending from the corporeal to the spiritual and from the earthly to the heavenly, killed Sisera, who, as we have already said above, symbolizes the man of carnal or animal vices, for Sisera's name means "vision of a horse," concerning which Scripture teaches: "Do not become like horses and mules, in which there is no understanding."[7] She killed him with a stake, then, which is to say that she overthrew him by the power and cunning of the wood of the cross. Nor is it without reason that the stake is described as having pierced his jaws, for that mouth which spoke of carnal things and that doctrine which preferred the glory of the flesh, deceiving and persuading the human race, by secular wisdom and by the idolatry of comfort, to live for selfish delights and pleasure, that very mouth, I say, is pierced and penetrated by the wood of the cross, in as much as the "broad and easy way" of pleasure which is preached by philosophy has been exposed by Christ, who showed that the "way of our salvation is narrow and difficult."[8] [Thus], Jael the church sent Sisera the king of vices to his everlasting sleep covered with skins, that is, lulled to sleep by the mortification of his members.[9] HOMILIES ON JUDGES 5.5.[10]

GREAT DEEDS ARE GOD'S WORK. SALVIAN THE PRESBYTER: We read that when God wished it clearly understood that great deeds were done by him, they were done through a few or through the lowliest, lest the work of his heavenly hand be attributed to human strength. In this way the leader Sisera, before whom the Hebrew army trembled, was laid low by a woman. THE GOVERNANCE OF GOD 7.8.[11]

---

[4]NPNF 2 10:399*. [5]Judg 4:9. [6]See Eph 3:10. [7]Ps 32:9 (31:9 LXX). [8]See Mt 7:13. [9]See Col 3:5. [10]GCS 30:495-96. [11]FC 3:195*.

5:1-31 THE SONG OF DEBORAH AND BARAK

¹*Then sang Deborah and Barak the son of Abino-am on that day:*
    ²*"That the leaders took the lead in Israel,*
        that the people offered themselves willingly,
            bless[d] the LORD!
    ³*"Hear, O kings; give ear, O princes;*

> to the LORD I will sing,
>> I will make melody to the LORD, the God of Israel." . . .
> [12]"Awake, awake, Deborah!
>> Awake, awake, utter a song!
>> Arise, Barak, lead away your captives,
>>> O son of Abino-am.
> [13]Then down marched the remnant of the noble;
>> the people of the LORD marched down for him[f] against the mighty.

d Or You who offered yourselves willingly among the people, bless   f Gk: Heb me

OVERVIEW: The saints encourage one another, but every mind should be held captive to the obedience of Christ (PROCOPIUS). Victory over one's adversaries prompts melodic praise. The kings to which Deborah directs her song are understood to be believers who have Christ reigning in them (ORIGEN).

5:1-3 Making Melody to the Lord

VICTORY PROMPTS A SONG. ORIGEN: The fourth song is in the book of Judges. Concerning it there is written, "And Deborah and Barak the son of Abinoam sang on that day, saying, 'That the princes took the lead in Israel, that the people offered themselves willingly, bless the Lord! Hear, O kings, give ear, O governors!'" and the rest. And the person who sings this ought to be a bee, whose product is used by kings and ordinary people for their health. For "Deborah," who sings this song, means "bee." Moreover, Barak is with her; and his name means "flashing." And this song is sung after a victory, because no one can sing of what is perfect unless he has conquered his adversaries. Furthermore, it is said in this song, "Awake, awake, Deborah! Stir up the thousands of the people. Awake, awake, utter a song! Awake, Barak!" But you will find these matters more fully discussed in the homilies we have given on the book of Judges. COMMENTARY ON THE SONG OF SONGS, PROLOGUE.[1]

5:3 Hear, O Kings

A ROYAL PRIESTHOOD. ORIGEN: Hear, O kings. She names them "kings" who are called together to hear the word of God. You should rejoice, people of God, at this emblem of your nobility. It is not as just any people that you are called to hear the word of God, but as a king, for to you it was said, "You are a royal, priestly race, a people for God's possession."[2] Because you are kings, therefore, Christ our Lord is rightly called the "King of kings and the Lord of lords."[3] However, as you revel in this title of your nobility, you should also learn what each one of you must do to be a king. Let me outline it for you briefly. You are made a king if Christ reigns in you, for he is called a king by reigning. If also in you, therefore, the soul reigns and the body submits, if you put the concupiscence of the flesh under of yoke of your command, if you subdue every kind of vice by the tight bridle of your sobriety, then you who know how to reign are also rightly called a "king." HOMILIES ON JUDGES 6.3.[4]

5:12-13 Arise, Deborah!

I CAN DO ALL THINGS THROUGH CHRIST. PROCOPIUS OF GAZA: "Awake, Awake, Deborah!" Increase righteousness, establish the people, arise for the glory of God and the salvation of the people. "Gathering strength, arise Barak!" Arise and establish [the people] as was said to Moses, "Stand by me."[5] David likewise said, "Our feet

[1]OSW 238. [2]1 Pet 2:9. [3]1 Tim 6:15; Rev 19:16. [4]GCS 30:501. [5]Ex 38:21.

stand in your courts, O Jerusalem."[6] "He set my feet upon the rock."[7] Therefore, gathering strength, arise and say, "I can do all things through Christ who strengthens me!"[8] "You are my strength and my song, O Lord." But also you, Deborah, strengthen Barak. For the saints also give courage to us in the power of the Lord, instructing our souls against our enemies. But every mind should be held captive to the obedience of Christ.[9] And if, Deborah, you should fall in your work, like what happened to Jonathan [when he tasted the honey],[10] may your soul be strengthened by the sweet taste of prophecy. COMMENTARY ON JUDGES 5.12.[11]

---

[6]Ps 121:2 LXX. [7]Ps 40:2 (39:2 LXX). [8]Phil 4:13. [9]2 Cor 10:5. [10]Cf. 1 Sam 14:27ff. [11]PG 87.1:1056.

6:1-10 MIDIANITE OPPRESSION

[1]*The people of Israel did what was evil in the sight of the* LORD; *and the* LORD *gave them into the hand of Midian seven years.* [2]*And the hand of Midian prevailed over Israel; and because of Midian the people of Israel made for themselves the dens which are in the mountains, and the caves and the strongholds.*

OVERVIEW: As the people of Israel were handed over to physical enemies when they neglected God's commandments, so Christians, as the spiritual Israel, may expect to face demonic powers when they forsake God's grace (ORIGEN).

6:1 The Lord Delivers Israel to Midian

THE SPIRITUAL ISRAEL. ORIGEN: The "land was at rest" as long as sin was at rest. But the land is said to be disturbed, meaning those who inhabit the land, when the souls of the people began to move and to dislocate in sin. This is why the text was written this way: "The land was at rest for forty years. And the sons of Israel did evil in the sight of the Lord, and the Lord delivered them into the hand of Midian for seven years. And Midian ruled over Israel." As long as there was justice in the land, therefore, that is, in those who inhabited the land, the land is said to be at rest. But when iniquity arose and "they did evil in the sight of the Lord," then the Lord is said to have delivered them into the hand of Midian for seven years. Nor are the Midianites said to have ruled over the people of the Lord as long as they observed the commandments of the Lord. But when they began to neglect the divine mandates, the hand of their enemy became stronger and more powerful against them. Yet, whereas their bodily enemies arose and strengthened against them when the first people failed, against us, on the other hand, who are called the spiritual Israel, a spiritual enemy will arise and the hand of demons will be strengthened when we neglect the commandments of God and hold the precepts of Christ in contempt, and we will be delivered to our own enemies when we forsake God's grace. HOMILIES ON JUDGES 7.1.[1]

---

[1]GCS 30:504-5.

6:11-18 THE LORD CALLS GIDEON

> [11]Now the angel of the LORD came and sat under the oak at Ophrah, which belonged to Joash the Abiezrite, as his son Gideon was beating out wheat in the wine press, to hide it from the Midianites. [12]And the angel of the LORD appeared to him and said to him, "The LORD is with you, you mighty man of valor."

OVERVIEW: Gideon's selection as deliverer and his threshing in the winepress prefigure Christ's incarnation and the refinement of the saints (AMBROSE). It is in the church that the final separation between the good grain of holiness and the chaff of sin takes place (CAESARIUS OF ARLES).

6:11-12 The Angel of the Lord Appears to Gideon

PREFIGURING THE FUTURE INCARNATION. AMBROSE: When Jerubbaal,[1] as we read, was beating out wheat under an oak, he received a message from God in order that he might bring the people of God from the power of strangers into liberty. Nor is it a matter of wonder if he was chosen for grace, seeing that even then, being appointed under the shadow of the holy cross and of the adorable Wisdom in the predestined mystery of the future incarnation, he was bringing forth the visible grains of the fruitful corn from their hiding places and was [mystically] separating the elect of the saints from the refuse of the empty chaff. For these elect, as though trained with the rod of truth, laying aside the superfluities of the old man together with his deeds, are gathered in the church as in a winepress. For the church is the winepress of the eternal fountain, since from it wells forth the juice of the heavenly Vine. ON THE HOLY SPIRIT 1, PROLOGUE 1.[2]

THE CHURCH AS WINEPRESS. CAESARIUS OF ARLES: When Gideon, the son of Joash, was beating the grain of wheat with a rod under an oak tree, he merited to hear an angel promise that he would deliver God's people from the power of their enemies. It is no wonder that he was chosen for a special grace, when by the predestined mystery of the future incarnation he was even then seated under the shade of the cross of holy and venerable wisdom. He was bringing the tangible grains of a fruitful field out of their concealment, separating choice holy men from the rubbish of useless chaff. Putting aside the superfluities of the old man and his actions by treating them with the rod of experienced truth, they are assembled in the church as in a winepress. The church is the winepress of the eternal fountain in which abounds the fruit of the heavenly vine. SERMON 117.1.[3]

---

[1]Gideon; cf. Judg 6:32. [2]NPNF 2 10:93*. [3]FC 47:177*.

6:19-24 GIDEON SACRIFICES TO THE LORD

[19]So Gideon went into his house and prepared a kid, and unleavened cakes from an ephah of flour; the meat he put in a basket, and the broth he put in a pot, and brought them to him under the oak and presented them. [20]And the angel of God said to him, "Take the meat and the unleavened cakes, and put them on this rock, and pour the broth over them." And he did so. [21]Then the angel of the LORD reached out the tip of the staff that was in his hand, and touched the meat and the unleavened cakes; and there sprang up fire from the rock and consumed the flesh and the unleavened cakes; and the angel of the LORD vanished from his sight.

OVERVIEW: As the fire consumes Gideon's offering to the angel of God, the sacrament of the body and blood of Christ, which spiritually purifies Christians, is anticipated (AMBROSE, GREGORY THE GREAT).

6:19-21 The Angel of God Burns Gideon's Offering

THE ROCK AS THE BODY OF CHRIST. AMBROSE: Gideon, moved by that message, when he heard that though thousands of the people failed, God would deliver his own from their enemies by means of one man, offered a kid, and according to the word of the angel, laid its flesh and the unleavened cakes upon the rock and poured the broth upon them. And as soon as the angel touched them with the end of the staff which he bore, fire burst forth out of the rock, and so the sacrifice which he was offering was consumed. By which it seems clear that that rock was a figure of the body of Christ, for it is written: "They drank of that rock that followed them, and that rock was Christ."[1] This certainly refers not to his Godhead but to his flesh, which watered the hearts of the thirsting people with the perpetual stream of his blood.

Even at that time was it declared in a mystery that the Lord Jesus in his flesh would, when crucified, do away the sins of the whole world, and not only the deeds of the body but the desires of the soul. For the flesh of the kid refers to sins of deed, the broth to the enticements of desire, as it is written: "For the people greedily lusted, and said, 'Who shall give us flesh to eat?' "[2] That the angel then stretched forth his staff and touched the rock, from which fire went out, shows that the flesh of the Lord, being filled with the divine Spirit, would burn away all the sins of human frailty. Wherefore, also, the Lord says, "I have come to send fire upon the earth."[3] ON THE HOLY SPIRIT 1, PROLOGUE 2-3.[4]

CRUCIFYING THE FLESH. GREGORY THE GREAT: "But I say to you that whoever looks on a woman lustfully has committed adultery with her already in his heart."[5] "The pus is wiped off,"[6] therefore, when sin is not only severed from the deed but also from the thought. It is hence that Jerubbaal saw the angel when he was winnowing corn from the chaff, at whose request he immediately prepared a kid and set it upon a rock and poured over it the broth of the flesh, which the angel touched with a rod and fire came out of the rock and consumed it. For what else is it to beat corn with a rod, but to separate the grains of virtues from the chaff of vices with an upright judgment? But to those that are thus employed the angel presents himself, in that the Lord is more ready to communicate interior truth to the extent that

---

[1]1 Cor 10:4. [2]Num 11:4. [3]Lk 12:49. [4]NPNF 2 10:93*. [5]Mt 5:28. [6]See Job 2:8.

people are more earnest in ridding themselves of external things. And he orders a kid to be killed, that is, every appetite of the flesh to be sacrificed, and the flesh to be set upon a rock and its broth to be poured upon it. Whom else does the rock represent except him of whom it is said by Paul, "And that rock was Christ"?[7] We "set flesh upon the rock," then, when in imitation of Christ we crucify our body. He too pours the broth of the flesh over it who, in following the conduct of Christ, empties himself even of the mere thoughts of the flesh themselves. For the "broth" of the dissolved flesh is in a manner "poured

upon the rock" when the mind is emptied of the flow of carnal thoughts too. Yet the angel directly touches it with a rod, in that the might of God's assistance never deserts our striving. And fire issues from the rock and consumes the broth and the flesh, in that the Spirit, breathed upon us by the Redeemer, lights up the heart with so fierce a flame of remorse that it consumes everything in it that is unlawful either in deed or in thought. MORALS ON THE BOOK OF JOB 3.30.[8]

---

[7]1 Cor 10:4. [8]LF 18:169-70*.

6:25-32 THE ASHERAH AND THE ALTAR OF BAAL

[25]*That night the LORD said to him, "Take your father's bull, the second bull seven years old, and pull down the altar of Baal which your father has, and cut down the Asherah that is beside it;* [26]*and build an altar to the LORD your God on the top of the stronghold here, with stones laid in due order; then take the second bull, and offer it as a burnt offering with the wood of the Asherah which you shall cut down." * [27]*So Gideon took ten men of his servants, and did as the LORD had told him; but because he was too afraid of his family and the men of the town to do it by day, he did it by night.*

OVERVIEW: By sacrificing the bull, which is a type of Christ, Gideon foreshadowed the sole capacity of Jesus' sacrifice to bring redemption and the future cessation of sacrifices (AMBROSE).

6:25-27 An Altar to the Lord Replaces Idol Worship

THE END OF SACRIFICES. AMBROSE: Then the man, instructed and foreknowing what was to be, observes the heavenly mysteries, and therefore, according to the warning, killed the bull destined for idols by his father, and himself offered to God another bull seven years old. By doing this he most plainly showed that after the coming of the Lord

all Gentile sacrifices should be done away and that only the sacrifice of the Lord's passion should be offered for the redemption of the people. For that bull was, in a type, Christ, in whom, as Isaiah said, dwelled the fullness of the seven gifts of the Spirit.[1] This bull Abraham also offered when he saw the day of the Lord and was glad.[2] He it is who was offered at one time in the type of a kid,[3] at another in that of a sheep, at another in that of a bull. Of a kid, because he is a sacrifice for sin; of a sheep, because he is an unresisting victim; of a bull, because he is a victim without blemish. ON THE HOLY SPIRIT 1, PROLOGUE 4.[4]

---

[1]Is 11:2. [2]Jn 8:56. [3]Lev 4:23, 28. [4]NPNF 2 10:93-94*.

6:33-40 THE FLEECE AND THE DEW

³⁶*Then Gideon said to God, "If thou wilt deliver Israel by my hand, as thou hast said,* ³⁷*behold, I am laying a fleece of wool on the threshing floor; if there is dew on the fleece alone, and it is dry on all the ground, then I shall know that thou wilt deliver Israel by my hand, as thou hast said."* ³⁸*And it was so. When he rose early next morning and squeezed the fleece, he wrung enough dew from the fleece to fill a bowl with water.* ³⁹*Then Gideon said to God, "Let not thy anger burn against me, let me speak but this once; pray, let me make trial only this once with the fleece; pray, let it be dry only on the fleece, and on all the ground let there be dew."* ⁴⁰*And God did so that night; for it was dry on the fleece only, and on all the ground there was dew.*

OVERVIEW: Gideon asked for another sign, not due to lack of faith but in order to signify divine mysteries. The fleece was placed on a threshing floor to symbolize a plentiful harvest of virtues from among the Gentiles. The dew wrung out of the fleece into a basin prefigures the Lord's washing of his disciples' feet (AMBROSE). The absence of dew on the fleece illustrates how, in former times, God's justice was manifested in the law (AUGUSTINE). The appearance of dew symbolizes Jesus' ministry, first to the Jews, then to the Gentiles (AUGUSTINE, CAESARIUS OF ARLES). As the Lord was to come down like rain upon a fleece, the dew is recognized as the divine Word (ORIGEN, AMBROSE). God's truth, like dew, ceased to fall upon Israel and began to water the rest of the world (JEROME). Like moisture in a cloud, the dew-filled fleece represents God's grace hidden within Israel, whereas the dew on the floor represents the manifestation of God's grace through Christ. Since grace is no longer hidden but openly manifested, Christians who contend that righteousness is a result of nature are in error and without excuse (AUGUSTINE). Mary, the mother of the lamb of God, is recognized in the fleece (MAXIMUS OF TURIN).

6:36-40 Gideon Asks God for Signs of Victory

SPEAKING IN MYSTERIES. AMBROSE: Someone perhaps will enquire whether Gideon does not seem to have been lacking in faith, seeing that after being instructed by many signs he asked [for] still more. But how can he seem to have asked as if doubting or lacking in faith, who was speaking in mysteries? He was not doubtful then, but careful so that we would not doubt. For how could he be doubtful whose prayer was effectual? And how could he have begun the battle without fear, unless he had understood the message of God? For the dew on the fleece signified the faith among the Jews, because the words of God come down like the dew. ON THE HOLY SPIRIT 1, PROLOGUE 6.[1]

A PLENTIFUL HARVEST. AMBROSE: Nor was it without a reason that he put the fleece neither in a field nor in a meadow, but in a threshing floor, where the harvest of the wheat is: "For the harvest is plenteous, but the laborers are few;"[2] because, through faith in the Lord, there was about to be a harvest fruitful in virtues. ON THE HOLY SPIRIT 1, PROLOGUE 10.[3]

WASHING THE DISCIPLES' FEET PREFIGURED. AMBROSE: Nor, again, was it without a reason that he dried the fleece of the Jews and put the dew from it into a basin, so that it was filled with

---

[1]NPNF 2 10:94*. [2]Lk 10:2. [3]NPNF 2 10:94*.

water, yet he did not himself wash his feet in that dew. The prerogative of so great a mystery was to be given to another. He was being waited for who alone could wash away the filth of all. Gideon was not great enough to claim this mystery for himself, but "the Son of man came not to be ministered to, but to minister."[4] Let us, then, recognize in whom these mysteries are seen to be accomplished. Not in holy Gideon, for they were still at their commencement. Therefore the Gentiles were surpassed, for dryness was still upon the Gentiles, and therefore did Israel surpass them, for then did the dew remain on the fleece.

Let us come now to the gospel of God. I find the Lord stripping himself of his garments and girding himself with a towel, pouring water into a basin, and washing the disciples' feet.[5] That heavenly dew was this water, this was foretold, namely, that the Lord Jesus Christ would wash the feet of his disciples in that heavenly dew. ON THE HOLY SPIRIT 1, PROLOGUE 11-12.[6]

THE LAW AND THE FLEECE. AUGUSTINE: Again on this subject[7] it is written: "For through the law comes the knowledge of sin. But now, apart from the law, the justice of God is made manifest, being witnessed by the law and the prophets."[8] When he says "made manifest" he shows that it had existed but was like the dew for which Gideon asked; then it was not visible on the fleece, but now it is made manifest on the ground around. Therefore, since law without grace could only strengthen rather than kill sin—as it is written: "The sting of death is sin and the strength of sin is the law"[9]—and as many flee to grace for refuge from the face of sin which had been so enthroned, to grace lying manifest, as it were, on the ground, so at that time few fled to it [grace] for refuge, invisible as it were, on the fleece. Indeed, this division of times belongs to the depth of the riches of the wisdom and of the knowledge of God, of which it is said: "How incomprehensible are his judgments and how unsearchable his ways!"[10] LETTER 177.[11]

DEW SIGNIFIES JESUS' MINISTRY. AUGUSTINE: "And he shall come down like rain into a fleece, and like drops distilling upon the earth."[12] He has reminded and admonished us that what was done by Gideon the judge has its end in Christ. He asked the Lord for a sign, that a fleece laid on the floor should alone be rained upon and the floor should be dry; and again, that the fleece alone should be dry and the floor should be rained upon; and so it happened. This dry fleece, which lay upon a floor in the midst of the whole round world, signified the former people Israel. Therefore, Christ came down like rain upon the fleece while the floor remained dry; concerning this he said, "I was sent only to the lost sheep of the house of Israel."[13] There [in Israel] he selected a mother through whom he would receive the [bodily] form of a servant in order to appear to humanity: there he gave this command to the disciples, saying, "Don't go in the direction of the nations or enter into the cities of the Samaritans: go first to the lost sheep of the house of Israel."[14] When he said, go "first" to them, he also showed that afterward, when the floor was to be rained upon, they would also go to other sheep who were not of the former people of Israel. Concerning these he says, "I have other sheep which are not of this fold; I need to bring in them also, that there may be one flock and one Shepherd."[15] For this reason the apostle also says, "For I say that Christ was a minister of the circumcision for the truth of God, to confirm the promises of the patriarchs."[16] Thus rain came down upon the fleece, while the floor remained dry. Regarding this he continues, "so that the nations should glorify God for his mercy,"[17] and, when the time arrived, that what he says by the prophet should be fulfilled, "a people whom I have not known has served me, in listening attentively it has obeyed me."[18] We now understand that the nation

---

[4]Mt 20:28. [5]Jn 13:8. [6]NPNF 2 10:94-95*. [7]That is, how divine law and grace relate to human nature. [8]Rom 3:20-21. [9]1 Cor 15:56. [10]Rom 11:33. [11]FC 30:104. [12]Ps 71:6 LXX. [13]Mt 15:24. [14]Mt 10:5-6. [15]Jn 10:16. [16]Rom 15:8. [17]Rom 15:9. [18]Ps 18:43-44 (17:43-44 LXX).

of the Jews has remained dry of Christ's grace, and all the nations throughout the whole round world are being rained upon by clouds full of Christian grace. He has indicated this rain with another phrase, as he says that "drops [are] distilling" no longer upon the fleece but "upon the earth." For what else is rain but drops distilling? I think that the above [Jewish] nation is signified as a fleece either because they were to be stripped of the authority of teaching—just as a sheep is stripped of its skin—or because he was hiding that same rain in a secret place and did not desire that it should be preached to those who were not circumcised, that is, to be revealed to uncircumcised nations. EXPLANATIONS OF THE PSALMS 72.9.[19]

THE DEW OF A HEAVENLY VISITATION. CAESARIUS OF ARLES: Now, although Gideon was brave and confident, still he sought fuller proofs of victory from the Lord, saying, "If indeed you are going to save Israel through me, as you promised, O Lord, I am putting this woolen fleece on the threshing floor. If dew comes on the fleece, while all the ground is dry, I shall know that you will save the people through me, as you promised." That is what took place. Afterwards, he added that the second time dew should pour over all the ground and only the fleece be dry; and so it happened. The dew on the fleece was faith in Judea, for the words of God descend as dew; for this reason Moses says, "May my discourse be awaited like the rain, and my words descend like the dew."[20] Thus, when the whole world was dried up from the unproductive heat of Gentile superstition, then there was the dew of a heavenly visitation upon the fleece, that is, in Judea. However, after "the lost sheep of the house of Israel"[21] (foreshadowing, I think, the figure of the fleece of the Jews) refused the fountain of living water, the dew of faith dried up in the hearts of the Jews, and that divine stream turned its path to the hearts of the Gentiles. For this reason, the whole world is now moist with the dew of faith, but the Jews destroyed their prophets and advis-

ers. It is no wonder that they submit to the dryness of faithlessness, since the Lord God deprived them of the fruitful rains of the prophets, saying, "I will command the clouds not to send rain upon that vineyard."[22] Salutary is the rain of the prophetic cloud, as David said: "He shall be like rain coming down on the meadow, like showers watering the earth."[23] The sacred writings of the whole world promised us this rain which watered the world at the advent of our Lord and Savior with the dew of the divine spirit. Thus, the dew has already come, and also the rain; the Lord came and brought with him heavenly showers. For this reason, we who thirsted before now drink, and by an interior drinking [we] absorb that divine spirit. Therefore, holy Gideon foresaw that by perceiving faith, even tribes and nations would drink the true heavenly dew. SERMON 117.4.[24]

THE DEW OF THE WORD. ORIGEN: But now let's see why, in the first sign, "dew fell upon the fleece, whereas the ground was dry," and in the second sign, "dew fell upon the ground, while the fleece remained dry," an indication which Gideon accepted as a pledge that the Lord would save Israel through his hand. The rationale for this mystery is to be seen in what I remember from one of our preceding books, which characterized the people of Israel as a "fleece," with the surrounding ground being the Gentiles, while the dew that fell "upon the fleece" was the word of God written for this people alone.[25] For only to Israel did the dew of the divine law arrive, whereas all the surrounding nations remained dry, none of them being infused with the moisture of divine locution. In the second sign, however, where he asked that the dew fall on the ground and that the fleece remain dry, a completely different rationale can be observed. We should see this entire people, who were gathered together from nations

---

[19]NPNF 1 8:329**. [20]Deut 32:2. [21]Mt 15:24. [22]See Is 5:6. [23]Ps 72:6 (71:6 LXX). [24]FC 47:179-80*. [25]See Ps 72:6 (71:6 LXX).

around the world, now having within themselves the divine dew; see them infused with the dew of Moses, irrigated by the word of the prophets; see them green from evangelical and apostolic water. The fleece, however, that is, the Jewish people, suffers aridity and dryness in the word of God, according to which it is written: "The children of Israel will be for a long time without king, without prince, without prophet; they will have no altar, no victim, no sacrifice."[26] You can see how they remain arid, how they are stricken with drought of the word of God. . . . Even the seventy-first psalm, as I have often discussed with them, moves me to this conclusion because, when it describes the advent of Christ, it foretells his coming as rain on a fleece and as showers on the earth. Here in Judges a fleece is mentioned and in the psalm, also, "fleece" is the word chosen. For he will "descend like rain," it says, "on a fleece." He descends, therefore, on that fleece of the people of circumcision and "like showers upon the earth," meaning that our Lord Jesus Christ descends on the remainder of the earth, dripping upon us and bringing the "dew of heaven"[27] to us Gentiles also, that we too may drink who were on the previously arid surrounding land. HOMILIES ON JUDGES 8.4.[28]

THE DEW OF THE DIVINE WORD. AMBROSE: But what does this mean: "Until the day on which the Lord shall send rain on the earth"? except that he, too, "shall come down like rain upon a fleece, and like the drops that water the earth."[29] In this passage the mystery of the old history is disclosed where Gideon, the warrior of the mystic conflict, receiving the pledge of future victory, recognized the spiritual sacrament in the vision of his mind, that that rain was the dew of the divine Word, which first came down on the fleece, when all the earth was parched with continual drought, and by a second true sign, moistened the floor of all the earth with a shower, while dryness was upon the fleece. CONCERNING WIDOWS 3.18.[30]

THE DRYNESS OF ISRAEL. JEROME: The truth of the Lord reaches even to the clouds. The clouds are the apostles and prophets; to them he gave the command not to rain upon Israel. This is in agreement with history as recorded in the book of Judges, where it speaks of the fleece that was dry while rain fell upon the rest of the world. It means that Israel is dry and the rain is pouring down over the whole world. HOMILIES ON THE PSALMS 24 (Ps 96).[31]

CHRIST, THE SWEETNESS OF DEW. AUGUSTINE: What did Gideon's fleece signify? It is like the nation of the Jews in the midst of the world, which had the grace of sacraments, not indeed openly manifested, but hidden in a cloud or in a veil, like the dew in the fleece. The time came when the dew was to be manifested in the floor; it was manifested, no longer hidden. Christ alone is the sweetness of dew: him alone you do not recognize in Scripture, for whom Scripture was written. But yet, "they have heard all the words of your mouth." EXPLANATIONS OF THE PSALMS 138.7.[32]

GRACE HIDDEN, THEN MANIFESTED. AUGUSTINE: But some, like the Jews in former times, both wish to be called Christians, and—still ignorant of God's righteousness—desire to establish their own, even in our own times of open grace, of the full revelation of grace that was previously hidden, that is, in the times of grace now manifested in the floor, which had before lay hidden in the fleece. . . . Gideon, one of the righteous men of old, asked for a sign from the Lord, and said, "I pray, Lord, that this fleece which I put on the floor would be wet with dew, and that the floor would be dry." And it was so. The fleece was wet with dew while the whole floor was dry. In the morning he wrung out the fleece in a basin—since grace is given to the humble—and you

---

[26]Hos 3:4. [27]See Gen 27:28; Deut 33:13; Is 45:8; Dan 4:12ff. [28]GCS 30:511-12. [29]Ps 71:6 LXX. [30]NPNF 2 10:394*. [31]FC 48:193*. [32]NPNF 1 8:634*.

know what the Lord did to his disciples [with water] in a basin.[33] He asked for yet another sign: "O Lord, I [pray] that the fleece would be dry, and the floor wet with dew." And it was so. Consider how, in the time of the Old Testament, grace was hidden in a cloud, as the rain in the fleece. Note also the time of the New Testament: if you consider the nation of the Jews, you will find it like the dry fleece, whereas the whole world, like that floor, is full of grace, not hidden but manifested. Therefore we are greatly compelled to grieve for our brothers who strive against openly manifested, rather than hidden, grace. There is allowance for the Jews, but what shall we say of Christians? For what reason are you enemies of Christ's grace? Why do you rely on yourselves? Why are you unthankful? Why did Christ come? Wasn't [human] nature here before, which you only deceive by your excessive praise? Wasn't the law here? But the apostle says, "If righteousness comes through the law, then Christ died in vain."[34] What the apostle says of the law,

we say regarding nature concerning these people. "If righteousness comes through [human] nature, then Christ died in vain." SERMON 81.9.[35]

COMPARING MARY WITH FLEECE. MAXIMUS OF TURIN: Rightly, then, do we compare Mary with fleece—she who conceived the Lord in such a way that she absorbed him with her whole body; nor did she undergo a rending of that same body, but she was tender in submission and firm in chastity. Rightly, I say, is Mary compared with fleece—she from whose offspring saving garments are woven for the people. Clearly Mary is fleece since from her tender womb came forth the Lamb who himself, bearing his mother's wool (that is, flesh), covers the wounds of all peoples with a soft fleece. For every wound of sin is covered with the wool of Christ, tended by the blood of Christ, and, so that it may receive health, clothed in the garment of Christ. SERMON 97.3.[36]

---

[33]See Jn 13.   [34]Gal 2:21.   [35]NPNF 1 6:503-4**.   [36]ACW 50:261.

7:1-8 THE REDUCTION OF GIDEON'S ARMY

[1]*Then Jerubbaal (that is, Gideon) and all the people who were with him rose early and encamped beside the spring of Harod; and the camp of Midian was north of them, by the hill of Moreh, in the valley.*

[2]*The* LORD *said to Gideon, "The people with you are too many for me to give the Midianites into their hand, lest Israel vaunt themselves against me, saying, 'My own hand has delivered me.'* [3]*Now therefore proclaim in the ears of the people, saying, 'Whoever is fearful and trembling, let him return home.'" And Gideon tested them;[i] twenty-two thousand returned, and ten thousand remained. . . .*

[5]*So he brought the people down to the water; and the* LORD *said to Gideon, "Every one that laps the water with his tongue, as a dog laps, you shall set by himself; likewise every one that kneels down to drink." [6]And the number of those that lapped, putting their hands to their mouths, was three hundred men; but all the rest of the people knelt down to drink water. [7]And the* LORD *said to*

Gideon, "With the three hundred men that lapped I will deliver you, and give the Midianites into your hand; and let all the others go every man to his home."

i Cn: Heb *and depart from Mount Gilead*

OVERVIEW: As a lesson to all who would boast in their own strength, Gideon's army is reduced so that God would be proved the victor (SALVIAN). As the Lord had Gideon send home those who were afraid to fight, Christ purges his camp of fearful followers (ORIGEN). Kneeling and drinking from the stream allegorically refers to the submission to the power of God and to drinking from the unadulterated waters of the orthodox doctrine (GREGORY THE GREAT). The three hundred men, who lapped the water as dogs, signify the sign of the cross. These are praised as good dogs for their good behavior in guarding against the church's enemies (AUGUSTINE, BEDE). By drinking in this manner they demonstrate their knowledge that temperance is developed by limiting the intake of water (EVAGRIUS OF PONTUS). Gideon's trumpets and lighted torches inside pitchers allegorically symbolize the mystery of the Trinity (AMBROSE).

7:1-2 Preparing for the Battle

GLORYING AGAINST GOD. SALVIAN THE PRESBYTER: Against the Midianites, also, who, as the book of Judges relates, had filled all places like locusts, Gideon was ordered to lead a few men into battle. It was not that he did not have many in his army, but that he was forbidden to lead many into battle, lest the multitude might claim for itself some share of the victory. Hence, when he had gathered thirty thousand armed fighters, the Lord spoke thus to him: "the people with you are too many, and the Midianites shall not be given into their hands."

What happened next? He left only three hundred fighters to the man who was about to fight against countless thousands of barbarians. Indeed, he ordered the line of soldiers to be reduced to the smallest number in order that their fewness would not permit them to realize any credit from the prosecution of the divinely waged war. Why the Lord acted thus, he himself very clearly stated, saying, "lest Israel glory against me and say, 'I am saved by my own strength.'" Let them hear, I say, let all the unjust and the presumptuous hear. Let all the powerful hear what God says when he says, "Lest Israel glory against me and say, 'I am saved by my own strength.'"

I say, let them hear, all those who hurl blasphemies and statements contrary to the above, let them who place their hope in human beings hear these things. God says that all who presume they can be liberated by their own strength speak against him. THE GOVERNANCE OF GOD 7.8-9.[1]

7:3 Whoever Is Fearful

CULLING OUT THE FEARFUL AND ANXIOUS. ORIGEN: Does not the leader of our army, the Lord and Savior Jesus Christ, call out now to his soldiers and say, Whoever is "fearful and anxious of heart," let him not come to war with me? For this is also what he says in the Gospels in other words but with the same meaning: "Whoever does not take his own cross and come after me is not worthy of me,"[2] and again: "Whoever does not renounce all that he has cannot be my disciple."[3] Is not Christ thus culling out the fearful and anxious and sending them from his camp? . . . But don't let such a life of warfare turn you away; there really is nothing difficult, nothing arduous or impossible in it. HOMILIES ON JUDGES 9.1.[4]

7:5-7 Those Who Lapped Will Attack

ONLY THE UPRIGHT QUALIFY. GREGORY THE

---

[1]FC 3:196*. [2]Mt 10:38; Lk 14:27. [3]Lk 14:33. [4]OSF 225.

GREAT: And they were brought to the river to drink the waters; and whoever drank the waters with bended knees were removed from the struggle of war. For by the waters is designated the doctrine of wisdom, but by the unbended knee righteous conduct. Therefore those who are reported to have bent their knees while drinking the water retired from the strife of battles, having been forbidden because Christ proceeds to battle against the enemies of the faith with those who, when they drink the streams of doctrine, do not distort the uprightness of their actions. For all are said at that time to have drunk the water, but not all [are said] to have stood with unbended knee. And those who bent their knees while they were drinking the waters were rejected because, as the apostle witnesses, "It is not the hearers of the law who are just before God, but the doers of the law will be justified."[5] For since weakness of conduct is, as we have said, signified by this very bending of the knees, it is rightly said again by Paul: "Lift up the hands that droop and the feeble knees and make straight steps with your feet."[6] Therefore those who proceed under Christ as their leader to battle, are those who exhibit in their conduct that which they profess with their mouth, who drink spiritually the streams of doctrine and yet are not carnally distorted by wicked works. MORALS ON THE BOOK OF JOB 30.25.[7]

LAPPING LIKE DOGS. AUGUSTINE: Dogs are commendable, not abominable. They observe fidelity toward their master, and before his house they bark against enemies. He has not simply said "of dogs" but "of your dog." Nor are their teeth praised, but their tongue is: for it was not indeed to no purpose, not without a great mystery, that Gideon was bidden to lead those alone who should lap the water of the river like dogs. Of such sort not more than three hundred among so great a multitude were found. In this number is the sign of the cross because of the letter T [tau], which signifies three hundred in the Greek numeral characters. EXPLANATIONS OF THE PSALMS 68.29.[8]

PRAISEWORTHY DOGS. AUGUSTINE: Dogs should not always be taken in an evil sense; otherwise the prophet would not blame "dogs not able to bark and loving to dream."[9] Doubtless they would be praiseworthy dogs if they both knew how to bark and loved to watch. And certainly those three hundred men—a most sacred number according to the letter of the cross[10]— would not have been chosen to win the victory because they lapped water as dogs do, unless some great mystery were signified. Good dogs watch and bark to protect their house and their master, their flock and their shepherd. Finally, even here in the praises offered by the church, when a selection is made from this prophecy, it is the tongue of dogs that is mentioned, not their teeth. LETTER 149.[11]

OBTAINING TEMPERANCE. EVAGRIUS OF PONTUS: Limiting one's intake of water helps a great deal to obtain temperance. This was well understood by the three hundred Israelites accompanying Gideon just when they were preparing to attack Midian. PRAKTIKOS 17.[12]

THE FIRE OF GOD. AMBROSE: For the same reason[13] was it that when Gideon was about to overcome the Midianites, he commanded three hundred men to take pitchers, and to hold lighted torches inside the pitchers, and trumpets in their right hands. Our predecessors have preserved the explanation received from the apostles, that the pitchers are our bodies, fashioned of clay, which do not know fear if they burn with the fervor of the grace of the Spirit, and bear witness to the passion of the Lord Jesus with a loud confession of the voice. Who, then, can doubt the divinity of the Holy Spirit, since where the grace of the Spirit is, there the manifestation of the divinity

---

[5]Rom 2:13. [6]Heb 12:12. [7]LF 31:417*. [8]NPNF 1 8:295*. [9]Is 56:10. [10]As C is the symbol for 100 and is the initial letter of crux, or cross, 300 (CCC) would be most sacred. [11]FC 20:247*. [12]CS 4:21. [13]Namely, as Ambrose was arguing immediately heretofore, that God the Father, Son, and Holy Spirit are all fire, as revealed variously at the burning bush to Moses and at Pentecost, inter alia.

appears. By this evidence we infer not a diversity but the unity of the divine power. For how can there be a severance of power, where the effect of the working in all is one? Neither can there be the grace of the sacraments where there is no forgiveness of sins. What, then, is that fire? Not certainly one made up of common twigs or roaring with the burning of the reeds of the woods, but that fire which improves good deeds like gold and consumes sins like stubble. This is undoubtedly the Holy Spirit, who is called both the fire and light of the countenance of God: light as we said above: "The light of your countenance has been sealed upon us, O Lord."[14] What is, then, the light that is sealed, but that of the seal of the Spirit, believing in whom, "you were sealed," he says, "with the Holy Spirit of promise."[15] And as there is a light of the divine countenance, so, too, does fire shine forth from the countenance of God, for it is written: "A fire shall burn in his sight."[16] For the grace of the day of judgment shines beforehand, that forgiveness may follow to reward the service of the saints. O the great fullness of the Scriptures, which no one can comprehend with human genius! O greatest proof of the divine unity! For how many things are pointed out in these two verses! ON THE HOLY SPIRIT 1.167-70.[17]

VICTORY THROUGH THE CROSS. BEDE: Just as the six hundred years of life which Noah completed prior to entering the ark[18] designate the perfection of faith and confession of those who approach the church's sacraments of heavenly grace and perpetual reward, so also does the three hundred and fifty years that he lived after the great flood[19] typify the perfection of those who, having received the sacraments of life, zealously and faithfully serve the Lord until death. For we say that three hundred, because it is denoted in Greek by the letter *tau*, which is written in the shape of a cross, most aptly signifies those who resolve not to glory except in the cross of our Lord Jesus Christ.[20] Hence Gideon, at the Lord's command and with his assistance, conquered the innumerable army of the Midianites with three hundred men, thus teaching figuratively that by faith in the Lord's cross we will be victorious in the wars waged against us both by this world and by our own vices. ON GENESIS 2.9.[21]

---

[14]Ps 4:6 LXX. [15]Eph 1:13. [16]Ps 50:3 (49:3 LXX). [17]NPNF 2 10:112*. The critical edition in CSEL 79 numbers the paragraphs differently, 147-50 here. The sentence "Neither can there be the grace of the sacraments where there is no forgiveness of sins" is included here but was left untranslated and omitted by NPNF. [18]See Gen 7:6. [19]See Gen 9:28. [20]See Gal 6:14. [21]CCL 118A:140.

7:9-25 GIDEON ATTACKS THE MIDIANITES

[13]*When Gideon came, behold, a man was telling a dream to his comrade; and he said, "Behold, I dreamed a dream; and lo, a cake of barley bread tumbled into the camp of Midian, and came to the tent, and struck it so that it fell, and turned it upside down, so that the tent lay flat."* [14]*And his comrade answered, "This is no other than the sword of Gideon the son of Joash, a man of Israel; into his hand God has given Midian and all the host."*

[15]*When Gideon heard the telling of the dream and its interpretation, he worshiped; and he*

returned to the camp of Israel, and said, "Arise; for the LORD has given the host of Midian into your hand." . . .

[19]*So Gideon and the hundred men who were with him came to the outskirts of the camp at the beginning of the middle watch, when they had just set the watch; and they blew the trumpets and smashed the jars that were in their hands.* [20]*And the three companies blew the trumpets and broke the jars, holding in their left hands the torches, and in their right hands the trumpets to blow; and they cried, "A sword for the LORD and for Gideon!"* [21]*They stood every man in his place round about the camp, and all the army ran; they cried out and fled.* . . .

[25]*And they took the two princes of Midian, Oreb and Zeeb; they killed Oreb at the rock of Oreb, and Zeeb they killed at the wine press of Zeeb, as they pursued Midian; and they brought the heads of Oreb and Zeeb to Gideon beyond the Jordan.*

OVERVIEW: Gideon is a type of Christ, while Gideon's victorious army is a type of the victorious martyrs who won their battle in Christ's name (GREGORY THE GREAT). The names of Midian's princes reveal mysteries of the Savior (JEROME).

7:15 The Lord Gives Victory Over Midian

GIDEON TYPIFIES CHRIST. GREGORY THE GREAT: I think it will not be amiss if we consider at greater length this war of the Midianites, which was intentionally introduced by the prophet in comparison with the coming of the Lord.[1] For in the book of Judges Gideon is described as having fought against the Midianites. . . . Why then is it that such a battle is brought forward by the prophet, and why is victory in that battle compared with the coming of our Redeemer? Did the prophet intend to point out to us that that victorious battle under the command of Gideon was a type of the coming of our Redeemer? Such deeds were doubtless there wrought, which, the more they exceed the usual mode of fighting, are the less removed from the mystery of prophecy. For whoever went forth to battle with pitchers and lamps? Who, when going against arms, ever abandoned his arms? These things would have been truly absurd to us, had they not been terrible to the enemies. But we have learned by the evidence of the victory itself not to regard these things which were done as of little account. Gideon,

therefore, coming to battle, signifies to us the coming of our Redeemer, of whom it is written: "Lift up, O princes, your gates, and be lifted up you everlasting doors, and the King of glory shall come in. Who is this King of glory? The Lord strong and mighty. The Lord mighty in battle."[2] He prophesied of our Redeemer not only by his doings but also by his name. For Gideon is interpreted "going about in the womb." For our Lord embraces all things by the power of his majesty, and yet he came through the grace of the dispensation assuming the nature of a human being in the womb of the Virgin. Who then is he who goes about in the womb except almighty God, redeeming us by his own dispensation, embracing all things by his divinity and taking a human's nature in the womb? In the womb he was both incarnate and not confined because he was both within the womb by the substance of his infirmity and beyond the world by the power of his majesty. MORALS ON THE BOOK OF JOB 30.25.[3]

7:20 Advancing with Trumpets and Torches

AN ARMY OF GLITTERING MARTYRS. GREGORY THE GREAT: They go forth therefore to battle with trumpets, with lamps and with pitchers.

---

[1]Cf. Is 9:4, "For the yoke of his burden, and the staff of his shoulder, the rod of his oppressor, you have broken as in the day of Midian." [2]Ps 24:7-8 (23:7-8 LXX). [3]LF 31:415-16*.

This, as we have said, was an unusual order of battle. They sounded with the trumpets, and the pitchers were held in their left hands. But lamps were placed within the pitchers; but, when the pitchers were broken, the lamps appeared, and by their flashing light the frightened enemies are put to flight. The trumpets signify, therefore, the loud voice of preachers, the lamps the brightness of their miracles, and the pitchers the frailty of their bodies. For our leader led forth with him to the contest of preaching, so as by making light of their bodily safety would overthrow their enemies by dying and would overcome their swords, not by arms, not by words, but by patience. For our martyrs came armed under their leader to battle, but armed with trumpets, with pitchers, with lamps. And they sounded with their trumpets when preaching. They broke their pitchers when exposing their bodies to dissolution by the swords of the enemy in their suffering. They shone forth with lamps when, after the dissolution of their bodies, they flashed forth with miracles. And their enemies were presently put to flight, because, when they beheld the bodies of dead martyrs glittering with miracles, they were overpowered by the light of truth and believed that which they had impugned. They sounded therefore with the trumpets that the pitchers might be broken; the pitchers were broken that the lamps might appear; the lamps appeared that the enemies might be put to flight. That is, the martyrs preached until their bodies were dissolved in death; their bodies were dissolved in death that they might shine forth with miracles; they shone forth with miracles that they might overthrow their enemies with divine light, so that they might no longer stand up and resist God but fear him and submit to him. MORALS ON THE BOOK OF JOB 30.25.[4]

7:25 Oreb and Zeeb Are Killed

GIDEON'S VICTORY. JEROME: They who were glorying in their army, whose king was the Assyrian and who used to boast "I will scale the heavens,"[5] not only fell down to earth but on the ground became dung.

"Make their nobles." What nobles? Those who fight against your people. "Like Oreb and Zeeb; all their chiefs like Zebah and Zalmunna."[6] I suppose you have read in the book of Judges the story of Gideon, who is also called Jerubbaal, how he outwitted those four kings while fighting for the people of God and put an end to them. And notice the kind of nobles these Midianites are who abandoned the judgment of God: "Oreb and Zeeb; all their chiefs like Zebah and Zalmunna." Who would dream that such words contain mysteries of the Savior? The philosophers read them and smile; the rhetoricians read them and sneer. Not only the rhetoricians, however, but the Jews, too; they have not the key to their treasures, for a veil covers their eyes.[7] "Oreb" means a "hole in which a snake lurks"; "Zeeb" equals "wolf." Mark, now, the names of the chiefs of Christ's opponents: "Zebah," "victim or spoil that the wolf will strangle"; and "Zalmunna," "masters of malice." See, then, the divine secrets hidden away in names? HOMILIES ON THE PSALMS 15 (Ps 82).[8]

---

[4]LF 31:417-18*. [5]Is 14:13. [6]Ps 82:11 LXX. [7]2 Cor 3:15. [8]FC 48:115-16*.

[8:1-35 THE DEFEAT OF THE MIDIANITES]

[9:1-6 ABIMELECH SEEKS KINGSHIP]

9:7-15 JOTHAM'S PARABLE

[7]When it was told to Jotham, he went and stood on the top of Mount Gerizim, and cried aloud and said to them, "Listen to me, you men of Shechem, that God may listen to you. [8]The trees once went forth to anoint a king over them; and they said to the olive tree, 'Reign over us.' [9]But the olive tree said to them, 'Shall I leave my fatness, by which gods and men are honored, and go to sway over the trees?' [10]And the trees said to the fig tree, 'Come you, and reign over us.' [11]But the fig tree said to them, 'Shall I leave my sweetness and my good fruit, and go to sway over the trees?' [12]And the trees said to the vine, 'Come you, and reign over us' [13]But the vine said to them, 'Shall I leave my wine which cheers gods and men, and go to sway over the trees?' [14]Then all the trees said to the bramble, 'Come you, and reign over us.' [15]And the bramble said to the trees, 'If in good faith you are anointing me king over you, then come and take refuge in my shade; but if not, let fire come out of the bramble and devour the cedars of Lebanon.' "

OVERVIEW: Although fictitious, fables in secular and sacred writings communicate a message through metaphor and should not be regarded as lies (AUGUSTINE). Jotham's parable recounts the history of God's involvement with humanity and foretells the future reign of chastity (METHODIUS).

9:8-15 The Trees and the Bramble

TRUTH IN FICTION. AUGUSTINE: And no one has been so illiterate as to think that similar fables of Aesop, related for the same purpose, ought to be called lies. But also in the sacred writings such passages are found, as in the book of Judges the trees look for a king to rule over them and speak to the olive and the fig and the vine and the bramble. Surely, all this is invented in order that we may reach the matter intended by means of a narrative [that is] fictitious, to be sure, but bearing a true and not a false signification. AGAINST LYING 13.28.[1]

THE FUTURE REIGN OF CHASTITY. METHOD-IUS: But lest I should appear to some to be so-phistical, and to conjecture these things from mere probabilities, and to babble, I will bring forward to you, O virgins, from the Old Testament, written prophecy from the book of Judges, to show that I speak the truth, where the future reign of chastity was already clearly foretold. . . .

Now it is clear that these things are not said of trees growing out of the earth. Inanimate trees

---

[1]FC 16:162*.

cannot be assembled in council to choose a king since they are firmly fixed to the earth by deep roots. But on the whole these things are narrated concerning souls that—before the incarnation of Christ—luxuriated too deeply in transgressions, who approach God as beggars asking for mercy so that they may be governed by his pity and compassion. This mercy is what Scripture expresses by the figure of the olive, because oil is of great advantage to our bodies: it takes away our fatigue and ailments and offers light. For all lamplight increases when nourished by oil. So also God's mercies entirely dispel death, assist the human race and nourish the light of the heart. Consider the laws [which were in effect] from the first created man successively on to Christ. Weren't they imaginatively set forth in these words by the Scripture, in opposition to which the devil has deceived humanity? In it the fig tree has been associated with the command given to the man in paradise, because, when he was deceived, he covered his nakedness with the leaves of a fig tree;[2] and the vine [has been related] to the instruction given to Noah at the time of the deluge, because he was mocked when overpowered by wine.[3] The olive signifies the law given to Moses in the desert, because the prophetic grace, the holy oil, had failed from their inheritance when they broke the law. Lastly, the bramble aptly refers to the law

that was given to the apostles for the salvation of the world: by their instruction we have been taught virginity, which is the only figure that the devil has not been able to make into a deceptive image. For this reason, also, the four Gospels have been given, because God has four times given the gospel to the human race[4] and has instructed them by four laws, the times of which are clearly known by the diversity of the fruits. For the fig tree, on account of its sweetness and richness, represents the delights of man, which he had in paradise before the fall. Indeed, as we shall afterwards show, the Holy Spirit[5] frequently takes the fruit of the fig tree as an emblem of goodness. But the vine, on account of the gladness produced by wine and the joy of those who were saved from wrath and from the deluge, signifies the change produced from fear and anxiety into joy.[6] Moreover, the olive, on account of the oil that it produces, indicates the compassion of God, who again, after the deluge, bore patiently when people turned aside to ungodliness, so that he gave them the law and manifested himself to some, and nourished by oil the light of virtue, which is now almost extinguished. BANQUET OF THE TEN VIRGINS 10.2.[7]

---

[2]Gen 3:7. [3]Gen 9:22. [4]That is, with Adam, Noah, Moses, and Christ. [5]Jer 8:13. [6]Joel 2:22. [7]ANF 6:348*.

[9:16-25 JOTHAM'S CURSE]

[9:26-45 GAAL LEADS A REVOLT]

9:46-57 THE DEATH OF ABIMELECH

[50]*Then Abimelech went to Thebez, and encamped against Thebez, and took it.* [51]*But there was a strong tower within the city, and all the people of the city fled to it, all the men and women, and shut themselves in; and they went to the roof of the tower.* [52]*And Abimelech came to the tower, and fought against it, and drew near to the door of the tower to burn it with fire.* [53]*And a certain woman threw an upper millstone upon Abimelech's head, and crushed his skull. . . .* [56]*Thus God requited the crime of Abimelech, which he committed against his father in killing his seventy brothers.*

Overview: Abimelech's ultimate failure to become king exemplifies the illusory benefit of human wisdom (BASIL).

9:50-53 *Abimelech at the Tower of Thebez*

THE PROFIT OF HUMAN WISDOM. BASIL THE GREAT: The homicide Abimelech, bastard son of Gideon, killed the seventy legitimate sons, and, thinking he had hit upon a ruse for securing his grasp on the royal power, he destroyed his accomplices in the crime. He, however, was in turn destroyed by them and in the end was slain with a stone cast by a woman's hand. . . . In short, countless examples teach us that the profit of human wisdom is illusory, for it is a meager and lowly thing and not a great and preeminent good. On Humility.[1]

---

[1]FC 9:478*.

[10:1-9 PHILISTINE OPPRESSION]

[10:10-18 ISRAEL RETURNS TO THE LORD]

[11:1-11 JEPHTHAH'S LEADERSHIP IS SOUGHT]

[11:12-28 JEPHTHAH'S MESSAGE TO THE AMMONITES]

11:29-33 JEPHTHAH'S VOW AND VICTORY

³⁰And Jephthah made a vow to the LORD, and said, "If thou wilt give the Ammonites into my hand, ³¹then whoever comes forth from the doors of my house to meet me, when I return victorious from the Ammonites, shall be the LORD's, and I will offer him up for a burnt offering." ³²So Jephthah crossed over to the Ammonites to fight against them; and the LORD gave them into his hand. ³³And he smote them from Aroer to the neighborhood of Minnith, twenty cities, and as far as Abelkeramim, with a very great slaughter. So the Ammonites were subdued before the people of Israel.

OVERVIEW: God caused Jephthah's daughter to meet him so that he and others would be fearful of making a rash vow and sacrificing a fellow human being (EPHREM, JEROME). Augustine reasons that the wording of Jephthah's vow indicates that he intended to sacrifice a human being.

11:30-31 Jephthah Makes a Vow to the Lord

ON HUMAN SACRIFICE. EPHREM THE SYRIAN: People imitate those who do good deeds, therefore, not out of love for these good deeds but because of their utility.... The king of Moab took note of Jephthah.[1] But, because it was his firstborn and a human being rather than an animal that he killed, God took pity on him, since he did it in affliction and not through love. In the case of Jephthah, if it had been one of his servants who had been first to encounter him, he would have killed him. But, in order that people would not engage in the sacrifice of their fellow human beings, he caused his own daughter to meet him, so that others would be afraid, lest they offer human beings by vow to God. **COMMENTARY ON TATIAN'S DIATESSARON 10.3.**[2]

A RASH VOW. JEROME: And whereas he [Jovin-

ianus] prefers the fidelity of the father Jephthah to the tears of the virgin daughter, that corroborates our point. For we are not commending virgins of the world so much as those who are virgins for Christ's sake. Most Hebrews blame the father for the rash vow he made, "If you will indeed deliver the children of Ammon into my hand, then it shall be that whatsoever comes out of the doors of my house to meet me, when I return in peace from the children of Ammon, it shall be for the Lord's, and I will offer it up for a burnt offering." Supposing (the Hebrews say) a dog or an ass had met him, what would he have done? Their meaning is that God so ordered events that he who had improvidently made a vow should learn his error by the death of his daughter. **AGAINST JOVINIANUS 1.23.**[3]

HUMAN SACRIFICE INTENDED. AUGUSTINE: With these words [of his vow] at any rate Jephthah did not vow some kind of animal that he could offer as a whole burnt offering according to the law; it is neither customary now nor was it in the past that cattle would run to meet generals returning victoriously from war. As far as mute

---

[1]2 Kings 3:26-27. [2]ECTD 166*. [3]NPNF 2 6:363*.

animals are concerned, dogs often run to meet their masters and sport with them in fawning servitude. But Jephthah could not have been thinking about dogs in his vow, because it would seem that he would have vowed not only something unlawful but also something contemptible and unclean according to the law. It would have been an insult to God. Nor does he say, "I will offer as a whole burnt offering whatever will come out of the doors of my house to meet me." He says, "I will sacrifice whoever comes out of my house." Thus, there can be no doubt that he was thinking of nothing else than a human being—not his only daughter, however. Yet who would have been able to surpass her in her father's eyes except perhaps his wife? QUESTIONS ON JUDGES 49.6.[4]

---

[4]CCL 33:360-61.

11:34-40 JEPHTHAH FULFILLS HIS VOW

[34]*Then Jephthah came to his home at Mizpah; and behold, his daughter came out to meet him with timbrels and with dances; she was his only child; beside her he had neither son nor daughter.* [35]*And when he saw her, he rent his clothes, and said, "Alas, my daughter! you have brought me very low, and you have become the cause of great trouble to me; for I have opened my mouth to the* LORD, *and I cannot take back my vow."* [36]*And she said to him, "My father, if you have opened your mouth to the* LORD, *do to me according to what has gone forth from your mouth, now that the* LORD *has avenged you on your enemies, on the Ammonites."* [37]*And she said to her father, "Let this thing be done for me; let me alone two months, that I may go and wander*[p] *on the mountains, and bewail my virginity, I and my companions."* [38]*And he said, "Go." And he sent her away for two months; and she departed, she and her companions, and bewailed her virginity upon the mountains.* [39]*And at the end of two months, she returned to her father, who did with her according to his vow which he had made. She never known a man. And it became a custom in Israel* [40]*that the daughters of Israel went year by year to lament the daughter of Jephthah the Gileadite four days in the year.*

p Cn: Heb *go down*

OVERVIEW: Scripture lacks an evaluation of Jephthah's vow and its fulfillment in order to exercise the minds of those who seek the righteousness and law of God (AUGUSTINE). The apparent cruelty of the sacrifice of Jephthah's daughter begs for spiritual explanation, which is found in its symbolism of the shedding of the blood of the martyrs (ORIGEN). God was not carnally pleased by whole burnt offerings but by the meaning these sacrifices carried and the future they foreshadowed (AUGUSTINE). As this example shows, it is sometimes contrary to duty to fulfill a promise (AMBROSE). By not preventing the vow's fulfillment, God exhibits clemency, not cruelty, because the instance ensured that it would never be repeated (CHRYSOSTOM). The virgin's demeanor and resolve turn an otherwise grievous error into a pious sacrifice (AMBROSE). Augustine distinguishes between the literal sacrifice of a human being, which is displeasing to God, and the sacrificing of one's own well-being for the sake of righteousness.

11:34-38 *Celebration Turns to Grief*

SCRIPTURE'S SILENCE PROVIDES MENTAL EXERCISE. AUGUSTINE: The Scriptures do not seem to pass judgment on this vow and its fulfillment as it does quite clearly in the case of Abraham, when he was ordered to sacrifice his son and did so. Rather the Scriptures seem to have only recorded the matter and left it to the reader to evaluate, just as in the case of Judah, Jacob's son, who in ignorance lay with his daughter-in-law but committed fornication by the very act, because he thought her to be a prostitute. The Scriptures never approve nor disapprove of the act explicitly but let the matter stand, to be evaluated and contemplated after consulting the righteousness and law of God. Therefore, the Scriptures of God do not offer any comment in either the vow or its fulfillment, so that our mind might be put to work to pass judgment on this matter and so that we might now say that such a vow displeased God and led to the punishment that his only daughter, of all people, ran out to meet her father. QUESTIONS ON JUDGES 49.7.[1]

DEFENDING SACRIFICE. ORIGEN: The remaining sacrifices, of which those relating to the law are a symbol, are akin to this sacrifice. But in addition, the other sacrifices akin to this sacrifice seem to me to be the shedding of the blood of the noble martyrs. It was not in vain that the disciple John saw them standing beside the heavenly altar.[2] "But who is wise, that he shall understand these things? Or intelligent, and he shall know them?"[3]

Now comprehend, even if to a limited extent, the more spiritual sense of such sacrifices which cleanse those for whom they are offered; one must understand the sense of the sacrifice of the daughter of Jephthah who was offered as a burnt offering because of the vow of him who conquered the children of Ammon. She who was offered as a burnt offering consented to this vow, for, when her father said, "I have opened my mouth to the Lord against you," she said to him, "And if you have opened your mouth to the Lord against me, perform your vow."

Such accounts give an appearance of great cruelty to God to whom such sacrifices are offered for humanity's salvation. We need a generous and perceptive spirit in order to refute the reproaches made against providence and, at the same time, to make a defense of all the sacrifices insofar as they are rather mysterious and beyond human nature. COMMENTARY ON THE GOSPEL OF JOHN 6.276-78.[4]

11:39-40 *Jephthah Honors His Vow*

SACRIFICE AS SHADOW OF REALITY TO BE REVEALED. AUGUSTINE: As regards to the fact that Jephthah sacrificed his daughter to God as a whole burnt offering, these are the facts: he had vowed that if he were to obtain the victory, he would offer as a whole burnt offering whoever would come out of his house and meet him; because he had vowed this and won the battle and his daughter had been the one to meet him first, he fulfilled his vow. This event has become a great and rather difficult question to settle both for some who investigate the matter with piety and genuinely seek to know what this passage means and for some who out of ignorant impiety oppose the Holy Scriptures and call this a horrible misdeed that the God of the law and prophets would have delighted in sacrifices, yes, even human sacrifices. First let us reply to their calumnies by noting that the whole burnt offerings of cattle did not delight the God of the law and the prophets—or

---

[1]CCL 33:361. [2]Rev 6:9. [3]Hos 14:9 (14:10 LXX). [4]FC 80:243*.

as I prefer to say, the God of Abraham, Isaac and Jacob. What pleased God about those sacrifices was that they were full of meaning and a foreshadowing of future things. We, however, have the very substance which was foreshadowed by these sacrifices that he wished to commend to us. Moreover, there was also a very pertinent reason why those sacrifices have been changed so that they no longer are commanded but even forbidden: it is so that we may not think that God is pleased by such sacrifices according to some carnal passion. QUESTIONS ON JUDGES 49.1.[5]

FULFILLING AN OATH. AMBROSE: It is also sometimes contrary to duty to fulfill a promise or to keep an oath. As was the case with Herod, who swore that whatever was asked he would give to the daughter of Herodias, and so allowed the death of John, that he might not break his word.[6] And what shall I say of Jephthah, who offered up his daughter in sacrifice, she having been the first to meet him as he returned home victorious; whereby he fulfilled the vow which he had made that he would offer to God whatever should meet him first. It would have been better to make no promise at all than to fulfill it in the death of his daughter. DUTIES OF THE CLERGY 1.50.264.[7]

ONE DEATH PREVENTS OTHERS. CHRYSOSTOM: For Jephthah likewise, when he had promised that the first thing that met him, after a victorious battle, he would sacrifice, fell into the snare of child murder; for his daughter first meeting him, he sacrificed her, and God did not forbid it. And I know, indeed, that many of the unbelievers impugn us of cruelty and inhumanity on account of this sacrifice; but I should say that the concession in the case of this sacrifice was a striking example of providence and clemency; and that it was in care for our race that he did not prevent that sacrifice. For if after that vow and promise he had forbidden the sacrifice, many also who were subsequent to Jephthah, in the expectation that God would not receive their vows, would have

increased the number of such vows, and proceeding on their way would have fallen into child murder. But now, by suffering this vow to be actually fulfilled, he put a stop to all such cases in the future. And to show that this is true, after Jephthah's daughter had been slain, in order that the calamity might be always remembered and that her fate might not be consigned to oblivion, it became a law among the Jews that the virgins assembling at the same season should bewail during forty[8] days the sacrifice which had taken place; in order that renewing the memory of it by lamentation, they should make all people wiser for the future; and that they might learn that it was not after the mind of God that this should be done, for in that case he would not have permitted the virgins to bewail and lament her. And that what I have said is not conjectural, the event demonstrated; for after this sacrifice, no one vowed such a vow to God. Therefore also he did not indeed forbid this; but what he had expressly commanded in the case of Isaac, that he directly prohibited,[9] plainly showing through both cases that he does not delight in such sacrifices. HOMILIES CONCERNING THE STATUES 14.7.[10]

A PIOUS SACRIFICE. AMBROSE: Never shall I be led to believe that the leader Jephthah made his vow otherwise than without thought, when he promised to offer to God whatever should meet him at the threshold of his house on his return. For he repented of his vow, as afterwards his daughter came to meet him. He tore his clothes and said, "Alas, my daughter, you have entangled me, you have become a source of trouble for me." And though with pious fear and reverence he took upon himself the bitter fulfillment of his cruel task, yet he ordered and left to be observed an annual period of grief and mourning for future times. It was a hard vow, but far more bitter was its fulfillment, while he who carried it out had the greatest cause to mourn. Thus it became a

---

[5]CCL 33:358. [6]Mt 14:6ff. [7]NPNF 2 10:42-43. [8]Some manuscripts read "four" as the text. [9]Gen 22:12. [10]NPNF 1 9:434*.

rule and a law in Israel from year to year, as it says: "that the daughters of Israel went to lament the daughter of Jephthah the Gileadite four days in a year." I cannot blame the man for holding it necessary to fulfill his vow, but yet it was a wretched necessity which could only be solved by the death of his child. . . .

What, then, in the case of esteemed and learned people is full of marvel, that in the case of a virgin is found to be far more splendid, far more glorious, as she says to her sorrowing father, "Do to me according to that which has proceeded out of your mouth." But she asked for a delay of two months in order that she might go about with her companions upon the mountains to bewail fitly and dutifully her virginity now given up to death. The weeping of her companions did not move her, their grief did not prevail upon her, nor did their lamentations hold her back. She did not allow the day to pass, nor did the hour escape her notice. She returned to her father as though returning according to her own desire, and of her own will [she] urged him on when he was hesitating, and acted thus of her own free choice, so that what was at first an awful chance became a pious sacrifice. DUTIES OF THE CLERGY 3.12.78, 81.[11]

LITERAL HUMAN SACRIFICE PROHIBITED.
AUGUSTINE: But we rightly ask whether human sacrifices must have foreshadowed future events. . . . But if this were true, this type of sacrifice would not displease God. But in fact the Scriptures themselves clearly testify that human sacri-

fices displease him. For when God wanted and commanded all the firstborn to belong to him and to be his, he nonetheless wanted the firstborn of humankind to be redeemed by their parents, so that they would not entrust their firstborn children to God through immolation. . . .

Now clearly God loves and rewards those sacrifices when a just man endures injustice and struggles for the truth even to the point of death or when he is killed by enemies whom he has offended for righteousness' sake, as he has returned them good for evil, that is, love instead of hatred. . . . In imitation of Abel, thousands of martyrs have struggled for the truth to the point of death and have been sacrificed by savage enemies. The Scripture says of them, "God has tested them like gold in a furnace and he has accepted them as a whole burnt offering."[12] So too the apostle says, "I am being sacrificed."[13]

But that is not how Jephthah made a whole burnt offering to the Lord out of his daughter. Rather he offered her as a literal sacrifice in the way that it was commanded for animals to be offered and forbidden for humans to be sacrificed. What he did seems rather similar to what Abraham did. In that instance the Lord gave him a special command that this ought to be done. He did not order him by way of a general commandment that such sacrifices should take place at some time. Indeed, the general rule prohibited it. QUESTIONS ON JUDGES 49.2-4.[14]

---

[11]NPNF 2 10:80-81*. [12]Wis 3:6. [13]2 Tim 4:6. [14]CCL 33:358-60.

[12:1-7 EPHRAIM AND GILEAD FIGHT]

[12:8-15 THE JUDGESHIPS OF IBZAN, ELON, AND ABDON]

13:1-7 THE BIRTH OF SAMSON FORETOLD

[1]And the people of Israel again did what was evil in the sight of the LORD; and the LORD gave them into the hand of the Philistines for forty years.

[2]And there was a certain man of Zorah, of the tribe of the Danites, whose name was Manoah; and his wife was barren and had no children. [3]And the angel of the LORD appeared to the woman and said to her, "Behold, you are barren and have no children; but you shall conceive and bear a son. [4]Therefore beware, and drink no wine or strong drink, and eat nothing unclean, [5]for lo, you shall conceive and bear a son. No razor shall come upon his head, for the boy shall be a Nazirite to God from birth; and he shall begin to deliver Israel from the hand of the Philistines." [6]Then the woman came and told her husband, "A man of God came to me, and his countenance was like the countenance of the angel of God, very terrible; I did not ask him whence he was, and he did not tell me his name; [7]but he said to me, 'Behold, you shall conceive and bear a son; so then drink no wine or strong drink, and eat nothing unclean, for the boy shall be a Nazirite to God from birth to the day of his death.' "

OVERVIEW: Philistine oppression was God's instrument to turn the Hebrews from pride to dependence upon divine aid (AMBROSE). Samson's miraculous nativity portends his future renown (BEDE). From his beginning Samson is to be admired for the amazing feats of strength he accomplished in his youth, which brought credence to the angel's prophecy (AMBROSE).

13:1 The Philistines Oppress Israel

SUCCESS PUFFS UP THE MIND. AMBROSE: For many years the Philistines held the Hebrews in subjection after their surrender, for they had lost the prestige of faith by which their fathers had gained victory. Yet the mark of their election and the ties of their heritage had not been entirely obliterated by their Creator. But, because they were often puffed up by success, he delivered them for the most part into the power of the enemy, so that with manly dignity they would seek from heaven the remedy of their ills. We submit to God at a time when we are overwhelmed by other reverses; success puffs up the mind. This is proved not only in other matters but especially in that change of fortune by which success returned again from the Philistines to the Hebrews. LETTER 35.[1]

13:2-7 The Angel of the Lord Visits Manoah's Wife

---

[1]FC 26:177.

A MIRACULOUS NATIVITY. BEDE: Thus Jacob, the patriarch Joseph, Samson, [who was] the bravest of the chieftains, and Samuel, [who was] the most distinguished of the prophets, [all] had as their progenitors [mothers who were] for a long time barren in body but always fruitful in virtues. In this way their dignity would be known from the miraculous nativity of those who were born, and it might be proven that they would be famous in their lives, since at the very outset of their lives they transcended the norms of the human condition. HOMILIES ON THE GOSPELS 2.19.[2]

A GREAT HERO AROSE. AMBROSE: When the spirit of the Hebrews had been so crushed by long and injurious subjection that no one with manly vigor dared to encourage them to freedom, there arose in their behalf a great hero, Samson, whose destiny was ordained by God's words. He was not numbered with the many, but outstanding among the few; he was without question easily reckoned as surpassing all in bodily strength. We must regard him with great admiration from the very beginning, not because he gave great evidence of temperance and sobriety from boyhood by abstaining from wine, nor because as a Nazarite he was ever faithful to guard his sacred trust, with locks unshorn, but because from his youth—a period of softness in others, but truly remarkable in him—he worked amazing deeds of strength, perfect beyond the measure of human nature. By his deeds he soon gained credence for that divine prophecy. For no slight cause had such great graces preceded him that an angel came down to foretell to his parents his unexpected birth, the leadership he would hold and the protection he would give his people who had been tormented so long by the oppressive rule of the Philistines.

His godfearing father was of the tribe of Dan, of no low station in life, preeminent among others. His mother, a barren woman, was not unfruitful in the virtues of the soul. She was worthy to receive into the dwelling of her soul the vision of an angel, whose command she obeyed and whose words she fulfilled. She did not permit herself to know even the secrets of God without her husband's sharing of them; she told him that a man of God had appeared to her, of wondrous beauty, bringing her a prophecy that a child would be born. Because she trusted his promises she shared with her husband her trust in these heavenly pledges. LETTER 35.[3]

---

[2]CS 111:192. [3]FC 26:177-78*.

13:8-14 THE ANGEL OF THE LORD RETURNS

[8]*Then Manoah entreated the LORD, and said, "O, LORD, I pray thee, let the man of God whom thou didst send come again to us, and teach us what we are to do with the boy that will be born."*

OVERVIEW: Manoah's desire for an angelic visitation reveals his desire for a divine favor, not his jealousy (AMBROSE).

13:8 Manoah Entreated the Lord

A FAVOR FROM HEAVEN. AMBROSE: When he

learned them [the promises spoken by the angel], he devoutly begged God in prayer that he might also be granted the favor of a vision, saying, "O Lord, let your angel come to me."

I do not think, as a certain author has supposed, that he did this out of jealousy for his wife, who was remarkable for her beauty, but rather because he was moved by a desire for a favor from heaven and wished to share the benefit of the heavenly vision. One depraved by vices of the soul would not have found such favor with the Lord that an angel would return to his house, give the admonition which the fulfilling of the prophecy entailed, be suddenly raised in the form of a glowing flame, and depart. This vision, which so frightened the husband, the wife interpreted more auspiciously, turning it to joy and removing his anxiety. She said that to see God was a proof of favor, not of ill will. LETTER 35.[1]

---

[1]FC 26:178-79*.

13:15-20 MANOAH SACRIFICES TO THE LORD

[15]Manoah said to the angel of the LORD, "Pray, let us detain you, and prepare a kid for you." [16]And the angel of the LORD said to Manoah, "If you detain me, I will not eat of your food; but if you make ready a burnt offering, then offer it to the LORD. (For Manoah did not know that he was the angel of the LORD.) [17]And Manoah said to the angel of the LORD, "What is your name, so that, when your words come true, we may honor you?" [18]And the angel of the LORD said to him, "Why do you ask my name, seeing it is wonderful?" [19]So Manoah took the kid with the cereal offering, and offered it upon the rock to the LORD, to him who works[r] wonders.[s] [20]And when the flame went up toward heaven from the altar, the angel of the LORD ascended in the flame of the altar while Manoah and his wife looked on; and they fell on their faces to the ground.

r Gk Vg: Heb and working   s Heb wonders, while Manoah and his wife looked on

---

OVERVIEW: The angel's instructions to Manoah show that worship should be directed to God alone (ATHANASIUS). The only name that signifies the divine nature is the unspeakable wonder that arises in the heart concerning it (GREGORY OF NYSSA). Bestowed by God, the name "catholic" is "wonderful" in meaning (PACIAN OF BARCELONA). God's greater ability to use all of creation in order to speak is assured since even angels and men can use natural substances to communicate their thoughts (AUGUSTINE).

13:16 An Offering to the Lord

WORSHIP BELONGS TO GOD ALONE. ATHANASIUS: Therefore to God alone appertains worship, and this the very angels know, that though they excel other beings in glory, yet they are all creatures and not to be worshiped, but worship the Lord. Thus Manoah, the father of Samson, wishing to offer sacrifice to the angel, was thereupon hindered by him, saying, "Offer not to me, but to God." On the other hand, the Lord is worshiped even by the angels; for it is written: "Let all the angels of God worship him."[1] FOUR DISCOURSES AGAINST THE ARIANS 2.16.23.[2]

13:18 Why Do You Ask My Name?

UNSPEAKABLE WONDER. GREGORY OF NYSSA: And so, too, the word that was spoken to Manoah shows the fact that the Divinity is not comprehensible by the significance of his name, because, when Manoah asks to know his name, that when the promise has come actually to pass, he may by name glorify his benefactor, he says to him, "Why do you ask this? It also is wonderful"; so that by this we learn that there is one name significant of the divine nature—the wonder, namely, that arises unspeakably in our hearts concerning it. AGAINST EUNOMIUS 8.1.[3]

THE NAME CATHOLIC. PACIAN OF BARCELONA: Concerning the name Catholic I answered fully and in a conciliatory manner.[4] For I said that it mattered to neither one of us what the other was called. But if you demanded to know the meaning of the name, whatever it might be, it is "wonderful"—whether it means "one in all" or "one above all" or, an interpretation I have not mentioned previously, "the king's child"—that is, the Christian people. Certainly this name, which has endured for so many centuries, was not bestowed upon us by ourselves but by God. And truly I rejoice that, although you may have preferred other names, you agree that the name belongs to us. And what if you were to deny this? Then nature would cry out. Or if you still have doubts, let us say nothing about it. We will both be that

which we are called, under the witness of the antiquity of the name. If, however, quite stubbornly you continue to ask, take care lest that "man of might" may exclaim to you, "Why do you ask my name? The name itself is wonderful." I then sensibly added that we ought not to consider whence Catholics acquired this name, because neither was it traditionally considered to represent a charge against the Valentinians if they were named after Valentinus, nor against the Phrygians, if from Phrygia, nor against the Novatians, if after Novatian. LETTER 2.2.[5]

13:20 The Angel of the Lord Ascends in the Flame

ALL THINGS ARE SUBJECT TO GOD. AUGUSTINE: For if an angel is able to use air, mist, cloud, fire, and any other natural substance or physical species; and a person [is able] to use, face, tongue, hand, pen, letters, or any other means for the purpose of communicating the secret things of his own mind: in a word, if, though he is human, he sends human messengers, and he says to one, "Go," and he goes; and to another, "Come," and he comes; and to his servant, "Do this," and he does it";[6] with how much greater and more effectual power does God—to whom, as Lord, all things are subject—use both angel and man in order to declare whatever pleases him? EXPLANATIONS OF THE PSALMS 78.5.[7]

---

[1]Heb 1:6. [2]NPNF 2 4:360-61. [3]NPNF 2 5:200-201*. [4]In his second letter to the Novatianist Sympronian, Pacian continues to defend and elaborate upon the meaning and use of the label Catholic. [5]FC 99:28. [6]See Lk 7:8. [7]NPNF 1 8:368*.

13:21-25 THE BIRTH OF SAMSON

²¹*The angel of the* Lord *appeared no more to Manoah and to his wife. Then Manoah knew that he was the angel of the* Lord. ²²*And Manoah said to his wife, "We shall surely die, for we have seen God."* ²³*But his wife said to him, "If the* Lord *had meant to kill us, he would not have accepted a burnt offering and a cereal offering at our hands, or shown us all these things, or now announced to us such things as these."* ²⁴*And the woman bore a son, and called his name Samson; and the boy grew, and the* Lord *blessed him.* ²⁵*And the Spirit of the* Lord *began to stir him in Mahaneh-dan, between Zorah and Eshta-ol.*

Overview: Manoah's response to the angelic visit shows that even a vision of God overwhelms human beings, let alone God's actual nature (Gregory of Nazianzus). It was the Spirit's presence and guidance that enabled Samson to accomplish his feats of strength. That it is said that the Lord departed from Samson later shows that the Spirit and the Lord are one and the same (Ambrose). Samson, as a vessel of the spirit of the Lord, was filled with God's strength (Caesarius of Arles).

13:22 We Shall Surely Die

A Vision of God. Gregory of Nazianzus: Must you not show respect for Manoah, the Old Testament judge.... Manoah was overwhelmed by the sight of God in a vision. "Wife," he said, "we are lost, we have seen God"—meaning by this that even a vision of God is too much for human beings, let alone God's nature. Theological Orations 2 (28).19.[1]

13:25 The Spirit of the Lord

The Spirit's Guidance. Ambrose: And why should I speak of all one by one? Samson, born by the divine promise, had the Spirit accompanying him, for we read, "The Lord blessed him, and the Spirit of the Lord began to be with him in the camp." And so foreshadowing the future mystery, he demanded a wife of the aliens, which, as it is written, his father and mother did not know about, because it was from the Lord. And rightly was he esteemed stronger than others, because the Spirit of the Lord guided him, under whose guidance he alone put to flight the foreign peoples, and at another time inaccessible to the bite of the lion, he, unconquerable in his strength, tore the lion apart with his hands. Would that Samson had been as careful to preserve grace, as he was strong to overcome the beast! On the Holy Spirit 2, Prologue 5.[2]

The Lord Is the Spirit. Ambrose: Above, you read that "the Lord blessed him, and the Spirit of the Lord began to go with him." Farther on it is said, "And the Spirit of the Lord came upon him." Again he says, "If I be shaven, my strength will depart from me."[3] After he was shaven, see what the Scripture says: "The Lord," it says, "departed from him."[4]

You see, then, that he who went with him, himself departed from him. The same is, then, the Lord, who is the Spirit of the Lord, as also the apostle says: "The Lord is the Spirit, now where the Spirit of the Lord is, there is liberty."[5] On the Holy Spirit 2.1.17-18.[6]

---

[1]FGFR 235. [2]NPNF 2 10:115*. [3]Judg 16:17. [4]Judg 16:20. [5]2 Cor 3:17. [6]NPNF 2 10:117*.

STRENGTH FOUND IN THE SPIRIT. CAESARIUS OF ARLES: The strength which Samson possessed, dearly beloved, came from the grace of God rather than by nature, for if he had been naturally strong his power would not have been taken away when his hair was cut. Where, then, was that most powerful strength, except in what the Scripture says: "The Spirit of the Lord walked with him"? Therefore, his strength belonged to the Spirit of the Lord. In Samson was the vessel, but the fullness was in the Spirit. A vessel can be filled and emptied. Moreover, every vessel has its perfection from something else, and so in Paul grace was commended when he was called a vessel of election.[7] SERMON 118.2.[8]

---

[7]See Rom 9:21-23. [8]FC 47:183.

14:1-4 SAMSON DEMANDS A PHILISTINE WIFE

[1]*Samson went down to Timnah, and at Timnah he saw one of the daughters of the Philistines.* [2]*Then he came up, and told his father and mother, "I saw one of the daughters of the Philistines at Timnah; now get her for me as my wife."* [3]*But his father and mother said to him, "Is there not a woman among the daughters of your kinsmen, or among all our people, that you must go to take a wife from the uncircumcised Philistines?" But Samson said to his father, "Get her for me; for she pleases me well."*

OVERVIEW: Samson, who is determined to marry a Timnite woman, hopes to flee the deceitful lust of youth or desires an occasion to break Philistine tyranny in Ambrose's retelling of his judgeship.

14:1-3 A Daughter of the Philistines

A MARRIAGE REQUEST. AMBROSE: Samson, then graced by such favors from heaven, turned his thoughts to marriage as soon as he reached manhood, whether because he detested in his mind the free and familiar manner of deceitful lust in the young, or because he was seeking a reason for loosing from the necks of his people the power and harsh tyranny of the Philistines. Going down, therefore, to Thamnatha[1] [Timnah] (this is the name of a city in that country which then was inhabited by the Philistines), he saw a maiden of pleasing appearance and beautiful countenance. He asked his parents, who were guiding him on his way, to ask her in marriage for him. They did not realize that his purpose was so set that, if the Philistines refused her to him, he would become very angry, nor that they, if they gave their consent, would be bringing an end to the wrong treatment of the conquered. Since from intercourse a sense of equality and kindness grows apace, and, if offense is given, the desire for revenge becomes deeper, his parents thought that he should avoid her because she was a stranger. In vain did they try to change his purpose by lawful objections; finally, then, they gave their consent to the wishes of their son. LETTER 35.[2]

---

[1]LXX. [2]FC 26:179.

14:5-9 SAMSON SLAYS A LION

⁵*Then Samson went down with his father and mother to Timnah, and he came to the vineyards of Timnah. And behold, a young lion roared against him;* ⁶*and the Spirit of the Lord came mightily upon him, and he tore the lion asunder as one tears a kid; and he had nothing in his hand. But he did not tell his father or his mother what he had done.* ⁷*Then he went down and talked with the woman; and she pleased Samson well.* ⁸*And after a while he returned to take her; and he turned aside to see the carcass of the lion, and behold, there was a swarm of bees in the body of the lion, and honey.* ⁹*He scraped it out into his hands, and went on, eating as he went; and he came to his father and mother, and gave some to them, and they ate. But he did not tell them that he had taken the honey from the carcass of the lion.*

OVERVIEW: Surprised by a lion while on his way to visit his betrothed, Samson's strength is his only weapon against it. On his return home, he discovers honey in its carcass, which he carries off as a fitting gift for his bride (AMBROSE). The lion can be understood to prefigure Christ in whose mouth the sweet word of God is found, and to prefigure the Gentiles who believed as those who have become the body of Christ (CAESARIUS OF ARLES).

14:5-9 Samson's Secret

THE LION AND THE HONEY. AMBROSE: Samson obtained his request and upon his return to visit his promised bride he turned off the road for a short while; there a lion came out of the woods to meet him, a truly fierce beast, because released from the forest. No comrade, no weapon was ready at hand; the shame of fleeing and an inner sense of power gave him courage. As the lion rushed upon him he caught it in his arms and killed it with his grasp, leaving it lying there beside the road on a heap of forest wood. The spot was thick with the grassy growth of fodder and planted, too, with vineyards. He felt sure that the spoils of a savage beast would be of little importance to his beloved spouse, because the times of such events [as marriage] are made charming not by savage trophies but by genteel joys and festal garlands. Later, upon his return along the same road, he stumbled upon a honeycomb in the lion's belly, and carried it off as a gift to his parents and the maiden, for such gifts suit a bride. After he had tasted the honey, he gave them the honeycomb to eat, but he did not disclose where it came from. LETTER 35.[1]

THE LION IS CHRIST. CAESARIUS OF ARLES: Many of the fathers have spoken a great deal about this lion, beloved brothers, and all of them have said what is fitting and in accord with the facts. Some have said that the lion prefigured Christ our Lord. Truly, this is very appropriate, for to us Christ is a lion in whose mouth we found the food of honey after his death.[2] What is sweeter than the Word of God? Or what is stronger than his right hand? In whose mouth after death is there food and bees, except his in whose word is the good of our salvation and the congregation of the Gentiles? The lion can further be understood as the Gentiles who believed. First, it was a body of vanity, but is now the body of Christ in which the apostles like bees stored the honey of wisdom gathered from the dew of heaven and the flowers of divine grace. Thus,

---

[1]FC 26:179-80. [2]The LXX locates the honey in the lion's "mouth."

food came out of the mouth of the one who died; because nations which were as fierce as lions at first, accepted with a devout heart the word of God which they received and produced the fruit

of salvation. SERMON 119.1.[3]

---

[3]FC 47:189-90.

14:10-14 SAMSON'S RIDDLE AND WAGER

[12]*And Samson said to them, "Let me now put a riddle to you; if you can tell me what it is, within the seven days of the feast, and find it out, then I will give you thirty linen garments and thirty festal garments;* [13]*but if you cannot tell me what it is, then you shall give me thirty linen garments and thirty festal garments." And they said to him, "Put your riddle, that we may hear it."* [14]*And he said to them,*

"Out of the eater came something to eat.

Out of the strong came something sweet."

And they could not in three days tell what the riddle was.

OVERVIEW: The conversion of the Gentiles is prophesied in the story of Samson's interactions with the lion. Likewise, his riddle and wager contain mysteries regarding Christ (AMBROSE). Prefiguring the Jews, Samson killed the lion of the tribe of Judah, who gives believers the spiritual food of his honey (CAESARIUS OF ARLES).

14:14 Samson's Riddle

AN UTTERANCE OF PROPHECY. AMBROSE: And perhaps this was not only a prodigy of valor, but also a mystery of wisdom, an utterance of prophecy. For it does not seem to have been without a purpose that, as he was going to his marriage, a roaring lion met him, which he tore asunder with his hands, in whose body, when about to enjoy the wished-for wedlock, he found a swarm of bees, and took honey from its mouth, which he gave to his father and mother to eat. The people of the Gentiles who believed had honey; the people that were previously savage are now the people of Christ.

Nor is the riddle without mystery, which he set forth to his companions: "Out of the eater came forth meat, and out of the strong came forth sweetness." And there was a mystery up to the point of the three days in which its answer was sought in vain, which could not be made known except by the faith of the church, on the seventh day, the time of the law being completed, after the passion of the Lord. For thus you find that the apostles did not understand, "because Jesus was not yet glorified."[1] ON THE HOLY SPIRIT 2, PROLOGUE 6-7.[2]

THE LION OF JUDAH. CAESARIUS OF ARLES: Since sacred Scripture can be understood and interpreted in many ways as a pearl, Christ himself is not unfittingly regarded as the lion. . . . But he was victorious in his triumph over the devil through his death on the cross. Indeed, he is both the lion and the lion's cub: a lion because equal to

---

[1]Jn 7:39. [2]NPNF 2 10:116*.

the Father; the lion's cub because the Son of the Father who was killed by his own will and rose again by his own power. Of him it is written: "Who will disturb him?"[3] Voluntarily offering his father the sacrifice of his body for us, he who is most high forever takes up the life which he himself had laid down, as he testifies. That Samson says, "Out of the eater came forth food, and out of the strong came forth sweetness," is fittingly applied to Christ. By his teaching he both chews over the spiritual food of his honey and in his

promises gives it to us. In still another way this can be understood concerning Christ. This lion, that is, Christ from the tribe of Judah, victoriously descended into hell to snatch us from the mouth of the hostile lion. For this reason he hunts in order to protect, seizes in order to free, leads people captive in order to restore them when freed to their eternal country. SERMON 119.2.[4]

---

[3]Gen 49:9. [4]FC 47:190-91*.

14:15-20 THE DECEIT OF THE TIMNITES

[15]*On the fourth[t] day they said to Samson's wife, "Entice your husband to tell us what the riddle is, lest we burn you and your father's house with fire. Have you invited us here to impoverish us?"* [16]*And Samson's wife wept before him . . .* [17]*and on the seventh day he told her, because she pressed him hard. Then she told the riddle to her countrymen.* [18]*And the men of the city said to him on the seventh day before the sun went down,*

"What is sweeter than honey?
What is stronger than a lion?"
And he said to them,

"If you had not plowed with my heifer,
you would not have found out my riddle."
[19]*And the Spirit of the LORD came mightily upon him, and he went down to Ashkelon and killed thirty men of the town, and took their spoil and gave the festal garments to those who had told the riddle. In hot anger he went back to his father's house.*

t Gk Syr: Heb *seventh*

OVERVIEW: The story of Samson's riddle and wager is recounted to exemplify the danger of marrying a woman who is a stranger to the faith. The events illustrate life coming forth from death, in which the presence of honey symbolizes the remnant's salvation according to the election of grace (AMBROSE). As part of the Old Testament, the prophetic nature of Samson's actions removes any

questions concerning his righteousness. His riddle signifies Christ's resurrection and the salvation of the Gentiles, while the heifer represents the church that received the secrets of the faith (CAESARIUS OF ARLES).

14:18-19 The Wager Is Settled

A DANGEROUS MARRIAGE. AMBROSE: Why should I mention many examples? Of the many, I shall set forth one, and by the mention of this one it may be clear how dangerous it is to marry a woman who is a stranger [to the faith]. Who more than the Nazarite, Samson, ever was mightier and from the cradle more endowed with strength by the Spirit of God? Yet he was betrayed by a woman and because of her he was unable to stay in God's good favor. . . .

By chance one day, during a nuptial feast, the young people at the banquet challenged one another to a game of question and answer. And while one caught up the other with spicy banter, as is the custom on such occasions, the contest, which had begun in fun, grew heated. Then Samson proposed the question to his fellow guests: "Out of the eater came forth meat, and out of the strong came forth sweetness." He promised as the reward for their wisdom that those who guessed it should have thirty shirts and the same number of coats, for that was the number of men present, but if they did not solve it they should pay a forfeit.

Since they could not untie the knot and solve the riddle, they prevailed upon his bride, using repeated threats and constant entreaty, that she ask her husband for the answer to the question as a mark of his devotion in return for her love. Truly terrified in mind, or perhaps in the plaintive manner of a woman, she began her supposedly loving complaints, pretending that she was sorely grieved that her husband did not love her: she who was his life partner and confidant did not know her husband's secret and was treated like the rest of his friends and not entrusted with her husband's secret. She even said, "You hate me and do not love me whom until now you have deceived."

These and other remarks overcame him, and, weakened by her womanly charms, he revealed to his beloved the riddle which he had proposed. She in turn revealed it to her countrymen. Seven days later, before sunset, which was the time agreed for the solving of the riddle, they gave the answer which they had learned and which they expressed thus: "What is stronger than a lion? What is sweeter than honey?" And he answered that nothing is more treacherous than woman, saying, "If you had not ploughed with my heifer, you would not have found out my riddle." Immediately he went down to Ashkelon, killed thirty men, stripped off their garments and gave them as the reward he had promised to those who had solved the riddle. LETTER 35.[1]

MYSTERY AND MEANING. AMBROSE: "What," answer they, "is sweeter than honey, and what is stronger than a lion?" To which he replied, "If you had not farmed with my heifer, you would not have found out my riddle." O divine mystery! O manifest sacrament! We have escaped from the slayer, we have overcome the strong one. The food of life is now there, where before was the hunger of a miserable death. Dangers are changed into safety, bitterness into sweetness. Grace came forth from the offense, power from weakness, and life from death.

There are, however, those who think, on the other hand, that the wedlock could not have been established unless the lion of the tribe of Judah had been slain; and so in his body, that is, the church, bees were found who store up the honey of wisdom, because after the passion of the Lord the apostles believed more fully. This lion, then, Samson as a Jew killed, but in it he found honey, as in the figure of the heritage which was to be redeemed, that the remnant might be saved according to the election of grace.[2]

"And the Spirit of the Lord," it is said, "came upon him, and he went down to Ascalon, and killed thirty men of them." For he could not fail to carry off the victory who saw the mysteries. And so in the garments they receive the reward of wisdom, the badge of intercourse, who resolve and answer the riddle. ON THE HOLY SPIRIT 2, PROLOGUE 8-10.[3]

---

[1]FC 26:176-81*. [2]Rom 11:5. [3]NPNF 2 10:116*.

A MATTER OF PROPHECY. CAESARIUS OF ARLES: Let us see further what kind of a parable Samson proposed to the strangers. "Out of the eater came forth food," he said, "and out of the strong came forth sweetness." This parable was revealed, carried to friends and solved. Samson was defeated. If he was a just man, the fact is well hidden and the justice of the man is deep down. For since he is read to have been overcome by the flattery of a woman and went in to a harlot, his merits seem to totter in the eyes of those who do not understand so well the secrets of truth. Indeed, he is commanded by a precept of the Lord to take the harlot as his wife. Perhaps we can say that in the Old Testament this was not blameworthy or disgraceful, seeing that whatever was said or done was a matter of prophecy. SERMON 118.2.[4]

CHRIST AND THE CHURCH. CAESARIUS OF ARLES: As to the question implied in the words "Out of the eater came forth food, and out of the strong came forth sweetness," what else does it signify but Christ rising from the dead? Truly, out of the eater, that is, from death which devours and consumes all things, came forth that food which said, "I am the bread that has come down from heaven."[5] The Gentiles were converted and received the sweetness of life from him whom human iniquity loaded with bitterness and offered bitter vinegar and gall as a drink. Thus, from the mouth of the dead lion, that is, from the death of Christ who lay down and slept like the lion, there proceeded a swarm of bees, that is, of Christians. When Samson said, "If you had not ploughed with my heifer, you would not have solved my riddle," this heifer is the church which had the secrets of our faith revealed to her by her husband. By the teaching and preaching of the apostles and saints, she spread to the ends of the earth the mysteries of the Trinity, the resurrection, judgment and the kingdom of heaven, promising the rewards of eternal life to all who understand and know them. SERMON 118.3.[6]

---

[4]FC 47:183. [5]Jn 6:41. [6]FC 47:185*.

15:1-8 SAMSON'S REVENGE

[1]*After a while, at the time of wheat harvest, Samson went to visit his wife with a kid; and he said, "I will go in to my wife in the chamber." But her father would not allow him to go in.* [2]*And her father said, "I really thought that you utterly hated her; so I gave her to your companion. Is not her younger sister fairer than she? Pray take her instead."* [3]*And Samson said to them, "This time I shall be blameless in regard to the Philistines, when I do them mischief."* [4]*So Samson went and caught three hundred foxes, and took torches; and he turned them tail to tail, and put a torch between each pair of tails.* [5]*And when he had set fire to the torches, he let the foxes go into the standing grain of the Philistines, and burned up the shocks and the standing grain, as well as the olive orchards.* [6]*Then the Philistines said, "Who has done this?" And they said, "Samson, the son-in-law of the Timnite, because he has taken his wife and given her to his companion." And the*

Philistines came up, and burned her and her father with fire. ⁷And Samson said to them, "If this is what you do, I swear I will be avenged upon you, and after that I will quit." ⁸And he smote them hip and thigh with great slaughter; and he went down and stayed in the cleft of the rock of Etam.

OVERVIEW: Angered by the loss of his bride, Samson wreaks public revenge over his personal insult, which ultimately results in her death (AMBROSE). The friend who married his betrothed prefigures all heretics who attempt to possess the Lord's bride (CAESARIUS OF ARLES). Enduring a famine brought on by God, the Philistines, who were terrified of Samson, perished after their crops were burned (EPHREM).

The activity of the foxes is likened to the spread of heresy. As the foxes entered and burned the cornfields, false doctrine cunningly scattered heresy in the church (PRUDENTIUS). Believers are admonished to avoid the deceits of the foxes of perverse teachings by being wise as serpents and as simple as doves (MAXIMUS OF TURIN). The foxes, whose tails represent the results of heresy, destroy the good works of those who are seduced by them and are themselves destroyed by the fire they bear (CAESARIUS OF ARLES).

15:1-8 Samson Retaliates for the Loss of His Bride

A WRONG AVENGED. AMBROSE: Moreover, Samson did not live with the girl whose treachery he had discovered but, instead, returned home to his own country. But the maid, in fear and dread of the wrath of one so wronged, afraid lest his wrath be vented on her, agreed to marry another man, one whom Samson considered a friend of his, a bridal companion on his wedding day. Even though their union was offered as an excuse, she did not escape the peril of his hatred. When this became known and he was denied an opportunity of going to his wife, for her father said that she had married someone else, but that he might, if he wished, marry her sister, sorely stung with wrong, he made plans to wreak public revenge in

anger over his personal affront. He caught three hundred foxes and, at the end of summer when the grain was ripe in the fields, coupled them tail to tail and fastened torches between their tails, tying them with unbreakable knots. Then, to avenge the affront, he sent them into the standing corn fields which the Philistines had cut. The foxes, driven mad by the fire, spread the blaze wherever they ran and burned the corn stalks. Greatly disturbed by their loss, for their entire harvest had perished, the owners went and told their leaders. They dispatched men to the Thamnathite[1] [Timnite] woman, who had given her troth to more than one husband, and also to her house and parents. They said that she was the cause of her own destruction and harm, but that it was not right for the husband who was wronged to avenge himself by injuring the whole people. LETTER 35.[2]

HERETICS PREFIGURED. CAESARIUS OF ARLES: Then follow the words "Samson was angry because a friend married his wife." This friend prefigured all heretics. It is a great mystery, my brothers. Heretics who divide the church have wanted to marry the wife of the Lord and carry her away. By departing from the church and the Gospels, they attempt through adulterous wickedness to seize the church, that is, the body of Christ, as their portion. For this reason that faithful servant and friend of the Lord's bride says, "I betrothed you to one spouse, that I might present you a chaste virgin to Christ."[3] Moreover, through the zeal of faith and a rebuke he touches the person of his wicked companion: "And I fear lest, as the serpent seduced Eve, so your minds may be corrupted from the truth which is in

---

[1]LXX. [2]FC 26:181-82*. [3]2 Cor 11:2.

Christ Jesus."[4] Who are the companions, that is, the heretical deserters who want to seize the Lord's spouse, unless Donatus, Arius, Manichaeus,[5] and other vessels of error and perdition? SERMON 118.4.[6]

15:4-5 Foxes with Torches Burn Philistine Crops

THE TERROR OF SAMSON. EPHREM THE SYRIAN: Just as those who travel about in the pathless desert tremble at serpents on the ground, and those who travel on the pathways are also terrified of vipers that hide on the paths, so were the Philistines, who traveled on paths and in the pathless desert, terrified of Samson. "To bite the horse's heels and throw its rider backward."[7] It was during the great famine, which God had brought upon the Philistines, that Samson burned their crops by means of foxes, for fire was carried on their bodies like a rider on its horse. Then the Philistines keeled over from lack of bread and then fell backwards from lack of nourishment. ON GENESIS 42.9.[8]

LESSONS FROM MIGHTY DEEDS. PRUDENTIUS:
Samson resistless because of his hair is attacked
    by a lion;
When he killed the wild beast, from its mouth
    there flowed streams of honey,[9]
And from an ass's jawbone comes forth a fountain of water:[10]
Folly with water overflows and virtue with
    sweetness.
Samson catches three hundred foxes and arms
    them with firebrands,
Which he ties to their tails, and he lets them
    go into the cornfields
Of the Philistines to burn their crops: thus the
    fox of false doctrine
Cunningly scatters the flames of heresy over
    our vineyards.
SCENES FROM SACRED HISTORY 17-18.[11]

THE FOXES OF FALSE TEACHING. MAXIMUS OF TURIN: Let us avoid, then, brothers, let us avoid the pestilential deceits of the insidious foxes [heretics]. Let us avoid the deadly frauds of wicked persons lest, like the foxes which that famous strong man Samson once sent into the Philistines' fields, bearing torches on their tails that burned up everything with their flames, the foxes of perverse teachings in like manner either get hold of the fruits of our fields by deceitful traps or consume them by burning flames. Let us, therefore, as we read, be simple and clever—that is to say, simple as doves and clever as serpents, so that the cleverness of the serpents might protect the simplicity of the doves. SERMON 41.5.[12]

THE CONSEQUENCES OF HERESY. CAESARIUS OF ARLES: Now let us see what Samson did when he was injured by his friend in the person of his wife. He took foxes, that is, adulterous friends of whom it is said in the Canticle of Canticles, "Catch us the foxes, the little foxes that damage the vineyards."[13] What does it mean, "catch"? It means seize, convict, repress them, lest the vines of the church be destroyed. What else does it mean to catch foxes, except to convict heretics with the authority of the divine law, to fasten and fetter them with the testimony of holy Scripture as with chains? Samson caught the foxes and put torches of fire on their tails after they were coupled. What do the tails of the foxes tied together signify? What are foxes' tails except the results of heresy (for their first appearance is flattering and deceitful) bound fast, that is, condemned and dragging fire in their trail? Moreover, they

---

[4]2 Cor 11:3. [5]Caesarius criticizes the heretical teachings of these men for leading the church astray. Donatists believed that the purity of the church meant that it was a congregation of saints alone. Therefore, if a bishop lapsed under persecution but later repented he was to be excluded as a minister of the church because of the magnitude of his sin. Arius stressed the human nature of Christ to the exclusion of his divinity. Unlike the Father, he argued, Christ had a beginning and was therefore the foremost of God's creations. Manichaeans held the dualist view that good and evil were discrete yet equal forces that battled eternally. [6]FC 47:185-86*. [7]Gen 49:17. [8]FC 91:205-6*. [9]Judg 14:8 LXX. [10]Judg 15:19 LXX. [11]FC 52:184-85. [12]ACW 50:103*. [13]Song 2:15.

destroy the fruits and good works of those who consent to their seductions. People are told, Do not listen to heretics, do not consent to them or be seduced by them. They reply, Why? Has not that one or so and so listened to heretics? Has not that other Christian committed such vices, such adultery, or such robbery? And what evil has befallen him? Those are the first appearances of the foxes, and souls that are seduced pay attention; the fire is behind them. Nothing has happened to him now, it is said. Since nothing has gone before, will nothing be dragged after? He is sure to come to the fire which follows. Do you think further that the heretics drag along the fire with which to burn the fruits of their enemies but are not themselves burned? Doubtless, when the foxes burned the harvest they, too, were burned. This judgment will come back upon the heretics; what they do not see now they have behind them. They delight people with their flattery and show themselves at first free from restraint. But at the judgment of God their tails are bound, that is, they drag fire upon themselves afterwards, since wickedness preceded their punishment. SERMON 118.4.[14]

---

[14]FC 47:186-87*.

15:9-17 THE MEN OF JUDAH BRING SAMSON TO THE PHILISTINES

[9]*Then the Philistines came up and encamped in Judah, and made a raid on Lehi.* [10]*And the men of Judah said, "Why have you come up against us?" They said, "We have come up to bind Samson, to do to him as he did to us."* [11]*Then three thousand men of Judah went down to the cleft of the rock of Etam, and said to Samson, "Do you not know that the Philistines are rulers over us? What then is this that you have done to us?" And he said to them, "As they did to me, so have I done to them."* [12]*And they said to him, "We have come down to bind you, that we may give you into the hands of the Philistines." And Samson said to them, "Swear to me that you will not fall upon me yourselves."* [13]*They said to him, "No; we will only bind you and give you into their hands; we will not kill you." So they bound him with two new ropes, and brought him up from the rock.*

[14]*When he came to Lehi, the Philistines came shouting to meet him; and the Spirit of the LORD came mightily upon him, and the ropes which were on his arms became as flax that has caught fire, and his bonds melted off his hands.* [15]*And he found a fresh jawbone of an ass, and put out his hand and seized it, and with it he slew a thousand men.* [16]*And Samson said,*

"With the jawbone of an ass,
heaps upon heaps,
with the jawbone of an ass
have I slain a thousand men."

OVERVIEW: Succumbing to Philistine pressure and discounting Samson's desire for revenge, a group of men from Judah bind him and deliver him to his enemies. Seizing the jawbone of an ass, Samson slaughters the Philistines and wins a great victory yet fails to give God glory (AMBROSE). The dry bones of the ass prefigured the Gentiles, who became instruments of justice in the holy hands of Christ the true Samson (CAESARIUS OF ARLES).

15:9-13 The Men of Judah Deliver Samson to the Philistines

SAMSON'S CAPTURE. AMBROSE: Samson still did not content himself with this wrong against the Philistines, nor was he content with what he had done in revenge. He slaughtered them in a great orgy of bloodshed, and many died by the sword. He then went to Elam to a stream in the desert. The rock there was a fortification belonging to the tribe of Judah. The Philistines, who did not dare attack him or to climb the steep and hazardous fortification, denounced the tribe of Judah and rose up, urging the tribe to battle. They saw that justice would be done otherwise, if the men, who were their subjects and paid tribute, seemed about to lose a rightful and fair treatment in public affairs just because of another's crime. In consolation, they demanded that they hand over the perpetrator of such a crime and on this condition they would be unharmed.

The men of the tribe of Judah, hearing this stipulation, gathered three thousand of their men and went up to him, maintaining that they were the subjects of the Philistines and had to obey them, not from choice but through fear of danger. They put the blame for their deed upon those who had the right to force them. Then he said, "And what form of justice is it, O race of the sons of Abraham, that the wrong of first betrothing and then stealing my spouse should be my punishment, and that one may not avenge with impunity a wrong done to one's home? Are you stooping in submission to little domestic slaves?

Will you make yourselves agents of another's insolence and turn your own hands upon yourselves? If I must die for the sorrow which is understandably mine, I will gladly die at the hands of the Philistines. My home has been assailed, my wife has been harassed. If I may not live without their evil deeds, at least I may die without crimes being committed by my people. Have I not returned an injury which I received? Have I inflicted it? Consider whether the exchange was a fitting one. They complain of damage to their crops; I, the loss of my wife. Compare sheaves of wheat and the marital union. They have themselves seen proof of my pain, the injuries which they have avenged. See what service they consider you worthy of. They want the one put to death whom they thought should be avenged, whom they injured, and to whom they gave the weapon of revenge. If you bring my neck to bend to the proud, hand me over to the enemy, but do not yourselves kill me. I do not shrink from death, but I dread your being contaminated. If you yield to those insolent men through fear, bind my hands with cords. Defenseless though they be, they will find their weapons in the knotted cords. Surely, the enemy must think you have made sufficient payment of your promise if you deliver me alive into their power."

In answer, the three thousand who had climbed up the mountain gave him an oath that they would not use force against his life provided he would wear chains, so that they could hand him over and free themselves of the crime with which they were charged. LETTER 35.[1]

15:14-16 Samson Slays with the Jawbone of an Ass[2]

KILLING WITH A JAWBONE. AMBROSE: When he had received their pledge, Samson left the cave and abandoned his rocky fortification. When he saw the strong Philistines approaching to take him, although he was bound with double cords,

---

[1]FC 26:182-83. [2]See also Theodoret's comment for 1 Sam 17:47.

he groaned in spirit and broke his bonds. Then, seizing the jawbone of an ass lying there, he struck a thousand men and put the rest to flight in a magnificent display of strength, while battle lines of armed men fell back before a single defenseless man. Any and all who dared to approach him were slain with easy effort. Flight staved off death for the rest. Thus, even today, the place is called Agon, because there Samson won a great victory by his overwhelming strength.

I wish that he had been as controlled in victory as he was strong against the enemy! But, as usually happens, a soul unused to good fortune, which ought to have attributed the outcome of the engagement to God's favor and protection, attributed it to himself, saying, "With the jawbone of an ass I have destroyed . . . a thousand men." He neither erected an altar nor sacrificed a victim to God, but, failing to sacrifice and taking glory to himself, he called the place "the killing of the jawbone" to immortalize his triumph with an everlasting name. LETTER 35.[3]

THE ASS PREFIGURES THE GENTILES. CAESARIUS OF ARLES: Now when Samson destroyed a thousand men with a jawbone from the body of an ass, the Gentiles were prefigured in the ass; for thus Scripture speaks concerning both Jews and Gentiles: "An ox knows its owner, and an ass its master's manger."[4] Before the coming of Christ all the Gentiles were torn to pieces by the devil and lay scattered like dry bones from the ass's body, but when Christ the true Samson came, he seized them all in his holy hands. He restored them by the hands of his power, and with them overcame his and our adversaries. Thus, we who had given our members to the devil before so that he might kill us, were seized by Christ and became instruments of justice unto God. SERMON 119.4.[5]

---

[3]FC 26:183-84*. [4]Is 1:3. [5]FC 47:192*.

15:18-20 THE LORD PROVIDES WATER

[18]*And he was very thirsty, and he called on the LORD and said, "Thou hast granted this great deliverance by the hand of thy servant; and shall I now die of thirst, and fall into the hands of the uncircumcised?"* [19]*And God split open the hollow place that is at Lehi, and there came water from it; and when he drank, his spirit returned, and he revived. Therefore the name of it was called En-hakkore;*[v] *it is at Lehi to this day.*

v That is The spring of him who called

OVERVIEW: Since by God's will water poured from the jawbone of an ass, it is believable that fragrant ointment flows from the relics of martyrs (JOHN OF DAMASCUS). After feeling a great thirst, Samson calls out to God and atones for his boasting of victory through prayer (AMBROSE). The fountain that results from prayer is recognized in those who have believed in the Lord (CAESARIUS OF ARLES).

15:18-19 God Provides for Samson's Thirst

IN DEFENSE OF RELICS. JOHN OF DAMASCUS: In the relics of the saints the Lord Christ has provided us with saving fountains which in many ways pour out benefactions and gush with fragrant ointment. And let no one disbelieve. For, if by the will of God water poured out of the precipitous living rock in the desert, and for the thirsty Samson from the jawbone of an ass,[1] is it unbelievable that fragrant ointment should flow from the relics of the martyrs? Certainly not, at least for such as know the power of God and the honor which the saints have from him. ORTHODOX FAITH 4.15.[2]

HUMILITY MAKES ATONEMENT. AMBROSE: Soon Samson began to feel a fierce thirst; there was no water, and he could no longer stand to bear his thirst. Knowing that to attain human help would not be easy and that it would be difficult without divine aid, he called upon and begged almighty God. He did not think God would help him because of his offense against him, and because he had unwisely and carefully attributed any success to himself. No, he even assigned the victory to almighty God, saying, "You have given this very great deliverance into the hand of your servant, and it has been my help. And behold! Because I die of thirst, I am placed by my need of water into the power of those over whom you gave me a great triumph." Then God's mercy opened the earth when Samson threw down the jawbone, and a stream issued from it, and Samson drank and resumed his spirit and called the place "the invoking of the spring." Thus, by his prayer, he atoned for his vaunting of victory. LETTER 35.[3]

RIVERS OF LIVING WATER. CAESARIUS OF ARLES: Although we had been dried up because of lack of the dew of God's grace, we merited to be changed into fountains and rivers. At that time Samson prayed and a fountain issued from the jawbone. This fact is clearly fulfilled in us, for the Lord himself said, "He who believes in me, from within him there shall flow rivers of living water."[4] SERMON 119.4.[5]

---

[1]The use of the same word in the Hebrew for the jawbone and the town (Lehi) has led to confusion on the source of the gushing water, which the LXX denotes as the jawbone. [2]FC 37:368*. [3]FC 26:184-85*. [4]Jn 7:38. [5]FC 47:192.

16:1-3 SAMSON ESCAPES FROM GAZA

[1]*Samson went to Gaza, and there he saw a harlot, and he went in to her.* [2]*The Gazites were told, "Samson has come here," and they surrounded the place and lay in wait for him all night at the gate of the city. They kept quiet all night, saying, "Let us wait till the light of the morning; then we will kill him."* [3]*But Samson lay till midnight, and at midnight he arose and took hold of the doors of the gate of the city and the two posts, and pulled them up, bar and all, and put them on his shoulders and carried them to the top of the hill that is before Hebron.*

OVERVIEW: Repulsed by the cowardice of his people, Samson lodges in enemy territory. During the night he is surrounded and escapes by carrying the columns of the house up a mountain that faces Hebron (AMBROSE). The event is understood allegorically as Christ's going out from the lower world, destroying its defenses and ascending into the kingdom of heaven (GREGORY THE

GREAT). Samson's lodging with a harlot mystically foreshadows Christ's descent into hell, after which he removes its gates and ascends to heaven (CAESARIUS OF ARLES).

16:1-3 Samson Evades the Gazites

A FEAT OF GREAT STRENGTH. AMBROSE: When in the course of events he had brought an end to the war with the Philistines, despising his people's cowardice and scorning the enemy bands, Samson went off to Gaza. This city was in the territory of the Philistines, and he lived there in a certain lodging house. The people of Gaza immediately took note and hastily surrounded his lodging place, putting a guard at all the doorways so that he could not plan to flee by night. When Samson became aware of their preparations, he anticipated the plot they had laid for the nighttime, and taking hold of the columns of the house, lifting all the wood framework and the weight of the tower on his strong shoulders, he carried them up to the top of a high mountain which faced Hebron, where the Hebrew people dwelled. LETTER 35.[1]

FORESHADOWING THE REDEEMER. GREGORY THE GREAT: Samson, in the book of Judges, foreshadowed this by his deeds. When he had entered Gaza, a city of the Philistines, they immediately knew of his entry. They quickly surrounded the city with a blockade and assigned guards, and they rejoiced at having now apprehended Samson who was so extremely strong. But we know what Samson did. At midnight he carried off the gates of the city and ascended to the top of the hill. Whom, dearly beloved, whom does Samson foreshadow by his deed but our Redeemer? What does the city of Gaza signify if not the lower world? What is indicated by the Philistines except the faithlessness of the Jews? When they saw that the Lord was dead and his body had been laid in the sepulcher, they assigned guards there.[2] They were happy that they caught and held him, who shone out as the creator of life, behind the defense of the lower world, as Samson had been held in Gaza. Samson not only went out at midnight but even carried off the gates of the city, because our Redeemer, rising before it was light, not only went out free from the lower world but even destroyed its very defenses. He bore the gates and went up to the top of the hill, because by rising he carried off the defenses of the lower world, and by ascending he passed into the kingdom of heaven. FORTY GOSPEL HOMILIES 21.[3]

HE DESCENDED INTO HELL. CAESARIUS OF ARLES: When Samson went in to the harlot, he was impure if he did so without reason, but if he did so as a prophet it is a mystery. If he did not enter in order to lie with the woman, perhaps he did so because of a mystery. We do not read that he was intimate with her. . . . See how it is not recorded in Scripture that he was united to the harlot whom he had visited, but it is written that he slept. . . . He took away the city gates through which he had gone in to the harlot and carried them to a mountain. What does this mean? Hell and love for a woman Scripture joins together; the house of the harlot was an image of hell. It is rightly considered as hell, for it rejects no one but draws to itself all who enter. At this point we recognize the actions of our Redeemer. After the synagogue to which he had come was separated from him through the devil, they shaved his head, that is, they crucified him on the site of Calvary, and he descended into hell. Then, his enemies guarded the place where he slept, that is, the sepulcher, and wanted to seize him although they could not see him. . . . The words "he arose and left at midnight" signify that he arose in secret. He had suffered openly, but his resurrection was revealed only to his disciples and certain other people. Thus, all saw the fact that he went in, but the fact that he arose just a few knew, remembered and felt. Moreover, he removed the city gates. That is, he took away the gates of hell. What does it mean to remove the gates of hell,

---

[1]FC 26:185*. [2]Mt 27:62-66. [3]CS 123:162-63*.

except to take away the power of death? He took it away and did not return it. Furthermore, what did our Lord Jesus Christ do after he had taken away the gates of death? He went up to the top of a mountain. Truly, we know that he both arose and ascended into heaven. SERMON 118.5.[4]

[4]FC 47:187-88*.

16:4-9 SAMSON AND DELILAH

[4]*After this he loved a woman in the valley of Sorek, whose name was Delilah.* [5]*And the lords of the Philistines came to her and said to her, "Entice him, and see wherein his great strength lies, and by what means we may overpower him, that we may bind him to subdue him; and we will each give you eleven hundred pieces of silver."* [6]*And Delilah said to Samson, "Please tell me wherein your great strength lies, and how you might be bound, that one could subdue you."* [7]*And Samson said to her, "If they bind me with seven fresh bowstrings which have not been dried, then I shall become weak, and be like any other man."* [8]*Then the lords of the Philistines brought her seven fresh bowstrings which had not been dried, and she bound him with them.* [9]*Now she had men lying in wait in an inner chamber. And she said to him, "The Philistines are upon you, Samson!" But he snapped the bowstrings, as a string of tow snaps when it touches the fire. So the secret of his strength was not known.*

OVERVIEW: Although imbued with great power and spiritual blessing, Samson was rejected by God because he defiled his body through union with a harlot (ISAAC OF NINEVEH). Still heedless of his ancestors' customs, Samson marries Delilah, a foreigner and a prostitute. By conniving to learn the secret of his strength for profit, her love of money leads to his loss of God's favor (AMBROSE).

16:4-9 Delilah Attempts to Subdue Samson

SAMSON'S REJECTION. ISAAC OF NINEVEH: Why was the mighty man Samson rejected by God, he who was set apart and consecrated to God while still in the womb; whose birth was announced by an angel, like John, the son of Zacharias; who was granted great power and worked great wonders [and who by the supernatural strength which God poured into his body smote a thousand men with the jawbone of an ass and became a savior and judge to Israel]? Was it not because he defiled his holy members by union with a harlot? For this reason God departed from him and surrendered him to his enemies. ASCETICAL HOMILIES 10.[1]

DELILAH'S TEMPTATION. AMBROSE: But when with free and untrammeled gait he passed not only beyond the limits of his home country but also the boundaries which his ancestors had been taught to observe by custom, he soon found that he was playing with death. With small faith he contracted a marriage with a foreign-born wife

[1]AHSIS 75*.

and should have been cautious then or later. But he did not refrain from again forming a union, this time with Delilah, who was a prostitute. Out of love for her he caused her to tempt him with the wiles of an enemy. For the Philistines came to her and each man promised her eleven hundred pieces of silver if she would find out in what lay the source of his strength. If they but possessed this secret, he could be surrounded and taken.

She who had once prostituted herself for money, cleverly and craftily amid the banquet cups and the charms of her love, in admiration, as it were, of his preeminent bravery, began to question him about it and to ask him how it was he so excelled others in strength. Then, too, as though she were fearful and anxious, she begged him to tell his beloved what bond precisely would put him in the power of another. But he was still prudent and strong-willed, and he countered deceit with deceit against the harlot's treachery, saying that if he were bound with supple green boughs[2] he would be as weak as other men. When they learned this, the Philistines had Delilah put boughs on him like chains while he slept. Then, as if suddenly awakened, the hero felt his famed and customary strength, broke his bonds and fought back against the many who had their strength untrammeled. LETTER 35.[3]

MONEY IS SEDUCTIVE. AMBROSE: Overcome by love of money, Achan led to destruction all the people of the fathers. So Joshua the son of Nun, who could stay the sun from setting, could not stay the love of money in people from creeping on. At the sound of his voice the sun stood still, but love of money stayed not. When the sun stood still, Joshua completed his triumph, but when love of money went on, he almost lost the victory.

Why? Did not the woman Delilah's love of money deceive Samson, the bravest man of all? So he who had torn apart the roaring lion with his hands; who, when bound and handed over to his enemies, alone, without help, burst his bonds and killed a thousand of them;[4] who broke the cords interwoven with sinews as though they were but the slight threads of a net; he, I say, having laid his head on the woman's knee, was robbed of the decoration of his victory-bringing hair, that which gave him his might. Money flowed into the lap of the woman, and the favor of God forsook the man.[5]

Love of money, then, is deadly. Money is seductive, as it defiles those who have it and does not help those who do not. DUTIES OF THE CLERGY 2.26.130-32.[6]

---

[2]What the RSV translates as "bowstrings" in 1 Sam 15:7-8 are fresh cords that have not been dried.   [3]FC 26:185-86.   [4]Judg 15:14-15.   [5]Judg 16:20.   [6]NPNF 2 10:63*.

16:10-17 THE SECRET OF SAMSON'S STRENGTH REVEALED

[10]And Delilah said to Samson, "Behold, you have mocked me, and told me lies; please tell me how you might be bound." [11]And he said to her, "If they bind me with new ropes that have not been used, then I shall become weak, and be like any other man." [12]So Delilah took new ropes and bound him with them, and said to him, "The Philistines are upon you, Samson!" And the men

lying in wait were in an inner chamber. But he snapped the ropes off his arms like a thread.

¹³*And Delilah said to Samson, "Until now you have mocked me, and told me lies; tell me how you might be bound." And he said to her, "If you weave the seven locks of my head with the web and make it tight with the pin, then I shall become weak, and be like any other man."* ¹⁴*So while he slept, Delilah took the seven locks of his head and wove them into the web.*ʷ *And she made them tight with the pin, and said to him, "The Philistines are upon you, Samson!" But he awoke from his sleep, and pulled away the pin, the loom, and the web.*

¹⁵*And she said to him, "How can you say, 'I love you,' when your heart is not with me? You have mocked me these three times, and you have not told me wherein your great strength lies."* ¹⁶*And when she pressed him hard with her words day after day, and urged him, his soul was vexed to death.* ¹⁷*And he told her all his mind, and said to her, "A razor has never come upon my head; for I have been a Nazirite to God from my mother's womb. If I be shaved, then my strength will leave me, and I shall become weak, and be like any other man."*

w Compare Gk: Heb lacks *and make it tight . . . into the web*

OVERVIEW: After repeated attempts, Delilah succeeds in tricking Samson to reveal the secret of his strength as a Nazirite. Delilah's persuasive speech illustrates that polished discourse penetrates the soul. Samson's power was not found in the hairs of his head but in the grace of God's spirit (AMBROSE). Perceiving Delilah to represent the law of the flesh, the story is introduced as a lesson to a young man to avoid the evil counsel of fleshly desires (PAULINUS OF NOLA). Samson signifies what Christ did and what he suffered: as both the Son of God and the Son of man; and, as both the head and the body of the church (CAESARIUS OF ARLES).

16:10-17 Samson Yields to Delilah's Persistence

HIS WEAKNESS DISCOVERED. AMBROSE: After a short time, Delilah, like one who had been made fun of, began to complain passionately and to ask again and again what his real skill was, demanding proof of his affection for her. Samson, still strong of purpose, laughed at her tricks and suggested to her that if he were bound with seven brand-new ropes he would come into the power of his enemy. This also was tried, in vain. The third time he pretended that she had drawn him out regarding the mystery, but in reality, being nearer to a fall, he said that his strength would leave him if seven hairs of his head were cut and woven into a coverlet. This, too, deceived the tricksters.

Later, when the woman boldly deplored the fact that he mocked her so many times and when she lamented that she was unworthy to be entrusted with her lover's secret and a betrayal, she gained his confidence by her tears. And just since it was due that a man of bravery who had been invincible all this time should pay the price, he opened up the wounded recesses of his soul: the strength of God was in him; he was holy to the Lord and by his command he let his hair grow, for, if he cut it, he would cease to be a Nazarene[1] and would lose the use of his strength! When the Philistines discovered his weakness, through the woman, they gave her, the slave of their price, the reward for the treachery and thus concluded the affair. LETTER 35.[2]

THE POWER OF SPEECH. AMBROSE: Adam was

[1]Judg 13:5. Ambrose appears to be following a variant of the LXX. [2]FC 26:186-87.

beguiled by speech,[3] and Samson was overcome by a word; in truth, nothing penetrates the soul so much as polished discourse and, on the other hand, nothing is so biting as discourse of a harsher tenor. Although they have overcome the torments that were brought to bear against them, many persons have not withstood harsh discourse. THE PRAYER OF JOB AND DAVID 2.3.8.[4]

IS GOD CONCERNED WITH HAIR? AMBROSE: Is that, then, Samson who broke ropes twisted with thongs, and new cords like weak threads? Is that Samson who did not feel the bonds of his hair fastened to the beam, so long as he had the grace of the Spirit? He, I say, after the Spirit of God departed from him, was greatly changed from that Samson who returned clothed in the spoils of the foreigners, but fallen from his greatness on the knees of a woman, caressed and deceived, is shorn of his hair.

Was, then, the hair of his head of such importance that, so long as it remained, his strength should endure unconquered, but when his head was shorn the man should suddenly lose all his strength? It is not so, nor may we think that the hair of his head has such power. There is the hair of religion and faith; the hair of the Nazarite perfect in the law, consecrated in sparingness and abstinence, with which she (a type of the church), who poured ointment on the feet of the Lord, wiped the feet of the heavenly Word,[5] for then she knew Christ also after the flesh. That hair it is of which it is said: "Your hair is as flocks of goats,"[6] growing on that head of which it is said: "The head of the man is Christ."[7] And in another place: "His head is as fine gold, and his locks like black pine trees."[8]

And so, also, in the Gospel our Lord, pointing out that some hairs are seen and known, says, "But even the hairs of your head are all numbered,"[9] implying, indeed, acts of spiritual virtues, for God does not take care for our hair. Though, indeed, it is not absurd to believe that literally, seeing that according to his divine Majesty nothing can be hidden from him.

But what does it profit me, if God himself knows all my hairs? That rather abounds and profits me, if the watchful witness of good works rewards me with the gift of eternal life. And, in fine, Samson himself, declaring that these hairs are not mystical, says: "If I be shorn, my strength will depart from me." ON THE HOLY SPIRIT 2, PROLOGUE 13-16.[10]

AVOID FLESHLY DESIRES. PAULINUS OF NOLA: Like the famed Samson, whose power lay in the strength of his hair, whose locks were endowed with sacred might, he must throttle and bring low the lion by means of the strong arms of prayers and pluck the sweet fruit of notable victory from its dead mouth.

But this triumph must be a lesson to him not to make alliances with foreigners. That woman of another race I interpret as the law of the flesh, so wily with its alluring nets. If this law proves stronger than the law of the mind, it will drag him into the dominion of sin. The evil counsel of its pleasant words weakens with its deceitful guile the male spirit. It blinds the eyes of the mind and shaves the head; it plunders and disarms faith. I would not have our boy a Samson in this respect, becoming involved in a love encounter immediately followed by captivity, enervation and blindness, even though the strong Samson later recovered his strength when his hair grew again. For he was led by the hand from the mill to be the sport of the vaunting enemy, and though physically blind he used his mind's eye and summoned God to take vengeance. Then, when his hair restored his strength, he brought down that house of the enemy. Once his hands, more powerful than any stone, gripped the pillars of the house in their fierce embrace, the roof collapsed upon him when its props were torn from the earth. Yet even in his death God's powerful hero involved the foe in destruction, and by a glorious death [he] avenged the disgrace of his life as a

[3]Gen 3:6. [4]FC 65:357. [5]Jn 11:2. [6]Song 4:1. [7]1 Cor 11:3. [8]Song 5:11. [9]Mt 10:30. [10]NPNF 2 10:116-17*.

slave. He had lived a life of subservience under an exultant foe, but even as he fell he conquered the eclipsed enemy, destroying more thousands at his death than he had killed in his life.

I pray that our son[11] may imitate Samson's death by his own, that while remaining in the flesh he may conquer that flesh and live for God, subduing the sins of the flesh. I would not have him devoting his heart in enslavement to the flesh's joys as to the wiles of that criminal woman, to become subsequently the property of the foe, stripped of the strength of grace. POEM 24.529-581.[12]

SAMSON SIGNIFIES CHRIST. CAESARIUS OF ARLES: What was the meaning of Samson? If I say he signified Christ, it seems to me that I speak the truth. However, the thought immediately occurs to anyone who reflects: Was Christ overcome by the flattery of a woman? How is Christ understood to have gone in to a prostitute? Then, again, when did Christ have his head uncovered or his hair shaved, himself robbed of courage, bound, blinded and mocked? Watch, faithful soul. Notice why it is Christ, not only what Christ did, but also what he suffered. What did he do? He worked as a strong man and suffered as a weak one. In the one person I understand both qualities; I see the strength of the Son of God and the weakness of the Son of man. Moreover, when the Scriptures extol him, Christ is entire, both head and body. Just as Christ is the head of the church, so the church is his body; and in order that it might not be alone, it is the whole Christ with the head. Now the church contains within itself both strong and weak members. It has some who are fed on bread alone, and others who must still be nourished with milk. There is a further fact which must be admitted: in association at the sacraments, the imparting of baptism or participation at the altar, the church has both just and unjust people. At present the body of Christ is a threshing floor, as you know, but afterwards it will be a granary. While it is a threshing floor, it does not refuse to tolerate chaff, but when the time of storage comes it will separate the wheat from the chaff. Thus, some things Samson did as the head and others as the body, but all in the person of Christ. Inasmuch as Samson performed virtues and miracles, he prefigured Christ, the head of the church. When he acted prudently, he was an image of those who live justly in the church, but when he was overtaken and acted carelessly, he represented those who are sinners in the church. The prostitute whom Samson married is the church[13] which committed fornication with idols before knowing one God, but which Christ afterwards united to himself. However, when she was enlightened and received faith from him, she even merited to learn the mysteries of salvation through him, and he further revealed to her the mysteries of heavenly secrets. SERMON 118.3.[14]

---

[11]Paulinus instructs Cytherius and his wife regarding the appropriate development of their son, who was an aspirant to the priesthood. [12]ACW 40:234-36. [13]Israel. [14]FC 47:184-85*.

16:18-22 THE PHILISTINES SUBDUE SAMSON

[18]*When Delilah saw that he had told her all his mind, she sent and called the lords of the Philistines. . . .* [19]*She made him sleep upon her knees; and she called a man, and had him shave off the*

seven locks of his head. Then she began to torment him, and his strength left him. [20]*And she said, "The Philistines are upon you, Samson!" And he awoke from his sleep, and said, "I will go out as at other times, and shake myself free." And he did not know that the LORD had left him.* [21]*And the Philistines seized him and gouged out his eyes, and brought him down to Gaza, and bound him with bronze fetters; and he ground at the mill in the prison.*

OVERVIEW: Betrayed by Delilah, Samson awakens to find himself powerless. Samson's seven locks of curls signify the grace that comes from the Spirit in seven parts (GREGORY OF NYSSA). With hair that prefigures the covering Christ had in the law, the elements of the story of Samson's capture symbolize Christ's betrayal, suffering, and resurrection (CAESARIUS OF ARLES).

16:19-21 Samson Is Shaved and Blinded

SEVEN LOCKS OF CURLS. GREGORY OF NYSSA: But the one who has taken root as "a fruitful olive tree in the house of God"[1] composes those words against the tyrant which we have heard in the psalm, saying, "Why do you glory in evil, you who are mighty in iniquity," whose "tongue" is "like a sharp razor."[2] It was by means of these two things that [Samson] was led off, after [Delilah] had removed the beauty of his hair and cut off the "seven locks of curls" in which our strength lies. Now you will by all means understand the meaning of the spiritual curls from the number seven, just as Isaiah has enumerated the grace which comes from the Spirit in seven parts.[3] If these are cut off, as happened in the case of Samson, the destruction of the "eyes" follows, and one becomes a laughing stock to foreigners when they are drunk. ON THE INSCRIPTIONS OF THE PSALMS 2.13.183.[4]

STRENGTH IN A COVERING. CAESARIUS OF ARLES: Now what does it mean that Samson possessed strength in his hair? Notice this carefully, too, brothers. He did not have strength in his hand, his foot, his chest, not even in his head, but in his hair. What is hair? If we perceive it, the apostle answers us after being questioned, "Hair is a covering";[5] and Christ had strength in a covering, when the shadows of the old law protected him. For this reason the hair of Samson was a covering, since it was seen and understood in Christ at different times. What does it mean that Samson's secret was betrayed and his head was shaved? The law was despised and Christ suffered. They would not have killed Christ if they had not contemned the law, for they knew that it was not right for them to kill him. They told the judge, "It is not lawful for us to put anyone to death."[6] Samson's head was shaved, the secrets were exposed, the covering was removed; Christ who lay hidden was revealed. Moreover, the hair was restored and again covered the head, because the Jews were unwilling to recognize Christ when he was risen. He was in a mill, blinded and in a prison house. The prison or mill is the labor of this world. The blindness of Samson indicates people who are blinded by their infidelity and do not recognize Christ exercising his power or ascending into heaven. SERMON 118.6.[7]

---

[1]Ps 52:8 (51:8 LXX). [2]Ps 52:1-2 (51:1-2 LXX). [3]Is 11:2. [4]*GNTIP* 179-80. [5]1 Cor 11:15. [6]Jn 18:31. [7]FC 47:188-89*.

16:23-31 THE DEATH OF SAMSON

²³Now the lords of the Philistines gathered to offer a great sacrifice to Dagon their god, and to rejoice; for they said, "Our god has given Samson our enemy into our hand." ²⁴And when the people saw him, they praised their god; for they said, "Our god has given our enemy into our hand, the ravager of our country, who has slain many of us." ²⁵And when their hearts were merry, they said, "Call Samson, that he may make sport for us." So they called Samson out of the prison, and he made sport before them. They made him stand between the pillars; ²⁶and Samson said to the lad who held him by the hand, "Let me feel the pillars on which the house rests, that I may lean against them." ²⁷Now the house was full of men and women; all the lords of the Philistines were there, and on the roof there were about three thousand men and women, who looked on while Samson made sport.

²⁸Then Samson called to the LORD and said, "O Lord GOD, remember me, I pray thee, and strengthen me, I pray thee, only this once, O God, that I may be avenged upon the Philistines for one of my two eyes." ²⁹And Samson grasped the two middle pillars upon which the house rested, and he leaned his weight upon them, his right hand on the one and his left hand on the other. ³⁰And Samson said, "Let me die with the Philistines." Then he bowed with all his might; and the house fell upon the lords and upon all the people that were in it. So the dead whom he slew at his death were more than those whom he had slain during his life. ³¹Then his brothers and all his family came down and took him and brought him up and buried him between Zorah and Eshta-ol in the tomb of Manoah his father. He had judged Israel twenty years.

OVERVIEW: In response to the Philistines' insults, Samson calls to the Lord so that he may avenge himself. Despising his own death, he attains a triumph that surpasses all previous victories, yet his story warns against marriage to unbelievers (AMBROSE). Distinguished from a prayer, Samson's final words are an example of the Spirit's intercession (ORIGEN). Like Samson, sinners may destroy their adversaries, or vices, through repentance. By renouncing the devil, who resides upon the pillars of our sins, Christ's servants will cause his dominion to cease. With arms spread out, Samson's manner of death portrays Christ's crucifixion and the redemption he accomplished (CAESARIUS OF ARLES). After poetically comparing the fates of Samson and Adam, the former is recognized as a type of the death Christ the high Priest (EPHREM).

16:23-30 Samson Is Brought to the Philistine Lords

SAMSON'S FINAL TRIUMPH. AMBROSE: With the passage of time his hair began to grow; then, during a crowded banquet of the Philistines, Samson was brought from prison and shown before the people. About three thousand men and women were there. They taunted him with cruel remarks, they surrounded him with mocking jests which he bore with greater stamina and beyond what his blind appearance suggested, for he was a man of great native strength. To live and to die are functions of nature, but mockery belongs to the baseborn. The wish arose in him, therefore, either to compensate for such insults by revenge or preclude any more insults by death. He pretended that he could no longer support himself, because of the weakness of his body and the knots of his shackles, and he asked a servant boy, who was guiding his steps, to put him near the pillars which supported the house. Placed there, he grasped with both hands the support of the entire building and, while the Philistines were intent upon the sacrifices of the feast in honor of their god Dagon, through whom they thought the adversary had come into their hands, accounting the woman's treachery among the benefits of heaven, he called to the Lord, saying, "Lord, once more remember your servant so that I may revenge myself on the Gentiles for my two eyes. Do not allow them to give glory to their gods, because with their help they have got me in their power. I count my life as of no worth. Let my soul die with the Philistines, so that they may know that my weakness no less than my strength is deadly."

So he shook the columns with mighty force and loosened and shattered them. The crash of the roof came next and fell on him and hurled headlong all those who were looking on from above. There in great confusion lay heaps of men and women. Though slain, Samson attained his wished-for triumph, greater than all his former victories, and a death not inglorious or lacking luster. Although he was unassailable here and hereafter, and was not to be compared in his life with men who experienced war, in his death Samson conquered himself and made his invincible soul despise death, giving no thought to the end of life which all people fear.

Through his valor he ended his days with numerous victories and found the captive not undone but triumphing. The fact that he was outwitted by a woman must be attributed to his nature, not to his person; his condition was human rather than his fault. He was overwhelmed and yielded to the enticements of sin. And when Scripture bears witness that he killed more in death than when he possessed the light of life, it seems that Samson was made a captive more to work the ruin of his adversaries than to become cast down or counted less. He never

experienced degradation, for his grave was more famous than had been his power. Finally, he was overwhelmed and buried not by weapons but by the dead bodies of his enemies, covered with his own triumph, leaving to posterity a glorious renown. Those people of his, whom he had found captive, he ruled in liberty for twenty years. Then, entombed in the soil of his native land, he left behind the heritage of liberty.

Because of this example, men should avoid marriage with those outside the faith, lest, instead of love of one's spouse, there be treachery. LETTER 35.[1]

THE SPIRIT'S INTERCESSION. ORIGEN: The Spirit, therefore, "asks" and "intercedes,"[2] but we "pray." And Joshua's words commanding the sun to stand over [Gibeon] seem to me to be an intercession also. . . . And in Judges, Samson in my opinion said in intercession: "Let me die with the foreigners—when he bent in his strength and the house fell upon the princes and all the people that were there." Even though it is not written that Joshua and Samson "interceded" but that they "said," nevertheless their words seem to be an "intercession," which we must judge to be different from a "prayer," if we are to give words their proper meaning. ON PRAYER 14.5.[3]

REPENTANCE DESTROYS SINS. CAESARIUS OF ARLES: Furthermore, the fact that after Samson's hair grew again he recovered his former strength and seizing the pillars destroyed the house of his enemies together with its builders, is also seen today in the case of some sinners. If they destroy their vices by repentance and provide a place for virtue, the likeness and figure of Samson is fulfilled in them. Then is accomplished in them what is written concerning Samson: "Those he killed at his death were more than those he had killed during his lifetime." It is true, brothers. A greater number of sins is destroyed by repentance than is known to be overcome at a time when one

---

[1]FC 26:187-89. [2]Rom 8:26. [3]ACW 19:56*.

seems to be free from offenses. Now we should not notice with indifference that at the death of Samson all his enemies were killed. Thus, may our adversaries also be destroyed at our death. Brothers, the apostle says, "Mortify your members, which are on earth: lust, evil desire and covetousness (which is a form of idol worship)."[4] Let drunkenness and pride die in us, envy be extinguished, anger appeased and malice rejected. If we endeavor to kill all these things with God's help, like Samson we can destroy our adversaries by dying to sins and vices. SERMON 119.5.[5]

RENOUNCE THE DEVIL. CAESARIUS OF ARLES: Now that splendor which was restored in Samson and was covered at his death I think fits every servant of Christ. If someone is overtaken by some sin and in a salutary manner has recourse to the remedies of repentance, with the restoration of grace there returns the face of a good conscience, like the hair which grew again. Thus, it becomes possible for the merits of faith like very strong muscles of courage to attack and overthrow the enemy's pillars which support the hostile house. What are these pillars of the enemy's house except our sins upon which the house of the devil rests, where he feasts as victor and mocks our minds if they have been captivated? Therefore, we eject this enemy from his house by the destruction and death of our flesh. Our enemy is enclosed within us; he daily wages an internal war inside. As long as we sometimes assent to him, in accord with the evil agreement of our will he gains power over us. With our vices against us as his accomplices within, he attacks our exterior ministry, so that when we hand over to him our members for works of iniquity we are killed by our own sword, as is usually said. However, we ought to remember the agreement which we promised in return for the grace of baptism, when we were buried together with Christ in the mystery of the cross: that we would renounce the devil, his ostentatious displays and his works. Let us no longer live in this world as we have been; in fact, let us no longer live to ourselves but let Christ live in us. When he has been

restored to the honor of the head, the house of the devil will fall, and all our enemies will die with our sins in eternal destruction. SERMON 119.3.[6]

THE CRUCIFIXION PREFIGURED. CAESARIUS OF ARLES: "Therefore his enemies brought him to play the buffoon before them." Notice here an image of the cross. Samson extends his hands spread out to the two columns as to the two beams of the cross. Moreover, by his death he overcame his adversaries, because his sufferings became the death of his persecutors. For this reason Scripture concludes as follows: "Those he killed at his death were more than those he had killed during his lifetime." This mystery was clearly fulfilled in our Lord Jesus Christ, for at his death he completed our redemption which he had by no means publicly announced during his life: who lives and reigns forever and ever. Amen. SERMON 118.6.[7]

16:31 Samson Is Buried in His Father's Tomb

SAMSON'S RELEASE AND DEATH. EPHREM THE SYRIAN:

> Satan the tyrant outwitted Samson with a
>   woman,
> the same tyrant outwitted Adam with a
>   woman:
> Samson had to grind at the mill, Adam had to
>   labor wearily on the soil;
> Samson prayed to be released,
> whereas we pray to grow old in our misery.
> Blessed is he who delivered Samson, releasing
>   him from the grinding.
>
> Samson is a type of the death of Christ the
>   high priest:
> Samson's death returns prisoners to their
>   towns,
> whereas the High Priest's death has returned
>   us to our heritage.

HYMNS ON PARADISE 13.12-13.[8]

---

[4]Col 3:5. [5]FC 47:193*. [6]FC 47:191-92*. [7]FC 47:189*. [8]HOP 173.

[17:1-13 MICAH'S IDOLATRY]

[18:1-10 THE DANITES SEEK AN INHERITANCE]

[18:11-20 THE THEFT OF MICAH'S GODS]

[18:21-31 THE DANITES CAPTURE LAISH]

19:1-9 THE LEVITE AND HIS CONCUBINE

¹*In those days, when there was no king in Israel, a certain Levite was sojourning in the remote parts of the hill country of Ephraim, who took to himself a concubine from Bethlehem in Judah. ²And his concubine became angry with^a him, and she went away from him to her father's house at Bethlehem in Judah, and was there some four months. ³Then her husband arose and went after her, to speak kindly to her and bring her back. He had with him his servant and a couple of asses. And he came^b to her father's house; and when the girl's father saw him, he came with joy to meet him. ⁴And his father-in-law, the girl's father, made him stay, and he remained with him three days; so they ate and drank, and lodged there. ⁵And on the fourth day they arose early in the morning, and he prepared to go; but the girl's father said to his son-in-law, "Strengthen your heart with a morsel of bread, and after that you may go." ⁶So the two men sat and ate and drank together; and the girl's father said to the man, "Be pleased to spend the night, and let your heart be merry." ⁷And when the man rose up to go, his father-in-law urged him, till he lodged there again. ⁸And on the fifth day he arose early in the morning to depart; and the girl's father said, "Strengthen your heart, and tarry until the day declines." So they ate, both of them. ⁹And when the man and his concubine*

and his servant rose up to depart, his father-in-law, the girl's father, said to him, "Behold, now the day has waned toward evening; pray tarry all night. Behold, the day draws to its close; lodge here and let your heart be merry; and tomorrow you shall arise early in the morning for your journey, and go home."

a Gk Old Latin: Heb *played the harlot against*   b Gk: Heb *she brought him*

Overview: A story of deplorable behaviors begins with a Levite and his concubine who, offended by her husband's chiding, returns to her father's house. Seeking to reconcile, he goes to her father's and enjoys warm hospitality. After attempting to depart numerous times, he finally leaves with his wife during the evening of the seventh day (Ambrose).

19:1-9 At the Home of the Concubine's Father

Lodging with Relatives. Ambrose: How full of pitiful traits is this story! A man, it says, a Levite, had taken to himself a wife, who I suppose was called a concubine from the word *concubitus*. She some time afterwards, as is likely to happen, offended at certain things, returned to her father and was with him four months. Then her husband arose and went to the house of his father-in-law to reconcile himself with his wife, to win her back and take her home again. The woman ran to meet him and brought her husband into her father's house.

The maiden's father rejoiced and went to meet him, and the man stayed with him three days, and they ate and rested. On the next day the Levite arose at daybreak but was detained by his father-in-law, that he might not so quickly lose the pleasure of his company. Again on the next and the third day the maiden's father did not allow his son-in-law to start [his journey], until their joy and mutual regard was complete. But on the seventh day, when it was already drawing to a close, after a pleasant meal, having urged the approach of the coming night, so as to make him think he ought to sleep among friends rather than strangers, he was unable to keep him, and so let him go together with his daughter. Duties of the Clergy 3.19.111-12.[1]

A Cordial Visit and Delayed Departure. Ambrose: A Levite, more courageous than wealthy, lived in the region of Mount Ephrem, for his tribe was allotted a landed possession far removed in place of the right of inheritance. He took a wife from the tribe of Bethlehem of Judah. While they felt the first attraction of their love deeply and equally, he continued to burn with unbounded desire for his wife. Yet her ways were different. His passion for her intensified until he inwardly seethed with desire. Yet, because there was a difference in their ages, and because he felt—either because she seemed to love him less or due to the violence of his pain—that she didn't consider him her equal, he used to criticize her. Frequently quarreling followed, and the offended wife gave back the keys of the house and went home.

After the fourth month slipped by her husband, who was overwhelmed with love and had nothing else to hope for, went to her, trusting that the young girl's heart would be softened on the advice of her parents. His father-in-law met him at the door and brought him into the house. He reconciled his daughter and, in order that he might send them away more joyous, kept them three days while he prepared a sort of nuptial banquet. Although the man wanted to depart, he kept him a fourth day, offering him excuses of civility, devising delays. In his desire to add a fifth day as well, he found new reasons for delaying

[1]NPNF 2 10:85-86*.

them, while the husband, unwilling to thwart the father's affection of its desire to keep his daughter, though he was at last promised an opportunity for setting forth, postponed it to midday so that they would start out well fortified with food. Even after dinner, the father wished to find some delay, saying that evening was now approaching. At last he acquiesced, though reluctantly, to the entreaties of his son-in-law. LETTER 33.[2]

---

[2]FC 26:164-65.

19:10-21 THE LEVITE LODGES IN GIBEAH

¹¹When they were near Jebus, the day was far spent, and the servant said to his master, "Come now, let us turn aside to this city of the Jebusites, and spend the night in it." ¹²And his master said to him, "We will not turn aside into the city of foreigners, who do not belong to the people of Israel; but we will pass on to Gibe-ah." ¹³And he said to his servant, "Come and let us draw near to one of these places, and spend the night at Gibe-ah or at Ramah." ¹⁴So they passed on and went their way; and the sun went down on them near Gibe-ah, which belongs to Benjamin, ¹⁵and they turned aside there, to go in and spend the night at Gibe-ah. And he went in and sat down in the open square of the city; for no man took them into his house to spend the night.

¹⁶And behold, an old man was coming from his work in the field at evening; the man was from the hill country of Ephraim, and he was sojourning in Gibe-ah; the men of the place were Benjaminites. ¹⁷And he lifted up his eyes, and saw the wayfarer in the open square of the city; and the old man said, "Where are you going? and whence do you come?" ¹⁸And he said to him, "We are passing from Bethlehem in Judah to the remote parts of the hill country of Ephraim, from which I come. I went to Bethlehem in Judah; and I am going to my home;ᶜ and nobody takes me into his house. ¹⁹We have straw and provender for our asses, with bread and wine for me and your maidservant and the young man with your servants; there is no lack of anything." ²⁰And the old man said, "Peace be to you; I will care for all your wants; only, do not spend the night in the square." ²¹So he brought him into his house, and gave the asses provender; and they washed their feet, and ate and drank.

c Gk Compare 19.29. Heb *to the house of the* LORD

OVERVIEW: As darkness descends, the Levite rejects his servant's suggestion and refuses to lodge among the Jebusites. In search of shelter, the company proceeds to Gibeah, a city of the tribe of Benjamin, where no lodging is found except for the home of an elderly fieldworker (AMBROSE).

19:11-21 *Levite Prefers Gibeah over Jebus*

LODGING IN GIBEAH. AMBROSE: When some

little progress was made, though night was threatening to come on, and they were close by the town of the Jebusites, on the slave's request that his lord should turn aside there, he refused, because it was not a city of the children of Israel. He meant to get as far as Gibeah, which was inhabited by the people of the tribe of Benjamin. But when they arrived there was no one to receive them with hospitality, except a stranger of advanced age—when he had looked upon them he asked the Levite, "Where are you going and from where have you come?" On his answering that he was traveling and was making for Mount Ephraim and that there was no one to take him in, the old man offered him hospitality and prepared a meal. DUTIES OF THE CLERGY 3.19.113.[1]

THE EVENTS RETOLD. AMBROSE: He set out on his journey in happy spirits because he had recovered his dearly beloved wife. One servant was with him, and as day was already declining they sped on their way with swift steps. The woman rode on an ass; her husband felt no weariness, taking joy in his desire and lightening his journey with talk at times with the woman, at times with the slave. When at length they neared Jerusalem, about thirty stades away, a place inhabited then by Jebusites, the servant boy suggested that they turn into the city, especially since night makes even safe places suspect and one must guard against the uncertainties of darkness, and particularly since the inhabitants of this locality were not of the children of Israel. They should beware lest treachery be done with hostile design, for the night's darkness is opportune enough for any tricksters to perpetrate evil. But his master did not care for the servant's idea of seeking lodging among foreigners, since Gaba[2] [Gibeah] and

Rama, cities of Benjamin, were not far distant. His strong will overrode the servant's suggestion, as though advice takes its value from one's condition [of birth] rather than that through advice a lowly condition may be raised. The sun was now setting and he agreed reluctantly to go into the city [Gibeah], for he was overtaken by evening. The Gabanites lived there, unfriendly, harsh, unbearable people, who could stand anything but to receive people hospitably. Indeed, it would have been much more suitable had the Levite not sought hospitality in Gaba [Gibeah]. That his treatment be utterly offensive, he found on entering the city that there was no inn. And when he sat on the road imploring the mercy of these strangers, an old man from the fields happened to stumble on him, for evening had compelled him to leave his work in the fields at night. Seeing him, he asked where he was from and where he was going. He answered, "I came from Bethlehem of Judah, I am going to Mount Ephrem, and my wife is here with me. But I have learned that there is no one here to give hospitality and provide us a chance to rest." He needed no food or drink for himself nor food for his flock, but they had been refused the hospitality of shelter. They had everything; only a bare lodging was needed. To this the old man kindly and calmly said, "Peace to you! Come in as my guest and fellow citizen, for I am also from the region of Mount Ephrem, and here is a lodging place; someone who lived here a long time laid its foundations." Having received them into his home, he attentively and carefully provided for his guests and entertained them. LETTER 33.[3]

---

[1]NPNF 2 10:86*. [2]LXX. [3]FC 26:165-66.

19:22-30 THE DEATH OF THE CONCUBINE

²²As they were making their hearts merry, behold, the men of the city, base fellows, beset the house round about, beating on the door; and they said to the old man, the master of the house, "Bring out the man who came into your house, that we may know him." ²³And the man, the master of the house, went out to them and said to them, "No, my brethren, do not act so wickedly; seeing that this man has come into my house, do not do this vile thing. ²⁴Behold, here are my virgin daughter and his concubine; let me bring them out now. Ravish them and do with them what seems good to you; but against this man do not do so vile a thing." ²⁵But the men would not listen to him. So the man seized his concubine, and put her out to them; and they knew her, and abused her all night until the morning. And as the dawn began to break, they let her go. ²⁶And as morning appeared, the woman came and fell down at the door of the man's house where her master was, till it was light. . . .

²⁹And when he entered his house, he took a knife, and laying hold of his concubine he divided her, limb by limb, into twelve pieces, and sent her throughout all the territory of Israel. ³⁰And all who saw it said, "Such a thing has never happened or been seen from the day that the people of Israel came up out of the land of Egypt until this day; consider it, take counsel, and speak."

OVERVIEW: Inflamed with lust for the Levite's wife, wicked townsmen surround the house. Seeking to shield his guest from injury, the old man offers his daughter and the concubine, but to no avail. The Levite's concubine is delivered to them and is abused all night. Showing her care for her husband by preserving her remains for him, she dies at the door (AMBROSE). By way of comparison this offense and its aftermath, although grievous, is considered less injurious than the atrocities committed against the church, which bring its canons and ordinances into jeopardy (ATHANASIUS).

19:22-26 The Men of Gibeah Abuse the Concubine

VIOLENCE PREVAILED. AMBROSE: And when they were satisfied and the tables were removed, vile men rushed up and surrounded the house. Then the old man offered these wicked men his daughter, a virgin, and the concubine with whom she shared her bed, only that violence might not be inflicted on his guest. But when reason did no good and violence prevailed, the Levite parted from his wife, and they knew her and abused her all that night. Overcome by this cruelty or by grief at her wrong, she fell at the door of their host where her husband had entered, and died, with the last effort of her life guarding the feelings of a good wife so as to preserve for her husband at least her mortal remains. DUTIES OF THE CLERGY 3.19.114.[1]

SUBJECTED TO VIOLENCE. AMBROSE: The old man kept urging them to be glad and kept inviting them to drink more wine so that they would forget their cares, when all of a sudden they were surrounded by young men of Gaba[2] [Gibeah], given to lust, all lacking esteem for moderation. The woman's beauty had bewitched them and thrown them into utter folly. They were capti-

---

[1]NPNF 2 10:86*. [2]LXX.

vated by her beauty and, because of the old man's age and lack of help, with high hope of getting her, they demanded the woman and kept pounding at the door.

The old man, going out, begged them not to defile his guest's stay with a base crime, contemplating violation of a privilege reverenced even by savage nations of barbarous peoples; they could not insultingly mistreat a fellow tribesman of his, legitimately born, a married man, without causing wrath in their heavenly judge. When he saw that he was making little headway, he added that he had a maiden daughter and he offered her to them, with great sorrow, since he was her parent, but with less damage to the favor he owed his guest. He considered a public crime more tolerable than private disgrace. Driven by a wave of fury and inflamed by the incentive of lust, their desire for the young woman's beauty increased the more she was denied them. Deprived of all righteousness, they mocked his fair words, considering the old man's daughter an object of contempt in that she was offered with less feeling of ill will toward the crime.

Then, when pious entreaties availed nothing and the aged hands were hopelessly extended in vain, the woman was seized and all that night was subjected to violence. When day brought an end to the outrage, she went back to the door of their lodging, where she would not ask to see her husband, whom she thought she must now forego, ashamed at her pitiable condition. Yet, to show her love for her husband, she who had lost her chastity lay down at the door of the lodging, and there in pitiable circumstance came an end to her disgrace. The Levite, coming out, found her lying there and thought that she dared not lift her head for shame. He began comforting her, since she had succumbed to such injury not willingly but unwillingly. He bade her rise and go home with him. Then, as no answer came, he called her loudly as though to rouse her from sleep. LETTER 33.[3]

19:29-30 The Concubine Is Cut into Twelve Pieces

IS THE DISGRACE SHARED? ATHANASIUS: Our sufferings have been dreadful beyond endurance, and it is impossible to describe them in suitable terms; but in order that the dreadful nature of the events which have taken place[4] may be more readily apprehended, I have thought it good to remind you of a history out of the Scriptures. It happened that a certain Levite was injured in the person of his wife; and, when he considered the exceeding greatness of the pollution (for the woman was a Hebrew, and of the tribe of Judah), being astounded at the outrage which had been committed against him, he divided his wife's body, as the holy Scripture relates in the book of Judges, and sent a part of it to every tribe in Israel, in order that it might be understood that an injury like this pertained not to himself only, but extended to all alike; and that if the people sympathized with him in his sufferings, they might avenge him; or if they neglected to do so, might bear the disgrace of being considered thenceforth as themselves guilty of the wrong. The messengers whom he sent related what had happened; and they that heard and saw it, declared that such things had never been done from the day that the children of Israel came up out of Egypt. So every tribe of Israel was moved, and all came together against the offenders, as though they had themselves been the sufferers; and at last the perpetrators of this iniquity were destroyed in war and became a curse in the mouths of all: for the assembled people considered not their kindred blood but regarded only the crime they had committed. . . . For my object in reminding you of this history is this, that you may compare those ancient transactions with what has happened to us now, and perceiving how much these last exceed the other in cruelty, may be filled with greater indignation on account

---

[3]FC 26:166-67. [4]Athanasius details the outrage that was precipitated by the "violent and uncanonical" arrival of "the Arian" Gregory, who was appointed to replace him as the see of Alexandria. Like the Levite's summons of the tribes of Israel against Benjamin, this encyclical letter was written to all the bishops of the Catholic church to gain their support.

of them, than were the people of old against those offenders. For the treatment we have undergone surpasses the bitterness of any persecution; and the calamity of the Levite was but small when compared with the enormities which have now been committed against the church; or rather such deeds as these were never before heard of in the whole world or the like experienced by any one. For in that case it was but a single woman that was injured and one Levite who suffered wrong; now the whole church is injured, the priesthood insulted, and worst of all, piety is persecuted by impiety. On that occasion the tribes were astounded, each at the sight of part of the body of one woman; but now the members of the whole church are seen divided from one another and are sent abroad some to you, and some to others, bringing word of the insults and injustice which they have suffered. Be therefore also moved, I beseech you, considering that these wrongs are done to you no less than to us; and let every one lend his aid, as feeling that he is himself a sufferer, lest shortly ecclesiastical canons and the faith of the church be corrupted. For both are in danger, unless God shall speedily by your hands amend what has been done amiss and the church be avenged on its enemies. For our canons and our forms were not given to the churches at the present day but were wisely and safely transmitted to us from our forebears. Neither had our faith its beginning at this time, but it came down to us from the Lord through his disciples. That therefore the ordinances which have been preserved in the churches from old time until now, may not be lost in our days, and the trust which has been committed to us required at our hands; rouse yourselves, brothers, as being stewards of the mysteries of God, and seeing them now seized upon by others. ENCYCLICAL LETTER 1.[5]

---

[5]NPNF 2 4:92-93*.

[20:1-11 ISRAEL GATHERS AGAINST GIBEAH]

20:12-18 THE BENJAMINITES PREPARE TO FIGHT

[12]*And the tribes of Israel sent men through all the tribe of Benjamin, saying, "What wickedness is this that has taken place among you?* [13]*Now therefore give up the men, the base fellows in Gibeah, that we may put them to death, and put away evil from Israel." But the Benjaminites would not listen to the voice of their brethren, the people of Israel.* [14]*And the Benjaminites came together out of the cities to Gibe-ah, to go out to battle against the people of Israel.*

OVERVIEW: Before charging into war, on the advice of wise men, the Israelites first discussed the charge, set conditions for the guilty and determined to seek only the perpetrators from among the Benjaminites so that the whole tribe would not be punished for the vile deeds of a few men (AMBROSE).

20:12-13 The Israelites Seek the Guilty Benjaminites

THE GUILTY ARE SOUGHT. AMBROSE: When he realized that she was dead, he lifted her onto the mule and brought her home; then, dividing her limbs into twelve parts, he sent one to each of the tribes of Israel. In great distress over this, all the people met at Mizpah, and there, learning of the abominable deed from the Levite, desired to go to war, deciding that it was unlawful for anyone to go to his tent until vengeance was taken on the authors of this deed. With courage they rushed into battle, but the advice of wiser men changed their purpose as they decided not to engage the citizens in war but to put the charge to the test first with words and to determine the conditions for the guilty. Nor did it seem fair that the cost of a few men's crimes should fall on all and that the private sins of young men should make the safety of the citizenry fall. So they sent men to demand that the Gabanites[1] [Gibeonites] give up those guilty of this crime, and, if they did not do so, let them know that to have defended such a crime was not less than to have committed it. LETTER 33.[2]

---

[1]LXX. [2]FC 26:167-68*.

[20:19-28 ISRAEL ATTACKS THE BENJAMINITES]

20:29-48 ISRAEL AMBUSHES THE BENJAMINITES

[29]*So Israel set men in ambush round about Gibe-ah....*
[38]*Now the appointed signal between the men of Israel and the men in ambush was that when they made a great cloud of smoke rise up out of the city* [39]*the men of Israel should turn in battle. Now Benjamin had begun to smite and kill about thirty men of Israel; they said, "Surely they are smitten down before us, as in the first battle."* [40]*But when the signal began to rise out of the city in a column of smoke, the Benjaminites looked behind them; and behold, the whole of the city went up in smoke to heaven.* [41]*Then the men of Israel turned, and the men of Benjamin were dismayed, for they saw that disaster was close upon them.* [42]*Therefore they turned their backs before the men of Israel in the direction of the wilderness; but the battle overtook them, and those who came out of the cities destroyed them in the midst of them.* [43]*Cutting down[e] the Benjaminites, they pursued them and trod them down from Nohah[f] as far as opposite Gibe-ah on the east.* [44]*Eighteen thousand men of Benjamin fell, all of them men of valor.* [45]*And they turned and fled toward the wilderness*

to the rock of Rimmon; five thousand men of them were cut down in the highways, and they were pursued hard to Gidom, and two thousand men of them were slain. ⁴⁶So all who fell that day of Benjamin were twenty-five thousand men that drew the sword, all of them men of valor. ⁴⁷But six hundred men turned and fled toward the wilderness to the rock of Rimmon, and abode at the rock of Rimmon four months. ⁴⁸And the men of Israel turned back against the Benjaminites, and smote them with the edge of the sword, men and beasts and all that they found. And all the towns which they found they set on fire.

e Gk: Heb *surrounding*   f Gk: Heb *(at their) resting place*

OVERVIEW: War between the people of Israel and Benjamin ensued, ultimately resulting in Benjamin's defeat. The great regard our forebears had for virtue is exhibited by their readiness to wage war against those who had violated chastity and their persistence in battle (AMBROSE). Benjaminites were saved from total destruction through divine providence, so that Paul could call himself Benjaminite (JEROME).

20:40-48 The Benjaminites Are Defeated

THE VIOLATION OF CHASTITY AVENGED.
AMBROSE: When this [what had happened to the concubine] became known, (to be brief) almost all the people of Israel broke out into war. The war remained doubtful with an uncertain issue, but in the third engagement the people of Benjamin were delivered to the people of Israel, and being condemned by the divine judgment [they] paid the penalty for their widely immoral behavior....

And when at first the people of Israel were defeated, yet unmoved by fear at the reverses of the war, they disregarded the sorrow the avenging of chastity cost them. They rushed into the battle ready to wash out with their own blood the stains of the crime that had been committed. DUTIES OF THE CLERGY 3.19.115-16.[1]

CHASTITY DEFENDED. AMBROSE: After you found out what transpired in our court, you kept to yourself; therefore, I now summon, as it were, part of my own soul, for I have a friendly yet sorrowful complaint against you for the outrage done to chastity. Was it necessary for an unsurpassed, unheard-of case of virginity to be subjected to a sentence? Could it not have been dismissed? In other words, unless with injury to herself she had been handed over from honored modesty to an indecent surrender of her body, though she offered strong proof regarding herself, she would be exposed to ridicule and marked out as a wanton individual! You have tendered this privilege to virginity, honor of a sort, to which they are pleased to be summoned and invited who plan to recover this boon! Thus, they lose the liberty of a common reputation, nor do they protect themselves by the statutes of sacred or public law; they may not ask their accuser or oppose an informer but may only put on shamelessness and expose themselves to harm.

Our ancestors did not think chastity so to be despised; rather, they showed it such reverence that they would wage war on violators of modesty. In fact, so great was their desire for revenge that all the tribe of Benjamin would have been destroyed unless the six hundred who remained out of the war had been protected by a natural hill. This is the expression found in the account of the sacred lesson whose meaning it is profitable to consider. LETTER 33.[2]

THE DESTRUCTION OF BENJAMIN. AMBROSE: A proud retort was made, and plans for peace were changed to war. In the first and second en-

---

[1]NPNF 2 10:86*.   [2]FC 26:163-64*.

counters, when many were harmed by a few, the Israelites considered yielding, since the battles were so unfavorable. There were four hundred thousand men warring against twenty-five thousand of the tribe of Benjamin, and they strove with seven hundred Gabanites[3] [Gibeonites] experienced in war. When two battles were unfavorable, Israel with eager spirit did not lose hope of victory nor of vengeance for the hope they had fostered.

Superior in cause and number they yet fell back defeated in the battle's outcome, and, feeling that God was offended, they tried with fasting and much weeping to gain a reconciliation of heaven's favor. Begging the Lord's peace, they returned more boldly to war, and they to whom prayer had given courage and who had entertained much hope were now able to do what they planned. On a pretext of withdrawing their front lines, setting ambushes at night in the rear of the city, where a segment of the enemy was located, they followed as some retired and thus were provided with an opportunity for invading the unprotected city. Fires were quickly set and flared up while raging flames and waves of heat revealed the sight of the taken city. Their spirits broken, they faced the enemy. The men of Benjamin who thought they were shut in and surrounded, even before they were invaded from the rear, began scattering and fleeing to the desert, while Israel pressed after with doubled force and pursued them as they wandered in rout.

About twenty-five thousand were slain, therefore, that is, almost all the men of Benjamin except six hundred who seized a fortification on a rough cliff and by virtue of its situation and with the help of nature and partly through fear were a terror to their victors. Success advises caution; in adversity, revenge is esteemed rather than victory. Not even a minority of the women stayed clear of that struggle, but all the women of the tribe of Benjamin, along with boys and girls of every age, were wiped out by sword or fire, and an oath was taken that no one would give his daughter to a man of that tribe in marriage, so that all chance of repairing the name was abolished. LETTER 33.[4]

PROVIDENTIAL ESCAPE. JEROME: At Gibeah also, now a complete ruin, she[5] stopped for a little while remembering its sin, and the cutting of the concubine into pieces, and how in spite of all this three hundred men of the tribe of Benjamin were saved[6] that in after days Paul might be called a Benjamite. LETTER 108.8.[7]

---

[3]LXX. [4]FC 26:168-69*. [5]Paula, the mother Eustochium and the subject of this letter of consolation from Jerome sent to her daughter shortly after her death. [6]According to Judg 20:47, the number of the escaped Benjaminites was six hundred. [7]NPNF 2 6:198.

21:1-7 THE TRIBE'S FUTURE IS THREATENED

[1]Now the men of Israel had sworn at Mizpah, "No one of us shall give his daughter in marriage to Benjamin." [2]And the people came to Bethel, and sat there till evening before God, and they lifted up their voices and wept bitterly. [3]And they said, "O LORD, the God of Israel, why has this come to pass in Israel, that there should be today one tribe lacking in Israel?" [4]And on the morrow the people rose early, and built there an altar, and offered burnt offerings and peace offerings. [5]And

the people of Israel said, "Which of all the tribes of Israel did not come up in the assembly to the LORD?" For they had taken a great oath concerning him who did not come up to the LORD to Mizpah, saying, "He shall be put to death." ⁶And the people of Israel had compassion for Benjamin their brother, and said, "One tribe is cut off from Israel this day. ⁷What shall we do for wives for those who are left, since we have sworn by the LORD that we will not give them any of our daughters for wives?"

OVERVIEW: Our forebears' regard for virtue is further exhibited by their vow to refuse to give their daughters in marriage to the tribe of Benjamin, a fitting punishment that ensured they would enter a union by rape rather than the sacrament of marriage. With the war's end, wrath turns to grief as the people of Israel lament the potential loss of the tribe of Benjamin and consider how to remedy the unfortunate situation (AMBROSE).

21:1 No Daughters Will Be Given to Benjamin

FOREBEARS' REGARD FOR VIRTUE. AMBROSE: What regard for virtue our forefathers had to avenge by a war the wrongs of one woman which had been brought on her by her violation at the hands of profligate men! No, when the people were conquered, they vowed that they would not give their daughters in marriage to the tribe of Benjamin! That tribe had remained without hope of posterity, had they not received leave of necessity to use deceit. And this permission does not seem to fail in giving fitting punishment for violation, since they were only allowed to enter on a union by a rape, and not through the sacrament of marriage. And indeed it was right that they who had broken another's intercourse should themselves lose their marriage rites. DUTIES OF THE CLERGY 3.19.110.[1]

21:2-7 The Israelites Have Compassion on Benjamin

ANGER TURNS TO GRIEF. AMBROSE: The end of the war was also the end of their wrath, and anger turned to sorrow. Then, putting off their armor, the men of Israel met together and wept much and celebrated a fast, grieving that one tribe of their brothers had perished and a strong band of people had been wiped out. They had warred rightly against the authors of the crime because of the cost of the sin, but the people had turned unhappily against their own flesh and each was afflicted with civil war. The outpouring of tears moved their minds to compassion and stirred their feelings; the plan conceived in anger was gone. Sending legates to the six hundred men of Benjamin, who for four months guarded themselves on the top of sheer rocks and by the desert's barrenness, which was dangerous for a mass of attackers, they lamented their common hardship in losing their fellow tribesmen, relatives and allies. Yet the hope of renewing the tribe was not utterly destroyed, and they consulted together how they might agree on a pledge of faith and one tribe not perish, severed from the body. LETTER 33.[2]

---

[1]NPNF 2 10:85*. [2]FC 26:169*.

[21:8-15 WIVES ARE SOUGHT IN JABESH-GILEAD]

21:16-25 WIVES ARE SOUGHT IN SHILOH

[16]*Then the elders of the congregation said, "What shall we do for wives for those who are left, since the women are destroyed out of Benjamin?"* [17]*And they said, "There must be an inheritance for the survivors of Benjamin, that a tribe be not blotted out from Israel.* [18]*Yet we cannot give them wives of our daughters." For the people of Israel had sworn, "Cursed be he who gives a wife to Benjamin."* [19]*So they said, "Behold, there is the yearly feast of the LORD at Shiloh, which is north of Bethel, on the east of the highway that goes up from Bethel to Shechem, and south of Lebonah."* [20]*And they commanded the Benjaminites, saying, "Go and lie in wait in the vineyards,* [21]*and watch; if the daughters of Shiloh come out to dance in the dances, then come out of the vineyards and seize each man his wife from the daughters of Shiloh, and go to the land of Benjamin. . . . "*

[25]*In those days there was no king in Israel; every man did what was right in his own eyes.*

OVERVIEW: The severity of the sentence against Benjamin is moderated by the forebears so that the tribe might not perish (AMBROSE). Applied to present circumstances, that "there was no king in Israel" is understood to mean that quarreling and discord in the church is a result of turning away from the one true God and King of the universe (BASIL).

21:17-21 *Preserving an Inheritance for Benjamin*

SEVERITY MODERATED. AMBROSE: The sentence, further, was that none of the people of the ancestors should give his daughter in marriage to [members of Benjamin's tribe]. This was confirmed by a solemn oath. But relenting at having laid so hard a sentence on their brothers, they moderated their severity so as to give them in marriage those maidens that had lost their parents, whose fathers had been slain for their sins, or to give them the means of finding a wife by a

raid. Because of the villainy of so foul a deed, they who had violated another's marriage rights were shown to be unworthy to ask for marriage. But for fear that one tribe might perish from the people, they connived at the deceit. DUTIES OF THE CLERGY 3.19.115.[1]

21:25 *There Was No King in Israel*

BEING LED BY THE LORD. BASIL THE GREAT: After a long time spent in this state of indecision[2] and while I was still busily searching for the cause I have mentioned, there came to my mind the book of Judges, which tells how each man did what was right in his own eyes and gives the reason for this in these words: "In those days there was no king in Israel." With these words in mind, then, I applied also to the present circumstances

---

[1]NPNF 2 10:86*. [2]Basil's experience led him to conclude that whether in secular or sacred contexts, poor leadership and/or the failure to respect one source of authority leads to discord and division.

that explanation which, incredible and frightening as it may be, is quite truly pertinent when it is understood; for never before has there arisen such discord and quarreling as now among the members of the church in consequence of their turning away from the one, great and true God and only King of the universe. Each person, indeed, abandons the teachings of our Lord Jesus Christ and arrogates to himself authority in dealing with certain questions, making his own private rules and preferring to exercise leadership in opposition to the Lord to being led by the Lord. PREFACE ON THE JUDGMENT OF GOD.[3]

---

[3]FC 9:38*.

RUTH

1:1-14 NAOMI AND HER FAMILY

¹In the days when the judges ruled there was a famine in the land, and a certain man of Bethlehem in Judah went to sojourn in the country of Moab, he and his wife and his two sons. ²The name of the man was Elimelech and the name of his wife Naomi, and the names of his two sons were Mahlon and Chilion; they were Ephrathites from Bethlehem in Judah. They went into the country of Moab and remained there. ³But Elimelech, the husband of Naomi, died, and she was left with her two sons. ⁴These took Moabite wives; the name of the one was Orpah and the name of the other Ruth. They lived there about ten years; ⁵and both Mahlon and Chilion died, so that the woman was bereft of her two sons and her husband.

⁶Then she started with her daughters-in-law to return from the country of Moab, for she had heard in the country of Moab that the LORD had visited his people and given them food. . . . ⁸But Naomi said to her two daughters-in-law, "Go, return each of you to her mother's house. May the LORD deal kindly with you, as you have dealt with the dead and with me. . . . ¹⁴Then they lifted up their voices and wept again; and Orpah kissed her mother-in-law, but Ruth clung to her.

OVERVIEW: Elimelech's involuntary exile was due to the famine, which resulted from disobedience (JEROME). Ruth is included in Jesus' genealogy because her righteousness exceeded the law (AMBROSE). Ruth was greatly rewarded for comforting Naomi: she became ancestor of Christ himself (JEROME). Orpah's faithlessness and Ruth's fidelity symbolize the disharmony between those in the world who pursue death versus salvation (PAULINUS OF NOLA).

1:1-4 Elimelech's Family Goes to Moab

THE CAUSE OF ELIMELECH'S EXILE. JEROME: The Hebrews' tradition is that this is he in whose time the sun stood still, on account of those who did not keep the law, so that, when they had seen such a miracle, they should turn to the Lord God. And because they scorned to do such a thing, therefore the famine grew worse, and he who seemed foremost in the tribe of Judah not only was expelled from his native land with his wife and sons, made helpless by famine, but even continued in that same exile with his sons. HEBREW QUESTIONS ON CHRONICLES.[1]

KINSHIP OF MIND AND DEEDS. AMBROSE: If, therefore, we know that Tamar was included in the Lord's genealogy on account of mystery,[2] we ought also to conclude, without doubt, that Ruth was not omitted for a similar reason,[3] which the holy apostle seems to sense when he foresees in

---

[1]MEIT (Ruth), 31*; PL 23:1373. [2]See Mt 1:3. [3]See Mt 1:5.

the Spirit that the calling of foreign nations will be accomplished through the gospel, saying that the law was given not for the just but for the unjust.[4] For how did Ruth, when she was a foreigner, marry a Jew? And for what reason did the Evangelist believe that this marriage, which was forbidden by the weight of the law, should be included in the genealogy of Christ? Did the Savior therefore descend from an illegitimate heritage? Unless you return to the apostolic principle that the law was not given for the just but for the unjust, then, his genealogy would seem to be deformed, given that Ruth was a foreigner and a Moabite, whereas the law of Moses prohibits marriage to Moabites and excludes them from the church, as it is written: "No Moabite shall enter the church of the Lord even to the third and fourth generation forever."[5] Hence, how did she enter the church unless because she was made holy and immaculate by deeds [moribus] that go beyond the law? For if the law was given for the irreverent and sinners, then surely Ruth, who exceeded the limits of the law and entered the church and was made an Israelite and deserved to be counted among the honored figures in the Lord's genealogy, chosen for kinship of mind, not of body, is a great example for us, because she prefigures all of us who were gathered from the nations for the purpose of joining the church of the Lord. We should emulate her, therefore, who merited by her deeds this privilege of being admitted to his society, as history teaches, so that we also, by our deeds and accompanying merits, might be chosen for election to the church of the Lord. . . . When Naomi said to her, "Behold, your sister-in-law has already returned to her people and to her god, and so should you," Ruth responded, "May it not befall me to leave you and to go back to my god, for wherever you go, I shall go, and I will dwell where you dwell. Your people will be my people and your God will be my God; I will die where you die and I will be buried where you are buried."[6] Thus, the two of them went on to Bethlehem. When Boaz, David's great-grandfather, came to know her deeds,

therefore, and her holiness in relation to her mother-in-law and her respect for the dead and her reverence for God, he chose her to be his wife. EXPOSITION OF THE GOSPEL OF LUKE 3.[7]

ANCESTOR OF CHRIST. JEROME: You call to mind Blaesilla's companionship, her conversation and her endearing ways; and you cannot endure the thought that you have lost them all. I pardon you the tears of a mother, but I ask you to restrain your grief.[8] When I think of the parent, I cannot blame you for weeping, but when I think of the Christian and the recluse, the mother disappears from my view. Your wound is still fresh, and any touch of mine, however gentle, is more likely to inflame than to heal it. Yet why do you not try to overcome by reason a grief which time must inevitably assuage? Naomi, fleeing because of famine to the land of Moab, there lost her husband and her sons. Yet when she was thus deprived of her natural protectors, Ruth, a stranger, never left her side. And see what a great thing it is to comfort a lonely woman: Ruth, for her reward, is made an ancestor of Christ.[9] Consider the great trials which Job endured, and you will see that you are over-delicate. Amid the ruins of his house, the pains of his sores, his countless bereavements, and, last of all, the snares laid for him by his wife, he still lifted up his eyes to heaven and maintained his patience unbroken. I know what you are going to say "All this befell him as a righteous man, to try his righteousness." Well, choose which alternative you please. Either you are holy, in which case God is putting your holiness to the proof; or else you are a sinner, in which case you have no right to complain. For if so, you endure far less than your deserts. LETTER 39.5.[10]

1:14 Ruth Clung to Naomi

THE GREAT CONFLICT. PAULINUS OF NOLA: Next

---

[4]See 1 Tim 1:9. [5]Deut 23:3. [6]Ruth 1:15-17. [7]SC 45:136-138. [8]Jerome writes to console Paula after the death of Blaesilla, a recent convert. [9]Mt 1:5. [10]NPNF 2 6:52.

pass with eager eyes to Ruth, who with one short book separates eras—the end of the period of the judges and the beginning of Samuel. It seems a short account, but it depicts the symbolism of the great conflict when the two sisters separate to go their different ways. Ruth follows[11] after her holy mother-in-law, whereas Orpah abandons her; one daughter-in-law demonstrates faithlessness, the other fidelity. The one puts God before country, the other puts country before life. Does not such disharmony continue through the universe, one part following God and the other falling headlong through the world? If only the two groups seeking death and salvation were equal! But the broad road seduces many, and those who glide on the easy downward course are snatched off headlong by sin which cannot be revoked.[12] POEMS 27.511.[13]

---

[11]The LXX has "followed" rather than "clung." [12]See Mt 7:13. [13]ACW 40:289-90*.

1:15-22 THE RETURN TO BETHLEHEM

[16]But Ruth said, "Entreat me not to leave you or to return from following you; for where you go I will go, and where you lodge I will lodge; your people shall be my people, and your God my God; [17]where you die I will die, and there will I be buried. May the LORD do so to me and more also if even death parts me from you." [18]And when Naomi saw that she was determined to go with her, she said no more.

[19]So the two of them went on until they came to Bethlehem. And when they came to Bethlehem, the whole town was stirred because of them; and the women said, "Is this Naomi?" [20]She said to them, "Do not call me Naomi,[a] call me Mara,[b] for the Almighty has dealt very bitterly with me. [21]I went away full, and the LORD has brought me back empty. Why call me Naomi, when the LORD has afflicted[c] me and the Almighty has brought calamity upon me?"

a That is *Pleasant*　b That is *Bitter*　c Gk Syr Vg: Heb *testified against*

OVERVIEW: Ruth prefigures the Christian church as she was called from the Gentiles and, through her confession of the true God, joined the company of patriarchs and saints (ISIDORE OF SEVILLE). We may enter the company of the elect, as she did, through pious behavior (AMBROSE). Virtuous Ruth, although a foreigner, merits a place in the genealogy of the Lord due to her actions towards Naomi (JEROME). Ruth's outstanding loyalty is praiseworthy (THEODORET). Boaz married Ruth on account of her great faith (INCOMPLETE WORK ON MATTHEW). Understood allegorically, Naomi represents the Christian soul who laments her lost righteousness and exile from the face of the Lord (GREGORY THE GREAT).

1:16 Your God Shall Be My God

RUTH PREFIGURES CHRISTIAN CHURCH. ISIDORE OF SEVILLE: Now let us look at Ruth, for she is a type of the church. First she is a type because she is a stranger from the Gentile people who renounced her native land and all things belonging to it. She made her way to the land of Israel. And when her mother-in-law forbade her from coming with her she persisted, saying, "Wherever you go,

I shall go; your people shall be my people; and your God shall be my God. Whichever land receives you as you die, there I too shall die." This voice without doubt shows that she is a type of the church. For the church was called to God from the Gentiles in just this way: leaving her native land (which is idolatry) and giving up all earthly associations, she confessed that he in whom the saints believed is the Lord God; and that she herself will go where the flesh of Christ ascended after his passion; and that on account of his name she would suffer in this world unto death; and that she will unite with the community of the saints, that is, the patriarchs and the prophets. This company, by virtue of which she [Ruth] might be joined to the longed-for saints from the lineage of Abraham, Moses revealed to us in the canticle, saying, "Rejoice, you nations, with his people, (that is, people of the Gentiles), pour forth what you believe; exult with those who were first chosen for eternal joy."[1] ON RUTH.[2]

KINSHIP OF SOUL. AMBROSE: Ruth entered the church and was made an Israelite, and [she] deserved to be counted among God's greatest servants; chosen on account of the kinship of her soul, not of her body. We should emulate her because, just as she deserved this prerogative because of her behavior, [we] may be counted among the favored elect in the church of the Lord. Continuing in our Father's house, we might, through her example, say to him who, like Paul or any other bishop, [who] calls us to worship God, your people are my people, and your God my God. EXPOSITION OF THE GOSPEL OF LUKE 3.30.[3]

MERIT FOR SOLACING THE DESERTED. JEROME: Ruth, a foreigner, did not leave Naomi's side. See how much merit there is in standing by the deserted in solace. From her seed, Christ is born. LETTER 39.5.[4]

PRAISEWORTHY LOYALTY. THEODORET OF CYR: The constancy of Ruth, who because of the piety of her spirit and the memory of her husband pre-ferred to her parents a woman worn out in old age and laboring in poverty, is praiseworthy. QUESTIONS ON RUTH.[5]

THE MERITS OF RUTH'S FAITH. INCOMPLETE WORK ON MATTHEW: Boaz married Ruth on account of the merits of her faith, because she scorned her own people and land and nation and chose Israel, and because she did not despise her mother-in-law, a widow like herself, and an exile; but she was led by desire to her [Naomi's] people rather than to her [Ruth's] own. She rejected the god of her native land and chose the living God, saying to her mother-in-law, "Do not oppose me." HOMILY 1.[6]

1:20 Do Not Call Me Naomi

HER SORROW. GREGORY THE GREAT: In describing loftily the sweetness of contemplation, you have renewed the groans of my fallen state, since I hear what I have lost inwardly while mounting outwardly, though undeserving, to the summit of rule. Know then that I am stricken with so great sorrow that I can scarcely speak; for the dark shadows of grief obscure the eyes of my soul. Whatever is beheld is sad, whatever is thought delightful appears to my heart lamentable. For I reflect on what a dejected height of external advancement I have ascended in falling from the lofty summit of my rest. And, being sent for my faults into the exile of employment from the face of my Lord, I say with the prophet, in the words, as it were of destroyed Jerusalem, "He who should comfort me has departed far from me."[7] . . . For I, my good man, have, as it were, lost my children, since through earthly cares I have lost works of righteousness. Therefore "call me not Naomi, that is lovely; but call me Mara, for I am full of bitterness." LETTER 1.6.[8]

---

[1]Rom 15:10. [2]MEIT (Ruth), 7*. [3]MEIT (Ruth), 32*; SC 45:137. [4]MEIT (Ruth), 35; CSEL 54:304-5. [5]MEIT (Ruth), 32; PG 80:521, no. 348. [6]MEIT (Ruth), 32; PG 56:619. [7]Lam 1:16. [8]NPNF 2 12:76.

2:1-7 RUTH GLEANS IN BOAZ'S FIELD

[1]*Now Naomi had a kinsman of her husband's, a man of wealth, of the family of Elimelech, whose name was Boaz.* [2]*And Ruth the Moabitess said to Naomi, "Let me go to the field, and glean among the ears of grain after him in whose sight I shall find favor." And she said to her, "Go, my daughter."*

OVERVIEW: The widow Naomi, who properly trained her daughter-in-law Ruth, receives the benefit of her assistance as payment for pious instruction (AMBROSE).

2:2 Ruth Sets Out to Glean

THE FRUIT OF GOOD INSTRUCTION. AMBROSE: Does the widow Naomi seem to you of small account, who supported her widowhood on the gleanings from another's harvest, and who, when heavy with age, was supported by her daughter-in-law? It is a great benefit both for the support and for the advantage of widows that they so train their daughters-in-law as to have in them a support in full old age, and, as it were, payment for their teaching and reward for their training.

For to her who has well taught and well instructed her daughter-in-law a Ruth will never be wanting who will prefer the widowed life of her mother-in-law to her father's house, and if her husband also be dead, will not leave her, will support her in need, comfort her in sorrow and not leave her if sent away; for good instruction will never know need. So that Naomi, deprived of her husband and her two sons, having lost the offspring of her fruitfulness, did not lose the reward of her pious care, for she found both a comfort in sorrow and a support in poverty. CONCERNING WIDOWS 6.33.[1]

---

[1]NPNF 2 10:396-97*.

2:8-23 BOAZ TREATS RUTH KINDLY

[8]*Then Boaz said to Ruth, . . .* [11]*"All that you have done for your mother-in-law since the death of your husband has been fully told me, and how you left your father and mother and your native land and came to a people that you did not know before.* [12]*The LORD recompense you for what you have done, and a full reward be given you by the LORD, the God of Israel, under whose wings you have come to take refuge!". . .*

[17]*So she gleaned in the field until evening; then she beat out what she had gleaned, and it was about an ephah of barley. . . .* [19]*And her mother-in-law said to her, "Where did you glean today? And where have you worked? Blessed be the man who took notice of you." So she told her mother-*

in-law with whom she had worked, and said, "The man's name with whom I worked today is Boaz." ²⁰And Naomi said to her daughter-in-law, "Blessed be he by the LORD, whose kindness has not forsaken the living or the dead!"

OVERVIEW: Boaz teaches us the virtues of generosity and kindness in his actions toward Ruth. God generously rewarded Ruth's virtues as she was deemed worthy to be an ancestor of Jesus. Naomi pronounced prophetic blessing upon the anonymous benefactor (THEODORET).

2:12 The Lord Recompense You

A GENEROUS MINISTER OF KINDNESS. THEODORET OF CYR: The story of Boaz also teaches us about virtue. For he not only liberally shares his grain with Ruth but also consoles her with words. Not only does he share food with her but also was himself the minister of his kindness; so that whoever does not order another person to be his minister, but prepares the flour and bread himself, will have given very liberally indeed. QUESTIONS ON RUTH.[1]

DIVINE REWARD FOR RUTH'S VIRTUES. THE-ODORET OF CYR: The blessing followed as Boaz said it would. For Ruth received the full reward from God, so that she was the progenitor of the blessing of the nations. QUESTIONS ON RUTH.[2]

2:20 Naomi Utters a Blessing

A THANKFUL HEART. THEODORET OF CYR: With a heart thankful for the remembrance of kindness, Naomi rewarded the absent benefactor of her daughter-in-law with a blessing. For she said, "May he who has acknowledged you be blessed, for he has filled an empty soul by doing what he did. He took notice not of poverty but only of the Lawgiver, who ordered that widows be shown care." QUESTIONS ON RUTH.[3]

---

[1]MEIT (Ruth), 32-33; PG 80:521, no. 348 [2]MEIT (Ruth), 33; PG 80:521, no. 348. [3]MEIT (Ruth), 33; PG 80:521, nos. 348-49.

3:1-18 RUTH AND BOAZ AT THE THRESHING FLOOR

¹Then Naomi her mother-in-law said to her, "My daughter, should I not seek a home for you, that it may be well with you? ²Now is not Boaz our kinsman, with whose maidens you were? See, he is winnowing barley tonight at the threshing floor. ³Wash therefore and anoint yourself, and put on your best clothes and go down to the threshing floor; but do not make yourself known to the man until he has finished eating and drinking. ⁴But when he lies down, observe the place where he lies; then, go and uncover his feet and lie down; and he will tell you what to do." . . .

⁶So she went down to the threshing floor and did just as her mother-in-law had told her. ⁷And when Boaz had eaten and drunk, and his heart was merry, he went to lie down at the end of the heap of grain. Then she came softly, and uncovered his feet, and lay down. ⁸At midnight the man was startled, and turned over, and behold, a woman lay at his feet! [9]*He said, "Who are you?" And she answered, "I am Ruth, your maidservant; spread your skirt over your maidservant, for you are next of kin."* [10]*And he said, "May you be blessed by the Lord, my daughter; you have made this last kindness greater than the first, in that you have not gone after young men, whether poor or rich.* [11]*And now, my daughter, do not fear, I will do for you all that you ask, for all my fellow townsmen know that you are a woman of worth.* [12]*And now it is true that I am a near kinsman, yet there is a kinsman nearer than I.* [13]*Remain this night, and in the morning, if he will do the part of the next of kin for you, well; let him do it; but if he is not willing to do the part of the next of kin for you, then, as the Lord lives, I will do the part of the next of kin for you. Lie down until the morning."*

Overview: Naomi's advice to Ruth is moral and dictated by the desire to keep the memory of the dead. Ruth's marriage is free from voluptuous impulses (Theodoret). Ruth exemplifies a great number of virtues, including faith, piety, obedience and chastity, while Boaz embodies humility, chastity and faith (Incomplete Work on Matthew).

3:1-4 Naomi Instructs Ruth to Approach Boaz

Naomi's Advice. Theodoret of Cyr: What does Naomi suggest to her daughter-in-law? When Ruth heard her mother-in-law saying, "Our neighbor is a true man," she was reminded of his great kindness and thought to want him [to be] married to her in law, so that she might keep up the memory of the dead. Therefore, she [Naomi] suggests to her that she sleep at Boaz's feet, not she might sell her body (for the words of the narrative signify the opposite); rather, she trusts the man's temperance and judgment. Moreover, the actions corroborate the words. Questions on Ruth.[1]

3:10 Boaz Utters a Blessing

The Chaste Matrimony. Theodoret of Cyr: He praised Ruth's deed and, moreover, he did not betray temperance, but he kept to the law of nuptial congress.[2] "You show by your deed," he said, "that this was not done out of voluptuous-

ness. In fact, you might have gone to those who are young and blooming, with only the intent of enjoying voluptuousness, but you went to the man who stands in place of a father to you." Twice indeed, he calls her daughter. Questions on Ruth.[3]

3:11-13 Boaz Assents to Ruth's Request

Ruth's and Boaz's Virtues. Incomplete Work on Matthew: Unless God's inspiration had been in Ruth, she would not have said what she said or done what she did. What is praised in her first? A love of the tribe of Israel,[4] or obedience, or faith? She desired to have sons[5] out of the seed of Israel and become one of the people of God. Simplicity [is praised] also, because she came in under Boaz's coverlet voluntarily. She feared neither that he would perhaps spurn her, as a just man might spurn a lascivious woman, nor that he might deceive her and, worse, despise a deceived woman, as many men might have done. But, obeying her mother-in-law's plans, she confidently believed that God would prosper her action, knowing her conscience, because lust did not push her to it but rather religion was her encouragement.

---

[1]MEIT (Ruth), 33; PG 80:521, 524, no. 349. [2]No sex before marriage. [3]MEIT (Ruth), 34; PG 80:524, nos. 349-50. [4]PG text adds "or simplicity." [5]PG text reads "A love of the tribe of Israel because she desired to have sons."

What, however, is praised in Boaz? Humility, chastity and religion. Humility indeed and chastity, because he did not touch her as a lascivious man would [touch] a girl or abhor her as a chaste man would a lascivious girl, but as soon as he had heard her speak of the law, he ascribed her actions to religion. Nor did he despise her as a rich man would a pauper, nor was he in awe of her, as a mature man might be of a young woman; but, more experienced in faith than in body, he proceeded in the morning to the gate, calling the neighborhood together and prevailing not by the law of kinship to her but, rather, by the favor of being the chosen one of God.[6] HOMILY 1.[7]

---

[6]They were married not because it was the law and Boaz was the closer relative but in spite of the law, because God willed it. [7]MEIT (Ruth), 34*; PG 56:619.

4:1-6 BOAZ AT THE CITY GATE

[1]*And Boaz went up to the gate and sat down there; and behold, the next of kin, of whom Boaz had spoken, came by. So Boaz said, "Turn aside, friend; sit down here"; and he turned aside and sat down.* [2]*And he took ten men of the elders of the city, and said, "Sit down here"; so they sat down.* [3]*Then he said to the next of kin, "Naomi, who has come back from the country of Moab, is selling the parcel of land which belonged to our kinsman Elimelech.* [4]*So I thought I would tell you of it, and say, Buy it in the presence of those sitting here, and in the presence of the elders of my people. If you will redeem it, redeem it; but if you will not, tell me, that I may know, for there is no one besides you to redeem it, and I come after you." And he said, "I will redeem it."* [5]*Then Boaz said, "The day you buy the field from the hand of Naomi, you are also buying Ruth[e] the Moabitess, the widow of the dead, in order to restore the name of the dead to his inheritance."* [6]*Then the next of kin said, "I cannot redeem it for myself, lest I impair my own inheritance. Take my right of redemption yourself, for I cannot redeem it."*

e Old Latin Vg: Heb of Naomi and from Ruth

OVERVIEW: The story of Boaz and Ruth prefigures the coming of John the Baptist, which anticipates the union of Christ and his chaste bride, the church, who is called from among the Gentiles (ISIDORE OF SEVILLE). The manner in which Boaz proceeds with the marriage clearly testifies about his chastity (THEODORET) and was an act of piety (INCOMPLETE WORK ON MATTHEW).

4:1-6 Boaz Speaks with the Elders

THE BRIDE, BRIDEGROOM AND BEST MAN PREFIGURED. ISIDORE OF SEVILLE: When Ruth entered the land of Israel with her mother-in-law, it was provided (on account of the merits of her prayers) that she be married to a man of the lineage of Abraham and whom, indeed, she at first believed to be her closest kinsman. He [the nearest kinsman] said that he could not marry her and, when he had withdrawn, Boaz was married to her, with the witness of ten elders. He [Boaz] who previously confessed himself unable to marry that same woman was united with her and was blessed by those ten elders.

It is thought that this passage prefigures John the Baptist who, when he himself was thought by the people of Israel to be Christ and was asked who he was, did not deny who he was but confessed it, saying that he was not Christ. And those who were sent persisted in these inquiries about who he was. He answered, "I am the voice crying in the desert."[1] He confessed the good news about the Lord, saying, "He who has the bride is the bridegroom." He showed that he himself was the friend of the groom [the best man], since he added, "Truly, the friend of the groom is he who stands and hears him and rejoices on account of the groom's voice."[2] And so they thought he was Christ, because they did not understand that Christ had come on the day of the visitation[3] and that he who was earlier promised by the prophets' voices was the church's bridegroom. But just as he told her he was not her kinsman but then afterwards Ruth was united with Boaz, so Christ, who is the true bridegroom of the church, whom the sayings of all the prophets proclaim, was deemed worthy, from all Gentile nations, to claim the church, to present to God the Father unnumbered people throughout the whole orb of the world, because his kinsman took off the sandals. ON RUTH.[4]

THE CHASTITY OF BOAZ. THEODORET OF CYR: The man was so virtuous that he did not rush

into a marriage outside the law, but he spoke with his neighbors about the marriage. However, his words are also worthy of admiration. For his first words were not about the marriage but about the possession of fields, etc. Moreover, when, on account of the prospective marriage he [the relative] in fact refused the contract for the land and indeed took off his sandal and gave it to Boaz, in accordance with the law, Boaz then took Ruth to be his wife. Furthermore, because he was not serving lust, he took her in the spirit that one should take a wife, and his words also showed themselves worthy of praise, You are witnesses today, etc. "I do not," he said, "transgress the law in marrying a Moabite woman; rather, I diligently fulfill divine law, so that the memory of the dead is not extinguished." QUESTIONS ON RUTH.[5]

BOAZ'S MARRIAGE IS AN ACT OF PIETY. INCOMPLETE WORK ON MATTHEW: Boaz took Ruth to be his wife because of the merits of her faith, so that a royal nation might be born out of so holy a marriage. For Boaz, an old man, did not take a wife for himself but for God; not on account of his corporeal passions but on account of the justice of the law, to revive the seed of his kinsman, not serving love so much as religion. He was old in age but youthful in faith. HOMILY 1.[6]

---

[1]Jn 1:19-27. [2]Jn 3:28-29. [3]Lk 1:40-45. [4]MEIT (Ruth), 7*. [5]MEIT (Ruth), 34-35*; PG 80:524-25, nos. 350-51. [6]MEIT (Ruth), 35; PG 56:619.

4:7-12 BOAZ REDEEMS NAOMI'S PROPERTY

[7]*Now this was the custom in former times in Israel concerning redeeming and exchanging: to confirm a transaction, the one drew off his sandal and gave it to the other, and this was the manner of attesting in Israel.* [8]*So when the next of kin said to Boaz, "Buy it for yourself," he drew off his*

sandal. [9]*Then Boaz said to the elders and all the people, "You are witnesses this day that I have bought from the hand of Naomi all that belonged to Elimelech and all that belonged to Chilion and to Mahlon.* [10]*Also Ruth the Moabitess, the widow of Mahlon, I have bought to be my wife, to perpetuate the name of the dead in his inheritance, that the name of the dead may not be cut off from among his brethren and from the gate of his native place; you are witnesses this day."* [11]*Then all the people who were at the gate, and the elders, said, "We are witnesses. May the LORD make the woman, who is coming into your house, like Rachel and Leah, who together built up the house of Israel. May you prosper in Ephrathah and be renowned in Bethlehem;* [12]*and may your house be like the house of Perez, whom Tamar bore to Judah, because of the children that the LORD will give you by this young woman."*

OVERVIEW: Although Boaz desires to marry Ruth, the law of kinsman redemption seems to prevent such a union. Ruth must first seek her dead husband's nearest next of kin to satisfy the law (AMBROSE). The marriage of Ruth and Boaz has a profound symbolic meaning; it prefigures salvation of all peoples in Christ and his church (ISIDORE OF SEVILLE, CHRYSOSTOM). The elders' blessing of Ruth's marriage is prophetic as it looks toward the birth of Jesus in Bethlehem (THEODORET).

4:7-12 The Transaction Confirmed

THE CUSTOM OF REDEMPTION. AMBROSE: For, by the law, when a man died, the marriage bond with his wife was passed on to his brother or other male next of kin, in order that the seed of the brother or next of kin might renew the life of the house. And so it was that Ruth, though she was foreign-born, had possessed a husband of the Jewish people who had left a kinsman of near relation. Although she was seen and loved by Boaz while gleaning and maintaining herself and her mother-in-law with what she gleaned, she could not become the wife of Boaz until she had first loosed the shoe from him whose wife she ought, by the law, to have become.

The story is a simple one, but deep are its hidden meanings, for that which was done was the outward signs of something more. If indeed we should stretch the sense so as to fit the letter

exactly, we should almost find the words an occasion of a certain shame and horror, that we should regard them as intending and conveying the thought of common bodily intercourse. Rather it was the foreshadowing of one who was to arise from the Jewish people—whence Christ was, after the flesh—who should, with the seed of heavenly teaching, revive the seed of his dead kinsman, that is to say, the people, and to whom the precepts of the law, in their spiritual significance, assigned the sandal of marriage, for the espousals of the church. ON THE CHRISTIAN FAITH 3.69-70.[1]

CHRIST, THE TRUE BRIDEGROOM. ISIDORE OF SEVILLE: It was an old custom that if a groom wished to divorce his bride he took off his sandal and this was the sign of the divorce. Consequently, he was ordered to take off his sandals, lest he approach the church wearing sandals like a bridegroom; for this office was reserved for Christ, who is the true bridegroom. However, the blessing of the ten elders showed that all Gentile peoples were saved and blessed in the name of Christ. For *iota* signifies ten in Greek, and this first letter will signify the name of the Lord Jesus in full; which shows, as we said, that all peoples are saved through him and are blessed. Therefore, let no one doubt these things that were said, since it may be seen that they were everywhere and

---

[1]NPNF 2 10:253*.

from the beginning prefigured by antecedent figures; and they were clearly fulfilled in this way through the advent of the Lord; and which were superfluous, being completed in this way by the accord of all voiced in truth; and by all "figures" of the holy Scriptures, which he who promised [them] fulfilled through his son, Jesus Christ our Lord, king, and redeemer and savior, with whom is honor and glory from age to age. Amen. ON RUTH.[2]

FORSAKING A PRIOR WAY OF LIFE. CHRYSOSTOM: Those things which happened to Ruth should be seen as figures. For she was an outsider and had fallen into extreme penury; but Boaz, seeing her, did not despise her on account of her poverty, nor was he horrified on account of her impiety; even as Christ received the church, who was both a stranger and laboring, in need of great good things. Ruth is not joined with her consort before forsaking her parents and her nation and her native land: never was anyone so much ennobled by marriage. Thus the church was not made loveable to her spouse before she had forsaken her prior customs. The prophet says, "Forget your people."[3] HOMILIES ON THE GOSPEL OF MATTHEW 3.[4]

PROPHETIC BENEDICTION OF THE ELDERS. THEODORET OF CYR: The elders confirmed the marriage with a blessing, saying, "The Lord made this woman," etc. Moreover, "So that she may be an example of virtue in Ephrathah," they predicted the salvific birth through which Bethlehem was made famous among all people. QUESTIONS ON RUTH.[5]

---

[2]MEIT (Ruth), 7-8*. [3]Ps 45:10 (44:10 LXX). [4]MEIT (Ruth), 35*; PG 57:35-36. [5]MEIT (Ruth), 35; PG 80:525, no. 351-52.

4:13-22 THE BIRTH OF OBED

[13]*So Boaz took Ruth and she became his wife; and he went in to her, and the LORD gave her conception, and she bore a son. [14]Then the women said to Naomi, "Blessed be the LORD, who has not left you this day without next of kin; and may his name be renowned in Israel! [15]He shall be to you a restorer of life and a nourisher of your old age; for your daughter-in-law who loves you, who is more to you than seven sons, has borne him." [16]Then Naomi took the child and laid him in her bosom, and became his nurse. [17]And the women of the neighborhood gave him a name, saying, "A son has been born to Naomi." They named him Obed; he was the father of Jesse, the father of David.*

OVERVIEW: Ruth's love for God, exhibited in her boldness and humility, is rewarded with the privilege of bearing Christ (EPHREM). The union of Boaz, the son of Abraham, with Ruth, a foreigner, prefigures the marriage of the Son of God to the Gentile-born church (THEOPHYLACT).

4:13-17 The Lord Provides a Next of Kin

RUTH'S LOVE REWARDED. EPHREM THE SYR-

IAN: Let Tamar rejoice that her Lord has come, for her name announced the son of her Lord, and her appellation called you to come to her.

By you honorable women made themselves contemptible, [you] the One who makes all chaste. She stole you at the crossroads, [you] who prepared the road to the house of the kingdom. Since she stole life, the sword was insufficient to kill her.

Ruth lay down with a man on the threshing floor for your sake. Her love was bold for your sake. She teaches boldness to all penitents. Her ears held in contempt all [other] voices for the sake of your voice.

The fiery coal that crept into the bed of Boaz went up and lay down. She saw the Chief Priest hidden in his loins, the fire for his censer. She ran and became the heifer of Boaz. For you she brought forth the fatted ox.

She went gleaning for love of you; she gathered straw. You repaid her quickly the wage of her humiliation: instead of ears [of wheat], the Root of kings, and instead of straw, the Sheaf of Life that descends from her. HYMNS ON THE NATIVITY 9.12-16.[1]

FOREIGNERS NOT EXCLUDED. THEOPHYLACT: And Boaz begat Obed of Ruth. Ruth was a foreigner, but nevertheless she was married to Boaz. So, too, the church is from among the Gentiles. For like Ruth, these Gentiles had been foreigners and outside the covenants, yet they forsook their people, their idols and their father, the devil. And as Ruth was wed to Boaz of the seed of Abraham, so too was the church taken as bride by the Son of God. EXPLANATION OF MATTHEW 1.3-4.[2]

---

[1]CWS 126-27. [2]EBT 16.

1 SAMUEL

1:1-2 ELKANAH AND HIS WIVES

¹*There was a certain man of Ramathaim-zophim of the hill country of Ephraim, whose name was Elkanah the son of Jeroham, son of Elihu, son of Tohu, son of Zuph, an Ephraimite. ²He had two wives; the name of the one was Hannah, and the name of the other Peninnah. And Peninnah had children, but Hannah had no children.*

OVERVIEW: Unlike sinners, who possess divided personalities, the just are praised for their internal peace and their unity of heart with others like them. As Peninnah and Hannah symbolize conversion and grace, the wives of the patriarchs are most fittingly understood as figures for virtues, hence Elkanah had sons by conversion and sons by grace (ORIGEN). Samuel is a type of Christ (CYPRIAN).

1:1 There Was a Certain Man

THE JUST ARE ONE. ORIGEN: Is not this very thing a reason for praising the just person, that one can say of him: "There was one man"? We who are still sinners cannot acquire that title of praise because each of us is not one but many. For looking at me is the face of one who is now angry, and then sad, a little later happy, and then disturbed and then gentle, at times concerned with the things of God and actions leading to eternal life, but shortly after doing things based on greed or the glory of this world. You can see, then, that he who was thought to be one is not one at all; but there seem to be as many persons in him as there are customs. . . . But as for the just, not only is each said to be one but they are, all together,

said to be one. And why shouldn't they all be called one, who were described as being of "one heart and soul"[1]? They constantly contemplate one wisdom, are of one affection and disposition, reverence one God, confess one Jesus Christ as Lord, are filled with one Spirit of God. They are rightly called not just one [thing] but "one person," as the apostle indicated when he said, "All the runners compete, but only one receives the prize."[2] HOMILIES ON 1 KINGS 1.4.[3]

1:2 Elkanah Had Two Wives

WIVES AS FIGURES FOR VIRTUES. ORIGEN: In this [figurative] way, therefore, I think the marriages of the elders are interpreted more fittingly; in this way the unions entered by the patriarchs in their now final and weakened age are understood nobly; in this way I hold the necessary begetting of children should be reckoned. For young men are not so well fitted as old men for such marriages and for offspring of this kind. For to the extent that someone is feeble in the flesh, to such an extent will he be stronger in virtue of the soul and more fit for the embraces of wisdom. So

---

[1]Acts 4:32. [2]1 Cor 9:24. [3]OSF 281*.

also that just man Elkanah in the Scriptures is reported to have had two wives at the same time, one of whom was called Peninnah, the other Hannah, that is, "conversion" and "grace." And first, indeed, he is said to have had sons by Peninnah, that is, of conversion, and later by Hannah, that is, of grace.

And indeed the Scripture designates the progress of the saints figuratively by marriages. Whence also you can, if you wish, be a husband of marriages of this kind. For example, if you freely practice hospitality, you will appear to have taken her as your wife. If you shall add to this care of the poor, you will appear to have obtained a second wife. But if you should also join patience to yourself and gentleness and the other virtues, you will appear to have taken as many wives as the virtues you enjoy.

Thence it is, therefore, that Scripture recounts that some of the patriarchs had many wives at the same time, that others took other wives when previous wives had died. The purpose of this is to indicate figuratively that some can exercise many virtues at the same time; others cannot begin those which follow before they have brought the former virtues to perfection. HOMILIES ON GENESIS 11.2.[4]

SAMUEL A TYPE OF THE MESSIAH. CYPRIAN: That the church which before had been barren should have more children from among the Gentiles than what the synagogue had had before. Isaiah said, "Rejoice, O barren one, that barest not; break forth and shout, who has not been in labor, for the deserted one will have more children than she who has a husband. . . ."[5] So also, to Abraham, when his first son was born of a bondwoman, Sarah remained long barren, but later, in her old age, bore him her promised son Isaac, who was a type of the Christ. Jacob also took two wives: the elder, Leah, with weak eyes, was a type of the synagogue; the younger and beautiful Rachel, a type of the church, who also remained long barren and afterwards brought forth Joseph, who also was himself a type of Christ. And in 1 Kings [Samuel] it is said that Elkanah has two wives: Peninnah, with her sons; and Hannah, barren, from whom is born not according to the order of generation but according to the mercy and promise of God, when she had prayed in the temple; and Samuel, being born, was a type of Christ. Again in 1 Kings [Samuel]: "The barren has born seven; and she who had many children has grown weak."[6] To QUIRINUS: TESTIMONIES AGAINST THE JEWS 1.20.[7]

---

[4]FC 71:170-71*. [5]Is 54:1. [6]1 Sam 2:5. [7]ANF 5:512-13**.

1:3-8 HANNAH'S GRIEF

[3]Now this man used to go up year by year from his city to worship and to sacrifice to the LORD of hosts at Shiloh, where the two sons of Eli, Hophni and Phinehas, were priests of the LORD. [4]On the day when Elkanah sacrificed, he would give portions to Peninnah his wife and to all her sons and daughters; [5]and, although[a] he loved Hannah, he would give Hannah only one portion, because the LORD had closed her womb. [6]And her rival used to provoke her sorely, to irritate her, because the LORD had closed her womb. [7]So it went on year by year; as often as she went up to the house of

the Lord, she used to provoke her. Therefore Hannah wept and would not eat. ⁸And Elkanah, her husband, said to her, "Hannah, why do you weep? And why do you not eat? And why is your heart sad? Am I not more to you than ten sons?"

a Gk: Heb obscure

Overview: The highest values may be learned from witnessing Hannah's patience while enduring suffering as she waited for God's timing (Chrysostom). "Rivalry" has several meanings (Verecundus). Weeping and fasting for want of a child, Hannah is an example of watchfulness in prayer serves as a model for Christians (Chrysostom). Her fast, which demonstrates reverential awe, is the means by which she obtained a son (Tertullian).

1:5 The Lord Had Closed Her Womb

God's Purpose for Suffering. Chrysostom: Let us not take this with a grain of salt; instead let us learn also from this the highest values, and when we fall foul of some disaster, even if we are suffering grief and pain, even if the trouble seems insupportable to us, let us not be anxious or beside ourselves but wait on God's providence. He is well aware, after all, when is the time for what is causing us depression to be removed—which is what happened in her case as well. It was not out of hatred, in fact, or of revulsion that he closed her womb, but to open to us the doors on the values the woman possessed and for us to espy the riches of her faith and realize that he rendered her more conspicuous on that account. . . . Extreme the pain, great the length of grief—not two or three days, not twenty or a hundred, not a thousand or twice as much; instead, "for a long time," it says, for many years the woman was grieving and distressed, the meaning of "for a long time." Yet she showed no impatience, nor did the length of time undermine her values, nor the reproaches and abuse of her rival; instead, she was unremitting in prayer and supplication, and what was most remarkable of all, showing in particular her love for God, was

the fact that she was not simply anxious to have this very child for herself but to dedicate the fruit of her womb to God, offer the first fruits of her own womb and receive the reward for this fine promise. Homilies on Hannah 1.[1]

1:6 Her Rival Provoked Her

Envy. Verecundus: The word *rival [aemulare]* has a threefold meaning.[2] First, it means to emulate *[imitari]*, as in "Seek after the greater gifts."[3] We also read, "It is good that you always be emulated for the good."[4] Second, it is to envy *[invidere]*, even one's enemy, as was said through Samuel to Saul: "God has taken the kingdom from you and has given it to your rival *[aemulo]*."[5] Peninnah, moreover, who played the role of the synagogue, was envied by Hannah because Hannah had not begotten a child in her barrenness. "Hannah's rival *[aemula]* afflicted and agitated her severely." The term *rival* here indicates enmity or envy. But "agitated" signifies "oppressed" *[obprimebat]*, a metaphorical expression drawn from the act of choking on a piece of meat that one has suddenly regurgitated. Third, *aemulare* means "to anger," as was demonstrated when the apostle said, "Shall we be angered *[aemulamur]* by the Lord? Are we stronger than he?"[6] In other words, it means to provoke a temper. Commentary on the Canticle of Deuteronomy 22.8.[7]

1:7-8 Hannah Wept and Would Not Eat

---

[1]COTH 1:74-75. [2]The text upon which Verecundus here comments, apparently a conflation of Deuteronomy 32:16-21, reads, "They envied me in their idols, not in God; they provoked my wrath with their idols." [3]1 Cor 12:31. [4]Gal 4:18. [5]1 Sam 15:28. [6]1 Cor 10:22. [7]CCL 93:38-39.

Watchfulness in Prayer. Chrysostom: Would you like to understand what watchfulness in prayer is? Go to Hannah, listen to her very words, "Adonai Eloi Sabaoth."[8] No, rather, hear what preceded those words; "they all rose up,"[9] says the history, "from the table," and she did not give herself right away to sleep or to repose. She appears to me even when she was sitting at the table to have partaken lightly and not to have been made heavy with food. Otherwise she could never have shed so many tears. When we are fasting and foodless, we hardly pray in such a manner, or rather never pray in this way. Much more Hannah would not ever have prayed in this fashion after a meal, unless even at the meal she had been like those that do not eat. Let men be ashamed at the example of this woman. Let those be ashamed who are suing and grasping for a kingdom, at her, praying and weeping for a little child. Homilies on Ephesians 24.[10]

The Power of Fasting. Tertullian: Thus a Godward fast is a work of reverential awe. By its means also Hannah the wife of Elkanah making suit, barren as she had been beforetime, easily obtained from God the filling of her belly, empty of food, with a son, indeed, and a prophet. On Fasting 7.[11]

---

[8]1 Sam 1:20. [9]1 Sam 1:9. [10]NPNF 1 13:170*. [11]ANF 4:106*.

1:9-11 HANNAH'S VOW AT SHILOH

[9]*After they had eaten and drunk in Shiloh, Hannah rose. Now Eli the priest was sitting on the seat beside the doorpost of the temple of the* Lord. [10]*She was deeply distressed and prayed to the* Lord, *and wept bitterly.* [11]*And she vowed a vow and said, "O* Lord *of hosts, if thou wilt indeed look on the affliction of thy maidservant, and remember me, and not forget thy maidservant, but wilt give to thy maidservant a son, then I will give him to the* Lord *all the days of his life, and no razor shall touch his head."*

Overview: Hannah exhibits great confidence by boldly approaching the heavenly King directly with her request (Chrysostom). Similarity between the Lord's prayer and Hannah's is found in the request for deliverance from evil (Augustine). Like water on hard ground, Hannah's tears softened her infertile womb. Through her tears, suffering and vow, Hannah demonstrates exemplary behavior. Out of great reverence, she asked God for one son whom she promises to return, content with the reward of laboring for God's priest (Chrysostom).

1:9 Eli the Priest

Hannah's Great Confidence. Chrysostom: You see, just as a widow who is destitute and all alone, much abused and wronged, will often not be alarmed at the imminent triumphal procession of emperor, bodyguards, shield bearers, horses, and all the rest of his advance retinue, but without need of a patron will brush past them all and with great confidence accost the emperor, exaggerating her own situation under pressure of her sense of need, so too this woman was not embarrassed, was not ashamed, though the priest was sitting there, to make her request in person and with great confidence approach the king. Instead, under the impulse of desire and in her mind ascending to heaven as though she saw God himself, she addressed him this way with complete ardor. Homilies on Hannah 1.[1]

1:10-11 Hannah Prays and Vows to the Lord

Deliverance from Evil. Augustine: There were two women with the honored name of Anna:[2] one married, who gave birth to holy Samuel; the other a widow, who recognized the Saint of saints when he was still an infant. The married one prayed with grief of soul and affliction of heart, because she had no sons. In answer to her prayer Samuel was given to her, and she offered him to God as she had vowed in her prayer to do. It is not easy to see how her prayer agrees with the Lord's Prayer, except, perhaps, in those words, "Deliver us from evil," because it seemed no slight evil to be married and to be deprived of the fruit of marriage, when the sole purpose of marriage is the begetting of children. Letter 130.[3]

Floods of Tears. Chrysostom: What did she say? Instead of saying anything at first, she began with wailing and shed warm floods of tears. And just as, when rain storms fall, even the harder ground is moistened and softened and easily bestirs itself to produce crops, so too did this happen in the case of this woman: as though softened by the flood of tears and warmed with the pangs, the womb began to stir in that wonderful fertility. Homilies on Hannah 1.[4]

Hannah's Example. Chrysostom: "And she stood," it says, "before the Lord"; and what are her words? "Adonai, Lord, Eloi Sabaoth!" and this is, being interpreted, "O Lord, the God of Hosts." Her tears went before her speech. By

these she hoped to prevail with God to bend to her request. Where tears are, there is always affliction also; where affliction is, there is great wisdom and attentiveness. She continues, "If you will indeed look on the affliction of your handmaid and will give to your handmaid a male child, then I will give him to the Lord all the days of his life." She said not "for one year" or "for two" as we do; nor did she say, "If you will give me a child, I will give you money"; but, "I give back to you the very gift itself entirely, my firstborn, the son of my prayer." Truly here was a daughter of Abraham. He gave when it was demanded of him. She offers even before it is demanded. Homilies on Ephesians 24.[5]

A Wealth of Reverence. Chrysostom: Take note of the woman's reverence: she did not say, "If you give me three, I shall give you two;" or "if two, I shall give you one." Instead, "If you give me one, I shall dedicate the offspring wholly to you." "He will not drink wine or strong drink." She had not yet received the child and was already forming a prophet, talking about his upbringing and making a deal with God. What wonderful confidence on a woman's part! Since she could not make a deposit on account of not having anything, she pays the price from what is coming to her. Just as many farmers who are living in extreme poverty but have no money to buy a calf or sheep, get them on credit from their masters by pledging to pay the price from the crops that are due, just so did she do, too—or rather much more: she did not take her son from God on credit but on condition of returning him wholly to him once again and reaping the fruit of his upbringing. She regarded it as sufficient reward, you see, to devote her labors to God's priest. Homilies on Hannah 1.[6]

---

[1]COTH 1:76-77. [2]"Hannah" as it appears in Greek translation. [3]FC 18:399. [4]COTH 1:77. [5]NPNF 1 13:170*. [6]COTH 1:78.

1:12-18 ELI BLESSES HANNAH

[12]*As she continued praying before the* Lord, *Eli observed her mouth.* [13]*Hannah was speaking in her heart; only her lips moved, and her voice was not heard; therefore Eli took her to be a drunken woman.* [14]*And Eli said to her, "How long will you be drunken? Put away your wine from you."* [15]*But Hannah answered, "No, my lord, I am a woman sorely troubled; I have drunk neither wine nor strong drink, but I have been pouring out my soul before the* Lord." . . . [17]*Then Eli answered, "Go in peace, and the God of Israel grant your petition which you have made to him."*

Overview: Our hearts, rather than our voices, cry out to God as Hannah's did (Caesarius of Arles). Women should emulate Hannah's example by singing and praying quietly in church (Cyril of Jerusalem). Tears shed in private are esteemed as appropriate and effective (Chrysostom). God hears the inward, silent prayer (Clement of Alexandria). Hannah, who typifies the church, exhibits faith that the Lord hears the heart's cry through her silent prayer (Cyprian). God's delay in fulfilling Hannah's desire displays providential kindness since affliction develops character and makes the heart wise (Chrysostom).

1:13-14 Hannah's Unspoken Prayer

Silent Prayer. Caesarius of Arles: As often as we apply ourselves to prayer, dearly beloved, we should above all pray in silence and quiet. If a man wants to pray aloud, he seems to take the fruit of prayer away from those who are standing near him. Only moans and sighs and groans should be heard. Indeed our prayer ought to be like that of holy Hannah, the mother of blessed Samuel, of whom it is written that "she prayed, shedding many tears, and only her lips moved, but her voice was not heard at all." Let everyone hear and imitate this, especially those who pray aloud without any embarrassment and in such a chattering fashion that they do not allow those near them to pray. Therefore, let us pray, as I said, with sighs and moans and groans, in accord with the words of the prophet: "I roared with the groaning of my heart."[1] Let us pray, I repeat, not with a loud voice but with our hearts crying out to God. Sermon 72.2.[2]

Women Are to Emulate Hannah. Cyril of Jerusalem: Let the virgins likewise form a separate band, singing hymns or reading; silently, however, so that while their lips speak, no other's ears may hear what they say. For, "I suffer not a woman to speak in church."[3] Let the married woman imitate them: let her pray and her lips move but her voice not be heard. So shall Samuel come among us: your barren soul, that is to say, shall bring forth the salvation of "God who has heard your prayers." For that is the meaning of "Samuel." Catechetical Lectures, Procatechesis 14.[4]

Secret Tears. Chrysostom: For I seek those tears which are shed not for display but in compunction; those which trickle down secretly and in closets and in sight of no person, softly and noiselessly; those which arise from a certain depth of mind, those shed in anguish and in sorrow, those which are for God alone. Such were Hannah's, for "her lips moved," it is said, "but her voice was not heard." Her tears alone uttered a cry more clear than any trumpet. And because of this, God also opened her womb and made the

---

[1]Ps 38:8 (37:8 LXX). [2]FC 31:339*. [3]1 Cor 14:34. [4]FC 61:81.

hard rock a fruitful field. Homilies on the Gospel of Matthew 6.8.[5]

Conversation with God. Clement of Alexandria: Prayer is, then, to speak more boldly, a conversation with God. Though whispering, consequently, and not opening the lips, we speak in silence, yet we cry inwardly. For God hears continually the whole inward conversation. Stromateis 7.7.[6]

God Hears the Heart. Cyprian: This Hannah does in the first book of Kings [Samuel], portraying a type of the church, [she] prays to God not with a noisy petition but silently and modestly within the very recesses of her heart. She spoke with a hidden prayer but with manifest faith. She did not speak with the voice but with the heart, because she knew that so the Lord hears, and she effectually obtained what she sought, because she asked with faith. Divine Scripture declares this, saying, "She spoke in her heart and her lips moved, but her voice was not heard, and the Lord heard her." The Lord's Prayer 5.[7]

Win Greater Favor from God. Chrysostom: At home her rival mocked her. She went into the temple, and the priest's boy abused her and the priest upbraided her. She fled the storm at home, entered port and still ran into turbulence. She went to get a remedy, and not only did not get it but received an additional burden of taunts, and the wound instead was opened up again. You are aware, of course, how distressed souls are susceptible to abuse and insult: just as bad wounds cannot stand the slightest contact with the hand but become worse, so too the soul that is disturbed and upset has problems with everything and is stung by a chance remark. The woman, on the contrary, was not like that, even in this case with the boy abusing her.[8] Had the priest been intoxicated, the insults would not have been so surprising; his high rank and heavy responsibility convinced her against her will to

keep her composure. But in fact she was not even upset with the priest's boy, and hence she won God's favor even further. Should we too be abused and suffer countless misadventures, let us put up nobly with those who insult us, and we shall thus win greater favor from God. Homilies on Hannah 2.[9]

The Testing of Affliction. Chrysostom: But observe even after this her deep reverence. "Only her lips moved, but her voice," it says, "was not heard." And in this way does the one who would gain his request draw near to God; not consulting his ease, nor gaping, nor lounging, nor scratching his head, nor with utter listlessness. So was not God able to grant, even without any prayer at all? So did he not know the woman's desire even before she asked? And yet had he granted it before she asked, then the woman's earnestness would not have been shown, her virtue would not have been made manifest, she would not have gained so great a reward. So that the delay is not the result of envy or of witchcraft but of providential kindness. When therefore you hear the Scripture saying that "the Lord had shut up her womb" and that "her rival deeply provoked her," consider that it is his intention to prove the woman's seriousness. For observe that she had a husband devoted to her, for he said, "Am I not better to you than ten sons?" "And her rival," it says, "deeply provoked her," that is, reproached her, insulted her. And yet she never once retaliated, nor uttered imprecation against her, nor said, "Avenge me, for my rival reviles me." The other had children, but this woman had her husband's love to make amends. With this at least he even consoled her, saying, "Am I not better to you than ten sons?"

But let us look again at the deep wisdom of this woman. "And Eli," it says, "thought she was drunk." Yet observe what she says to him also, "No, do not count your handmaid for a daughter

---

[5]NPNF 1 10:41*. [6]ANF 2:534*. [7]FC 36:130*. [8]In the LXX, the charge of drunkenness comes from Eli's servant. [9]COTH 1:87-88.

of Belial, for out of the abundance of my complaint and my provocation have I spoken up till now." Here is truly the proof of a contrite heart, when we are not angry with those that revile us, when we are not indignant against them, when we reply only in self-defense. Nothing renders the

heart so wise as affliction; nothing is there so sweet as "godly mourning."[10] Homilies on Ephesians 24.[11]

---

[10]2 Cor 7:10. [11]NPNF 1 13:170*.

1:19-28 SAMUEL'S BIRTH AND PRESENTATION AT SHILOH

[19]*They rose early in the morning and worshiped before the Lord; then they went back to their house at Ramah. And Elkanah knew Hannah his wife, and the Lord remembered her;* [20]*and in due time Hannah conceived and bore a son, and she called his name Samuel, for she said, "I have asked him of the Lord."* . . .

[24]*And when she had weaned him, she took him up with her, along with a three-year-old bull,*[b] *an ephah of flour, and a skin of wine; and she brought him to the house of the Lord at Shiloh; and the child was young.*

b Gk Syr: Heb *three bulls*

Overview: Women and men alike are urged to emulate Hannah as she faced intolerable calamity with faith and zeal toward God (Chrysostom). Hannah, who strove in prayer to overcome her barrenness, is a model of diligence and faithfulness (Augustine).

1:20 Hannah Bore a Son

Emulate Hannah's Faith. Chrysostom: Let the men among us emulate her, let the women among us imitate her: the woman is teacher of both sexes. Those who are sterile, let them not despair; those who are mothers, let them bring up in this fashion the children they have borne; and let everyone emulate this woman's faith in giving birth and zeal following the birth. I mean, what could reveal sounder values than the way she meekly and nobly put up in such a manner with an

intolerable calamity and did not desist until she had escaped the disaster and discovered a remarkable and baffling outcome of the problem, finding no helper or ally here below. In fact, she experienced the Lord's lovingkindness—hence she made her approach on her own and achieved what she wanted. That is to say, the remedy for that depression depended not on human help but on divine grace. Homilies on Hannah 2.[1]

1:24 Hannah Brings Samuel to the House of the Lord

A Model of Wholehearted Prayer. Augustine. Considering all these things, and whatever else the Lord shall have made known to you in this matter, which either does not occur to

---

[1]*COTH* 1:82-83.

me or would take too much time to state here, strive in prayer to overcome this world: pray in hope, pray in faith, pray in love, pray earnestly and patiently, pray as a widow belonging to Christ. For although prayer is, as he has taught, the duty of all his members, that is, of all who believe in him and are united to his body, a more assiduous attention to prayer is found to be specially enjoined in Scripture upon those who are widows. Two women of the name of [Hannah] are honorably named there—the one, Elkanah's wife, who was the mother of holy Samuel; the other, the widow who recognized the Most Holy One when he was yet a babe. [Hannah], though married, prayed with sorrow of mind and brokenness of heart because she had no sons; and she obtained Samuel and dedicated him to the Lord, because she vowed to do so when she prayed for him. LETTER 130.16[2]

---

[2]NPNF 1 1:468*.

2:1-10 HANNAH'S PRAYER

[1]*Hannah also prayed and said,*
   "My heart exults in the Lord;
      my strength is exalted in the Lord.
   My mouth derides my enemies,
      because I rejoice in thy salvation.
[2]*"There is none holy like the* Lord,
      there is none besides thee;
   there is no rock like our God.
[3]*Talk no more so very proudly,*
      let not arrogance come from your mouth;
   for the Lord *is a God of knowledge,*
      and by him actions are weighed.
[4]*The bows of the mighty are broken,*
      but the feeble gird on strength.
[5]*Those who were full have hired themselves out for bread,*
      but those who were hungry have ceased to hunger.
   The barren has borne seven,
      but she who has many children is forlorn.
[6]*The* Lord *kills and brings to life;*
      he brings down to Sheol and raises up.
[7]*The* Lord *makes poor and makes rich;*
      he brings low, he also exalts.

⁸*He raises up the poor from the dust;*
* he lifts the needy from the ash heap,*
to make them sit with princes
* and inherit a seat of honor.*
For the pillars of the earth are the Lord's,
* and on them he has set the world.*
⁹*"He will guard the feet of his faithful ones;*
* but the wicked shall be cut off in darkness;*
* for not by might shall a man prevail.*
¹⁰*The adversaries of the* Lord *shall be broken to pieces;*
* against them he will thunder in heaven.*
The Lord *will judge the ends of the earth;*
* he will give strength to his king,*
* and exalt the power of his anointed."*

OVERVIEW: More than simply offering her praise, Hannah portrayed the role of God's grace and the Christian religion when she uttered her prophetic prayer (AUGUSTINE). Hannah's glory, or horn, is secure because it has been exalted by God rather than human beings (CHRYSOSTOM). True glory is found not in wisdom or strength or riches but by knowing that the Lord is God (BASIL). Unlike humans, who are given existence through the divine will, God owes his existence to no other (ORIGEN). Since it is the flesh that is killed through death, it is the flesh that is revived by the resurrection (TERTULLIAN). Scripture foretells the return of Christ and his future judgment of all (EUSEBIUS). That the Lord will justify or condemn at the end sobers the proud and gives hope to the penitent (FRUCTUOSUS OF BRAGA).

2:1-10 Hannah Rejoices in Prayer

HANNAH THE PROPHET. AUGUSTINE: Are these words going to be regarded as simply the words of one mere woman giving thanks for the birth of her son? Are people's minds so turned away from the light of truth that they do not feel that the words poured out by this woman transcend the limit of her own thoughts? Surely, anyone who is appropriately moved by the events whose fulfillment has already begun, even in this earthly pilgrimage, must listen to these words and observe and recognize that through this woman (whose very name, Hannah, means "God's grace"[1]), there speaks, by the spirit of prophecy, the Christian religion itself, the City of God itself, whose king and founder is Christ. There speaks, in fact, the grace of God itself, from which the proud are estranged so that they fall, with which the humble are filled so that they rise up, which was in fact the chief theme that rang out in her hymn of praise. Now it may be that someone will be ready to say that the woman didn't utter a prophecy but merely praised God in an outburst of exultation for the son who was granted in answer to her prayer. If so, what is the meaning of this passage, "He has made weak the bow of the mighty ones, and the weak have girded themselves with strength. Those who were full of bread have been reduced to want, and the hungry have passed over the earth. Because the barren woman has given birth to seven, while she who has many children has become weak." Had Hannah herself really borne seven children, although she was barren?

---

[1]Hebrew *hānan* means "show favor" or "be gracious."

She had only one son when she spoke these words; and even afterwards she did not give birth to seven, or to six, which would have made Samuel the seventh. She had in fact three male and two female children. And then observe her concluding words, spoken among that people at a time when no one had yet been king over them: "He gives strength to our kings and will exalt the horn of his anointed." How is it that she said this, if she was not uttering a prophecy?

Therefore, let the church of Christ speak, the "city of the great king,"[2] the church that is "full of grace,"[3] fruitful in children. Let it speak the words that it recognizes as spoken prophetically about itself, so long ago, by the lips of this devout mother, "My heart is strengthened in the Lord; my horn is exalted in my God." Her heart is truly strengthened and her horn truly exalted, because it is "in the Lord her God," not in herself, that she finds strength and exaltation. CITY OF GOD 17.4.[4]

2:1 My Strength Is Exalted in the Lord

THE PERMANENCE OF GOD'S EXALTATION. CHRYSOSTOM: What is the meaning of "my horn"? Scripture frequently employs this phrase, remember, as when it says, "His horn was exalted" and "The horn of his anointed was exalted."[5] So what on earth does "horn" mean? Force, glory, prominence, using a metaphor from the brute beasts: God implanted in them only the horn by way of glory and weaponry, and if they lose it, they lose most of their force; and like a soldier without weapons a bull without horns is also easily disposed of. So by this the woman means nothing other than this, my glory is exalted. How is it exalted? "In my God," she says. Hence the exaltation is also secure, having a firm and permanent root: while glory from human beings corresponds to the baseness of those glorifying, and so is very liable to disappear, God's glory is not like that, remaining forever permanent. HOMILIES ON HANNAH 4.[6]

2:2 There Is None Other Than God

ONLY GOD TRULY EXISTS. ORIGEN: "Be holy, for I also am holy."[7] But however much one might advance in sanctity, however much purity and sincerity one might acquire, a human being cannot be holy like the Lord, because he is the bestower of sanctity, the human being its receiver, he is the fountain of sanctity, the human being the drinker from the fountain, he is the light of sanctity, the human being the contemplator of the holy light. Thus "there is none holy like the Lord, there is none besides thee." What it means to say "There is none besides thee," I do not understand. If it had said, "There is no God but you" or "There is no creator but you" or had added something like this, there would be no problem. But if it now says "There is none besides thee," this is what it seems to me to mean here: none of those things which are possess their existence by nature. You alone, O Lord, are the one to whom your existence has not been given by anyone. Because all of us, that is the whole creation, did not exist before we were created; thus, that we are, is [due to] the will of the Creator. And because there was a time when we were not, it is not wholly right if it is said of us, without qualification, that we exist.... For the shadow is nothing in comparison with the body; and in comparison with the fire, smoke too is nothing. HOMILIES ON 1 KINGS 1.11.[8]

2:3 Speak Not Proudly

TRUE GLORY. BASIL THE GREAT: No sensible person, then, will be proud of his wisdom ... but will follow the excellent advice of blessed Hannah and of the prophet Jeremiah, "Let not the wise man glory in his wisdom and let not the strong man glory in his strength and let not the rich man glory in his riches." But what is true glory and what makes one great? "In this," says the prophet, "let him that glories, glory, that he understands

[2]Ps 48:2 (47:2 LXX). [3]Lk 1:28 Vg. [4]CG 717*. [5]See Ps 75:10 (74:10 LXX); 1 Sam 2:10. [6]COTH 1:113*. [7]See Lev 20:26; Mt 5:48. [8]OSF 52*.

and knows that I am the Lord."[9] This constitutes the pinnacle of human dignity, this is his glory and greatness: truly to know what is great and to cleave to it, and to seek after glory from the Lord of glory. On Humility.[10]

2:6 The Lord Kills and Brings to Life

Resurrection of the Flesh. Tertullian: Certainly his making alive is to take place after he has killed. As, therefore, it is by death that he kills, it is by the resurrection that he will make alive. Now it is the flesh which is killed by death; the flesh, therefore, will be revived by the resurrection. Surely if killing means taking away life from the flesh, and its opposite, reviving, amounts to restoring life to the flesh, it must needs be that the flesh rise again, to which the life, which has been taken away by killing, has to be restored by vivification. On the Resurrection of the Flesh 28.[11]

2:10 The Lord Will Judge

Christ's Return. Eusebius of Caesaria: These words refer to the return of Christ or to the return of God to heaven. His teaching [will be] heard like thunder by all, and holy Scripture foretells his future judgment of all afterwards. And after this it is said that the Lord will give strength to our kings. And these would be the apostles of Christ, of whom it is written in Psalm 67: "The Lord will give a word to the preachers of the gospel with much power." Here, also, he mentions Christ by name, humanly known as our Savior, whose horn he says shall be exalted, meaning his invisible power and kingdom. For it is usual for Scripture to call a kingdom a "horn." It is found also in Psalm 88: "And in my name shall his horn be exalted." Proof of the Gospel 1.4.16.[12]

Judgment at the End. Fructuosus of Braga: For it is written: "He himself shall judge the ends of the earth." The Lord justifies or condemns each person at the end and considers the outcome of all things, so that not even the sinner, if he or she truly repents, need despair of forgiveness, nor should the just person have confidence in his own sanctity. General Rule for Monasteries 19.[13]

---

[9]Jer 9:24. [10]FC 9:478-79*. [11]ANF 3:565. [12]POG 1:212-13*. [13]FC 63:203.

2:11-21 THE MINISTRY OF SAMUEL AND ELI'S CORRUPT SONS

[12]*Now the sons of Eli were worthless men; they had no regard for the LORD.* [13]*The custom of the priests with the people was that when any man offered sacrifice, the priest's servant would come, while the meat was boiling, with a three-pronged fork in his hand,* [14]*and he would thrust it into the pan, or kettle, or caldron, or pot; all that the fork brought up the priest would take for himself.[c] So they did at Shiloh to all the Israelites who came there.* [15]*Moreover, before the fat was burned, the priest's servant would come and say to the man who was sacrificing, "Give meat for the priest to roast; for he will not accept boiled meat from you, but raw."* [16]*And if the man said to him, "Let*

them burn the fat first, and then take as much as you wish," he would say, "No, you must give it now; and if not, I will take it by force." [17]*Thus the sin of the young men was very great in the sight of the LORD; for the men treated the offering of the LORD with contempt.*

[18]*Samuel was ministering before the LORD, a boy girded with a linen ephod.* [19]*And his mother used to make for him a little robe and take it to him each year, when she went up with her husband to offer the yearly sacrifice.* [20]*Then Eli would bless Elkanah and his wife, and say, "The LORD give you children by this woman for the loan which she lent to[d] the LORD"; so then they would return to their home.*

[21]*And the LORD visited Hannah, and she conceived and bore three sons and two daughters. And the boy Samuel grew in the presence of the LORD.*

c Gk Syr Vg: Heb *with it* d Or *for the petition which she asked of*

OVERVIEW: Samuel serves as one example among many of saints who suffered due to the faithlessness of their own people (AUGUSTINE). Imitate the faith of Hannah, who fulfilled her vow by offering her firstborn to God (JEROME).

2:12-17 The Wickedness of Eli's Sons

GODLY TOLERATION. AUGUSTINE: Samuel bore with the wicked sons of Eli, his debased sons whom the people would not bear and who were thereupon accused by divine truth or disciplined by divine wrath; finally he bore with the people themselves in their pride and rejection of God. . . . Let them read who wish, and who can, the heavenly language. They will find that all the saints have had to tolerate among their own people those who were recognized as servants and friends of God. LETTER 43.[1]

2:21 Hannah Bears More Children

IMITATE HANNAH'S FAITH. JEROME: When Hannah had once offered in the tabernacle the son whom she had vowed to God, she never took him back: for she thought it unbecoming that one who was to be a prophet should grow up in the same house with her who still desired to have other sons. Accordingly after she had conceived him and given him birth, she did not venture to come to the temple alone or to appear before the Lord empty but first paid to him what she owed, and then, when she had offered up that great sacrifice, she returned home; and because she had borne her firstborn for God, she was given five children for herself. Do you marvel at the happiness of that holy woman? Imitate her faith. LETTER 107.13.[2]

[1]FC 12:202*. [2]LCC 5:344.

2:22-26 ELI CONFRONTS HIS SONS' EVIL WAYS

[22]*Now Eli was very old, and he heard all that his sons were doing to all Israel, and how they lay with the women who served at the entrance to the tent of meeting.* [23]*And he said to them, "Why do you do such things? For I hear of your evil dealings from all the people.* [24]*No, my sons; it is no good*

report that I hear the people of the LORD spreading abroad. [25]*If a man sins against a man, God will mediate for him; but if a man sins against the LORD, who can intercede for him?" But they would not listen to the voice of their father; for it was the will of the LORD to slay them.*

OVERVIEW: The case of Eli, who failed to exercise sufficient zealousness regarding his wicked sons, illustrates God's condemnation of all disobedience (BASIL). That blasphemy against the Holy Spirit and God is unpardonable reveals the divine nature of the Holy Spirit (NICETAS OF REMESIANA). Like the priest Eli, who understood what sins could be expiated according to the law, the apostles and their followers prescribe or prohibit sacrifice for sins (ORIGEN). The sin that leads to death is a current sin for which no repentance has been offered (PACIAN OF BARCELONA).

2:22-25 The Wickedness of Eli's Sons

THE CONDEMNATION OF DISOBEDIENCE.
BASIL THE GREAT: Because their father [Eli] did not chastise them with enough severity . . . he moved the forbearance of God to wrath so great that foreign peoples rose up against them and killed those sons of his in war in one day. His entire nation, furthermore, was vanquished, and a considerable number of his people fell. Now, this happened even with the ark of the holy covenant of God nearby—an unheard of thing—so that the ark, which it was not lawful at any time for the Israelites or even for all their priests themselves to touch and which was kept in a special place, was carried hither and yon by impious hands and was put in the shrines of idols instead of the holy temples. Under such circumstances one can readily conjecture the amount of laughter and mockery that was inflicted upon the very name of God by these foreigners. Add to this, also, that Eli himself is recorded to have met a most pitiable end after hearing the threat that his seed would be removed from the priestly dignity; and so it happened.

Such, then, were the disasters which befell that nation. Such griefs did the father suffer because of the iniquity of his sons, even though no accusation was ever made against Eli's personal life. Moreover, he did not bear with those sons of his silence, but he earnestly exhorted them not to persist longer in those same wicked deeds, saying, "Do not act this way, my sons; for I hear no good report concerning you." And to stress the enormity of their sin, he confronted them with an alarming view of their perilous state. "If one man shall sin against another," he said, "they will pray for him to the Lord; but if a man shall sin against God, who shall pray for him?" Yet, as I said, because he did not exercise a suitable rigor of zeal in their regard, the disaster recounted above took place. And so I find throughout the Old Testament a great many instances of this kind illustrating the condemnation of all disobedience. PREFACE ON THE JUDGMENT OF GOD.[1]

2:25 Sin Against God

THE NATURE OF THE HOLY SPIRIT. NICETAS OF REMESIANA: The sin of one who blasphemes against the Holy Spirit is unpardonable. Compare with this judgment what is said in the book of Kings [Samuel]: "If one man shall sin against the Lord, who shall pray for him?" Thus, it is one and the same sin whether we blaspheme against the Holy Spirit or against God, and it is inexpiable. Hence, the nature of the Holy Spirit begins to dawn in our minds. THE POWER OF THE HOLY SPIRIT 17.[2]

PRIESTLY AUTHORITY AND FORGIVENESS.
ORIGEN: The law prohibits priests in the case of certain sins from offering a sacrifice to gain people forgiveness for the transgressions for which

---

[1]FC 9:46-47*. [2]FC 7:37-38*.

sacrifices are made. For though the priest has authority to make an offering for certain inadvertent sins or transgressions, nevertheless he does not offer a burnt offering and a sin offering for adultery, deliberate murder, or any other graver fault. Therefore, it is in the same way that the apostles and those like the apostles, since they are priests according to the great High Priest, have received knowledge of God's healing and know, since they are taught by the Spirit, for what sins sacrifice must be offered and when and how; and they know for what sins it is wrong to do this. Thus, Eli the priest, when he knew that his sons Hophni and Phinehas were sinning, realizing he could in no way contribute to the forgiveness of their sins, acknowledged it as a hopeless case and said, "If a man sins against a man, they will pray for him; but if he sins against he Lord, who will pray for him?" ON PRAYER 28.9.[3]

SIN THAT LEADS TO DEATH. PACIAN OF BAR-

CELONA: "Eli the priest speaks, stating, 'If a man sins against another man, they shall offer entreaties on his behalf; but if he sins against God, who shall offer entreaties on his behalf?'" In the same way John writes, "If anyone knows that his brother commits a sin which does not lead to death, he shall implore [God] on his behalf, and God shall give him life. Indeed, there is a sin that leads to death; I do not say that you should pray about that."[4] You see that all of this refers to sins still remaining, not to those persons who have at any time sinned and have begun to repent before anyone asks on their behalf. It is too long a task for us to go over such instances. Observe every one of the sins for which the Lord makes threats; you will at once see that they are current ones. LETTER 3.16.2.[5]

---

[3]OSW 151*. [4]1 Jn 5:16. [5]FC 99:57*.

2:27-36 THE LORD REJECTS ELI'S HOUSE

[27]*And there came a man of God to Eli, and said to him, "Thus the LORD has said, 'I revealed[e] myself to the house of your father when they were in Egypt subject to the house of Pharaoh. [28]And I chose him out of all the tribes of Israel to be my priest, to go up to my altar, to burn incense, to wear an ephod before me; and I gave to the house of your father all my offerings by fire from the people of Israel. [29]Why then look with greedy eye at[f] my sacrifices and my offerings which I commanded, and honor your sons above me by fattening yourselves upon the choicest parts of every offering of my people Israel?' [30]Therefore the LORD the God of Israel declares: 'I promised that your house and the house of your father should go in and out before me for ever'; but now the LORD declares: 'Far be it from me; for those who honor me I will honor, and those who despise me shall be lightly esteemed. [31]Behold, the days are coming, when I will cut off your strength and the strength of your father's house, so that there will not be an old man in your house.'"*

e Gk Tg: Heb *Did I reveal*   **f** Or *treat with scorn* Gk: Heb *kick at*

Overview: Giving honor to priests, although a burden to them with respect to the future, shows honor to God (Chrysostom). Eli's negligence regarding his sons illustrates how a policy of equality, rather than of discipline, causes evil to increase (Gregory the Great). As one who brings about good and not evil, God confers glory upon the good and allows evil to work out its own punishment (Ambrose). As God's friends, the duty of those whom God has honored is to continue to give honor to God (Chrysostom). The saints, who will receive a heavenly crown, also receive honor in the present life (Jerome). Honoring God benefits the individual and not God: the one who honors God pursues virtue and receives God's honor. Parents must discipline their children appropriately to ensure that they are not held liable for the errors of their offspring (Chrysostom).

2:27-28 Chosen to Be Priests

Honor the Priest. Chrysostom: For with respect to the future, they [rulers] will not be benefited by the honor done them but receive the greater condemnation; neither will they be injured as to the future by ill treatment but will have the more excuse. But all this I desire to be done for your own sakes. For when rulers are honored by their people, this too is reckoned against them; as in the case of Eli it is said, "Did I not choose him out of his father's house?" But when they are insulted, as in the instance of Samuel, God said, "They have not rejected you, but they have rejected me."[1] Therefore insult is their gain, honor their burden. What I say, therefore, is for your sakes, not for theirs. He that honors the priest will honor God also; and he who has learned to despise the priest will sooner or later insult God. Homilies on 2 Timothy 2.[2]

2:29 Why Honor Your Sons Above Me?

A Policy of Discipline. Gregory the Great: Sometimes, though, greater evil ensues when in the case of wicked persons a policy of equality is adhered to rather than of discipline. Eli, for example, overcome by misguided affection and unwilling to chastise his delinquent sons, struck both himself and his sons before the strict judge with a cruel sentence, for the divine utterance was, "You have honored your sons rather than me." Pastoral Care 2.6.[3]

2:30 Those Who Honor Me

The Glory of the Good. Ambrose: If we regard the sentence passed on him [the serpent] to be in the nature of a condemnation, God did not condemn the serpent in order to cause injury to humans. He pointed out what was to happen in the future.[4] . . . What we are to expect can in some measure be gathered from our knowledge of what has been written: "Whoever shall glorify me, him will I glorify, and he that despises me shall be despised." God brings to pass what is good, not what is evil, as his words can teach you that he confers glory and disregards punishment. "Whoever shall glorify me," he says, "him will I glorify," thus declaring that the glory of the good is the purpose of his work. And concerning "him that despises me," he did not say I shall deprive of glory, but that he shall be deprived of glory. He did not avow that injury to them [Adam and Eve] would be the result of his action but pointed out what was to come. On Paradise 15.74.[5]

The Duty of God's Friends. Chrysostom: If he [the Lord] says, "Those who honor me I will honor, and those that despise me shall be lightly esteemed," then we should reflect on what he requires of us also. True, it is to the praise of his glory that he saves those who are his enemies, yet those who have become his friends should continue to act as his friends. For if they were to return to their former state of enmity all [that

---

[1]1 Sam 8:7. [2]NPNF 1 13:481*. [3]ACW 11:65-66*. [4]Gen 3:14-15. [5]FC 42:352-53.

had been borne of their friendship] would be rendered futile and purposeless. There is not another baptism or a second reconciliation but "a certain fearful expectation of judgment which shall devour the adversaries."[6] If we intend—at the same time—to be at enmity with him and yet claim his forgiveness, we shall never be rid of enmity, wantonness and depravity, and [we will] be blind to the sun of righteousness which has risen. . . . But once you have tasted the goodness and the honey, if you abandon them and return to your own vomit, what else are you doing but bringing forward evidence of excessive hatred and contempt? Homilies on Ephesians 2.[7]

Honor in the Present Life. Jerome: A pearl will shine in the midst of squalor, and a gem . . . will sparkle in the mire. This is what the Lord promised when he said, "Those who honor me I will honor." Others may understand this of the future when sorrow shall be turned into joy and when, although the world shall pass away, the saints shall receive a crown which shall never pass. But I for my part see that the promises made to the saints are fulfilled even in this present life. Letter 66.7.[8]

The Fruit of Honoring God. Chrysostom: In honoring him, therefore, we do honor to ourselves. He who opens his eyes to gaze on the light of the sun receives delight himself, as he admires the beauty of the star but does no favor to that luminary nor increases its splendor, for it continues [to be] what it was; much more is this true with respect to God. He who admires and honors God does so to his own salvation, and highest benefit; and how? Because he follows after virtue and is honored by him. For "them that honor me," he says, "I will honor." Homilies on 1 Timothy 4.[9]

2:31 I Will Cut off Your Strength

Disciplining Children. Chrysostom: Hence I beg you to offer a hand to our children lest we ourselves become liable for what is committed by them. Are you not aware of what happened to old Eli for not properly correcting his sons' shortcomings? I mean, when a disease requires surgery, it rapidly becomes incurable if the physician is bent on treating it with skin ointments and does not apply the appropriate remedy. In just the same way it behooved that old man to take appropriate action regarding his sons' failing, but by being guilty of excessive tolerance he too shared in their punishment. Homilies on Genesis 59.20.[10]

---

[6]Heb 10:27. [7]NPNF 1 13:57**. [8]NPNF 2 6:137*. [9]NPNF 1 13:421*. [10]FC 87:176*.

3:1-9 THE LORD CALLS SAMUEL

[2]*At that time Eli, whose eyesight had begun to grow dim, so that he could not see, was lying down in his own place;* [3]*the lamp of God had not yet gone out, and Samuel was lying down within the temple of the Lord, where the ark of God was.* [4]*Then the Lord called, "Samuel! Samuel!"*[i] *and he said, "Here I am!"* [5]*and ran to Eli, and said, "Here I am, for you called me." But he said, "I did not call; lie down again." So he went and lay down.* [6]*And the Lord called again, "Samuel!" and*

Samuel arose and went to Eli, and said, "Here I am, for you called me." But he said, "I did not call, my son; lie down again." [7]Now Samuel did not yet know the Lord, and the word of the Lord had not yet been revealed to him. [8]And the Lord called Samuel again the third time. And he arose and went to Eli, and said, "Here I am, for you called me." Then Eli perceived that the Lord was calling the boy. [9]Therefore Eli said to Samuel, "Go, lie down; and if he calls you, you shall say, 'Speak, Lord, for thy servant hears.'" So Samuel went and lay down in his place.

i Gk See 3.10: Heb *the* LORD *called Samuel*

Overview: "Temple of the Lord" signifies the tabernacle in which the ark of covenant was placed (Theodore of Mopsuestia). It pleases God for the young to benefit from the teaching of elders (Cassian).

3:3 Within the Temple of the Lord

Powerful Presence. Theodore of Mopsuestia: It says "The Lord is in his holy temple,"[1] as if it had been appropriate to say "The Lord is his help." For the Lord's name alone is commonly inserted as an indication of assistance. But here the psalmist intends to indicate that there is one who lives in the temple and is used for defense and protection, in whom it is able to stand firm securely in hope against all treachery. But what it calls the temple is the tabernacle in which the ark of God was placed, for the temple had not yet been built. That the tabernacle may be called the temple, the testimony of Kings [Samuel] clearly instructs, since the construction of the temple had not begun at the time: "And Samuel was lying down in the temple of God, in which the ark of God was located." Expositions on Psalms, Psalm 10.[2]

3:4-9 Samuel Hears His Name Called

On Learning from Elders. John Cassian: And therefore by no means let the ignorance or shallowness of one old man or of a few deter you and cut you off from that salutary path about which we have spoken and from the traditions of our forebears. The clever enemy misuses their gray hairs to deceive the young. But everything should be revealed to the elders without any obfuscating embarrassment, and from them one may confidently receive both healing for one's wounds and examples for one's way of life. Thanks to them we shall experience the same assistance and a like result if we strive to aim at nothing whatsoever by our own judgment and presumption.

Finally, it is evident that this understanding is greatly pleasing to God, for not without reason do we find this same instruction even in holy Scripture. Thus, the Lord did not desire of himself to teach the boy Samuel through divine speech, once he had been chosen by his own decision, but he was obliged to return twice to the old man. He willed that one whom he was calling to an intimate relationship with himself should even be instructed by a person who had offended God, because he was an old man. And he desired that one whom he judged most worthy to be selected by himself should be reared by an old man so that the humility of him who was called to a divine ministry might be tested and so that the pattern of this subjection might be offered as an example to young men. Conference 2.13.12-2.14.[3]

[1]Ps 11:4 (10:5 LXX). [2]CCL 88A:56. [3]ACW 57:98-99*.

3:10-21 THE LORD REVEALS HIMSELF TO SAMUEL

¹⁰And the LORD came and stood forth, calling as at other times, "Samuel! Samuel!" And Samuel said, "Speak, for thy servant hears." ¹¹Then the LORD said to Samuel, "Behold, I am about to do a thing in Israel, at which the two ears of every one that hears it will tingle. ¹²On that day I will fulfil against Eli all that I have spoken concerning his house, from beginning to end. ¹³And I tell him that I am about to punish his house for ever, for the iniquity which he knew, because his sons were blaspheming God,ʲ and he did not restrain them. ¹⁴Therefore I swear to the house of Eli that the iniquity of Eli's house shall not be expiated by sacrifice or offering for ever."

j Another reading is *for themselves*

OVERVIEW: Through Eli's example we learn that extending kindness to the wicked betrays the truth, assaults the community and harms the one who extends it (BASIL). Likewise, failure to vindicate thoroughly God's laws brings grievous punishment (CHRYSOSTOM). The Lord manifests his wrath upon all who transgress his statutes, even upon genuine servants who have lived righteously for many years (ISAAC OF NINEVEH).

3:13 Eli Failed to Restrain His Sons

MISTAKEN KINDNESS. BASIL THE GREAT: Benevolence to such persons is like that mistaken kindness of Eli which he was accused of showing his sons, contrary to the good pleasure of God. A feigned kindness to the wicked is a betrayal of the truth, an act of treachery to the community and a means of habituating oneself to indifference to evil. THE LONG RULES 28.[1]

ZEALOUSNESS FOR GOD'S LAWS. CHRYSOSTOM: For no one of those who are now rich will stand up for me there when I am called to account and accused, as not having thoroughly vindicated the laws of God with all due earnestness. For this is what ruined that admirable old man, though the way he lived his own life provided no reason for blame: yet for all that, because he overlooked the treading under foot of God's laws he was chastised with his children and paid that grievous penalty. And if, where the absolute authority of nature was so great, he who failed to treat his own children with due firmness endured so grievous a punishment; what indulgence shall we have, freed as we are from that dominion and yet ruining all by flattery? HOMILIES ON THE GOSPEL OF MATTHEW 17.6.[2]

LOVE FOR THE LORD'S STATUTES. ISAAC OF NINEVEH: For what reason did wrath and death come upon the house of the priest Eli, the righteous elder who was eminent for forty years in his priesthood? Was it not because of the iniquity of his sons Hophni and Phinehas? For neither did he sin, nor did they with his assent, but it was because he did not have the zeal to demand from them the Lord's vindication and he loved them more than the statutes of the Lord. Lest someone surmise that the Lord manifests his wrath only upon those who pass all the days of their life in iniquities, behold how for this unseemly sin he manifests his zeal against his genuine servants, against priests, judges, rulers, people consecrated to him, to whom he entrusted the working of miracles, and he does not overlook their transgression of his statutes. ASCETICAL HOMILIES 10.[3]

---

[1]FC 9:290*. [2]NPNF 1 10:123*. [3]AHSIS 75*.

4:1-9 ISRAEL ATTACKS THE PHILISTINES

[1]*Now Israel went out to battle against the Philistines; they encamped at Ebenezer, and the Philistines encamped at Aphek. . . .*

[6]*And when they learned that the ark of the LORD had come to the camp,* [7]*the Philistines were afraid; for they said, "A god has come into the camp." And they said, "Woe to us! For nothing like this has happened before.* [8]*Woe to us! Who can deliver us from the power of these mighty gods? These are the gods who smote the Egyptians with every sort of plague in the wilderness."*

OVERVIEW: The Philistines testify that God has selected one nation, Israel, to teach all others the knowledge of God (THEODORET).

4:8 The Philistines Fear the Ark of the Lord

SPREADING HIS MAJESTY. THEODORET OF CYR: For he selected this one nation to teach the knowledge of God to all the others. ... The Philistines also testified to this. They feared the presence of the ark and said to one another, "This is the God who struck Egypt. Woe to us Philistines." Then God gave the ark to the Philistines to convict his people of transgressing the law. For he could not make those who flagrantly broke the law its upholders. But in giving the ark he safeguarded his majesty, teaching the Philistines that it was sinful men they had conquered and not God. ON DIVINE PROVIDENCE 10.49-50.[1]

---

[1]ACW 49:150.

4:10-18 THE CAPTURE OF THE ARK OF GOD

[10]*So the Philistines fought, and Israel was defeated. . . .* [11]*And the ark of God was captured; and the two sons of Eli, Hophni and Phinehas, were slain.*

[12]*A man of Benjamin ran from the battle line, and came to Shiloh the same day, with his clothes rent and with earth upon his head.* [13]*When he arrived, Eli was sitting upon his seat by the road watching, for his heart trembled for the ark of God. And when the man came into the city and told the news, all the city cried out.* [14]*When Eli heard the sound of the outcry, he said, "What is this uproar?" Then the man hastened and came and told Eli. . . .* [18]*When he mentioned the ark of God, Eli fell over backward from his seat by the side of the gate; and his neck was broken and he died, for he was an old man, and heavy. He had judged Israel forty years.*

OVERVIEW: The tabernacle erected by the Lord is to be inhabited by the innocent in hands and pure in heart (ORIGEN). A bishop's chastity must extend to his children (JEROME). Eli failed in his essential pastoral duty to correct the sinners and was punished severely (CAESARIUS OF ARLES).

4:11 The Ark of God Was Captured

INHABITING THE TABERNACLE. ORIGEN: How will it be true to say about that [earthly] tabernacle that only "the innocent in hands and pure in heart, who did not receive his soul in vain,"[1] will inhabit it, when the history of the kings transmits that the worst priests, "sons of pestilence," have dwelt in the tabernacle of God and the ark of the covenant itself also was captured by foreigners and detained with the impious and profane? From all of this it is evident that the prophet felt in a far different sense about this tabernacle[2] in which he says that only "the innocent in hands and pure in heart, who did not receive his soul in vain nor do evil to his neighbor and did not accept reproach against his neighbor" will dwell.[3] It is necessary, therefore, that the inhabitant of this tabernacle which the Lord erected, not man, be such a person. HOMILIES ON EXODUS 9.2.[4]

4:18 Eli Dies

CHASTITY REQUIRED. JEROME: See what chastity is required in a bishop! If his child is unchaste, he himself cannot be a bishop, and he offends God in the same way as did Eli the priest, who had indeed rebuked his sons, but because he had not put away the offenders, fell backwards and died before the lamp of God went out. AGAINST JOVINIANUS 1.35.[5]

ESSENTIAL PUNISHMENT. CAESARIUS OF ARLES: Harsh preaching provides remedies for souls that are sick and arranges adornments for the healthy. What the Holy Spirit threatens the Lord's priests through the prophet is not a slight matter. "If you do not declare to the wicked his iniquity," he says, "I will require his blood at your hand,"[6] and again: "cry, do not cease; lift up your voice like a trumpet, and show my people their sins."[7] ... For this reason, dearly beloved, I absolve my conscience in the sight of God as often as I mention with humility a few words for the salvation of your soul. Indeed, I fear and shudder at the example of Eli, the priest, for, when he heard that his sons were committing adultery, he pretended to kill them or to suspend them from communion, but only gently admonished them, saying, "My sons, it is no good report that I hear about you. If one man shall sin against another, the priest will pray for him; but if the priest himself sins, who shall pray for him?"[8] Now, in spite of this admonition, he fell backwards from his stool and died of a broken neck, and his name was blotted out of the book of life, because he did not punish his sons with great severity. SERMON 5.[9]

---

[1]Ps 24:4 (23:4 LXX). [2]Origen suggests that the prophet is speaking of an eternal tabernacle rather than the one initiated in the wilderness, which is an imperfect representation of the heavenly one. [3]Ps 24:4; 15:3 (23:4; 14:3 LXX). [4]FC 71:336. [5]NPNF 2 6:373*. [6]Is 58:1. [7]Lk 19:23, 30. [8]1 Sam 2:24-25. [9]FC 31:32-33*.

4:19-22 THE BIRTH OF ICHABOD

[19]*Now his daughter-in-law, the wife of Phinehas, was with child, about to give birth. And when she heard the tidings that the ark of God was captured, and that her father-in-law and her hus-*

band were dead, she bowed and gave birth; for her pains came upon her. [20]And about the time of her death the women attending her said to her, "Fear not, for you have borne a son." But she did not answer or give heed. [21]And she named the child Ichabod, saying, "The glory has departed from Israel!" because the ark of God had been captured and because of her father-in-law and her husband.

Overview: The pain of giving birth, which is likened to the pain of hell, is rarely associated with holy women in Scripture (Jerome). The unmourned death of Phinehas' widow is perceived as one among many in accordance with the psalmist's account (Cassiodorus).

4:19-20 The Wife of Phinehas Gives Birth

Labors of Death. Jerome: Read the Scriptures and you will never find holy women bearing children in pain, with the exception of Rachel, who, when she was on a journey and in the hippodrome, that is, in the course for horses which had been sold to Egypt,[1] suffered while delivering her son, whom his father later called "son of the right hand."[2] Eve, when she was expelled from paradise and was told "You will bear children in pain,"[3] is described as experiencing pain in childbirth. The wife of Phinehas, who was bent over and could not stand erect, like the woman whom the devil bound in the gospel,[4] gave birth after she had heard that the ark of God was captured and her people were destroyed. But Sarah, because she was holy and postmenopausal,[5] said to Isaac when he was born: "God has made laughter for me, for whoever hears about this will congratulate me."[6] The pains, therefore, which overcame the tower of the flock,[7] are the pains of hell and the pains of death, which surrounded and attacked even the Savior but were never able to overtake him, as he himself says in Psalm 17:5: "The pains of death surrounded me and the torrents of evil shook me and the pains of hell attacked me." Commentary on Micah 2.4.[8]

The Fate of Many Widows. Cassiodorus: "Their priests fell by the sword and their widows were not mourned."[9] We read that during the captivity the sons of the priest Eli were put to the sword by the foreigners. The wife of one of them thus widowed suddenly gave birth and prematurely died. So it happened that his widow went wholly unmourned, since they were all preoccupied by the widespread deaths. We must believe that this fate befell many widows among the people, since divine authority has cited a plurality of widows, and we know that no detail recorded is useless. Exposition of the Psalms 77.64.[10]

[1]Cf. 2 Macc 5:1-4. [2]Benjamin; see Gen 35:16-20. [3]Gen 3:16. [4]See Lk 13:10-16. [5]See Gen 18:11. [6]Gen 21:6. [7]See Gen 35:21; Mic 4:8. [8]CCL 76:475-76. [9]Ps 78:64 (77:64 LXX). [10]ACW 52:271*.

5:1-5 THE ARK OF GOD IN THE HOUSE OF DAGON

[1]When the Philistines captured the ark of God, they carried it from Ebenezer to Ashdod; [2]then the Philistines took the ark of God and brought it into the house of Dagon and set it up beside

Dagon. ³And when the people of Ashdod rose early the next day, behold, Dagon had fallen face downward on the ground before the ark of the Lord. So they took Dagon and put him back in his place. ⁴But when they rose early on the next morning, behold, Dagon had fallen face downward on the ground before the ark of the Lord, and the head of Dagon and both his hands were lying cut off upon the threshold; only the trunk of Dagon was left to him. ⁵This is why the priests of Dagon and all who enter the house of Dagon do not tread on the threshold of Dagon in Ashdod to this day.

OVERVIEW: The presence of religious articles, such as the ark or books of the law and prophets, does not make the temple holy (CHRYSOSTOM). Dagon's temple, void of its idol after its second fall before the ark of the Lord, remains a reminder of God's justice for succeeding generations (THEODORET).

5:2-5 Dagon Falls

THE PRESENCE OF THE ARK. CHRYSOSTOM: In short, if you believe the place is holy because the law and the books of prophets are there, then it is time for you to believe that idols and the temples of idols are holy. Once, when the Jews were at war, the people of Ashdod conquered them, took their ark and brought it into their own temple. Did the fact that it contained the ark make their temple a holy place? By no means! It continued to be profane and unclean, as the events immediately proved. For God wanted to teach the enemies of the Jews that the defeat was not due to God's weakness but to the transgressions of those who worshiped him. And so the ark, which had been taken as booty in war, gave proof of its own power in an alien land by twice throwing the idol to the ground so that the idol was broken. The ark was so far from making that temple a holy place that it even openly attacked it. DISCOURSES AGAINST JUDAIZING CHRISTIANS 6.7.1.[1]

FALSE GODS AND THE TRUE GOD ARE DISTINGUISHED. THEODORET OF CYR: So Dagon who was adored as God by them (although he was a dumb, senseless idol) was made to fall before the ark, and God prepared to stage a spectacle for the spectators, so that the Philistines might perceive the difference between false god and true God.

In their folly, they raised him up again only to see him fallen a second time and brought to his knees, so to speak. Behaving thus with singular stupidity and reluctant to recognize the difference, they were taught by experience not to run to excess. Having learned their lesson, they returned to their senses, shook off their drunken ignorance and returned the ark, as was fitting, to its proper admirers, having honored it with votive offerings. They confessed their chastisements and instructed those who received it about the manner of its return. ON DIVINE PROVIDENCE 10.50-51.[2]

A REMINDER FOR SUCCEEDING GENERATIONS. CHRYSOSTOM: And now is not the first time, but he has performed these amazing marvels from time immemorial. It is not pertinent to enumerate them all; I shall mention what seems to resemble these events most closely. Once when the Jews waged war in Palestine with certain foreigners and the enemy was victorious and took the ark of God, they dedicated it as the choice part of the spoils to one of their local idols named Dagon; and, as soon as the ark was brought in, the statue fell down and lay on its face. Since they did not comprehend God's mighty power from this fall but set it up and again placed it on its pedestal, when they appeared the next day at dawn they observed that it was no longer simply fallen but also quite broken. The arms, detached from the shoulders, were flung onto the threshold of the temple, with the feet; and the rest of the

---

[1]FC 68:172*. [2]ACW 49:150-51.

statue was scattered in another place in pieces. . . . Therefore the place, which is able to exist for a long time, receives the blow and reminds each succeeding generation that those who do such things are ordained by law to suffer such things

even if they do not pay the penalty at once; which is exactly what happened in the case of this temple. Discourse on Blessed Babylas 116.[3]

---

[3]FC 73:144-45.

5:6-12 THE LORD AFFLICTS THE PHILISTINES

[6]*The hand of the Lord was heavy upon the people of Ashdod, and he terrified and afflicted them with tumors, both Ashdod and its territory.* [7]*And when the men of Ashdod saw how things were, they said, "The ark of the God of Israel must not remain with us; for his hand is heavy upon us and upon Dagon our god."*

Overview: Gregory the Great offers an allegorical interpretation of the affliction suffered by the people of Ashdod that signifies two kinds of death. Those who have witnessed Christ's power and continue in their idolatrous ways are not simply ignorant of Scripture's precepts but actively refuse to learn them, to their own peril (Bede).

5:6 The Hand of the Lord Was Heavy

Two Kinds of Death. Gregory the Great: And this explains how they died. It is said that each one died when he went out to purge his bowels and was bitten in the inner part of his buttocks by mice.[1] Now this wound is shown here in a literal fashion, but it is united with an allegorical exposition. For in its literal meaning, it refers to the illness caused by the hand of the Lord and the bites of the mice, which led to the outcome of death. It is said that the hand of the Lord weighed heavily upon the inhabitants of Ashdod because they were being killed by the mouse bites. In giving this passage its spiritual meaning, however, we recognize two kinds of deaths: the first kind of death is that by which

sinners die to righteousness when they sin; the second kind of death is that by which the righteous deliver themselves from the sins in which they had lived and repent of them. The first kind of death enters into human hearts whenever the devil persuades someone to sin. The second kind of death is effected by the virtue of almighty God. Therefore, we must give attention to both kinds of death in this place as they are alluded to spiritually. The one type of death, by which sinners arise when they repent of their sins is alluded to by the words "The hand of the Lord was heavy upon the inhabitants of Ashdod." But that type of death by which the Gentiles offered themselves as slaves to impurity and sin is alluded to when the people of Ashdod were bitten by the mice and died. A mouse, after all, is an unclean animal and could not be eaten according to the law. Therefore, what else could the mice refer to except to demons? And what else is being bitten by mice

---

[1]The gnawing is inferred from the offering of golden tumors, or hemorrhoids, and golden mice. The LXX specifies that the tumors were in their "secret parts" in 1 Samuel 5:3, 9 and notes an abundance of mice in 1 Samuel 5:6 and 1 Samuel 6:1.

except being wounded by the penalty for sin? But they were bitten by the mice when they went out to purge their bowels. Now what does it mean to purge one's bowels other than to reveal the stench of a wretched reputation by one's obedience to sin? Thus, whoever went out to purge his bowels died by the bites of the mice, for by his sinning in plain sight of others he showed them an example of depravity, and he himself was also detained for eternal death by his dire obligations to the demons. SIX BOOKS ON 1 KINGS 3.78.[2]

5:7 Ashdod Recognizes the Lord's Affliction

CHOOSING IGNORANCE. BEDE: When those who delight in idolatry see the power of Christ against their own gods, they do not wish to embrace faith in him, lest on account of their faith alone they be compelled to reject the whole pantheon of their gods. When false Christians see that because of their faith in Christ the sins which they love are now forbidden to them, they ward off with all their might the very piety called forth by their faith, so that they might not end up being ordered at the behest of their faith to quench the desires they serve instead of God. The citizens of Ashdod are worthy of the name of excessiveness, dissoluteness and passions, since they do not want to know the precepts of sacred Scripture so that they do not have to carry them out, once they have learned them. Just as our Lord said that those who fail to carry out his will out of ignorance shall receive fewer blows of the scourge than those who knew it, so they do not wish to know what things they ought to do. They do not understand that there is a great difference between simply being ignorant and refusing to learn what you have studied and ought to know. FOUR BOOKS ON 1 SAMUEL 1.5.[3]

---

[2]CCL 144:241-42. [3]CCL 119:49.

6:1-9 THE ARK'S RETURN IS PLANNED

[2]And the Philistines called for the priests and the diviners and said, "What shall we do with the ark of the LORD? Tell us with what we shall send it to its place." [3]They said, "If you send away the ark of the God of Israel, do not send it empty, but by all means return him a guilt offering. Then you will be healed, and it will be known to you why his hand does not turn away from you." [4]And they said, "What is the guilt offering that we shall return to him?" They answered, "Five golden tumors and five golden mice, according to the number of the lords of the Philistines; for the same plague was upon all of you and upon your lords. [5]So you must make images of your tumors and images of your mice that ravage the land, and give glory to the God of Israel; perhaps he will lighten his hand from off you and your gods and your land. . . . [7]Now then, take and prepare a new cart and two milch cows upon which there has never come a yoke, and yoke the cows to the cart, but take their calves home, away from them. [8]And take the ark of the LORD and place it on the cart, and put in a box at its side the figures of gold, which you are returning to him as a guilt offering. Then send it off, and let it go its way. [9]And watch; if it goes up on the way to its own land, to

Beth-shemesh, then it is he who has done us this great harm; but if not, then we shall know that it is not his hand that struck us, it happened to us by chance."

Overview: Like the Philistines who were gnawed alive by mice, so God afflicts sinners in the afterlife (Cassiodorus). To accomplish divine purposes, God fits the means of revelation to the subject (Chrysostom).

6:4-5 A Guilt Offering

A Perennial Reproach. Cassiodorus: We read in the first book of Kings [Samuel] that because of the damage done to the consecrated ark the foreigners were smitten on their hinder parts, so that they even suffered the dreadful fate of being gnawed alive by mice.[1] This remains a perennial reproach on them, because no other was punished in this way. Similarly he afflicts sinners in the afterlife . . . they are so devoured by mice when the devil's hostile troop surrounds them. Exposition of the Psalms 77.66.[2]

6:9 A Test

The Fittingness of Means. Chrysostom: For this reason he [Paul] says, "To the Jews I became as a Jew, to those without law, as one without law, to those that are under the law, as under the law."[3] Thus God does too, as in the case of the wise men, he does not conduct them by an angel, nor a prophet, nor an apostle, nor an evangelist, but how? By a star.[4] For as their art made them conversant with these, he made use of such means to guide them. So [he does] in the case of the oxen that drew the ark. "If it goes up by the way of his own coast, then he has done this great evil to us," as their prophets suggested. Do these prophets then speak the truth? No; but he refutes and confounds them out of their own mouths. Homilies on Titus 3.[5]

---

[1]See Gregory the Great's comment at 1 Sam 5:6. [2]ACW 52:272*. [3]1 Cor 9:20-21. [4]Mt 2:1-11. [5]NPNF 1 13:528-29*.

6:10-21 THE ARK ARRIVES IN BETH-SHEMESH

[10]*The men did so, and took two milch cows and yoked them to the cart, and shut up their calves at home.* [11]*And they put the ark of the Lord on the cart, and the box with the golden mice and the images of their tumors.* [12]*And the cows went straight in the direction of Beth-shemesh along one highway, lowing as they went; they turned neither to the right nor to the left, and the lords of the Philistines went after them as far as the border of Beth-shemesh.* [13]*Now the people of Beth-shemesh were reaping their wheat harvest in the valley; and when they lifted up their eyes and saw the ark, they rejoiced to see it.* [14]*The cart came into the field of Joshua of Beth-shemesh, and stopped there. A great stone was there; and they split up the wood of the cart and offered the cows as a burnt offering to the Lord.*

Overview: Symbolized by milk cows, the faithful of the church carry the ark of God in their hearts as they journey without deviation toward God (Gregory the Great). When the cows halted at the farm of Hoshea, a man sharing Joshua's former name, it was revealed they were guided by the powerful name of Jesus (Justin Martyr) upon a straight and narrow path to salvation (Gregory the Great).

6:10-14 Cows Bring the Ark to Joshua's Field

Cows Signify the Faithful. Gregory the Great: We know that when the ark of the Lord was returned from the land of the Philistines to the land of the Israelites, it was placed on a cart. They yoked cows that had recently borne young to the cart, and shut up their calves at home. "And the cows went straight on over the way that leads to Beth-shemesh, keeping to the one road, lowing as they went; they turned neither to the right nor to the left." What do these cows represent but the faithful of the church? When they ponder the sacred precepts, it is as if they are carrying the ark of the Lord placed upon them. We should also notice that they are described as having recently borne young. Many who are inwardly set on the way toward God are externally bound by their unspiritual feelings, but they do not turn aside from the right road because they are carrying the ark of God in their hearts.

The cows were going to Beth-shemesh, a name meaning "house of the sun." The prophet says, "For you who fear the Lord, the sun of righteousness shall rise."[1] If we are moving on toward the dwelling place of the everlasting sun, we do right not to turn aside from the route toward God on account of our unspiritual feelings. We must consider with all our energy that the cows yoked to God's cart moan as they go, lowing from their depths, but do not turn aside from their road. So surely must God's preachers, so must all believers within holy church do. They must be compassionate toward their neighbors through their love, while not deviating from God's way through their

compassion. Forty Gospel Homilies 37.[2]

Walking the Straight and Narrow Path. Gregory the Great: For it is not that holy people do not love their fleshly kin, to give them all things necessary, but they subdue this very fondness within themselves from love of spiritual things, in order so to temper it by the control of discretion, that they may be never led by it, even in a small measure and in the very least degree, to deviate from the straight path. And these are well conveyed to us by the representation of the cows, which going along towards the hilly lands under the ark of the Lord, proceed at one and the same time with fondness and with hardened feeling; as it is written, "And the men did so: and took two milk cows and tied them to the cart and shut up their calves at home; and they laid the ark of the Lord upon the cart." And soon after: "And the cows took the straight way to the way of Beth-shemesh, and they went along by one way, lowing as they went, and did not turn aside to the right hand or to the left." For observe, when the calves were shut up at home, the cows, which are fastened to the wagon bearing the ark of the Lord, moan and go their way, they give forth lowings from deep within, and yet [they] never alter their steps from following the path. They feel love indeed shown by compassion but never bend their necks behind. Thus, they must go on their way, who, being placed under the yoke of the sacred law, henceforth carry the Lord's ark in interior knowledge, so as never to deviate from the course of righteousness which they have entered upon, in order to take compassion on the necessities of relatives. For Beth-shemesh is rendered "the house of the sun." Thus to go to Beth-shemesh with the ark of the Lord placed on them is in company with heavenly knowledge to draw near to the seat of light eternal. But we are then really going on toward Beth-shemesh when, in walking the path of righteousness, we never turn aside onto the adjoining side-paths of error, not

[1]Mal 4:2. [2]CS 123:329-30.

even for the sake of the affection we bear for our offspring. MORALS ON THE BOOK OF JOB 7.30.[3]

GUIDED BY THE NAME OF JESUS. JUSTIN MARTYR: One of these, I think, I must now mention, because it will help to give you a better understanding of Jesus, whom we acknowledge as Christ the Son of God, who was crucified, arose from the dead, ascended into heaven and will come to judge every person who ever lived, even back to Adam himself. You certainly know that when the tabernacle of testimony was carried off by the enemies who inhabited the region of Ashdod, and a dreadfully incurable plague had broken out among them, they decided to place the tabernacle upon a cart to which they yoked cows that had recently borne calves, in order to determine whether they had been plagued by God's power because of the tabernacle, and whether it

was God's will that it be returned to the place from which they had taken it. In the execution of this plan, the cows, without any human guidance, proceeded not to the place from where the tabernacle had been taken but to the farm of a man named Hoshea (the same name as his whose name was changed to Jesus [Joshua], as was said above, and who led your people into the promised land and distributed it among them by lot). When the cows came to this farm, they halted. Thus it was shown to you that they were guided by the powerful name [of Jesus], just as the survivors among your people who fled Egypt were guided into the promised land by him whose name was changed from Hoshea to Jesus [Joshua]. DIALOGUE WITH TRYPHO 132.[4]

---

[3]LF 18:398-99*. [4]FC 6:352-53*.

7:1-11 THE PHILISTINES ATTACK
ISRAEL AT MIZPAH

[2]*From the day that the ark was lodged at Kiriath-jearim, a long time passed, some twenty years, and all the house of Israel lamented after the LORD.*

[3]*Then Samuel said to all the house of Israel, "If you are returning to the LORD with all your heart, then put away the foreign gods and the Ashtaroth from among you, and direct your heart to the LORD, and serve him only, and he will deliver you out of the hand of the Philistines."* [4]*So Israel put away the Baals and the Ashtaroth, and they served the LORD only.*

[5]*Then Samuel said, "Gather all Israel at Mizpah, and I will pray to the LORD for you."* [6]*So they gathered at Mizpah, and drew water and poured it out before the LORD, and fasted on that day, and said there, "We have sinned against the LORD." And Samuel judged the people of Israel at Mizpah.*

OVERVIEW: The ark's twenty-year rest in Kiriath-jearim represents a time of spiritual contemplation (GREGORY THE GREAT). Samuel's priesthood prefigures Jesus' as he instructs the people to re-

direct their works and their hearts towards God (BEDE). In Scripture, the use of "alone" or "only" with reference to God distinguishes the true God from false gods, rather than from the Son or the

Spirit (Basil). As the Israelites prevailed over their physical enemies by fasting, so spiritual enemies may be overcome by observing the commands of heaven (Leo).

7:2 The Ark Remained for Twenty Years

The Contemplative Life. Gregory the Great: Because we relate the perfection of the ark to the perfection of the contemplative life, the ark of God remained in Kiriath-jearim, since the learned minds of those who contemplate achieve with delight the gift of their very learning, namely, the brightness of above revealed to them. For twenty years the ark of God remained there, for the elect souls are transported to the pinnacle of innermost exaltation. Thus, they have the number ten, which stands for the perfection of knowledge, but then the number twenty for the delight in things above. For the multiplication of days can be related to the increase of spiritual virtues. Since this is the reason why the days were multiplied and it was expressly stated and asserted that it was the twentieth year: the more richly the elect minds of those who contemplate grazed on the thoughts above, the more fully they would be adorned with the glories of the spiritual virtues.

Now what does it mean when it is said that all Israel "lay at rest after the Lord in the twentieth year," except that the height of the perfection of the elect does not consist in the might of a good work but in the virtue of contemplation? To rest after the Lord is to cling to the imitation of our Redeemer with invincible love. And, if someone contemplates those inexpressible joys of our citizenship above but does not learn to love mightily—for often he can be diverted to love of the world—he by no means rests for the Lord. Thus, when the ark remained in Kiriath-jearim and the days were prolonged, all of Israel rested after the Lord. Surely, while the knowledge of the mind of the elect was raised up into the experience of divine delight, and while the lights of the spiritual virtues gathered beneath the light of restored glory, Israel was able to hold on all the more tenaciously to the imitation of our Lord, to the degree that they, illuminated by the immense lights of virtue, were not able to perceive those shadows by which they were divided from the light. Thus Israel is said to be well off as they rested after the Lord, for they saw God. The higher the contemplative individual was carried into divine matters, the further they departed from human affairs. They held those mightily in check and so by no means could they be conquered. Six Books on 1 Kings 3.141-142.[1]

7:3 Return to the Lord

Jesus' Priesthood Prefigured. Bede: "However, Samuel said to the whole house of Israel, 'If you are returning to the Lord with your whole heart, remove the foreign gods from your midst.'" This passage and whatever follows up to the statement that "he built there an altar to the Lord" shows in a figurative manner how the Lord taught in Judea, performed miracles, suffered, rose and ascended into heaven and sent the grace of the Holy Spirit, thus making not only the Jews but also the Gentiles partakers of his mercy. Therefore, after Eli had died and Samuel had assumed the priesthood, Samuel told the whole house of Israel to remove the foreign gods from their midst.

He said, "And prepare your hearts for the Lord and serve him alone, and he will deliver you from the hand of the Philistines." The Lord, the author of a new priesthood which is manifested in the flesh according to the order of Melchizedek, teaches the whole house of Israel, that is, the church made up of those desiring to see God, to remove from themselves the traditions of the Pharisees. He teaches them not only to prepare works (a thing that the law also taught) but also to prepare their very hearts for serving the Lord alone. He said, "You have heard that it was said by the fathers . . . I, however say to you,"[2] for in

---

[1]CCL 144:276-77.

this way they would be able to be freed from all their enemies in the life to come. Four Books on 1 Samuel 1.7.[3]

7:4 Israel Put Away the Baals and the Ashtaroth

The Lord Alone. Basil the Great: God alone is substantially and essentially God. When I say "alone," I set forth the holy and uncreated essence and substance of God. For the word *alone* is used in the case of any individual and generally of human nature. In the instance of Paul, that he alone was caught into the third heaven and "heard unspeakable words that are not lawful for a man to utter,"[4] and of human nature, as when David says, "as for man his days are as grass,"[5] not meaning any particular man but human nature generally; for every human is short-lived and mortal. So we understand these words to be said of the nature, "who alone has immortality"[6] and "to God only wise,"[7] and "none is good save one, that is God,"[8] for here "one" means the same as alone. . . . In Scripture "one" and "only" are not predicated of God to mark distinction from the Son and the Holy Spirit but to exclude the unreal gods falsely so called. As for instance, "The Lord alone did lead them and there was no strange god with them,"[9] and "then the children of Israel did put away Baalim and Ashtaroth and served the Lord only." Letter 8.3.[10]

7:6 Israel Fasted

Triumph Through Fasting. Leo the Great: At one time the Hebrew people and all the Israelite tribes, because of the offensiveness of their sins, were held under the heavy domination of the Philistines. In order to be able to overcome

their enemies, as the sacred history shows, they restored strength of soul and body with a self-imposed fast. They had judged rightly that they deserved that hard and wretched subjection because of neglect of God's commandments and the corruption of their lives, and that in vain did they fight with weapons unless they had first made war on their sins. By abstaining, therefore, from food and drink they imposed the penalty of severe punishment on themselves, and to conquer their enemies, they first conquered the enticement of gluttony in themselves. In this way it happened that the fierce adversaries and harsh masters yielded to those who were fasting whom they had overcome when they had been full.

We too, dearly beloved, situated as we are among many struggles and battles, if we wish to overcome our enemies in the same way, we may be healed by the same practice. Indeed, our situation is the same as theirs, seeing that they were attacked by bodily adversaries, we by spiritual enemies. If our spiritual enemies may be overcome by the correction of our lives bestowed on us through the grace of God, even the force of our bodily enemies will also give way to us. They will be weakened by our correction, since not their merits but our own sins made them onerous to us.

Therefore, dearly beloved, in order that we may be able to overcome our enemies, let us seek divine help by observing the commands of heaven, knowing that in no other way can we prevail over our foes except by prevailing over ourselves as well. Sermon 39 (Recension a) 1-2.[11]

---

[2]Mt 5:21-22. [3]CCL 119:60. [4]2 Cor 12:4. [5]Ps 103:15 (102:15 LXX). [6]1 Tim 6:16. [7]Rom 16:27. [8]Lk 18:19. [9]Deut 32:12 LXX. [10]NPNF 2 8:117*. [11]FC 93:166-67*.

7:12-17 RESTORATION AND PEACE DURING SAMUEL'S JUDGESHIP

[12]*Then Samuel took a stone and set it up between Mizpah and Jeshanah,*[l] *and called its name Ebenezer;*[m] *for he said, "Hitherto the LORD has helped us."*

l Gk Syr: Heb *Shen*   m That is *Stone of help*

OVERVIEW: Ebenezer, meaning "the stone of help," signifies Christ in fulfillment of Psalm 117:22 (JEROME). The erection of the stone symbolizes how conversion shifts one's focus from earthly happiness to spiritual (AUGUSTINE).

7:12 Samuel Sets Up a Stone

THE STONE OF HELP. JEROME: "That stone which the builders rejected has become the cornerstone."[1] That is the stone that is called Ebenezer in the book of Kings [Samuel]. That stone is Christ. The name Ebenezer, moreover, means "the stone of help." HOMILIES ON THE PSALMS 46 (Ps 133).[2]

PURSUING SPIRITUAL HAPPINESS. AUGUSTINE: For we may be sure that the very aim of those who pass over [from Israelite to Christian] is transformed from the old to the new, so that the aim of each is no longer the attainment of material felicity but spiritual happiness. That explains the action of the great prophet Samuel himself, before he had anointed King Saul.

Samuel cried out to the Lord on behalf of Israel, and God heard him; and when he offered a whole burnt offering, and the foreigners approached to do battle with the people of God, the Lord thundered over them, and they were thrown into confusion and panic as they faced Israel, and so they were overcome. Then Samuel took a stone and set it up between the old and the new Mizpah and gave it the name Ebenezer, which means "the stone of the helper." And he said, "So far the Lord has helped us."[3]

Now Mizpah means "aim." That "stone of the helper" is the mediation of the Savior, through whom we must pass over from the old Mizpah to the new, that is, from the aim which looked for material bliss—a false bliss, in a material kingdom—to the aim which looks for spiritual bliss, the really true bliss, in the kingdom of heaven. And since there is nothing better than this, God helps us "so far." CITY OF GOD 17.7.[4]

---

[1]Ps 118:22 (117:22 LXX). [2]FC 48:351*. [3]1 Sam 7:9-12 LXX. [4]CG 733*.

8:1-9 ISRAEL DEMANDS A KING

¹*When Samuel became old, he made his sons judges over Israel.* ²*The name of his first-born son was Joel, and the name of his second, Abijah; they were judges in Beer-sheba.* ³*Yet his sons did not walk in his ways, but turned aside after gain; they took bribes and perverted justice.*

⁴*Then all the elders of Israel gathered together and came to Samuel at Ramah,* ⁵*and said to him, "Behold, you are old and your sons do not walk in your ways; now appoint for us a king to govern us like all the nations."* ⁶*But the thing displeased Samuel when they said, "Give us a king to govern us." And Samuel prayed to the* LORD. ⁷*And the* LORD *said to Samuel, "Hearken to the voice of the people in all that they say to you; for they have not rejected you, but they have rejected me from being king over them."*

OVERVIEW: Samuel, as the father of faithless sons, exemplifies how the merits of a father do not atone for a child's transgressions (JEROME). Since God may grant or decline a request for a thing that will bring harm confirms that we sometimes do not know how to pray as we should (AUGUSTINE). That God avenges his priests is illustrated in the appointment of King Saul after the people's rejection of Samuel (CYPRIAN). Perfect obedience is due one's bishop: to contradict mocks God (IGNATIUS).

8:3 Samuel's Sons Take Bribes

PERSONAL CULPABILITY. JEROME: But possibly you flatter yourself[1] that since the bishop who has made you a deacon is a holy man, his merits will atone for your transgressions. I have already told you that the father is not punished for the son or the son for the father. "The soul that sins shall itself die."[2] Samuel too had sons who forsook the fear of the Lord and "turned aside after lucre" and iniquity. LETTER 147.10.[3]

8:4-7 The Lord Hears the People's Demand

PATIENCE AND PRAYER. AUGUSTINE: To some, indeed, who lack patience, the Lord God, in his wrath, grants them what they ask, just as, on the other hand, he refused it to his apostle, in his mercy. We read what and how the Israelites asked and received, but, when their lust had been satisfied, their lack of patience was severely punished.[4] And when they asked, he gave them a king, as it is written, according to their heart, but not according to his heart.... These things are written that no one may think well of himself if his prayer is heard, when he has asked impatiently for what it would be better for him not to receive, and that no one may be cast down and may despair of the divine mercy toward him if his prayer has not been heard, when he has, perhaps, asked for something which would bring him more bitter suffering if he received it or would cause his downfall if he were ruined by prosperity. In such circumstances, then, we know not what we should pray for as we ought. LETTER 130.[5]

GOD AVENGES HIS PRIESTS. CYPRIAN: And that we may know that this voice of God came forth with his true and greatest majesty to honor and avenge his priests.... In the book of Kings [Samuel] also when Samuel, the priest, was despised, as you know, by the people of the Jews

---

[1]Sabinianus, a deacon who is called upon to repent of his sins in this letter from Jerome. [2]Ezek 18:4, 20. [3]NPNF 2 6:294*. [4]Num 11:1-34. [5]FC 18:396-97.

on account of his old age, the angry Lord cried out and said, "They have not rejected you, but they have rejected me." And to avenge this, he raised over them King Saul, who afflicted them with grave injuries and trod under foot and pressed the proud people with all insults and punishments that the priest scorned might be avenged on the proud people by divine vengeance. LETTER 3.1.[6]

MOCKING GOD. PSEUDO-IGNATIUS: It is becoming, therefore, that you also should be obedient to your bishop and contradict him in nothing; for it is a fearful thing to contradict any such person. For no one does [by such conduct] deceive him that is visible but does [in reality] seek to mock him that is invisible, who, however, cannot be mocked by anyone. And every such act has respect not to man but to God. For God says to Samuel, "They have not mocked you, but me." LETTER TO THE MAGNESIANS 3.[7]

---

[6]FC 51:7*. [7]ANF 1:60*.

8:10-22 SAMUEL WARNS OF THE WAYS OF THE KING

[10]*So Samuel told all the words of the LORD to the people who were asking a king from him.* [11]*He said, "These will be the ways of the king who will reign over you: he will take your sons and appoint them to his chariots and to be his horsemen, and to run before his chariots;* [12]*and he will appoint for himself commanders of thousands and commanders of fifties, and some to plow his ground and to reap his harvest, and to make his implements of war and the equipment of his chariots.* [13]*He will take your daughters to be perfumers and cooks and bakers.* [14]*He will take the best of your fields and vineyards and olive orchards and give them to his servants.* [15]*He will take the tenth of your grain and of your vineyards and give it to his officers and to his servants.* [16]*He will take your menservants and maidservants, and the best of your cattle*[o] *and your asses, and put them to his work.* [17]*He will take the tenth of your flocks, and you shall be his slaves.* [18]*And in that day you will cry out because of your king, whom you have chosen for yourselves; but the LORD will not answer you in that day."*

o Gk: Heb *young men*

OVERVIEW: Bishops, who bear greater responsibilities than kings, should receive greater benefits from their charges (APOSTOLIC CONSTITUTIONS). Desiring that the people would reconsider their request, Samuel describes the king's ways, thus demonstrating his wisdom and God's lovingkind-ness (CHRYSOSTOM). Those who possess too many servants are likened to the unfeeling tyrant warned of by the prophet Samuel (CLEMENT OF ALEXANDRIA).

8:11-17 *The Ways of the King*

Esteem for Priests. Apostolic Constitutions: Account bishops worthy to be esteemed [as] your rulers and your kings, and bring them tribute as to kings; for by you they and their families ought to be maintained. As Samuel made constitutions for the people concerning a king, in the first book of Kings [Samuel], and Moses did so concerning priests in Leviticus, so do we also make constitutions for you concerning bishops. For if there the multitude distributed the inferior services in proportion to so great a king, should not the bishop, therefore, all the more now receive from you those things which are determined by God for the sustenance of himself and of the rest of the clergy belonging to him? But if we may add somewhat further, let the bishop receive more than the other received of old: for he only managed military affairs, being entrusted with war and peace for the preservation of people's bodies; but the other is entrusted with the exercise of the priestly office in relation to God, in order to preserve both body and soul from dangers. Constitutions of the Holy Apostles 2.4.34.[1]

The Lovingkindness of God. Chrysostom: And observe the wisdom of the prophet, or rather the lovingkindness of God. For because he wished to turn them from their desire, bringing together a number of difficult things he asserted what would be true of their future king, as, for instance, that he would make their wives grind at the mill, require the men to serve as shepherds and drivers of mules; for he described all the service appertaining to the kingdom in minute detail. Homilies on 2 Corinthians 24.3.[2]

Unfeeling Tyrants. Clement of Alexandria: I must now ... express my disapproval of the possession of too many slaves. People resort to servants to escape work and waiting on themselves. ... The Word has given a complete description of these offenders when he promised through the prophet Samuel that the people who were demanding a king would have not a kind master but one who would be an unfeeling tyrant, given over to immorality, "who will take," he said, "your daughters to make him ointments and to be his cooks and bakers," who will rule by law of war and not be zealous for the administration of peace. Christ the Educator 3.4.26-27.[3]

---

[1]ANF 7:412*. [2]NPNF 1 12:392*. [3]FC 23:220-22.

9:1-2 SAUL, SON OF KISH

[1]*There was a man of Benjamin whose name was Kish, the son of Abiel, son of Zeror, son of Becorath, son of Aphiah, a Benjaminite, a man of wealth;* [2]*and he had a son whose name was Saul, a handsome young man. There was not a man among the people of Israel more handsome than he; from his shoulders upward he was taller than any of the people.*

Overview: Saul's ancestry demonstrates that the tribe of Jemini and the tribe of Benjamin are one and the same (Jerome).

9:1-2 Saul's Ancestry and Qualities

One and the Same Tribe. Jerome: The name

Benjamin is a combination, then, of two words, son and right hand: *ben* means "son" and *jamin* means "right hand."

Let us remember once for all that the tribe of Benjamin was called Jemini. We read in the book of Kings [Samuel], where it speaks of Saul, the words "Now there was a man of Benjamin whose name was Saul, the son of Kish, the son of Abiel, son of Jethra, son of Jether, son of Gera, son of

Jemini," and immediately following, it says, a man of Jemini, that is, from the tribe of Jemini, or Benjamin.[1] . . . Now why have I said all this? To show that the tribe of Jemini was the tribe of Benjamin. HOMILIES ON THE PSALMS 3 (Ps 7).[2]

---

[1]Scripture reference is conflated with 2 Sam 19:16; 1 Kings 2:5, 8, 32.
[2]FC 48:28*.

9:3-10 SAUL SEARCHES FOR LOST ASSES

[3]*Now the asses of Kish, Saul's father, were lost. So Kish said to Saul his son, "Take one of the servants with you, and arise, go and look for the asses."* . . . [5]*When they came to the land of Zuph, Saul said to his servant who was with him, "Come, let us go back, lest my father cease to care about the asses and become anxious about us."* [6]*But he said to him, "Behold, there is a man of God in this city, and he is a man that is held in honor; all that he says comes true. Let us go there; perhaps he can tell us about the journey on which we have set out."* . . . [9] *(Formerly in Israel, when a man went to inquire of God, he said, "Come, let us go to the seer"; for he who is now called a prophet was formerly called a seer.)* [10]*And Saul said to his servant, "Well said; come, let us go." So they went to the city where the man of God was.*

OVERVIEW: That the term *seer* was synonymous with "prophet" shows that sight is an attribute of the spirit as well as the physical body (AUGUSTINE). Prophets warranted this name by foreseeing future events (HIPPOLYTUS) and Christ. As the eyes of the church, those who perceive God's mysteries in Holy Writ are deemed seers (JEROME).

9:9 A Prophet Was Called a Seer

SPIRITUAL SIGHT. AUGUSTINE: I wonder how that opinion could have arisen whereby sight is thought to belong to bodies only. But, from whatever habit of speech that opinion may have come, the holy Scriptures are not accustomed to speak

thus; they attribute vision not only to the body but also to the spirit, and more to the spirit than to the body. Otherwise they would not have been right in giving the name *seers* to the prophets who saw the future not by bodily but by spiritual sight. LETTER 147.50.[1]

PROPHETS FORESAW THE FUTURE. HIPPOLYTUS: For with what reason should the prophet be called a prophet, unless he in spirit foresaw the future? For if the prophet spoke of any chance event, he would not be a prophet then in speaking of things which were under the eye of all. But one who sets forth in detail things yet to be, was

---

[1]FC 20:219.

rightly judged a prophet. Wherefore prophets were with good reason called from the very first "seers." On the Antichrist 2.[2]

Prophets Foresaw Christ. Jerome: In him [Christ] are hidden all the treasures of wisdom and knowledge.[3] He also who was hidden in a mystery is the same that was foreordained before the world. Now it was in the law and in the prophets that he was foreordained and prefigured. For this reason too the prophets were called seers, because they saw him whom others did not

see. Letter 53.4.[4]

The Eyes of the Church. Jerome: The church has real eyes: manifestly its churchmen and teachers who see in holy Writ the mysteries of God, and to them applies the scriptural appellation of "seer." It is correct, then, to call these seers the eyes of the church. Homilies on Matthew 85.[5]

---

[2]ANF 5:205. [3]See Col 2:3. [4]NPNF 2 6:98*. [5]FC 57:196-97.

9:11-21 SAUL AND SAMUEL MEET

[15]Now the day before Saul came, the Lord had revealed to Samuel: [16]"Tomorrow about this time I will send to you a man from the land of Benjamin, and you shall anoint him to be prince over my people Israel. He shall save my people from the hand of Philistines; for I have seen the affliction of [q] my people, because their cry has come to me.". . . [18]Then Saul approached Samuel in the gate, and said, "Tell me where is the house of the seer?" [19]Samuel answered Saul, "I am the seer; go up before me to the high place, for today you shall eat with me, and in the morning I will let you go and will tell you all that is on your mind. . . . [21]Saul answered, "Am I not a Benjaminite, from the least of the tribes of Israel? And is not my family the humblest of all the families of the tribe of Benjamin? Why then have you spoken to me in this way?"

q Gk: Heb lacks *the affliction of*

Overview: Since the anointing of kingship precedes the reception of other honorific titles, it best defines what the title of Christ means (Gregory of Nyssa). Rather than being an excuse for errors, receiving honor should motivate godliness (Chrysostom).

9:16 Prince over Israel

The Kingship of Christ. Gregory of

Nyssa: However, since the rank of kingship underlies all worth and power and rule, by this title the royal power of Christ is authoritatively and primarily indicated (for the anointing of kingship, as we learn in the historical books, comes first), and all the force of the other titles depends on that of royalty. For this reason, the person who knows the separate elements included under it also knows the power encompassing these elements. But it is the kingship itself which declares what the title of Christ means. ON PERFECTION.[1]

9:21 *From the Least of the Tribes*

GREAT HONOR IS NO EXCUSE FOR ERRORS.
CHRYSOSTOM: I will give you a proof of what I maintain, from the case of a kingdom, which does not weigh as heavily with God as the priesthood. Saul, that son of Kish, was not himself at all ambitious of becoming a king but was going in quest of his asses and came to ask the prophet about them. The prophet, however, proceeded to speak to him of the kingdom, but not even then did he run greedily after it, though he heard about it from a prophet, but drew back and deprecated it, saying, "Who am I, and what is my father's house?" What then? When he made a bad use of the honor which had been given him by God, were those words of his able to rescue him from the wrath of him who had made him king? And was he able to say to Samuel, when rebuked by him: "Did I greedily run and rush after the kingdom and sovereign power? I wished to lead the undisturbed and peaceful life of ordinary men, but you dragged me to this post of honor. Had I remained in my low estate, I should easily have escaped all these stumbling blocks, for if I were one of the obscure multitude, I should never have been set forth on this expedition, nor would God have committed to my hands the war against the Amalekites, and if I had not had it committed to me, I should not have sinned this sin." But all such arguments are weak as excuses, and not only weak but perilous, inasmuch as they rather kindle the wrath of God. For he who has been promoted to great honor by God must not advance the greatness of his honor as an excuse for his errors but should make God's special favor toward him the motive for further improvement; whereas he who thinks himself at liberty to sin because he has obtained some uncommon dignity, what does he but study to show that the lovingkindness of God is the cause of his personal transgression, which is always the argument of those who lead godless and careless lives. But we ought to be on no account thus minded, nor to fall away into the insane folly of such people, but be ambitious at all times to make the most of such powers as we have, and to be reverent both in speech and thought. ON THE PRIESTHOOD 4.1.[2]

---

[1]FC 58:97-98. [2]NPNF 1 9:61*.

9:22-27 SAUL ENJOYS THE HOSPITALITY OF SAMUEL

[22]Then Samuel took Saul and his servant and brought them into the hall and gave them a place at the head of those who had been invited, who were about thirty persons. [23]And Samuel said to the cook, "Bring the portion I gave you, of which I said to you, 'Put it aside.'" [24]So the cook took up the leg and the upper portion[r] and set them before Saul; and Samuel said, "See, what was kept is set before you. Eat; because it was kept for you until the hour appointed, that you might eat with the guests."[s]

So Saul ate with Samuel that day. [25]And when they came down from the high place into the city, a bed was spread for Saul[t] upon the roof, and he lay down to sleep. [26]Then at the break of *dawn[u] Samuel called to Saul upon the roof, "Up, that I may send you on your way." So Saul arose, and both he and Samuel went out into the street.*

[27]As they were going down to the outskirts of the city, Samuel said to Saul, "Tell the servant to pass on before us, and when he has passed on stop here yourself for a while, that I may make known to you the word of God."

r Heb obscure   s Cn: Heb *saying, I have invited the people*   t Gk: Heb *and he spoke with Saul*   u Gk: Heb *and they arose early and at break of dawn*

Overview: The best teacher and leader knows how to manage both lofty and ordinary affairs (Gregory the Great). Bede contemplates how the relationship between Samuel and Saul prefigures that of John the Baptist and Jesus. Like Jesus, Saul partakes of hidden food. In descending from the high place to the city, teaching for both the strong and the weak is symbolized. Like Samuel the prophet, John confesses that another is the Lord's anointed after the dawning of a new grace. Their entering the streets anticipates the public aspect of Jesus' and John's ministries. As Saul tarries at Samuel's request, Jesus remains a little while in the world in order to fulfill the words of the prophets.

9:24-25 Samuel and Saul Dine and Descend to the City

The True Leader. Gregory the Great: Whoever is received into the eminent office of dispensing pastoral care ought to have in the very sublimity of his rank both the true loftiness of his own life and compassion for the weaknesses of others. Therefore, Saul went with Samuel into the heights and then descended into the town. Let the ruler know how to conduct lofty things, but let him also know how to manage ordinary things. Let him say with Paul, "Our manner of living is in the heavens."[1] But let him also say with us, "Wretched man that I am! Who will free me from this mortal body? For I see another law in my members that fights against the law of my mind and takes me captive by the law of sin."[2] He is a true ruler, when he speaks wisdom among the perfect; he descends into the town when he arranges carnal matters and

says, "Because of fornication let each man have his own wife and each woman her husband."[3] He is in the heights when he says, "No creature will be able to separate us from the love of God which is in Christ Jesus,"[4] but he descends into the town when he says, "I became weak to the weak that I might win the weak. I became all things to all people."[5] Therefore, Samuel brought Saul to the heights and led him down into the town. For when the greatest men put in order the pinnacle of the holy church, namely, those whom they place at the very pinnacle of the church, they teach them to live in a distinguished manner, to preach clearly, to be strict with themselves but more gentle with those under their care, to attend to their own salvation so that they can be weak with the weak. I meant that they are weak by letting their mind feel compassion on the weak rather than by being idle due to some internal malady. For if a teacher suffers from idleness of mind, he is not able to encourage the spiritually feeble and bedridden. Six Books on 1 Kings 4.141.[6]

Jesus and John the Baptist Prefigured. Bede: "And Saul ate with Samuel on that day. And he went down from the high place into the city."[7] And the Lord preached with John [the Baptist] at a time when grace shone until John was cast into prison. The Lord said about those people who would believe in him, "I have a food to eat which you do not know."[8] John and the Lord

---

[1]Phil 3:20. [2]Rom 7:23-24, inverted. [3]1 Cor 7:2. [4]Rom 8:39. [5]1 Cor 9:22. [6]CCL 144:368-69. [7]In this passage Bede interprets the actions of Samuel and Saul to portend the work of John the Baptist and Jesus, respectively. [8]Jn 6:32.

did not hand down commands only to the perfect by ascending to the heights of virtues but also to the weak by condescending to general matters. To the perfect they said, "Sell what you own and give alms,"[9] but to the weak they said, "You shall not murder; you shall not commit adultery."[10] Four Books on 1 Samuel 2.9.[11]

9:26 Samuel Calls to Saul at Dawn

THE DAWNING OF A NEW GRACE. BEDE: "And he spoke with Saul on the sun porch[12] atop the house. For when he had arisen early and it had already grown light, Samuel called to Saul on the sun porch, saying, 'Arise that I might send you.'" John spoke with the Lord in the light that came from recognizing his divinity. It is called a sun porch because it receives the rays of the sun first before the lower portions of the building. Without doubt, then, the sun porch represents those hearts for whom the sun of righteousness has arisen as they have been lifted up from earthly desires by the fear of God. For when John commenced with the beginning of the dispensation for which he was sent and when the new light of grace gradually began to shine clearly in the world, the very same John confessed that Jesus was the Christ, the Son of God, but that he himself had been sent before him. John desired with the full intent of his mind that Christ would rise in the flesh to perform his divine works and let John rest at the right time from his office of forerunner to Christ. Four Books on 1 Samuel 2.9.[13]

IN PLAIN SIGHT. BEDE: "And Saul arose and the two departed, namely, Saul and Samuel." So too

Jesus "manifested his glory and his disciples believed in him."[14] The two, namely, Jesus and John, set out and departed from their secret contemplation of the divine will to show the miraculous works in plain sight. Four Books on 1 Samuel 2.9.[15]

9:27 Samuel Prepares to Share God's Word with Saul

FULFILLING THE WORDS OF THE PROPHETS. BEDE: "And when they had descended to the edge of the city, Samuel said to Saul, 'Tell the lad to go on ahead of us and pass over, but you stay here a little bit so that I may tell you the word of the Lord.'" Although the Lord took on humility and poverty for us and showed himself as a despised man and the least among the citizens of the world and taught that his followers ought also to be poor in spirit, nonetheless he did not at once undergo death, although often godless men were plotting it, but according to the oracles of the prophets. It was the prophets' duty (and John too is to be counted a prophet) to precede him and be his obedient servants and to call their hearers to pass over from vices to virtues, from death to life. However, Christ himself stood still in the world for a little while as those prophets were departing until he could fulfill the word of the father concerning himself declared to his faithful through the prophets. Four Books on 1 Samuel 2.9.[16]

---

[9]Lk 12:33. [10]Mt 19:18. [11]CCL 119:85. [12]The *solarium* usually refers to the top of the house, which was frequently used for living space. Here *solarium* is translated as "sun porch" to convey Bede's play on words. [13]CCL 119:85. [14]Jn 2:11. [15]CCL 119:85. [16]CCL 119:85.

10:1-8 SAUL IS ANOINTED KING

[1]Then Samuel took a vial of oil and poured it on his head, and kissed him and said, "Has not the LORD anointed you to be prince over his people Israel? And you shall reign over the people of the LORD and you will save them from the hand of their enemies round about. And this shall be the sign to you that the LORD has anointed you to be prince[w] over his heritage."

w Gk: Heb lacks *over his people Israel? And you shall . . . to be prince*

OVERVIEW: The grace of the spirit descended with the oil as the prophet of old fulfilled the ministry of anointing God's chosen one (CHRYSOSTOM). Unlike Saul's anointing from an earthen vessel, the supremacy of the Christian's anointing is found in its likeness to David's anointing from a horn (HIPPOLYTUS).

10:1 Samuel Pours Oil on Saul's Head

ANOINTED WITH OIL AND GRACE. CHRYSOSTOM: Furthermore, whenever someone had to be chosen and anointed, the grace of the Spirit would wing its way down and the oil would run on the forehead of the elect. Prophets fulfilled these ministries. DISCOURSES AGAINST JUDAIZING CHRISTIANS 6.4.3.[1]

A DIFFERENT ANOINTING. HIPPOLYTUS: And of all people, we Christians alone are those who . . . celebrate the mystery and are anointed there with the unspeakable chrism from a horn, as David (was anointed), not from an earthen vessel, he says, as (was) Saul, who held converse with the evil demon of carnal concupiscence. THE REFUTATION OF ALL HERESIES 5.4.[2]

---

[1]FC 68:160. [2]ANF 5:58*.

10:9-16 SAUL PROPHESIES AND RETURNS HOME

[9]When he turned his back to leave Samuel, God gave him another heart; and all these signs came to pass that day. [10]When they came to Gibe-ah,[z] behold, a band of prophets met him; and the spirit of God came mightily upon him, and he prophesied among them. [11]And when all who knew him before saw how he prophesied with the prophets, the people said to one another, "What has come over the son of Kish? Is Saul also among the prophets?"

z Or *the hill*

OVERVIEW: The Spirit of God acts in many ways—mental understanding, visions and ecsta-sies (AUGUSTINE). That an evil or divine spirit may influence a man, as Saul's life illustrates, proves the soul's autonomous existence (TERTULLIAN).

10:10 *The Spirit of God Came upon Saul*

SEEING AND UNDERSTANDING. AUGUSTINE: First, you ask that I explain how it can be said in the first book of Kings [Samuel], "The Spirit of the Lord came upon Saul," when it is said elsewhere "There was an evil spirit from the Lord in Saul."[1] Thus it is written: "And it happened that when he turned his back to depart from Samuel, God gave Saul another heart, and all the signs came to pass on that day. Then he came to the hill and, behold, a chorus of prophets met him on the way and the Spirit of God came upon him and he prophesied among them." But Samuel had already predicted this when he anointed him.[2] About that, I don't think that there is any question. For "the Spirit blows where he wills,"[3] and no one's soul can be fouled by contact with the Spirit of prophecy, for it extends everywhere on account of its purity. Yet, it does not affect everyone in the same way; the Spirit's infusion in some people confers images of things, others are granted the mental fruit of understanding, others are given both by inspiration, and still others know nothing. But the Spirit works through infusion in two ways. The first way comes during sleep, and not only to saints, but even Pharaoh and King Nebuchadnezzar saw what neither of them was able to understand but both of them were able to see.[4] The second way is through demonstration in ecstasy (which some Latins translate as "trembling"—astonishingly idiosyncratic, but close in meaning nonetheless), where the mind is separated from the bodily senses so that the human spirit, which is assumed by the divine Spirit, might be free of perceiving and intuiting ideas, as, for instance, when it was shown to Daniel what he had not understood and, to Peter, the sheet let down from heaven by its four corners, who only later recognized what this vision represented.[5] One way is through the mental fruit of understanding, when the significance and relevance of the things demonstrated through images is revealed, which is a more certain prophecy, for the apostle calls such prophecy "greater,"[6] as Joseph deserved to understand but Pharaoh only to see, and as Daniel explained to the king that he saw but did not know. But since the mind is affected in such a fashion that it does not understand ideas of things by conjectural examination but intuits the things themselves, as wisdom and justice and every divine form are understood to be immutable, it does not pertain to the prophecy about which we are now concerned. ON VARIOUS QUESTIONS TO SIMPLICIAN 2.1.1.[7]

10:11 *Is Saul Among the Prophets?*

THE EXISTENCE OF THE SOUL. TERTULLIAN: It is possible for an evil spirit to influence a person. The spirit of God later turned Saul into another man, that is, into a prophet, when people said, "What is this that has happened to the son of Kish? Is Saul also among the prophets?" But the evil spirit also turned him into another man, in other words, into a renegade. For some time Judas was numbered among the chosen [apostles], even becoming the keeper of the purse. He was then not yet a traitor, but he was dishonest. Later, the devil entered into his soul.

Therefore, if neither the spirit of God nor the devil enters into the soul of man at the birth of the soul, then the soul must exist separately before the accession of either spirit. If it exists alone, then it is simple and uncompounded in substance and it breathes simply as a result of the substance which it received from God. ON THE SOUL 11.5-6.[8]

---

[1] 1 Sam 16:15; 18:10; 19:9. [2] See 1 Sam 10:1-6. [3] Jn 3:8. [4] See Dan 2. [5] See Acts 10:9ff. [6] 1 Cor 14:5. [7] CCL 44:58-59. [8] FC 10:204*.

10:17-24 THE LOT REVEALS THE LORD'S CHOICE FOR A KING

²⁰Then Samuel brought all the tribes of Israel near, and the tribe of Benjamin was taken by lot. ²¹He brought the tribe of Benjamin near by its families, and the family of the Matrites was taken by lot; finally he brought the family of the Matrites near man by man,ᵃ and Saul the son of Kish was taken by lot. But when they sought him, he could not be found. ²²So they inquired again of the Lord, "Did the man come hither?"ᵇ and the Lord said, "Behold, he has hidden himself among the baggage." ²³Then they ran and fetched him from there; and when he stood among the people, he was taller than any of the people from his shoulders upward. ²⁴And Samuel said to all the people, "Do you see him whom the Lord has chosen? There is none like him among all the people." And all the people shouted, "Long live the king!"

a Gk: Heb lacks *finally . . . man by man*   b Gk: Heb *Is there yet a man to come hither?*

Overview: The benefit of a low estate and danger of a high estate are made evident by Saul's initial reluctance to accept the kingdom and his subsequent pride. Although Saul is chosen as good according to the limited human insight, he is wicked in the omniscient sight of God (Gregory the Great).

10:21-23 Saul Is Chosen by Lot

The Danger of a High Estate. Gregory the Great: It is common experience that in the school of adversity the heart is forced to discipline itself; but when one has achieved supreme rule, it is at once changed and puffed up by the experience of his high estate.

It was thus that Saul, realizing at first his unworthiness, fled from the honor of governing but presently assumed it and was puffed up with pride. By his desire for honor before the people and wishing not to be blamed before them, he alienated him who had anointed him to be king. Pastoral Care 1.3.[1]

10:24 Whom the Lord Has Chosen

Hay in the Sight of God, yet Chosen in the View of the People. Gregory the Great: But I see we must enquire how this Behemoth,[2] who eats hay like an ox, is said to destroy the life of the spiritual, when, as was said before, by the word *hay* is designated the life of the carnal. His food also will no longer be choice, if, in eating hay, he seizes the carnal. But it occurs at once in reply, that some people are both hay in the sight of God and among people are counted under the name of holiness, when their life displays one thing before the eyes of men and before the divine judgment their conscience intends another. They therefore in the opinion of men are "elect," but in the accurate judgment of the Lord are "hay." Was not Saul hay in the sight of God, of whom the prophet Samuel said to the people, "You surely see him whom the Lord has chosen," and of whom it is just said above, "He is choice and good"?[3] For he whom the sinful people deserved was both reprobate in the sight of God and yet in the order of causes was choice and good. Morals on the Book of Job 32.13.[4]

---

[1]ACW 11:26. [2]See Job 40:15, "Behold, Behemoth, which I made as I made you; he eats hay like an ox." [3]See 1 Sam 9:2. [4]LF 31:525*.

10:25-27 SAMUEL CONTINUES
TO GUIDE THE PEOPLE

[25]Then Samuel told the people the rights and duties of the kingship; and he wrote them in a book and laid it up before the LORD. Then Samuel sent all the people away, each one to his home. [26]Saul also went to his home at Gibe-ah, and with him went men of valor whose hearts God had touched. [27]But some worthless fellows said, "How can this man save us?" And they despised him, and brought him no present. But he held his peace.

OVERVIEW: The irresistibility of God's will is demonstrated in that those whose hearts had been touched by God followed Saul while those whose hadn't been touched refused. That God acted upon human hearts in order to create earthly kingdoms defends the argument that God inclines the heart to salvation to create a heavenly one (AUGUSTINE).

10:26-27 Reaction to Saul Is Mixed

THE SUPREMACY OF GOD'S WILL. AUGUSTINE: Accordingly, there is no doubt that human wills cannot resist the will of God, "who has done whatever he pleased in heaven and on earth,"[1] and who has even "done the things that are to come."[2] Nor can the human will prevent him from doing what he wills, seeing that even with human wills he does what he wills, when he wills to do it. Take, for instance, the case of Saul. When God willed to give the kingdom to Saul, was it in the power of the Israelites to subject themselves to him or not to subject themselves? In a sense, yes; but not in such a way that they were able to resist God himself. As a matter of fact, God carried the matter through by means of the wills of people themselves, having, as he undoubtedly does, the almighty power to bend human hearts in whatever direction he pleases. So it is written: "And Samuel sent away all the people, everyone to his own house. Saul also departed to his own house in Gibeah; and there went with him a part of the army, whose hearts God had touched. But the children of Belial said, 'Shall this fellow be able to save us?' And they despised him, and brought him no presents." Surely, no one will say that any of the children of Belial, whose hearts God had not so touched, did go with him. ADMONITION AND GRACE 14.45.[3]

GOD MOVES HUMAN WILLS TO SALVATION. AUGUSTINE: In vain also do they object that what we have established from Scripture in the books of Kings [which includes Samuel] and Chronicles—that when God wills the accomplishment of something which ought not to be done except by people who will it, their hearts will be inclined to will this, with God producing this inclination, who in a marvelous and ineffable way works also in us that we will—is not pertinent to the subject with which we are dealing. What else is this but to contradict without saying anything? Unless perhaps they gave you some explanation of why it seems this way to them, but you have chosen not to mention it in your letters.[4] But what that explanation could be, I do not know. Do our brothers perhaps think that because we have shown that God so acted in the human hearts and led the wills of those whom it pleased him to lead, that Saul or

---

[1]Ps 135:6 (134:6 LXX). [2]Is 45:11 LXX. [3]FC 2:299*. [4]This treatise is in response to two lengthy letters, one from Prosper and the other from Hilary, seeking Augustine's response to theological issues relating to the relationship of salvation and the freedom of the will.

David was established as king, these examples are not pertinent to the subject, since it is one thing to reign temporally in this world and another to reign eternally with God? Do they suppose, accordingly, that God moves the wills of those whom he has wished to the creation of earthly kingdoms but that he does not move them to the attainment of a heavenly kingdom? Predestination of the Saints 20.42.[5]

[5]FC 86:268*.

11:1-15 SAUL'S VICTORY OVER THE AMMONITES

[1]*Then Nahash the Ammonite went up and besieged Jabesh-gilead; and all the men of Jabesh said to Nahash, "Make a treaty with us, and we will serve you."* [2]*But Nahash the Ammonite said to them, "On this condition I will make a treaty with you, that I gouge out all your right eyes, and thus put disgrace upon all Israel."* [3]*The elders of Jabesh said to him, "Give us seven days respite that we may send messengers through all the territory of Israel. Then, if there is no one to save us, we will give ourselves up to you."* [4]*When the messengers came to Gibe-ah of Saul, they reported the matter in the ears of the people; and all the people wept aloud. . . .*

[6]*And the spirit of God came mightily upon Saul when he heard these words, and his anger was greatly kindled. . . .* [11]*And on the morrow Saul put the people in three companies; and they came into the midst of the camp in the morning watch, and cut down the Ammonites until the heat of the day; and those who survived were scattered, so that no two of them were left together.*

Overview: By taking the right eye from the men of Jabesh, Nahash sought to render them powerless as the right eye is understood to perceive heavenly realities. The wise consult the fathers (Bede). Saul's division of his army into three companies symbolizes the fasts of the law, the prophets and the gospel (Gregory the Great).

11:1-2 Nahash Threatens Jabesh

The Right Eye. Bede: Some of the faithful people in the church often consented to be genuinely and lovingly allied with and to serve obediently teachers whom they deemed to be as "wise as serpents" in their frequent meditation on the Scriptures, but these preservers of peace in the church did not know that these teachers were not as "innocent as doves."[1] But because there is nothing hidden which will not be revealed these "creators of falsehoods" and "worshipers of false doctrines"[2] immediately showed themselves not to have the eyes of their heart illuminated. They were unable to say, "Our eyes are like doves,"[3] but on the contrary they long to take away the right eyes of their hearers, that is, the perception of heavenly and supernal contemplation, and to turn them aside to view only evil and perverse matters and to render them powerless in the war which we wage "against spiritual powers of iniquity in heavenly places."[4] For this reason Nahash wanted

[1]Mt 10:16. [2]Is 45:16. [3]Song 1:14. [4]Eph 6:12.

to deprive the men of Jabesh of their right eyes so that they would not be able to see anything they needed to see for their defense against the enemy since they would have covered the left side of their face with their shields in battle. Four Books on 1 Samuel 2.11.[5]

11:3 The Elders Ask for a Respite

Wisdom and the Spirit. Bede: Certain wiser individuals were more cautious in not trusting the heretics and recognized in them the ancient dragon or serpent speaking in them (that is to say, the devil or Satan as in various writings of Paul or even as Christ himself spoke in his parables). These wiser individuals said, "Do not compel us to believe your new doctrine until we read through the writings of the fathers and inquire of the sevenfold Holy Spirit, who was given to the church as its light. If there will not be anything in them which will defend our faith, we will come out to you and leave behind the inner catholic unity and instead ally ourselves with you who have already left it and assail it. Then we will listen to you in that matter, even if it is against us." "They went out from us but they were not of us; for if they had been of us, they would certainly have remained with us."[6] They said these things, however, not as if they would ever agree on any condition, but because they were most convinced of the soundness of the faith of their fathers and were confident that they would completely conquer the heretics in this exchange. Four Books on 1 Samuel 2.11.[7]

11:11 Saul Defeats the Ammonites

Three Fasts Symbolized. Gregory the Great: The people were divided into three parts, so that we might not strike the serpent Nahash in one battle line alone. The people were divided into three parts so that they might reveal the fruit and dignity of sacred fasting. By fasting we are called back to the contemplation of the holy Trinity, which we lost by eating the forbidding fruit. The people were also divided into three groups because this act commended the fasts of the law, the prophets and the gospel. When Moses was deemed worthy to receive the law, he twice fasted for forty days. When Elijah escaped the hand of Jezebel, he came to Mount Horeb on the strength of one meal that sufficed him for forty days. Our Lord and Savior Jesus Christ fasted for forty days in the wilderness and did not eat any food of any kind. Therefore, Saul divided the people into three parts in order to promote the fasts of the law, the prophets and the gospel as an example for those abstaining from food. Six Books on 1 Kings 5.20.[8]

---

[5]CCL 119:94. [6]Jn 2:19. [7]CCL 119:94-95. [8]CCL 144:428-29.

12:1-5 SAMUEL ADDRESSES THE PEOPLE

[1]*And Samuel said to all Israel, "Behold, I have hearkened to your voice in all that you have said to me, and have made a king over you. . . . *[3]*Here I am; testify against me before the Lord and before his anointed. Whose ox have I taken? Or whose ass have I taken? Or whom have I defrauded? Whom have I oppressed? Or from whose hand have I taken a bribe to blind my eyes*

with it? Testify against me[c] and I will restore it to you." [4]They said, "You have not defrauded us or oppressed us or taken anything from any man's hand." [5]And he said to them, "The Lord is witness against you, and his anointed is witness this day, that you have not found anything in my hand." And they said, "He is witness."

c Gk: Heb lacks *Testify against me*

Overview: Samuel's appeal for testimony against himself prompts varied comments. Samuel speaks in order to instruct Saul to be meek and gentle (Chrysostom). Samuel clears himself of any wrongdoing near the end of his lengthy ministry (Irenaeus). Samuel teaches that a priest must avoid covetousness (Jerome).

12:3-5 The People Attest to Samuel's Righteousness

Instructing the King to Gentleness. Chrysostom: For Samuel also put together a high panegyric upon himself, when he anointed Saul, saying, "Whose ass have I taken, or calf, or shoes? Or have I oppressed any of you?" And yet no one finds fault with him. And the reason is because he did not say it by way of setting off himself, but because he was going to appoint a king, he wishes under the form of a defense [of himself] to instruct him to be meek and gentle. . . . But when he saw that they [the people] would not be hindered by any of these things [the ways of the king] but were incurably distempered, he thus both spared them and composed their king to gentleness. Therefore he also takes him to witness. For indeed no one was then bringing suit or charge against Saul that he needed to defend himself, but Samuel said those things in order to make him better. And therefore also he added, to take down his pride, "If you will listen, you and your king," such and such good things shall be yours, "but if you will not listen, then the reverse of all." Homilies on 2 Corinthians 24.3.[1]

A Good Conscience. Irenaeus: In this way, too, Samuel, who judged the people so many years and bore rule over Israel without any pride, in the end cleared himself. . . . In this strain also the apostle Paul, inasmuch as he had a good conscience, said to the Corinthians, "For we are not as many [are], who corrupt the Word of God: but in sincerity, but as from God, in the sight of God we speak in Christ."[2] "We have injured no one, corrupted no one, circumvented no one."[3] Against Heresies 4.26.4.[4]

Avoiding Covetousness. Jerome: That a priest must avoid covetousness even Samuel teaches when he proves before all the people that he has taken nothing from any one. Letter 69.9.[5]

---

[1]NPNF 1 12:392*. [2]2 Cor 2:17. [3]2 Cor 7:2. [4]ANF 1:497-98*. [5]NPNF 2 6:148*.

12:6-18 ISRAEL'S WICKEDNESS AND THE LORD'S FIDELITY RECOUNTED

⁶And Samuel said to the people, . . . ¹⁶"Now therefore stand still and see this great thing, which the Lord will do before your eyes. ¹⁷Is it not wheat harvest today? I will call upon the Lord, that he may send thunder and rain; and you shall know and see that your wickedness is great, which you have done in the sight of the Lord, in asking for yourselves a king." ¹⁸So Samuel called upon the Lord, and the Lord sent thunder and rain that day; and all the people greatly feared the Lord and Samuel.

Overview: As Samuel brought thunder and rain through prayer, so also the genuine disciple of Jesus will receive the rain of the soul (Origen). Like Moses, Samuel prevents God from venting his wrath against the people by means of his persistent entreaty (Jerome).

12:16-18 Samuel Calls on the Lord for a Sign

Accomplished Through Prayer. Origen: That mighty deed Samuel is said to have accomplished through prayer is something that everyone who genuinely relies on God can accomplish spiritually even now, since he has become worthy of being heard. . . . For every saint and genuine disciple of Jesus is told by the Lord, "Lift up your eyes, and see how the fields are already white for harvest. He who reaps receives wages and gathers fruit for eternal life."[1] In this time of harvest the Lord does "a great thing" before the eyes of those who hear the prophets. For when the one adorned with the Holy Spirit calls to the Lord, God gives from heaven thunder and rain that waters the soul, so that he who once was in evil may stand in great awe of the Lord and his minister of goodness, manifested as venerable and august by the requests that are heard. And Elijah, who shut up heaven for the wicked for three and a half years, later opened it. This, too, is always accomplished for everyone who through prayer receives the rain of the soul, since the heavens were previously deprived of it because of his sin. On Prayer 13.5.[2]

The Works of Samuel. Jerome: As a matter of fact, the works Moses did, Samuel did too. Moses resisted God and prevented him from destroying his people when God said to him, "Let me alone, that I may strike this people."[3] Just see the power of Moses! What does God say to him? Let me alone; you are compelling me, your prayers, as it were, restrain me; your prayers hold back my hand. I shoot an arrow; I hurl a javelin; and your prayers are the shield of the people. Let me alone that I might strike down this people. Along with this, consider the compassionate kindness of God. When he says, "Let me alone," he shows that if Moses will continue to importune him, he will not strike. If you, too, will not let me alone, I shall not strike; let me alone, and I shall strike. In other words, what does he say? Do not cease your persistent entreaty, and I shall not strike.

Let us see if Samuel persistently importuned God in this way. We read in the book of Kings [Samuel] that he prevented God from venting his wrath against the people, and although it was harvest time, the Lord sent rain, thunder and lightning. What does Scripture say in Samuel?

---

[1]Jn 4:35-36. [2]OSW 108. [3]See Ex 32:10.

"And there came hailstones and struck down the Philistines."[4] See how wise the fire, how wise the hail! Where Samuel is, the thunderbolts do not dare to strike, for they see the prophet of God, they see the Levite. Samuel's hands were threatening the thunderbolts. He was praying, and the lightning strokes were held back. Why have I said all this? Because Moses and Aaron and Samuel with different titles performed the same mighty deeds. Let us bless the Lord to whom be glory forever and ever. Homilies on the Psalms 26 (Ps 98).[5]

[4]See Josh 10:11. [5]FC 48:211-12*.

12:19-25 COVENANT BLESSINGS AND CURSES RECOUNTED

[20]*And Samuel said to the people, "Fear not; you have done all this evil, yet do not turn aside from following the Lord, but serve the Lord with all your heart;* [21]*and do not turn aside after*[i] *vain things which cannot profit or save, for they are vain.* [22]*For the Lord will not cast away his people, for his great name's sake, because it has pleased the Lord to make you a people for himself.* [23]*Moreover as for me, far be it from me that I should sin against the Lord by ceasing to pray for you; and I will instruct you in the good and the right way."*

i Gk Syr Tg Vg: Heb *because after*

Overview: Samuel's affection for his charges, demonstrated by his ceaseless prayer on their behalf, shows that the one who loves Christ also loves his flock. Prayer brings great profit when it is coupled with action (Chrysostom). Regarding prayer, Samuel is revered because he interceded even for his enemies (Gregory the Great).

12:23 Samuel Promises to Continue His Ministry

Love for Christ's Flock. Chrysostom: For he who loves Christ also loves his flock. . . . David in this way came to be king, having been seen first to be affectionately-minded toward them. So much indeed, though yet young, did he grieve for the people, as to risk his life for them, when he killed that barbarian.[1] . . . And Samuel too was very affectionate; when it was that he said, "But God forbid that I should sin in ceasing to pray to the Lord for you." In like way Paul also, or rather not in like way but even in a far greater degree, burned toward all his subjects. Homilies on Romans 29.[2]

Prayer Profits with Action. Chrysostom: What did Samuel profit Saul? Did he not mourn for him even to his last day, and not merely pray for him only? What did he profit the Israelites? Did he not say, "God forbid that I should sin in ceasing to pray for you"? Did they not all perish? Do prayers then, you say, profit nothing? They profit even greatly: but it is when we also do something. For prayers indeed cooperate and assist, but

[1]Goliath. [2]NPNF 1 11:545*.

a man cooperates with one that is operating and assists one that is himself also working. But if you remain idle, you will receive no great benefit. Homilies on 1 Thessalonians 1.[3]

Interceding for Enemies. Gregory the Great: Why is it that Moses and Samuel are preferred to all the other fathers in this matter of making requests if it is not that these two alone in the whole history of the Old Testament are said to have prayed earnestly even for their ene-mies? One of them the people attacked with stones, and yet he prayed to his Lord for those who were stoning him.[4] The other was deposed from his position of leadership, and yet when he was asked to make supplication he yielded, saying, "Far be it from me that I should sin against the Lord by ceasing to pray for you." Forty Gospel Homilies 27.[5]

---

[3]NPNF 1 13:326*. [4]Ex 17:4. [5]CS 123:218.

13:1-14 SAUL DISOBEYS THE LORD'S COMMANDMENT

[5]And the Philistines mustered to fight with Israel, thirty thousand chariots, and six thousand horsemen, and troops like the sand on the seashore in multitude; they came up and encamped in Michmash, to the east of Beth-aven. . . . [7]Saul was still at Gilgal, and all the people followed him trembling.

[8]He waited seven days, the time appointed by Samuel; but Samuel did not come to Gilgal, and the people were scattering from him. [9]So Saul said, "Bring the burnt offering here to me, and the peace offerings." And he offered the burnt offering. [10]As soon as he had finished offering the burnt offering, behold, Samuel came; and Saul went out to meet him and salute him. [11]Samuel said, "What have you done?" And Saul said, "When I saw that the people were scattering from me, and that you did not come within the days appointed, and that the Philistines had mustered at Michmash, [12]I said, 'Now the Philistines will come down upon me at Gilgal, and I have not entreated the favor of the Lord'; so I forced myself, and offered the burnt offering." [13]And Samuel said to Saul, "You have done foolishly; you have not kept the commandment of the Lord your God, which he commanded you; for now the Lord would have established your kingdom over Israel for ever. [14]But now your kingdom shall not continue; the Lord has sought out a man after his own heart; and the Lord has appointed him to be prince over his people, because you have not kept what the Lord commanded you."

Overview: Reverence for superiors is taught as seen in Saul's failure and subsequent dishonor for failing to wait for Samuel (Ignatius). This instance in Saul's life illustrates the prohibition and penalty of the meddling of duties, which have been prescribed by tradition (Apostolic Constitutions). This little step along the path toward the superstition of witchcraft was brought about by the devil's subtle guidance (Chrysostom).

As Samuel's presence was required to bring benefit from the offering, so the laity will not labor in vain if they are dependent upon the priest (Apostolic Constitutions).

Rather than conveying that Saul would have reigned forever if he had not sinned, God's words declare his intention that Saul's kingdom would symbolize an everlasting one (Augustine). The events of Saul's and David's lives find striking parallels in the life of Christ (Aphrahat). David's description as a man after God's own heart, as distinguished from Saul, sparks observations. Although characterized so favorably, David is cognizant of his own sinfulness (Clement of Rome). He warrants this description as one whose sin was not imputed to him due to his penitence and holy humility (Augustine). His response to trials after the pattern of the Lord proves the reference to be true (Hilary). Remarkably, David attains to New Testament values of clemency while in the old dispensation (Chrysostom). That an avowed Christian follows a teaching does not make it orthodox since any, even a person after God's heart, can turn from right rule (Tertullian).

13:11-12 Saul Explains Why He Offered the Sacrifice

Reverence for Superiors. Pseudo-Ignatius: Saul also was dishonored because he did not wait for Samuel the high priest. It behooves you, therefore, also to reverence your superiors. Letter to the Magnesians 3.[1]

Meddling of Duties. Apostolic Constitutions: Now this we all in common do charge you, that every one remain in that rank which is appointed him, and do not transgress his proper bounds; for they are not ours but God's. . . . And those things which are allotted for the high priests to do, those might not be meddled with by

the priests; and what things were allotted to the priests, the Levites might not meddle with; but every one observed those ministrations which were written down and appointed for them. And if any would meddle beyond the tradition, death was his punishment. And Saul's example does show this most plainly, who, thinking he might offer sacrifice without the prophet and high priest Samuel, drew upon himself a sin and a curse without remedy. Nor did even his having anointed him king discourage the prophet. Constitutions of the Holy Apostles 8.5.46.[2]

Little by Little. Chrysostom: And mark it, he [the devil] desired to bring Saul into [the] superstition of witchcraft. But if he had counseled this at the beginning, the other would not have given heed; for how should he, who was even driving them out? Therefore gently and by little and little he leads him on to it. For when he had disobeyed Samuel and had caused the burnt offering to be offered, when he was not present, being blamed for it, he says, "The compulsion from the enemy was too great," and when he ought to have bewailed, he felt as though he had done nothing.

Again God gave him the commands about the Amalekites, but he transgressed these too. Then he proceeded to his crimes about David, and thus slipping easily and little by little he did not stop, until he came to the very pit of destruction and cast himself in. Homilies on the Gospel of Matthew 86.3.[3]

13:13-14 Samuel States the Consequences of Disobedience

Laboring in Vain. Apostolic Constitutions: As, therefore, it was not lawful for one of another tribe, that was not a Levite, to offer anything or to approach the altar without the priest, so also do you do nothing without the bishop; for if any one does anything without the bishop, he

---

[1]ANF 1:60*. [2]ANF 7:499. [3]NPNF 1 10:513*.

does it to no purpose. For it will not be esteemed as of any avail to him. For as Saul, when he had offered without Samuel, was told, "It will not avail for you," so every person among the laity, doing anything without the priest, labors in vain. Constitutions of the Holy Apostles 2.4.27.[4]

An Everlasting Kingdom. Augustine: In the same vein, take the words Samuel said to Saul.... These words are not to be taken to mean that God had intended for Saul himself to reign forever and subsequently had decided otherwise on account of Saul's sins (for God knew Saul was going to sin). They mean merely that God had planned for him to have such a kingdom as would typify an everlasting kingdom. Hence the added precision: "But your kingdom shall not continue."

The kingdom which Saul's kingdom symbolized has continued and will continue—but not for Saul; for neither was he personally destined to rule forever, nor was even his progeny after him (at least in the sense of his blood successors following one after another) to make good the pledge "forever." City of God 17.6.[5]

13:14 David, Man After God's Heart

Comparing David with Jesus. Aphrahat: Also David was persecuted, as Jesus was persecuted. David was anointed by Samuel to be king instead of Saul who had sinned; and Jesus was anointed by John to be high priest instead of the priests, the ministers of the law. David was persecuted after his anointing; and Jesus was persecuted after his anointing. David reigned first over one tribe only and afterwards over all Israel; and Jesus reigned from the beginning over the few who believed on him, and in the end he will reign over all the world. Samuel anointed David when he was thirty years old; and Jesus when about thirty years old received the imposition of the hand from John. David wedded two daughters of the king; and Jesus wedded two daughters of kings, the congregation of the people and the congregation of the Gentiles. David repaid good to

Saul his enemy; and Jesus taught, "Pray for your enemies."[6] David was the heart of God; and Jesus was the Son of God. David received the kingdom of Saul his persecutor; and Jesus received the kingdom of Israel his persecutor. David wept with dirges over Saul his enemy when he died; and Jesus wept over Jerusalem,[7] his persecutor, which was to be laid waste. David handed over the kingdom to Solomon and was gathered to his people; and Jesus handed over the keys to Simon[8] and ascended and returned to him who sent him. For David's sake, sins were forgiven to his posterity; and for Jesus' sake sins are forgiven to the nations. Demonstration 21.13.[9]

No One Is Pure. Clement of Rome: What shall we say of the celebrated David, to whom God said, "I have found a man after my own heart, David the son of Jesse, in eternal mercy I have anointed him."[10] But even he says to God, "Have mercy on me, O God, according to your great mercy, and according to the multitude of your tender mercies blot out my iniquity. Wash me yet more from my iniquity, and cleanse me from my sin; for I knew my iniquity, and my sin is always before me."[11] 1 Clement 18.[12]

Sin and Humility. Augustine: You ask, "Why did the Lord, undoubtedly having foreknowledge of the future, say 'I choose David according to my own heart,' although this very man committed such serious sins?"[13] As a matter of fact, if we understand this statement concerning David himself, who was king of Israel after Saul had been condemned and slain, it was especially because God has foreknowledge of the future that he foresaw in him such great holiness and such true repentance, that he numbered him among those of whom he himself said, "Blessed are they whose iniquities are forgiven and whose

---

[4]ANF 7:410*. [5]FC 24:41-42*. [6]Lk 6:28. [7]See Lk 19:41. [8]Mt 16:19. [9]NPNF 2 13:397-98*. [10]See Ps 89:20 (88:21 LXX); Acts 13:22. [11]Ps 51:1-3 (50:1-5 LXX). [12]FC 1:24*. [13]Cf. 1 Sam 16:7; 1 Kings 8:16; Acts 13:23.

sins are covered. Blessed is the one to whom the Lord has not imputed sin."[14] Therefore, since God foreknew that he would sin and would wash his sins away by holy humility, why should he not say, "I have found David according to my own heart?" He was not going to impute sin to him who was doing so many good acts and living in such great holiness and by this same holiness offering the sacrifice of a contrite spirit for his sins. For all these reasons, it has very truthfully been said, "I have found David according to my heart." For, although the fact that he sinned was not according to God's heart, the fact that he atoned for his sins with a fitting penitence was according to God's heart. Only this, then, in him was not according to God's heart, which God did not impute [David's sins] to him. So, when this has been removed, that is, has not been imputed, what remains but that it be very truthfully said, "I have found David according to my own heart"? Eight Questions of Dulcitius 5.[15]

After God's Own Heart. Hilary of Poitiers: The doctrines of the gospel were well known to holy and blessed David in his capacity of prophet, and although it was under the law that he lived his bodily life, he yet filled, as far as in him lay, the requirements of the apostolic concern and justified the witness borne to him by God in the words: I have found a man after my own heart, David, the son of Jesse. He did not avenge himself upon his foes by war,[16] he did not oppose force of arms to those that laid wait for him, but after the pattern of the Lord, whose name and whose meekness alike he foreshadowed, when he was betrayed he entreated, when he was in danger he sang psalms, when he incurred hatred he rejoiced; and for this cause he was found a man after God's own heart. Homilies on Psalm 53(54).1.[17]

An Exemplar of Clemency. Chrysostom: So whom should we cite in discoursing on clemency? Who else than the one receiving testimony from on high and especially remarkable in this case? "I found in David, son of Jesse," Scripture says, remember, "a man after my own heart." Now, when God gives his opinion, there are no grounds left for opposition: that verdict is proof against corruption, God judging not from favor or from hatred but making his decision on the mere virtue of the soul. It is not for this reason alone, however, that we cite him, that he received the verdict from God, but also because he is one of those nourished in the old dispensation. You see, while there is nothing remarkable for anyone in the ages of grace to be found free of resentment, forgiving enemies their sins and sparing abusers—that is, after the death of Christ, after such wonderful forgiveness of sins, after the directives redolent of sound values—in the old dispensation, by contrast, when the law permitted an eye to be plucked out for an eye, a tooth for a tooth, and vengeance to be taken on the wrongdoer in equal terms, who amongst the listeners is not struck by someone found to surpass the norm of the commandments and attain to New Testament values? Homilies on David and Saul 1.[18]

Enduring to the End. Tertullian: And is it surprising that a person previously of good repute should afterwards fall? Saul, though good beyond all others, was afterwards overthrown by jealousy. David, a good man after the Lord's heart, was afterwards guilty of murder and adultery. Solomon, whom the Lord had endowed with all grace and wisdom, was led by women into idolatry. To remain without sin was reserved for the Son of God alone. If then a bishop or deacon, a widow, a virgin or a teacher, or even a martyr, has lapsed from the Rule of Faith, must we conclude that heresy possesses the truth? Do we test the faith by persons or person by the faith? No one is wise, no one is faithful, no one worthy of honor unless he is a Christian, and no one is a Christian unless he perseveres to the end. Prescriptions Against Heretics 3.[19]

---

[14]Ps 32:1-2 (31:1-2 LXX). [15]FC 16:463*. [16]The qualities Hilary extols in David are those he exhibited in his encounters with Saul. [17]NPNF 2 9:243*. [18]COTH 1:10-11. [19]LCC 5:32.

13:15-23 THE ISRAELITES AND PHILISTINES PREPARE FOR BATTLE

[19]Now there was no smith to be found throughout all the land of Israel; for the Philistines said, "Lest the Hebrews make themselves swords or spears"; [20]but every one of the Israelites went down to the Philistines to sharpen his plowshare, his mattock, his axe, or his sickle;[m] [21]and the charge was a pim for the plowshares and for the mattocks, and a third of a shekel for sharpening the axes and for setting the goads."[n] [22]So on the day of the battle there was neither sword nor spear found in the hand of any of the people with Saul and Jonathan; but Saul and Jonathan his son had them. [23]And the garrison of the Philistines went out to the pass of Michmash.

m Gk: Heb *plowshare*   n The Heb of this verse is obscure

OVERVIEW: Fear, which pervaded the Israelite army due to Saul's disobedience, was compounded by a shortage of iron weaponry, which was a product of the Philistines' exclusive trade (SULPICIUS SEVERUS). This state of affairs symbolizes the enemy's efforts to prevent the church from putting on the armor of God. Those who went to the Philistines' smiths represent those who turn from God's word to earthly teaching. The Israelites' lack of arms represents those who, out of laziness, fail to prepare for spiritual battles (BEDE).

13:19-21 The Philistines' Exclusive Knowledge of Forging

SHORTAGE OF COURAGE AND WEAPONS. SULPICIUS SEVERUS: For, as a result of the king's sin [Saul's offering of the sacrifice], fear had pervaded the whole army. The camp of the enemy, which was lying at no great distance, showed them how real the danger was, and no one had the courage to think of going out to battle: most had absconded to the marshes. For besides the lack of courage on the part of those who felt that God was alienated from them on account of the king's sin, the army was in the greatest need of iron weapons; so much so that nobody, except Saul and Jonathan his son, is said to have pos-

sessed either sword or spear. For the Philistines, as conquerors in the former wars, had deprived the Hebrews of the use of arms, and no one had had the power of forging any weapon of war or even making any implement for rural purposes. SACRED HISTORY 1.33.[1]

A SMITH OF SPIRITUAL ARMS. BEDE: The reason for this is rather obvious. It clearly offers the enemy an opportunity to devastate the land, that is to say, to corrupt the virtues of the church, if there is no teacher and smithy of the spiritual arms which the apostle teaches we must employ against the fiery darts of the evil one. For the wicked tempters take care with all their might to keep us from putting on the armor of God so that the two-edged sword might not appear in our hands and exact vengeance upon them. FOUR BOOKS ON 1 SAMUEL 2.13.[2]

TURNING FROM THE WORD OF GOD. BEDE: Today some also leave the heights of God's Word to which they ought to have ascended and listened to. Instead they go down and hear worldly fables and doctrines of demons. Deprived of all spiritual knowledge, they meet to read logicians, teachers of rhetoric and the poets of the Gentiles

---

[1]NPNF 2 11:86-87*.   [2]CCL 119:112.

to exercise their earthly talents, just as the unarmed men of Israel went to the smiths of the Philistines to sharpen their iron tools for use in the woods or fields. Four Books on 1 Samuel 2.13.[3]

13:22-23 As the Philistines Approach

Spiritual Laziness. Bede: Although the day of battle against the hostile powers daily looms, many are content with their rustic life and few set forth properly armed for this battle with a suitable reading or hearing of the Scriptures. Thus our spiritual enemy, aided by our laziness, daily does to us what the physical enemy of Israel is described as having done at that time. . . .

Because Israel did not have arms, it abandoned the country to its enemies. We too grant our enemy an opportunity by our laziness in reading or consulting spiritual teachers, just as the Israelites did by their neglect of making arms or seeking Israelite smiths for them. Consequently, the enemy uses the opportunity to bring in their weapons of godlessness against the other virtues, just as the Philistines invaded the boundaries of the holy land. (The fact that Michmash was besieged refers to humility and subjugation.) But we must not summon the experience of human arts to repel the arms of this most foul enemy, but we must summon the exhortation of the heavenly teachers as the grace of the Holy Spirit aids us. Four Books on 1 Samuel 2.13.[4]

---

[3]CCL 119:112. [4]CCL 119:112-13.

14:1-23 JONATHAN LEADS A VICTORIOUS RAID

[1]One day Jonathan the son of Saul said to the young man who bore his armor, "Come, let us go over to the Philistine garrison on yonder side." But he did not tell his father. [2]Saul was staying in the outskirts of Gibe-ah under the pomegranate tree which is at Migron; the people who were with him were about six hundred men, [3]and Ahijah the son of Ahitub, Ichabod's brother, son of Phinehas, son of Eli, the priest of the Lord in Shiloh, wearing an ephod. And the people did not know that Jonathan had gone. . . .
[6]And Jonathan said to the young man who bore his armor, "Come, let us go over to the garrison of these uncircumcised; it may be that the Lord will work for us; for nothing can hinder the Lord from saving by many or by few." . . . [11]So both of them showed themselves to the garrison of the Philistines; and the Philistines said, "Look, Hebrews are coming out of the holes where they have hid themselves." [12]And the men of the garrison hailed Jonathan and his armor-bearer, and said, "Come up to us, and we will show you a thing." And Jonathan said to his armor-bearer, "Come up after me; for the Lord has given them into the hand of Israel." [13]Then Jonathan climbed up on his hands and feet, and his armor-bearer after him. And they fell before Jonathan, and his armorbearer killed them after him; [14]and that first slaughter, which Jonathan and his armor-bearer made, was of about twenty men within as it were half a furrow's length in an acre[r] of land. [15]And

---

there was a panic in the camp, in the field, and among all the people; the garrison and even the raiders trembled; the earth quaked; and it became a very great panic. . . .

²³*So the Lord delivered Israel that day; and the battle passed beyond Beth-aven.*

r *Heb* yoke

OVERVIEW: Jonathan urges his armor bearer to go with him into battle like an excellent teacher urges obedient disciples to conquer vices. Withholding news of virtuous plans from the spiritually immature has many benefits. Saul's tarrying in Gibeah represents both zeal for the Lord and imperfection as he lacks complete victory over vices (BEDE). While others were cowering, Jonathan and his armor bearer boldly and successfully attacked the Philistine outpost, sending their army into confusion (SULPICIUS SEVERUS).

14:1 The Philistine Garrison

ENCOURAGING VICTORY OVER VICES. BEDE: Jonathan's name means "gift of the dove." His armor bearer refers to the teachers endowed with the grace of the Spirit, the disciples who obediently carry arms not made of flesh but arms made mighty for God. Their youth is renewed like that of an eagle. A certain day to begin their battle represents the sudden inspiration of supernal light against the trials of the enemy. On a certain day Jonathan urges his armor bearer to join him in crossing over to the Philistines and their garrison, since every perfect teacher, suddenly regarded by heavenly grace, urges the hearts of his pious hearers to conquer the onslaughts of vices. FOUR BOOKS ON 1 SAMUEL 2.14.[1]

DEALING WITH THE SPIRITUALLY IMMATURE. BEDE: When Jonathan was about to go to the camp of the Philistines, he kept his plan hidden from his father and the rest of the people. Just as it is always most appropriate to avail oneself of the counsel of spiritual people, so it is also useful to keep hidden from carnal individuals great and virtuous undertakings, when planning or beginning them. We do this so that their fear

might not break us and scare us while the desire of our mind is still tender; we also do this so that they themselves might not begin to do the very same things in emulation of us when they are not yet up to the task; and we also do this so that their imperfect praise might not degrade the integrity of our spiritual undertaking. For the following words relate that Saul at this juncture and the people who were with him had not yet attained spiritual maturity. FOUR BOOKS ON 1 SAMUEL 2.14.[2]

14:2 Saul Near Gibeah

TARRYING IN GIBEAH. BEDE: For a person of virtue comes to the conclusion that he tarried in Gibeah, that is, on the hill, that he tarried under the pomegranate tree and that he had six hundred companions. As we already noted before, the hill portrays the height of the virtues, the shade of the pomegranate tree the protection of the cross of our Lord, the number of the six hundred soldiers those made complete in hope and work. But the fact that he sat at the outskirts of the hill and that the tree by whose shade he was protected was located in Migron, that is, in the throat, are signs of a less than perfect mind. That is to say, his mind had not yet scaled the walls of virtues, although he much desired them. His mind confessed with his mouth the mystery of the Lord's passion, but he was not yet strong enough to imitate it. But if we follow the ancient translators and read Megiddo ("Tempter") instead of Migron, we still come to the same meaning. There are those who are endowed with the right faith and ablaze with the desires of just works but who do not cease to undergo harsh struggles

---

[1]CCL 119:113. [2]CCL 119:113.

against vices that tempt them. Four Books on 1 Samuel 2.14.[3]

14:11-14 *Attacking a Philistine Outpost*

Jonathan's Daring Exploit. Sulpicius Severus: In these circumstances [with few weapons and Saul's fearful army], Jonathan, with an audacious design and with his armor bearer as his only companion, entered the camp of the enemy, and having slain about twenty of them, [he]

spread a terror throughout the whole army. And then, through the appointment of God, taking themselves to flight, they neither carried out orders nor kept their ranks but placed all the hope of safety in flight. Saul, perceiving this, hastily drew forth his men, and pursuing the fugitives, obtained a victory. Sacred History 1.33.[4]

---

[3]CCL 119:113-14. [4]NPNF 2 11:87*.

14:24-30 JONATHAN BREAKS SAUL'S OATH

[24]*And the men of Israel were distressed that day; for Saul laid an oath on the people, saying, "Cursed be the man who eats food until it is evening and I am avenged on my enemies." So none of the people tasted food.* [25]*And all the people[u] came into the forest; and there was honey on the ground.* [26]*And when the people entered the forest, behold, the honey was dropping, but no man put his hand to his mouth; for the people feared the oath.* [27]*But Jonathan had not heard his father charge the people with the oath; so he put forth the tip of the staff that was in his hand, and dipped it in the honeycomb, and put his hand to his mouth; and his eyes became bright.* [28]*Then one of the people said, "Your father strictly charged the people with an oath, saying 'Cursed be the man who eats food this day.'" And the people were faint.* [29]*Then Jonathan said, "My father has troubled the land; see how my eyes have become bright, because I tasted a little of this honey.* [30]*How much better if the people had eaten freely today of the spoil of their enemies which they found; for now the slaughter among the Philistines has not been great."*

u Heb *land*

Overview: The seriousness of proclaiming a solemn fast to the Lord is illustrated. Although victorious and ignorant of the proclamation, its binding nature is seen in Jonathan's conviction by lot and near execution (Jerome, Tertullian).

14:24-26 *Saul Proclaims a Fast*[1]

A Binding Oath. Jerome: Saul, as it is written

in the first book of Kings [Samuel], pronounced a curse on him who ate bread before the evening, and until he had avenged himself upon his enemies. So none of his troops tasted any food while all the people of the land ate. And so binding was a solemn fast once it was proclaimed to the Lord, that Jonathan, to whom the victory was due, was

---

[1]See also Augustine's comment for 1 Sam 28:3.

taken by lot and could not escape the charge of sinning in ignorance, and his father's hand was raised against him, and the prayers of the people barely saved him. Against Jovinianus 2.15.[2]

Convicted of Gluttony. Tertullian: At all events, Saul himself, when engaged in battle, clearly enjoined this duty: "Cursed (be) the man who shall have eaten bread until evening, until I am avenged against my enemy"; and his whole company did not taste (food), and (yet) the whole earth was breakfasting![3] So solemn a sanction,

moreover, did God confer on the edict which enjoined that station, that Jonathan the son of Saul, although it had been in ignorance of the fast having been appointed till a late hour that he had allowed himself a taste of honey, was both presently convicted, by lot . . . and with difficulty was exempted from punishment through the prayer of the people: for he had been convicted of gluttony, although of a simple kind. On Fasting 10.[4]

---

[2]NPNF 2 6:399*. [3]The LXX adds to verse twenty-four that "all the land was dining." [4]ANF 4:109*.

14:31-42 THE LOT REVEALS JONATHAN'S GUILT

[31]*They struck down the Philistines that day from Michmash to Aijalon. And the people were very faint;* [32]*the people flew upon the spoil, and took sheep and oxen and calves, and slew them on the ground; and the people ate them with the blood.* [33]*Then they told Saul, "Behold, the people are sinning against the Lord, by eating with the blood." And he said, "You have dealt treacherously; roll a great stone to me here."* [34]*And Saul said, "Disperse yourselves among the people, and say to them, 'Let every man bring his ox or his sheep, and slay them here, and eat; and do not sin against the Lord by eating with the blood.'" So every one of the people brought his ox with him that night, and slew them there.* [35]*And Saul built an altar to the Lord; it was the first altar that he built to the Lord.*

v Gk: Heb *this day*

Overview: The peoples' seizing and eating of the spoils of war represents the thoughts and actions of the arrogant who exult in carnal pleasures (Gregory the Great). The Israelites' eating of bloody meat typifies lazy teachers who fail to draw catechists away from earthly and fleshly allurements (Bede).

14:31-32 The People Eat Animals with the Blood

The Ways of the Proud. Gregory the

Great: It is also the custom of the arrogant to not let their self-esteem keep quiet whenever the tongues of others grow silent in praising them. Indeed, while all the others keep quiet, the arrogant shouts aloud, for in his heart he carries around one who broadcasts his great worth. Therefore, the following words are readily applied to such people: "And the people turned to the spoils and brought sheep, cows and calves. They slaughtered them on the ground, and the people ate them with their blood." If anyone cultivates many reasons for his innocence and boasts about them, he takes sheep. When someone thinks about his labors of preaching and collects in his memory whatever has been useful as he spoke to others or cultivated the earth, he takes cattle as booty. When he is elated from the fact that the impulses of wantonness upon the mind have been restrained and reduced, he takes calves. For there are two commandments that bring great praise to the just: the splendor of chastity and the light of good works. When an arrogant individual is exalted in his own estimation, he is said to have stolen sheep and calves. Sheep refer to the innocence of good works, calves to the mortification of bodily passion. Clearly, he added cattle to these, for he is not perfectly exalted if he thinks that he is in any way weak or powerless. He had already been great in his own opinion as far as he estimated his chastity and good works, but he raised himself in the arrogance of even fuller exaltation when he thought himself perfect in the labor of preaching.

But afterwards he wrote about the end to which all these things lead: "And they slaughtered them on the ground." To slaughter sheep, cows and calves on the ground is to exult with carnal joy and a conscience bereft of virtues. Thus God spoke about the proud and arrogant in the book of Hosea: "He turned away their sacrificial offerings into the deep."[1] Indeed, they plunge their victims into the deep when they do not raise up the heavenly offerings of virtues to the heavens in gratitude, but they yield their sacrifices to the earth through their quest for vain praise. Therefore, these words are well applied to them: "The people ate the sacrifices with their blood." The food of the mind is its own internal joy. What, then, does eating with blood signify except to refuse to remove by any means striving for vain praise from the internal appetite of the mind? The blood is removed when the mind removes the striving for vanity from the joy of a good work. For the mind of a godly sort knows to rejoice in a good work, since he rejoices to draw near to the heavenly beings through his good works, but he avoids letting those works be seen at the time as he carries out those works. Then to eat with

blood is to take the joy of a good work and mix it with a longing for vanity. Clearly, when praise is offered by others, then it is sincere food even for the arrogant. But when no one else praises them, the conscience of the haughty swells up, it violently snatches as loot the praise nobody else voluntarily offers. SIX BOOKS ON 1 KINGS 5.143-144.[2]

LAZY TEACHERS. BEDE: When it is said that the people ate the animals with their blood, one ought not the think that they ate the meat bloody and raw. After all, it is not human nature but the nature of wild animals to do that. Rather, once the herds had been killed, they began cooking or roasting the meat before it had been properly drained, and so they ate meat not yet fully purged of blood. This practice, however, refers to lazy teachers who, just as we see today, are wearied by the time-consuming task of catechizing, offer to God through their teaching a number of people whom they have delivered by their preaching from demonic errors and pagan rituals. They attempt to imitate him to whom it was said, when animals of every sort were lowered from the heavens, "Kill and eat."[3] But just as the Israelites slaughtered animals on the ground and ate them with the blood, so these teachers do not draw them from earthly senses and the allurements of flesh and blood. Perhaps they are less than perfect teachers; perhaps they see virtue less than perfectly. They hasten to incorporate into the members of the church people who are still accustomed to vice and not yet well grounded in performing virtues. They do this contrary to the example of the first pastor of the church who, seated in the upper room, that is, at the highest pinnacle of his living and teaching, was ordered to kill and eat offerings purified by God. And one should note how less than perfect and weak is the perfection of the human mind. Jonathan achieved so many and so great works and was the instigator of such a great victory, but in ignorance [he] committed a fault by

---

[1]Hos 5:2. [2]CCL 144:506-7. [3]Acts 10:13.

letting his stomach steal food. After all the people had with due deliberation observed the time of fasting and after they had overcome their enemies in one day, the Israelites themselves were overcome in turn by gluttony. But because the temptation of the stomach is manifold, it enticed Jonathan, who ate before he should have, and it persuaded the Israelites to eat what is not appropriate, although it was an appropriate time. FOUR BOOKS ON 1 SAMUEL 2.14.[4]

[4]CCL 119:122.

14:43-52 JONATHAN'S LIFE IS SPARED

[43]*Then Saul said to Jonathan, "Tell me what you have done." And Jonathan told him, "I tasted a little honey with the tip of the staff that was in my hand; here I am, I will die."* [44]*And Saul said, "God do so to me and more also; you shall surely die, Jonathan."* [45]*Then the people said to Saul, "Shall Jonathan die, who has wrought this great victory in Israel? Far from it! As the LORD lives, there shall not one hair of his head fall to the ground; for he has wrought with God this day." So the people ransomed Jonathan, that he did not die.*

OVERVIEW: Exposed by the lot, Jonathan's confession is met with the intercession and prayers of the people, which deliver him from death (JEROME), which he deserved through succumbing to unbounded desire (GREGORY THE GREAT). As Saul overcame his enemies through abstinence, so Christians must avoid the honey of the pleasures and vices of the world (MAXIMUS OF TURIN).

14:43-45 Jonathan's Confession and Consequences

DELIVERED THROUGH INTERCESSION. JEROME: Jonathan tasted of a honeycomb on a rod, and his eyes were enlightened, and his life was in danger because he acted through ignorance. For Scripture testifies to the fact that he did not know that his father had given strict orders that no one was to taste any food until the victory of the Lord was accomplished. However, the Lord was so angered that the lot disclosed him hiding, and he confessed openly, saying, "I did but taste a little honey with the end of the rod, which was in my hand, and behold I must die." And he was subsequently delivered through the intercession and prayers of the people, who said to Saul, "Shall Jonathan die, who has wrought this great salvation in Israel? This must not be. As the Lord lives, not one hair of his head shall fall to the ground, for he has wrought with God this day. And the people delivered Jonathan, and he did not die." DEFENSE AGAINST THE PELAGIANS 1.38.[1]

FIVE WAYS OF GLUTTONY. GREGORY THE GREAT: It should also be known that the vice of gluttony tempts us in five ways. For it sometimes anticipates the seasons of want, but sometimes [it] does not anticipate them but seeks for daintier food. Sometimes it looks for those things, which must be taken, to be prepared more care-

[1]FC 53:288-89*.

fully; but sometimes it agrees with both the quality of, and the season for, its food, but exceeds, in the quantity of what is to be taken, the measure of moderate refreshment. But sometimes that which it longs for is even of a baser kind, and yet it sins more fatally through the heat of unbounded desire. For Jonathan deserved in truth the sentence of death from the mouth of his father, because in taking honey he anticipated the time which had been fixed for eating. MORALS ON THE BOOK OF JOB 30.18.[2]

VICTORY THROUGH ABSTINENCE. MAXIMUS OF TURIN: It is no light sin, as I have said, to violate the appointed fast. In order to demonstrate this briefly by examples, we read in the book of Kings [Samuel] that when Saul the king of Israel was waging war against the foreigners he proclaimed a fast for his entire army, and when all were abstaining he began to fight against the opposing forces. This is obviously a good king, who overcame his enemies not so much by arms as by devotion and who fought more by piety than with spears. When, therefore, Saul had proclaimed a day's abstinence for all his men and his son Jonathan, unaware of the command, had tasted some honeycomb into which the tip of his staff had been dipped as the victorious army was proceeding into the midst of the enemy, suddenly such indignation was aroused that the victory was delayed and the Divinity offended. And neither was an end put to the war nor a prophetic response given to the king. From this we understand that Saul used to overcome his enemies not so much by the might of his soldiers as by the abstinence of his soldiers. And so by the sin of one person guilt is laid upon all, and by the crime of one person weakness is produced in all, for the army's strength failed when the observance of the fast failed. But since Saul recognized the sin from the fact that the Divinity had been offended, he immediately said that Jonathan should not be pardoned but that the sin which he admitted should be atoned for by the shedding of his blood. See how religious was the behavior of Saul the king, who desired to pacify the offended Lord even by the slaying of his kin! And see what guilt attaches to the broken fast, which is only punished by the shedding of blood! And if the unwitting Jonathan is delivered over to death because he broke the fast proclaimed by his father, what would a person deserve who knowingly broke the fast proclaimed by Christ? Therefore, brothers, let us most carefully observe the fast that has been decreed for us so that we may overcome our spiritual and fleshly enemies. For we have, as you know, fleshly enemies as well. Let us fast, then, so that our army, like Saul's, might overcome and seize them, and let us not having determined to abstain, turn away for a honeycomb. For a honeycomb is, so to speak, the pleasure and vices of the world, which, as it is written, are sweet in the throat for a time, to be sure, but in the end are more bitter than gall. SERMON 69.4.[3]

---

[2]LF 31:405. [3]ACW 50:170-71*.

15:1-9 SAUL'S DISOBEDIENCE
IN THE DEFEAT OF AMALEK

⁷And Saul defeated the Amalekites, from Havilah as far as Shur, which is east of Egypt. ⁸And he took Agag the king of the Amalekites alive, and utterly destroyed all the people with the edge of the sword. ⁹But Saul and the people spared Agag, and the best of the sheep and of the oxen and of the fatlings, and the lambs, and all that was good, and would not utterly destroy them; all that was despised and worthless they utterly destroyed.

OVERVIEW: Failure to dispense punishment, which is a sacred charge of the magisterial office, has a contaminating effect on those governed (APOSTOLIC CONSTITUTIONS).

15:8-9 Saul Spared Agag and the Best of the Livestock[1]

DO NOT SPARE THOSE WHO DESERVE PUNISHMENT. APOSTLIC CONSTITUTIONS: But he who does not consider these things, will, contrary to justice, spare him who deserves punishment; as Saul spared Agag, and Eli[2] his sons, "who knew not the Lord." Such a one profanes his own dignity and that church of God which is in his parish. Such a one is esteemed unjust before God and holy men, as affording occasion of scandal to many of the newly baptized and to the catechumens; as also to the youth of both sexes, to whom a woe belongs, add "a millstone about his neck,"[3] and drowning, on account of his guilt. For, observing what a person their governor is, through his wickedness and neglect of justice they will grow skeptical, and, indulging the same disease, will be compelled to perish with him; as was the case of the people joining with Jeroboam,[4] and those which were in the conspiracy with Korah.[5] CONSTITUTIONS OF THE HOLY APOSTLES 2.10.[6]

---

[1]See also Augustine's comment for 1 Samuel 28:3. [2]1 Sam 2. [3]Mt 18:6-7. [4]1 Kings 12. [5]Num 16. [6]ANF 7:399*.

15:10-16 SAMUEL CONFRONTS SAUL

¹⁰The word of the LORD came to Samuel: ¹¹"I repent that I have made Saul king; for he has turned back from following me, and has not performed my commandments." And Samuel was angry; and he cried to the LORD all night.

OVERVIEW: God's revulsion over making Saul king demonstrates that promises should not be clung to stubbornly and that God deals with individuals on the basis of their actions in the present, not the future (CASSIAN). Rather than signifying wrongdoing, God's "repentance," which must not be taken literally (AUGUSTINE) serves to further incriminate and condemn Saul (TERTULLIAN).

15:11 I Repent That I Have Made Saul King[1]

PROMISES TO BE TEMPERED BY REASON. JOHN CASSIAN: These texts declare that we should not cling stubbornly to our promises, but that they should be tempered by reason and judgment, that what is better should always be chosen and preferred and that we should pass over without any hesitation to whatever is proven to be more beneficial. This invaluable judgment also teaches us above all that, although each person's end may be known to God before he was born, he so disposes everything with order and reason and, so to say, human feelings, that he determines all things not by his power or in accordance with his ineffable foreknowledge but, based upon the deeds of human beings at the time, either rejects them or draws them or daily pours out grace upon them or turns them away.

The choosing of Saul also demonstrates that this is so. Although, indeed, the foreknowledge of God could not be ignorant of his miserable end, he chose him from among many thousands of Israelites and anointed him king. In doing this he rewarded him for his deserving life at the time and did not take into consideration the sin of his future transgression. And so after he became reprobate, God as it were repented of his choice and complained of him with, so to speak, human words and feelings, saying, "I repent that I set up Saul as king, because he has forsaken me and not carried out my words." And again: "Samuel grieved over Saul, because the Lord repented that he had set up Saul as king over Israel."[2] CONFERENCE 17.25.14-15.[3]

GOD'S CONFESSION INCRIMINATES SAUL. TERTULLIAN: Furthermore, with respect to the repentance which occurs in his conduct you interpret it with similar perverseness just as if it were with fickleness and improvidence that he

repented, or on the recollection of some wrongdoing; because he actually said, "I repent that I have set up Saul to be king," very much as if he meant that his repentance savored of an acknowledgment of some evil work or error. Well, this is not always implied. For there occurs even in good works a confession of repentance, as a reproach and condemnation of the man who has proved himself unthankful for a benefit. For instance, in this one case of Saul, the Creator, who had made no mistake in selecting him for the kingdom and endowing him with his Holy Spirit, makes a statement respecting the goodness of his person, how that he had most fitly chosen him as being at that moment the choicest man, so that (as he says) there was not one like him among the children of Israel. Neither was he ignorant how he would afterwards turn out. For no one would bear you out in imputing lack of foresight to that God whom, since you do not deny him to be divine, you allow to be also foreseeing; for this proper attribute of divinity exists in him. However, he did, as I have said, burden the guilt of Saul with the confession of his own repentance; but as there is an absence of all error and wrong in his choice of Saul, it follows that this repentance is to be understood as upbraiding another rather than as self-incriminating. AGAINST MARCION 2.24.[4]

ANALOGICAL LANGUAGE. AUGUSTINE: Again, there are some things which are praiseworthy in people but cannot be present in God, such as shame, which is a prominent trapping of the state of sin, as is the fear of God. For not only in the Old Testament books is it praised, but the apostle also says, "perfecting holiness in the fear of God,"[5] none of which is to be found in God. Therefore, just as certain praiseworthy human qualities are not rightly predicated of God, so also are certain contemptible human qualities properly said to be in God, not as they are found

---

[1]See also comment for 1 Samuel 15:35. [2]1 Sam 15:35. [3]ACW 57:608-9*. [4]ANF 3:315*. [5]2 Cor 7:1.

in people but only in a very different manner and for different reasons. For shortly after the Lord had said to Samuel, "I repent that I have made Saul king," Samuel himself said of God to Saul: "He is not like a man, that he should repent."[6] This clearly demonstrates that even though God said "I repent," it is not to be taken according to the human sense, as we have already argued at length. On Various Questions to Simplician 2.2.5.[7]

---

[6]1 Sam 15:29. [7]CCL 44:80-81.

15:17-23 THE LORD REJECTS SAUL AS KING

[17]And Samuel said, "Though you are little in your own eyes, are you not the head of the tribes of Israel? The Lord anointed you king over Israel. [18]And the Lord sent you on a mission, and said, 'Go, utterly destroy the sinners, the Amalekites, and fight against them until they are consumed.' [19]Why then did you not obey the voice of the Lord? Why did you swoop on the spoil, and do what was evil in the sight of the Lord?" [20]And Saul said to Samuel, "I have obeyed the voice of the Lord, I have gone on the mission on which the Lord sent me, I have brought Agag the king of Amalek, and I have utterly destroyed the Amalekites. [21]But the people took of the spoil, sheep and oxen, the best of the things devoted to destruction, to sacrifice to the Lord your God in Gilgal." [22]And Samuel said,

"Has the Lord as great delight in burnt offerings and sacrifices,
as in obeying the voice of the Lord?
Behold, to obey is better than sacrifice,
and to hearken than the fat of rams.
[23]For rebellion is as the sin of divination,
and stubbornness is as iniquity and idolatry.
Because you have rejected the word of the Lord,
he has also rejected you from being king."

Overview: Saul exemplifies how power corrupts: humility is commonly replaced with pride when one receives an affluence of subordinates (Gregory the Great). Answering an accusation of wrongdoing by citing instances of good conduct, instead of refuting the charge or confessing, plainly shows wrongdoing and the awareness of guilt (Athanasius). Lack of discretion twisted Saul's thinking so that he believed his offering, which was an act of disobedience, would be rewarded (Cassian). The law is fulfilled not by burnt offerings but through obedience and offering words of praise (Athanasius). In no need of offerings, God enjoined observances in the law on account of the people in order to occasion their obedience (Irenaeus). The payment due those who offer counsel by which sin may be corrected is fervency in reading, hearing and obeying the word of God (Origen). Taking refuge in excuses, rather than humbly confessing one's guilt, is the greatest of faults (Cassiodorus).

15:17 The Lord Anointed You King over Israel

Power and Pride. Gregory the Great: Thus Saul, after merit of humility, became swollen with pride, when in the height of power: for his humility he was preferred, for his pride rejected; as the Lord attests, who says, "When you were little in your own sight, did I not make you the head of the tribes of Israel?" He had before seen himself little in his own eyes, but, when propped up by temporal power, he no longer saw himself little. For, preferring himself in comparison with others because he had more power than all, he esteemed himself great above all. Yet in a wonderful way, when he was little with himself, he was great with God; but, when he appeared great with himself, he was little with God. Thus commonly, while the mind is inflated from an affluence of subordinates, it becomes corrupted to a flux of pride, the very summit of power being pander to desire. Pastoral Care 2.6.[1]

15:19-21 Saul Defends His and the People's Actions

Unmitigated Disobedience. Athanasius: And when Saul was charged with negligence and a breach of the law, he did not benefit his cause by alleging his conduct on other matters. For a defense on one count will not operate to obtain an acquittal on another count. But if all things should be done according to law and justice, one must defend himself in those particulars wherein he is accused and must either disprove the past or else confess it with the promise that he will desist and do so no more. But if he is guilty of the crime and will not confess, but in order to conceal the

truth speaks on other points instead of the one in question, he shows plainly that he has acted amiss and is conscious of his delinquency. Letter to the Bishops of Egypt 1.11.[2]

The Eye of Discretion. John Cassian: Finally, because he never had this eye of discretion, he who by God's judgment first deserved to rule over the people of Israel was cast out of his kingdom like something dark out of a healthy body. Having been deceived by the darkness and error of this light, he decided that his own sacrifices were more acceptable to God than obedience to Samuel's command, and in the very act by which he had hoped that he would propitiate the divine majesty he committed sin instead. Conference 2.3.1.[3]

15:22 To Obey Is Better Than Sacrifice

The Fulfillment of the Law. Athanasius: Samuel, that great man, no less clearly reproved Saul, saying, "Is not the word better than a gift?" For hereby one fulfills the law and pleases God, as he says, "The sacrifice of praise shall glorify me."[4] Let one "learn what this means, I will have mercy, and not sacrifice,"[5] and I will not condemn the adversaries. Festal Letter 19.5.[6]

On Sacrifice and Obedience. Irenaeus: Moreover, the prophets indicate in the fullest manner that God did not stand in need of their slavish obedience but that it was on their own account that he enjoined certain observances in the law. And again, that God did not need their oblation but [merely demanded it], on account of the one who offers it, the Lord taught distinctly, as I have pointed out. For when he perceived that they were neglecting righteousness, and abstaining from the love of God, and imagining that God was to be propitiated by sacrifices and the other typical observances, Samuel spoke thus to them:

---

[1]NPNF 2 12:15*. [2]NPNF 2 4:228*. [3]ACW 57:86. [4]Ps 50:23 (49:23 LXX). [5]Mt 9:13; Hos 6:6. [6]NPNF 2 4:546*.

"God does not desire whole burnt offerings and sacrifices, but that his voice is obeyed. Behold, a ready obedience is better than sacrifice, and to heed than the fat of rams." Against Heresies 4.17.1.[7]

The Cost of Correction. Origen: Therefore, when different prophets or different apostles should give to those who sin the counsel by which they can correct or amend the sin, they rightly will seem to have sold rams to them for sacrifice. But how much do they charge the buyers? It is, I think, the cost of reading zealously, of hearing with vigilance the word of God, and above all, I think, the most diligent obedience, about which the Lord says, "I prefer obedience to sacrifice; and hearing what I say rather than whole burnt offerings." Homilies on Leviticus 4.5.6.[8]

15:23 Rebellion Is Like the Sin of Divination

Taking Refuge in Excuses. Cassiodorus: This is the greatest fault under which humanity labors, that after sinning they take refuge in excuses rather than prostrate themselves with repentant confession. Clearly such wickedness is to be reckoned amongst the worst sins, for its true source also seems to occasion slower progress by the sinner towards repentance. As the first book of Kings [Samuel] has it: "It is like the sin of witchcraft to rebel, and like the crime of idolatry to refuse to obey." Exposition of the Psalms 140.4.[9]

---

[7]ANF 1:482**. [8]FC 83:77. [9]ACW 53:394*.

15:24-33 SAUL CONFESSES HIS SIN

[24]And Saul said to Samuel, "I have sinned; for I have transgressed the commandment of the Lord and your words, because I feared the people and obeyed their voice. [25]Now therefore, I pray, pardon my sin, and return with me, that I may worship the Lord." [26]And Samuel said to Saul, "I will not return with you; for you have rejected the word of the Lord, and the Lord has rejected you from being king over Israel." [27]As Samuel turned to go away, Saul laid hold upon the skirt of his robe, and it tore. [28]And Samuel said to him, "The Lord has torn the kingdom of Israel from you this day, and has given it to a neighbor of yours, who is better than you. [29]And also the Glory of Israel will not lie or repent; for he is not a man, that he should repent."

Overview: That God discerned a difference in the hearts of Saul and David teaches that this is where the kingdom of heaven resides: hearts, rather than words, exhibit faith (Augustine). Although the law of obedience helps overcome the fear of office, which trusts that God rewards faithfulness through sanctification, there is no such relief from the danger of disobedience

(Gregory of Nazianzus).

Saul's consequence for tearing Samuel's cloak illustrates that the church is to be governed not by political leaders but by spiritual ones (John of Damascus). Saul's rejection, which applied to his posterity since he reigned as long as David did, signified that the Christ would not come from his lineage. Following a translation of the Greek, it is understood that this figuratively represents the tearing of the kingdom "from" Israel in the New Testament with Christ's advent (AUGUSTINE).

15:24 I Have Sinned

A DIFFERENCE IN THE HEART. AUGUSTINE: Saul, too, when he was reproved by Samuel, said, "I have sinned." Why, then, was he not considered fit to be told, as David was, that the Lord had pardoned his sin? Is there favoritism with God? Far from it. While to the human ear the words were the same, the divine eye saw a difference in the heart. The lesson for us to learn from these things is that the kingdom of heaven is within us[1] and that we must worship God from our inmost feelings, that out of the abundance of the heart the mouth may speak, instead of honoring him with our lips, like the people of old, while our hearts are far from him. We may learn also to judge people, whose hearts we cannot see, only as God judges, who sees what we cannot, and who cannot be biased or misled. AGAINST FAUSTUS, A MANICHAEAN 22.67.[2]

15:26 The Lord Has Rejected You

THE DANGER OF DISOBEDIENCE. GREGORY OF NAZIANZUS: Moreover, to distinguish still more clearly between them, we have, against the fear of office, a possible help in the law of obedience, inasmuch as God in his goodness rewards our faith, and makes a perfect ruler of the one who has confidence in him, and places all his hopes in him; but against the danger of disobedience I know of nothing which can help us, and of no ground to encourage our confidence. For we should fear that we will have to hear these words concerning those who have been entrusted to us: "I will require their souls at your hands"; and, "Because you have rejected me, and [have] not been leaders and rulers of my people, I also will reject you, that I should not be king over you"; and, "As you refused to listen to my voice, and turned a stubborn back, and were disobedient, so

shall it be when you call upon me, and I will not regard nor hear your prayer."[3] IN DEFENSE OF HIS FLIGHT TO PONTUS, ORATION 2.113.[4]

15:27-28 Saul Tears Samuel's Robe as He Departs

THE GOVERNMENT OF THE CHURCH. JOHN OF DAMASCUS: Political prosperity is the business of emperors; the condition of the church is the concern of shepherds and teachers. Any other method is piracy, brothers. Saul tore Samuel's cloak, and what was the consequence? God tore the kingdom away from him and gave it to David the meek. . . . We will obey you, O emperor, in those matters which pertain to our daily lives: payments, taxes, tributes; these are your due, and we will give them to you. But as far as the government of the church is concerned, we have our pastors, and they have preached the word to us; we have those who interpret the ordinances of the church. ON DIVINE IMAGES 2.12.[5]

THE REJECTION OF SAUL'S POSTERITY. AUGUSTINE: Again Saul sinned by disobedience, and again Samuel addressed to him the Lord's word: "Inasmuch, therefore, as you have rejected the word of the Lord, the Lord has also rejected you as king." And again, because of the same sin, when Saul admitted it and sought pardon, beseeching Samuel to go back with him and appease God, the prophet said, "I will not return with you, because you have rejected the word of the Lord, and the Lord has rejected you as king over Israel." And Samuel turned about to go away; but he grabbed hold of the skirt of his mantle, and it tore. And Samuel said to him, "The Lord has torn the kingdom from Israel from your hand this day and has given it to your neighbor who is better than you, and Israel shall be divided in two. But the triumpher in Israel will not spare

---

[1]Lk 17:21. [2]NPNF 1 4:298*. [3]Zech 7:11, 13. [4]NPNF 2 7:226-27*. Gregory is here struggling with his own vocational ambivalence, which was later overcome. [5]ODI 59-60*.

and will not be moved to repentance; for he is not a man that he should repent. He threatens and does not persist."

Actually, the man to whom these words were spoken, "The Lord shall reject you as king over Israel," and, "The Lord has torn the kingdom of Israel from you this day," ruled over Israel for forty years—for the same duration as David did—and he heard this pronouncement in the early part of his reign. Accordingly, we are to understand it to mean that no one of Saul's posterity was to rule after him—an admonition to look to David's stock whence was to stem, according to the flesh, Jesus Christ, the Mediator between God and humanity. CITY OF GOD 17.7.[6]

THE KINGDOM FROM ISRAEL. AUGUSTINE: In many Latin versions we find one of the above verses in the following form: "The Lord has torn the kingdom of Israel from your hand." But I have quoted from the Greek text: "The Lord has torn the kingdom from Israel from your hand"—the expression "from Israel" being equivalent to "from your hand." In this way, Samuel stood figuratively for the people of Israel which was to lose the kingdom when our Lord Jesus Christ would come to reign—spiritually, not carnally—in the New Testament. The reference to him in the words "and he has given it to your neighbor" is an allusion to the racial relationship, for Christ in the flesh derived from Israel just as did Saul. CITY OF GOD 17.7.[7]

---

[6]FC 24:43-44*. [7]FC 24:44*.

15:34-35 SAMUEL GRIEVES OVER SAUL

[34]*Then Samuel went to Ramah; and Saul went up to his house in Gibe-ah of Saul.* [35]*And Samuel did not see Saul again until the day of his death, but Samuel grieved over Saul. And the LORD repented that he had made Saul king over Israel.*

OVERVIEW: Scripture's anthropomorphic language, which is not as a fact descriptive of God, helps to instill godliness and humility (GREGORY OF NYSSA). Good people, like Samuel, grieve for the sins of others (JEROME).

15:35 The Lord Repented That He Had Made Saul King[1]

GOD'S HUMAN ASCRIPTIONS. GREGORY OF NYSSA: Holy Scripture is often accustomed to attributing expressions to God such that seem quite like our own, for example, "The Lord was angry, and he was grieved because of their sins";[2] and again, "He repented that he had anointed Saul king" . . . and besides this, it makes mention of his sitting, and standing, and moving, and the like, which are not as a fact connected with God but are not without their use as an accommodation to those who are under teaching. For in the case of the too unbridled, a show of anger restrains them by fear. And to those who need the medicine of repentance, it says that the Lord repents along with them of the evil, and those who grow insolent through prosperity it warns, by God's repentance in respect to Saul, that their

---

[1]See also comment for 1 Samuel 15:11. [2]See Ps 106:40 (105:40 LXX).

good fortune is no certain possession, though it seems to come from God. Answer to Eunomius's Second Book.[3]

Zeal for Souls. Jerome: I am induced to write to you,[4] a stranger to a stranger, by the entreaties of that holy servant of Christ, Hedibia, and of my daughter in the faith Artemia, once your wife but now no longer your wife but your sister and fellow servant. Not content with assuring her own salvation, she has sought yours also, in former days at home and now in the holy places. She is anxious to emulate the thoughtfulness of the apostles Andrew and Philip, who, after Christ had found them, desired in their turn to find, the one his brother Simon and the other his friend Nathanael.[5] . . . So of old Lot desired to rescue his wife as well as his two daughters, and refusing to leave blazing Sodom and Gomorrah until he was himself half on fire, tried to lead forth one who was tied and bound by her past sins.[6] But in her despair she lost her composure, and looking back became a monument of an unbelieving soul. Yet, as if to make up for the loss of a single woman, Lot's glowing faith set free the whole city of Zoar. In fact, when he left the dark valleys in which Sodom lay and came to the mountains the sun rose upon him as he entered Zoar or the little city; so-called because the little faith that Lot possessed, though unable to save greater places, was at least able to preserve smaller ones. . . . Good people have always sorrowed for the sins of others. Samuel of old lamented for Saul because he neglected to treat the ulcers of pride with the balm of penitence.[7] And Paul wept for the Corinthians who refused to wash out with their tears the stains of fornication.[8] Letter 122.[9]

---

[3]NPNF 2 5:292-93**. [4]This letter is addressed to Rusticus. Rusticus and Artemia, his wife, made a vow of continence and broke it. Artemia proceeded to Palestine to do penance for her sin, and Rusticus promised to follow her. However, he failed to do so, and Jerome was asked to write this letter in the hope that it might induce him to fulfill his promise. [5]See Jn 1:41-45. [6]See Gen 19:15-26. [7]See 1 Sam 15:25. [8]See 2 Cor 2:4. [9]NPNF 2 6:225.

16:1-5 THE LORD INSTRUCTS SAMUEL TO ANOINT A NEW KING

[1]*The* Lord *said to Samuel, "How long will you grieve over Saul, seeing I have rejected him from being king over Israel? Fill your horn with oil, and go; I will send you to Jesse the Bethlehemite, for I have provided for myself a king among his sons."*

Overview: David, who was anointed as king and prophet, prefigures Christ, the anointed One, the King of Kings, and the High Priest (Lactantius). Gregory the Great expounds the spiritual meaning of anointing leaders with an oil-filled horn.

16:1 Fill Your Horn with Oil

David's Kingly Anointing Prefigures Christ's. Lactantius: The Jews had before been directed to compose a sacred oil, with which those who were called to the priesthood or to the kingdom might be anointed. And as now the robe of purple is a sign of the assumption of royal dignity among the Romans, so with them the anointing with the holy oil conferred the title and power of king. But since the ancient Greeks used the word *chriesthai* to express the art of anointing, which they now express by *anleiphesthai*, as the verse of Homer shows, "But the attendants washed, and anointed them with oil"; on this account we call him Christ, that is, the Anointed, who in Hebrew is called the Messiah. Epitome of the Divine Institutes 4.7.[1]

A Full Horn of Oil. Gregory the Great: We have touched on these things as they pertain to the literal meaning; now let us see the election of our nobles as we look at the meaning beneath the literal one. When Samuel was told to fill the horn with oil, what else could it mean than this: he who is to be selected as a pastor in the holy church must not be someone clearly known as a transgressor but must be commended by wondrous praise as an example to others. The horn, you see, is the spear of an animal. But the authority and rebuke of even the highest bishop is nothing but his weapon. Indeed, they strike with their horn, whenever they lock horns with sinners as they issue their rebukes. They strike with their horn whenever they sharply confute sinners. The

horn is filled with oil, then, whenever the loftiness of preachers does not have the harshness of threats but the allurements of grace. Or the horn is filled with oil when both the sublimity of the heights and the virtue of unction are given to a chosen pastor at the same time, that is, when he both ascends to a high degree, but the one who is taken into the heights is filled with the riches of merits. The priests were anointed with a full horn of oil, inasmuch as they arrived at the highest degree with a full possession of graces. When a fire is lit in a lamp of oil, the oil of the teacher is the love of the heart. A fire is lit in it, for the virtue and grace of the Holy Spirit burns in the richness of the mouth. Since a teacher ought to have the richness of great love, the king is said to have been anointed with a full horn of oil when he was ordered to be anointed. The fullness of the horn refers to the perseverance of the graces. For those who fail before they reach the end are not worthy to be anointed with a full horn of oil. Six Books on 1 Kings 6.65.[2]

---

[1]ANF 7:106. [2]CCL 144:588-89.

16:6-13 SAMUEL ANOINTS DAVID

⁶*When they came, he looked on Eliab and thought, "Surely the Lord's anointed is before him."* ⁷*But the Lord said to Samuel, "Do not look on his appearance or on the height of his stature, because I have rejected him; for the Lord sees not as man sees; man looks on the outward appearance, but the Lord looks on the heart.". . .* ¹¹*And Samuel said to Jesse, "Are all your sons here?" And he said, "There remains yet the youngest, but behold, he is keeping the sheep." And Samuel said to Jesse, "Send and fetch him; for we will not sit down till he comes here."* ¹²*And he sent, and brought him in. Now he was ruddy, and had beautiful eyes, and was handsome. And the Lord said, "Arise, anoint him; for this is he."* ¹³*Then Samuel took the horn of oil, and anointed him in the midst of his brothers; and the Spirit of the Lord came mightily upon David from that day forward. And Samuel rose up, and went to Ramah.*

OVERVIEW: In his search for the Lord's anointed, Samuel's favorable appraisal of Jesse's older sons evidences the weakness of the human mind (Jerome). Like all falsehood, artificial beautification of one's body must be abhorrent to God, who places more importance on the beauty of the soul (Clement of Alexandria). Since only God can judge the heart, Christians should refrain from judging ministers based upon their credentials (Gregory of Nazianzus). The eyes of the Lord are superior to those of humans because God sees the condition of the heart (Tertullian). The psalms of David are prophetic in nature because his inspiration came from none other than the Holy Spirit (Cassiodorus).

16:6-7 The Lord Looks on the Heart

The Weakness of Human Reasoning. Jerome: He goes to Bethlehem and considers every son of Jesse to be the very person that the Lord was looking for.... He makes the same mistake in each case, and he is reproved in each case, giving evidence of the weakness of the human mind.[1] Defense Against the Pelagians 1.38.[2]

Artificial Beautification. Clement of Alexandria: They have gone beyond the limits of impropriety. They have invented mirrors to reflect all this artificial beautification of theirs, as if it were nobility of character or self-improvement. They should, rather, conceal such deception with a veil. It did the handsome Narcissus no good to gaze on his own image, as the Greek myth tells us. If Moses forbade his people to fashion any image to take the place of God, is it right for these women to study their reflected images for no other reason that to distort the natural features of their faces?

In much the same way, when Samuel the prophet was sent to anoint one of the sons of Jesse as king, and when he brought out his chrism as soon as he saw the oldest son, admiring his handsomeness and height, Scripture tells us, "The Lord said to him: 'Look not on his counte-

nance, nor on the height of his stature, because I have rejected him. For man sees those things that appear, but the Lord beholds the heart.'" He finally anointed not the one who was fair in body but the one who was fair of soul. If the Lord places more importance on beauty of soul than on that of the body, what must he think of artificial beautification when he abhors so thoroughly every sort of lie? "We walk by faith, not by sight."[3] Christ the Educator 3.2.11-12.[4]

Refrain from Judging. Gregory of Nazianzus: Do not say, "I do not mind a mere priest, if he is a celibate, and a religious [person], and of angelic life; for it would be a sad thing for me to be defiled even in the moment of my cleansing." Do not ask for credentials of the preacher or the baptizer. For another is his judge and the examiner of what you can't see. For humans look on the outward appearance, but the Lord looks on the heart. On Holy Baptism, Oration 40.26.[5]

The Eyes of the Lord. Tertullian: You are human, and so you know other people only from the outside. You think as you see, and you see only what your eyes let you see. But "the eyes of the Lord are lofty."[6] "Man looks on the outward appearance, God looks on the heart." So "the Lord knows them that are his"[7] and roots up the plant which he has not planted. He shows the last to be first, he carries a fan in his hand to purge his floor. Let the chaff of light faith fly away as it pleases before every wind of temptation. So much the purer is the heap of wheat which the Lord will gather into his garner. Prescriptions Against Heretics 3.[8]

16:13 The Spirit of the Lord Came upon David

---

[1]Contrary to the biblical text, Samuel's appraisal of Eliab is extended to his brothers. [2]FC 53:289. [3]2 Cor 5:7. [4]FC 23:208-9*. [5]NPNF 2 7:369*. [6]4 Esdr 8:20. [7]2 Tim 2:19. [8]LCC 5:32-33.

PSALMS ARE PROPHECY. CASSIODORUS: So clearly holy David was filled with heavenly inspiration, and not through human actions, the birth of twins, angels, visions, a dream, a cloud and a voice from heaven, or any other way of that kind. As the first book of Kings [Samuel] says of him: "And the spirit of the Lord came upon David from that day forward." The Lord himself too says in the Gospel: "If David in the spirit calls him Lord, how do you say he is his son?" By these words we realize that the psalms were clearly expressions of prophecy through the holy Spirit. EXPOSITION OF THE PSALMS, PREFACE 1.[9]

[9]ACW 51:27*.

16:14-23 AN EVIL SPIRIT TORMENTS SAUL

[14]*Now the Spirit of the LORD departed from Saul, and an evil spirit from the LORD tormented him.* [15]*And Saul's servants said to him, "Behold now, an evil spirit from God is tormenting you.* [16]*Let our lord now command your servants, who are before you, to seek out a man who is skilful in playing the lyre; and when the evil spirit from God is upon you, he will play it, and you will be well."* [17]*So Saul said to his servants, "Provide for me a man who can play well, and bring him to me."* [18]*One of the young men answered, "Behold, I have seen a son of Jesse the Bethlehemite, who is skilful in playing, a man of valor, a man of war, prudent in speech, and a man of good presence; and the LORD is with him."* [19]*Therefore Saul sent messengers to Jesse, and said, "Send me David your son, who is with the sheep."* . . . [23]*And whenever the evil spirit from God was upon Saul, David took the lyre and played it with his hand; so Saul was refreshed, and was well, and the evil spirit departed from him.*

OVERVIEW: As evidenced by Saul's torment by an evil spirit and David's anointed harp playing, the Holy Spirit does not continually remain with those who receive the Spirit (APHRAHAT). Those who fall from the Spirit through acts of wickedness may be restored through repentance; otherwise, they remain subject to evil (ATHANASIUS). God's role in inflicting Saul through the evil spirit assures us that God curbs the spirit of pride (JEROME). God grants the devil power to inflict trials on humans in order to bring about their sanctification or punishment (TERTULLIAN). The efficacious and immediate work of the Holy Spirit is exhibited in the lives of our ancestors in the faith (GREGORY THE GREAT). By playing a harp, which symbolized the cross, David sung the passion and subdued the spirit of the devil (NICETAS OF REMESIANA). Do not imagine that the concupiscence of the flesh is a good merely because it is sometimes restrained by music (AUGUSTINE). That David's harp expelled the demon from Saul reveals the virtue of the beautiful discipline of music (CASSIODORUS). David's soothing of Saul's madness with sweet tones symbolizes how the saints can dispel the raving anger of leaders with gentle words (GREGORY THE GREAT). The symbolism of the singing advises that we must strive to subjugate the various passions that arise in us as our circumstances change (Gregory of Nyssa).

16:14-15 An Evil Spirit Torments Saul

The Presence of the Holy Spirit. Aphrahat: I will instruct you of that which is written, that the Spirit is not at every time found with those that receive it. For it is written about Saul, that the Holy Spirit, which he received when he was anointed, departed from him, because he grieved it, and God sent to him instead of it a vexing spirit. And whenever he was afflicted by the evil spirit, David used to play upon the harp, and the Holy Spirit, which David received when he was anointed, would come, and the evil spirit that was vexing Saul would flee from before it. So the Holy Spirit that David received was not found with him at every time. As long as he was playing the harp, then it used to come. Demonstration 6.16.[1]

Falling from the Spirit. Athanasius: Therefore, when a person falls from the Spirit for any wickedness, if he repents after his fall, the grace remains irrevocably to the one who is willing; otherwise he who has fallen is no longer in God (because that Holy Spirit and Paraclete which is in God has deserted him), but this sinner shall be in him to whom he has subjected himself, as took place in Saul's instance; for the Spirit of God departed from him and an evil spirit was afflicting him. Four Discourses Against the Arians 3.25.25.[2]

The Spirit of Pride. Jerome: Again, that you may be sure that God curbs the spirit of pride, recall how the good spirit of God departed from Saul and an evil spirit troubled him. Holy Writ says, "And an evil spirit of God troubled him," a spirit from God. Does God, then, have an evil spirit? Not at all. God had withdrawn so that afterwards an evil spirit might trouble Saul. In that sense, the spirit of God is called evil. Finally, holy David, knowing that God could take away

the spirit of princes, entreats him, "And do not take your holy spirit from me."[3] Homilies on the Psalms 9 (Ps 75).[4]

The Power of the Devil. Tertullian: The devil has power that might be called his own, only over such as no longer belong to God, the heathen whom he considers once for all as a drop in a bucket, as dust on the threshing floor, as spittle in the mouth—and, as such, totally handed over to the devil as a quite useless possession.

Otherwise, he may do nothing by his own right, against those who dwell in the house of God, because the cases that are noted in Scripture show us when—that is, for what reasons—he may touch them. The right to tempt a person is granted to the devil, either for the sake of a trial, as in the texts cited above, whether God or the devil initiates the plan, or for the purpose of the reprobation of a sinner, who is handed over to the devil as to an executioner. This was the case with Saul. "The spirit of the Lord departed from Saul, and an evil spirit from the Lord troubled and stifled him." Again, it may happen in order to humble a person, as Paul tells us that there was given him a thorn, a messenger of Satan, to buffet him,[5] and even this sort of thing is not permitted for the humiliation of holy ones through torment of the flesh, unless it be done so that their power to resist may be perfected in weakness. On Flight in Time of Persecution 2.6-7.[6]

16:18 David's Musical and Spiritual Gifting Are Renowned

The Work of the Spirit. Gregory the Great: It is agreeable to lift up eyes of faith to the power of this Worker, and to look here and there at our ancestors in the Old and New Testaments. With the eyes of faith open on David, Amos, Daniel, Peter, Paul and Matthew, I wish to analyze the nature of the workman, the Holy Spirit. But I

---

[1]NPNF 2 13:372-73*. [2]NPNF 2 4:407**. [3]Ps 51:11 (50:11 LXX). [4]FC 48:66-67*. [5]2 Cor 12:7. [6]FC 40:280-81*.

fail in my analysis. The Spirit filled a boy who played upon a harp and made him a psalmist, a shepherd and herdsman who pruned sycamore trees and made him a prophet,[7] a boy given to abstinence and made him a judge of mature men,[8] a fisherman and made him a preacher,[9] a persecutor and made him the teacher of the Gentiles,[10] a tax collector and made him an evangelist.[11]

What a skillful workman this Spirit is! There is no question of delay in learning. It no sooner touches the mind in regard to anything it chooses than it teaches; its very touch is teaching. It changes a human mind in a moment to enlighten it; suddenly what it was it no longer is, suddenly it is what it was not. FORTY GOSPEL HOMILIES 30.[12]

16:23 The Evil Spirit Departs When David Plays the Lyre

THE PASSION SUBDUED THE SPIRIT. NICETAS OF REMESIANA: After this, you will find plenty of men and women, filled with a divine spirit, who sang of the mysteries of God. Among these was David. As a boy, he was given a special call to this office, and by God's grace he became the prince of singers and left us a treasury of song. He was still a boy when his sweet, strong song with his harp subdued the evil spirit working in Saul. Not that there was any kind of power in the harp, but, with its wooden frame and the strings stretched across, it was a symbol of the cross of Christ. It was the passion that was being sung, and it was this which subdued the spirit of the devil. LITURGICAL SINGING 4.[13]

THE INSTRUCTION OF MUSIC. AUGUSTINE: You, a man of the church, ought to be better instructed by the music of the church than by Pythagoras.[14] Think what David's lyre did for Saul, who was harassed by an evil spirit but recovered from this disturbance when the holy man played his lyre; beware of thinking the concupiscence of the flesh is a good merely because it is sometimes checked by musical sounds. AGAINST JULIAN 5.5.23.[15]

THE POWER OF MUSIC. CASSIODORUS: The discipline of music incorporates great power and knowledge which brings delight; teachers of secular literature, through the generosity of God who grants all that is useful, have made it possible through theoretical texts to ascertain what was earlier regarded as hidden from view in the nature of the world. The first division of this discipline, then, is into harmonics, rhythmics and metrics. The second division, that of musical instruments, is between percussion, strings and wind. The third division is into six harmonies, the fourth into fifteen tones. In this way the virtue of this most beautiful discipline is unfolded by such distinctions drawn by people of old. We read in secular works that many miracles were brought forth by these measures. But we need say nothing of this fabulous material; we read that by means of David's tuneful harp the demon was expelled from Saul. The divine reading attests that the walls of Jericho at once collapsed at the din of trumpets. So there is no doubt that sounds of music, at the Lord's command or with his permission, have unleashed great forces. EXPOSITION OF THE PSALMS 80.4.[16]

SWEET TONES OF THE HARP. GREGORY THE GREAT: Indeed, we should not disregard the fact that whenever the evil spirit possessed Saul, David took his harp and soothed his madness. What is symbolized by Saul but the pride of the mighty and what by David but the lowly life of the saints? As often, therefore, as Saul was possessed by the unclean spirit, his madness was soothed by David's singing. So, too, whenever the disposition of people in power is turned to raving anger by pride, it is proper that we should recall them to a healthy frame of mind by gentle words, sweet tones of the harp, as it were. PASTORAL CARE 3.2.[17]

---

[7]Amos 7:14-15. [8]Dan 1:8, 2:48. [9]Mt 4:19. [10]Acts 9:1-20. [11]Lk 5:27-28. [12]CS 123:244-45. [13]FC 7:68*. [14]In his *Counsels*, Cicero recounts an incident where Pythagoras requests a flute player to sing a slow and grave song in order to calm the licentiousness stirred by earlier melodies. [15]FC 35:267. [16]ACW 52:295. [17]ACW 11:94.

The Subjugation of Passions. Gregory of Nyssa: Once when he came to Saul, who was frenzied and out of his right mind, he healed him by soothing his passions with song, so that Saul's understanding returned to him again in accordance with nature. The goal, then, of the symbolism of the singing is clear from these words. It recommends that we achieve the subjugation of those passions which arise in us in various ways from the circumstances of life. On the Inscriptions of the Psalms 1.3.24.[18]

---

[18]GNTIP 92.

17:1-11 GOLIATH SEEKS A CHALLENGER

[1]Now the Philistines gathered their armies for battle. . . . [3]And the Philistines stood on the mountain on the one side, and Israel stood on the mountain on the other side, with a valley between them. [4]And there came out from the camp of the Philistines a champion named Goliath, of Gath, whose height was six cubits and a span. [5]He had a helmet of bronze on his head, and he was armed with a coat of mail, and the weight of the coat was five thousand shekels of bronze. [6]And he had greaves of bronze upon his legs, and a javelin of bronze slung between his shoulders. [7]And the shaft of his spear was like a weaver's beam, and his spear's head weighed six hundred shekels of iron; and his shield-bearer went before him.

Overview: Scripture, foreseeing that heresy would arise from within the church, describes Goliath as being positioned "on this side" (Paulus Orosius). Whereas Goliath's protection was external, David's more effectual protection came through his faith (Chrysostom).

17:3-7 The Philistine Champion, Goliath of Gath

Heresy Within the Church. Paulus Orosius: Yet there stands Goliath, monstrous in his pride, swollen with his earthly power, confident that he can do everything by himself, with his head, hands and entire body clad in much bronze, having his own armor bearer behind him who, though he does not himself fight, nevertheless furnishes this Goliath with all kinds of aid in bronze and iron. And it is not surprising if Scripture, foreseeing our present situation, comments appropriately when it says, "The Philistines were standing on top of the mountain on this side," since the individual who is attacking the [Pelagian] heresy[1] is now being banished from the church, while the heretic is found to be nourished at its very breast! Because of this, it is so stated by the Holy Spirit that on the other side Israel was standing, while on this side, the enemy. And such is often the way. For even King David, who was always the righteous father toward his unrighteous son, having laid aside his royal robes, was forced to flee from Jerusalem, whereupon the tyrant Absalom immediately entered.[2] There

---

[1]Pelagius maintained that humans were born sinless and could choose to live sinless lives by responding to God's commands autonomously, that is, without further dependence upon divine assistance beyond that which the commands imparted. [2]See 2 Sam 15:16-17; 16:15.

now stands Goliath—oh, what sorrow!—on this side, that is, within the church; and he not only stands but even offers challenges. And at the same time, over the course of many days, he reproaches holy Israel for its well-known fear of God. Defense Against the Pelagians 2.[3]

Fortified by Faith. Chrysostom: In my discourse I showed that Goliath was protected by the power of his weapons and the strength of a full set of armor, whereas David had none of that panoply. But he was fortified by his faith.

Goliath had the external protection of his glittering breastplate and shield; David shone from within with the grace of the Spirit. This is why a boy prevailed over a man, this is why the one wearing no armor conquered the one fully armed, this is why the shepherd's hand crushed and destroyed the bronze weapons of war. Against the Anomoeans 11.4-5.[4]

---

[3]FC 99:117. [4]FC 72:272.

17:12-23 DAVID ENTERS THE BATTLE CAMP

[12]*Now David was the son of an Ephrathite of Bethlehem in Judah, named Jesse, who had eight sons. . . .* [13]*The three eldest sons of Jesse had followed Saul to the battle. . . .*

[17]*And Jesse said to David his son, "Take for your brothers an ephah of this parched grain, and these ten loaves, and carry them quickly to the camp to your brothers;* [18]*also take these ten cheeses to the commander of their thousand. See how your brothers fare, and bring some token from them."*

[19]*Now Saul, and they, and all the men of Israel, were in the valley of Elah, fighting with the Philistines.* [20]*And David rose early in the morning, and left the sheep with a keeper, and took the provisions, and went, as Jesse had commanded him; and he came to the encampment as the host was going forth to the battle line, shouting the war cry.*

Overview: The refreshment David brings to his brothers typifies the perfect humility Christ brought to his disciples (Bede). By sending David with food to look for his brothers, Jesse typified God the Father, who sent Jesus to free humanity from the devil's power. David's arrival and subsequent battle with Goliath symbolize Christ's advent and victory over the devil (Caesarius of Arles).

17:17-18 Jesse Sends David to His Brothers

Christ's Perfect Humility. Bede: The whole nation of the faithful Hebrews was saying to their Lord and Savior who would be born from their seed, as they sighed for his advent with earnest desire, "Take these, I beg you, to refresh and aid your people in spiritual warfare. They are your brothers because you deigned to be born from their midst according to the flesh. Amid their camps worn out by daily warfare, take, I say, the form of perfect humility in the body and guardianship of the law, although you in no wise need to submit voluntarily to its demands." For the parched grain refers to a distressed spirit and a contrite and humiliated heart. The ephah is a measure which holds three amphoras and points to the spirit, soul and body perfected and joined together by humility—whether of our Lord or of each of the elect. This parched grain of humility appeared in the Lord by his own power and volition so that he might build the same in us, but really such humility cannot be brought about except by being placed between the upper and lower grindstones, that is, through fear and hope. Now the ten loaves brought by David clearly point to the food that comes from keeping the decalogue, which we have not by our own powers but by the gift of giver. After he himself was placed under the law for us, he also made the burdens of the law bearable, just as by his humility (which he did not have to show) he taught us to be humble because of the great debt which we will never be able to pay back. But turn, he says, to the gentleness of the decalogue, full of milk (so to say). Just as it is well suited for infants to build up the vigor of their spiritual minds, so it can also refresh and comfort every great and outstanding general of the heavenly army. For after our longed-for Lord, mighty in deed, gave bread and barley groats to his brothers, he brought down cheese to the commander. This occurred after he showed the example of his patience and humility before the magistrates of the Jews and after he did not abolish but fulfilled the commandments of the law and prophets and commanded them to his disciples. These he established and appointed as rulers of the church. "He opened their minds to understand the Scriptures."[1] FOUR BOOKS ON 1 SAMUEL 3.17.[2]

THE MYSTERY OF THE TRINITY. CAESARIUS OF ARLES: Just as this happened, then, in the blessed patriarchs, Isaac and Jacob, dearest brothers, so we know it was prefigured in Jesse the father of David; for when he sent his son David to look for his brothers, he seems to have typified God the Father. Jesse sent David to search for his

brother, and God sent his only-begotten Son of whom it is written: "I will proclaim your name to my brothers."[3] Truly, Christ had come to seek his brothers, for he said, "I was not sent except to the lost sheep of the house of Israel."[4]

"And Jesse said to David his son, 'Take an ephah of flour, and ten little cheeses, and go see your brothers.'" An ephah, brothers, is a quantity of three measures, and in three measures is understood the mystery of the Trinity. Blessed Abraham knew this mystery well; for when he merited to perceive the mystery of the Trinity in the three persons under the holm-oak of Mamre, he ordered three measures of flour to be mixed. It is three measures, and for this reason Jesse gave this amount to his son. In the ten little cheeses we recognize the decalogue of the Old Testament. Thus, David came with the three measures and ten cheeses, in order to visit his brothers who were in battle, because Christ was to come with the decalogue of the law and the mystery of the Trinity to free the human race from the power of the devil. SERMON 121.1-2.[5]

17:19-20 David Arrives at the Encampment

CHRIST THE TRUE DAVID. CAESARIUS OF ARLES: As David came, he found the Jewish people located in the valley of Terebinth in order to fight against the Philistines, because Christ the true David was to come in order to lift up the human race from the valley of sins and tears. They stood in a valley facing the Philistines. They were in a valley, because the weight of their sins had pressed them down. However, they were standing but did not dare to fight against their adversaries. Why did they not dare to do so? Because David who typified Christ had not yet arrived. It is true, dearly beloved. Who was able to fight against the devil before Christ our Lord freed the human race from his power? Now the word *David* is interpreted as strong in hand; and

---

[1]Lk 24:45. [2]CCL 119:151. [3]Ps 22:22 (21:22 LXX). [4]Mt 15:24. [5]FC 47:199*.

what is stronger, brothers, than he who conquered the whole world, armed with a cross but not a sword? Furthermore, the children of Israel stood against their adversaries for forty days. Because of the four seasons and the four parts of the world, those forty days signify the present life in which the Christian people do not cease to fight against Goliath and his army, that is, the devil and his angels. Moreover, it would be impossible to conquer, if Christ the true David had not come down with his staff which is the

mystery of the cross. Truly, the devil was free before the advent of Christ, dearly beloved; but at his coming Christ did to him what is recorded in the Gospel: "No one can enter the strong man's house, and plunder his goods, unless he first binds the strong man."[6] For this reason Christ came and bound the devil. Sermon 121.5.[7]

---

[6]Mt 12:29. [7]FC 47:200-201*.

17:24-30 DAVID LEARNS OF THE REWARD FOR GOLIATH'S DEATH

[24]*All the men of Israel, when they saw the man, fled from him, and were much afraid.* [25]*And the men of Israel said, "Have you seen this man who has come up? Surely he has come up to defy Israel; and the man who kills him, the king will enrich with great riches, and will give him his daughter, and make his father's house free in Israel."* [26]*And David said to the men who stood by him, "What shall be done for the man who kills this Philistine, and takes away the reproach from Israel? For who is this uncircumcised Philistine, that he should defy the armies of the living God?"* [27]*And the people answered him in the same way, "So shall it be done to the man who kills him."*

[28]*Now Eliab his eldest brother heard when he spoke to the men; and Eliab's anger was kindled against David, and he said, "Why have you come down? And with whom have you left those few sheep in the wilderness? I know your presumption, and the evil of your heart; for you have come down to see the battle."* [29]*And David said, "What have I done now? Was it not but a word?"*

Overview: David's good sense, self-restraint and boldness demonstrate the great strength of the one who is protected by help from on high (Chrysostom). In chiding David, Eliab signified the Jewish people who jealously slandered Christ, who came for the salvation of the human race (Caesarius of Arles).

17:26-29 David's Questioning Angers Eliab

From on High. Chrysostom: If you don't mind, however, let us refer to a theme in our preaching earlier, so that by bringing the whole story to mind we may learn that nothing is stronger than the person protected by help from on high, and nothing is more vulnerable than the person deprived of this help, surrounded though he may be with countless armies. So this man David, quite young though he was and living in his father's house on account of his immaturity, heard the call of destiny for his virtue to become conspicuous; he was urged by his father to observe his brothers; he obeyed and was sent off to them. So, after coming on the scene to observe them, he saw the battle line drawn against the foreigner Goliath and the whole people of Saul's company withdrawing in fright and the king himself placed in particular danger. For a while he was happy to be an onlooker and went to see the strange and unusual sight of one person pitted against so many thousands. But his brothers could not tolerate the manliness of his bearing; they were moved to hatred and said to him, "Have you come for no other reason than to see the war." You haven't really come to observe us.

Notice, however, his good sense and great restraint. Instead of saying anything rash to them, anything harsh, he extinguished the flame of their hatred; he mollified their hatred by saying, "Isn't it only a word?" I mean, surely you haven't observed me taking position in the ranks? I simply wanted to watch and find out the source of this man's extraordinary frenzy. "After all, who is this foreigner who reproaches the ranks of the living God?" Then, on hearing the man's awful arrogance and the unspeakable cowardice of those who had gone with Saul, he said, "What will be given to the man who cuts off his head?" He showed great boldness of spirit through these words and caused amazement in every one. Realizing this, Saul sent for the young man, who had experience of nothing other than shepherding, and when he saw his age he made fun of him. Then he learned from him how he dealt with bears when they raided his flocks; you see, this remarkable young man was obliged to describe this, not out of a wish to blow his own trumpet

but because he had no choice if the king was to be inspired with courage and to have regard not for the poor impression he gave but for the faith concealed within him and the assistance from on high that made the young man stronger than the grown-ups, the unarmed stronger than the armed men, the shepherd than the soldiers. HOMILIES ON GENESIS 46.9-10.[1]

DEVILISH ENVY. CAESARIUS OF ARLES: Now when David came, one of his brothers rebuked him, saying, "Why did you leave those few sheep and come to the battle?" This elder brother, maliciously chiding David who typified our Lord, signified the Jewish people who jealously slandered Christ the Lord even though he had come for the salvation of the human race, for they frequently chastised him with many insults. "Why did you leave the sheep and come to the battle?" Does it not seem to you as though through his lips the devil is speaking in envy of the salvation of humankind? It is as though he said to Christ: "Why did you leave the ninety-nine sheep who had strayed and come looking for the one which was lost, in order that you might call him back to your sheepfold, after freeing him with the staff of the cross from the hand of the spiritual Goliath, that is, from the power of the devil?" "Why did you leave those few sheep?" He spoke the truth, although in a wicked and haughty spirit. Jesus intended to leave the ninety-nine sheep, as was already said, in order to seek the one and to bring it back to his sheepfold, that is, to the company of the angels. SERMON 121.3.[2]

---

[1]FC 87:8-9*. [2]FC 47:199-200*.

17:31-40 DAVID VOLUNTEERS TO FIGHT GOLIATH

[31]*When the words which David spoke were heard, they repeated them before Saul; and he sent for him.* [32]*And David said to Saul, "Let no man's heart fail because of him; your servant will go and fight with this Philistine."* [33]*And Saul said to David, "You are not able to go against this Philistine to fight with him; for you are but a youth, and he has been a man of war from his youth."* [34]*But David said to Saul, "Your servant used to keep sheep for his father; and when there came a lion, or a bear, and took a lamb from the flock,* [35]*I went after him and smote him and delivered it out of his mouth; and if he arose against me, I caught him by his beard, and smote him and killed him.* [36]*Your servant has killed both lions and bears; and this uncircumcised Philistine shall be like one of them, seeing he has defied the armies of the living God."* [37]*And David said, "The Lord who delivered me from the paw of the lion and from the paw of the bear, will deliver me from the hand of this Philistine." And Saul said to David, "Go, and the Lord be with you!"* [38]*Then Saul clothed David with his armor; he put a helmet of bronze on his head, and clothed him with a coat of mail.* [39]*And David girded his sword over his armor, and he tried in vain to go, for he was not used to them. Then David said to Saul, "I cannot go with these; for I am not used to them." And David put them off.* [40]*Then he took his staff in his hand, and chose five smooth stones from the brook, and put them in his shepherd's bag or wallet; his sling was in his hand, and he drew near to the Philistine.*

OVERVIEW: We must beg Christ, the spiritual David, to abolish all evil high councils when battling Satan (ORIGEN). David's killing of both lion and bear prefigures the Lord's victory over the devil when he descended into hell to free the saints from his jaws (CAESARIUS OF ARLES). Rather than arming himself as those he saw around him, David wisely chose weaponry appropriate for his stature and youth (CASSIAN).

17:34-37 David Recounts Killing Lions and Bears

TAKING HOLD OF THE LION. ORIGEN: But as David who took hold of the beard seized the lion, so let us beg the spiritual David, Christ, when taking hold of the lion, to abolish also every Sanhedrin of beasts. FRAGMENTS ON JEREMIAH 28.1.[1]

THE DEVIL PREFIGURED. CAESARIUS OF ARLES: When David had been anointed by blessed Sam-

uel before he came here, he had killed a lion and a bear without any weapons, as he himself told King Saul. Both the lion and the bear typified the devil, for they had been strangled by the strength of David for having dared to attack some of his sheep. All that we read prefigured in David at that time, dearly beloved, we know was accomplished in our Lord Jesus Christ; for he strangled the lion and the bear when he descended into hell to free all the saints from their jaws. Moreover, listen to the prophet entreating the person of our Lord: "Rescue my soul from the sword, my loneliness from the grip of the dog. Save me from the lion's mouth."[2] Since a bear possesses his strength in his paw and a lion has his in his mouth, the same devil is prefigured in those two beasts. Thus, this was said concerning the person of Christ, in order that his sole church might be removed from the hand, that is, the power or

---

[1]FC 97:296. [2]Ps 22:20-21 (21:20-21 LXX).

mouth of the devil. Sermon 121.4.[3]

17:38-40 David Dresses for Battle

Appropriate Weaponry. John Cassian: We sometimes see a bad example drawn from good things. For if someone presumes to do the same things but not with the same disposition and orientation or with unlike virtue, he easily falls into the snares of deception and death on account of those very things from which others acquire the fruits of eternal life. That brave boy who was set against the most warlike giant in a contest of arms would certainly have experienced this if he had put on Saul's manly and heavy armor, with which a person of more robust age would have laid low whole troops of the enemy. This would undoubtedly have imperiled the boy, except that with wise discretion he chose the kind of weaponry that was appropriate for his youth and armed himself against the dreadful foe not with the breastplate and shield that he saw others outfitted with but with the projectiles that he himself was able to fight with. Conference 24.8.1-2.[4]

[3]FC 47:200*. [4]ACW 57:830.

17:41-47 GOLIATH JEERS AT DAVID

[41]*And the Philistine came on and drew near to David, with his shield-bearer in front of him. . . .* [45]*Then David said to the Philistine, "You come to me with a sword and with a spear and with a javelin; but I come to you in the name of the Lord of hosts, the God of the armies of Israel, whom you have defied.* [46]*This day the Lord will deliver you into my hand, and I will strike you down, and cut off your head; and I will give the dead bodies of the host of the Philistines this day to the birds of the air and to the wild beasts of the earth; that all the earth may know that there is a God in Israel,* [47]*and that all this assembly may know that the Lord saves not with sword and spear; for the battle is the Lord's and he will give you into our hand."*

Overview: As simple weapons prove victorious, so defenders of true religion need arguments that plainly proclaim the truth without causing strife. Onlookers who object to this means should remain silent (Theodoret).

17:47 The Lord Saves Not with Sword and Spear

Plainly Proclaim the Truth. Theodoret of Cyr: And we need only the Lord's goodness to stay the storm.[1] Easy it is for him to stay it, but we are unworthy of the calm, yet the grace of his patience is enough for us, so that with good fortune by it we may get the better of our foes. So the divine apostle has taught us to pray "for he will with the temptation also make a way to escape that you may be able to bear it."[2] But I beseech your godliness to stop the mouths of the objectors and make them understand that it is

[1]In this letter to Bishop Irenaeus, Theodoret defends the language he uses to describe Mary's role as the mother of the divine/human Jesus. [2]1 Cor 10:13.

not for them who stand, as the phrase goes, out of range, to scoff at men fighting in the ranks and giving and receiving blows; for what does it matter which weapon the soldier uses to strike down his antagonists? Even the great David did not use a panoply when he killed the aliens' champion,[3] and Samson killed thousands on one day with the jawbone of an ass.[4] Nobody grumbles at the victory, nor accuses the conqueror of cowardice, because he wins it without brandishing a spear or covering himself with his shield or throwing darts or shooting arrows. The defenders of true religion must be criticized in the same way, nor must we try to find language which will stir strife, but rather arguments which plainly proclaim the truth and make those who venture to oppose it ashamed of themselves. LETTER 16.[5]

---

[3]1 Sam 17. [4]Judg 15:16. [5]NPNF 2 3:255*.

17:48-49 DAVID FELLS GOLIATH WITH A STONE

[48]*When the Philistine arose and came and drew near to meet David, David ran quickly toward the battle line to meet the Philistine.* [49]*And David put his hand in his bag and took out a stone, and slung it, and struck the Philistine on his forehead; the stone sank into his forehead, and he fell on his face to the ground.*

OVERVIEW: By fighting only when compelled to do so and by rejecting the weapons of others, David exhibited both prudence and fortitude in battle (AMBROSE). The faith that trusts Christ and regards God alone as highest prevails over all weapons (PAULINUS OF NOLA). David killed Goliath with a stone, which symbolizes the power of Christ, in a battle that figuratively teaches the superiority of heavenly weapons over earthly ones (MAXIMUS OF TURIN). In order to be victorious in battle we must take hold of the spiritual stone, or Christ, which prevailed over Goliath (CHRYSOSTOM).

17:49 David Strikes Goliath on His Forehead

PRUDENCE COMBINED WITH FORTITUDE. AMBROSE: David never waged war unless he was driven to it. Thus prudence was combined in him with fortitude in the battle. For even when about to fight single-handed against Goliath, the enormous giant, he rejected the armor with which he was laden. His strength depended more on his own arm than on the weapons of others. Then, at a distance, to get a stronger throw, with one cast of a stone, he killed his enemy. DUTIES OF THE CLERGY 1.35.177.[1]

FAITH PREVAILS OVER WEAPONS. PAULINUS OF NOLA: Having trust in Christ, consigning everything to the God of powers, regarding God alone as all that is highest—this has always been efficacious in achieving every good. This is the faith that has prevailed over all weapons. This was the strength that made that slight boy great, for he grew stronger by spurning weapons and brought low the armed giant by the power of a stone. POEMS 26.150.[2]

---

[1]NPNF 2 10:30*. [2]ACW 40:259.

HEAVENLY WEAPONS. MAXIMUS OF TURIN: Therefore, brothers, let us arm ourselves with heavenly weapons for the coming judgment of the world: let us gird on the breastplate of faith, protect ourselves with the helmet of salvation, and defend ourselves with the word of God as with a spiritual sword.[3] For the one who is arrayed with these weapons does not fear present disturbance and is not afraid of future judgment, since holy David, protected with this devotion, killed the very strong and armed Goliath without weapons and struck down the warlike man, girt about with defenses on all sides, by the strength of his faith alone. For although holy David did not put on a helmet, strap on a shield, or use a lance, he killed Goliath. He killed him, however, not with an iron spear but with a spiritual sword, for although he appeared weaponless in the eyes of human beings, yet he was adequately armed with divine grace. But the spiritual sword itself was not a sword, since it was not by the sword but by a stone that Goliath died when he was struck down. We read in the Scriptures that Christ is figuratively designated by the word *stone*, as the prophet says: "The stone that the builders rejected has become the head of the corner."[4] Therefore, when Goliath is struck by a stone, he is struck down by the power of Christ. And in what part of the body is he struck? On the forehead, for when the sacrilegious man is struck, there Christ was absent, and where his end comes upon him, there the sign of salvation is not to be found. For although Goliath was protected by weapons on all sides, still his forehead was exposed to death because it did not carry the Savior's seal, and therefore he is slain in the spot where he is found to be bare of God's grace.

But there is no one who does not realize that this took place figuratively. For David had also put on armor beforehand but, since he was so heavy and awkward in it that he could hardly walk, he removed it at once, signifying that the weapons of this world are vain and superfluous things and that the person who chooses to involve himself in them will have no unimpeded road to heaven, since he will be too heavy and encumbered to walk. At the same time this teaches us that victory is not to be hoped for from arms alone but is to be prayed for in the name of the Savior. SERMON 85.3.[5]

THE POWER OF THE SPIRITUAL STONE. CHRYSOSTOM: Therefore, let us take in our hands that stone, I mean the cornerstone, the spiritual rock. If Paul could think in these terms of the rock in the desert, no one will in any way feel resentment against me if I understand David's stone in the same sense. In the case of the Jews in the desert, it was not the nature of the visible stone but the power of the spiritual stone which sent forth those streams of water.[6] So, too, in David's case, it was not the visible stone but the spiritual stone which sank into the barbarian's head. This is why, at that time, I promised that I would say nothing based on rational arguments. "Our weapons are not merely carnal but spiritual, demolishing sophistries and reasoning and every proud height that raises itself against the knowledge of God."[7] AGAINST THE ANOMOEANS 11.6.[8]

---

[3]See Eph 6:14-17. [4]Ps 118:22 (117:22 LXX). [5]ACW 50:204-5*. [6]See Ex 17:6. [7]See 2 Cor 10:4-5. [8]FC 72:272-73*.

17:50-58 THE PHILISTINES FLEE

[50]*So David prevailed over the Philistine with a sling and with a stone, and struck the Philistine, and killed him; there was no sword in the hand of David.* [51]*Then David ran and stood over the Philistine, and took his sword and drew it out of its sheath, and killed him, and cut off his head with it. When the Philistines saw that their champion was dead, they fled.*

OVERVIEW: As David used Goliath's sword to slay him, so the Lord transforms sinners into instruments of righteousness (BEDE). David demonstrates how the one who wears God's armor and fights for Christ's glory may be victorious and remain with the truth (AUGUSTINE).

17:50-51 David Beheads the Philistine

WEAPONS OF RIGHTEOUSNESS. BEDE: The only ministers of the Lord's Word through whom the Lord might teach and so break the arrogance of the devil are individuals whom the Lord himself has victoriously snatched away from the devil, for all are by nature sons of wrath, conceived in iniquity and given birth by their mothers in sin. Since this is the case, he unexpectedly appeared and overcame the enemy. Just like a strong man strips the armor of his weaker opponent, so he took away all his weapons in which he had trusted. As the enemy had used people as his weapons to slaughter the souls of the wretched, so now the Savior has transformed these very same people into weapons of righteousness and uses them to cut off the head of iniquity from its body. That is to say, he compels sinners who have been converted to the faith to condemn Satan and to renounce all his works and all his evil ways. Moreover, it is correctly said that David took the sword first with his hand and then drew it from its sheath to kill the Philistine. For first the Lord comes in his desire to snatch away each great and brave defender of the demonic realm; then he draws him from the hidden recesses of errors into the light of liberating grace; and thus through this convert he allows others to be snatched out of the devil's realm and corrected. But even when we meet and dispute with the madness of the heretics and convince them that they are "fabricators and worshipers of lies and perverse doctrines"[1] by using nothing other than the reasons of their argument and the testimonies of the Scriptures which they themselves had purposed to use to seduce us, we clearly cut down the arrogance of the giant with his own sword. FOUR BOOKS ON 1 SAMUEL 3.17.[2]

THE ARMOR OF GOD. AUGUSTINE: But our armor is Christ; it is that which the apostle Paul prescribes when, writing to the Ephesians, he says, "Take unto you the whole armor of God, that you may be able to withstand in the evil day;" and again, "Stand, therefore, having your loins gird about with truth, and having on the breastplate of righteousness; and your feet shod with the preparation of the gospel of peace; above all, taking the shield of faith, wherewith you shall be able to quench all the fiery darts of the wicked: and take the helmet of salvation, and the sword of the Spirit, which is the word of God."[3] Armed with these weapons, king David went forth in his day to battle. Taking from the torrent's bed five smooth rounded stones, he proved that, even amidst all the eddying currents of the world, his feelings were free both from roughness and from defilement. Drinking of the brook by the way, and therefore lifted up in spirit, he cut off the head of Goliath, using the proud enemy's own

---

[1]Job 13:4. [2]CCL 119:161. [3]Eph 6:13-17.

sword as the fittest instrument of death, smiting the profane boaster on the forehead and wounding him in the same place in which Uzziah was smitten with leprosy when he presumed to usurp the priestly office;[4] the very place also in which shines the glory that makes the saints rejoice in the Lord, saying, "The light of your countenance is sealed upon us, O Lord."[5] Let us therefore also say, "My heart is fixed, O God, my heart is fixed: I will sing and give praise: awake up, my glory; awake, psaltery and harp; I myself will awake early";[6] that in us may be fulfilled that word,

"Open thy mouth wide, and I will fill it";[7] and, "The Lord shall give the word with great power to them that publish it."[8] I am well assured that your prayer as well as mine is that in our contending, the victory may remain with the truth. For you seek Christ's glory, not your own: if you are victorious, I also gain a victory if I discover my error. LETTER 75.2.[9]

---

[4]2 Chron 26:19. [5]Ps 4:6 LXX. [6]Ps 57:7-8 (56:7-8 LXX). [7]Ps 81:10 (80:10 LXX). [8]Ps 67:11 LXX. [9]NPNF 1 1:333-34*.

18:1-5 JONATHAN'S COVENANT WITH DAVID

[1]*When he had finished speaking to Saul, the soul of Jonathan was knit to the soul of David, and Jonathan loved him as his own soul. [2]And Saul took him that day, and would not let him return to his father's house. [3]Then Jonathan made a covenant with David, because he loved him as his own soul. [4]And Jonathan stripped himself of the robe that was upon him, and gave it to David, and his armor, and even his sword and his bow and his girdle.*

OVERVIEW: That Jonathan's soul was knit to David's teaches that the soul is free and naturally tends to exist wherever the mind and imagination are (GREGORY THAUMATURGUS). Jonathan's covenant with David prefigures the covenant of love and peace between Christ and the church (BEDE).

18:1 Jonathan and David

THE SOUL IS FREE. GREGORY THAUMATURGUS: Jonathan was not knit to David as a whole, but his "soul," the higher parts, which are not cut off when the apparent and visible elements have been cut off from a person and which will not be coerced by any means, for they never move involuntarily. For the soul is free and not imprisoned in any way. . . . For in its primary sense, it is its

nature to be wherever the mind is, and if it seems to you to be in a room, you are imagining it there in some secondary sense. So it is never prevented from being in whatever place it wishes to be; but rather, in actual fact, it can only be, and reasonably be thought to be, where the works proper to itself alone are found, and relative to that. ADDRESS OF THANKSGIVING TO ORIGEN 6.85-87.[1]

18:3-4 Jonathan Covenants with David

A COVENANT OF LOVE AND PEACE. BEDE: Christ and the church have made a covenant of mutual love and peace, for the church in its more perfect members loves him so much that it has

---

[1]FC 98:104-5.

been ready to die for him, thinking it just to give itself, body and soul, for him who for its redemption deigned to put on our human flesh and soul, although he was very God of very God. For it is written, "the Word became flesh"[2] and "the Lord is the upholder of my soul."[3] Finally, by its martyrs the church strips itself of the flesh which it had worn and gives it in obedience to Christ. [The church] has not any virtue of talent of its own at all, but depends devotedly on the will of

his work. It relies on him even for acumen and skill in speaking and for the diligence to set forth arguments truthful in faith and reason against the wiles of those who are not soundly wise. It relies on him even for preserving the glory of its chastity and spotless honor for his love. Four Books on 1 Samuel 3.18.[4]

---

[2]Jn 1:14. [3]Ps 54:4. [4]CCL 119:164.

18:6-11 SAUL BECOMES WARY OF DAVID

[6]*As they were coming home, when David returned from slaying the Philistine, the women came out of all the cities of Israel, singing and dancing, to meet King Saul, with timbrels, with songs of joy, and with instruments[z] of music. [7]And the women sang to one another as they made merry,*

> *"Saul has slain his thousands,*
> *and David his ten thousands."*

[8]*And Saul was very angry, and this saying displeased him; he said, "They have ascribed to David ten thousands, and to me they have ascribed thousands; and what more can he have but the kingdom?" [9]And Saul eyed David from that day on.*

[10]*And on the morrow an evil spirit from God rushed upon Saul, and he raved within his house, while David was playing the lyre, as he did day by day. Saul had his spear in his hand; [11]and Saul cast the spear, for he thought, "I will pin David to the wall." But David evaded him twice.*

z Or *triangles,* or *three-stringed instruments*

Overview: Saul exemplifies one who is envious of his own good, since David's victory over Goliath delivered his army from the enemy and saved them from embarrassment (Basil). The passion of envy dulled Saul's mind, leading him to regard his benefactor as his enemy. Placing his own soul in peril, Saul's wicked response to David's greater praise illustrates the dreadfulness of envy (Chrysostom). Saul's fate cautions believers against envying another's success (Apostolic Constitutions). While faithful humans are prone to fall, as

Saul demonstrates, the Son of God resisted all sin (Tertullian). Since all creatures are subject to God's discretion, both the transgressor and the just may be tested by the devil (Cassiodorus).

18:7 A Song of Victory

Envious of One's Own Good. Basil the Great: Why do you grieve, my friend, when you yourself have suffered no misfortune? Why are you hostile to someone who is enjoying prosperity, when he has in no way caused your own possessions to decrease? If you are vexed even upon receiving a kindness [from the object of your spite], are you not quite clearly envious of your own good? Saul is an example of this. He made David's great favors to himself a motive for enmity with him. First, after he had been cured of insanity by the divine and melodious strains of David's harp, he attempted to run his benefactor through with a spear. Then, on another occasion, it happened that he and his army were delivered from the hands of the enemy and saved from embarrassment before Goliath. In singing the triumphal songs commemorating this victory, however, the dancers attributed to David a tenfold greater share in the achievement, saying, "Saul killed his thousands and David his ten thousands." For this one utterance and because truth itself was its witness, Saul first attempted murder and tried to slay David by treachery, then forced him to flee. CONCERNING ENVY.[1]

THE PASSION OF ENVY. CHRYSOSTOM: But now notice in this incident how much trouble the passion of envy caused: when the king saw this young man enjoying such popularity and the dancing crowds calling out, "Saul's conquests ran into thousands, David's into tens of thousands," he didn't take kindly to their words . . . but overwhelmed by envy, he now repaid his benefactor with the opposite treatment, and the one whom he should have recognized as his savior and benefactor he endeavored to do away with. What an extraordinary degree of frenzy! What excess of madness! The man who had won him the gift of life and had freed his whole army from the foreigner's rage he now suspected as an enemy, and, instead of the man's good deeds remaining fresh in his memory and prevailing over passion, the clarity of his thinking was dulled with envy as though by a kind of drunkenness, and he regarded his benefactor as his enemy.

That is what the evil of this passion is like, you see: it first has a bad effect on the person giving birth to it. HOMILIES ON GENESIS 46.13-14.[2]

THE NATURE OF ENVY. CHRYSOSTOM: For envy is a fearful, a fearful thing, and persuades people to despise their own salvation. In this way did both Cain destroy himself, and again, before his time, the devil who was the destroyer of his father. So did Saul invite an evil demon against his own soul; yet when invited, he soon envied his physician. For such is the nature of envy; he knew that he was saved, yet he would rather have perished than see him that saved him have honor. What can be more grievous than this passion? One cannot err in calling it the devil's offspring. And in it is contained the fruit of vainglory, or rather its root also, for both these evils are apt mutually to produce each other. And thus in truth it was that Saul even thus envied, when they said, "David smote by ten thousands." What could be more senseless? For why do you envy? Tell me! "Because such a one praised him"? Yet surely you ought to rejoice. Besides, you do not know even whether the praise is true. And do you therefore grieve because without being admirable he has been praised as such? And yet you ought to feel pity. For if he is good, you ought not to envy him when praised, but you should praise along with those that speak well of him; but if not such, why are you galled? HOMILIES ON 2 CORINTHIANS 24.4.[3]

THE SIN OF JEALOUSY. APOSTOLIC CONSTITUTIONS: You shall not be a hypocrite, lest your "portion be with them."[4] You shall not be ill-natured or proud, for "God resists the proud."[5] "You shall not accept persons in judgment; for the judgment is the Lord's." "You shall not hate any man; you shall surely reprove your brother, and not become guilty on his account";[6] and, "Reprove a wise man, and he will love you."[7] Eschew all evil, and all that is like it: for he says, "Abstain from injustice, and trembling shall not come close to you."[8] Do not grow angry quickly, or spiteful, or passionate, or furious or daring,

---

[1]FC 9:466*. [2]FC 87:10-11. [3]NPNF 1 12:393*. [4]Mt 24:51. [5]1 Pet 5:5. [6]Deut 1:17; Lev 19:17. [7]Prov 9:8. [8]Is 54:14.

lest you undergo the fate of Cain, and of Saul and of Joab. The first of these killed his brother Abel, because Abel was found to be preferred before him with God, and because Abel's sacrifice was preferred;[9] the second persecuted holy David, who had slain Goliath the Philistine, being envious of the praises of the women who danced; the third killed two generals of armies—Abner of Israel and Amasa of Judah.[10] CONSTITUTIONS OF THE HOLY APOSTLES 7.5.[11]

18:8 Saul Was Angry

THE GOOD MAN SUBVERTED BY ENVY. TERTULLIAN: It is usual, indeed, with persons of a weaker character, to be so built up in confidence by certain individuals who are caught by heresy, as to topple over into ruin themselves. How does it come to pass, they ask, that this woman or that man, who were the most faithful, the most prudent and the most approved in the church, have gone over to the other side? Who that asks such a question does not in fact reply to it himself, to the effect that men whom heresies have been able to pervert ought never to have been esteemed prudent or faithful or approved? This again, I suppose, is an extraordinary thing, that one who

has been approved should afterwards fall back? Saul, who was good beyond all others,[12] is afterwards subverted by envy. David, a good man "after the Lord's own heart,"[13] is guilty afterwards of murder and adultery.[14] Solomon, endowed by the Lord with all grace and wisdom, is led into idolatry by women.[15] For to the Son of God alone was it reserved to persevere to the last without sin.[16] PRESCRIPTIONS AGAINST HERETICS 3.[17]

18:10 An Evil Spirit Came upon Saul

ALL CREATURES ARE SUBJECT. CASSIODORUS: It was also through a wicked angel that the transgressor was tempted in the account of the book of Kings [Samuel], where it says "The evil spirit from God came upon Saul." Just men, too, like Job and the apostle Paul and others of that kind were tried by the devil. It is clear that all created things are subject to the discretion or command of the Creator. EXPOSITION OF THE PSALMS 77.49.[18]

---

[9]Gen 4. [10]2 Sam 3, 20. [11]ANF 7:466-67*. [12]See 1 Sam 9:2. [13]1 Sam 13:14. [14]See 2 Sam 11. [15]See 1 Kings 11:4. [16]See Heb 4:15. [17]ANF 3:244. [18]ACW 52:267*

18:12-19 DAVID GROWS IN POPULARITY

[14]And David had success in all his undertakings; for the LORD was with him. [15]And when Saul saw that he had great success, he stood in awe of him. [16]But all Israel and Judah loved David; for he went out and came in before them.

[17]Then Saul said to David, "Here is my elder daughter Merab; I will give her to you for a wife; only be valiant for me and fight the LORD's battles." For Saul thought, "Let not my hand be upon him, but let the hand of the Philistines be upon him." [18]And David said to Saul, "Who am I, and who are my kinsfolk, my father's family in Israel, that I should be son-in-law to the king?"

OVERVIEW: Saul's two daughters typify two portions of the Jewish people: those who would follow Christ the Lord and the religious leaders who feigned respect in order to trap him with their questions (BEDE). Amazed at the greatness of God's lovingkindness, David considers himself unworthy of the blessings revealed to him (SYMEON THE NEW THEOLOGIAN).

18:17 Saul Offers Merab to David

TWO PORTIONS OF THE JEWS. BEDE: Because Saul was anointed with a holy chrism and given governorship over the kingdom, he preserved himself as a type of Christ. At that time we understood his two daughters to be two peoples, which were begotten by the twofold faith and love for Christ for salvation, namely, of the body and the mind, and made perfect by discipline. We understood the elder daughter to refer to the synagogue and the younger daughter the church. However, because the circumstances have changed in this passage, inasmuch as David represents Christ the Lord and Saul represents the people of the Jews who envied him, the older daughter who was promised but not given, means that portion of the same people which is more numerous and powerful and was promised to the brave and desirable bridegroom. When the predecessors of that portion of the Israelites (that is to say, the scribes, priests, Pharisees and elders of the people) came together to hear him, they called him a good teacher—and what is more, a singularly learned teacher. They wanted to learn to simply test him so, they browbeat him with many a question. And yet that portion of Israel was not given to Christ but to another, when the same teachers, seeking to be called rabbi by men, compelled those they could to listen to them. Now the younger daughter who by her devotion deserved to be given to David is surely that portion of the Jewish people that is less esteemed owing to their lesser numbers and despised posi-tion but that prefers to follow, love and hear their Lord and Savior rather than the scribes and experts in the law. They hear Christ say, "Do not fear, little flock, for it has pleased your Father to give you the kingdom."[1] Therefore, the Pharisees and other leaders of the Jews said to Christ, "Look, we entrust to you that larger part of the synagogue which has been subjected to us. Go ahead and teach it. Only see to it that you be brave in soul and fight with the word for the freedom of the people to whom it was commanded to preserve the law of God and to serve him alone. For 'we know that you are truthful and that you do not favor anyone nor do you regard any individual but you teach the way of the Lord in truth. Now is it lawful for us to pay taxes to Caesar or should we not give it?' "[2] However, they said these things while the servants of Herod were present so that, if he should have forbidden them to pay taxes, they themselves would have seemed not to be responsible for his death, if the Herodians would have punished him. FOUR BOOKS ON 1 SAMUEL 3.18.[3]

18:18 Who Am I?

AMAZED BY GOD'S GOODNESS. SYMEON THE NEW THEOLOGIAN: As [David] looks on the greatness of God's lovingkindness, he is struck with amazement. He considers himself with all his soul to be unworthy of the vision of such goodness and does not wish to look closely at them or fully understand them. He is constrained by trembling, fear and reverence to cry, "Who am I, Lord, and what is my father's house, that you should reveal such mysteries to me, unworthy as I am, and have wondrously made me not only to have a vision of such good things, but even to participate and share in them!" DISCOURSES 14.4.[4]

---

[1]Lk 12:32. [2]Mk 12:14. [3]CCL 119:170. [4]SNTD 190-91.

18:20-30 MICHAL BECOMES DAVID'S WIFE

²⁰*Now Saul's daughter Michal loved David; and they told Saul, and the thing pleased him.*
²¹*Saul thought, "Let me give her to him, that she may be a snare for him, and that the hand of the Philistines may be against him." Therefore Saul said to David a second time,^a "You shall now be my son-in-law." ²²And Saul commanded his servants, "Speak to David in private and say, 'Behold, the king has delight in you, and all his servants love you; now then become the king's son-in-law.'"*
²³*And Saul's servants spoke those words in the ears of David. And David said, "Does it seem to you a little thing to become the king's son-in-law, seeing that I am a poor man and of no repute?"*
²⁴*And the servants of Saul told him, "Thus and so did David speak." ²⁵Then Saul said, "Thus shall you say to David, 'The king desires no marriage present except a hundred foreskins of the Philistines, that he may be avenged of the king's enemies.'" Now Saul thought to make David fall by the hand of the Philistines.*

a Heb *by two*

OVERVIEW: Since God is good and the creator of only good things, Saul was not evil by nature but acted out of an evil will (SYMEON THE NEW THEOLOGIAN).

18:20-25 Saul Offers Michal to David

AN EVIL WILL. SYMEON THE NEW THEOLOGIAN: Why did Saul seek to apprehend and kill David whom he had formerly honored as himself and greatly loved as a benefactor? Was it by nature or out of an evil will? Obviously it was out of ill will. No one is born evil by nature, since God did not create evil works but things that were very good. Or, rather, he did so since he is good, and that not by disposition and choice but in nature and in truth. DISCOURSES 4.2.¹

¹*SNTD* 72.

19:1-7 SAUL SEEKS DAVID'S LIFE

¹*And Saul spoke to Jonathan his son and to all his servants, that they should kill David. But Jonathan, Saul's son, delighted much in David. ²And Jonathan told David, "Saul my father seeks to kill you; therefore take heed to yourself in the morning, stay in a secret place and hide yourself;*
³*and I will go out and stand beside my father in the field where you are, and I will speak to my father about you; and if I learn anything I will tell you." ⁴And Jonathan spoke well of David to Saul his father, and said to him, "Let not the king sin against his servant David; because he has*

*not sinned against you, and because his deeds have been of good service to you; *[5]*for he took his life in his hand and he slew the Philistine, and the* Lord *wrought a great victory for all Israel. You saw it, and rejoiced; why then will you sin against innocent blood by killing David without cause?"* *[6]*And Saul hearkened to the voice of Jonathan; Saul swore, "As the* Lord *lives, he shall not be put to death."*

Overview: David exemplifies a true martyr, that is, someone who is persecuted for righteousness' sake (Augustine). Bede understands the episode of Saul's threatening of David allegorically: Saul's threat prefigures the Sanhedrin's command to the apostles to not teach in Jesus' name; Jonathan represents the apostles who implored Christ to hide in the hearts of believers while they preached on his behalf; and Saul's vow that David would not be killed signifies the Jews' faithful affirmation of the enduring presence of Christ's church.

19:1 Saul Speaks of Killing David

Suffering for the Sake of Righteousness. Augustine: But true martyrs are such as those of whom the Lord says, "Blessed are those who are persecuted for righteousness' sake."[1] It is not, therefore, those who suffer persecution for their unrighteousness and for the divisions which they impiously introduce into Christian unity, but those who suffer for righteousness' sake, that are truly martyrs. For Hagar also suffered persecution at the hands of Sarah;[2] and in that case she who persecuted was righteous, and she who suffered persecution was unrighteous. Are we to compare with this persecution which Hagar suffered to the case of holy David, who was persecuted by unrighteous Saul? Surely there is an essential difference, not in respect of his suffering but because he suffered for righteousness' sake. The Correction of the Donatists 2.9.[3]

19:1-3 Jonathan Warns David

The Apostles' Plea. Bede: The leaders of the Jews and the elders and scribes spoke to the apostles and strictly commanded them not to speak or teach in the name of Jesus.[4] . . .

Moreover, the apostles loved Christ mightily and, as they counted the abusive attacks of the treacherous, they asked him to defend his church and to save his name and to stay in the church in a hidden manner and to hide in the hearts of the believers away from the consternation of men. They said, "As you dwell in the flowering minds of the pious—for here is a field full of aroma and grace which the Lord has blessed—we will speak and teach this people in your name, and those among it who prefer to believe rather than remain in unbelief we will announce to your holy church so that as each one knows the state of each individual, he will know to ally himself with the faithful and to preserve himself from the unbelievers." Four Books on 1 Samuel 3.19.[5]

19:4-6 Saul Relents

The Church Will Endure. Bede: When the people of the Jews heard the voice of the apostles preaching, they were calmed down from the anger of their earlier fury and declared in a true affirmation of faith that the church of Christ would never be able to be wiped out from their midst and that the memory of him who is before all ages and endures for eternity would never perish. Four Books on 1 Samuel 3.19.[6]

---

[1]Mt 5:1. [2]Gen. 16:6. [3]NPNF 1 4:636. [4]Acts 4:18. [5]CCL 119:174-75. [6]CCL 119:175.

19:8-10 DAVID ELUDES SAUL A SECOND TIME

⁹Then an evil spirit from the LORD came upon Saul, as he sat in his house with his spear in his hand; and David was playing the lyre. ¹⁰And Saul sought to pin David to the wall with the spear; but he eluded Saul, so that he struck the spear into the wall. And David fled, and escaped.

OVERVIEW: David's evasion of Saul's attempt at impaling him with a cross-like spear figuratively depicts the distinction between Jesus' humanity and deity (GREGORY OF NYSSA). When we are listening to divine song and doing good works, we ensure that the Spirit will not depart from us (CHRYSOSTOM).

19:9-10 *Saul Again Tries to Impale David*

BOTH CHRIST AND KING. GREGORY OF NYSSA: Now it is certainly obvious what the sequence is looking to through the figures of the story. The one of David is predicted by means of David, and the one who was anointed signifies the Christ. And the lyre is a human instrument, but the song which comes from it is the Word which has been made manifest to us through the one who was made flesh, whose work is to destroy the derangement that comes from demons so that "the gods of the nations" may no longer be "demons."[1]

That king, however, who had the demons in himself, when the spirits withdrew at the song of him who adapted his instrument to this purpose, smote him with his spear (now a spear is wood which has been equipped with iron), but the wall received the spear instead of him. And we think that the wall is the earthly building, by which we understand the body, in relation to which we see the wood of the cross and the iron. But that David, who is both Christ and king, is without suffering. For the deity does not experience the cross and the nails. ON THE INSCRIPTIONS OF THE PSALMS 2.16.269-70.[2]

THE HARP OF DAVID. CHRYSOSTOM: As also, on the other hand, if we have no works, the Spirit flies away. But if we are deserted by the Spirit, we shall also halt in our works. For when this has gone, the unclean one comes. This is plain from Saul. For what if he does not choke us as he did him, still he strangles us in some other way by wicked works. We have need then of the harp of David, that we may charm our souls with the divine songs, both these, and those from good actions. Since if we do the one only, and while we listen to the charm, war with the charmer by our actions, as he did of old, the remedy will even turn to judgment to us, and the madness become the more furious. For before we heard, the wicked demon was afraid lest we should hear it and recover. But even when after hearing it, we continue the same as we were, this is the very thing to rid him of his fear. Let us sing then the psalm of good deeds, that we may cast out the sin that is worse than the demon. HOMILIES ON ROMANS 28.[3]

---

[1]Ps 95:5 LXX. [2]*GNTIP* 208. [3]NPNF 1 11:539-40*.

19:11-17 MICHAL HELPS DAVID TO ESCAPE

[11]*That night Saul[x] sent messengers to David's house to watch him, that he might kill him in the morning. But Michal, David's wife, told him, "If you do not save your life tonight, tomorrow you will be killed." [12]So Michal let David down through the window; and he fled away and escaped. [13]Michal took an image[c] and laid it on the bed and put a pillow[d] of goats' hair at its head, and covered it with the clothes. [14]And when Saul sent messengers to take David, she said, "He is sick." [15]Then Saul sent the messengers to see David, saying, "Bring him up to me in the bed, that I may kill him." [16]And when the messengers came in, behold, the image[c] was in the bed, with the pillow[d] of goats' hair at its head. [17]Saul said to Michal, "Why have you deceived me thus, and let my enemy go, so that he has escaped?" And Michal answered Saul, "He said to me, 'Let me go; why should I kill you?'"*

x Gk Old Latin: Heb *escaped that night.* [11]*And Saul* c Heb *teraphim* d The meaning of the Hebrew word is uncertain

OVERVIEW: The greatness of David's patience, exhibited by his fleeing the king's presence in hopes that he would repent, stands out in sharp contrast to Saul's persistence in evil (GREGORY OF NYSSA). As David is shut up in his house and surrounded by Saul's men, Christ's temporary entombment is signified (CASSIODORUS). The absence of David signifies the resurrection of the Lord from the empty tomb (GREGORY OF NYSSA). In times of both war and peace, a temporary deception on behalf of a larger truth is at times justifiable in public and private life (CHRYSOSTOM).

19:11-12 David Escapes During the Night

PATIENCE IN SUFFERING. GREGORY OF NYSSA: The story relates how, when the vehement emotion of the demonic spirit had settled on Saul and the holy David quieted the disturbance of the passion by means of his psaltery, Saul found the spear that was standing by him, aimed it straight at David and hurled it against his benefactor. David, however, avoided the attack on himself by means of the divine alliance, and the assault of the spear fixed itself deeply in the wall. He fled the royal dwellings and was in his own house, in the hope that repentance would alter the king's anger. But Saul placed his spearmen around David's house and ordered the executioners to kill him. He barely escaped the dangers by letting himself down into the open through a window and avoiding detection by the guard. ON THE INSCRIPTIONS OF THE PSALMS 2.16.264.[1]

THE TOMB AND THE GUARDS. CASSIODORUS: "Then Saul sent and watched his house to kill him." This too is fittingly associated with the Lord's passion, for house indicates the tomb where he rested in a three-day death. The Jews' leaders sent men to guard it, to destroy so to say the fame of his name, so that by some trick it should not be claimed that he rose again, an eventuality which Christ had been heard earlier proclaiming. It was better that his enemies should of their own accord desire to condemn this, for it allowed the whole world to acknowledge the fact more certainly. The evidence which the unwilling witness offers is beyond doubt; it cannot be called partisan when confirmed by the guilty person. EXPOSITION OF THE PSALMS 58.1.[2]

---

[1]*GNTIP* 206-7. [2]ACW 52:51*.

19:13-17 *Michal Deceives Saul's Messengers*

The Lord's Resurrection Prefigured.
Gregory of Nyssa: Now Michal's name means
"reign," because sin reigned over our nature up to
that time.[3] And at the very time he himself was
born, he [the Lord in the figure of David] went
out through a window. And the window indicates
the return to the light again of the one who made
himself known to those sitting in darkness and
the shadow of death.[4]

And his image is seen on the bed. For the angel
says to those seeking the Lord in the tomb, "Why
do you seek the living with the dead? He is not
here; he is risen."[5] "Behold the place" in which he
lay.[6] Those seeking the Lord saw the tomb in
which he was buried empty of the body of the one
they were seeking. Only the burial sheets were in
it. We think, therefore, that the image of David
on the bed signifies the resurrection of the Lord
in the tomb, through which the true averting of
our death through expiatory sacrifice occurs. On

the Inscriptions of the Psalms 2.16.272-73.[7]

The Need of Deceit. Chrysostom: And not
in war only, but also in peace the need of deceit
may be found, not merely in reference to the
affairs of the state but also in private life, in the
dealings of husband with wife and wife with husband, son with father, friend with friend, and also
children with a parent. For the daughter of Saul
would not have been able to rescue her husband
out of Saul's hands except by deceiving her father.
And her brother, wishing to save him whom she
had rescued when he was again in danger, made
use of the same weapon as the wife. On the
Priesthood 1.8.[8]

---

[3]The Hebrew verb *mālak*, which means "to be king," is apparently in
view. The spelling in the LXX may have contributed to this misunder-
standing. [4]Mt 4:16. [5]Lk 24:5; Mt 28:6. [6]Mt 28:6; Mk 16:6.
[7]*GNTIP* 209*. [8]*NPNF* 1 9:37.

19:18-24 DAVID FLEES TO SAMUEL AT RAMAH

[18]Now David fled and escaped, and he came to Samuel at Ramah, and told him all that Saul
had done to him. And he and Samuel went and dwelt at Naioth. [19]And it was told Saul, "Behold,
David is at Naioth in Ramah." [20]Then Saul sent messengers to take David; and when they saw the
company of the prophets prophesying, and Samuel standing as head over them, the Spirit of God
came upon the messengers of Saul, and they also prophesied. [21]When it was told Saul, he sent other
messengers, and they also prophesied. And Saul sent messengers again the third time, and they also
prophesied. [22]Then he himself went to Ramah, and came to the great well that is in Secu; and he
asked, "Where are Samuel and David?" And one said, "Behold, they are at Naioth in Ramah."
[23]And he went from[f] there to Naioth in Ramah; and the Spirit of God came upon him also, and as
he went he prophesied, until he came to Naioth in Ramah. [24]And he too stripped off his clothes,
and he too prophesied before Samuel, and lay naked all that day and all that night. Hence it is
said, "Is Saul also among the prophets?"

f Gk: Heb lacks *from*

Overview: It is like water to the soul to be motivated to pursue godliness by the examples of ancient history (Bede). As David fled from the contagion of a cruel and treacherous man, the perfect soul renounces the vices in material goods and cleaves to God. Fleeing from sin is glorious, not shameful (Ambrose). As Saul demonstrates, possessing the spirit of prophecy does not indicate that one is God's child. Not unlike Caiaphas, Saul had the gift of prophecy yet without charity (Augustine). Fortuitous circumstance is sometimes the cause of prophecy, as indicated by the unexpected prophecies of Saul and his men (Origen). Saul illustrates how a person may unwittingly advocate for the one that he was contending against (Gregory of Nyssa).

19:18 David Flees to Samuel

David Replaces Saul. Bede: David was allotted the kingdom of the Israelites in place of Saul. He was a humble, innocent and gentle exile, yet he was for a long time tormented by [Saul's] unjust persecution. . . . Whoever upon hearing these things begins to strive after humility and innocence and to drive pride and envy from his heart, has, as it were, found a draught of the clearest water, by which he may be refreshed. But if he recognizes that Saul signifies those who persecute, and David signifies Christ and the church; and if he recognizes that on account of the [persecutors'] lack of faith, both their material and spiritual sovereignty has been destroyed, while the reign of Christ and the church will always remain; [with this understanding] he will perceive a cup of wine made from the water, for he will know that he is reading not only about that king but about his own life and reign, where before he read [the story] as if it were an ancient history about others. Homilies on the Gospels 1.14.[1]

Flight from Vice. Ambrose: Moreover the perfect soul turns away from matter, shuns and rejects everything that is excessive or inconstant or wicked, and neither sees nor approaches this earthly defilement and corruption. It is attentive to things divine but shuns earthly matter. But its flight is not to depart from the earth but to remain on earth, to hold to justice and temperance, to renounce the vices in material goods, not their use. Holy David fled from the face of Saul, not indeed to depart from the earth but to turn away from the contagion of a cruel, disobedient and treacherous man. He fled, cleaving to God, just as he himself said, "My soul has stuck fast to you."[2] Isaac, or the Soul 3.6.[3]

A Glorious Flight. Ambrose: Therefore let us not be ashamed to flee, for this flight is a glorious one, to flee from the face of sin. . . . Thus did David, too, flee from the face of King Saul, and from the face of Absalom.[4] Indeed, in his flight he brought about an increase of holiness, for he spared a treacherous assailant and sought after a parricide. Flight from the World 4.19.[5]

19:20-24 Saul and His Messengers Prophesy

The Children of God. Augustine: For all who do not love God are strangers, are antichrists. And though they come to the churches, they cannot be numbered among the children of God. That fountain of life does not belong to them. To have baptism is possible even for a bad person; to prophesy is possible even for a bad person. We find that king Saul prophesied: he was persecuting holy David, yet he was filled with the spirit of prophecy and began to prophesy. Homilies on 1 John 7.6.[6]

The Cause of Prophecy. Origen: Now, it seems to me that fortuitous circumstance also is sometimes the cause of prophesying, as is true in the present case of Caiaphas.[7] He was high priest of that year [in which] Jesus was to die for the people that the whole nation might not perish.[8]

---

[1]CS 110:141*. [2]Ps 63:8 (62:8 LXX). [3]FC 65:14. [4]2 Sam 15:14. [5]FC 65:296. [6]NPNF 1 7:503*. [7]See Jn 18:14. [8]See Jn 18:13.

For although others were high priests ... no one prophesies except the high priest of the year in which Jesus was to suffer.

And it was fortuitous circumstance that caused the messengers of Saul to prophesy when they were sent to David, along with Saul himself. For it is as if the fact that they were seeking David became the cause of their prophecy, such as it was, as has been recorded. COMMENTARY ON THE GOSPEL OF JOHN 28.175-76.[9]

PROPHECY WITHOUT CHARITY. AUGUSTINE: The book of Kings [Samuel] gives us an example about prophecy.[10] Saul was the persecutor of David. When he was persecuting him, he sent guards to drag him away to punishment, and those who were sent to bring David to be slain found him among the prophets; and Samuel was there too.... So he had fled to the place where besides Samuel, the most distinguished of all the prophets, there were also many other prophets. Pushing their way among them, while they were prophesying, came the emissaries of Saul, to drag him off, as I said, to death. The spirit of God leaped upon them and they began to prophesy, having come to lead a holy and just man of God to the execution block and snatch him away from among the prophets. They were suddenly filled with the spirit of God and turned into prophets. It's possible this happened because of their innocence; after all, they hadn't come of their own accord to arrest him but had been sent by their king. And perhaps they had indeed come to the place where David was but weren't going to do what Saul had told them to; perhaps they too were intending to stay there. Because such things even happen today. Sometimes a bailiff is sent by high authority to drag somebody out of the church; he dare not act against God, and in order not to face execution himself he stays there, in the place he was sent, to haul someone out of it. So you could say, pleasantly surprised and relieved, that these men suddenly became prophets because they were innocent; the very gift of prophecy bore witness to their innocence. They came

because they were sent, but they weren't going to do what that bad man had told them to. Let us believe that about them.

Others were sent; the Spirit of God leaped on them too, and they too began to prophesy. Let's count them too with the first lot as being quite innocent. A third lot were sent; the same happened to them too; let them all be innocent. When they delayed and what Saul had ordered wasn't done, he came himself. Was he too innocent? Was he also sent by some authority, and not ill-intentioned of his own free will? Yet the Spirit of God leaped on him too, and he began to prophesy. There you are, Saul is prophesying, he has the gift of prophecy, but he has not got charity. He has become a kind of instrument to be touched by the Spirit, not one to be cleansed by the Spirit. The Spirit of God, you see, touches some hearts to set them prophesying, and yet does not cleanse them.... And so the Spirit of God did not cleanse Saul the persecutor, but all the same it touched him to make him prophesy.

Caiaphas, the chief priest, was a persecutor of Christ; and yet he uttered a prophecy when he said, "It is right and proper that one man should die, and not the whole nation perish." The Evangelist went on to explain this as a prophecy and said, "He did not, however, say this of himself, but being high priest, he prophesied."[11] Caiaphas prophesied, Saul prophesied; they had the gift of prophecy, but they didn't have charity. Did Caiaphas have charity, considering he persecuted the Son of God, who was brought to us by charity? Did Saul have charity, who persecuted the one by whose hand he had been delivered from his enemies, so that he was guilty not only of envy but also of ingratitude? So we have proved that it is possible for you to have prophesy and not to have charity. But prophecy does you no good, according to the apostle: "If I do not have charity," he says, "I am nothing."[12] He doesn't say, "Prophesy is nothing," or "Faith is nothing," but

---

[9]FC 89:328. [10]1 Samuel through 2 Kings were known as 1 Kings through 4 Kings in the LXX and Vg. [11]Jn 11:50-51. [12]1 Cor 13:2.

"I myself am nothing, if I don't have charity." So while he has great gifts, he is nothing; although he has great gifts, he is nothing; because these great gifts which he has, he doesn't have to his benefit but to his condemnation. It isn't a great thing to have great gifts; but it is a great thing to use great gifts well; but you don't use them well if you haven't got charity. The fact is, it is only a good will that uses anything well; but there cannot be a good will where charity is not to be found. SERMON 162A.[13]

OVERCOME BY GRACE. GREGORY OF NYSSA: For by the arguments by which he [Eunomius] endeavors to destroy the truth, he is often himself unwittingly drawn into an advocacy of the very doctrines against which he is contending. Some such thing the history tells us concerning Saul ... when moved with wrath against the prophets, he was overcome by grace and was found as one of the inspired (the Spirit of prophecy willing, as I suppose, to instruct the apostate by means of himself) whence the surprising nature of the event became a proverb ... history records such an expression by way of wonder, "Is Saul also among the prophets?" AGAINST EUNOMIUS 3.4.[14]

---

[13]WSA 3 5:153-54. [14]NPNF 2 5:145.

20:1-11 DAVID RETURNS TO JONATHAN

Then David fled from Naioth in Ramah, and came and said before Jonathan, "What have I done? What is my guilt? And what is my sin before your father, that he seeks my life?" [2]And he said to him, "Far from it! You shall not die. Behold, my father does nothing either great or small without disclosing it to me; and why should my father hide this from me? It is not so." [3]But David replied,[g] "Your father knows well that I have found favor in your eyes; and he thinks, 'Let not Jonathan know this, lest he be grieved.' But truly, as the LORD lives and as your soul lives, there is but a step between me and death." [4]Then said Jonathan to David, "Whatever you* say, I will do for you."

g Gk: Heb *swore again*   *Heb *napšĕka*; Gk *psychē*

OVERVIEW: The apostle Paul uses the word *flesh* to refer to the depraved will, not to posit a contrast between the body and the soul (CHRYSOSTOM).

20:4 Whatever You Say, I Will Do for You

THE FLESH IS THE DEPRAVED WILL. CHRYSOSTOM: Here[1] some make the charge that the apostle has divided the human being into two parts, and that he states that a human's combined essence conflicts with itself, and that the body has a contest with the soul.[2] But this is clearly not so, for by "the flesh" he does not mean the body; if he did, what would be the sense of the clause immediately following, "for it lusts," he says,

---

[1]Gal 5:17. [2]This conflict would be affirmed by Hellenistic dualists, who believed that matter (i.e., the body) was evil while the spirit or soul was good.

"against the Spirit"? Yet the body does not move but is moved, is not an agent but is acted upon. How then does it lust, for lust belongs to the soul not to the body, for in another place it is said, "My soul longs,"[3] and, "Whatever your soul[4] desires, I will even do it for you" . . . and "So my soul pants."[5] Therefore when Paul says, "the flesh lusts against the Spirit," he means that the flesh is not the human body but the depraved will, as where he says, "But you are not in the flesh, but in the Spirit,"[6] and again, "Those who are in the flesh cannot please God."[7] COMMENTARY ON GALATIANS 5.[8]

---

[3]Ps 84:2 (83:2 LXX). [4]Gk *psyche*. [5]Ps 42:1 (41:1 LXX). [6]Rom 8:9. [7]Rom 8:8. [8]NPNF 1 13:40-41*.

20:12-25 JONATHAN'S PLAN TO TEST SAUL'S INTENTIONS

[12]*And Jonathan said to David, "The LORD, the God of Israel, be witness![i] When I have sounded my father, about this time tomorrow, or the third day, behold, if he is well disposed toward David, shall I not then send and disclose it to you?* [13]*But should it please my father to do you harm, the LORD do so to Jonathan and more also, if I do not disclose it to you, and send you away, that you may go in safety. May the LORD be with you, as he has been with my father."*

i Heb lacks *be witness*

OVERVIEW: David trusted Jonathan, a man of good will, even though he foresaw Saul's intentions more clearly (AMBROSE).

20:12-13 Jonathan Promises to Disclose Saul's Intentions

A MAN OF GOOD WILL. AMBROSE: But good will also goes together with generosity, for generosity really starts from it, seeing that the habit of giving comes after the desire to give. But generosity may be distinguished from good will. For where generosity is lacking, there good may abide—the parent, as it were, of all in common, uniting and binding friendships together. It is faithful in counsel, joyful in times of prosperity, and in times of sorrow sad. So it happens that any one trusts himself to the counsels of a man of good will rather than to those of a wise one, as David did. For he, though he was the more far-seeing, agreed to the counsels of Jonathan, who was the younger. DUTIES OF THE CLERGY 1.32.167.[1]

---

[1]NPNF 2 10:28*.

20:26-42 JONATHAN HELPS DAVID ESCAPE

²⁶Yet Saul did not say anything that day; for he thought, "Something has befallen him; he is not clean, surely he is not clean." ²⁷But on the second day, the morrow after the new moon, David's place was empty. And Saul said to Jonathan his son, "Why has not the son of Jesse come to the meal, either yesterday or today?" ²⁸Jonathan answered Saul, "David earnestly asked leave of me to go to Bethlehem; ²⁹he said, 'Let me go; for our family holds a sacrifice in the city, and my brother has commanded me to be there. So now, if I have found favor in your eyes, let me get away, and see my brothers.' For this reason he has not come to the king's table."

³⁰Then Saul's anger was kindled against Jonathan, and he said to him, "You son of a perverse, rebellious woman, do I not know that you have chosen the son of Jesse to your own shame, and to the shame of your mother's nakedness? ³¹For as long as the son of Jesse lives upon the earth, neither you nor your kingdom shall be established. Therefore send and fetch him to me, for he shall surely die." ³²Then Jonathan answered Saul his father, "Why should he be put to death? What has he done?" ³³But Saul cast his spear at him to smite him; so Jonathan knew that his father was determined to put David to death. ³⁴And Jonathan rose from the table in fierce anger and ate no food the second day of the month, for he was grieved for David, because his father had disgraced him.

Overview: By referring to David as the "son of Jesse," Saul attempted to diminish David's glory by putting his low birth on display. Despite his father's severe reproach, Jonathan demonstrates the nature of love in his affection for David (Chrysostom). As Jonathan exemplifies, a friendship that seeks virtue is rightly to be preferred to wealth, power and personal safety. Saul attempted to spear Jonathan because he thought that his son esteemed David's friendship more highly than his family's (Ambrose).

20:27 Saul Asks About David's Absence

The Son of Jesse. Chrysostom: As for Saul, he hated and abhorred David so much after the countless good services which he had done, after his brilliant triumphs, and the salvation which he had wrought in the matter of Goliath, that Saul could not bear to mention him by his own name but called him after his father. For once when a festival was at hand, and Saul, having devised some treachery against him and contrived a cruel plot, did not see him arrive— "where," said he, "is the son of Jesse?" He called him by his father's name because he thought to damage the distinguished position of that righteous man by a reference to his low birth—a miserable and despicable thought. For certainly, even if he had some accusation to bring against the father this could in no way injure David. For each man is answerable for his own deeds, and by these he can be praised and accused. But, as it was, not having any evil deed to mention, Saul brought forward his low birth, expecting by this means to throw his glory into the shade, which in fact was the height of folly. For what kind of offence is it to be the child of insignificant and humble parents? Saul, however, did not understand true wisdom in these things. Homily to Those Who Had Not Attended the Assembly 6.[1]

---

[1]NPNF 1 9:230*.

20:30-34 Saul's Anger Against Jonathan

LOVE AND SHAME. CHRYSOSTOM: For love "does nothing unseemly," but as it were with certain golden wings covers up all the offenses of the beloved. Thus also Jonathan loved David and heard the scorn of his father as one . . . "who has nothing of a man, but lives to the shame of himself and the mother who bore you." What then? Did he grieve at these things, and hide his face and turn away from his beloved [David]? No, quite the contrary; he displayed his fondness as an ornament. And yet the one was at that time a king, and a king's son, even Jonathan; the other a fugitive and a wanderer, David. But not even in this circumstance was he ashamed of his friendship. "For love does not act inappropriately." This is its remarkable quality that it not only does not suffer the injured to grieve and feel irritated but even disposes him to rejoice. Accordingly, the one of whom we are speaking, after all these things, just as though he had a crown put on him, went away and fell on David's neck. For love does not know what sort of thing shame is. Therefore it glories in those things for which another hides his face. The shame is in "not knowing how to love" rather than "incurring danger and enduring all for the beloved" when you do love. HOMILIES ON 1 CORINTHIANS 33.2.[2]

A FRIENDSHIP THAT SEEKS VIRTUE.
AMBROSE: For that commendable friendship which maintains virtue is to be preferred most certainly to wealth or honors or power. It is not apt to be preferred to virtue indeed, but to follow after it. So it was with Jonathan, who for his affection's sake avoided neither his father's displeasure nor the danger to his own safety. DUTIES OF THE CLERGY 3.21.124.[3]

GREAT ESTEEM FOR DAVID. AMBROSE: Who would not have loved him [David], when they saw how dear he was to his friends? For as he truly loved his friends, so he thought that he was loved as much in return by his own friends. No, parents put him even before their own children, and children loved him more than their parents. Therefore Saul was very angry and strove to strike Jonathan his son with a spear because he thought that David's friendship held a higher place in his esteem than either filial piety or a father's authority. DUTIES OF THE CLERGY 2.7.36.[4]

---

[2]NPNF 1 12:196**. [3]NPNF 2 10:87*. [4]NPNF 2 10:49*.

21:1-6 AHIMELECH AIDS DAVID

[1]*Then came David to Nob to Ahimelech the priest; and Ahimelech came to meet David trembling, and said to him, "Why are you alone, and no one with you?"* [2]*And David said to Ahimelech the priest, "The king has charged me with a matter, and said to me, 'Let no one know anything of the matter about which I send you, and with which I have charged you.' I have made an appointment with the young men for such and such a place.* [3]*Now then, what have you at hand? Give me five loaves of bread, or whatever is here."* [4]*And the priest answered David, "I have no common bread at hand, but there is holy bread; if only the young men have kept themselves from women."*

[5]And David answered the priest, "Of a truth women have been kept from us as always when I go on an expedition; the vessels of the young men are holy, even when it is a common journey; how much more today will their vessels be holy?" [6]So the priest gave him the holy bread; for there was no bread there but the bread of the Presence, which is removed from before the Lord, to be replaced by hot bread on the day it is taken away.

Overview: Even if we are utterly alone, if we possess God's grace we are the most secure of all (Chrysostom). Although lying, as well as other base behaviors, was permissible for the holy men of old, it is utterly forbidden by the gospel (Cassian). David was allowed to eat the holy bread because, although not a priest in the formal sense, he was considered one since he was a temple of the Holy Spirit (Ephrem). Christ and his disciples assuaged their hunger by breaking the sabbath. This finds warrant in David's procurement of the holy bread, which illustrates the dispensation from fasting allowed to the sabbath day (Tertullian). By eating the holy loaves, David shows that he foresaw the prophetic mysteries of a new grace (Ambrose). As David's son, Christ is testified to in Scripture as both king and priest by David's kingship and priestly act of eating the show bread (Augustine).

21:1 David Goes to Nob

The Greatest Security. Chrysostom: In similar fashion, whenever we have God on our side, even if we are utterly alone, we will live more securely than those who dwell in the cities. After all, the grace of God is the greatest security and the most impregnable fortification. To prove to you how the person who, in fact, lives utterly alone turns out to be more secure and efficacious than a person living in the middle of cities and enjoying plenty of human assistance, let us see how David, though shifting from place to place and living like a nomad, was protected by the hand from above, whereas Saul, who in fact was in the middle of cities and had armies at his command, bodyguards and shieldbearers as well, still spent each day in fear and dread of enemy assaults. Whereas the one man, although alone and with no one else in his company, had no need of assistance from human beings, the other, by contrast, needed his help, despite wearing a diadem and being clad in purple. The king stood in need of the shepherd; the wearer of the crown had need of the peasant. Homilies on Genesis 46.8.[1]

21:2 David Lies to Ahimelech the Priest

Lying Utterly Forbidden. John Cassian: No wonder that these dispensations were uprightly made use of in the Old Testament and that holy men sometimes lied in praiseworthy or at least in pardonable fashion, since we see that far greater things were permitted them because it was a time of beginnings. For what is there to wonder at that when the blessed David was fleeing Saul and Ahimelech the priest asked him, "Why are you alone, and no one is with you?" he replied and said, "The king gave me a commission and said, Let no one know the reason why you were sent, for I have also appointed my servants to such and such a place"? And again: "Do you have a spear or a sword at hand? For I did not bring my sword and my weapons with me because the king's business was urgent"? Or what happened when he was brought to Achish, the king of Gath, and made believe that he was insane and raging, and "changed his countenance before them, and fell down between their hands, and dashed himself against the door of the gate, and his spittle ran down his beard"?[2] For, after all, they lawfully enjoyed flocks of wives and concubines, and no sin was imputed to them on this ac-

---

[1]FC 87:8. [2]1 Sam 21:13.

count. Besides that, they also frequently spilled their enemies' blood with their own hands, and this was held not only to be irreprehensible but even praiseworthy.

We see that, in the light of the gospel, these things have been utterly forbidden, such that none of them can be committed without very serious sin and sacrilege. Likewise we believe that no lie, in however pious a form, can be made use of by anyone in a pardonable way, to say nothing of praiseworthily, according to the words of the Lord: "Let your speech be yes, yes, no, no. Whatever is more than these is from the evil one."[3] The apostle also agrees with this: "Do not lie to one another."[4] CONFERENCE 17.18.1-2.[5]

21:3-6 Ahimelech Offers David the Holy Bread

DAVID THE PRIEST. EPHREM THE SYRIAN: Our Lord put forward the clear example of David, who was not accused either over this, as he was over something else. It was not permissible, he said, for David to eat [the holy bread] since he was not a priest. However, he was a priest, because he was a temple of the Spirit. Because they did not understand this, he openly proved them wrong with regard to their own [position]: "The priests were defiling the sabbath in the temple, and they were not guilty of sin."[6] Another element is depicted for us there. Before David was persecuted, he partook of the bread with authority. COMMENTARY ON TATIAN'S DIATESSARON 5.24.[7]

A SABBATH DISPENSATION. TERTULLIAN: When the disciples had been hungry on the sabbath and had plucked some ears [of grain] and rubbed them in their hands, they violated the holy day by so preparing their food. Yet Christ excuses them and even became their accomplice in breaking the sabbath.[8] . . . For from the Creator's Scripture and from the purpose of Christ there is derived a vivid precedent from David's example when he went into the temple on the sabbath and provided food by boldly breaking up the show bread. Even he remembered that this privilege (the dispensation from fasting) was allowed on the sabbath from the very beginning, from when the sabbath itself was instituted. For although the Creator had forbidden that the manna should be gathered for two days, he permitted it on only one occasion—the day before the sabbath—so that the previous day's provision of food might free them from fasting on the following sabbath. Therefore the Lord had good reason for pursuing the same principle in the "annulling" of the sabbath (since that is the word which people will use). He had good reason, too, for expressing the Creator's will, when he bestowed the privilege of not fasting on the sabbath.[9] In short, might he have—right then and there—put an end not only to the sabbath but to the Creator himself if he had commanded his disciples to fast on the sabbath, as this would have been contrary to the intention of the Scripture and of the Creator's will. But is he alien from the Creator because he did not directly defend his disciples but excuses them? Or because he interposes human need, as if deprecating censure? Or because he maintains the honor of the sabbath as a day which is to be free from gloom rather than from work? Or because he puts David and his companions on a level with his own disciples in their fault and their validation? Or because he is pleased to endorse the Creator's indulgence? Or because he is himself good according to his example—is he therefore alien from the Creator? AGAINST MARCION 4.12.[10]

CHRIST EXCUSES. AMBROSE: Even if they accuse, yet Christ excuses,[11] and he makes the souls that he wishes, that follow him, similar to David, who ate the loaves of proposition outside of the law—for even then he foresaw in his mind the prophetic mysteries of a new grace. ISAAC, OR THE SOUL 6.56.[12]

---

[3]Jas 5:12. [4]Col 3:9. [5]ACW 57:596-97. [6]Mt 12:5. [7]ECTD 106*. [8]See Mt 12:1-8. [9]See Ex 16:4-5. [10]ANF 3:362-63**. [11]Lk 6:3-5. [12]FC 65:46*.

Both King and Priest. Augustine: In many other testimonies of the divine Scriptures, Christ appears both as king and as priest. With good reason, therefore, he is declared to be David's son more frequently than he is said to be Abraham's son. Matthew and Luke have both affirmed this: the one viewing him [David] as the person from whom, through Solomon, his [Jesus'] lineage can be traced down, and the other taking him [David] for the person to whom, through Nathan, his [Jesus'] genealogy can be carried up. So he [David] did represent the role of a priest, although he was patently a king, when he ate the show bread. For it was not lawful for any one to eat that, except the priests alone. Harmony of the Gospels 1.3.5.[13]

---

[13]NPNF 1 6:79**.

21:7-15 DAVID FLEES TO ACHISH, KING OF GATH

[10]And David rose and fled that day from Saul, and went to Achish the king of Gath. [11]And the servants of Achish said to him, "Is not this David the king of the land? Did they not sing to one another of him in dances,

'Saul has slain his thousands,
and David his ten thousands'?"
[12]And David took these words to heart, and was much afraid of Achish the king of Gath. [13]So he changed his behavior before them, and feigned himself mad in their hands, and made marks on the doors of the gate, and let his spittle run down his beard.

Overview: Scripture's figurative expressions and actions, like David's pretense of insanity, should be judged as prophecies, which are veiled to exercise the mind and to increase their meaning (Augustine). Signifying a great mystery, David's spittle represents the Scriptures flowing with abundant strength (Cassiodorus).

21:13 David Feigns Insanity

A Figurative Expression. Augustine: All these modes of expression will be thought lies, if a figurative expression or action is to be considered a lie. But, if it is not a lie when signs signifying one thing are put for another to serve the understanding of a truth, certainly that should not be judged a lie either which Jacob did or said to his father in order to be blessed, or what Joseph said in sporting with his brothers,[1] or David's pretense of insanity, or other signs of the same kind. They should be judged as prophetic expressions and actions set forth for the understanding of those things which are true. Those things are veiled in figures, in garments as it were, in order that they may exercise the mind of the pious inquirer and not become cheap for being bare and obvious. Although we have learned their meaning stated openly and plainly in other places, still, when they are dug out of obscurity, they are somehow recreated in our knowledge and thus become sweet. A student is not hindered because they are shrouded in this way. On the contrary,

---

[1]Gen 42.

294

they are rendered more acceptable: for being remote they are more ardently desired, and for being desired they are more joyfully discovered. AGAINST LYING 10.24.[2]

EVIDENCE OF A GREAT MYSTERY. CAS-SIODORUS: When Saul was pursuing David, David fled to king Achish, and since through the motive of jealousy he was suspected there, he carefully changed his countenance, covering his face with spittle so that he would be thought to be diabolically possessed and thus released unharmed as an object of pity. But these and other deeds were accomplished by David as evidence of a great mystery, for he showed that the spittle, which represented the holy Scriptures,

was running down his beard, that is, had great strength. The significance of these things led to the substitution of the name of Abimelech, meaning "kingdom of my father," for Achish, to whom David had fled. Clearly this incident aptly refers to the Lord Christ, through whom the glorious Father with most holy devotion undertook service to the world. The expression "who dismissed him" refers to king Abimelech; "and he went his way" means that David departed to another region because, as we have said, he had begun to be suspected. EXPOSITION OF THE PSALMS 33(34).1.[3]

---

[2]FC 16:154. [3]ACW 51:324-25*.

22:1-5 DAVID GAINS SUPPORT AND FLEES TO JUDAH

[1]*David departed from there and escaped to the cave of Adullam; and when his brothers and all his father's house heard it, they went down there to him.* [2]*And every one who was in distress, and every one who was in debt, and every one who was discontented, gathered to him; and he became captain over them. And there were with him about four hundred men.*

OVERVIEW: David's presence in the cave is analogous to the bodily existence of the just, who are engaged repeatedly in spiritual battles (AMBROSE). The flight of those who are persecuted speaks volumes against those who persecute, only later to become the persecutor's undoing (ATHANASIUS). Bede reads the story of David's escape as an allegory for Christ and the church: As relatives and discontents join David, the elect and the repentant who come to Christ are signified while the four hundred men suggest the unity of the four Gospels.

22:1-2 David's Escape and Growing Contingent

THE STRUGGLES OF THE JUST. AMBROSE: For the just engage in many struggles. Does an athlete contend only once? How often, after he has won many victor's crowns, is he overcome in another contest! How often it happens that one who has frequently gained the victory sometimes hesitates and is held fast in uncertainty! And it frequently comes to pass that a brave man is contending with brave men and greater struggles arise, where proofs of strength are greater. Thus, when David sought to flee to avoid the adversary, he also did not find his wings.[1] He was driven here and there in an uncertain struggle. . . . But David is still in the cave—that is, in the flesh—in the cavern of his body, as it were, as he fights with King Saul, the son of hardness, and with the power of that spiritual prince who is not visible but is comprehensible. FLIGHT FROM THE WORLD 5.28.[2]

FLIGHT FROM PERSECUTION. ATHANASIUS: For if it is a bad thing to flee, it is much worse to persecute. The one party hides himself to escape death, the other persecutes with a desire to kill. It is written in the Scriptures that we ought to flee; but he that seeks to destroy transgresses the law and also is himself the occasion of the other's flight. If then they [the Arians] reproach me with my flight, let them be more ashamed of their own persecution. Let them cease to conspire, and those who flee will immediately cease to do so. But they, instead of giving up their wickedness, are employing every means to obtain possession of my person, not perceiving that the flight of those who are persecuted is a strong argument against those who persecute. For no one flees from the gentle and the humane, but from the cruel and the evil-minded.

"Every one that was in distress and every one that was in debt" fled from Saul and took refuge with David. But this is the reason why these men [those persecuting Athanasius] desire to cut off those who are in concealment, that there may be no evidence forthcoming of their own wickedness. But in this their minds seem to be blinded with their usual error. For the more the flight of their enemies becomes known, so much the more notorious will be the destruction or the banishment which their treachery has brought upon them. So whether they kill them outright, their death will be the more loudly noised abroad

against them, or whether they drive them into banishment, they will but be sending forth everywhere monuments of their own iniquity. DEFENSE OF HIS FLIGHT 8.[3]

CLINGING TO CHRIST AND HIS TEACHING. BEDE: When Christ stays among the humble, all the elect come down to him by humbling themselves. They come whether they are men, who are his brothers because he himself was made man, or angels, who are most of all his father's house and the place of the dwelling of his glory. Also they come who are pressed down by the awareness of their sin and long by their bitter tears of penance to be washed and freed from their debt, that is, the debt of sin which the devil bestowed on them. With Christ as their leader, they hope to be brought into the joys of the kingdom.

"And about four hundred men joined him." All who stand in the faith cling to the Lord, as they behave bravely, strengthen their hearts and are called to hope for, seek and obtain the realms of heaven through the teaching of the gospel. This doctrine is sealed in the most beautiful unity of the four books. The number hundred is often sought as the first fruitful number after so many preceding fruitless numbers, just as it is said that when the labors here below have been completed, God opens the entrance to the kingdom above. It is well worth noting that the events in the cave of Adullum, which we have explained as we had the strength, can be applied to the early church. Consequently they are not unbecoming to be appropriated to the state of the whole church. For whatever things have special application to our age, that is, the age of the Gentiles, have a view to the church. FOUR BOOKS ON 1 SAMUEL 3.22.[4]

---

[1]See Ps 139:9 (138:9 LXX). [2]FC 65:303*. [3]NPNF 2 4:257-58*. [4]CCL 119:204.

22:6-10 SAUL LEARNS OF DAVID'S ACTIONS

⁷And Saul said to his servants who stood about him, "Hear now, you Benjaminites; will the son of Jesse give every one of you fields and vineyards, will he make you all commanders of thousands and commanders of hundreds, ⁸that all of you have conspired against me? No one discloses to me when my son makes a league with the son of Jesse, none of you is sorry for me or discloses to me that my son has stirred up my servant against me, to lie in wait, as at this day." ⁹Then answered Doeg the Edomite, who stood by the servants of Saul, "I saw the son of Jesse coming to Nob, to Ahimelech the son of Ahitub, ¹⁰and he inquired of the LORD for him, and gave him provisions, and gave him the sword of Goliath the Philistine."

OVERVIEW: As a tender of mules, which signify the evil, sterile nature that is not of God's creation, Doeg represents the wicked angel who draws human souls to evil (GREGORY OF NYSSA).

22:9-10 *Doeg the Edomite*

THE WICKED ANGEL. GREGORY OF NYSSA: I am taught through these words that whenever understanding guides my life like it did the life of the great David, that this carries me through to the end of the victory. And then I grieve especially for Doeg, the tyrant of my salvation, whenever I am in the house of the priest and when the attendant of the mules[1] plots against me secretly because he no longer has the power to come to grips with me face to face, by informing the one who thirsts for my blood that I am staying with the priest.

It's obvious what the mules represent, which this Edomite has charge over. He tends that sterile nature which has no room for God's blessing that sets fruitfulness in the creature in the beginning by saying "increase and multiply."[2] Multiplication in evil, like the continuation of the species of mules, is not of God. As the animal is always begun anew, this sterile nature of the creature is produced by trickery and is achieved underhandedly by means of the nature itself.

But the goal intended by the Word is obvious in what has been said. For if everything that the Lord made was very good,[3] and the mule is not part of what was made in creation, it is obvious that "mule" has been used by the story to indicate evil. Its existence does not come from God, and it lacks the ability to propagate in order to make its characteristic nature endure. As the mule is unable to maintain its nature by itself, so evil lacks the ability to remain forever or preserve itself. Like with mules, another evil comes into being when it is created by another, when what is noble and splendid in our nature, and perhaps also haughty, sinks to the desire for a union which is ass-like and irrational.

That foreigner Doeg, then, who became the messenger to Saul against David, the herdsman of the sterile herd of mules, is the wicked angel who draws the human soul to evil through the various passions of sin. Whenever he sees that the soul is in the house of the true priest, being unable to strike it with the kicks of the mules, he informs the ruler of wickedness, "the spirit which is at work in the sons of disobedience."[4] ON THE INSCRIPTIONS OF THE PSALMS 2.13.179-82.[5]

---

[1]The LXX describes Doeg as the tender of Saul's mules (1 Sam 21:7; 22:9). [2]Gen 1:28. [3]Gen 1:31. [4]Eph 2:2. [5]*GNTIP* 178-79**.

22:11-23 THE CITY OF NOB IS ATTACKED

[11]*Then the king sent to summon Ahimelech* the priest, the son of Ahitub, and all his father's house, the priests who were at Nob; and all of them came to the king. . . . [16]And the king said, "You shall surely die, Ahimelech, you and all your father's house." [17]And the king said to the guard who stood about him, "Turn and kill the priests of the* LORD; *because their hand also is with David, and they knew that he fled, and did not disclose it to me." But the servants of the king would not put forth their hand to fall upon the priests of the* LORD. [18]*Then the king said to Doeg, "You turn and fall upon the priests." And Doeg the Edomite turned and fell upon the priests, and he killed on that day eighty-five persons who wore the linen ephod. [19]And Nob, the city of the priests, he put to the sword; both men and women, children and sucklings, oxen, asses and sheep, he put to the sword.*

* LXX *Abimelech*

OVERVIEW: Doeg the Edomite, whose name means "earthquakes," is rightly understood as a figure for the antichrist who will make martyrs and disturb the whole world (CASSIODORUS). Those who persecuted David and the son of David share a common guilt for shedding innocent blood (EPHREM). Doeg and David represent earthly and heavenly persons, respectively (AUGUSTINE). Jerome looks into the meaning of ephod and related textual problems.

22:18-19 Doeg Kills the Priests of Nob

DOEG THE ANTICHRIST. CASSIODORUS: When David was fleeing from Saul, he came to the priest Abimelech. He was received by him and obtained the loaves of proposition[1] and the sword with which he had slain Goliath. The loaves of proposition denoted his role as priest, the consecrated sword his future rank as most powerful king. The Edomite Doeg happened to be there in charge of the mules and reported everything to King Saul. Then Saul was angry and caused Abimelech and the other priests of the same city to be slain by Doeg. This Doeg through whom such events occurred was called the Edomite from the name of his land. The names combined, according to the authority of the fathers,[2] mean

"earthquakes." Such meaning attached to the names is rightly related to the acts of antichrist, for Doeg the Edomite was the foe of David, just as antichrist will be the enemy of Christ. Doeg destroyed priests; antichrist will make martyrs. Doeg through the meaning of his name denotes earthquakes; antichrist will disturb the whole world when with sacrilegious presumption he will constrain it to worship his name.[3] So antichrist is rightly understood by the name of Doeg the Edomite, since he is seen to be similar to him in these striking parallels. EXPOSITION OF THE PSALMS 51.1-2.[4]

CORRELATING PAST EVENTS. EPHREM THE SYRIAN: Indeed, when Saul heard that the priests had helped David unwittingly, he had them brought to him, and he killed them. It was fitting for you too that innocent blood be hung about your neck, as was Saul's case. But the Son of David escaped from your hands amid the Gentiles. David was persecuted by Saul, just as the Son was by Herod.[5] The priests were slain because of David, and the infants because of our

---

[1]The holy bread (1 Sam 21:6). [2]Cf. Jerome and Augustine. [3]Cassiodorus seems to be following Cyril of Jerusalem *Catechetical Lectures* 15.11ff. [4]ACW 52:1*. [5]See Mt 2.

Lord.[6] Abiathar escaped from the priests, as John did from the infants.[7] In [the person of] Abiathar the priesthood of the house of Eli was brought to an end, and in John the prophecy of the sons of Jacob was terminated.[8] COMMENTARY ON TATIAN'S DIATESSARON 3.3.[9]

THE EARTHLY VERSUS THE HEAVENLY. AUGUSTINE: While the holy man David was on the run from Saul's persecution, he fled to a place where he thought he would be safe. He passed by the house of a priest named Ahimelech and accepted loaves from him. In so doing, he acted in the role not of a king only, but of a priest too, because he ate the bread of the presence which "it was unlawful for anyone other than the priests to eat," as the Lord reminds us in the Gospel.[10] Saul, when later he began to hunt him, was angry with his retainers because none of them was willing to betray David. The story has just been read from the book of the Kingdoms [Samuel]. But there was a man present that day named Doeg, who was an Edomite and the principal herdsman in Saul's service; he too had come to Ahimelech the priest. He was present again when Saul raged against his followers because none of them would betray David. Doeg revealed where he had seen him. Saul immediately sent for the priest and all his family to be brought before him, and [he] ordered that they be killed. Not one of Saul's entourage dared raise a hand against the priests of the Lord, even under orders from the king. But this Doeg, who had betrayed David's whereabouts, was like Judas; he did not recoil from his evil purpose but persisted in bringing forth fruit from that same root even to the end, the kind of fruit typical of a rotten tree. So at the king's order Doeg killed the priest and all his family, and afterwards the city of the priests was demolished. We have seen, then, that this man Doeg was the enemy of both David the king and Ahimelech the priest. Doeg was a single person, but he represents a whole class of people. Similarly David embodies both king and priest, like one man with a dual personality, though the human race is one.

So too at the present time and in our world let us recognize these two groups of people, so that what we sing, or hear sung, may profit us. Let us recognize Doeg still with us today, as we recognize the kingly and priestly body today, and so we shall recognize the body that is opposed to king and priest still. Notice from the outset how mysteriously significant their names are. Doeg is said to mean "movement," and Edomite means "earthly." Already you can see what kind of people this "movement," this Doeg, symbolizes: the kind that does not remain stable forever but is destined to be moved elsewhere. As for "earthly": why expect any fruit from an earthly person? But the heavenly humans will last forever. So, to put it briefly, there is an earthly kingdom in this world today, but there is also a heavenly kingdom. Each of them has its pilgrim citizens, both the earthly kingdom and the heavenly, the kingdom that is to be uprooted and the kingdom that is to be planted for eternity. EXPLANATIONS OF THE PSALMS 51.[11]

HOLY EPHOD. JEROME: You put in the front of your letter what would be pleasing, that it is written in the book of 1 Kings [Samuel]: "Samuel served as a boy before the Lord, girded in a linen ephod and having a small duplicate cloak which his mother had made for him and would bring to him day after day when she went up with her husband to offer sacrifice on the day of sacrifice."[12] Thus you inquire about this linen ephod with which the coming prophet will also be girded, namely, whether it will be a girdle, or, as many believe, some type of clothing. And if you clothe him, how will it be bound together? And why is the adjective *linen* added after the ephod? You also wrote down to be read the following: "And a man of God came to Eli and said to him, 'Thus says the Lord: "I revealed myself to the house of your father when they were in the land of Egypt serving in the house

[6]Mt 2:16. [7]That is, John the Baptist was not killed by Herod's order (Mt 2:16). [8]Mt 11:13. [9]ECTD 75. [10]Mt 12:4. [11]WSA 3 17:14-16*. [12]1 Sam 2:18-19.

of Pharaoh and I chose the house of your father from all the tribes of Israel to be my priest, that they might go up to my altar and burn incense and wear ephods." ' "[13] You took as an exemplar of the entire order of the book to follow that passage where Doeg the Edomite killed the priests at the king's command. "Doeg of Syrus turned," the Scripture says, "and fell upon the priests of the Lord and killed on that day three hundred and five men," or, as the Hebrew reads, "eighty-five men," all wearing ephods.

And Nob, the city of priests, he killed with the edge of the sword, men and women, infants and toddlers, calves and foals and sheep, all to the edge of the sword. But Abiathar, one of the sons of Ahimelech, son of Ahitub, was saved and fled after David. I will not delay now except to anticipate the textual problem where we read "all wearing ephods," but the Hebrew has "all wearing linen ephods." You will learn in what follows why I say this. And add this to it: Abiathar, son of

Ahimelech, fled to David and went down with David to Keilah, having the ephod in his hand. Then, Saul abandoned his pursuit when David came to Keilah, where, because it was feared that Saul would arrive and besiege the city, David said to Abiathar, "Bring down the ephod of the Lord." These are excerpts from the book of Kings [Samuel] pushing you to transcend the book of Judges, in which Micah from Mt. Ephraim gave eleven hundred pieces of silver to his mother, which he had promised, who is said to have made graven and molten images out of them.[14] Notice also that in a short while it is called ephod and teraphim, since surely if it is a girdle or a type of clothing, it cannot also be a graven or molten image. Acknowledge the error of almost all Latin thinkers who allege that the ephod and teraphim, named later, were part of the molten images made from this silver which Micah had given to his mother. LETTER 29.[15]

---

[13]1 Sam 2:27-28. [14]See Judg 17:1-6. [15]CCL 54:234-35.

23:1-18 DAVID RESCUES KEILAH FROM THE PHILISTINES

[5]And David and his men went to Keilah, and fought with the Philistines, and brought away their cattle, and made a great slaughter among them. So David delivered the inhabitants of Keilah. . . .

[12]Then said David, "Will the men of Keilah surrender me and my men into the hand of Saul?" And the LORD said, "They will surrender you." [13]Then David and his men, who were about six hundred, arose and departed from Keilah, and they went wherever they could go. . . . [14]And David remained in the strongholds in the wilderness, in the hill country of the Wilderness of Ziph. And Saul sought him every day, but God did not give him into his hand.

OVERVIEW: Bede interprets David's dwelling in the wilderness as an allegory for Christ's presence in the hearts of tested believers in an arid age.

23:14 David Lives in the Wilderness of Ziph

STRONGHOLDS OF THE HEARTS. BEDE: "But

David tarried in the strongholds of the desert and stayed in the hill country of the wilderness of Ziph." After Christ dismisses those who had nominally accepted the faith, he tarries instead in the strongholds of the hearts of those who for the mighty and living God [exist] amid the aridness of this present age. He tarries with them when they come and appear before the face of God. He gladly remains in them whose heart, raised on

high and removed from the allurements of the world and hidden in blessed solitude, rejoices in the unfailing budding and flowering of the virtues. For Ziph means "flower" or "bud." Four Books on 1 Samuel 4.23.[1]

---

[1]CCL 119:216.

23:19-29 SAUL PURSUES DAVID IN THE WILDERNESS OF MAON

[19]*Then the Ziphites went up to Saul at Gibe-ah, saying, "Does not David hide among us in the strongholds at Horesh, on the hill of Hachilah, which is south of Jeshimon?* [20]*Now come down, O king, according to all your heart's desire to come down; and our part shall be to surrender him into the king's hand." . . .*

Now David and his men were in the wilderness of Maon, in the Arabah to the south of Jeshimon. [25]*And Saul and his men went to seek him. And David was told; therefore he went down to the rock which is[v] in the wilderness of Maon. And when Saul heard that, he pursued after David in the wilderness of Maon.* [26]*Saul went on one side of the mountain, and David and his men on the other side of the mountain; and David was making haste to get away from Saul, as Saul and his men were closing in upon David and his men to capture them,* [27]*when a messenger came to Saul, saying, "Make haste and come; for the Philistines have made a raid upon the land."* [28]*So Saul returned from pursuing after David, and went against the Philistines; therefore that place was called the Rock of Escape.* [29w]*And David went up from there, and dwelt in the strongholds of En-gedi.*

v Gk: Heb *and dwelt*   w Ch 24.1 in Heb

Overview: Bede explains the allegorical significance of the Ziphites' words to Saul: Christ, in the person of David, dwells in the minds of those who hold firmly to the faith while false brothers, represented by the Ziphites, aid the church's enemies. While David was persecuted explicitly, Christ is often persecuted secretly through impiety and heresy (Ephrem).

23:19 The Ziphites Tell Saul Where David Is Hiding

The Church and Her Persecutors. Bede: Often false brothers abandon the budding and flowering of their virtues and instead arise and go to the arrogant enemies of the faith. They go to them to help the enemies destroy the church.

They despise the simplicity of the faithful and in a manner of speaking they say to the persecutors, "Does not Christ dwell among us in the very safe hearts of the people?" It is not without meaning that it was said, "on the hill of Hachilah," that is, "the hill of one who takes hold of her." For where is it more pleasing for the spirit of Christ to dwell than in the heights of a mind which takes hold of the faith firmly? Such a mind is "on the favorable side[1] of the desert" because of the many favorable things belonging to eternal life and so abandons the joys of the world and all its ostentation. For whoever resists the enticements of this world for merely temporal or earthly gain ought not to be said to have turned to the favorable side of the desert, but to the unfavorable side, where our desirable king is not wont to live, but rather our detestable enemy. And the residents of Ziph tell Saul all these things whenever those feigning faith betray to the open persecutors of the church either the mysteries of the faith or those who worship them. Through their perverse mind they differ from the persecutors in acknowledging the faith, but they are one at heart with them in their hatred of the faith. The more profoundly they know the mysteries of Christ (just as the men of Ziph knew the hiding places of David), the more wickedly they aid those who attempt to besiege the church from without. Four Books on 1 Samuel 4.23.[2]

23:24-29 Saul Pursues David and His Company

Persecuted by Saul. Ephrem the Syrian: This is what happened to Paul.[3] For the potency of the light suddenly surprised his feeble eyes and injured them. But the greatness of the voice brought low his strength and entered his ears and opened them. . . . For the voice did not plough up the ears, as the light injured the eyeballs. Why? But because it was necessary that he should hear but not see. Therefore the doors of hearing were opened by the voice as by a key: but the doors of sight were shut by the light that should open them. Why then was it necessary that he should hear? Clearly because by that voice our Lord was able to reveal himself as being persecuted by Saul. For he was not able to show himself by sight as being persecuted; for there was no way whereby this should be, that the son of David should be seen fleeing and Saul pursuing after him. For this happened in very deed with that first Saul and with the first David. The one was pursuing; the other was being persecuted; they both of them saw and were seen, each by the other. But here the ear alone could hear of the persecution of the Son of David; the eye could not see that he was being persecuted. Homily on Our Lord 32.[4]

---

[1]The Hebrew word for "south" (and the word the Vg uses to translate it) means "right" (as if the observer is facing east with his right side to the south). In the Latin idiom (as well as in the Hebrew), the right hand was considered lucky (i.e., "favorable") and the left hand unlucky, which lends to Bede's play on words. [2]CCL 119:218-19. [3]Acts 9:3-9. [4]NPNF 2 13:318-19*.

24:1-7 DAVID SPARES SAUL'S LIFE

[1]When Saul returned from following the Philistines, he was told, "Behold, David is in the wilderness of En-gedi." [2]Then Saul took three thousand chosen men out of all Israel, and went to seek

David and his men in front of the Wildgoats' Rocks. [3]*And he came to the sheepfolds by the way, where there was a cave; and Saul went in to relieve himself. Now David and his men were sitting in the innermost parts of the cave.* [4]*And the men of David said to him, "Here is the day of which the* LORD *said to you, 'Behold, I will give your enemy into your hand, and you shall do to him as it shall seem good to you.'" Then David arose and stealthily cut off the skirt of Saul's robe.* [5]*And afterward David's heart smote him, because he had cut off Saul's skirt.* [6]*He said to his men, "The* LORD *forbid that I should do this thing to my lord, the* LORD's *anointed, to put forth my hand against him, seeing he is the* LORD's *anointed."* [7]*So David persuaded his men with these words, and did not permit them to attack Saul. And Saul rose up and left the cave, and went upon his way.*

OVERVIEW: By hiding in a cave from Saul, David prefigured the hiddenness of the Lord's divinity in the incarnation (CASSIODORUS). Entering the cave, Saul prefigures the devil, who discharges corruption and filth into a world of imperfect light (JEROME). Exhibiting great forbearance in refusing to harm the Lord's anointed, David conquered his anger with reason and the fear of God (GREGORY OF NYSSA). That David was highly extolled for sparing the life of one man suggests greater blessing will be the reward of the one who liberates many from oppression (ENNODIUS). David exercised his authority to kill against his own anger, rather than against his persecutor (GREGORY OF NYSSA). David deeply revered the Lord's anointed because of the reality of the one Saul typified. Following David's example, a Christian judge must punish sin lovingly, exercising the office with healing, and not vengeance, as the goal (AUGUSTINE). By the grace of God David offered, as if a priest, an excellent sacrifice of gentleness and clemency in sparing Saul's life (CHRYSOSTOM). Although not practical at the time, David's virtuous act in sparing Saul became useful when he reigned: it inspired his subjects to loyalty (AMBROSE).

24:3 Saul Unknowingly Enters David's Hideout

THE CHARACTER OF THE LORD. CASSIODORUS: David, as we have said, took on the character of the Lord Savior, and so what was to take place at the Lord's passion is now recounted of him.

David was not to be effaced from the kingdom allotted to him, just as the inscription of the Lord's title could not be changed. The psalmist added, "When he fled from Saul into the cave."[1] This incident seems to be very similar in the cases of both David and the Lord. Just as David in fleeing from Saul hid in a cave, so the Lord Savior's divinity is known to have been hidden within the temple of his body from the unfaithful Jews. In this way the individual events concerning David and Christ are shared by them in this respect. EXPOSITION OF THE PSALMS 56.1.[2]

THE WORLD AND THE DEVIL. JEROME: Saul, unaware of David's hiding place, also entered the cave in order to take care of his needs, I presume.... Accordingly, this psalm of David[3] is accepted for certain in the name of the Lord; Saul appears as the devil, and the cave becomes this world. The devil, furthermore, does not discharge any good into this world, but only dung and corruption. Then, too, the cave symbolizes this world because its light is very imperfect when compared with the light of the future world, albeit the Lord, on coming into this world as light, brightens it up considerably. That is why the apostle, in relation to the Father, speaks of him "who is the brightness of his glory."[4] Now just as David entered the cave in his flight from Saul, the Lord, too, has come

---

[1]Ps 57:1 (56:1 LXX). [2]ACW 52:38. [3]Ps 142 (141 LXX). [4]See Heb 1:3.

into this world and has suffered persecution. Homilies on the Psalms 52 (Ps 141).[5]

24:4-5 David Cuts off a Piece of Saul's Robe

Trained in Forbearance. Gregory of Nyssa: When, therefore, he was alone and had removed his robe and laid it down somewhere beside him, the light from the mouth of the cave made him visible to those hidden within the darkness. All of David's companions wanted to rush upon the enemy and avenge themselves on the one who had come to kill them, since God had given the enemy into the hands of those who were being pursued for slaughter. But David forbade them to attack, considering an assault against their king unlawful. He drew his own sword from its sheath and imperceptibly stood behind Saul. There was no witness to his undertaking against Saul, for the darkness in the cave concealed his appearance and prevented scrutiny of what was happening. When, then, he could have driven his whole sword through Saul's heart from behind with one blow, he neither touched his body nor was he about to. But he secretly cut off the end of his robe with his sword, so that the garment might be a witness later of his clemency toward Saul and prove the power that he had had to strike a blow against Saul's body by means of the cut at its end.

By this it became obvious that David had been trained in forbearance. When he held the bare sword in his palm, and the body of his enemy lay under his hand, he had the power to kill him, but he conquered his anger with reason, and his power to strike the blow with the fear of God. Not only did he become superior to his own anger, but he also restrained his shield bearer who was eager to murder Saul, addressing him with that saying famous in song, "Destroy not the anointed of the Lord." On the Inscriptions of the Psalms 2.14.227-28.[6]

A Praiseworthy Act. Ennodius: You have grounds for complaint against the leaders of our people, since you are redeeming those whom they very often permitted to be taken captive or even themselves reduced to servitude.[7] Scripture gives us an example of singular praise when it extols David to the very skies because, having his enemy Saul in his power, he spared him, cutting off but the hem of his robe as evidence of both the opportunity that was his and of his loyalty. Good God, how munificently will You reward the deed of this man who now negotiates for the liberation of so many oppressed souls, you who have exalted David for sparing the life of a single man! Life of St. Epiphanius.[8]

The Authority to Kill. Gregory of Nyssa: This is why the coming together of Saul, who was in pursuit of murder, and of David, who was shunning murder, in the cave is described after many events which it had preceded. The authority to kill was reversed in this event, since the one who was being pursued for execution had authority over the slaughter of his killer, and although he had the right, so far as retribution against his enemy was concerned, he stayed his power so far as consisted with the right and killed his own anger in himself instead of his enemy. On the Inscriptions of the Psalms 2.14.224.[9]

Reverence for the Anointed One. Augustine: In the same way, Saul's kingdom foreshadowed one that should last forever, though he personally was reprobate and rejected. The very oil with which he was anointed (the chrism by token of which he was called a "Christ"[10]) must be understood symbolically as pointing to a profound mystery. David himself so religiously respected this anointed state that he was conscience-stricken when, in a dark cave where Saul had entered to ease himself, David came up, unseen, from behind and cut off a tiny piece of Saul's robe. David did this merely to have evidence later how he had spared Saul when he could have

---

[5]FC 48:374. [6]*GNTIP* 194-95*. [7]This is Epiphanius's response to a king who promises the release of Italian captives. [8]FC 15:337. [9]*GNTIP* 193. [10]Gk: "anointed one."

killed him, thus hoping to disabuse Saul of the idea which drove him implacably to pursue David as his foe. Nevertheless, David quaked with fear that perhaps merely by so touching Saul's garments he was guilty of sacrilege. . . . Such deep religious reverence was paid to this foreshadowing figure, not for what it was in itself but precisely because of the reality it typified. CITY OF GOD 17.6.[11]

24:6-7 David Persuades His Men Not to Harm Saul

JUDGE WITH LOVE. AUGUSTINE: As a Christian judge, you must play the part of a loving father, you must show anger for wrongdoing but remember to make allowance for human weakness; do not indulge your inclination to seek vengeance for the vile acts of sinners, but direct your effort to the cure of the sinners' wounds. . . . There is also that well-known example of forbearance on the part of holy David, when his enemy was delivered into his hands and he spared him, an example which shines with greater luster from the fact that he had power to act otherwise. Do not, then, let your power of punishment make you harsh, when the necessity of inquiry did not shake your spirit of mildness. LETTER 133.[12]

AN EXCELLENT SACRIFICE. CHRYSOSTOM: It was not without God's influence, you see, that he [David] succeeded in prevailing over those frenzied men [his soldiers who wished to kill Saul]: the grace of God was found on the inspired man's

lips, adding a sort of inducement to those words. It was, however, no slight contribution that David also made: since he had formed them in the past, consequently in the critical moment he found them ready and willing. It was not as leader of troops, you see, but as priest he commanded them, and that cave was a church on that occasion: like someone appointed as bishop, he delivered a homily to them, and after this homily he offered a kind of remarkable and unusual sacrifice, not sacrificing a calf, not slaying a lamb, but—what was of greater value than these—he offered to God gentleness and clemency, sacrificing irrational resentment, slaying anger and mortifying the limbs that are on the earth. He acted as victim, priest and altar: everything came from him—the thought that offered gentleness and clemency, the clemency and gentleness and the heart in which they were offered. HOMILIES ON DAVID AND SAUL 2.[13]

VIRTUE PREFERRED. AMBROSE: What a virtuous action that was, when David wished rather to spare the king his enemy, though he could have injured him! How useful, too, it was, for it helped him when he succeeded to the throne. For all learned to be faithful to their king and not to seize the kingdom but to fear and reverence him. Thus what is virtuous was preferred to what was useful, and then usefulness followed on what was virtuous. DUTIES OF THE CLERGY 3.9.60.[14]

---

[11]FC 24:41*. [12]FC 20:7-8. [13]COTH 1:27-28. [14]NPNF 2 10:77*.

24:8-15 DAVID REVEALS HIMSELF TO SAUL

[8]*Afterward David also arose, and went out of the cave, and called after Saul, "My lord the king!" And when Saul looked behind him, David bowed with his face to the earth, and did obei-*

sance. [9]And David said to Saul, "Why do you listen to the words of men who say, 'Behold, David seeks your hurt'? [10]Lo, this day your eyes have seen how the Lord gave you today into my hand in the cave; and some bade me kill you, but I[x] spared you. I said, 'I will not put forth my hand against my lord; for he is the Lord's anointed.' [11]See, my father, see the skirt of your robe in my hand; for by the fact that I cut off the skirt of your robe, and did not kill you, you may know and see that there is no wrong or treason in my hands. I have not sinned against you, though you hunt my life to take it. . . . [14]After whom has the king of Israel come out? After whom do you pursue? After a dead dog! After a flea! [15]May the Lord therefore be judge, and give sentence between me and you, and see to it, and plead my cause, and deliver me from your hand."

x Gk Syr Tg: Heb *you*

Overview: David emerged from the cave with heavenly spoils of mortified resentment and unnerved rage. In relation to Saul, he fulfills the apostolic law of honoring others above himself (Chrysostom). Like David, the one of excellent virtue fights against the passions, not the people of his own race (Gregory of Nyssa). The degree of one's exaltation to glory is paralleled to one's humility (Cassiodorus).

24:8-11 David Calls to Saul

Heavenly Trophies. Chrysostom: When he had offered this excellent sacrifice, then, achieved the victory and omitted nothing needed for a trophy, the cause of the problem, Saul, arose and left the cave, all unaware of what had gone on. "David also left behind him," looking in the direction of heaven with eyes now free of concern, and more satisfied on that occasion than when he had overthrown Goliath and cut off the savage's head. It was, in fact, a more conspicuous victory than the former one, the spoils more majestic, the booty more glorious, the trophy more commendable. In the former case he needed a sling, stones and battle line, whereas in this case thought counted for everything, the victory was achieved without weapons, and the trophy was erected without blood being spilt. He returned, therefore, bearing not a savage's head but resentment mortified and rage unnerved—spoils he deposited not in Jerusalem but in heaven and the city on high. Homi-

lies on David and Saul 2.[1]

A Rivalry of Respect. Chrysostom: So what did David reply? "Your servant, my lord the king." A contest and rivalry then developed as to which one would pay greater respect to the other: one admitted the other to kinship, the other called him lord. What he means is something like this: I am interested in one thing only, your welfare and the progress of virtue. You called me child, and I love and am fond of you if you have me as a servant, provided you set aside your resentment, provided you do not suspect me of any evil or think me to be scheming and warring against you. He fulfilled that apostolic law, note, that bids us excel ourselves in showing one another honor, unlike the general run of people, whose disposition is worse than beasts' and who cannot bear to be the first to greet their neighbor, having the view that they are shamed and insulted if they share a mere greeting with someone. Homilies on David and Saul 3.[2]

Fighting Against the Passions. Gregory of Nyssa: Saul, therefore, came out of the cave unaware of what had happened, wearing the little garment which had been trimmed all around. David came out behind him in self-assurance, and having seized the hill lying above the cave in advance, held out the end [of Saul's robe] in his

---

[1]COTH 1:28. [2]COTH 1:51*.

hand. This was nothing other than a bloodless trophy against his enemies. And he cried out to Saul in a loud voice and told him about this new and marvelous heroism, which was unstained by the defilement of blood, in which the hero was victorious and the one defeated was saved from death. For David's excellence is not attested in the fall of his enemy, but the superiority of his power is made clearer in the salvation of his opponent from danger. He had such an excess of confidence that he did not think that his own salvation lay in the destruction of those arrayed against him, but even when those who plotted against him survived he was confident that no one would harm him.

But the Word teaches rather by this story that the one who excels in virtue does not fight bravely against those of his own race but fights against the passions. The anger in both men, then, was destroyed by such excellence as David had, in the one, when he destroyed his own wrath by means of reason and quenched the urge to take vengeance, and in the other, when Saul put to death his evil against David because of the clem-

ency which he had experienced. For one can learn from the story itself the kind of things Saul uttered afterwards to the victor when he was submerged in shame for what he had undertaken and demonstrated his spontaneous turning away from evil by his lament and tears.[3] ON THE INSCRIPTIONS OF THE PSALMS 2.14.229-30.[4]

24:14 Whom Do You Pursue?

THE HUMBLEST FLEA. CASSIODORUS: The Creator compares himself to the lowest of his creatures so that you may regard nothing as despicable which is known to have been fashioned by his agency. As Scripture has it, "God made all things very good."[5] Thus David too followed his Teacher and compared himself with the humblest flea; for the real power of religion is that the more an individual humbles himself after the model of the Creator, the more splendidly he is exalted to glory. EXPOSITION OF THE PSALMS 21.7.[6]

---

[3]1 Sam 24:16-21. [4]*GNTIP* 194-95*. [5]See Gen 1:31. [6]ACW 51:220.

24:16-22 SAUL CONFESSES DAVID'S RIGHTEOUSNESS

[16]*When David had finished speaking these words to Saul, Saul said, "Is this your voice, my son David?" And Saul lifted up his voice and wept.* [17]*He said to David, "You are more righteous than I; for you have repaid me good, whereas I have repaid you evil.* [18]*And you have declared this day how you have dealt well with me, in that you did not kill me when the LORD put me into your hands.* [19]*For if a man finds his enemy, will he let him go away safe? So may the LORD reward you with good for what you have done to me this day."*

OVERVIEW: David's words penetrated Saul's mind and transformed his anger into affection (CHRYSOSTOM). Saul's confession of David's right-

eousness, typologically understood, represents the elect Jews' confession of Christ (BEDE). As Saul illustrates, envy is the most savage form of hatred because it responds to favors with an increase of hostility (BASIL).

24:16 Is This Your Voice, My Son David?

DRIVING OUT RESENTMENT. CHRYSOSTOM: What then did Saul say? Having heard David saying, "See, here is the corner of your cloak in my hand," and everything else by which he mounted his defense along with this, he said, "Is this your voice, my child David?" O, what a great change had suddenly taken place: the one who could never bear even to call him by name, and instead hated the very mention of it, even admitted him to kinship, calling him "child." What could be more blessed than David, who turned the murderer into a father, the wolf into a lamb, who filled the furnace of anger with heavy dew, turned the tempest into tranquility and allayed all the inflammation of resentment? Those words of David, you see, penetrated the mind of that enraged man and effected this total transformation, as you can see from those words. He did not even say, "Are these your words, my son David?" but "Is this your voice, my child David?" He was now heartened by his very utterance. Just as a father hears the voice of his son returning from somewhere and is excited not only at the sight of him but also at the sound of his voice, so Saul too, when David's words penetrated and drove out the hostility, now recognized him as holy, and in setting aside one passion he was affected by another. That is to say, by driving out resentment he was affected by benevolence and fellow feeling. HOMILIES ON DAVID AND SAUL 3.[1]

24:17-19 Saul Publicly Recognizes David's Innocence

A CONFESSION OF CHRIST. BEDE: While the Lord taught through his apostles, the people of the Jews—or those in their midst who were predestined to eternal life—lifted up their voice to confess the truth which they had up until recently denied and sought to bury. They wore away the contaminations of original sin as they cleansed themselves with their tears befitting repentance. They confessed both the justice and the kindness of the Lord and recalled the faults caused by their own malice, for they themselves had ferociously handed over to death the author of every kindness, but he had been given over to death unjustly, although he was omnipotent and wished to save his killers and give them life rather than to destroy them. FOUR BOOKS ON 1 SAMUEL 4.24.[2]

THE MOST SAVAGE HATRED. BASIL THE GREAT: Not even this act of benevolence moved Saul, however. Again he gathered an army and again he set out in pursuit, until he was a second time apprehended by David in the cave where he more clearly revealed his own iniquity and made the virtue of David even more resplendent.[3] Envy is the most savage form of hatred. Favors render those who are hostile to us for any other reason more tractable, but kind treatment shown to an envious and spiteful person only aggravates his dislike. The greater the favors he receives, the more displeased and vexed and ill-disposed he becomes. CONCERNING ENVY.[4]

---

[1]*COTH* 1:48-49. [2]*CCL* 119:228. [3]It appears that Basil has reversed the order of this account and David's sparing of Saul in 1 Samuel 26. [4]*FC* 9:467.

25:1-8 DAVID SENDS MEN TO NABAL

[1]Then David rose and went down to the wilderness of Paran. [2]And there was a man in Maon, whose business was in Carmel. The man was very rich; he had three thousand sheep and a thousand goats. He was shearing his sheep in Carmel. [3]Now the name of the man was Nabal, and the name of his wife Abigail. The woman was of good understanding and beautiful, but the man was churlish and ill-behaved; he was a Calebite.

OVERVIEW: Nabal typifies the teachers of the law while Abigail represents the synagogue, which wisely understood and carried out the word of faith (BEDE).

25:3 Nabal and Abigail

THE FOOLISH AND THE WISE. BEDE: Nabal means "fool" and Abigail means "father's joy." Foolish was anyone skilled in the law, who had the key to knowledge but did not himself enter and prevented from entering those who wanted to. But the synagogue is rightly called "the Father's joy," inasmuch as it is said, "Rejoice because your names are written in heaven."[1] For in such circumstances she was very wise to understand the word of faith and she was respectable to carry out what she understood, although her teachers were harsh because of their unbelief, evil because of their evil manner of living and wicked because of their plotting treachery against the Lord. FOUR BOOKS ON 1 SAMUEL 4.25.[2]

[1]Lk 10:20. [2]CCL 119:232.

25:9-22 NABAL'S REFUSAL PROVOKES DAVID

[14]But one of the young men told Abigail, Nabal's wife, "Behold, David sent messengers out of the wilderness to salute our master; and he railed at them. [15]Yet the men were very good to us, and we suffered no harm, and we did not miss anything when we were in the fields, as long as we went with them. . . .
[21]Now David had said, "Surely in vain have I guarded all that this fellow has in the wilderness, so that nothing was missed of all that belonged to him; and he has returned me evil for good. [22]God do so to David[y] and more also, if by morning I leave so much as one male of all who belong to him."

y Gk Compare Syr: Heb the enemies of David

OVERVIEW: David's rash swearing should not be imitated, even though it was reconsidered, because it is an instance of anger prevailing over reason (AUGUSTINE). Vows made carelessly should be broken if fulfilling them would be a greater crime (BEDE).

25:21-22 *David Swears to Avenge Himself*

Against Swearing Rashly. Augustine: Indeed, because David swore that he would kill Nabal and then in more considerate forbearance did not, shall we say that we should imitate him by swearing rashly that we are going to do what we see later ought not to be done? But, just as fear confounded the one [Lot] so that he was willing to prostitute his daughters,[1] so did anger confound the other [David] so as to swear rashly. In short, if it were permitted us to make inquiry and ask them both why they did these things, the one could reply, "Fear and trembling are come upon me: and darkness has covered me,"[2] and the other also could say, "My eye is troubled through indignation."[3] And so we would not be surprised that the one in the darkness of fear and the other in the indignation of his eye did not see what ought to have been seen so as not to do what ought not to have been done.

Indeed, to the righteous David we might with reasonable justice say that he ought not to have become angry, not even with an ingrate who returned evil for good. Even if anger crept upon him, as it does upon a man, at least it ought not to have prevailed so far that he swore to do what he would either do in rage or not do and be forsworn. Against Lying 9.21-22.[4]

Break the Careless Oath. Bede: If it should perhaps happen that we swear carelessly to something which, if carried out, would have most unfortunate consequences, we should know that we should willingly change it [in accord with] more salutary counsel. There is an urgent necessity for us to break our oath, rather than turn to another more serious crime in order to avoid breaking our oath. David swore by the Lord to kill Nabal, a stupid and wicked man, and to destroy all his possessions; but at the first entreaty of the prudent woman Abigail, he quickly took back his threats, put back his sword into its scabbard, and did not feel that he had contracted any guilt by thus breaking his oath in this way. Homilies on the Gospels 2.[5]

---

[1]Gen 19:8. [2]Ps 55:5 (54:5 LXX). [3]See Ps 6:7. [4]FC 16:148-49*. [5]CS 111:233.

25:23-35 ABIGAIL DISSUADES DAVID
FROM TAKING REVENGE

[23]*When Abigail saw David, she made haste, and alighted from the ass, and fell before David on her face, and bowed to the ground.* [24]*She fell at his feet and said, "Upon me alone, my lord, be the guilt; pray let your handmaid speak in your ears, and hear the words of your handmaid." . . .*

[32]*And David said to Abigail, "Blessed be the Lord, the God of Israel, who sent you this day to meet me!* [33]*Blessed be your discretion, and blessed be you, who have kept me this day from bloodguilt and from avenging myself with my own hand!* [34]*For as surely as the Lord the God of Israel lives, who has restrained me from hurting you, unless you had made haste and come to meet me, truly by morning there had not been left to Nabal so much as one male."* [35]*Then David received*

from her hand what she had brought him; and he said to her, "Go up in peace to your house; see, I have hearkened to your voice, and I have granted your petition."

Overview: The wise yet courageous intervention of Abigail saved David from a gross sin (Ambrose). As it is clear that David's rash swearing should not be imitated, it is equally clear that the correction of such a decision should be pursued (Cassian).

25:23-24 Abigail Bows Before David

Wise Intervention Restrains Sinful Impulses. Ambrose: But before this David had already held back his armed hand in his indignation. How much greater it is not to revile again, than not to avenge oneself! The warriors, too, [who] prepared to take vengeance against Nabal, Abigail restrained by her prayers. From this we perceive that we ought not only to yield to timely entreaties but also to be pleased with them. So much was David pleased that he blessed her who intervened, because he was restrained from his desire for revenge. Duties of the Clergy 21.94.[1]

25:34-35 David Relents

Altering Promises. John Cassian: Further, we are taught at considerable length by other texts of Scripture, too, that we neither should nor can fulfill everything that we decide upon whether with tranquil or upset mind. In them we frequently read that holy men or angels or even almighty God himself altered the things that they had promised. For blessed David determined with the promise of an oath and said, "May God do this and add more to the enemies of David if, of all that belongs to Nabal, I leave one male until morning." But when his wife, Abigail, interceded and entreated on his behalf, David immediately ceased his threats, softened his words, and preferred to be considered a transgressor of his own intention than to be true to his oath by cruelly carrying it out. And he said, "As the Lord lives, unless you had come quickly to meet me, there would not have been left to Nabal one male until the morning light." As we do not at all consider the promptness of his rash vow, which proceeded from an upset and disturbed mind, as something to be imitated, so likewise we judge that the cessation and correction of the thing that was decided on is to be pursued. Conference 17.25.5-6.[2]

---

[1]NPNF 2 10:17**. [2]ACW 57:606*.

25:36-44 DAVID MARRIES ABIGAIL

[36]*And Abigail came to Nabal; and lo, he was holding a feast in his house, like the feast of a king. And Nabal's heart was merry within him, for he was very drunk; so she told him nothing at all until the morning light.* [37]*And in the morning, when the wine had gone out of Nabal, his wife told him these things, and his heart died within him, and he became as a stone.* [38]*And about ten days later the Lord smote Nabal; and he died.*

³⁹*When David heard that Nabal was dead, he said, "Blessed be the LORD who has avenged the insult I received at the hand of Nabal, and has kept back his servant from evil; the LORD has returned the evil-doing of Nabal upon his own head." Then David sent and wooed Abigail, to make her his wife. ⁴⁰And when the servants of David came to Abigail at Carmel, they said to her, "David has sent us to you to take you to him as his wife." ⁴¹And she rose and bowed with her face to the ground, and said, "Behold, your handmaid is a servant to wash the feet of the servants of my lord." ⁴²And Abigail made haste and rose and mounted on an ass, and her five maidens attended her; she went after the messengers of David, and became his wife.*

⁴³*David also took Ahino-am of Jezreel; and both of them became his wives.*

OVERVIEW: Following Abigail's laudable example, correction should be offered when the mind is not intoxicated in order for it to be of any benefit (GREGORY THE GREAT). Nabal's death after insulting David, who delayed avenging himself, shows that God judges the events of this world (SALVIAN). The marital union of David and Abigail signifies the mystery of the union of the church of the Gentiles with Christ (AMBROSE).

25:36-38 Nabal Dies

THE TIME FOR CORRECTION. GREGORY THE GREAT: It is better, however, that in correcting these people we shun them when their anger is actually seething; for when they are aroused, they do not perceive what is being said to them. But when they have been restored to their senses, they the more willingly accept words of counsel, as they blush for having been peacefully borne with. For to the mind that is intoxicated with frenzy, everything said that is right appears to be wrong. Wherefore, Abigail laudably did not speak to Nabal about his sin when he was intoxicated, and as laudably told him of it when he became sober. For it was precisely because he did not hear of his fault when drunk that he was able to recognize it. PASTORAL CARE 3.16.[1]

25:39 David Blesses God for Avenging Him

ALL THINGS ARE RULED BY GOD. SALVIAN THE PRESBYTER: Having proved by Holy Scrip-

ture that all things are both watched and ruled by God, it remains now for me to show that most things in this world are judged by his divine power. When the holy David had borne the affronts and insults of Nabal from Carmel, because David delayed vengeance, he was avenged at once by the very hand of God. Shortly thereafter, when his enemy had been defeated and killed by the hand of God, David said, "Blessed be the Lord who has judged the cause of my reproach at the hand of Nabal." THE GOVERNANCE OF GOD 2.3.[2]

25:40-43 David Takes Two Wives

A MYSTERY SIGNIFIED BY A MARITAL UNION. AMBROSE: David had two wives, Ahinoam the Jezreelite, and Abigail, whom he took later. The first was somewhat severe, the other full of mercy and graciousness, a kindly and generous soul who saw the Father with face unveiled, gazing on his glory. She received that heavenly dew of the grace of the Father, as her name is interpreted. What is the dew of the Father but the Word of God, which fills the hearts of all with the waters of faith and justice?

Beautifully does the true David say to this soul what was said to Abigail: "Blessed be the Lord God of Israel, who sent you this day to meet me, and blessed be your customs." And again he says to her, "Go in peace into your house, behold now

---

[1]ACW 11:139. [2]FC 3:60*.

I have heard your voice and have honored your face." In the Canticles, too, these are the words of the bridegroom to his bride: "Show me your face and let me hear your voice."[3]

Then she was sent away, since she had another husband who was called, in Hebrew, Nabal, which, in Latin, means foolish, harsh, unkind, ungentle, ungrateful, for he did not know how to show gratitude. Later, when her husband died, David the prophet took her as his wife, since she

was set free from the law of her husband. Through this union is signified the mystery of the church of the Gentiles which would believe, for, after losing her husband to whom she was at first united, she made her way to Christ, bringing a dowry of piety, of humility and of faith, and enriched with the heritage of mercy. LETTER 74.[4]

---

[3]Song 2:14. [4]FC 26:421-22*.

[26:1-5 SAUL PURSUES DAVID IN THE WILDERNESS OF ZIPH]

26:6-12 DAVID SPARES SAUL'S LIFE A SECOND TIME

[6]*Then David said to Ahimelech the Hittite, and to Joab's brother Abishai the son of Zeruiah, "Who will go down with me into the camp to Saul?" And Abishai said, "I will go down with you." [7]So David and Abishai went to the army by night; and there lay Saul sleeping within the encampment, with his spear stuck in the ground at his head; and Abner and the army lay around him. [8]Then said Abishai to David, "God has given your enemy into your hand this day; now therefore let me pin him to the earth with one stroke of the spear, and I will not strike him twice." [9]But David said to Abishai, "Do not destroy him; for who can put forth his hand against the LORD's anointed, and be guiltless?" [10]And David said, "As the LORD lives, the LORD will smite him; or his day shall come to die; or he shall go down into battle and perish. [11]The LORD forbid that I should put forth my hand against the LORD's anointed; but take now the spear that is at his head, and the jar of water, and let us go." [12]So David took the spear and the jar of water from Saul's head; and they went away. No man saw it, or knew it, nor did any awake; for they were all asleep, because a deep sleep from the LORD had fallen upon them.*

OVERVIEW: Saul's hostility toward David was inspired by the favors he received from David's hand (Basil). It is through the merit of patience in bearing sorrow and suffering that the saints attain their heavenly crowns (CYPRIAN). David's decision to suffer ill patiently, rather than entering his king-

313

ship by satisfying his anger, inspires awe (Gregory of Nyssa). Unlike David, who persuaded his men with reason, rulers who force their will by decree demonstrate that their wisdom is corrupted (Athanasius). As repeated blows are required to chisel letters deeply into stone, so the Holy Spirit repeatedly recalls to mind the works of holy people of the past in order to dissuade ungodly behavior (Gregory of Nyssa).

26:7 David and Abishai Find Saul Asleep

Favors Inspire Hostility. Basil the Great: If Saul had been asked the reason for his hostility, he would have been compelled to admit that it was the favors received from David's hand. Moreover, even though Saul had been found asleep by David during the very time that the latter was being pursued, and although Saul lay, an easy victim, before his enemy, his life was again spared by that just man, for he refrained from doing him violence. Concerning Envy.[1]

26:8-11 David Refuses to Kill Saul

Patience in Sorrow. Cyprian: But what great and wonderful and Christian patience is to be found in David from whom Christ descended according to the flesh! David often had the opportunity to kill King Saul, his persecutor, who was eager to destroy him. Yet when Saul was subject to him and in his power, David preferred to save his life and did not retaliate on his enemy but, on the contrary, even avenged him when he was killed. In short, many prophets have been killed, many martyrs have been honored with glorious deaths, and all have attained their heavenly crowns through the merit of patience, for a crown for sorrow and suffering cannot be obtained unless patience in sorrow and suffering precede. The Advantage of Patience 10.[2]

Suffer Ill Patiently. Gregory of Nyssa: But this is marvelous not only for the fact that he grants life to the one who is doing everything

against his life, but because David, although he had been anointed to the office of king and knew that he would not otherwise partake of that position unless Saul were out of the way, judged it better to suffer ill patiently in his private low estate than to enter upon the kingship by satisfying his anger against the one who had caused him grief. On the Inscriptions of the Psalms 2.16.266.[3]

Godly versus Human Wisdom. Athanasius: For the truth is not preached with swords or with darts, nor by means of soldiers, but by persuasion and counsel. But what persuasion is there where fear of the emperor[4] prevails? Or what counsel is there, when he who withstands them receives at last banishment and death? Even David, although he was a king and had his enemy in his power, did not prevent the soldiers by an exercise of authority when they wished to kill his enemy, but, as the Scripture says, David persuaded his men by arguments, and did not allow them to rise up and put Saul to death. But [the devil], being without arguments of reason, forces all men by his power, that it may be shown to all that their wisdom is not according to God but merely human, and that they who favor the Arian doctrines have indeed no king but Caesar; for by his means it is that these enemies of Christ accomplish whatsoever they wish to do. History of the Arians 4.33.[5]

Reminders for Times of Misfortune. Gregory of Nyssa: After that, the opportunity to kill the enemy presented itself to him twice. Once in the cave Saul fell into David's hands unawares, and again in the tent when he was relaxed in sleep. David stood over him when he was asleep, and when he could have satisfied all his anger by murdering the one who pursued him, he did not lay a hand on him himself, and he said to the one eager for the kill, "Do not destroy." The

---

[1]FC 9:466-67. [2]FC 36:273. [3]GNTIP 207. [4]Constantius, son of Constantine. [5]NPNF 2 4:281*.

voice which prevents destruction in the case of this man is obviously the voice of God.

For this reason, just as those who produce the more notable inscriptions on stones cut the characters deeply by frequently applying the chisel with blows to the carving of the letters, so the Holy Spirit contrives, by means of continuous repetition, that this great saying may become more distinct and quite clear on the stela[6] of our memory, so that this inscription, having been carved in us distinctly and without confusion, might be known well in the time of misfortunes. For, in my opinion, the goal of the economy of the Holy Spirit is to set forth the previous accomplishments of holy ones for guidance for the life after these accomplishments, the representation

leading us forward to good which is equal and similar. For whenever the soul swells with revenge against someone who is provoking it, and the blood around the heart boils with anger against the one who has grieved the soul, then, when one has looked up at this stela which the Holy Spirit set up for David, and has read the word on it which David uttered on behalf of him who was eager for his own blood, he will not fail to calm the troubled thoughts in his soul and appease his passion by his desire to imitate the same things. On the Inscriptions of the Psalms 2.15.246-47.[7]

---

[6]An upright stone slab or pillar bearing an inscription or design.
[7]GNTIP 200-201*.

26:13-20 DAVID REVEALS HIMSELF TO ABNER

[13]*Then David went over to the other side, and stood afar off on the top of the mountain, with a great space between them;* [14]*and David called to the army, and to Abner the son of Ner, saying, "Will you not answer, Abner?" Then Abner answered, "Who are you that calls to the king?"* [15]*And David said to Abner, "Are you not a man? Who is like you in Israel? Why then have you not kept watch over your lord the king? For one of the people came in to destroy the king your lord.* [16]*This thing that you have done is not good. As the Lord lives, you deserve to die, because you have not kept watch over your lord, the Lord's anointed. And now see where the king's spear is, and the jar of water that was at his head."*

Overview: Bede explains the typological significance of the passage: David's call to Abner from the mountaintop signifies Jesus who, in his heavenly kingdom, preaches to people of Israel through the apostles. The question he utters foreshadows the loss of the Israelite kingdom and temple worship. Parallel is found between the experiences and the suffering of David and the Son of David as both were persecuted by envy (Ephrem).

26:13-14 David Calls to Abner

A Great Space Between Them. Bede: Jesus has passed from this world to his Father and remains upon the heights of his Father's kingdom, clearly out of human sight, where a great distance exists between him who sat at the right hand of God now that he in the flesh had become victorious over everlasting death, and those wretched mortals and godless ones of this world who labored to fight against him. Nonetheless, as he preached through his apostles, he called out to the people of Israel and to the experts in the law and forced them to rouse themselves from the slumber of their guilty indolence and to answer him by believing in him. Abner, whose name means "lamp of the father," points to those who ought to have imparted the light of the truth of that time to the people. His father, Ner, which means "lamp," alludes to their teachers who excelled in kindling the light of knowledge of the law in a spiritual fashion and in revealing to the ordinary teachers and to the people at large. FOUR BOOKS ON 1 SAMUEL 4.26.[1]

26:16 See Where the King's Spear Is

THE LOSS OF THE KINGDOM. BEDE: The apostles say, "Now look, where is the scepter of your kingdom? You lost it on earth, and you have ceased to hope to find it in heaven. Where is your contemplative keeping of the law, for which you wholeheartedly thirsted and by which you boasted that you could wash your hands of your deeds and purify them from every filth of sin?" . . . Although all these things had not yet fully taken place in the days of the apostles, nonetheless they had already begun in part, both in the time before the apostles and while they were still alive, as anyone who reads history can discover. Finally, among the countless disasters which Herod the Great and his sons brought upon the Jews, they took away the sacred garb from the priests, they did not grant the priests permission to minister in their sacred garb, and they gutted the rules of the law about the priesthood and changed them

in turn to fit their own pleasure. Pilate defiled the temple by bringing in the images of Caesar during the middle of the night. He was simply following Herod's example of godlessness, since Herod had earlier profaned the temple by affixing a golden eagle on it and ordered any pious individual who tried to remove it to be burned alive. Caligula ordered the temple itself to be profaned, as well as all their synagogues, by offering pagan sacrifices there. He ordered it to be filled with statues and images and commanded them to worship him as a god. There is no end to listing all these ways in which both the worship and the political power of the Jews were curtailed until at last they perished altogether. FOUR BOOKS ON 1 SAMUEL 4.26.[2]

PERSECUTED BY ENVY. EPHREM THE SYRIAN: Envy persecuted David, and jealousy the Son of David. David was blocked up in the depths of the cave, and the Son of David in the depths of the underworld. It was imagined that David was guilty and despised, and that death was conquered and laid low. David cried out, "Where is your spear, O King?" and the Son of David, "Where is your victory, O Death?"[3] Saul hurled his spear against David, and, although it did not strike him, the wall was witness to its blow.[4] The crucifiers struck the Son of David with a lance,[5] and although his power was not injured, his body was a witness to their blow. David was not struck, nor was the Son of David injured. COMMENTARY ON TATIAN'S DIATESSARON 21.12.[6]

---

[1]CCL 119:246. [2]CCL 119:246. [3]1 Cor 15:55. [4]See 1 Sam 18:10-11. [5]See Jn 19:34. [6]ECTD 323.

26:21-25 SAUL CONFESSES HIS SIN

[21]Then Saul said, "I have done wrong; return, my son David, for I will no more do you harm, because my life was precious in your eyes this day; behold, I have played the fool, and have erred exceedingly." [22]And David made answer, "Here is the spear, O king! Let one of the young men come over and fetch it. [23]The LORD rewards every man for his righteousness and his faithfulness; for the LORD gave you into my hand today, and I would not put forth my hand against the LORD's anointed."

OVERVIEW: David's repentance, contrition of heart and obedience to the will of God secured his mercy in the eyes of God (AUGUSTINE).

26:23 Not Touching the Lord's Anointed

DAVID'S HUMILITY AND REPENTANCE SURPASS HIS SINS. AUGUSTINE: In the case of David also, we read of both good and bad actions. But where David's strength lay, and what the secret of his success was, is sufficiently plain, not to the blind malevolence with which Faustus assails holy writings and holy men, but to pious discernment, which bows to the divine authority and at the same time judges human conduct correctly. The Manichaeans[1] will find, if they read the Scriptures, that God rebukes David more than Faustus does.[2] But they will read also of the sacrifice of his penitence, of his surpassing gentleness to his merciless and bloodthirsty enemy, whom David, pious as he was brave, dismissed unhurt when now and again he fell into his hands. They will read of his memorable humility under divine chastisement, when the kingly neck was so bowed under the Master's yoke, that he bore with perfect patience bitter taunts from his enemy, though he was armed and had armed men with him. And when his companion was enraged at such things being said to the king and was on the point of requiting the insult on the head of the scoffer, he mildly restrained him, appealing to the fear of God in support of his own royal order and saying that this bad happened to him as a punishment from God, who had sent the man to curse him. AGAINST FAUSTUS, A MANICHAEAN 22.66.[3]

---

[1]Manichaeans held the dualist view that good and evil were discrete yet equal forces that battled eternally. [2]2 Sam 12. [3]NPNF 1 4:297*.

27:1-12 DAVID ESCAPES TO PHILISTINE TERRITORY

[1]And David said in his heart, "I shall now perish one day by the hand of Saul; there is nothing better for me than that I should escape to the land of the Philistines; then Saul will despair of seeking me any longer within the borders of Israel, and I shall escape out of his hand." [2]So David arose

and went over, he and the six hundred men who were with him, to Achish the son of Maoch, king of Gath. ³And David dwelt with Achish at Gath, he and his men, every man with his household, and David with his two wives, Ahino-am of Jezreel, and Abigail of Carmel, Nabal's widow. ⁴And when it was told Saul that David had fled to Gath, he sought for him no more.

OVERVIEW: Caution is urged against viewing all potentates as enemies of Christianity since Israel's history reveals that many foreign kings proved to be the friends of the patriarchs (AUGUSTINE). Gath is figuratively understood as the winepress of affliction, which causes the church to pour forth the merits of its saints like nectar (CASSIODORUS).

27:1-3 David and His Men Flee to Gath

PROVED THEIR FRIENDS. AUGUSTINE: "What," you say, "have you to do with the kings of this world, in whom Christianity has never found anything save envy toward it?" Having said this, you endeavored to reckon up what kings the righteous had found to be their enemies, and [you] did not consider how many more might be enumerated who have proved their friends. The patriarch Abraham was both most friendly treated, and presented with a token of friendship, by a king who had been warned from heaven not to defile his wife.[1] Isaac his son likewise found a king most friendly to him.[2] Jacob, being received with honor by a king in Egypt, went so far as to bless him.[3] What shall I say of his son Joseph, who, after the tribulation of a prison, in which his chastity was tried as gold is tried in the fire, being raised by Pharaoh to great honors, even

swore by the life of Pharaoh[4]—not as though puffed up with vain conceit but being not unmindful of his kindness. The daughter of a king adopted Moses.[5] David took refuge with a king of another race, compelled thereto by the unrighteousness of the king of Israel. THE LETTERS OF PETILIAN, THE DONATIST 2.93.204.[6]

THE WINEPRESS OF GATH. CASSIODORUS: "When the Philistines held him in Gath"; this is recounted in the text of the book of Kings [Samuel]. David was terrorized by attacks of Saul and thought that he would be hidden in the city of Gath among the Philistines. But we have said that all this is to be explained as mystical allegory. Gath denotes "winepress," the squeezing which every Christian endures, but then he makes the harvest most abundant when he has been pressed by the rods of afflictions. So the church reasonably and appropriately speaks in this heading. Though weighed down by the persecutions of the Philistines, that is, by outsiders, [the church] pours forth the deserving merits of its saints with abundant freedom as though they were liquid nectar. EXPOSITION OF THE PSALMS 55.1.[7]

---

[1]Gen 20. [2]Gen 26:6-11. [3]Gen 47:1-7. [4]Gen 39—41. [5]Ex 2:10. [6]NPNF 1 4:579. [7]ACW 52:30*.

28:1-7 THE PHILISTINES PREPARE
TO ATTACK ISRAEL

[3]*Now Samuel had died, and all Israel had mourned for him and buried him in Ramah, his own city. And Saul had put the mediums and the wizards out of the land.*

OVERVIEW: Having no flattery in its portraits, Scripture shows David and Saul to be both praiseworthy and blameworthy (AUGUSTINE).

28:3 Saul Had Expelled Mediums and Wizards

A FAITHFUL MIRROR. AUGUSTINE: As has been said already, the sacred record, like a faithful mirror, has no flattery in its portraits and either itself passes sentence upon human actions as worthy of approval or disapproval or leaves the reader to do so. And not only does it distinguish people as blameworthy or praiseworthy, but it also takes notice of cases where the blameworthy deserved praise, and the praiseworthy blame. Thus, although Saul was blameworthy, it was not the less praiseworthy in him to examine so carefully who had eaten food during the curse and to pronounce the stern sentence in obedience to the commandment of God.[1] So, too, he was right in banishing those that had familiar spirits and wizards out of the land. And although David was praiseworthy, we are not called on to approve or imitate his sins, which God rebukes by the prophet.[2] AGAINST FAUSTUS, A MANICHAEAN 22.65.[3]

---

[1] Sam 14. [2] 2 Sam 12. [3] NPNF 1 4:296-97*.

28:8-14 SAUL CONSULTS A MEDIUM

[8]*So Saul disguised himself and put on other garments, and went, he and two men with him; and they came to the woman by night. And he said, "Divine for me by a spirit, and bring up for me whomever I shall name to you."* . . . [11]*Then the woman said, "Whom shall I bring up for you?" He said, "Bring up Samuel for me." [12]When the woman saw Samuel, she cried out with a loud voice; and the woman said to Saul, "Why have you deceived me? You are Saul." [13]The king said to her, "Have no fear; what do you see?" And the woman said to Saul, "I see a god coming up out of the earth." [14]He said to her, "What is his appearance?" And she said, "An old man is coming up; and he is wrapped in a robe." And Saul knew that it was Samuel, and he bowed with his face to the ground, and did obeisance.*

Overview: To suggest that Samuel was not brought up by a medium is tantamount to saying that the Scripture's record of history is not true. Since the Holy Spirit speaks the words recorded in Scripture, their veracity is assured. Brought up by a medium, Samuel demonstrates that the God of the patriarchs is the God of the living. Samuel's presence in hades, like Jesus', demonstrates that every place is in need of Christ (Origen). Given the power to deceive, the witch of Endor brought forth Satan, who was transformed into Samuel, a man of light (Tertullian). Since souls survive after death, as Samuel's return proves, people should strive to be good so that their souls don't fall under a wicked power (Justin Martyr). That the soul rises in the form of a body is indicated by Samuel's appearance (Methodius). While the soul extends or contracts itself to fit the body, it does not similarly adapt to clothing. Samuel's appearance in bodily form suggests that the mind inhabits another [spiritual] body when it leaves its material one (Augustine).

28:11 Whom Shall I Bring Up for You?

Under the Sway of a Demon. Origen: Is it not the case then, if such a great man was under the earth and the medium did bring him up, that a little demon has sway over the soul of the prophet? What can I say? These things are recorded. Is it true or is it not true? To say that it is not true drives us to unbelief. It comes down on the heads of those who speak it. But to say it is true presents for us an enquiry and quandary.

And we well know that some among our brothers look askance at the Scripture and say, I do not believe in the medium. The medium says that she saw Samuel. She is lying! Samuel was not brought up. Samuel does not speak. Just as there are false prophets who say, "Thus says the Lord," and "The Lord did not speak,"[1] so too this little demon lies when it proclaims that it brings up the one pointed out by Saul. For, "whom shall I bring up?" He says, "Bring up Samuel for me." These things are said by those who state that this history is not true. Homily on 1 Kings 28.2.2-3.[2]

The Holy Spirit Speaks. Origen: For what is it which has been written? "And the woman said, Whom shall I bring up for you?" Whose expression is the one which says, "The woman said"? Is it the expression of the Holy Spirit, from whom the Scripture is believed to be recorded, or is it the expression of someone else? For the narrative expression, as those involved with all sorts of words also know, is above all the expression of the author. And the author for all of these words has not been believed to be a human, but the author is the Holy Spirit who moves humans. Homily on 1 Kings 28.4.2.[3]

28:13 I See a God Coming Up out of the Earth

The God of the Living. Origen: They [the Jews] reflected on the death of Abraham and the prophets, understanding that Samuel, too, when he was under the earth because of death, was brought up by a medium who thought the gods were somewhere below the earth and who said, "I saw gods[4] ascending from the earth." They had not, however, comprehended the life of Abraham and the prophets, nor that the God of Abraham, Isaac and Jacob was not the God of them as men who were dead, but as men who were alive.[5] Commentary on the Gospel of John 20.393.[6]

Every Place Has Need of Christ. Origen: Samuel in hades! Samuel, he who was special among the prophets, who was dedicated to God from his birth,[7] who before his birth is said to be in the temple, who at the same time he was weaned was clothed with the ephod and double cloak and became a priest of the Lord,[8] the child to whom the Lord when he speaks uttered his messages, he was brought up by a medium? . . .

---

[1]See Jer 2:2, 23:17. [2]FC 97:320-21*. [3]FC 97:322*. [4]The LXX translates the Hebrew, which could signify "god" or "gods," as plural. [5]See Mt 22:32. [6]FC 89:286. [7]1 Sam 1:11. [8]1 Sam 1:22; 2:18-19.

Why is Samuel in hades? . . .

Samuel comes up, and note that she does not say that she saw the soul of Samuel. She does not say she saw a man. She has been scared by this thing which she saw. What did she see? "I saw gods," she says, "coming up from the earth." And perhaps Samuel has not only come up in order just to prophesy to Saul, but it is likely, just as here "with the holy he will be holy, and with an innocent man he will be innocent,"[9] and with the one of the chosen he will be as one of the chosen, and here the ways of the holy are with the holy but not with the sinners. And if then at some point the way of life of the holy is with the sinners for the purpose of saving the sinners, so perhaps also you may speculate whether either the holy souls of the other prophets in the coming up of Samuel come up together or perhaps whether they were angels of their spirits[10]—the prophet says, "the angel who speaks in me"[11]—or whether they were angels who came up together with the spirits. And every [place] is filled with those who need salvation, and "are they not all ministering spirits sent forth to serve for the sake of those who are to obtain salvation?"[12] Why do you fear to say that every place has need of Jesus Christ? Those who have need of Christ have need of the prophets. But if he has no need of Christ, he has no need of those who prepare for the appearance and dwelling of Christ. HOMILY ON 1 KINGS 28.3.2, 7.1.[13]

28:14 Samuel's Appearance Prompts Saul's Obeisance

THE POWER TO DECEIVE. TERTULLIAN: Why, even now the followers of Simon [Magus][14] are so confident of their art that they undertake to bring back the souls of the prophets from hell. And this, I believe, because their power lies in their ability to deceive. This power was actually granted to the witch of Endor, who brought back the soul of Samuel after Saul had consulted God in vain. Apart from that case, God forbid we should believe that any soul, much less a prophet,

could be called forth by a demon. We are told that "Satan himself is transformed into an angel of light"[15]—and more easily into a man of light—and that at the end he will work marvelous signs and show himself as God, so much so that, "if possible, he will deceive even the elect."[16] He hardly hesitated to declare to Saul that he was the prophet [Samuel] in whom the devil was then dwelling.

So, you must not think that the spirit which created the apparition was different from the one who made Saul believe in it; but, the same spirit was in the witch of Endor and in the apostate [Saul], and so it was easy for him to suggest the lie that he had already made Saul believe. Saul's treasure, indeed, was then where his heart was,[17] where God most certainly was not. Thus, he saw only the devil, through whom he believed he would see Samuel, for he believed in the spirit who showed him the apparition. ON THE SOUL 57.7-9.[18]

SOULS SURVIVE AFTER DEATH. JUSTIN MARTYR: That souls survive I have shown to you from the fact that the soul of Samuel was called up by the witch, as Saul demanded. It appears also that all the souls of similar righteous people and prophets fell under the dominion of such powers, which is certainly to be inferred from the very facts in the case of that witch. For this reason God, by his Son, also teaches us—for whose sake these things seem to have been done—always to strive earnestly and at death to pray that our souls may not fall into the hands of any such power.[19] DIALOGUE WITH TRYPHO 105.[20]

CLOTHED IN A BODY. METHODIUS: And, therefore, if we inquire regarding the "tongue," and the "finger," and "Abraham's bosom," and the reclining there, it may perhaps be that the soul receives a form similar in appearance to its earthly body in

---

[9]Ps 18:25 (17:25 LXX). [10]See 1 Pet 3:19. [11]Zech 1:9. [12]Heb 1:14. [13]FC 97:321, 327*. [14]Simon the sorcerer; see Acts 8. [15]2 Cor 11:14. [16]Mt 24:24. [17]Mt 6:21. [18]FC 10:305*. [19]Lk 23:46. [20]ANF 1:252*.

the change. If, then, any one of those who have fallen asleep is recorded as having reappeared, he is seen in the same way and in the form that he had when he was in the flesh. Besides, when Samuel appeared, it is clear that, being seen, he was clothed in a body; and this must especially be admitted, if we are pressed by arguments which prove that the essence of the soul is incorporeal and is manifested by itself. ON THE RESURREC-TION 3.2.19.[21]

THE SEMBLANCE OF A BODY. AUGUSTINE: Why, then, did the rich man in hell crave for the drop of water?[22] Why did holy Samuel appear after his death (as you have yourself noticed) clothed in his usual garments? Did the one wish to repair the ruins of the soul, as of the flesh, by the aliment of water? Did the other quit life with his clothes on him? Now in the former case there was a real suffering, which tormented the soul, but not a real body, such as required food. The latter might have seemed to be clothed, not as being a true body but a soul only, having the semblance of a body with clothing. For although the soul extends and contracts itself to suit the members

of the body, it does not similarly adapt itself to the clothes, so as to fit its form to them. ON THE SOUL AND ITS ORIGIN 4.29.[23]

ANOTHER BODY TO ANIMATE. AUGUSTINE: I see no objection to saying that each mind has another body [*sōma pneumatikos*] when it leaves this solid one, and so the mind always has a body to animate, and in it crosses over, if there is any place to which necessity compels it to go, since, indeed, the angels themselves cannot be enumerated if they are not counted by bodies, as truth itself says in the Gospel: "I could ask my Father to send me twelve legions of angels";[24] and also since it is evident that Samuel was seen in the body when he was raised by the incantation of Saul, and since it is clear, according to the Gospel, that Moses, whose body was buried, came to the Lord on the mount when they stood together.[25] LETTER 158.[26]

---

[21]ANF 6:377*. [22]Lk 16:24. [23]NPNF 1 5:367*. [24]Mt 26:53. [25]Mt 17:3. [26]FC 20:358*.

28:15-25 SAMUEL PROPHESIES SAUL'S DEMISE

[15]*Then Samuel said to Saul, "Why have you disturbed me by bringing me up?" Saul answered, "I am in great distress; for the Philistines are warring against me, and God has turned away from me and answers me no more, either by prophets or by dreams; therefore I have summoned you to tell me what I shall do."* [16]*And Samuel said, "Why then do you ask me, since the LORD has turned from you and become your enemy?* [17]*The LORD has done to you as he spoke by me; for the LORD has torn the kingdom out of your hand, and given it to your neighbor, David.* [18]*Because you did not obey the voice of the LORD, and did not carry out his fierce wrath against Amalek, therefore the LORD has done this thing to you this day.* [19]*Moreover the LORD will give Israel also with you into the hand of the Philistines; and tomorrow you and your sons shall be with me; the LORD will give the army of Israel also into the hand of the Philistines."*

Overview: Samuel's presence in hades, like Christ's, in no way diminishes his holiness or purpose (Origen). His appearance and predictions regarding Saul's future show that some from the dead may be sent to the living (Augustine). Demons are incapable of prophesying God's great mysteries (Origen). The one who lets the guilty go unpunished despises God's judgment and urges the innocent to commit crimes (Ennodius).

28:15 Why Have You Disturbed Me?

The Holy Descended into Hades. Origen: If the prophets, the forerunners of Christ, all went down into hades before the Christ, so too Samuel has gone down there. For he does not merely go down, but he goes down as a holy man. Wherever the holy man may be, he is holy. Is Christ no longer Christ, since he was once in hades? Was he no longer Son of God, since he existed in an underworld place, "that every knee should bow in the name of Jesus Christ in heaven and on earth and under the earth"?[1] So, Christ was Christ even when he was below; that is to say, while he was in the place below, he was above in purpose. So too, the prophets and Samuel, even if they go down below where the souls are, they are able to be in a place below, but they are not below in purpose. Homily on 1 Kings 28.8.1.[2]

28:17-19 The Prophecies Concerning Saul

Visits from the Dead. Augustine: Also, some can be sent to the living from the dead, just as in the opposite direction divine Scripture testifies that Paul was snatched from the living into paradise.[3] Samuel the prophet, although dead, predicted future events to King Saul, who was alive, although some think that it was not Samuel himself who was able to be called forth by some magic, but that some spirit so allied with evil works had feigned a likeness to him—yet the book of Ecclesiasticus, which Jesus the son of Sir-

ach is said to have written, but because of some similarity of style is thought to be the work of Solomon, contains in praise of the fathers the fact that Samuel prophesied even though dead.[4] If there is objection to this book on the ground that it is not in the canon of ancient Hebrew Scripture, what are we going to say of Moses, who in Deuteronomy is certainly recorded as dead and again in the Gospel of Matthew is reported to have appeared to the living along with Elijah who did not die.[5] The Care to Be Taken for the Dead 15.18.[6]

Prophecy and Demons. Origen: Is a little demon capable of prophesying concerning the entire people of God that the Lord is about to deliver Israel? . . .

Can also a little demon know this, that after a king has been appointed with the anointing oil of a prophet, that tomorrow Saul and his sons with him will forfeit their lives? . . .

But I cannot give to a little demon such a great power that he can prophesy concerning Saul and the people of God and he can prophesy concerning David that he will become king. Homilies on 1 Kings 5.5, 5.8.[7]

28:18 Because You Did Not Obey the Lord

Letting the Guilty Go Unpunished. Ennodius: The need of severe measures tends to crush all gentleness and compassion of heart. The testimony of Scripture supports my assertion. We read that a sovereign sinned who spared an enemy appointed by heaven to be slain. His leniency brought upon him the penalty which his severity should have inflicted upon another. He who refuses to take vengeance, himself becomes its victim. He who, having an enemy in his power, pardons him, either makes light of or despises the weight of God's judgment. Rightly do they suffer punishment who have done wrong.

---

[1]Phil 2:10. [2]FC 97:329-30*. [3]See 2 Cor 12:2. [4]See Sir 46:16-20. [5]See Deut 34:5; Mt 17:3. [6]FC 27:377*. [7]FC 97:324-25, 330.

He who pardons present faults transmits them to posterity. As for . . . the patience of our Redeemer —mercy and grace embrace those whom the severity of the law forms. Never has a doctor restored a sick person to perfect health without first cutting away the putrid members and draw-ing out the filth hidden deep within. He who lets the guilty go unpunished urges the innocent to commit crimes.[8] LIFE OF ST. EPIPHANIUS.[9]

---

[8]In this portion of the dialogue, King Theodoric speaks to Epiphanius.
[9]FC 15:334-35*.

29:1-11 DAVID IS REMOVED FROM THE PHILISTINE RANKS

[2]As the lords of the Philistines were passing on by hundreds and by thousands, and David and his men were passing on in the rear with Achish, [3]the commanders of the Philistines said, "What are these Hebrews doing here? . . . [5]Is not this David, of whom they sing to one another in dances,

'Saul has slain his thousands,

and David his ten thousands'?"

[6]Then Achish called David and said to him, "As the LORD lives, you have been honest, and to me it seems right that you should march out and in with me in the campaign; for I have found nothing wrong in you from the day of your coming to me to this day. Nevertheless the lords do not approve of you. [7]So go back now; and go peaceably, that you may not displease the lords of the Phil-istines."

OVERVIEW: The Philistines' disdain for the Hebrews signifies the attitude of pagans toward Christians. Words that celebrate David's deeds, like the church's praises of Christ's faithfulness, evoke anger and fear in each one's enemies. Like Achish, who sent David on his way after confessing his uprightness, Gentile Christians praise Christ but resist entrusting the word to powerful pagans lest it result in persecution (BEDE).

29:3 What Are These Hebrews Doing Here?

PAGANS DESPISE PILGRIMS. BEDE: The pagans despise the life, fellowship and teaching of those who believe in Christ, who are rightly called Hebrews, that is, "pilgrims." For they know to pass over at the present time from vices to vir-tues, and in the future they hope to pass over from death to life. Looking from the summit of their heavenward mind, they know how to tran-scend the base desires of fleshly things and all the hostilities of the world. FOUR BOOKS ON 1 SAM-UEL 4.29.[1]

29:5 The Philistines Recall David's Valor for Israel

PRAISE EVOKES ANGER. BEDE: As the church among the Gentiles praises the faithfulness of

---

[1]CCL 119:259.

Christ through which it is awarded eternal life, the philosophers and high priests of idols are angered and fear to entrust themselves to him. They grieve that their own civilization and wisdom was destroyed by his word. They see clearly that the choir of the holy church celebrates his great triumph over the ancient enemy—a triumph such as no one else has ever been able to accomplish. As they come to understand the faith, they refuse to unite themselves to the members of Christ and refuse to submit themselves to his authority. Four Books on 1 Samuel 4.29.[2]

29:6 Achish Dismisses David

Praise and Persecution. Bede: Achish himself confesses that David was upright, innocent and good, like an angel of God, but he ordered him to depart from the battleline of the Philistines and to go his way in peace, since Achish did not wish to offend the princes of the Philistines. The throng of the faithful among the Gentiles praises, loves and proclaims the righteousness, mercy and holiness of Christ, since he had been sent by God to save the Gentiles. But they beg not to be forced to entrust the word to blasphemers, arrogant people and notorious idolaters, lest by chance they hear something and refuse to believe it and bring greater judgment against them. They ask their Lord, as it were, that he be content to rest in the peaceful and calm heart of the believers rather than to offer to the unbelievers an opportunity to persecute them as these opponents stir up trouble. Four Books on 1 Samuel 4.29.[3]

---

[2]CCL 119:259. [3]CCL 119:259.

30:1-10 DAVID RETURNS TO A PLUNDERED ZIKLAG

[1]*Now when David and his men came to Ziklag on the third day, . . . *[3]*they found it burned with fire, and their wives and sons and daughters taken captive.* [4]*Then David and the people who were with him raised their voices and wept, until they had no more strength to weep.*

Overview: Bede draws a parallel between David's weeping at finding Ziklag plundered to that of teachers who lament for those whose simple faith has been corrupted.

30:3-4 David and His Company Weep

Lamenting the Corruption of Faith. Bede: When the Lord came among his elect and the catholic teachers and saw the towers and roofs which once gleamed but now lay razed to the ground by the firebrand of heretical talk, he first moved his father with his prayers that the church be restored (as was fitting for him to do) and then he immediately attended to the undertaking of restoring it. The teachers lament the churches and souls entrusted to them, which they had begotten for God and nourished by the help but which had become corrupted from the simplicity of their faith when Christ's help was delayed for a time. This corresponds to how David's wives and children were led away captive, when his arrival was delayed for a time. But if his grace and aid had been present, they would not

have been able to seize everything. Four Books on 1 Samuel 4.30.[1]

---

[1]CCL 119:261.

30:11-20 DAVID OVERTAKES THE AMALEKITES

[11]They found an Egyptian in the open country, and brought him to David; and they gave him bread and he ate, they gave him water to drink, [12]and they gave him a piece of a cake of figs and two clusters of raisins. And when he had eaten, his spirit revived; for he had not eaten bread or drunk water for three days and three nights. [13]And David said to him, "To whom do you belong? And where are you from?" He said, "I am a young man of Egypt, servant to an Amalekite; and my master left me behind because I fell sick three days ago. [14]We had made a raid upon the Negeb of the Cherethites and upon that which belongs to Judah and upon the Negeb of Caleb; and we burned Ziklag with fire." [15]And David said to him, "Will you take me down to this band?" And he said, "Swear to me by God, that you will not kill me, or deliver me into the hands of my master, and I will take you down to this band."

[16]And when he had taken him down, behold, they were spread abroad over all the land, eating and drinking and dancing, because of all the great spoil they had taken from the land of the Philistines and from the land of Judah. [17]And David smote them from twilight until the evening of the next day; and not a man of them escaped, except four hundred young men, who mounted camels and fled.

Overview: David's encounter with the Egyptian servant is interpreted allegorically as the conversion of an outcast who is renewed by Christ (Gregory the Great) or as the experience of a person who escapes away from heretics to the church (Bede).

30:11-17 An Egyptian Servant

An Allegory of Conversion. Gregory the Great: The poor and the feeble, the blind and the lame, are called and come because the weak and the despised in this world are often quicker

to hear the voice of God, as in this world they have nothing to delight them.

The Egyptian servant of the Amalekites is a good example of this. When the Amalekites were plundering and moving about, he was left behind on the road sick and fainting from hunger and thirst. When David found him, he provided him with food and drink, and as soon as he revived he became David's guide, found the celebrating Amalekites, and with great bravery overthrew the people who had left him behind sick.

Amalekite means "a people that laps." What does "a people that laps" signify but the hearts of the worldly? Going about after the things of earth, it is as if they are lapping them up when they take delight in temporal things alone. A lapping people takes plunder, so to speak, when out of its love for earthly things it heaps up profit from others' losses. The Egyptian servant is left behind on the road sick, because all sinners, once they begin to grow weak from the situation of this world, soon come to be despised by worldly minds. David found him and provided him with food and drink, because the Lord, who is "brave in hand" (if we attribute to him the meaning of David's name), does not despise what the world has cast aside. Often he directs to the grace of his love those who are not strong enough to follow the world, and who are, so to speak, left behind on the road, holding out to them the food and drink of his word. It is as if he chooses them as guides for himself on the road when he makes them his preachers. When they bring Christ to the hearts of sinners, it is as if they are leading David upon the enemy, and, like David, they strike the celebrating Amalekites with the sword, because by the Lord's power they overthrow all the proud who had despised them in the world. Forty Gospel Homilies 36.[1]

Escaping from Heretics. Bede: It is a rule of the church to ask through its teachers about those who escape from the heretics and flee to it. They ask who they were before, what they

thought about the faith, where they will travel in spirit in the future and when they recognized that they opposed the heresies with all their mind and began to approve of the catholic faith. Then, once they have been reconciled, the church applies to them the sacraments of the catholic faith. This procedure is followed so that they may not seem to cast what is holy to the dogs or pearls before swine. The church asks, "To whom did you listen and from what body of Christians or to which body of Christians did you arrange to come?" Whoever truly wishes to escape the snares of the heretics must answer, "I confess that I was concealed in sins, sold to the heretics as I listened to them. But my teacher abandoned me, after he had filled me with his errors. When the heretics were waging war against the church, my teacher saw that I was less suitable for this battle because of some defect in my tongue or talent. He did not want, moreover, to take me with him into such a great conflict, inasmuch as we had sallied forth from the south, that is, from the light, had promised that our doctrine was complete and vivifying through the breath of the Holy Spirit, had led not a few Gentiles into our sect and had disturbed the very faith of the church in large measure." Four Books on 1 Samuel 4.30.[2]

---

[1]CS 123:318-19. [2]CCL 119:263-64.

30:21-31 THE DIVISION OF THE SPOIL

[21]*Then David came to the two hundred men, who had been too exhausted to follow David, and who had been left at the brook Besor; and they went out to meet David and to meet the people who were with him; and when David drew near to the people he saluted them.* [22]*Then all the wicked and base fellows among the men who had gone with David said, "Because they did not go with us, we will not give them any of the spoil which we have recovered, except that each man may lead*

away his wife and children, and depart." [23]*But David said, "You shall not do so, my brothers, with what the LORD has given us; he has preserved us and given into our hand the band that came against us.* [24]*Who would listen to you in this matter? For as his share is who goes down into the battle, so shall his share be who stays by the baggage; they shall share alike."*

OVERVIEW: Unity within the community is based upon the equal treatment of its members (HORSIESI).

30:21-24 All Receive a Share of the Spoils

A LIKE MEASURE FOR ALL. HORSIESI: Let there be no special food for anyone working in the kneading room. Let the food be the same for everyone, for those who bake and those who are appointed to any task, in accordance with what was established from the beginning by the father of the *koinōnia*, Apa, to whom God entrusted this great calling. If other fathers who have succeeded him have made canons granting special food to the bakers, they did so after Moses' manner, as we have learned in the Gospel that says, "Because of your hardness of heart, Moses has allowed you to repudiate your wives, but in the beginning it was not like this."[1] If, for some light fatigue, a man separates himself from his brother and differs from him in his food more than do those who are to leave for the harvest or for any other task at which they will have to endure the heat, let us not allow the brothers who have been appointed for any other task in the community to eat with these, since they have not set out to endure the heat and to work strenuously.

On the contrary, the unity of the *koinōnia* consists in a like measure for all, according to the saints' way of doing; thus David approached those who had not gone to war and spoke to them peacefully, giving them a share of the spoils equal to that received by those who had gone to war with him. He did not listen to those who were wicked and said, "We will not share with them." The Lord taught us likewise in the Gospel by the parable, when those who had "borne the weight of the day and the heat murmured, saying, 'Why have you treated us like those who have worked only an hour?'"[2] They, too, heard the reproach, "Is your eye evil because I am good?"[3] REGULATIONS 2.48.[4]

---

[1]Mt 19:8. [2]Mt 20:11-12. [3]Mt 20:15. [4]CS 48:214-15*.

31:1-13 SAUL, HIS SONS AND HIS ARMY PERISH

[1]*Now the Philistines fought against Israel; and the men of Israel fled before the Philistines, and fell slain on Mount Gilboa.* [2]*And the Philistines overtook Saul and his sons; and the Philistines slew Jonathan and Abinadab and Malchishua, the sons of Saul.* [3]*The battle pressed hard upon Saul, and the archers found him; and he was badly wounded by the archers.* [4]*Then Saul said to his armor-bearer, "Draw your sword, and thrust me through with it, lest these uncircumcised come and thrust me through, and make sport of me." But his armor-bearer would not; for he feared greatly. Therefore Saul took his own sword, and fell upon it.*

Overview: The Philistines' overtaking of Saul and his sons illustrates the corruptive power of heresies (Bede). Saul was struck by the spiritual arrows of the Lord (Verecundus). Saul's armor bearer mystically represents the teachers of the law whose weapons are the words of spiritual teaching (Bede).

31:2 The Philistines Overtook Saul and His Sons

The Master of Corruption. Bede: The nations that surrounded Judah rushed in with the sole intention of destroying the kingdom of Judah and of removing the sons of the kingdom from its midst. So too with their corruption they corrupted the high priests, scribes and Pharisees—and even the heretics. They forbade the sons of the kingdom (certainly, a reference to the leaders of that kingdom) from preaching or worshiping the grace of the Holy Spirit in their sincere heart. That is the meaning of their striking down Jonathan, "the gift of the dove." They forbade praising the Father through a worthy confession, who made us his sons not by nature but by adoption. The death of Abinadab pointed to this, for his name means "Father of his own volition." They resisted so that they would not believe in the salvation that was coming into the world through Christ's kingdom. The death of Malchishua pointed to this, since his name means "My king is my salvation." I believe that the philosopher who seduced Arius[1] killed Malchishua, as it were, just as the one who seduced Macedonius[2] killed Jonathan, and the one who seduced Mani[3] killed Abinadab. I say that because the master of corruption taught Arius to deny the omnipotence of Christ the king, Macedonius to detract from the gift of the Holy Spirit, and Mani to blaspheme the goodness of our great God. Four Books on 1 Samuel 4.31.[4]

31:3 Saul Badly Wounded

Arrows of the Lord. Verecundus: "I will inebriate my arrows with blood, and my sword will devour flesh."[5] These are the spiritual arrows of the Lord with which he strikes the heart of the human race and drains our spiritual blood. For just as Christ himself is called an arrow, chosen by the hand of the Father,[6] so also his apostles are named arrows metaphorically, whom his powerful bow dispersed throughout the entire breadth of the world. Perhaps Jonathan shot the same arrows as a sign that David should flee from the hand of his cruel king.[7] And Saul was struck by these very arrows, that such an obviously worthless king would be deprived of the Israelite kingdom. These are the arrows that drink the blood of our infidelity and carnal sins, for which reason it is said concerning them: "They will eat the sins of my people."[8] Commentary on the Ecclesiastical Canticles, On Deuteronomy 43.[9]

31:4 Saul Commands His Armor Bearer to Strike Him

Words of Spiritual Teaching. Bede: The armor bearer of Saul represents the teachers of the law, for just as the arms and arrows of the Philistines are the deceptions of depraved people, so in contrast the arms of the Israelites cannot be understood in any other way other than to refer mystically to the words of spiritual teaching by which the people of God ought to have protected themselves from all dangers. But when Saul had been wounded by the archers and was at the point of despair, he preferred to die by the sword of his armor bearer than by the sword of the uncircumcised. The chiefs of the kingdom of the Jews, once they had spent the course of their life in their sins and being at the point of death, preferred to perish as their teachers set aside the commandments of the law and taught them to do

---

[1]Arius was a priest from Alexandria, Egypt, who taught that Christ was not fully divine. [2]Macedonius was an Arian bishop of Constantinople. He is said to have denied the divinity of the Holy Spirit. [3]Mani was the founder of Manichaeism, a Gnostic religion. He taught an extreme form of dualism. [4]CCL 119:267. [5]Deut 32:42. [6]See Is 49:2. [7]See 1 Sam 20:35-42. [8]Hos 4:8. [9]CCL 93:61.

the same rather than to perish by consorting with the Gentiles and so defiling themselves, since they called the Gentiles profane and unclean. At last they feared even to enter the governor's residence "so that they might not be contaminated but be able to eat the Passover."[10] To be sure, that Passover ended up harming them by the very law which they had accepted, for they did not fear to contaminate that Passover with the blood of an innocent man. FOUR BOOKS ON 1 SAMUEL 4.31.[11]

---

[10]Jn 18:28. [11]CCL 119:268.

2 SAMUEL

[1:1-10 DAVID LEARNS OF SAUL'S DEATH]

1:11-16 DAVID ORDERS THE AMALEKITE'S DEATH

¹¹*Then David took hold of his clothes, and rent them; and so did all the men who were with him;* ¹²*and they mourned and wept and fasted until evening for Saul and for Jonathan his son and for the people of the LORD and for the house of Israel, because they had fallen by the sword.* ¹³*And David said to the young man who told him, "Where do you come from?" And he answered, "I am the son of a sojourner, an Amalekite."* ¹⁴*David said to him, "How is it you were not afraid to put forth your hand to destroy the LORD's anointed?"* ¹⁵*Then David called one of the young men and said, "Go, fall upon him." And he smote him so that he died.* ¹⁶*And David said to him, "Your blood be upon your head; for your own mouth has testified against you, saying, 'I have slain the LORD's anointed.'"*

Overview: David went beyond the law's command to pay back one's enemies in kind by mourning and avenging the death of Saul, his persecutor (CASSIAN). In the absence of laws that command taking a life, killing another is unlawful, even if done out of mercy (AUGUSTINE). Saul was the cause of his own death (JEROME).

1:14-16 David Orders the Death of the Amalekite

BEYOND THE PRECEPTS OF THE LAW. JOHN CASSIAN: We know that David went beyond the precepts of the law when, despite Moses' command to pay back one's enemies in kind, he not only did not do this but even embraced his persecutors in love, prayed devoutly to the Lord on their behalf, even wept mournfully for them and revenged them when they were slain. CONFERENCE 21.4.2.[1]

ON KILLING ANOTHER. AUGUSTINE: But when no laws or lawful authorities give command, it is not lawful to kill another, even if he wishes and asks for it and has no longer the strength to live, as is clearly proved by the Scripture in the book of Kings [Samuel], where King David ordered the slayer of King Saul to be put to death,

---

[1]ACW 57:720.

although he said that he had been importuned by the wounded and half-dead king to kill him with one blow and to free his soul struggling with the fetters of the body and longing to be released from those torments. LETTER 204.[2]

THE CAUSE OF HIS OWN DEATH. JEROME: Hence, "his blood will come upon him,"[3] that is, he will be the cause of his own death, according to which principle David said to the one who had announced Saul's death and had related that the king of Israel fell on his own sword: "Your blood be upon your head." Not by my sentence, but by the blood of Saul will your blood be spilled. COMMENTARY ON HOSEA 3.12.[4]

---

[2]FC 32:6*. [3]Hos 12:14. [4]CCL 76:140.

1:17-27 DAVID LAMENTS OVER SAUL AND JONATHAN

[17]*And David lamented with this lamentation over Saul and Jonathan his son . . .*
    [19]*"Thy glory, O Israel, is slain upon thy high places!*
        How are the mighty fallen!
    [20]*Tell it not in Gath,*
        publish it not in the streets of Ashkelon;
    lest the daughters of the Philistines rejoice,
        lest the daughters of the uncircumcised exult.

    [21]*"Ye mountains of Gilboa,*
        let there be no dew or rain upon you,
        nor upsurging of the deep![c]
    For there the shield of the mighty was defiled,
        the shield of Saul, not anointed with oil. . . .

    [25]*"How are the mighty fallen*
        in the midst of the battle!

    "Jonathan lies slain upon thy high places.
    [26]*I am distressed for you, my brother Jonathan;*
        very pleasant have you been to me;
            your love to me was wonderful,
            passing the love of women.

^{27}*"How are the mighty fallen,*
and the weapons of war perished!"

c Cn: Heb *fields of offerings*

OVERVIEW: As David desired to keep the news of
Saul's death from enemy ears, so Christians must
resist spreading news of another's failure or
downfall (CHRYSOSTOM). David's curse upon the
mountains of Gilboa demonstrates his profound
lamentation for Saul's death. Furthermore, it illustrates how nature testifies to the severe punishment awaiting the guilty (AMBROSE). The
mutual love of Jonathan and David, lamented at
Jonathan's death, characterized a wonderful and
exemplary friendship (CHRYSOSTOM).

1:20 Tell It Not in Gath

ON SPREADING RUMORS. CHRYSOSTOM: You
have heard David's lament for Saul. . . . If David
did not wish the matter paraded in public so that
it might not be a source of joy to his foes, so
much the more must we avoid spreading the story
to alien ears. Rather, we must not spread it even
among ourselves for fear that our enemies may
hear it and rejoice, for fear that our own may
learn of it and fall. We must hush it up and keep
it guarded on every side. Do not say to me, "I told
so-and-so." Keep the story to yourself. If you did
not manage to keep quiet, neither will he manage
to keep his tongue from wagging. DISCOURSES
AGAINST JUDAIZING CHRISTIANS 8.4.10.[1]

1:21 Let There Be No Dew or Rain

THE CONDEMNATION OF THE ELEMENTS.
AMBROSE: Nature, therefore, by withholding its
gifts from those places which were to be witnesses of a parricidal act and by its condemnation
of innocent soil, makes clear to us the severity of
the future punishments of the guilty. The very
elements are, therefore, condemned because of
the crime of people. Hence David condemned the
mountains, in which Jonathan and his father were

slain, to be punished with perpetual sterility, saying, "You mountains of Gilboa, let neither dew
nor rain come upon you, mountains of death."
CAIN AND ABEL 2.8.26.[2]

HOW ARE THE MIGHTY FALLEN. AMBROSE:
What a virtuous action was that when David
wished rather to spare the king his enemy, though
he could have injured him![3] How useful, too, it
was, for it helped him when he succeeded to the
throne. For all learned to observe faith in their king
and not to seize the kingdom but to fear and reverence him. Thus, what is virtuous was preferred to
what was useful, and then usefulness followed
from what was virtuous. But that he spared him
was a small matter; he also grieved for him when
slain in war and mourned for him with tears, saying, "You mountains of Gilboa, let neither dew nor
rain fall upon you; you mountains of death, for
there the shield of the mighty is cast away, the
shield of Saul. It is not anointed with oil but with
the blood of the wounded and the fat of the warriors. The bow of Jonathan turned not back, and
the sword of Saul returned not empty. Saul and
Jonathan were lovely and very dear, inseparable in
life, and in death they were not divided. They were
swifter than eagles, they were stronger than lions.
You daughters of Israel, weep over Saul, who
clothed you in scarlet with your ornaments, who
put on gold upon your apparel. How are the
mighty fallen in the midst of the battle! Jonathan
was wounded even to death. I am distressed for
you, my brother Jonathan; very pleasant have you
been to me. Your love came to me like the love of
women. How have the mighty fallen and the
longed-for weapons perished!" What mother could
weep thus for her only son as he wept here for his
enemy? Who could follow his benefactor with

---

[1]FC 68:220. [2]FC 42:427*. [3]See 1 Sam 24:10. [4]NPNF 2 10:77*.

such praise as that with which he followed the man who plotted against his life? How affectionately he grieved, with what deep feeling he bewailed him! The mountains dried up at the prophet's curse, and a divine power filled the judgment of him who spoke it. Therefore the elements themselves paid the penalty for witnessing the king's death. DUTIES OF THE CLERGY 3.9.[4]

1:25-26 David Laments Jonathan's Death

A WONDERFUL FRIENDSHIP. CHRYSOSTOM: I will now cite from the Scriptures a wonderful instance of friendship. Jonathan, the son of Saul, loved David, and his soul was so knit to him that David in mourning over him says, "Your love to me was wonderful, passing the love of women. You were wounded fatally." What then? Did Jonathan envy David? Not at all, though he had great reason. Why? Because, by the events he perceived that the kingdom would pass from himself to him, yet he felt nothing of the kind. He did not say, "This one is depriving me of my paternal kingdom," but he favored David obtaining the sovereignty; and he didn't spare his father for the sake of his friend. Yet let not any one think him a parricide, for he did not injure his father but restrained Saul's unjust attempts. He rather spared than injured him. He did not permit Saul to proceed to an unjust mur-

der. He was many times willing even to die for his friend, and far from accusing David, he restrained even his father's accusation. Instead of envying, Jonathan joined in obtaining the kingdom for him. Why do I speak of wealth? He even sacrificed his own life for David. For the sake of his friend, he did not even stand in awe of his father, since his father entertained unjust designs, but his conscience was free from all such [things]. Thus justice was conjoined with friendship.

Such then was Jonathan. Let us now consider David. He had no opportunity of returning the favor, for his benefactor was taken away before the reign of David and slain before he whom Jonathan had served came to his kingdom. What then? As far as it was allowed him and left in his power, let us see how that righteous man manifested his friendship. "Very pleasant," he says, "have you been to me, Jonathan; you were wounded fatally." Is this all? This indeed was no slight tribute, but he also frequently rescued from danger his son and his grandson, remembrance of the kindness of the father, and he continued to support and protect his children, as he would have done those of his own son. Such friendship I would wish all to entertain both toward the living and the dead. HOMILIES ON 2 TIMOTHY 7.[5]

---

[5]NPNF 1 13:503*.

2:1-11 JUDAH ANOINTS DAVID KING

[1]When they told David, "It was the men of Jabesh-gilead who buried Saul," [5]David sent messengers to the men of Jabesh-gilead, and said to them, "May you be blessed by the LORD, because you showed this loyalty to Saul your lord, and buried him! [6]Now may the LORD show steadfast love and faithfulness to you! And I will do good to you because you have done this thing. [7]Now therefore let your hands be strong, and be valiant; for Saul your lord is dead, and the house of Judah has anointed me king over them."

Overview: Christians should not fear how their bodies or those of other martyrs will be treated after they die (Augustine).

2:5 David Blesses the Men of Jabesh-gilead for Burying Saul

Love of One's Flesh. Augustine: The martyrs of Christ in their strivings for truth have conquered this love of one's flesh. . . . For, in all flesh that lacks life, the one who has left the body cannot be aware of injury to the lifeless body, nor can he who created it lose anything. But in the midst of what was being done to the bodies of the dead, although the martyrs were enduring them fearlessly with great fortitude, among the brothers there was great grief, because no opportunity was given to them to pay just dues at the burial of the saints. . . . And thus, although no misery came upon those who had been slain, in the dismemberment of their bodies, in the burning of their bones, in the scattering of their ashes, a great sorrow tortured those who were unable to bury anything of theirs, because they themselves in a certain manner felt for those who had no feeling in any manner, and where now there was no passion on the part of the one, there was wretched compassion on the part of the other.

Those men were praised and called blessed by King David who had bestowed the merciful kindness of burial on the dry bones of Saul and Jonathan, in keeping with that wretched compassion which I have mentioned. But, pray tell, what compassion is bestowed on those who have no feeling? Or should one think that the unburied were not able to cross the infernal river?[1] May this be far from the Christian belief! Otherwise, it worked out very badly for so great a multitude of martyrs whose bodies could not be buried, and for them truth emptily said, "Do not be afraid of those who kill the body and after that have nothing more that they can do,"[2] if they were able to do them such wrongs as to prevent their crossing over to the desired places. But, without any doubt, this is exceedingly false, for it is no hindrance to the faithful to be denied burial of the bodies. Also, it is of no advantage if burial is granted to the godless. Why, then, are those men said to have done an act of mercy in burying Saul and his son and blessed by good King David for this, unless it is because the hearts of the compassionate are favorably affected when they are concerned over the well-being of other bodies of the dead? Or is it because of that love which keeps one from ever hating his own flesh that they do not wish such things to happen after their own death to their own bodies, so that what they wish to be done for them when they shall have no feeling they care to do for others who now have no feeling, while they themselves still have feeling? The Care to Be Taken for the Dead 10-11.[3]

---

[1]This is a reference to Virgil's *Aeneid* 6.327. [2]Lk 12:4. [3]FC 27:364-66*.

2:12-23 ABNER AND JOAB ENGAGE IN BATTLE

[17]*And the battle was very fierce that day; and Abner and the men of Israel were beaten before the servants of David.*

[18]*And the three sons of Zeruiah were there, Joab, Abishai, and Asahel. Now Asahel was as*

swift of foot as a wild gazelle. . . . [22]*And Abner said again to Asahel, "Turn aside from following me; why should I smite you to the ground? How then could I lift up my face to your brother Joab?"* [23]*But he refused to turn aside; therefore Abner smote him in the belly with the butt of his spear, so that the spear came out at his back; and he fell there, and died where he was. And all who came to the place where Asahel had fallen and died, stood still.*

OVERVIEW: Abner's slaying of Asahel symbolizes how gentle and calm reasoning humbles the one driven by a violent frenzy (GREGORY THE GREAT).

2:22-23 Abner Slays Asahel

DRIVEN BY A VIOLENT FRENZY. GREGORY THE GREAT: But when the easily angered so attack others that it is impossible to shun them, they should not be smitten with open rebuke but sparingly with a certain respectful forbearance. We shall prove this better by citing the example of Abner. Scripture has it that when Asahel attacked him with vehement and inconsiderate haste, Abner said to Asahel, "Go off and do not follow me, lest I be obliged to strike you to the ground. . . . But he refused to listen to him, and would not turn aside. Therefore, Abner struck him with his spear, with a back stroke in the groin, and thrust him through, and he died." Of whom, then, did Asahel serve as a type, but of those who are driven headlong in a violent access of frenzy? Such people, when under the impulse of a like frenzy, are the more cautiously to be shunned, the more carried away they are in their madness. Therefore, too, Abner, who in our language is termed "lamp of the father," fled: that is to say, if the teacher, whose tongue symbolizes the heavenly light of God, perceives the mind of a person to be carried away along the rugged path of frenzy and refrains from bandying words with such an angered one, he is like one unwilling to strike a pursuer. But when easily angered people will not restrain themselves under any consideration, and, as it were, like Asahel, do not refrain from their mad pursuit, then it is necessary for those who try to check them in their frenzy, not on any account to allow their anger to be aroused but to show all possible calmness; and let them suggest discreetly that which will, as it were, by a side stroke pierce their frenzied mind.

Thus, when Abner made a stand against his pursuer, he pierced him, not with a direct thrust but with the reverse end of his spear. Of course, to strike with the sharp point is to oppose another with an attack of open rebuke, but to strike a pursuer with the reverse end of the spear is to touch the frenzied quietly and partially, and to overcome him, as it were, by sparing him. But Asahel falls down dead on the spot: that is, turbulent minds, on perceiving that they are shown consideration and, on the other hand, because they are touched in their hearts in consequence of being reasoned with calmly, fall down at once from the lofty place to which they had raised themselves. Those, therefore, who withdraw from their frenzied impulse under the stroke of gentleness, die, as it were, without being struck by the head of a spear. PASTORAL CARE 3.16.[1]

---

[1]ACW 11:139-40*.

[2:24-32 JOAB CEASES TO PURSUE ABNER]

3:1-5 DAVID'S STRENGTH GROWS

[1]*There was a long war between the house of Saul and the house of David; and David grew stronger and stronger, while the house of Saul became weaker and weaker.*

OVERVIEW: The weakening of Saul's house and the strengthening of David's is appropriated as a declaration of the decline of heretical teaching and the advance of correct teaching (CYRIL OF ALEXANDRIA). The case is different with Salvian: like the shift in power between Saul and David, God's judgment is evidenced in the flourishing of the "barbaric" Goths and Vandals and the demise of "faithful" Catholics.

3:1 David's House Grows Stronger

THE NUMBERS OF THE FAITHFUL INCREASE.
NESTORIUS: But you do well to cling to your anxiety for those scandalized, and I give thanks that your spirit, anxious over things divine, took thought of our affairs. But realize that you have been led astray by those condemned by the holy synod[1] as Manichaean sympathizers of the clerics who perhaps share your opinions. For the affairs of the church daily go forward, and the numbers of the faithful are so increasing through the grace of God that those who behold the multitudes of them repeat the words of the prophet, "The earth will be filled with the knowledge of the Lord, as much water would cover the seas,"[2]

since the teaching has shed its light upon the interest of the emperor, and, to put it briefly, one would very joyfully find fulfilled day by day among us the famous saying with regard to all the ungodly heresies and the correct teaching of the church, "The house of Saul went forth and grew weak. And the house of David went forth and was strengthened." LETTER 5.10.[3]

EVIDENCE OF GOD'S JUDGMENT. SALVIAN THE PRESBYTER: There is no need for us to discuss this point further, since the judgment of God is evident. Events prove what God judges about us and about the Goths and Vandals. They increase daily; we decrease daily. They prosper; we are humbled. They flourish; we are drying up. Truly there is said about us that saying which the divine Word spoke of Saul and David: "because David was strong and always growing more robust; the house of Saul grew less daily." As the prophet says, "For he is just, the Lord is just and his judgment is right."[4] THE GOVERNANCE OF GOD 7.11.[5]

---

[1]This is a reference to the condemnation of Philip, a presbyter of the church of Constantinople. [2]See Is 11:9. [3]FC 76:47-48*. [4]Ps 119:137 (118:137 LXX). [5]FC 3:201*.

3:6-19 ABNER SHIFTS HIS ALLEGIANCE TO DAVID

[12]*And Abner sent messengers to David at Hebron,[e] saying, "To whom does the land belong? Make your covenant with me, and behold, my hand shall be with you to bring over all Israel to you." [13]And he said, "Good; I will make a covenant with you; but one thing I require of you; that is, you shall not see my face, unless you first bring Michal, Saul's daughter, when you come to see my face." [14]Then David sent messengers to Ish-bosheth Saul's son, saying, "Give me my wife Michal, whom I betrothed at the price of a hundred foreskins of the Philistines."*

e Gk: Heb *where he was*

OVERVIEW: David anticipated the mercy of the new covenant when he took back his wife, Michal, who had been given in marriage to another man (AUGUSTINE).

3:14 Give Me My Wife Michal

ERADICATED BY THE MERCY OF GOD. AUGUSTINE: It appears harsh to you that after adultery, spouse should be reconciled to spouse. If faith is present, it will not be harsh. Why do we still regard as adulterers those who we believe have either been cleansed by baptism or have been healed by penance? Under the old law of God, no sacrifices wiped away these crimes, which, without a doubt, are cleansed by the blood of the new covenant. Therefore, in former times, it was for-bidden in every way to take back to oneself a woman sullied by another man, although David, as a figure of the New Testament, took back, without any hesitation, the daughter of Saul, whom the father of the same woman had given to another after her separation from David.[1] But now, afterwards, Christ says to the adulteress, "Neither will I condemn you. Go your way, and from now on sin no more."[2] Who fails to understand that it is the duty of the husband to forgive what he knows the Lord of both has forgiven, and that he should not now call her an adulteress whose sin he believes to have been eradicated by the mercy of God as a result of her penance? ADULTEROUS MARRIAGES 5.[3]

[1]1 Sam 25:44. [2]Jn 8:11. [3]FC 27:107*.

3:20-30 JOAB TAKES REVENGE ON ABNER

[20]*When Abner came with twenty men to David at Hebron, David made a feast for Abner and the men who were with him. [21]And Abner said to David, "I will arise and go, and will gather all Israel to my lord the king, that they may make a covenant with you, and that you may reign over all that your heart desires." So David sent Abner away; and he went in peace. . . .*

²⁶*When Joab came out from David's presence, he sent messengers after Abner, and they brought him back from the cistern of Sirah; but David did not know about it.* ²⁷*And when Abner returned to Hebron, Joab took him aside into the midst of the gate to speak with him privately, and there he smote him in the belly, so that he died, for the blood of Asahel his brother.* ²⁸*Afterward, when David heard of it, he said, "I and my kingdom are for ever guiltless before the Lord for the blood of Abner the son of Ner."*

OVERVIEW: David's manner of fulfilling his duty, which included admiration for an enemy's valor and retaliation for his treacherous murder, garnered the loyalty of the people. Anyone who kills the innocent—even if he is a king—must repent of the sin in order to obtain forgiveness (AMBROSE).

3:20 David Made a Feast for Abner

ADMIRING AN ENEMY'S VALOR. AMBROSE: He had bound the people to himself freely in doing his duty; first, when during the division among the people he preferred to live like an exile at Hebron rather than to reign at Jerusalem;[1] next, when he showed that he loved valor even in an enemy. He had also thought that justice should be shown to those who had borne arms against himself the same as to his own men. Again, he admired Abner, the bravest champion of the opposing side, while he was their leader and was yet waging war. Nor did he despise Abner when suing for peace, but honored him by a banquet. When killed by treachery, David mourned and wept for him. He followed him and honored his obsequies and evinced his good faith in desiring vengeance for the murder; for he handed on that duty to his son in the charge that he gave him, being anxious rather that the death of an inno-cent man should not be left unavenged than that any one should mourn for his own.[2] DUTIES OF THE CLERGY 2.7.33.[3]

3:28 David Professes His Innocence

KILLING THE INNOCENT. AMBROSE: Although he [Saul] was a king, he sinned if he killed the inno-cent. Finally, even David, when he was in posses-sion of his kingdom and had heard that an innocent man named Abner was slain by Joab, the leader of his army, said, "I and my kingdom are innocent now and forever of the blood of Abner the son of Ner," and he fasted in sorrow.

These things I have written not to disconcert you but that the example of kings may stir you to remove this sin from your kingdom, for you will remove it by humbling your soul before God.[4] You are a man, you have met temptation—con-quer it. Sin is not removed except by tears and penance. No angel or archangel can remove it; it is God himself who alone can say, "I am with you";[5] if we have sinned, he does not forgive us unless we do penance. LETTER 51.10-11.[6]

---

[1]2 Sam 2:11. [2]See 2 Sam 3:31-39. [3]NPNF 2 10:49*. [4]This letter was written about 390 to Emperor Theodosius to encourage his repen-tance for ordering a massacre in Thessolonica. [5]Mt 28:20. [6]FC 26:23-24*.

[3:31-39 DAVID MOURNS ABNER'S DEATH]

4:1-12 THE MURDER OF SAUL'S SON ISH-BOSHETH

[9]*But David answered Rechab and Baanah his brother, the sons of Rimmon the Be-erothite, "As the* LORD *lives, who has redeemed my life out of every adversity,* [10]*when one told me, 'Behold, Saul is dead,' and thought he was bringing good news, I seized him and slew him at Ziklag, which was the reward I gave him for his news.* [11]*How much more, when wicked men have slain a righteous man in his own house upon his bed, shall I not now require his blood at your hand, and destroy you from the earth?"* [12]*And David commanded his young men, and they killed them, and cut off their hands and feet, and hanged them beside the pool at Hebron. But they took the head of Ish-bosheth, and buried it in the tomb of Abner at Hebron.*

OVERVIEW: An unjust man, Ish-bosheth, was called "just," even while being unjust, because he was innocently killed (JEROME).

4:11-12 David Condemns Ish-bosheth's Murderers

THE WICKED AND THE JUST. JEROME: Ish-bosheth, the son of Saul, is killed through a ruse at the hands of Rechab and Baanah, the sons of Rimmon, the Beerothite. And, when they announced the news to David and showed him the head of his enemy, they were killed by David, who said, "Wicked men have slain a just man in his own house upon his bed." Ish-bosheth was certainly not a just man, and yet he is called a just man because he was innocently killed. DEFENSE AGAINST THE PELAGIANS 1.38.[1]

---

[1]FC 53:289*

5:1-5 ISRAEL ANOINTS DAVID KING

[1]*Then all the tribes of Israel came to David at Hebron, and said, "Behold, we are your bone and flesh."*

OVERVIEW: "Bone and flesh" signify the close unity of the tribes of Israel (CASSIAN) as well as David's close connection to his people (AMBROSE).

5:1 *We Are Your Bone and Flesh*

THE WORD FLESH IS USED WITH DIFFERENT MEANINGS. JOHN CASSIAN: We find that the word flesh is used in holy Scripture with many different meanings: for sometimes it stands for the whole person, that is, for that which consists of body and soul, as here: "And the Word was made flesh,"?[1] and "All flesh shall see the salvation of our God."[2] Sometimes it stands for sinful and carnal people, as here: "My spirit shall not remain in those men, because they are flesh."[3] Sometimes it is used for sins themselves, as here: "But you are not in the flesh but in the spirit,"[4] and again, "Flesh and blood shall not inherit the kingdom of God." Lastly there follows, "Neither shall corruption inherit incorruption."[5] Sometimes [as with David] it stands for unity and relationship, as here: "Behold we are your bone and your flesh," and the apostle says, "If by any means I may provoke to emulation them who are my flesh, and save some of them."[6] We must therefore inquire in which of these four meanings we ought to take the word flesh in this place. CONFERENCE 4.10.[7]

DAVID'S INTEGRITY. AMBROSE: What more should I say? He did not open his mouth to those planning deceit, and, as though he did not hear, he thought no word should be returned, nor did he answer their reproaches. When he was spoken of evilly, he prayed. When he was cursed, he blessed. He walked in simplicity of heart and fled from the proud. He was a follower of those unspotted from the world, one who mixed ashes with his food when bewailing his sins, and mingled his drink with weeping.[8] Worthily, then, was he called for by all the people. All the tribes of Israel came to him, saying, "Behold, we are your bone and your flesh. Also yesterday and the day before when Saul lived, and reigned, you were he that led out and brought in Israel. And the Lord said to you, you shall feed my people!" And why should I say more about him of whom the word of the Lord has gone forth to say: "I have found David according to my heart"[9] Who else always walked in holiness of heart and in justice as he did, so as to fulfill the will of God; for whose sake pardon was granted to his children when they sinned, and their rights were preserved to his heirs?[10] DUTIES OF THE CLERGY 2.7.35.[11]

---

[1]Jn 1:14. [2]Lk 3:6. [3]Gen 6:3. [4]Rom 8:9. [5]1 Cor 15:50. [6]Rom 11:14. [7]NPNF 2 11:333*. [8]Ps 102:9 (101:9 LXX). [9]Acts 13:22; cf. 1 Sam 13:14. [10]1 Kings 11:34. [11]NPNF 2 10:49*.

5:6-10 DAVID ATTACKS THE JEBUSITES

[6]*And the king and his men went to Jerusalem against the Jebusites, the inhabitants of the land, who said to David, "You will not come in here, but the blind and the lame will ward you off"—thinking, "David cannot come in here." [7]Nevertheless David took the stronghold of Zion, that is, the city of David. [8]And David said on that day, "Whoever would smite the Jebusites, let him get up the water shaft to attack the lame and the blind, who are hated by David's soul." Therefore it is said, "The blind and the lame shall not come into the house."*

OVERVIEW: Tertullian refutes the heretical claim of Marcion, who suggests that Christ is not really David's son given their opposite reactions to the blind, by emphasizing the difference in attitude of the ones who were blind.

5:8 The Blind and the Lame

THE SON OF DAVID. TERTULLIAN: For (here is one of Marcion's[1] antitheses): whereas David long ago, in the capture of Zion, was offended by the blind who opposed his admission (into the stronghold). In this respect (I should rather say) that they were a type of people equally blind,[2] who in later times would not admit Christ to be the son of David. So, on the contrary, Christ helped the blind man to show, by this act, that he was not David's son and how different in disposition he was, by being kind to the blind while David ordered them to be slain. If all this were so, why did Marcion allege that the blind man's faith was of such a worthless type? The fact is, the Son of David acted so that the antithesis must lose its point by its own absurdity. Those persons who offended David were blind, and the man who now presents himself as a beggar to David's son is afflicted with the same infirmity. Therefore the Son of David was appeased with some sort of satisfaction by the blind man when he restored him to sight, and added his approval of the faith which had led him to believe the very truth that he must gain the Son of David's help by earnest entreaty. But, after all, I suspect that it was the audacity (of the old Jebusites) which offended David, and not their malady. AGAINST MARCION 4.36.[3]

---

[1]Marcion did not consider the Old Testament authoritative for Christians since, he believed, the God it described was cruel and evil, making him unworthy of Christian reverence. [2]The Marcionites. [3]ANF 3:411*.

5:11-25 DAVID PREVAILS OVER THE PHILISTINES

[17]*When the Philistines heard that David had been anointed king over Israel, all the Philistines went up in search of David; but David heard of it and went down to the stronghold.* [18]*Now the Philistines had come and spread out in the valley of Rephaim.* [19]*And David inquired of the LORD, "Shall I go up against the Philistines? Wilt thou give them into my hand?" And the LORD said to David, "Go up; for I will certainly give the Philistines into your hand."*

OVERVIEW: While David's reliance upon the Lord's counsel and his success are noteworthy, so is the fortitude of those who courageously triumph against their foes unaided by armies (AMBROSE).

5:19 David Inquired of the Lord

GLORIOUS FORTITUDE. AMBROSE: After that [the killing of Goliath] he never entered on a war without seeking counsel of the Lord. Thus he was victorious in all wars, and even to his last years [he] was ready to fight. And when war arose with the Philistines, he joined battle with their fierce troops, being desirous of winning renown, while careless of his own safety.[1] But this is not the only kind of fortitude which is worthy of note. We consider their fortitude glorious, who, with greatness of mind, "through faith stopped the mouth of lions, quenched the violence of fire, escaped the edge of the sword, out of weakness were made strong,"[2] They did not gain a victory in common with many, surrounded by comrades and aided by the legions, but [they] won their triumph alone over their treacherous foes by the mere courage of their own souls. DUTIES OF THE CLERGY 1.35.177.[3]

[1]2 Sam 21:15. [2]Heb 11:33-34. [3]NPNF 2 10:30*.

6:1-5 CELEBRATION ACCOMPANIES MOVEMENT OF THE ARK

3And they carried the ark of God upon a new cart, and brought it out of the house of Abinadab
which was on the hill; and Uzzah and Ahio,[i] the sons of Abinadab, were driving the new cart[j]
4with the ark of God; and Ahio[i] went before the ark. 5And David and all the house of Israel were
making merry before the LORD with all their might, with songs[k] and lyres and harps and tambourines and castanets and cymbals.

i Or *and his brother* **j** Compare Gk: Heb *the new cart, and brought it out of the house of Abinadab which was on the hill* **k** Gk 1 Chron 13.8: Heb *fir-trees*

OVERVIEW: Like the symphony that accompanies the attainment of accord between God and the penitent, harmony in prayer has remarkable power (ORIGEN).

6:4-5 *Making Merry Before the Lord*

THE EFFICACY OF MUSICAL HARMONY. ORIGEN: "Again I say to you, if two of you agree on earth about anything they ask, it will be done for them."[1] Strictly speaking, the word *symphony* is used by musicians for the voices of harmony. For among musical tones, some harmonize with each other and others do not. But the Gospel is also familiar with this term as applied to music where it says, "He heard music *[symphōnias]* and dancing."[2] For it was fitting that, at the harmony that resulted between the father and his son who had been lost but was now found through his repentance, a symphony should be heard on the occasion of the rejoicing of the house. . . . Akin to this kind of symphony is what is written in the second book of Kings [Samuel] when the brothers of Aminadab "went before the ark, and David and the sons of Israel were playing before the face of the Lord on well-tuned instruments and in power and in songs."[3] For the "well-tuned instruments in power and in song" have in them that harmony of tones which is of such power that if only two people bring before the Father in heaven any request with that symphony which is found in divine and spiritual music, the Father grants it to them—which is most remarkable. COMMENTARY ON THE GOSPEL OF MATTHEW 14.1.[4]

[1]Mt 18:19. [2]Lk 15:25. [3]The LXX specifies "well-tuned" instruments. [4]*OSF* 306-7*.

6:6-11 THE LORD'S ANGER BURNS AGAINST UZZAH

⁶And when they came to the threshing floor of Nacon, Uzzah put out his hand to the ark of God and took hold of it, for the oxen stumbled. ⁷And the anger of the LORD was kindled against Uzzah; and God smote him there because he put forth his hand to the ark;¹ and he died there beside the ark of God. ⁸And David was angry because the LORD had broken forth upon Uzzah; and that place is called Perez-uzzah,ᵐ to this day. ⁹And David was afraid of the LORD that day; and he said, "How can the ark of the LORD come to me?" ¹⁰So David was not willing to take the ark of the LORD into the city of David; but David took it aside to the house of Obed-edom the Gittite.

l 1 Chron 13.10: Heb uncertain   m That is *The breaking forth upon Uzzah*

OVERVIEW: Uzzah's punishment for steadying the ark shows that nothing may be considered lightly when it pertains to God (SALVIAN). As the wrath of God was drawn down on Uzzah for intruding upon an office that was not his own, God's wrath will likewise advance against those who subvert the gospel (CHRYSOSTOM). Given the immediate judgment for irreverence in former times, God's present inaction is not ignorance but forbearance: judgment is being postponed to allow an opportunity for repentance (PACIAN OF BARCELONA). Although he was righteous and anointed by God, David feared a similar judgment after observing the Lord strike Uzzah for his ignorance (JEROME).

6:6-7 The Lord Strikes Uzzah

THE GREATNESS OF A LITTLE FAULT. SALVIAN THE PRESBYTER: We read in the law that even those who seem to have acted lightly against the sacred commandments have, nevertheless, been punished most severely.¹ This is that we might understand that nothing which pertains to God must be considered lightly, because even what seems to be very little in fault is made great by the injury to God. What did Uzzah, the Levite of God, do against the heavenly command when he tried to steady the tottering ark of the Lord?

There was nothing on this point prescribed by the law. Yet, immediately when he steadied the ark, he was struck down. Not that he was insolent in manner or undutiful in mind. Yet he was undutiful in his very act, because he went beyond his orders. THE GOVERNANCE OF GOD 6.10.²

ON SUBVERTING THE GOSPEL. CHRYSOSTOM: They [the Galatians] had, in fact, only introduced one or two commandments, circumcision and the observance of days, but he [Paul] says that the gospel was subverted, in order to show that a slight adulteration vitiates the whole. For as he who but partially pares away the image on a royal coin renders the whole spurious, so he who swerves ever so little from the pure faith soon proceeds from this to graver errors and becomes entirely corrupted. Where then are those who charge us with being contentious in separating from heretics and say that there is no real difference between us except what arises from our ambition? Let them hear Paul's assertion, that those who had but slightly innovated, subverted the gospel.³ . . . Don't you know that even under the old covenant, a man who gathered sticks on the sabbath, and transgressed a single commandment, and that not a great one, was punished

---

¹Ex 31:12-18. ²FC 3:168-69*. ³See Gal 1:7-9.

with death?[4] And that Uzzah, who supported the ark when on the point of being overturned, was struck suddenly dead, because he had intruded upon an office which did not pertain to him? Wherefore if to transgress the sabbath and to touch the falling ark drew down the wrath of God so signally as to deprive the offender of even a momentary respite, shall he who corrupts unutterably awe-inspiring doctrines find excuse and pardon? Assuredly not. A lack of zeal in small matters is the cause of all our calamities; and because slight errors escape fitting correction, great ones creep in. As in the body, a neglect of wounds generates fever, mortification and death; so in the soul, slight evils overlooked open the door to graver ones. COMMENTARY ON GALATIANS 1.[5]

GOD SEES BUT WAITS. PACIAN OF BARCELONA: When the people of the Hebrews were bringing back the ark of the Lord to Jerusalem, Uzzah, from the house of Abinadab the Israelite, who had touched the side of the ark without having examined his conscience, was slain. And yet he had drawn near not to take anything from it but to hold it up when it was leaning because of the stumbling of a young ox. So great a concern was there of reverence toward God that God did not accept bold hands even out of help. The Lord also proclaims the same thing, saying, "Everyone who is clean shall eat of the flesh, and whichever soul touches the flesh of the sacrifice of well-being and has his uncleanness upon him, that soul shall be cut off from his people."[6] Are these things which existed long ago, and now they do not happen in this way? What then? Has God ceased to care for what concerns us? Has he withdrawn beyond the view of the world, and does he look down from heaven upon no one? Is his forbearance really ignorance? God forbid, you will say. Therefore he sees what we do but he waits, indeed, and endures patiently, and he grants an opportunity for repentance and holds out his own Christ to postpone [the end], so that they whom he has redeemed may not readily perish. Understand this well, you sinner: you are observed by God; you can appease him if you want to. ON PENITENTS 6.3.[7]

6:8-9 David Grows Angry and Fearful

FEARING A SIMILAR JUDGMENT. JEROME: When the ark of the Lord was being transferred to Jerusalem, and the oxen kicked and made the wagon lean to one side, Uzzah, the Levite, reached out his hand to support the ark that had been tipped, and there follow immediately these words: "And the indignation of the Lord was enkindled against Uzzah, and God struck him there for his ignorance, and he died before the ark of God. And David was grieved because the Lord had struck Uzzah, and he was afraid of the Lord that day and said, 'How shall the ark of the Lord come to me?'" When David, who was a just man and a prophet and had been anointed as king, whom the Lord chose according to his own heart that he might do his will in all things, saw ignorance punished by the wrath of the Lord, he was afraid and was grieved; nor did he ask the Lord his reason for striking a man who was ignorant, but he feared a similar judgment happening to him. DEFENSE AGAINST THE PELAGIANS 1.38.[8]

---

[4]Num 15:32-36. [5]NPNF 1 13:7-8*. [6]Lev 7:19-20. [7]FC 99:77*. [8]FC 53:289-90.

6:12-15 THE ARK ENTERS THE CITY OF DAVID

[14]And David danced before the LORD with all his might; and David was girded with a linen ephod. [15]So David and all the house of Israel brought up the ark of the LORD with shouting, and with the sound of the horn.

OVERVIEW: David's joy was manifested in dancing when he recognized that the ark prefigured Mary and the Christ she would bear. So the union of Christ and the church should be celebrated by believers (MAXIMUS OF TURIN). That David danced does not condone Christian attendance at the theater, where lewd dancing is exhibited (NOVATIAN). David's dancing in front of the ark shows his humility before God (GREGORY THE GREAT).

6:14 David Danced Before the Lord

CELEBRATE WITH DANCING. MAXIMUS OF TURIN: For our vows are celebrated when the church is united to Christ, as John says: "The one who has the bride is the bridegroom."[1] Because of this marriage, therefore, it behooves us to dance, for David, at once king and prophet, is also said to have danced before the ark of the covenant with much singing. In high rejoicing he broke into dancing, for in the Spirit he foresaw Mary, born of his own line, brought into Christ's chamber, and so he says, "And he, like a bridegroom, will come forth from his chamber." Thus he sang more than the other prophetic authors because, gladder than the rest of them, by these joys he united those coming after him in marriage. And, by inviting us to his own vows in a more charming way than usual, having danced with such joy in front of the ark before his marriage, he taught us what we ought to do at those other vows. The prophet David danced, then. But what would we say that the ark was if not holy Mary, since the ark carried within it the tables of the covenant, while Mary bore the master of the same cove-

nant? The one bore the law within itself and the other the gospel, but the ark gleamed within and without with the radiance of gold, while holy Mary shone within and without with the splendor of virginity; the one was adorned with earthly gold, the other with heavenly. SERMON 42.5.[2]

ON ATTENDING THE THEATER. NOVATIAN: And that David danced before the Lord does in no way encourage faithful Christians to take seats in the theater. He did not distort his body in obscene movements and dance out the drama of Grecian libido. . . . Therefore, no approval whatever is given for spectators of illicit things. ON THE SPECTACLES 3.2.[3]

NOBLE THROUGH HUMILITY. GREGORY THE GREAT: But because secret pride of heart is reproved by this which Elihu says, "All who seem to themselves to be wise will not dare to contemplate him,"[4] it seems good to observe what great gifts of virtues David had obtained, and in all these with how firm a humility he maintained himself. For whom would it not puff up to break the mouths of lions,[5] to rend asunder the arms of bears,[6] to be chosen, when his elder brothers had been despised,[7] to be anointed to the government of the kingdom when the kings had been rejected, to slay with a single stone Goliath who was dreaded by all,[8] to bring back, after the destruction of the aliens, the numerous foreskins proposed by the king,[9] to receive at last the promised

---

[1]Jn 3:29. [2]ACW 50:106-7. [3]FC 67:125. [4]Job 37:24. [5]See Ps 58:6 (57:6 LXX). [6]See 1 Sam 17:34-36. [7]See 1 Sam 16. [8]See 1 Sam 17:49. [9]See 1 Sam 18:25.

kingdom, and to possess the whole people of Israel without any contradiction? And yet, when he brings back the ark of God to Jerusalem, he dances before the ark, mingled with the people, as though forgetful that he had been preferred to them all. And because, as is believed, it had been the custom of the common people to dance before the ark, the king wheels round in the dance, in service to God. Behold how he whom the Lord preferred specially above all despises himself beneath the Lord, both by equaling himself to the least and by displaying abject behavior. The power of his kingdom is not recalled to his memory. He does not fear to be of low stature in the eyes of his people by dancing. He does not remember, before the ark of him who had given him honor, that he had been preferred in honor above the rest. Before God he acted with the most extreme lowliness, in order to strengthen by his humility the bold deeds he had performed in the sight of people. What others think of his doings, I do not know; I am more surprised at

David dancing than fighting. For by fighting he subdued his enemies; but by dancing before the Lord he overcame himself. And when Michal, the daughter of Saul, still mad with pride at her royal descent, despised him when humbled, saying, "How glorious was the king of Israel today, uncovering himself before the handmaids of his servants, and made himself naked, as though one of the buffoons were naked," she immediately heard, "As the Lord lives, I will play before the Lord, who has chosen me rather than your father." And a little later he says, "And I will play and I will become more lowly than I have been, and I will be humble in my own eyes,"[10] as if he had said, I seek to become lowly before people because I seek to keep myself noble before the Lord through my humility. MORALS ON THE BOOK OF JOB 27.46.[11]

---

[10]2 Sam 6:20-22. [11]LF 23:256-57*.

6:16-23 MICHAL DESPISES DAVID

[16]*As the ark of the* LORD *came into the city of David, Michal the daughter of Saul looked out of the window, and saw King David leaping and dancing before the* LORD; *and she despised him in her heart.* . . . [18]*And when David had finished offering the burnt offerings and the peace offerings, he blessed the people in the name of the* LORD *of hosts,* [19]*and distributed among all the people, the whole multitude of Israel, both men and women, to each a cake of bread, a portion of meat,*[n] *and a cake of raisins. Then all the people departed, each to his house.*

[20]*And David returned to bless his household. But Michal the daughter of Saul came out to meet David, and said, "How the king of Israel honored himself today, uncovering himself today before the eyes of his servants' maids, as one of the vulgar fellows shamelessly uncovers himself!"* [21]*And David said to Michal, "It was before the* LORD, *who chose me above your father, and above all his house, to appoint me as prince over Israel, the people of the* LORD—*and I will make merry before the* LORD. [22]*I will make myself yet more contemptible than this, and I will be abased in your*[o] *eyes;*

but by the maids of whom you have spoken, by them I shall be held in honor." [23]*And Michal the daughter of Saul had no child to the day of her death.*

n Vg: Heb uncertain   o Gk: Heb *my*

OVERVIEW: David's prophetic dancing, which was offered humbly and without inhibition to God, was justified while Michal's censure was not. She, in turn, was censured by condemnation to barrenness (AMBROSE). Unlike the overindulgence of the Gentiles, which Plato is praised for denouncing, the sufficiency of Hebrew meals is understood from the food David distributed to his people (CLEMENT OF ALEXANDRIA). As David exemplifies, we will be blessed if we give thanks to God both in times of adversity and prosperity (LEANDER OF SEVILLE).

6:16 Michal Despised David

DANCING IN GOD'S HONOR. AMBROSE: But we also find praiseworthy bodily dancing in honor of God, for David danced before the ark of the Lord. Michal, however, the daughter of Saul, saw him dancing and beating a drum in the presence of the Lord and asked him, after receiving him into her home, "How is it honorable for the king of Israel to dance naked today in the presence of his maidservants?" And David answered Michal in the presence of the Lord: "Blessed be the Lord who chose me above your father and above his entire house to be established as prince over his people Israel. I will make merry in the presence of the Lord and run naked, and I will be lighthearted in your presence, and I will be honored by the maids with whom you called me naked." "And Michal," it says, "the daughter of Saul, had no children until the day she died." Thus, this is a clear lesson that the prophet who beats a drum and dances before the ark of the Lord is justified, whereas the one who reproves him is condemned to sterility. EXPOSITION ON PSALM 118.[1]

6:19 David Distributes Food to the People

EXTRAVAGANT LIVING CONDEMNED. CLEMENT OF ALEXANDRIA: So it is that he who of all philosophers so praised truth, Plato, gave new life to the dying ember of Hebrew philosophy by condemning a life spent in revelry. "When I arrived," he said, "what is here called a life of pleasure, filled with Italian and Syracusan meals, was very repulsive to me. It is a life in which one gorges oneself twice a day, sleeps not only during the night, and engages in all the pastimes that go with this sort of life. No one upon earth could ever become wise in this way, if from his youth he had followed such pursuits as these, nor would he ever attain in that way any reputation for an excellent physique."[2] Surely, Plato was not unacquainted with David, who, when he was settling the holy ark in the middle of the tabernacle of his city, made a feast for all his obedient subjects and "before the face of the Lord, distributed to all the multitude of Israel, both men and women, to everyone, a cake of bread and baked bread and pancakes from the frying pan."[3] This food sufficed, this food of Israel; that of the Gentiles is extravagance. CHRIST THE EDUCATOR 2.1.18.[4]

6:20-23 David Responds to Michal's Disdain

HUMBLED BEFORE GOD. AMBROSE: David was not ashamed when he danced before the ark of the covenant in the presence of all the people.... Yet, these actions of the body, though unseemly when viewed in themselves, become reverential under the aspect of holy religion, so that those who censure them drag their own souls into the net of censure. Thus, Michal censured David for dancing....

[1]CSEL 62:143. [2]Plato *Letter* 7. [3]The meaning of the Hebrew for the latter two foods is uncertain. [4]FC 23:109-10.

David did not blush at a woman's censure, nor was he ashamed to meet with reproach, because of his devotion to religion. He played before the Lord as his servant and pleased him the more in so humbling himself before God and laying aside his royal dignity, performing the humblest tasks for God like a servant. She who censured such dancing was condemned to barrenness and had no children by the king lest she should beget the proud. In truth, she had no continuance of posterity or of good deeds. LETTER 28.[5]

DAVID'S HUMBLE THANKSGIVING. LEANDER OF SEVILLE: You will be blessed if you give thanks to God both in adversity and in prosperity and if you consider the prosperity of this life as smoke and vapor that immediately vanishes.[6] David was a king, yet, in spite of having numerous treasures and ruling countless peoples with a strong hand, he sang of himself as humble and said, "I am afflicted in an agony from my youth."[7] And again, he said to the daughter of Saul, "I shall walk humbly, and I shall appear humbly before the Lord, who chose me rather than your father." Likewise, he also said, "I am a wayfarer of earth and a pilgrim like all my fathers."[8] THE TRAINING OF NUNS 23.[9]

---

[5]FC 26:145-46*. [6]See Ps 102:2 (101:4 LXX). [7]Ps 88:15 (87:15 LXX). [8]See Ps 39:12; 119:19 (38:12; 118:19 LXX). [9]FC 62:216-17*.

7:1-11 DAVID DESIRES TO BUILD A HOUSE FOR THE LORD

[1]*Now when the king dwelt in his house, and the* LORD *had given him rest from all his enemies round about,* [2]*the king said to Nathan the prophet, "See now, I dwell in a house of cedar, but the ark of God dwells in a tent."* [3]*And Nathan said to the king, "Go, do all that is in your heart; for the* LORD *is with you."*

[4]*But that same night the word of the* LORD *came to Nathan,* [5]*"Go and tell my servant David, 'Thus says the* LORD: *Would you build me a house to dwell in?* [6]*I have not dwelt in a house since the day I brought up the people of Israel from Egypt to this day, but I have been moving about in a tent for my dwelling.* [7]*In all places where I have moved with all the people of Israel, did I speak a word with any of the judges[p] of Israel, whom I commanded to shepherd my people Israel, saying, "Why have you not built me a house of cedar?" '"*

p 1 Chron 17.6: Heb *tribes*

OVERVIEW: The inconstancy of enlightenment of the spirit of prophecy is illustrated by Nathan's consent—and its subsequent withdrawal—to David's request to build a temple (GREGORY THE GREAT). The denial of David's request points to the fact that it is Christ who is the true temple of God (CYPRIAN).

7:3 Do All That Is in Your Heart

GOD THE SPIRIT MOVES WHERE HE PLEASES.

GREGORY THE GREAT: The spirit of prophecy does not enlighten the minds of the prophets constantly, Peter.[1] We read in sacred Scripture that the Holy Spirit breathes where he pleases,[2] and we should also realize that he breathes when he pleases. For example, when King David asked whether he could build a temple, the prophet Nathan gave his consent but later had to withdraw it. DIALOGUE 2.21.[3]

7:5 Would You Build Me a House?

CHRIST THE TEMPLE OF GOD. CYPRIAN: That Christ should be the house and temple of God, and that the old temple should cease, and the new one should begin. In the second book of Kings [Samuel]: "And the word of the Lord came to Nathan, saying, 'Go and tell my servant David, Thus says the Lord, You shall not build me a house to dwell in; but it shall be, when your days are fulfilled, and you sleep with your fathers, that I will raise up your seed after you, which shall come from your body, and I will prepare his kingdom. He shall build me a house in my name, and I will raise up his throne forever; and I will be a father to him, and he shall be a son to me, and his house shall obtain faith, and his kingdom [will be] forever in my sight.' "[4] Also in the Gospel the Lord says, "There shall not be left in the temple one stone upon another that shall not be thrown down."[5] And "After three days another shall be raised up without hands."[6] To QUIRINUS: TESTIMONIES AGAINST THE JEWS 1.15.[7]

---

[1]Using a common literary device, Gregory presents his teaching as a dialogue between himself and his deacon, Peter. [2]See Jn 3:8. [3]FC 39:88-89. [4]2 Sam 7:4-5, 12-16. [5]Mt 24:2. [6]Jn 2:19; Mk 14:58. [7]ANF 5:511**.

7:12-17 THE LORD'S PROMISE TO DAVID'S OFFSPRING

[12]"'When your days are fulfilled and you lie down with your fathers, I will raise up your offspring after you, who shall come forth from your body, and I will establish his kingdom. [13]He shall build a house for my name, and I will establish the throne of his kingdom for ever. [14]I will be his father, and he shall be my son. When he commits iniquity, I will chasten him with the rod of men, with the stripes of the sons of men; [15]but I will not take[q] my steadfast love from him, as I took it from Saul, whom I put away from before you. [16]And your house and your kingdom shall be made sure for ever before me; your throne shall be established for ever.'"

q Gk Syr Vg 1 Chron 17.13: Heb *shall not depart*

OVERVIEW: The Creator's promise regarding David's seed refers not to Solomon but to the coming of Christ from Mary and the perpetuity of his kingdom (TERTULLIAN). The tribe of Judah did not fail to continue until Christ, for whom the kingdom was reserved, came to rule in fulfillment of the Lord's promise to David (BASIL). As Scripture records many instances of God calling Israel and Solomon "my son," the title Son of God is rightly applied to Jesus (APHRAHAT). For the unbelieving Jew, repentance is urged since Jesus is shown to be the Messiah who was prophesied in the Old Testament (JUSTIN MARTYR).

7:12-13 God Will Establish the Kingdom Forever

CHRIST'S KINGDOM IS PROMISED. TERTULLIAN: That new dispensation, then, which is found in Christ now, will prove to be what the Creator then promised under the appellation of "the sure mercies of David,"[1] which were Christ's, inasmuch as Christ sprang from David, or rather his very flesh itself was David's "sure mercies," consecrated by religion, and "sure" after its resurrection. Accordingly the prophet Nathan, in the first [book] of Kings [Samuel], makes a promise to David for his seed, "which shall proceed," he says, "from your own body." Now, if you explain this simply of Solomon, you will send me into a fit of laughter. For David will evidently have brought forth Solomon! But is not Christ here designated the seed of David, as of that womb which was derived from David, that is, Mary's? Now, because Christ rather than any other was to build the temple of God, that is to say, a holy manhood, wherein God's Spirit might dwell as in a better temple, Christ rather than David's son Solomon was to be looked for as the Son of God. Then, again, the throne forever with the kingdom forever is more suited to Christ than to Solomon, a mere temporal king. AGAINST MARCION 3.20.[2]

AN INDESTRUCTIBLE KINGDOM. BASIL THE GREAT: However, the tribe of Judah did not fail until he came for whom it was reserved, who did not himself sit upon a material throne, for the kingdom of Judea had now been transferred to Herod, the son of Antipater, the Ascalonite, and to his sons, who divided Judea into four provinces when Pilate was governor and Tiberius held the power over the whole Roman province.[3] But his indestructible kingdom he calls the throne of David on which the Lord sat. He himself is "the expectation of nations,"[4] not of the least part of the world. "For there will be the root of Jesse," it is said,[5] "and he who rises up to rule the Gentiles, in him the Gentiles will hope." "For I have placed you for a covenant of the people, for a light of the Gentiles."[6] "And I shall establish," it is said, "his seed forever, and his throne as the days of the heavens." LETTER 236.[7]

7:14-15 The Lord Promises

THE SON OF GOD. APHRAHAT: Again, listen concerning the title Son of God, by which we have called him. They [the Jews] say that "though God has no son, you make that crucified Jesus, the firstborn son of God." Yet he called Israel "my firstborn" when he sent to Pharaoh through Moses and said to him, "Israel is my firstborn; I have said to you, let my son go to serve me, and if you are not willing to let (him) go, lo! I will slay your son, your firstborn."[8] And also through the prophet he testified concerning this and reproved them and said to the people, "Out of Egypt have I called my son. As I called them, so they went and worshiped Baal and offered incense to the graven images."[9] And Isaiah said concerning them, "Children have I reared and brought up, and they have rebelled against me."[10] And again it is written, "You are the children of the Lord your God."[11] And about Solomon he said, "He shall be a son to me, and I will be a Father to him." So also we call the Christ "the Son of God" because through him we have gained the knowledge of God; even as he called Israel my firstborn son and as he said concerning Solomon, "He shall be a son to me." DEMONSTRATION 17.4.[12]

MESSIANIC PROPHECIES. JUSTIN MARTYR: It would be much better for you, therefore, if, instead of being so contentious, you should repent before the great day of judgment comes, for then, as I showed from Scripture, all those of

---

[1]Is 55:3; Acts 13:34. [2]ANF 3:339*. [3]See Lk 3:1. [4]Gen 49:10 LXX. [5]Is 11:10 LXX. [6]See Is 42:6. [7]FC 28:169-70*. [8]Ex 4:22-23. [9]Hos 11:1-2. [10]Is 1:2. [11]Deut 14:1. [12]NPNF 2 13:387-88*.

your tribes who crucified Christ shall lament. Now, I have explained the meaning of the words "The Lord swore, [you are a priest forever] according to the order of Melchizedek."[13] I have also shown that the prophecy of Isaiah, "His burial has been taken away from the midst,"[14] referred to Christ, who was to be buried and to rise again. I have stated at length that this same Christ will be the judge of both the living and the dead. Further, Nathan spoke thus of him to David, "I will be his Father, and he shall be my Son, and I will not take my mercy away from him, as I did from those who were before him; and I will establish him in my house, and in his kingdom forever." And Ezekiel states that he shall be the only prince in this house, for he is the Son of God.[15] And do not suppose that Isaiah or the other prophets speak of sacrifices of blood or libations being offered on the altar at his second coming, but only of true and spiritual praises and thanksgivings. DIALOGUE WITH TRYPHO 118.[16]

---

[13]Ps 110:4 (109:4 LXX). [14]Is 53:8. [15]Ezek 44:3. [16]FC 6:329-30*.

7:18-29 DAVID PRAYS TO THE LORD

[18]*Then King David went in and sat before the* LORD, *and said, "Who am I, O Lord* GOD, *and what is my house, that thou hast brought me thus far?* [19]*And yet this was a small thing in thy eyes, O Lord* GOD; *thou hast spoken also of thy servant's house for a great while to come, and hast shown me future generations,*[r] *O Lord* GOD! [20]*And what more can David say to thee? For thou knowest thy servant, O Lord* GOD! [21]*Because of thy promise, and according to thy own heart, thou hast wrought all this greatness, to make thy servant know it.* [22]*Therefore thou art great, O* LORD *God; for there is none like thee, and there is no God besides thee, according to all that we have heard with our ears.* [23]*What other*[s] *nation on earth is like thy people Israel, whom God went to redeem to be his people, making himself a name, and doing for them*[t] *great and terrible things, by driving out*[u] *before his people a nation and its gods?*[v] [24]*And thou didst establish for thyself thy people Israel to be thy people for ever; and thou, O* LORD, *didst become their God.* [25]*And now, O* LORD *God, confirm for ever the word which thou hast spoken concerning thy servant and concerning his house, and do as thou hast spoken;* [26]*and thy name will be magnified for ever, saying, 'The* LORD *of hosts is God over Israel,' and the house of thy servant David will be established before thee.* [27]*For thou, O* LORD *of hosts, the God of Israel, hast made this revelation to thy servant, saying, 'I will build you a house'; therefore thy servant has found courage to pray this prayer to thee.* [28]*And now, O Lord* GOD, *thou art God, and thy words are true, and thou hast promised this good thing to thy servant;* [29]*now therefore may it please thee to bless the house of thy servant, that it may continue for ever before thee; for thou, O Lord* GOD, *hast spoken, and with thy blessing shall the house of thy servant be blessed for ever."*

r Cn: Heb *this is the law for man*   s Gk: Heb *one*   t Heb *you*   u Gk 1 Chron 17.21: Heb *for your land*   v Heb *before thy people, whom thou didst redeem for thyself from Egypt, nations and its gods*

Overview: The house God promises to build David is both the "house of David" and the "house of God" as it is the dwelling place of God and his people in eternal union. This house, built by living virtuously through God's enablement, will receive its final consecration when God establishes a permanent and peaceful home for his people (Augustine).

7:18-29 David Was Motivated to Pray

Building the House of God. Augustine: David, understanding this, says in the second book of Kings [Samuel] . . . "You did also speak of the house of your servant for a long time to come." And, further on, "And now begin and bless the house of your servant that it may endure forever," etc. At that time, David was about to beget his son through whom his lineage would be carried down to Christ; through whom, in turn, his house was to be everlasting—indeed, identified with the house of God. It was to be called the "house of David" because [it was] of David's stock and, simultaneously, the "house of God" because it was a temple to God made not of stones but of people. In this house God's people shall everlastingly dwell with their God and in

their God, and God with his people and in his people, God filling his people, his people filled with their God, so that "God may be all in all"[1]— the very same God being their prize in peace who was their strength in battle.

It was with this in view that, when Nathan had said, "And the Lord said to you, that you shall build him a house," David said further on, "Because you, O Lord of hosts, God of Israel, have revealed to the ear of your servant, saying, 'I will build you a house.'" This is a house which we build by living virtuously and which God builds by helping us to live virtuously, for "unless the Lord builds the house, those who build it labor in vain."[2]

Only, however, when this house receives its final consecration will the words God spoke by Nathan's lips come true: "And I will appoint a place for my people Israel, and I will plant them, and they shall dwell therein, and shall be disturbed no more: neither shall the children of iniquity afflict them any more as they did before, from the day that I appointed judges over my people Israel." City of God 17.12.[3]

---

[1]1 Cor 15:28. [2]Ps 127:1 (126:1 LXX). [3]FC 24:58-59*.

8:1-8 DAVID'S VICTORIES AND SPOIL

[1]*After this David defeated the Philistines and subdued them, and David took Metheg-ammah out of the hand of the Philistines.*

[2]*And he defeated Moab, and measured them with a line, making them lie down on the ground; two lines he measured to be put to death, and one full line to be spared. And the Moabites became servants to David and brought tribute.*

[3]*David also defeated Hadadezer the son of Rehob, king of Zobah, as he went to restore his power at the river Euphrates.* [4]*And David took from him a thousand and seven hundred horsemen, and twenty thousand foot soldiers; and David hamstrung all the chariot horses, but left*

enough for a hundred chariots. ⁵And when the Syrians of Damascus came to help Hadadezer king of Zobah, David slew twenty-two thousand men of the Syrians.

OVERVIEW: David's wars after ascending to the throne prefigure the Savior's victories over pagans and the faithless (CASSIODORUS). The measuring out of lines of Moabites, some for death and some for life, is understood in the persons of Orpah and Ruth, who represent the diverging paths of idolatry and true faith (JEROME).

8:1-5 David Defeats Israel's Enemies

A FIGURE OF THE LORD'S VICTORIES. CASSIODORUS: The history of the Kings [Samuel] recounts that David won these victories after he succeeded Saul in the kingship, and it seems inappropriate to introduce them into our ordered arrangement here since they are known to be recounted extensively there. But we must realize that these wars are a description in figure of the Lord Savior's victories which he wins throughout the whole world over pagans and the faithless. It is their words which this psalm[1] will utter, so that when truly dislodged from their old superstition they may deserve to be changed through the grace of the new man. EXPOSITION OF THE PSALMS 59.1-2.[2]

THE SIGNIFICANCE OF THE TWO LINES. JEROME: In the second book of Kings [Samuel], where David defeated the Moabites, Scripture records the measuring out of two separate lines for life and two for death.[3] The significance of setting aside some Moabites for life and others for death is made clear by the story of Orpah and Ruth. Orpah, who turned back to idolatry and her ancient country, was destined for death; Ruth, following her mother-in-law, whose name means "pleasant," says, "Your people shall be my people, and your God my God."[4] HOMILIES ON THE PSALMS, ALTERNATE SERIES 61 (Ps 15).[5]

---

[1]Ps 60 (59 LXX). [2]ACW 52:62*. [3]2 Sam 8:2 LXX. [4]Ruth 1:16. [5]FC 57:25*.

[8:9-18 DAVID'S NAME AND KINGDOM ARE ESTABLISHED]

[9:1-13 DAVID HONORS HIS COVENANT WITH JONATHAN]

[10:1-19 CONFLICTS ARISE WITH THE AMMONITES AND SYRIANS]

11:1-5 DAVID AND BATHSHEBA

[2]*It happened, late one afternoon, when David arose from his couch and was walking upon the roof of the king's house, that he saw from the roof a woman bathing; and the woman was very beautiful.* [3]*And David sent and inquired about the woman. And one said, "Is not this Bathsheba, the daughter of Eliam, the wife of Uriah the Hittite?"* [4]*So David sent messengers, and took her; and she came to him, and he lay with her. (Now she was purifying herself from her uncleanness.) Then she returned to her house.* [5]*And the woman conceived; and she sent and told David, "I am with child."*

OVERVIEW: Fascinated by Bathsheba's nudity, David illustrates how a man cannot use his eyes without danger, even in his own house (JEROME). Typifying the church of the faithful, Bathsheba's washing and union with David may be viewed in a spiritual sense as prefiguring the cleansing of baptism and union with Christ (CASSIODORUS, GREGORY THE GREAT). Given that the soul is the charioteer of the body, guiding it into purity or debauchery, the affairs of prudence depend upon the will, not one's age (CHRYSOSTOM).

11:2 David Sees a Beautiful Woman Bathing

THE USE OF THE EYES. JEROME: David was a man after God's own heart, and his lips had often sung of the Holy One, the future Christ. Yet as he walked upon his housetop he was fascinated by Bathsheba's nudity, and [he] added murder to adultery. Notice here how, even in his own house, a man cannot use his eyes without danger. Then repenting, he says to the Lord, "Against you, you only, have I sinned and done this evil in your sight."[1] Being a king he feared no one else. LETTER 22.12.[2]

A TYPE OF THE CHURCH. CASSIODORUS: For blessed Jerome among others points out that Bathsheba manifested a type of the church or of human flesh and says that David bore the mark of Christ; this is clearly apt at many points. Just as Bathsheba when washing herself unclothed in the brook of Kidron[3] delighted David and deserved to attain the royal embraces, and her husband was slain at the prince's command, so too the church, the assembly of the faithful, once it has cleansed itself of the foulness of sins by the bath of sacred baptism, is known to be joined to Christ the Lord. It was indeed appropriate in those days that the future mysteries of the Lord should be manifested by a deed of this kind, and that what people considered a blameworthy act should be shown to point in a spiritual sense to a great mystery. EXPOSITION OF THE PSALMS 50 (51).1-2.[4]

THE LITERAL FULFILLED BY THE SPIRITUAL. GREGORY THE GREAT: But who that hears of it, not only among believers but among unbelievers themselves also, does not utterly loathe this,

[1]Ps 51:4 (50:4 LXX). [2]NPNF 2 6:26*. [3]Cf. 2 Sam 15:23. [4]ACW 51:493*.

that David walking upon his roof lusted after Bathsheba, the wife of Uriah? Yet when he [Uriah] returns back from the battle, he bids him go home to wash his feet. Whereupon he answered at once, "The ark of the Lord dwells in tents; shall I then take rest in my house?"[5] David receives him to his own table and delivers to him letters, through which he would die. But who does David walking upon his roof typify if not him concerning whom it is written, "He has set his tent in the sun."[6] And what else is it to draw Bathsheba to himself, but to join to himself by a spiritual meaning the law of the letter, which was united to a carnal people? For "Bathsheba" means "the seventh well," surely, in that through the knowledge of the law, with spiritual grace infused, perfect wisdom is ministered to us. And whom does Uriah denote but the Jewish people, whose name is interpreted "My light from God"? Now because the Jewish people are raised high by receiving the knowledge of the law, they glory as though "in the light of God." But David took from this Uriah his wife and united her to himself, surely in that the strong-handed One, which is the meaning of "David," our Redeemer, showed himself in the flesh, while he made known that the law spoke in a spiritual sense concerning himself. In this way, because it was held according to the letter, he demonstrated that he took it from the Jewish people and joined it to himself, in that he declared himself to be proclaimed by it. Yet David asks Uriah to "go home to wash his feet," in that when the Lord came in the flesh, he asked the Jewish people to turn back to the home of the conscience and to wipe off with their tears the defilements of their deeds, that they would understand the precepts of the law in a spiritual sense and, finding the font of baptism after the grievous hardness of the commandments, have recourse to water after toil. MORALS ON THE BOOK OF JOB 3.28.[7]

THE AFFAIRS OF PRUDENCE. CHRYSOSTOM: It would be better for the sun to be extinguished than for David's words to be forgotten and not transmitted to others. He fell into adultery and envy. For he saw, he says, a beautiful woman bathing and became enamored of her; and later he succeeded in doing all that he fancied.

And the prophet was found in adultery, the pearl in mud. However, he did not yet understand that he had sinned, the passion ravaged him to such a great extent. Because, when the charioteer gets drunk, the chariot moves in an irregular, disorderly manner. What the charioteer is to the chariot, the soul is to the body. If the soul becomes darkened, the body rolls in mud. As long as the charioteer stands firm, the chariot drives smoothly. However, when he becomes exhausted and is unable to hold the reins firmly, you see this very chariot in terrible danger. This exact same thing happens to human beings. As long as the soul is sober and vigilant, this very body remains in purity. However, when the soul is darkened, this very body rolls in mud and in lusts.

Therefore, what did David do? He committed adultery; yet neither was he aware nor was he censured by anyone. This occurred in his most venerable years, so you may learn that, if you are indolent, not even old age benefits you, nor, if you are earnest, can youthful years seriously harm you. Behavior does not depend on age but on the direction of the will. . . .

So you may learn that the affairs of prudence rely upon the will and do not depend on age, just remember that David was found in his venerable years falling into adultery and committing murder; and he reached such a pathetic state that he was unaware that he had sinned, because his mind, which was the charioteer, was drunk from debauchery. HOMILIES ON REPENTANCE AND ALMSGIVING 2.2.4-7.[8]

11:3-4 David Sends for Bathsheba

---

[5] 2 Sam 11:11. [6] Ps 19:4 (18:5 LXX). [7] LF 18:166-67*. [8] FC 96:18-19*.

11:6-27 DAVID SENDS FOR URIAH

¹⁴In the morning David wrote a letter to Joab, and sent it by the hand of Uriah. ¹⁵In the letter he wrote, "Set Uriah in the forefront of the hardest fighting, and then draw back from him, that he may be struck down, and die."

OVERVIEW: Confidence in Scripture's truth, which is founded on divine authority, is not to be undermined by its record of the blameworthy conduct of certain otherwise praiseworthy persons (AUGUSTINE). David's earlier character and actions toward Saul, set in stark contrast to his treatment of Uriah, illustrate the greatness of his failure (GREGORY THE GREAT).

11:14-15 David Gives Joab Instructions

CONFIDENT IN SCRIPTURE'S TRUTH. AUGUSTINE: Surely, it is better to believe that the apostle Paul wrote something untruthful than that the apostle Peter did not act uprightly. If that is so, then let us say something abhorrent, that it is better to believe that the gospel lies than that Christ was denied by Peter;[1] and that the book of Kings [Samuel] lies than that a great prophet, so eminently chosen by the Lord God, committed adultery by coveting and seducing another man's wife and was guilty of a revolting murder by killing her husband. On the contrary, I will read the holy Scripture with complete certainty and confidence in its truth, founded as it is on the highest summit of divine authority; and I would rather learn from it that people were truly approved or corrected or condemned than allow my trust in the divine Word to be everywhere undermined because I fear to believe that the human conduct of certain excellent and praiseworthy persons is sometimes worthy of blame. LETTER 82.[2]

THE FAILURE OF DAVID. GREGORY THE GREAT: Well-pleasing in almost all of his actions in the judgment of him who had chosen him, so soon as the burden of his obligations was not upon him, he broke out into festering conceit and showed himself as harsh and cruel in the murder of a man as he had been weakly dissolute in his desire for a woman. And he who had known how in pity to spare the wicked learned afterwards without let or hesitation to pant for the death of even the good. At first he had, indeed, been unwilling to strike down his captive persecutor, but afterwards, with loss to his wearied army, he killed even his loyal soldier. His guilt would, in fact, have removed him a long way from the number of the elect, had not scourgings restored him to pardon. PASTORAL CARE 1.3.[3]

---

[1]Mt 26:69-75. [2]FC 12:393-94*. [3]ACW 11:26-27.

12:1-6 THE PARABLE OF THE RICH MAN
AND THE POOR MAN

¹*And the* Lord *sent Nathan to David. He came to him, and said to him, "There were two men in a certain city, the one rich and the other poor.* ²*The rich man had very many flocks and herds;* ³*but the poor man had nothing but one little ewe lamb, which he had bought. And he brought it up, and it grew up with him and with his children; it used to eat of his morsel, and drink from his cup, and lie in his bosom, and it was like a daughter to him.* ⁴*Now there came a traveler to the rich man, and he was unwilling to take one of his own flock or herd to prepare for the wayfarer who had come to him, but he took the poor man's lamb, and prepared it for the man who had come to him."* ⁵*Then David's anger was greatly kindled against the man; and he said to Nathan, "As the* Lord *lives, the man who has done this deserves to die;* ⁶*and he shall restore the lamb fourfold, because he did this thing, and because he had no pity."*

OVERVIEW: Nathan's shrewd manner of confronting David with his own words and then by open rebuke is an effective strategy for taking the powerful of this world to task (GREGORY THE GREAT). David's harsh verdict against Nathan's figurative rich man is met with his immediate and pointed indictment, yet David's prompt confession of guilt is met with assurance of the Lord's forgiveness and the repeal of his self-condemning sentence (CHRYSOSTOM). David's lust was a one-time sinful fall rather than a habit as suggested in the metaphor of the guest. Nathan used the sharp scalpel of David's own words to remove the diseased tissue of his heart (AUGUSTINE).

12:1-6 Nathan's Story and David's Judgment

CHALLENGING THE POWERFUL. GREGORY THE GREAT: But at times, in taking to task the powerful of this world, they are first to be dealt with by drawing diverse comparisons in a case ostensibly concerning someone else. Then, when they give a right judgment on what apparently is another's case, they are to be taken to task regarding their own guilt by a suitable procedure. Thus a mind puffed up with temporal power cannot possibly lift itself up against the reprover, for by its own judgment it has trodden on the neck of pride; and it cannot argue to defend itself, as it stands convicted by the sentence out of its own mouth.

Thus it was that Nathan the prophet, coming to chide the king, to all appearance asked his judgment in the case of a poor man against a rich man. The king first was to deliver judgment and then to hear that he was the culprit. Thus he was completely unable to deny the just sentence which he had personally delivered against himself. Therefore, the holy man, considering both the sinner and the king, aimed in that wonderful manner at convicting a bold culprit first by his own admission and then cut him by his rebuke. For a short while he concealed the person whom he was aiming at and then at once struck him when he had convicted him. His stroke would, perhaps, have had less force if he had chosen to castigate the sin directly the moment he began to speak. But by beginning with a similitude, he sharpened the rebuke which he was concealing. He came like a physician to a sick man, saw that his wound had to be incised, but was in doubt about the endurance of the patient. He, therefore, concealed the surgeon's knife under his coat, but drawing it out suddenly, pierced the wound, that the sick man might feel the knife before he saw it, for if he had first seen it, he might have refused to feel it. Pastoral Care 3.2.[1]

The Good of a Prompt Confession. Chrysostom: Therefore, Nathan went to David and wove a dramatic act for judgment. And what did he say? "My king, I want your judgment. There was a certain rich man and a certain poor one. The rich person possessed herds of cattle and many other flocks; and the poor one had one ewe that drank from his glass, ate from his table and slept in his embrace." Here Nathan revealed the genuine bond between a husband and wife. "When a certain stranger arrived, the rich man desired to keep his own animals, and he took the poor man's ewe and slaughtered her." Here, do you see how Nathan wove the dramatic act, mysteriously concealing the weapon in the glands of David's throat? Then what did the king say? Thinking that he had to pass judgment against someone else, he decided most severely. For such are human beings. When it concerns other people, they gladly and abruptly render decisions and publicize them. And what did David say? "As the Lord lives, the man who did this thing is worthy of death. And he shall restore the lamb fourfold." Therefore, what did Nathan reply? He did not allow the wound to be relieved for many hours; rather, he quickly stripped it naked and sharply embedded the knife deeply into it, so as not to rob it of the painful sensation. "You are the man, my king." What did the king say? "I have sinned against the Lord." He did not say, "Who are you who censures me? Who sent you to speak with such boldness? With what daring did you prevail?" He did not say anything of the sort; rather, he perceived the sin. And what did he say? "I have sinned against the Lord." Therefore, what did Nathan say to him? "And the Lord remitted your sin." You condemned yourself; I [God] remit your sentence. You confessed prudently; you annulled the sin. You appropriated a condemnatory decision against yourself; I repealed the sentence. Can you see that what is written in Scripture was fulfilled: "Be the first to tell of your transgres-

sion so you may be justified"[2] How toilsome is it to be the first one to declare the sin? Homilies on Repentance and Almsgiving 2.2.9.[3]

The Fleeting Character of David's Sin. Augustine: And with what moderation and self-restraint those men used their wives appears chiefly in this, that when this same king, carried away by the heat of passion and by temporal prosperity, had taken unlawful possession of one woman, whose husband also he ordered to be put to death, he was accused of his crime by a prophet, who, when he had come to show him his sin, set before him the parable of the poor man who had but one ewe lamb, and whose neighbor, though he had many, yet when a guest came to him, refused to take of his own flock but set his poor neighbor's one lamb before his guest to eat. And David's anger being kindled against the man, he commanded that he should be put to death and the lamb restored fourfold to the poor man; thus unwittingly condemning the sin he had wittingly committed. And when he had been shown this, and God's punishment had been announced against him, he wiped out his sin in deep penitence. But yet in this parable it was the adultery only that was indicated by the poor man's ewe lamb. About the killing of the woman's husband—that is, about the murder of the poor man himself who had the one ewe lamb—nothing is said in the parable, so that the sentence of condemnation is pronounced against the adultery alone. And hence we may understand with what temperance he possessed a number of wives when he was forced to punish himself for transgressing in regard to one woman. But in his case the immoderate desire did not take up its abode with him but was only a passing guest. On this account the unlawful appetite is called even by the accusing prophet, a guest. For he did not say that he took the poor man's ewe lamb to make a feast for his king, but for his guest. In the case of his son Solomon, however, this lust did not come

---

[1]ACW 11:94-95*. [2]Is 43:26. [3]FC 96:20-21*.

and pass away like a guest but reigned as a king. And about him Scripture is not silent but accuses him of being a lover of strange women; for in the beginning of his reign he was inflamed with a desire for wisdom, but after he had attained it through spiritual love, he lost it through carnal lust.[4] CHRISTIAN INSTRUCTION 3.21.[5]

DISEASED TISSUE IN DAVID'S HEART. AUGUSTINE: For I admit my wrongdoing, and my offense confronts me all the time.[6] "I have not thrust my deed behind my back; I do not look askance at others while forgetting myself; I do not presume to extract a speck of straw from my brother's eye while there is a timber in my own;[7] my sin is in front of me, not behind my back. It was behind me until the prophet was sent to me and put to me the parable of the poor man's sheep." What the prophet Nathan said to David was this: There was a certain rich man who had a large flock of sheep. His neighbor was a poor man who had only one little ewe lamb; she rested in his arms and was fed from his own dish. Then a guest arrived at the rich man's house. The rich

man took nothing from his flock; what he wanted was the little ewe lamb that belonged to his neighbor, so he slaughtered that for his guest. What does he deserve? Angrily David pronounced sentence. Obviously the king was unaware of the trap into which he had fallen, and he decreed that the rich man deserved to die and must make fourfold restitution for the sheep. It was a very severe view, and entirely just. But his own sin was not yet before his eyes; what he had done was still behind his back. He did not yet admit his own iniquity and hence would not remit another's. But the prophet had been sent to him for this purpose. He brought the sin out from behind David's back and held it before his eyes, so that he might see that the severe sentence had been passed on himself. To cut away diseased tissue in David's heart and heal the wound there, Nathan used David's tongue as a knife. EXPLANATIONS OF THE PSALMS 50.[8]

---

[4]See 1 Kings 11:1-8. [5]NPNF 1 2:565. [6]Ps 51:3 (50:3 LXX). [7]See Mt 7:3. [8]WSA 3 16:415.

12:7-12 NATHAN CONFRONTS DAVID

[7]Nathan said to David, "You are the man. Thus says the LORD, the God of Israel, 'I anointed you king over Israel, and I delivered you out of the hand of Saul; [8]and I gave you your master's house, and your master's wives into your bosom, and gave you the house of Israel and of Judah; and if this were too little, I would add to you as much more. [9]Why have you despised the word of the LORD, to do what is evil in his sight? You have smitten Uriah the Hittite with the sword, and have taken his wife to be your wife, and have slain him with the sword of the Ammonites. [10]Now therefore the sword shall never depart from your house, because you have despised me, and have taken the wife of Uriah the Hittite to be your wife.' [11]Thus says the LORD, 'Behold, I will raise up evil against you out of your own house; and I will take your wives before your eyes, and give them to your neighbor, and he shall lie with your wives in the sight of this sun. [12]For you did it secretly; but I will do this thing before all Israel, and before the sun.'"

OVERVIEW: Nathan's foretelling of the evils to befall David on account of his adultery and murder illustrate one of the three classes of prophecy, namely that which refers to the earthly Jerusalem as distinguished from the heavenly Jerusalem and from both the heavenly and earthly Jerusalem (AUGUSTINE). That God sees and judges actions committed in secret is proven by the exposure of David's grave sins, thereby warning sinners of impending punishment (SALVIAN). Although a virtuous man through whom Christ would descend, David was punished for his adultery, even though he was repentant and was declared forgiven (ISAAC OF NINEVEH).

12:10-12 Nathan Pronounces the Lord's Judgment

CLASSES OF PROPHECY. AUGUSTINE: Thus, the prophets' sayings are of three classes: one class refers to the earthly, a second to the heavenly Jerusalem, and a third to both simultaneously. It will be best to support this assertion with illustration. The prophet Nathan was sent to accuse King David of a grave sin and to foretell what evils were to befall him on this account. Now no one can fail to see that this prophecy refers to the earthly city. There are others like it, sometimes addressed to the people at large for their profit and well-being, and sometimes to an individual who merited a word from God to foreknow some event for the guidance of his temporal life. CITY OF GOD 17.3.[1]

GOD SEES AND JUDGES SECRET ACTIONS. SALVIAN THE PRESBYTER: But that you may clearly know that his censure and sacred considerations deal more with actions than with persons themselves, hear how God, the judge, who many times gave sentences favorable to his servant David, often gave decisions unfavorable to him. This happened in a transaction which did not involve many men, or perhaps, what would have aroused God more, in a transaction involving holy men. It happened in the instance of one man, a foreigner, where the action rather than the person demanded punishment.

When Uriah the Hittite, a member of a wicked race and of an unfriendly nation, had been killed, the divine Word was immediately passed to David, "You have killed Uriah, the Hittite, with the sword and have taken his wife to be your wife, and have slain him with the sword of the children of Ammon. Therefore the sword shall never depart from your house. Thus said the Lord, 'Behold, I will raise up evil against you out of your own house; and I will take your wives before your eyes and give them to your neighbor. For you did it secretly: but I will do this thing in the sight of all Israel and in the sight of the sun.'"

What do you say to this, you who believe that God does not judge our actions and who believe that he has no concern whatsoever for us? Do you not see that the eyes of God were never absent even from that secret sin through which David fell once? Learn from this that you are always seen by Christ, understand and know that you will be punished, and perhaps very soon, you, who, perhaps in consolation for your sins, think that our acts are not seen by God. You see that the holy David was unable to hide his sin in the secrecy of his inmost rooms; neither was he able to claim exemption from immediate punishment through the privilege of great deeds. What did the Lord say to him? "I will take your wives before your eyes, and the sword shall never depart from your house." THE GOVERNANCE OF GOD 2.4.[2]

TEMPORAL PUNISHMENT REMAINED. ISAAC OF NINEVEH: And David, who was a man after God's own heart, who because of his virtues was found worthy to generate from his seed the promise of the fathers and to have Christ shine forth from himself for the salvation of all the world, was he not punished because of adultery with a woman, when he held her beauty with his eyes and was pierced in his soul by that arrow? For it

---

[1]FC 24:21. [2]FC 3:61-62*.

was because of this that God raised up a war against him from within his own household, and he who came forth from his loins pursued him. These things befell him even after he had repented with many tears, such that he moistened his couch with his weeping, and after God

had said to him through the prophet, "The Lord has forgiven your sin."[3] Ascetical Homilies 10.[4]

[3] 2 Sam 12:13. [4] *AHSIS 75*.

12:13-14 DAVID CONFESSES HIS SIN

[13]*David said to Nathan, "I have sinned against the Lord." And Nathan said to David, "The Lord also has put away your sin; you shall not die. *[14]*Nevertheless, because by this deed you have utterly scorned the Lord,*[a] *the child that is born to you shall die."*

a Heb *the enemies of the* Lord

Overview: That, as king, David frankly confessed his sin and humbly repented in sackcloth and ashes admonishes the private person to offer no less of an expression of remorse (Cyril of Jerusalem). While Matthew presents Christ's kingly descent through Solomon, Luke presents his priestly ascent through Nathan, because it was through Nathan the prophet that David obtained the annulment of his sin (Augustine). Those who are rightly accused of a great sin may take heart that they will be forgiven if they admit their guilt as David did (Ambrose). While the reward of David's great penitence for his misdeed was the avoidance of eternal punishment, he did not merit full pardon: the child died because of David's sin (Salvian). That God responded differently to the similar confessions of David and Saul reveals the dissimilarity of their hearts. For the baptized who have deserted or violated the faith, forgiveness may be obtained through the heartfelt repentance exhibited in uttering a confession of sin, doing genuine penance and living good lives afterwards (Augustine). While we should be ashamed to sin, we should not be

ashamed to repent, as this is the means of deliverance and healing (Pacian of Barcelona). Confession alone is not sufficient for the penitent, but must be accompanied by correction and humility, as David exemplifies (Paulinus of Milan).

12:13-14 Nathan Responds to David's Admission of Guilt

An Example of Repentance. Cyril of Jerusalem: If you like, however, I will give you further examples relating to our condition. Come then to the blessed David, and take him for your example of repentance. Great as he was, he suffered a fall. It was in the afternoon, after his siesta, that he took a turn on the housetop and saw by chance what stirred his human passion. He fulfilled the sinful deed, but his nobility, when it came to confessing the lapse, had not perished with the doing of the deed. Nathan the prophet came, swift to convict, but now as a healer for his wound, saying, "The Lord was angry, and you have sinned." So spoke a simple subject to his reigning sovereign. But David, though king and robed in purple, did not take it amiss, for he had regard not to the rank of the speaker but to the majesty of him who sent him. He was not puffed up by the fact that guardsmen were drawn up all around him, for the angelic host of the Lord came to his mind and he was in terror "as seeing him who is invisible."[1] So he answered and said to the man that came to him, or rather, in his person, to the God whose messenger he was, "I have sinned against the Lord." You see this royal humility and the making of confession. Surely no one had been convicting him, nor were there many who knew what he had done. Swiftly the deed was done and immediately the prophet appeared as accuser. Lo! The sinner confesses his wicked deed, and as it was full and frank confession, he had the swiftest healing. For the prophet Nathan first threatened him, but then said immediately, "And the Lord has put away your sin." And see how quickly lovingkindness changes the face of God! Except that he first declares, "you have given great occasion to the enemies of the Lord to blaspheme" as though he said "you have many that are your foes because of your righteousness, from whom nevertheless, you were kept safe by your upright living. But as you have thrown away this best of armors, you have now, standing ready to strike, these foes that are risen up against you."

So then the prophet comforted David as we have seen, but that blessed man, though he received most gladly the assurance, "The Lord has put away your sin," did not, king as he was, draw back from penitence. Indeed he put on sackcloth in place of his purple robe, and the king sat in ashes on the bare earth instead of on his gilded throne. And in ashes he did not merely sit, but took them for eating, as he himself says, "I have eaten ashes as it were bread, and mingled my drink with weeping."[2] His lustful eye he wasted away with tears; as he says, "every night I wash my bed and water my couch with my tears."[3] And when his courtiers exhorted him to eat food, he would not, but prolonged his fast for seven whole days. CATECHETICAL LECTURES 2.11-12.[4]

THE ANNULMENT OF HIS SIN. AUGUSTINE: But just as Matthew, presenting Christ the king as if descending for the assumption of our sins, thus descends from David through Solomon, because Solomon was born of her with whom David had sinned, so Luke, presenting Christ the priest as if ascending after the destroying of sins, ascends through Nathan to David, because Nathan the prophet had been sent, and by his reproof the penitent David obtained the annulling of his sin. ON EIGHTY-THREE VARIED QUESTIONS 61.[5]

ON ADMITTING ONE'S GUILT. AMBROSE: Are you ashamed, sir,[6] to do as David did—David, the king and the prophet, the ancestor of Christ according to the flesh? He was told of the rich man who had a great number of flocks and yet, when a guest arrived, took the poor man's one ewe lamb and killed it; and when he recognized that he was himself condemned by the story, he said, "I have sinned against the Lord." Therefore do not take it ill, sir, if what was said to King David is said to you, "You are the man." For if you listen with attention and say, "I have sinned against the Lord," if you say, in the words of the royal prophet, "O come, let us worship and fall down, and weep before the Lord our Maker,"[7] then it will be said to you also, "Because you repented, the Lord has put away your sin; you shall not die." LETTER 51.7.[8]

ETERNAL PUNISHMENT AVERTED. SALVIAN THE PRESBYTER: You see what instant judgment so great a man suffered for one sin. Immediate condemnation followed the fault, a condemnation immediately punishing and without reservation, stopping the guilty one then and there and not deferring the case to a later date. Thus he did not say, "because you have done this, know that the

---

[1]Heb 11:27. [2]Ps 102:9 (101:9 LXX). [3]Ps 6:6. [4]LCC 4:87-88*. [5]FC 70:118-19. [6]The Emperor Theodosius. This letter was written about 390 to encourage his repentance for ordering a massacre in Thessalonica. [7]Ps 95:6 (94:6 LXX). [8]LCC 5:255*.

judgment of God will come and you will be tormented in the fire of hell." Rather, he said, "You shall suffer immediate punishment and shall have the sword of divine severity at your throat."

And what followed? The guilty man acknowledged his sin, was humbled, filled with remorse, confessed and wept. He repented and asked for pardon, gave up his royal jewels, laid aside his robes of gold cloth, put aside the purple, resigned his crown. He was changed in body and appearance. He cast aside all his kingship with its ornaments. He put on the externals of a fugitive penitent, so that his squalor was his defense. He was wasted by fasting, dried up by thirst, worn from weeping and imprisoned in his own loneliness. Yet this king, bearing such a great name, greater in his holiness than in temporal power, surpassing all by the prerogative of his antecedent merits, did not escape punishment though he sought pardon so earnestly.

The reward of this great penitence was such that he was not condemned to eternal punishment. Yet, he did not merit full pardon in this world. What did the prophet say to the penitent? "Because you have given occasion to the enemies of the Lord to blaspheme, the son that is born to you shall die." Besides the pain of the bitter loss of his son, God wished that there be added to the very loving father an understanding of this greatest punishment, namely, that the father who mourned should himself bring death to his beloved son, when the son, born of his father's crime, was killed for the very crime that had begotten him. The Governance of God 2.4.[9]

God Inspects Hearts. Augustine: Similarity of words, dissimilarity of hearts. We may hear the similarity of the words with our ears, but we can only know the dissimilarity of hearts by the angel's declaration. David sinned, and when he was rebuked by the prophet, he said, "I have sinned," and was immediately told, "Your sin has been forgiven you." Saul sinned, and when he was rebuked by the prophet, he said, "I have sinned," and his sin was not forgiven, but the wrath of

God remained upon him. What can this mean but similarity of words, dissimilarity of hearts? Human beings can hear words, God inspects hearts. Sermon 291.5.[10]

The Effectiveness of Three Syllables. Augustine: Baptized people, though, who are deserters and violators of such a great sacrament, if they repent from the bottom of their hearts, if they repent where God can see, as he saw David's heart, when on being rebuked by the prophet, and very sternly rebuked, he cried out after hearing God's fearsome threats and said, "I have sinned," and shortly afterward heard, "God has taken away your sin." Such is the effectiveness of three syllables. "I have sinned" is just three syllables; and yet in these three syllables the flames of the heart's sacrifice rose up to heaven. So those who have done genuine penance, and have been absolved from the constraints by which they were bound and cut off from the body of Christ, and have lived good lives after their penance, such as they ought to have lived before penance, and in due course have passed away after being reconciled, why, they too go to God, go to their rest, will not be deprived of the kingdom, will be set apart from the people of the devil. Sermon 393.1.[11]

No Shame in Repentance. Pacian of Barcelona: May we by all means be filled with revulsion for sin but not for repentance. May we be ashamed to put ourselves at risk but not to be delivered. Who will snatch away the wooden plank from the shipwrecked so that he may not escape? Who will begrudge the curing of wounds? Does David not say, "Every single night I will bathe my bed, I will drench my couch in my tears."[12] And again, "I acknowledge my sin, and my iniquity I have not concealed"[13] And further, "I said, 'I will reveal against myself my sin to my God,' and you forgave the wickedness of my

---

[9]FC 3:62-63*. [10]WSA 3 8:134*. [11]WSA 3 10:427*. [12]Ps 6:6. [13]Ps 32:5 (31:5 LXX).

heart"[14] Did not the prophet answer [David] as follows when, after the guilt of murder and adultery for the sake of Bathsheba, he was penitent? "The Lord has taken away from you your sin." Letter 1.5.3.[15]

Confession and Correction. Paulinus of Milan: Indeed, to the penitent himself confession alone does not suffice, unless correction of the deed follows, with the result that the penitent does not continue to do deeds which

demand repentance. He should even humble his soul just as holy David, who, when he heard from the prophet: "Your sin is pardoned," became more humble in the correction of his sin, so that "he did eat ashes like bread and mingled his drink with weeping."[16] The Life of St. Ambrose 9.39.[17]

---

[14]Ps 32:5 (31:5 LXX). [15]FC 99:23. [16]See Ps 102:9 (101:9 LXX). [17]FC 15:57.

12:15-19 THE CHILD DIES DESPITE DAVID'S FASTING

[15]And the Lord struck the child that Uriah's wife bore to David, and it became sick. [16]David therefore besought God for the child; and David fasted, and went in and lay all night upon the ground. [17]And the elders of his house stood beside him, to raise him from the ground; but he would not, nor did he eat food with them.

Overview: David's repentance and fasting, offered not for his sin's sake but for his child's, does not atone for sin but encourages abstinence from all evil (Chrysostom). That David's prayerful and humble repentance did not move the Lord to spare his child's life shows that no crime deserves greater guilt than those that give others cause for blasphemy (Salvian).

12:15-17 David Pleads to God for the Child's Life

Abstaining from All Evil. Chrysostom: And I do not say this to overturn fasting (God forbid!) but to exhort you that with fasting you do that which is better than fasting, the abstaining from all evil. David also sinned. Let us see then how he too repented. Three days he sat on ashes.

But this he did not for the sin's sake but for the child's, being as yet stupefied with that affliction. But he wiped away the sin by other means, by humbleness, contrition of heart, compunction of soul, by falling into this sin no more, by remembering it always, by bearing thankfully every thing that befalls him, by sparing those that grieve him, by forbearing to requite those who conspire against him; yes, even preventing those who desire to do this. Homilies on 2 Corinthians 4.6.[1]

Causing Others to Blaspheme. Salvian the Presbyter: How particularly difficult it is to atone for the evil deed of handing over the name of the Lord to the blasphemy of the heathen, we are instructed by the example of the most blessed

---

[1]NPNF 1 12:299*.

David who, because of the intercession of his acts of justice, deserved to evade eternal punishment for his offenses through one confession only. Yet he, with penance as his protector, was unable to obtain full pardon for his sin. When Nathan the prophet had said to David, who was confessing his own sins to him, "The Lord has taken away your sin, you shall not die," he added immediately, "nevertheless, because you have given occasion to the enemies of the Lord to blaspheme, for this word, the child that is born to you, shall die."

And what happened next? Having laid aside his crown and put away his jewels, all splendor of royal dignity being removed, he was relieved of the purple. For all his sins he shut himself up alone, weeping, filthy in sackcloth, soaked in tears and soiled with ashes, and sought the life of his little child with the voice of many lamentations and beat upon the Most Holy God with great fervor or prayer. Thus asking and imploring, he believed he could in this manner obtain what he sought from God. Yet he was unable to obtain his request through what is the most forceful aid to those who ask.

From this it can be understood that there is no crime deserving of greater guilt than to give to the heathen a reason for blaspheming. For, whoever has erred gravely without giving cause for blasphemy to others brings damnation to himself only, but he who makes others blaspheme drags many to death with himself, he will, of necessity, be guilty of as many as he shall have drawn into guilt. Not only this, whatever sinner so sins that he does not cause others to blaspheme by his sin, his sin is injurious only to him who sins, but does not insult the holy name of God with the sacrilegious curse of those who blaspheme. But he who, by his sin, causes others to blaspheme, his sin is, of necessity, beyond the measure of human crime, because he has done unthinkable harm to God through the curses of many. THE GOVERNANCE OF GOD 4.18.[2]

---

[2]FC 3:122-23.

12:20-23 DAVID CEASES TO FAST AND WEEP

[20]*Then David arose from the earth, and washed, and anointed himself, and changed his clothes; and he went into the house of the LORD, and worshiped; he then went to his own house; and when he asked, they set food before him, and he ate.* [21]*Then his servants said to him, "What is this thing that you have done? You fasted and wept for the child while it was alive; but when the child died, you arose and ate food."* [22]*He said, "While the child was still alive, I fasted and wept; for I said, 'Who knows whether the LORD will be gracious to me, that the child may live?'* [23]*But now he is dead; why should I fast? Can I bring him back again? I shall go to him, but he will not return to me."*

OVERVIEW: Wisely recognizing God's power to preserve or end life, David ceased his fasting with the assurance that he would one day go to be with his deceased child. Since deceased believers are with Christ, there is no reason for excessively grieving over them (AMBROSE). David's mourning shows his outstanding paternal affection, which is combined with wisdom (CHRYSOSTOM).

12:20-23 David Ends His Fast

CONFIDENCE IN GOD'S JUDGMENT. AMBROSE: Holy David lost two sons. One was guilty of incest, the other of fratricide.[1] To have had them caused him shame; to have lost them brought him grief. He also lost a third, a child whom he loved. He wept over him while he was still alive, but he did not long for him after he died. For so we read that when the boy fell sick, David besought the Lord for him and fasted and lay upon sackcloth, and, although the elders approached him and tried to make him get up from the ground, he resolved neither to rise nor to eat. After he learned that the boy was dead, however, he arose from the ground, bathed upon the spot, anointed himself, changed clothing, worshiped the Lord and took food. Since this seemed strange to his servants, he answered that while the child was still alive, he had rightly fasted and wept, because he justly thought that God might pity him and was certain that he who could restore the dead to life could surely preserve the life of one still living. But now that the child was dead, why should he fast, since he could not bring him back from death and restore him to life. "I shall go to him rather;" he said, "but he shall not return to me."

What greater consolation to a mourner! What a true judgment from a wise man! What wonderful wisdom exhibited by a servant! [Thus] no one should protest that some misfortune has befallen him and complain that he has been afflicted contrary to his merit. For who are you to proclaim your merit beforehand? Why do you desire to anticipate your judge? Why do you snatch the verdict from the mouth of him who is going to pronounce it? ON HIS BROTHER SATYRUS 2.25-26.[2]

NO REASON FOR EXCESSIVE GRIEF. AMBROSE: Thus David wept for his son who was about to die; he did not grieve for him when dead. He wept that he might not be snatched from him, but he ceased to weep when he was snatched away, for he knew that he was with Christ. And that you may know what I declare is true, he wept for his incestuous son Amnon[3] when he was killed, and he mourned for the parricide Absalom when he perished, saying, "My son Absalom, my son Absalom!"[4] He did not think the innocent son should be mourned, because he believed that the others had perished for their crime but that the latter would live on account of his innocence.

Therefore, you have no reason for grieving excessively over your brother. He was born a man, he was subject to human frailty. CONSOLATION ON THE DEATH OF EMPEROR VALENTINIAN 47-48.[5]

DAVID'S PATERNAL AFFECTION AND WISDOM. CHRYSOSTOM: King David loved his child and sat indeed in sackcloth and ashes, but he neither brought soothsayers nor enchanters (although there were such then, as Saul shows), but he made supplication to God. So you should do likewise: as that just man did, so you should do also; the same words you should say, when your child is dead, "I shall go to him, but he will not come to me."[6] This is true wisdom, this is affection. However much you may love your child, you will not love so much as he had then. For even though his child was born of adultery, yet that blessed man's love of the mother was at its height, and you know that the offspring shares the love of the parents. And so great was his love toward it, that he even wished it to live, though it would be his own accuser, but still he gave thanks to God. HOMILIES ON COLOSSIANS 9.[7]

---

[1]Amnon and Absalom, respectively. [2]FC 22:206-7*. [3]See 2 Sam 13:28-29. [4]2 Sam 18:33. [5]FC 22:286. [6]2 Sam 12:23. [7]NPNF 1 13:299*.

[12:24-31 THE BIRTH OF SOLOMON]

13:1-22 AMNON RAPES TAMAR, HIS SISTER

¹Now Absalom, David's son, had a beautiful sister, whose name was Tamar; and after a time Amnon, David's son, loved her. . . .

⁸So Tamar went to her brother Amnon's house, where he was lying down. And she took dough, and kneaded it, and made cakes in his sight, and baked the cakes. ⁹And she took the pan and emptied it out before him, but he refused to eat. And Amnon said, "Send out every one from me." So every one went out from him. ¹⁰Then Amnon said to Tamar, "Bring the food into the chamber, that I may eat from your hand." And Tamar took the cakes she had made, and brought them into the chamber to Amnon her brother. ¹¹But when she brought them near him to eat, he took hold of her, and said to her, "Come, lie with me, my sister." ¹²She answered him, "No, my brother, do not force me; for such a thing is not done in Israel; do not do this wanton folly. ¹³As for me, where could I carry my shame? And as for you, you would be as one of the wanton fools in Israel. Now therefore, I pray you, speak to the king; for he will not withhold me from you." ¹⁴But he would not listen to her; and being stronger than she, he forced her, and lay with her.

OVERVIEW: No conditions can assure that one's chastity will be preserved, not past abstinence, nor living in the presence of relatives (FRUCTUO-SUS OF BRAGA). Amnon's case shows that even close family relations are no safeguard against illicit passion (JEROME).

13:11-14 Amnon Forces Tamar

CHASTE LIVING. FRUCTUOSUS OF BRAGA: No man shall rely upon chastity in the past, for none whose hearts are tainted by women can become holier than David or wiser than Solomon. That none may assume that his chastity is safe in the presence of a woman related to him, let him remember how Tamar was corrupted by her brother Amnon when he pretended to be ill. Accordingly, both monks and nuns should live so chastely that they may have a good report, not only before God but also before people, and may leave to those who follow an example of sanctity. GENERAL RULE FOR MONASTERIES 17.[1]

HE BURNED WITH ILLICIT PASSION. JEROME: As if to show that near relationship is no safeguard, Amnon burned with illicit passion for his sister Tamar.[2] LETTER 22.12.[3]

---

[1]FC 63:201*. [2]2 Sam 8. [3]NPNF 2 6:26-27.

[13:23-29 ABSALOM TAKES REVENGE]

13:30-39 ABSALOM FLEES TO GESHUR

[34]*But Absalom fled. . . .* [35]*And Jonadab said to the king, "Behold, the king's sons have come; as your servant said, so it has come about."* [36]*And as soon as he had finished speaking, behold, the king's sons came, and lifted up their voice and wept; and the king also and all his servants wept very bitterly.* [37]*But Absalom fled, and went to Talmai the son of Ammihud, king of Geshur. And David mourned for his son day after day.* [38]*So Absalom fled, and went to Geshur, and was there three years.* [39]*And the spirit[h] of the king longed to go forth to Absalom; for he was comforted about Amnon, seeing he was dead.*

h Gk: Heb *David*

OVERVIEW: The first introduction of divine punishment for David's adultery and murder, which begins a series of great tribulations, is demonstrated in the slaying of Amnon (SALVIAN).

13:36-38 *Absalom Flees*

A SUCCESSION OF MISFORTUNES. SALVIAN THE PRESBYTER: This is the first introduction of divine punishment; the first but not the only one. A long series of great tribulations followed, and an almost unending succession of misfortunes scarcely left his house. Tamar was corrupted by the madness of Amnon, and Amnon was slain by Absalom. A grave crime was committed by one brother, but it was avenged more grievously by the other. In this way David, the father, was punished for the crimes of both. Two sons sinned, but three suffered for the crime of two; Tamar lost her virginity, and the loss of Absalom was mourned in Amnon. Indeed, you cannot tell for which of these two sons the loving father mourned more grievously: for him who was slain in this world by his brother's hand [Amnon] or for him who perished in the next because of killing by his own hand [Absalom]. THE GOVERNANCE OF GOD 2.5.[1]

---

[1]FC 3:63-64*.

14:1-17 THE WISE WOMAN OF TEKOA

[1]*And Joab sent to Tekoa, and fetched from there a wise woman. . . .*

[12]*Then the woman said, "Pray let your handmaid speak a word to my lord the king." He said, "Speak." [13]And the woman said, "Why then have you planned such a thing against the people of God? For in giving this decision the king convicts himself, inasmuch as the king does not bring his banished one home again. [14]We must all die, we are like water spilt on the ground, which cannot be gathered up again; but God will not take away the life of him who devises[i] means not to keep his banished one an outcast."*

i Cn: Heb *and he devises*

OVERVIEW: God's main purpose is not that humans should perish but that they should live forever (CASSIAN).

14:14 God's Preservation of Human Life

GOD'S UNCHANGING PURPOSE. JOHN CASSIAN: For God's purpose, according to which he did not make the human being to perish but to live forever, abides unchanging. When his kindness sees shining in us the slightest glimmer of good will, which he himself has in fact sparked from the hard flint of our heart, he fosters it, stirs it up and strengthens it with his inspiration, "desiring all to be saved and to come to the knowledge of the truth."[1] For, he says, "it is not the will of your Father who is in heaven that one of these little ones should perish."[2] And again he says, "God does not wish a soul to perish, but he withdraws and reflects, lest one who has been cast down perish utterly." CONFERENCE 13.7.[3]

[1]1 Tim 2:4. [2]Mt 18:14. [3]ACW 57:472.

[14:18-33 DAVID AND ABSALOM REUNITE]

15:1-6 ABSALOM TURNS THE ISRAELITES AWAY FROM DAVID

[2]*And Absalom used to rise early and stand beside the way of the gate; and when any man had a suit to come before the king for judgment, Absalom would call to him, and say, "From what city are*

you?" And when he said, "Your servant is of such and such a tribe in Israel," [3]Absalom would say to him, "See, your claims are good and right; but there is no man deputed by the king to hear you." [4]Absalom said moreover, "Oh that I were judge in the land! Then every man with a suit or cause might come to me, and I would give him justice." [5]And whenever a man came near to do obeisance to him, he would put out his hand, and take hold of him, and kiss him. [6]Thus Absalom did to all of Israel who came to the king for judgment; so Absalom stole the hearts of the men of Israel.

OVERVIEW: Absalom illustrates that nothing substantial or lasting is gained by attempting to ply others' hearts through feigned mildness, demonstrating that a right standard between mildness and harshness should be observed (AMBROSE). Prudence, which may be greatly hindered by wickedness, is required for the proper conduct of affairs. This is illustrated by the outcomes of the treacherous Absalom and guileless David (CHRYSOSTOM).

15:3-6 Absalom Steals the Hearts of the Israelites

A FALSE SHOW OF MILDNESS. AMBROSE: Moreover, due measure befits even our words and instructions, that it may not seem as though there was either too great mildness or too much harshness. Many prefer to be too mild, so as to appear to be good. But it is certain that nothing feigned or false can bear the form of true virtue; no, it cannot even last. At first it flourishes; then, as time goes on, like a flower it fades and passes away, but what is true and sincere has a deep root. . . .

Absalom was king David's son, known for his beauty, of splendid appearance and in the heyday of youth; so that no other man like him was found in Israel.[1] He was without a blemish from the sole of his foot to the crown of his head. He had his own chariot and horses and fifty men to run before him. He rose at early dawn and stood before the gate in the way, and whoever he knew to be seeking the judgment of the king, he called to himself, saying . . . "Is there no one given to you by the king to hear you? Who will make me a judge? And whosoever will come to me, that has

need of judgment, I will give him justice." With such words he cajoled them. And when they came to make obeisance to him, stretching forth his hand he took hold of them and kissed them. So he turned the hearts of all to himself. For flattery of this sort quickly finds its way to touch the very depths of the heart. DUTIES OF THE CLERGY 2.22.112-14.[2]

A HINDRANCE TO PRUDENCE. CHRYSOSTOM: For nothing is so necessary for the proper conduct of affairs as prudence; and there is no greater hindrance to prudence than wickedness and malice and hollowness. Look at people suffering from a liver ailment. How unsightly they are, with all their bloom withered away. How weak they are, and puny, and unfit for anything. So also are souls of this nature. What else is wickedness but a jaundice of the soul? Wickedness then has no strength in it. Indeed, it has none whatever. Will you mind that I again make what I am saying plain to you . . . by setting before you the portraits of a treacherous and a guileless man? Absalom was a treacherous man and "stole all the people's hearts." And observe how great was his treachery. "He went about," it says, "and said, 'Have you no justice?'" wishing to conciliate every one to himself. But David was guileless. What then? Look at the end of them both, look, how full of utter madness was the former! For inasmuch as he looked solely to the hurt of his father, in all other things he was blinded. HOMILIES ON EPHESIANS 15.[3]

---

[1]Cf. 2 Sam 14:25. [2]NPNF 2 10:60-61*. [3]NPNF 1 13:122-23*.

[15:7-18 ABSALOM USURPS THE THRONE]

[15:19-29 SUPPORTERS RALLY AROUND DAVID]

15:30-37 A PLAN TO FOIL AHITHOPHEL'S COUNSEL

[30]*But David went up the ascent of the Mount of Olives, weeping as he went, barefoot and with his head covered; and all the people who were with him covered their heads, and they went up, weeping as they went.* [31]*And it was told David, "Ahithophel is among the conspirators with Absalom." And David said, "O LORD, I pray thee, turn the counsel of Ahithophel into foolishness."*

OVERVIEW: By choosing to escape Absalom by way of the Mount of Olives, David invokes in his mind the Deliverer who would ascend from there into heaven. His deliverance, having sinned and repented, encourages our repentance (CYRIL OF JERUSALEM). The spectacle of David's flight as a pitiable and scorned outcast is rightly enumerated among the misfortunes that he suffered as part of God's judgment for his sins (SALVIAN). While Absalom chose to follow bad advice by his own will, he only did so because God answered David's prayer to this effect (AUGUSTINE). Since God is able to overrule the counsels of princes and nations, as he did the advice of Ahithophel, Christians who are threatened by these should appeal to the Lord for help (BASIL).

15:30 David Ascends the Mount of Olives

MINDFUL OF THE DELIVERER. CYRIL OF JERUSALEM: Again, after Absalom's rebellion, when David was in flight, with many possible routes before him, he chose to make his escape by the Mount of Olives, as good as invoking in his own mind the Deliverer who should from there ascend into the heavens. And when Shimei cursed him bitterly he said, "Let him be."[1] For he knew that forgiveness is for those who forgive. . . . As, then, brothers, you have many examples of people who have sinned and then repented and been saved, do you also make confession to the Lord with all your heart, so as to receive pardon of all your sins of the time past and be accounted worthy of the heavenly gift and inherit the heavenly kingdom with all the saints in Christ Jesus, to whom be glory, world without end. Amen. CATECHETICAL LECTURES 2.12, 20.[2]

A PUBLIC SPECTACLE. SALVIAN THE PRESBYTER: According to the word of God, misfortunes were piled up from this time on. The father suffered long from the treachery of his son. . . .

Is the spectacle of David's flight to be added to this account? Of such a nature was the flight that

---

[1]Cf. 2 Sam 16:11. [2]LCC 4:88-89*.

such a great king, of so great a reputation, greater and more honored than all other kings in the world, fled from his people with but a few servants. In comparison with his recent state, he was indeed poor; in comparison with his customary entourage, he was indeed alone. He fled in fear, disgrace and sorrow, "walking," says Scripture, "with head covered and barefoot." He was a witness of his former estate, an exile from his former self, almost one who lives after his own death. He was cast down so low that he received the scorn of his own servants, which is grave, or their pity, which is graver still. Sheba fed him, and Shimei did not fear to curse him in public.[3] He was so changed from his former self by God's judgment that he, whom the entire world had once feared, was insulted to his face by a single enemy. THE GOVERNANCE OF GOD 2.5.[4]

15:31 Turn the Counsel of Ahithophel into Foolishness

THE WILL AND THE LORD. AUGUSTINE: Was it not by Absalom's own will that he chose to follow advice that proved detrimental to him, though he only did so because the Lord had heard his father's prayer to this effect? ON GRACE AND FREE WILL 20.41.[5]

THE COUNSELS OF NATIONS. BASIL THE GREAT: Thus, then, the Lord knew how to bring to nothing the counsels of nations. We learned in the time of Ahithophel how he cast away the counsels of the princes, when David prayed, saying, "Infatuate the counsel of Ahithophel." Therefore, when you hear someone making great threats and announcing that he will bring upon you all sorts of ill treatment, losses, blows or death, look up to the Lord who brings to nothing the counsels of nations and rejects the devices of the people. HOMILIES ON THE PSALMS 32.6.[6]

---

[3]2 Sam 16. [4]FC 3:64-65*. [5]FC 59:300. [6]FC 46:240*.

16:1-4 DAVID MEETS ZIBA, SERVANT OF MEPHIBOSHETH

[1]*When David had passed a little beyond the summit, Ziba the servant of Mephibosheth met him, with a couple of asses saddled, bearing two hundred loaves of bread, a hundred bunches of raisins, a hundred of summer fruits, and a skin of wine. [2]And the king said to Ziba, "Why have you brought these?" Ziba answered, "The asses are for the king's household to ride on, the bread and summer fruit for the young men to eat, and the wine for those who faint in the wilderness to drink." [3]And the king said, "And where is your master's son?" Ziba said to the king, "Behold, he remains in Jerusalem; for he said, 'Today the house of Israel will give me back the kingdom of my father.'"*

OVERVIEW: David was deceived by Ziba, which should serve as a warning to all who are in authority to make sure they are not similarly deceived (THEODORET).

16:1-3 *Ziba Refreshes David and His Household*

It is Easy to be Deceived. Theodoret of Cyr: It ought not to excite astonishment that Constantine was so far deceived as to send so many great men into exile: for he believed the assertions of bishops of high fame and reputation, who skillfully concealed their malice. Those who are acquainted with the Sacred Scriptures know that the holy David, although he was a prophet, was deceived; and that too not by a priest, but by one who was a menial, a slave and a rascal. I mean Ziba, who deluded the king by lies against Mephibosheth, and thus obtained his land. It is not to condemn the prophet that I speak in this way; but that I may defend the emperor, by showing the weakness of human nature, and to teach that credit should not be given only to those who advance accusations, even though they may appear worthy of credit; but that the other party ought also to be heard, and that one ear should be left open to the accused. Ecclesiastical History 1.31.[1]

---

[1]NPNF 2 3:64.

16:5-14 DAVID ENDURES THE CURSING OF SHIMEI

[9]Then Abishai the son of Zeruiah said to the king, "Why should this dead dog curse my lord the king? Let me go over and take off his head." [10]But the king said, "What have I to do with you, you sons of Zeruiah? If he is cursing because the Lord has said to him, 'Curse David,' who then shall say, 'Why have you done so?' " [11]And David said to Abishai and to all his servants, "Behold, my own son seeks my life; how much more now may this Benjaminite! Let him alone, and let him curse; for the Lord has bidden him. [12]It may be that the Lord will look upon my affliction,[p] and that the Lord will repay me with good for this cursing of me today." [13]So David and his men went on the road, while Shime-i went along on the hillside opposite him and cursed as he went, and threw stones at him and flung dust.

p Gk Vg: Heb *iniquity*

Overview: By enduring Shimei's insults while fully able to silence them, David recognized the need for humility and acceptance of God's will as he exercised the utmost patience (Augustine). By refusing to be troubled by the cursing, David's exemplary silence and humility defend his good character better than action could (Ambrose). That God inclined the debased will of Shimei to curse David, rather than commanding him to do it, proves that God uses the hearts of even the wicked to assist the good (Augustine). David illustrated, in true evangelical spirit, the virtues of humility, justice and prudence as he thankfully endured abuse rather than taking offense at it (Ambrose). Although the holy may grow weary in maintaining justice, David's kindly acceptance of God's will provides encouragement (Jerome). When we nobly endure evil at the hands of others, as David did, it brings advantage as God reckons the ill treatment we suffer against our debt (CHRYSOSTOM).

16:9-13 David Allows Shimei to Continue His Cursing

PATIENT ENDURANCE. AUGUSTINE: By this patience we are supported even when we are in sound health, for, amid the stumbling blocks of this world, our true happiness is deferred. . . . With this patience holy David endured the insults of one abusing him, and, though he could easily have wreaked vengeance on him, he not only did not do this but even calmed another who was grieved and disturbed on his account and used his royal power to forbid rather than to exercise vengeance. He was not then suffering from any bodily disease or wound. But he did recognize the time of humility and accepted the will of God for whose sake he drank in the bitter reproach with the utmost patience. ON PATIENCE 9.8.[1]

IMITATE SILENCE AND HUMILITY. AMBROSE: What need is there to be troubled when we hear abuse? Why do we not imitate him who says, "I was dumb and humbled myself, and kept silence even from good words."[2] Or did David only say this, and not act up to it? No, he also acted up to it. For when Shimei the son of Gera reviled him, David was silent; and although he was surrounded with armed men he did not return the abuse, nor seek revenge: no, even when the son of Zeruiah spoke to him, because he wished to take vengeance on him, David did not permit it. He went on as though dumb and humbled; he went on in silence; nor was he disturbed, although called a bloody man, though he was conscious of his own gentleness. He therefore was not disturbed by insults, for he had full knowledge of his own good works.

He, then, who is quickly roused by wrong makes himself seem deserving of insult, even while he wishes to be shown not to deserve it. He who despises wrongs is better off than he who grieves over them. For he who despises them looks down on them, as though he doesn't feel them; but he who grieves over them is tormented, just as though he actually felt them. DUTIES OF THE CLERGY 1.6.21-22.[3]

GOD INCLINES THE HEART. AUGUSTINE: And was it not likewise of his own will that the wicked son of Gera cursed King David? And yet what does David say, full of true and deep and pious wisdom? What did he say to him who wanted to strike the reviler? "What," he said, "have I to do with you, you sons of Zeruiah? Let him alone and let him curse, because the Lord has said to him, 'Curse David.' Who, then, shall say, 'Why have you done so?'" And then the inspired Scripture, as if it would confirm the king's profound utterance by repeating it once more, tells us, "And David said to Abishai, and to all his servants, 'Behold, my son, who came forth from my body, seeks my life: how much more may this Benjamite do it! Let him alone, and let him curse; for the Lord has bidden him. It may be that the Lord will look on my humiliation and will requite me for his cursing this day.'" Now what prudent reader will fail to understand in what way the Lord bade this profane man to curse David? It was not by a command that he bade him, in which case his obedience would be praiseworthy; but he inclined the man's will, which had become debased by his own perverseness, to commit this sin, by his own just and secret judgment. Therefore it is said, "The Lord said to him." Now if this person had obeyed a command of God, he would have deserved to be praised rather than punished, as we know he was afterwards punished for this sin. Nor is the reason an obscure one why the Lord told him after this manner to curse David. "It may be," said the humbled king, "that the Lord will look on my humiliation and will requite me good for his cursing this day." See, then, what proof we have here that God uses the hearts of

---

[1]FC 16:243. [2]Ps 39:2 (38:2 LXX). [3]NPNF 2 10:4*.

even wicked people for the praise and assistance of the good. On Grace and Free Will 41.20.[4]

Blessing Those Who Curse. Ambrose: We can show, too, that holy David was like Paul in this same class of virtue. When . . . Shimei cursed him and charged him with heavy offenses, at the first he was silent and humbled himself, and was silent even about his good deeds, that is, his knowledge of good works. Then he even asked to be cursed; for when he was cursed he hoped to gain divine pity.

But see how he stored up humility and justice and prudence so as to merit grace from the Lord! At first he said, "Therefore he cursed me, because the Lord has said to him that he should curse." Here we have humility; for he thought that those things which are divinely ordered were to be endured with an even mind, as though he were but some servant lad. Then he said, "Behold, my son, who came forth of my body, seeks my life." Here we have justice. For if we suffer hard things at the hand of our own family, why are we angry at what is done to us by strangers? Lastly he says, "Let him alone that he may curse, for the Lord has bidden him. It may be that the Lord will look on my humiliation and requite me good for this cursing." So he bore not only the abuse but left the man unpunished when throwing stones and following him. No, even more. After his victory he freely granted him pardon when he asked for it.

I have written to show that holy David, in true evangelical spirit, was not only not offended but was even thankful to his abuser and was delighted rather than angered by his wrongs, for which he thought some return would be granted to him. But, though perfect, he sought something still more perfect. As a man he grew hot at the pain of his wrongs, but like a good soldier he conquered, he endured like a brave wrestler. Duties of the Clergy 1.48.245-47.[5]

Kindly Accept God's Will. Jerome: Have recourse, O Lord, always to your mercy, and sustain the weakness of my flesh by your divine assistance. "What have I to do," he says, "with you also, you sons of Zeruiah? Let Shimei curse. The Lord has bidden him to curse David. And who shall say to him, 'Why have you done so?'" For the will of God is not to be discussed but kindly accepted. . . . Therefore, the commandments of God are possible, which we know David had kept; and, yet, we find holy people growing weary in maintaining justice forever. Defense Against the Pelagians 2.20.[6]

Reckoned Towards Our Debt. Chrysostom: For if we suffer evil by human hands, we cut off no small part of our debt by nobly bearing what is done to us. Therefore we receive no injury; for God reckons the ill treatment towards our debt, not according to the principle of justice but of his lovingkindness; and for this cause he didn't relieve the one who suffered evil. . . . And when he bore with Shimei cursing him, David said, "Let him alone, that the Lord may see my abasement and requite me [with] good for this day." For when he doesn't aid us when we suffer wrong, then we are advantaged most of all; for he sets it to the account of our sins, if we bear it thankfully. Homilies on 2 Corinthians 23.7.[7]

---

[4]NPNF 1 5:461*. [5]NPNF 2 10:39*. [6]FC 53:327-28*. [7]NPNF 1 12:388-89**.

16:15-23 ABSALOM SEEKS AHITHOPHEL'S COUNSEL

[20]*Then Absalom said to Ahithophel, "Give your counsel; what shall we do?"* [21]*Ahithophel said to Absalom, "Go in to your father's concubines, whom he has left to keep the house; and all Israel will hear that you have made yourself odious to your father, and the hands of all who are with you will be strengthened."* [22]*So they pitched a tent for Absalom upon the roof; and Absalom went in to his father's concubines in the sight of all Israel.* [23]*Now in those days the counsel which Ahithophel gave was as if one consulted the oracle[r] of God; so was all the counsel of Ahithophel esteemed, both by David and by Absalom.*

r Heb *word*

OVERVIEW: David's shame, as an exiled king fleeing a murderous son, climaxes as Absalom's public incest brings defilement upon the king and his kingdom (SALVIAN).

16:21-22 Absalom Lays with David's Concubines

A PUBLIC DISGRACE. SALVIAN THE PRESBYTER: He was expelled from his kingdom and fled as an exile to escape murder. You do not know of a son more wicked and bloodthirsty. Because he could not kill his father in his attempt to murder him, he defiled him with incest. By heaping crime on crime, he achieved an incest beyond all incest. He committed in public a thing most shameful to his father, a crime which is abominable in secret. Not only his absent father was made to look hideous by his son's deadly crime, but the eyes of all were polluted by his public incest. THE GOVERNANCE OF GOD 2.5.[1]

[1]FC 3:64*.

17:1-4 AHITHOPHEL ADVISES ABSALOM TO ATTACK

[1]*Moreover Ahithophel said to Absalom, "Let me choose twelve thousand men, and I will set out and pursue David tonight.* [2]*I will come upon him while he is weary and discouraged, and throw him into a panic; and all the people who are with him will flee. I will strike down the king only,* [3]*and I will bring all the people back to you as a bride comes home to her husband. You seek the life of only one man,[s] and all the people will be at peace."* [4]*And the advice pleased Absalom and all the elders of Israel.*

s Gk: Heb *like the return of the whole (is) the man whom you seek*

OVERVIEW: Flattery, like that of Ahithophel which pleased Absalom, is opposed to humility (CHRYSOSTOM).

17:1-4 Ahithophel Advises an Immediate Attack

FLATTERY IS OPPOSED TO HUMILITY. CHRYSOSTOM: There is nothing so foreign to a Christian soul as haughtiness. Haughtiness, I say, not boldness nor courage, for these are agreeable. But these are one thing, and that is another; so too humility is one thing, and ignobility, flattery and adulation another. I will now, if you wish, give you examples of all these qualities. For these things which are contraries, seem in some way to be placed close together, as the tares are to the wheat and the thorns to the rose. But while babes might easily be deceived, those who are mature in truth and are skilled in spiritual husbandry know how to separate what is really good from the bad. Let me then lay before you examples of these qualities from the Scriptures. What is flattery and ignobility and adulation? Ziba flattered David out of season and falsely slandered his master.[1] Much more did Ahithophel flatter Absalom. But David was not like this but was humble. For the deceitful are flatterers, as when they say, "O king, live forever."[2] Again, what flatterers the magicians are. HOMILIES ON PHILIPPIANS 5.[3]

---

[1]2 Sam 14:1-3. [2]Dan 2:4. [3]NPNF 1 13:205**.

17:5-14 HUSHAI FRUSTRATES AHITHOPHEL'S ADVICE

[6]*And when Hushai came to Absalom, Absalom said to him, "Thus has Ahithophel spoken; shall we do as he advises? If not, you speak."* [7]*Then Hushai said to Absalom, "This time the counsel which Ahithophel has given is not good."* . . . [14]*And Absalom and all the men of Israel said, "The counsel of Hushai the Archite is better than the counsel of Ahithophel." For the LORD had ordained to defeat the good counsel of Ahithophel, so that the LORD might bring evil upon Absalom.*

OVERVIEW: God frustrated Ahithophel's counsel, which could have granted Absalom success, by influencing Absalom's heart to reject it (AUGUSTINE). Accomplished by the Lord's will, Hushai's deception of Absalom, which ensured the good purpose of David's safety and victory, is not blameworthy but approved by divine Scripture (CASSIAN).

17:14 The Lord Defeated the Counsel of Ahithophel

A DISINCLINATION TO GOOD COUNSEL. AUGUSTINE: Accordingly, as the Scripture says, "And by the command of the Lord the good counsel of Ahithophel was defeated, that the Lord might bring evil upon Absalom." The counsel of

Ahithophel was called "good" because it served his purpose for the time, since it favored Absalom over his father whom he had risen up against in rebellion. And it might well have destroyed him if the Lord had not frustrated Ahithophel's counsel by influencing the heart of Absalom to reject this counsel and to choose another which was not to his advantage. On Grace and Free Will 20.41.[1]

Good by Way of Deception. John Cassian: For what shall we say about Hushai's pious deception of Absalom for the sake of King David's safety which, although formulated with good will by the deceiver and cheater and

opposed to the well-being of the questioner, is approved by the text of divine Scripture that says, "By the will of the Lord the useful advice of Ahithophel was undone, so that the Lord might bring evil upon Absalom"? For what was accomplished with a right intention and pious judgment for a good purpose and conceived for the safety and religious victory of a man whose piety was pleasing to God, all by way of deception, could not be blamed. Conference 17.19.5.[2]

---

[1]FC 59:300*. [2]ACW 57:598*.

17:15-20 HUSHAI SENDS WORD TO DAVID

[15]Then Hushai said to Zadok and Abiathar the priests, "Thus and so did Ahithophel counsel Absalom and the elders of Israel; and thus and so have I counseled. [16]Now therefore send quickly and tell David, 'Do not lodge tonight at the fords of the wilderness, but by all means pass over; lest the king and all the people who are with him be swallowed up.'" [17]Now Jonathan and Ahima-az were waiting at En-rogel; a maidservant used to go and tell them, and they would go and tell King David; for they must not be seen entering the city. [18]But a lad saw them, and told Absalom; so both of them went away quickly, and came to the house of a man at Bahurim, who had a well in his courtyard; and they went down into it. [19]And the woman took and spread a covering over the well's mouth, and scattered grain upon it; and nothing was known of it. [20]When Absalom's servants came to the woman at the house, they said, "Where are Ahima-az and Jonathan?" And the woman said to them, "They have gone over the brook[u] of water." And when they had sought and could not find them, they returned to Jerusalem.

u The meaning of the Hebrew word is uncertain

Overview: Comparing the history of Hushai's role in aiding David with the seventh psalm, the name "son of Jemini" is understood as an ascription given to Hushai in honor of his valiant service to David (Basil). With the woman's deception of Absalom's servants as a case in

point, the apostle's charge to prefer the good of others over one's own well-being will undoubtedly necessitate lying on occasion (Cassian).

17:15-16 Hushai Gives the Priests a Message for David

Son of the Right Hand. Basil the Great:
For in the history, Hushai is mentioned as the
chief companion of David and the son of Arachi,
but in the psalm,[1] Hushai is the son of Jemini. Neither he nor any other of those appearing in the history was the son of Jemini. Perhaps he was called
the son of Jemini for this reason, because he displayed great valor and strength through a mere
pretense of friendship, going over, as he pretended,
to Absalom, but in reality thwarting the plans of
Ahithophel, a very skilled man, well trained in military affairs, who was giving his counsel. "The son
of Jemini" is interpreted "the son of the right
hand." By his proposals he prevented the acceptance of the plan of Ahithophel—that no time
should intervene in the affairs but that an attack
should be made immediately on the father while he
was unprepared— "in order that," as Scripture
says, "the Lord might bring all evils upon Absalom." At all events, he seemed to them to introduce more plausible reasons for postponement and
delay, while his real purpose was to give time to
David to gather his forces. Because of Hushai's
counsel he was acceptable to Absalom, who said,
"The counsel of Hushai the Archite is better than
the counsel of Ahithophel."

However, Hushai informed David through the
priests Zadok and Abiathar of the decision and
bade him not to camp in Araboth in the desert
but urged him to cross it. Since, then, he was on
the right hand of David through his good advice,
he obtained the name from his brave deed. Surely
it is because of this that he is called "son of Jemini," that is, "son of the right hand." It is a custom
of Scripture not only to give those who are more
wicked a name from their sin rather than from
their fathers but also to call the better sons from
the virtue characterizing them. Homilies on
the Psalms 7.1.[2]

17:19-20 A Woman Deceives Absalom's Servants

Loving May Necessitate Lying. John Cassian: And what shall we say about the deed of
the woman who received those who had been
sent to King David by the aforementioned
Hushai and who hid them in a well, spreading a
cover over the mouth of it and making believe
that she was drying barley? "They went on," she
said, "after having drunk a little water," and by
this trick she saved them from the hands of their
pursuers. Tell me, then, I ask you, what you
would have done if a similar situation had arisen
for you who now live under the gospel. Would
you have chosen to conceal them by a similar lie,
saying in the same way, "They went on after
having drunk a little water," thus fulfilling what
is commanded, "Do not spare [your help] to
save those who are being led to death and to
redeem those who are being slain"[3] Or by speaking the truth would you have given over those
who were hidden to those who were going to kill
them? What, then, of the apostle's words? "Let
no one seek what is [to] his own [benefit] but
rather [to] what is another's."[4] And, "Love does
not seek what is its own but rather what belongs
to others."[5] And what he says about himself, "I
do not seek what is beneficial to me but what is
beneficial to the many, so that they may be
saved."[6] For if we seek what is ours and wish to
hold on obstinately to what is beneficial to us,
we shall have to speak the truth even in difficulties of this sort, and we shall become guilty of
another's death. But if we fulfill the apostolic
command by placing what is helpful to others
ahead of our own well-being, without a doubt
the necessity of lying will be imposed upon us.
Conference 17.19.6-7.[7]

---

[1]The inscription of Ps 7 is translated in English as "Cush" rather than
"Hushai" (LXX "Chusi"). [2]FC 46:165-66*. [3]Prov 24:11. [4]1 Cor
10:24. [5]See 1 Cor 13:5; Phil 2:4. [6]1 Cor 10:33. [7]ACW 57:598-99*.

[17:21-29 DAVID CROSSES THE JORDAN]

18:1-8 DAVID'S ARMY GOES OUT AGAINST ISRAEL

[1]*Then David mustered the men who were with him, and set over them commanders of thousands and commanders of hundreds. . . .*

[6]*So the army went out into the field against Israel; and the battle was fought in the forest of Ephraim.* [7]*And the men of Israel were defeated there by the servants of David, and the slaughter there was great on that day, twenty thousand men.* [8]*The battle spread over the face of all the country; and the forest devoured more people that day than the sword.*

OVERVIEW: While sedition against royal power deserves punishment, opposing priestly authority warrants it more so (APOSTOLIC CONSTITUTIONS).

18:6-8 David's Army Attacks Absalom's

ON OPPOSING THE PRIESTHOOD. APOSTOLIC CONSTITUTIONS: Let us therefore, beloved, consider what sort of glory that of the seditious is, and what their condemnation [is]. For if he that rises up against kings is worthy of punishment, even though he is a son or a friend, how much more the one who rises up against the priests! For by how much the priesthood is more noble than the royal power, since its concern is for the soul, so much has the one a greater punishment who ventures to oppose the priesthood than the one who ventures to oppose the royal power, although neither of them goes unpunished. For neither did Absalom nor Abdadan[1] escape without punishment; nor Korah and Dathan.[2] The former rose against David, and strove concerning the kingdom; the latter against Moses, concerning preeminence. And they both spoke evil; Absalom of his father David, as of an unjust judge, saying to every one, "Your words are good, but there is no one that will hear you, and do justice. Who will make me a ruler?"[3] But Abdadan [said], "I have no part in David, nor any inheritance in the son of Jesse."[4] It is plain that he could not endure to be under David's government, of whom God spoke, "I have found David the son of Jesse, a man after my heart, who will do all my commands."[5] CONSTITUTIONS OF THE HOLY APOSTLES 6.1.2.[6]

---

[1]Variant of "Sheba." [2]Num 16. [3]2 Sam 15:3. [4]2 Sam 20:1. [5]Acts 13:22. [6]ANF 7:450**.

18:9-15 THE DEATH OF ABSALOM

[9]*And Absalom chanced to meet the servants of David. Absalom was riding upon his mule, and the mule went under the thick branches of a great oak, and his head caught fast in the oak, and he was left hanging*[y] *between heaven and earth, while the mule that was under him went on.* [10]*And a certain man saw it, and told Joab, "Behold, I saw Absalom hanging in an oak." . . .* [15]*And ten young men, Joab's armor-bearers, surrounded Absalom and struck him, and killed him.*

y Gk Syr Tg: Heb *was put*

Overview: The manner of Absalom's death, suspended in the air as his neck was entangled in branches, prefigures the death of Judas, the Lord's betrayer (Cassiodorus). The fate of those who usurped the authority of their superiors cautions against contradicting one's bishop, as all authority ultimately resides with God (Ignatius).

18:9 Absalom's Head Gets Caught in an Oak

Judas Prefigured. Cassiodorus: When Absalom was cruelly attacking his father David, the speed of his mule caused him to collide with a thick oak tree, and the branches wound round his neck so that he was suspended high in the air. This was a prefiguration of the Lord's betrayer. Just as Judas ended his life in the knot of a noose, so also David's persecutor breathed his last through the pressure on his throat. Exposition of the Psalms 3.1.[1]

18:14 Joab Kills Absalom

Reverence Your Superiors. Pseudo-Ignatius: It is becoming, therefore, that you also should be obedient to your bishop and contradict him in nothing, for it is a fearful thing to contradict any such person. For no one does [by such conduct] deceive him that is visible but does [in reality] seek to mock him that is invisible, who, however, cannot be mocked by anyone. And every such act has respect not to people but to God. For God says to Samuel, "They have not mocked you, but me."[2] And Moses declares, "For their murmuring is not against us but against the Lord God."[3] . . . Absalom, again, who had slain his brother, became suspended on a tree, and had his evil-designing heart thrust through with darts. In like manner was Abeddadan[4] beheaded for the same reason. Uzziah, when he presumed to oppose the priests and the priesthood, was smitten with leprosy.[5] Saul also was dishonored, because he did not wait for Samuel the high priest.[6] It is necessary for you, therefore, also to reverence your superiors. Letter to the Magnesians 3.[7]

---

[1]ACW 51:68*. [2]See 1 Sam 8:7. [3]Ex 16:8. [4]That is, Sheba. [5]2 Chron 26:19ff. [6]1 Sam 13:8-14. [7]ANF 1:60*.

18:16-30 RUNNERS BRING WORD TO DAVID

[17]And they took Absalom, and threw him into a great pit in the forest, and raised over him a very great heap of stones; and all Israel fled every one to his own home.

Overview: The ascents and descents described in the physical actions of the saints and the wicked typify their movement in relation to God (Ambrose). David, as he mourned Absalom's death, found consolation in the restoration of peace in his kingdom (Augustine).

18:17 Absalom's Burial

The God of the Mountains. Ambrose: What should I say of Peter, who went up to the roof at the sixth hour and learned there the mystery of the baptism of the Gentiles?[1] On the other hand, the murderer Absalom set up a pillar to himself in the valley of the king and was thrown into a ditch when he was slain. Thus the saints go up to the Lord, the wicked go down to sin; the saints are on the mountains, the guilty in the valleys, "For he is the God of the mountains and not the God of the valleys."[2] Letter 80.[3]

David's Paternal Affection for

Absalom. Augustine: But they, as we have sometimes said before in other places, do not charge themselves with what they do to us; while, on the other hand, they charge us with what they do to themselves. For which of our party is there who would desire, I do not say that one of them should perish but should even lose any of his possessions? But if the house of David could not earn peace on any other terms except that Absalom his son should have been slain in the war which he was waging against his father, although he had most carefully given strict injunctions to his followers that they should use their utmost endeavors to preserve him alive and safe, that his paternal affection might be able to pardon him on his repentance, what remained for him except to weep for the son that he had lost and to console himself in his sorrow by reflecting on the acquisition of peace for his kingdom? The Correction of the Donatists 8.32.[4]

[1]Acts 10:9. [2]1 Kings 20:28. [3]FC 26:448-49. [4]NPNF 1 4:645.

18:31-33 DAVID MOURNS FOR ABSALOM

[31]And behold, the Cushite came; and the Cushite said, "Good tidings for my lord the king! For the Lord has delivered you this day from the power of all who rose up against you." [32]The king said to the Cushite, "Is it well with the young man Absalom?" And the Cushite answered, "May the enemies of my lord the king, and all who rise up against you for evil, be like that young man." [33c]And the king was deeply moved, and went up to the chamber over the gate, and wept; and as he

went, he said, "O my son Absalom, my son, my son Absalom! Would I had died instead of you, O Absalom, my son, my son!"

c Ch 19.1 in Heb

OVERVIEW: With the record of the Cushite's words, the divine witness of Scripture proves that God judges not only by deeds and by examples but also by the very name and terms of judgment (SALVIAN). Having mourned the loss of his wicked sons but not his dead infant, the difference in David's actions is explained by his hope in the latter's resurrection (AMBROSE). Knowing that the opportunity for repentance had been eliminated, David mourned not for Absalom's death but for the punishment his adulterous and murderous son would endure (AUGUSTINE). The concern and sympathy of a good pastor are demonstrated by David's tremendous grief and desire to have endured death in Absalom's place (CHRYSOSTOM). As David mourned the loss of his wicked son and yet was consoled by the restoration of peace and unity his death brought, so the church responds to heretics who go out from its midst (AUGUSTINE).

18:31 The Cushite Brings News from the Battle

THE NAME AND TERMS OF JUDGMENT. SALVIAN THE PRESBYTER: When his rebellious son chased him from his kingdom, the Lord soon delivered David. Not only did the Lord deliver him, but [he] delivered him more fully than the one delivered wished. This was that God might show that the injustice is more grievous to himself than to those who suffer it. He who avenges beyond the wish of him who is being avenged, what else does he want understood than that he himself is being avenged in him for whom he is doing the avenging? Thus, when, for his attempted patricide, David's son being hanged on a cross not made by human hands, the Scripture says that the punishment, divinely brought on him, was thus announced: "I bring good tidings,

my lord, the king: for the Lord has judged on your behalf this day from the hand of all that have risen up against you."

You see how the Scriptures prove by divine witnesses that God judges not only by deeds and by examples, as I have already said, but does so today by the very name and terms of judgment. THE GOVERNANCE OF GOD 2.3-4.[1]

18:33 David Mourns for Absalom

GRIEF FOR THOSE FOREVER LOST. AMBROSE: That same David, I say, who had not wept for the innocent infant wept for the parricide when dead; the difference of his actions may not perhaps disturb those who cling to the words of Scripture. For at the last, when he was wailing and mourning, he said, "O my son Absalom, my son Absalom! Who will grant me to die for you!" But not only is Absalom the parricide wept over, Amnon is wept over. Not only is the incestuous wept over but is even avenged; the one by the scorn of the kingdom, the other by the exile of his brothers. The wicked is wept over, not the innocent. What is the cause? What is the reason? There is no little deliberation with the prudent and confirmation of results with the wise; for there is great consistency of prudence in so great a difference of actions, but the belief is one. He wept for those who were dead but did not think that he ought to weep for the dead infant,[2] for he thought that they were lost to him but hoped that the latter would rise again. ON BELIEF IN THE RESURRECTION 2.28.[3]

GRIEF OVER PUNISHMENT, NOT DEATH. AUGUSTINE: When King David had endured this affliction from his wicked and treacherous son,

[1]FC 3:60-61*. [2]2 Sam 12:22-23. [3]NPNF 2 10:178.

he had not only tolerated his uncontrolled passion but even lamented his death. He was not held ensnared by a carnal jealousy, since it was not the outrages inflicted on him, but rather the sins of his son that troubled him. For he had forbidden that his son be killed if he were conquered in order that opportunity for repentance might be reserved for him after he was vanquished. Since this was impossible, he did not grieve because of his bereavement in the death of his son but because he realized into what punishments such a wickedly adulterous and murderous soul was precipitated. CHRISTIAN INSTRUCTION 3.21.30.[4]

THE CONCERN OF A GOOD PASTOR. CHRYSOSTOM: So great is the concern and sympathy of a good pastor. For David was deeply moved at their falling, as when one's own children are killed. And on this ground he begged that the wrath might come upon himself. And in the beginning of the slaughter he would have done this, unless he had seen it advancing and expected that it would come to himself. When therefore he saw that this did not happen, but that the calamity was raging among them, he no longer forbore but was touched more than for Amnon his firstborn. For then he did not ask for death, but now he begs to fall in preference to the others. Such ought a ruler to be and to grieve rather at the calamities of others than his own. Some such thing he suffered in his son's case likewise, that you might see that he did not love his son more than his subjects. The youth was promiscuous and mistreated his father, yet still the father said, "Would that I might have died for you!" What do you say, you blessed one, you who are meekest of all men? Your son was set upon killing you and surrounded you with unnumbered ills. And when he had been removed, and the trophy was raised, do you then pray to be slain? Yes, he says, for it is not for me that the army has been victorious, but I am warred against more violently than before, and my insides are now more torn than before. HOMILIES ON ROMANS 29.[5]

THE CHURCH MOURNS THE LOSS OF HERETICS. AUGUSTINE: Now what are we to do, seeing how many, with the help of the Lord, find the way of peace through your[6] instrumentality? Surely we neither can nor ought to hold them back from this impulse toward unity, through fear that some, utterly hard and cruel to themselves, may destroy themselves by their own will, not ours. Indeed, we should pray that all who carry the standard of Christ against Christ and boast of the gospel against the gospel may forsake their wrong way and rejoice with us in the unity of Christ. But since God, by an inscrutable yet just disposition of his will, has predestined some of them to the ultimate penalty, undoubtedly it is better for some of them to perish in their own fires, while an incomparably greater number are rescued and won over from that deadly schism and separation, than that all should equally burn in the eternal fires of hell as a punishment for their accursed dissension. The church mourns their loss as holy David mourned the loss of his rebellious son about whose safety he had given orders with anxious love. He grieved over his son's death, with tearful utterance, although it was the penalty of a wicked impiety; but as his proud and wicked spirit departed to its own place, the people of God that had been divided by his tyranny recognized their king, and the completeness of their reunion consoled the grief of the father for the loss of his son. LETTER 204.[7]

---

[4]FC 2:141. [5]NPNF 1 11:546*. [6]This letter is addressed to Dulcitius, a Roman official in Africa who executed imperial decrees against the Donatists. [7]FC 32:4.

19:1-15 DAVID PREPARES
TO RETURN TO JERUSALEM

¹*It was told Joab, "Behold, the king is weeping and mourning for Absalom." ²So the victory that day was turned into mourning for all the people; for the people heard that day, "The king is grieving for his son." ³And the people stole into the city that day as people steal in who are ashamed when they flee in battle. ⁴The king covered his face, and the king cried with a loud voice, "O my son Absalom, O Absalom, my son, my son!"*

OVERVIEW: David mourned Absalom's eternal punishment rather than his bodily death (AUGUSTINE).

19:1-4 Victory Was Turned to Mourning

DAVID MOURNED OVER HIS IMPIOUS SON.
AUGUSTINE: But when king David had suffered this injury at the hands of his impious and unnatural son, he not only bore with him in his mad passion but mourned over him in his death. He certainly was not caught in the meshes of carnal jealousy, seeing that it was not his own injuries but the sins of his son that moved him. For it was on this account he had given orders that his son should not be slain if he were conquered in battle, that he might have a place of repentance after he was subdued. When he was baffled in this design, he mourned over his son's death, not because of his own loss but because he knew to what punishment so impious an adulterer and parricide had been hurried.[1] CHRISTIAN INSTRUCTION 3.21.[2]

---

[1]See also 2 Sam 16:22; 18:5. [2]NPNF 1 2:565.

19:16-30 THE OBEISANCE OF SHIMEI
AND MEPHIBOSHETH

²⁴*And Mephibosheth the son of Saul came down to meet the king. . . . ²⁶He answered, "My lord, O king, my servant deceived me; for your servant said to him, 'Saddle an ass for me,ᵍ that I may ride upon it and go with the king.' For your servant is lame. ²⁷He has slandered your servant to my lord the king. But my lord the king is like the angel of God; do therefore what seems good to you."*

g Gk Syr Vg: Heb *said, I will saddle an ass for myself*

OVERVIEW: Since even prophets may be deceived, it should come as no surprise that those who do not possess the gift of prophecy may err as well (GREGORY THE GREAT).

19:27 Mephibosheth Accuses His Servant of Slander

HUMANS MAKE MISTAKES. GREGORY THE GREAT: Why are you surprised, Peter,[1] that we who are but human make mistakes? Have you forgotten that it was David's reliance on the untruthful words of a servant that caused him to pronounce sentence against the innocent son of Jonathan?[2] And David had the spirit of prophecy. But, since David did this, we can be sure that in God's secret judgment he acted justly, even though we cannot see the justice of it with our human reason. Why should we be surprised, then, if we who are not prophets are sometimes led astray by deceitful people? An important point to consider is that the mind of a superior is distracted by a world of cares, and once the attention is preoccupied with a variety of matters it becomes less observant of details. One who is occupied with a multitude of affairs is all the more liable to be misled in regard to any one of them. DIALOGUE 1.4.[3]

---

[1]Using a common literary device, Gregory presents his teaching as a dialogue between himself and his deacon, Peter. [2]See also 2 Sam 16:3. [3]FC 39:23-24.

[19:31-43 DAVID CROSSES BACK OVER THE JORDAN]

20:1-10 SHEBA LEADS A REVOLT

[8]When they were at the great stone which is in Gibeon, Amasa came to meet them. Now Joab was wearing a soldier's garment, and over it was a girdle with a sword in its sheath fastened upon his loins, and as he went forward it fell out. [9]And Joab said to Amasa, "Is it well with you, my brother?" And Joab took Amasa by the beard with his right hand to kiss him. [10]But Amasa did not observe the sword which was in Joab's hand; so Joab struck him with it in the body, and shed his bowels to the ground, without striking a second blow; and he died.

OVERVIEW: The innumerable evils Joab suffered as a consequence of avenging himself demonstrates that vengeance is a sin to be avoided, even if it seems justified (CHRYSOSTOM). The wicked plot mischief in their hearts while deceiving with the words of their mouths (GREGORY THE GREAT).

20:9-10 Joab Stealthily Kills Amasa

ON AVENGING ONESELF. CHRYSOSTOM: Would you like that, in another way also, I should make what I say plainer? Let us look into their case, [to those] who avenge themselves even justly. For concerning the wrongdoers, that they are the most worthless of all people, warring against their own soul, is surely plain to every one.

But who avenged himself justly yet kindled innumerable ills and pierced himself through with many calamities and sorrows? The captain of David's host. For Joab both stirred up a grievous war and suffered unnumbered evils; not one of them would have happened had he but known how to exercise self-control. Let us flee therefore from this sin and neither in words nor deeds do our neighbors wrong. Homilies on the Gospel of Matthew 42.2.[1]

Malicious Deception. Gregory the Great: Thus also the wicked, because they have evil not

upon the tongue but under the tongue, in the words of their mouth they hold out sweet things, and in the thoughts of their heart are plotting mischief.[2] For it is hence that Joab held the beard of Amasa with his right hand, while secretly putting his left hand to his sword, he spilled out his bowels. For to hold the chin with the right hand is to caress as if in kindness. But he puts his left hand to his sword, who in secret strikes in malice. Morals on the Book of Job 15.11.[3]

---

[1]NPNF 1 10:271*. [2]See Job 20:12-13, upon which Gregory is commenting: "Though wickedness is sweet in his mouth, though he hides it under his tongue, though he is loath to let it go, and holds it in his mouth." [3]LF 21:179.

[20:11-26 THE DEATH OF SHEBA]

21:1-14 JUSTICE IS SOUGHT FOR THE GIBEONITES

[1]*Now there was a famine in the days of David for three years, year after year; and David sought the face of the Lord. And the Lord said, "There is bloodguilt on Saul and on his house, because he put the Gibeonites to death."* [2]*So the king called the Gibeonites.ᵐ Now the Gibeonites were not of the people of Israel, but of the remnant of the Amorites; although the people of Israel had sworn to spare them, Saul had sought to slay them in his zeal for the people of Israel and Judah. . .* [5]*They said to the king, "The man who consumed us and planned to destroy us, so that we should have no place in all the territory of Israel,* [6]*let seven of his sons be given to us, so that we may hang them up before the Lord at Gibeon on the mountain of the Lord."ᵐ And the king said, "I will give them."* . . .

[8]*The king took the two sons of Rizpah the daughter of Aiah, whom she bore to Saul, Armoni and Mephibosheth; and the five sons of Merabᵒ the daughter of Saul, whom she bore to Adri-el the son of Barzillai the Meholathite;* [9]*and he gave them into the hands of the Gibeonites, and they hanged them on the mountain before the Lord, and the seven of them perished together. They*

were put to death in the first days of harvest, at the beginning of barley harvest.

m Heb *the Gibeonites and said to them*   **n** Cn Compare Gk and 21.9: Heb *at Gibeah of Saul, the chosen of the* LORD   **o** Two Hebrew Mss Gk: Heb *Michal*

OVERVIEW: The treatment of the Gibeonites demonstrates that there are different grades within God's kingdom (JEROME).

21:2-9 The Gibeonites Avenge Themselves on Saul's Family

DIFFERENT GRADES IN GOD'S KINGDOM. JEROME: The Gibeonites met the children of Israel, and although other nations were slaughtered, they were kept for hewers of wood and drawers of water. And of such value were they in God's eyes that the family of Saul was destroyed for the wrong done to them. Where would you put them? Among the goats? But they were not slain, and they were avenged by the determination of God. Among the sheep? But holy Scripture says they were not of the same merit as the Israelites. You see then that they do indeed stand on the right hand but are of a far inferior grade. AGAINST JOVINIANUS 2.33.[1]

---

[1]NPNF 2 6:413.

21:15-22 BATTLES WITH THE PHILISTINES CONTINUE

[15]*The Philistines had war again with Israel, and David went down together with his servants, and they fought against the Philistines; and David grew weary.* [16]*And Ishbi-benob, one of the descendants of the giants, whose spear weighed three hundred shekels of bronze, and who was girded with a new sword, thought to kill David.* [17]*But Abishai the son of Zeruiah came to his aid, and attacked the Philistine and killed him. Then David's men adjured him, "You shall no more go out with us to battle, lest you quench the lamp of Israel."*

OVERVIEW: In order that cowardice is not imitated, priests must not flee danger out of fear but only do so when their preservation is necessary for the benefit of the church, as David's experience illustrates (AUGUSTINE). In physical and spiritual war the enemy endeavors most ardently to overthrow the general while his soldiers strive to protect him. Therefore, prayer is sought on behalf of spiritual leaders so that they and their charges will be preserved (CHRYSOSTOM).

21:17 You Shall Not Go with Us to Battle

ON FLEEING FROM DANGER. AUGUSTINE: At this point someone may say that the priests of God ought to flee from such threatening dangers in order to save themselves for the service of the church in more peaceful times. It is right for some to do this when others are not lacking to supply the ministry of the church, so that it is not wholly abandoned. This is what Athanasius did, as I said before; for the body of Catholic believers knew how necessary and how profitable it was for the church to retain in the flesh a man who had defended it by words and heart's love against the Arian heretics. But when the danger is common to all and there is more reason to fear that the priest's escape may be attributed to a dread of death rather than an intention of future help, and when he does more harm by the example of his flight than he would do good by his preservation, there is no justifiable reason for doing it. Finally, there was holy David, who did not trust himself to the dangers of battle lest the lamp of Israel, as it is there said, "should be put out"; but he did not take this course himself—he did it because his followers begged him to do it. Otherwise, he would have had many cowardly imitators who would believe that he acted thus at the bidding of his own fear, not for any motive of usefulness to others. LETTER 228.[1]

LEADERS FACE STRONGER ATTACKS. CHRYSOSTOM: Entreat God—for this cause entreat him. It is in our behalf indeed that it is done, but it is wholly for your sakes. For we [spiritual leaders] are appointed for your advantage, and for your interests we are concerned. . . .

For our enemy is violent. For each of you indeed anxiously thinks of his own interests, but we [think of] the concerns of all together. We stand in the part of the battle that is pressed on. The devil is more violently armed against us. For in wars too, the one who is on the opposite side endeavors before all others to overthrow the general. For this reason all his fellow combatants hasten there. For this reason there is much tumult, every one endeavoring to rescue him; they surround him with their shields, wishing to preserve his person. Hear what all the people say to David (I do not say this, as comparing myself to David, as I am not so mad, but because I wish to show the affection of the people for their ruler), "You shall go out no more; do not quench the lamp of Israel." See how anxious they were to spare the old man. I am greatly in need of your prayers. Let no one, as I have said, from an excessive humility deprive me of this alliance and succor. If our part is well approved, your own also will be more honorable. If our teaching flows abundantly, the riches will redound to you. HOMILIES ON 2 THESSALONIANS 4.[2]

---

[1]FC 32:147-48*. [2]NPNF 1 13:391*.

22:1-51 DAVID'S SONG OF DELIVERANCE

[1]And David spoke to the LORD the words of this song on the day when the LORD delivered him from the hand of all his enemies, and from the hand of Saul. [2]He said,
"The LORD is my rock, and my fortress, and my deliverer,
[3]my[p] God, my rock, in whom I take refuge,
my shield and the horn of my salvation,
my stronghold and my refuge,
my savior; thou savest me from violence. . . .

^{44}"Thou didst deliver me from strife with the peoples;^{v}
  thou didst keep me as the head of the nations;
  people whom I had not known served me.
^{45}Foreigners came cringing to me;
  as soon as they heard of me, they obeyed me.
^{46}Foreigners lost heart,
  and came trembling^w out of their fastnesses.

^{47}"The LORD lives; and blessed be my rock,
  and exalted be my God, the rock of my salvation,
^{48}the God who gave me vengeance
  and brought down peoples under me,
^{49}who brought me out from my enemies;
  thou didst exalt me above my adversaries,
  thou didst deliver me from men of violence.

^{50}"For this I will extol thee, O LORD, among the nations,
  and sing praises to thy name.
^{51}Great triumphs he gives^x to his king,
  and shows steadfast love to his anointed,
  to David, and his descendants for ever."

p Gk Ps 18.2: Heb lacks *my*   v Gk: Heb *from strife with my people*   w Ps 18.45: Heb *girded themselves*   x Another reading is *He is a tower of salvation*

OVERVIEW: Scripture's fifth song, uttered by David after being delivered from Saul's hand and from all his enemies, may be sung by those who are able to identify the enemies David defeated and the source of his worthiness of the Lord's help. Jesus did not come to produce incredulity among the Jews, but foretelling their unbelief, used it to call the Gentiles, as also prophesied in Scripture through Christ (ORIGEN). As prophets foretold the cessation of the old law and carnal circumcision, they likewise declared the coming of a new law and spiritual circumcision in "a people" formerly ignorant of God, that is, the Gentiles (TERTULLIAN). That David's house could not attain peace except through Absalom's death is paralleled to the church's relationship with heretics, which mourns their loss yet finds solace in the deliverance of many others (AUGUSTINE).

22:1-2 David Begins to Praise the Lord

ON SINGING SCRIPTURE'S FIFTH SONG. ORIGEN: The fifth song is in Second Samuel, when "David spoke to the Lord the words of this song on the day when the Lord delivered him from the hand of all his enemies and from the hand of Saul." He said, "The Lord is my rock, and my fortress, and my deliverer; my God will be my protector." If, then, you prove able to examine who are the enemies David defeats and overthrows in First and Second Samuel and how he was made worthy of deserving the Lord's help and of being delivered from enemies of this kind, then you will be able to sing this fifth song yourself. COMMENTARY ON THE SONG OF SONGS, PROLOGUE.[1]

---

[1]OSW 238.

22:44-45 David Recounts the Obedience of Foreign Nations

THE CALLING OF THE GENTILES. ORIGEN: "Did Jesus come into the world for this purpose, that we [the Jews] should not believe him?" To which we immediately answer that he did not come with the object of producing unbelief among the Jews; but knowing beforehand that such would be the result, he foretold it and made use of their unbelief for the calling of the Gentiles. For through their sin salvation came to the Gentiles, respecting whom the Christ who speaks in the prophecies says, "A people whom I did not know became subject to me: they were obedient to the hearing of my ear"; and, "I was found by those who did not seek me; I became manifest to those who did not inquire after me."[2] AGAINST CELSUS 2.78.[3]

OBEDIENCE OF THE UNCIRCUMCISED PROPH-ESIED. TERTULLIAN: Therefore as we have shown above that the coming cessation of the old law and of the carnal circumcision was declared, so, too, the observance of the new law and the spiritual circumcision has shone out into the voluntary obediences of peace. For "a people," he says, "whom I did not know has served me; in obedience of the ear it has obeyed me." Prophets made the announcement. But what is the people which was ignorant of God, but ours, who in days bygone did not know God? And who, in the hearing of the ear, paid attention to him, but we, who, forsaking idols, have been converted to God? AN ANSWER TO THE JEWS 3.[4]

22:47-51 David Extols the Lord's Love and Deliverance

COMFORT FOUND IN THE DELIVERANCE OF MANY. AUGUSTINE: But, as we have said elsewhere on occasion, these heretics refuse to take the blame for what they do to us and they lay the blame on us for what they do to themselves. Who of us would wish them to lose anything, much less that they be lost themselves? If the house of David could win peace in no other way than through the death of Absalom, David's son, in the war which he was carrying on against his father—although the latter had instructed his followers with great care to keep him safe and sound as far as it was possible for them to do so, that he might repent and receive pardon from his father's love—what was left for him but to weep over his son's loss and find comfort for his grief in the peace thus gained for his kingdom? In the same manner, then, our Catholic mother acts when others who are not her sons make war on her—because it is a fact that this little branch in Africa has been broken off from the great tree which embraces the whole world in the spreading of its branches—and although she is in labor with them in charity, that they may return to the root without which they cannot have true life, still, if she rescues so many others by losing some, especially when these fall by self-destruction, not by the fortune of war as Absalom did, she solaces the grief of her maternal heart and heals it by the deliverance of such numbers of people. LETTER 185.32.[5]

---

[2]Is 65:1. [3]ANCL 23:82-83*. [4]ANF 3:154-55*. [5]FC 30:172-73.

23:1-12 THE LAST WORDS OF DAVID

^{1}*Now these are the last words of David:*
  The oracle of David, the son of Jesse,
    the oracle of the man who was raised on high,
  the anointed of the God of Jacob,
    the sweet psalmist of Israel: ^{y}

  ^{2}*"The Spirit of the LORD speaks by me,*
    his word is upon my tongue.

y Or the favorite of the songs of Israel

OVERVIEW: Through examples drawn from Israel's history, Cyril of Jerusalem instructs his catechumens that the Holy Spirit will come upon them as well.

23:2 The Spirit of the Lord Speaks by Me

THE GRACE WILL COME. CYRIL OF JERUSALEM: In Moses' day the Spirit was given by the imposition of hands; and Peter imparted the Spirit by the imposition of hands. Upon you also, who are to be baptized, the grace will come. In what manner I do not say, for I do not anticipate the proper time. . . . We learn clearly in the book of Kings [Samuel], of Samuel and David, how by the Holy Spirit they prophesied and were leaders of the prophets. Samuel in fact was called the "seer." David says plainly: "The spirit of the Lord has spoken by me;" and in the psalms: "and do not take your holy spirit from me;"[1] and again: "May your good spirit guide me on level ground."[2] CATECHETICAL LECTURES 16.26, 28.[3]

---

[1]Ps 51:11 (50:11 LXX). [2]Ps 143:10 (142:10 LXX). [3]FC 64:92-93*.

23:13-39 THE BRAVERY OF DAVID'S MIGHTY MEN

^{13}*And three of the thirty chief men went down, and came about harvest time to David at the cave of Adullam, when a band of Philistines was encamped in the valley of Rephaim.* ^{14}*David was then in the stronghold; and the garrison of the Philistines was then at Bethlehem.* ^{15}*And David said longingly, "O that some one would give me water to drink from the well of Bethlehem which is by the gate!"* ^{16}*Then the three mighty men broke through the camp of the Philistines, and drew water out of the well of Bethlehem which was by the gate, and took and brought it to David. But he would not drink of it; he poured it out to the LORD, [17]and said, "Far be it from me, O LORD, that I should do this. Shall I drink the blood of the men who went at the risk of their lives?" Therefore he would not drink it. These things did the three mighty men.*

OVERVIEW: By pouring out the water his soldiers crossed enemy lines to obtain, David slaughtered his sinful lust through self-censure, an act which evidenced the strictness he possessed in dealing with his desires later in life (GREGORY THE GREAT). While the uncleanness of food is not a cause for concern, uncontrolled desire in regard to eating and drinking warrants diligence, as indicated by scriptural examples (AUGUSTINE). David's reason conquered his concupiscence, which bred an irrational longing for water from a cistern in Bethlehem, by causing him to recognize how he had jeopardized the lives of his soldiers (AMBROSE). Since the desire for food may become a deadly snare, it is wise to learn temperance and parsimony from the prayer and the examples of the ancients (LEANDER OF SEVILLE). David, in his anger at the lust that placed lives at risk, extinguished his lust by pouring the water out to the Lord, demonstrating how to be angry and yet refrain from sinning (CASSIAN).

23:14-17 Obtaining Water for David

SLAUGHTERING SINFUL DESIRES. GREGORY THE GREAT: Much later, David was sitting opposite the enemy lines and desired longingly to drink from the cistern. Chosen soldiers of his broke through the enemy troops and returned unharmed with the water the king had desired. But the man who had been taught by his chastisements immediately reproached himself for having endangered his soldiers by his desire for water. He poured it out, making a libation to the Lord, as it is written there: "He poured it out to the Lord." The water he poured out was changed into a sacrifice to the Lord, because he slaughtered his sin of eager desire by the penance of self-censure. The man who had once been unafraid to lust after another man's wife was later terrified at having desired

water. Since he remembered he had committed something forbidden, he was strict with himself and refrained even from what was allowed. FORTY GOSPEL HOMILIES 34.[1]

STRUGGLING AGAINST UNDISCIPLINED DESIRE. AUGUSTINE: I do not fear the uncleanness of food but only the uncleanness of uncontrolled desire. I know that Noah was permitted to eat every kind of meat which was edible;[2] that Elijah was nourished on meat;[3] that John, endowed with a marvelous abstinence, was not made unclean by partaking of living things, namely, the locusts which happened to be available as food.[4] And I know that Esau was led into error by his greed for lentils;[5] that David blamed himself for his craving for water; and that our King was tempted not by flesh but by bread.[6] Further, the people in the desert deserved to be reprimanded, not because they desired meat but because they murmured against the Lord as a result of this desire for meat.[7] Having been placed among these temptations, then, I struggle daily against undisciplined desire in eating and drinking. CONFESSIONS 10.31.46-47.[8]

REASON RESISTS LUST. AMBROSE: Further, what man can we consider finer and stronger than the holy David? He had desired water from the cistern of Bethlehem although it was cut off by a hostile army. That desire he was not able to remove, but he could mitigate it. For we do not find that the others lacked water, and the army was very large. And surely the king's need for water would have been much less, in view of the other springs nearby. But he suffered a kind of

---

[1]CS 123:295-96. [2]Gen 9:3. [3]1 Kings 17:6. [4]Mt 3:4. [5]Gen 25:30-34. [6]Mt 4:3. [7]Num 11:4. [8]FC 21:304-5*.

irrational longing and wanted that water which was walled in and surrounded by the enemy, so that it could not have been readily brought without great risk. Thus he said, "Who will get me a drink from the cistern that is in Bethlehem by the gate?" And when three men were found to break down the enemy camp and bring the water which he had desired with a very great desire, he knew that he had obtained that water at the cost of danger to others. He poured it out to the Lord, so that he might not seem to be drinking the blood of those who had brought it.

This incident is evidence that uncontrolled desire indeed comes before reason but that reason resists irrational desire. David suffered what is human—an irrational longing—but it is praiseworthy that he cheated the irrational desire in a rational manner with the remedy that was at hand. I praise the men who were ashamed at the desire of their king and preferred to bring his shameful action to an end even with danger to their own well-being. I praise the more him who was ashamed at the danger to others in his own desire and who compared to blood the water sought at the price of hazardous chance. At once, like a conqueror who had checked his desire, David poured out the water to the Lord, to show that he quenched his lust by the consolation found in his Word. JACOB AND THE HAPPY LIFE 1.1.3.[9]

LEARN TEMPERANCE FROM THE ANCIENTS.

LEANDER OF SEVILLE: A fish is caught by being enticed with a hook. A bird falls into a net while trying to get food. Animals that are tough by nature's endowment fall into a pit from desire to eat, and what nature does not soften, food deceives. Therefore, learn temperance and parsimony from the prayer and the examples of ancients: from prayer, because the Lord says,

"Lest your hearts be overburdened with self-indulgence and drunkenness";[10] from examples, because David was unwilling to drink the water he wanted, since he recognized the danger of being responsible for another's blood; and because Daniel scorned the feasts of kings and lived on vegetables.[11] What you possess in common with your companions should be acceptable to you and you should not cause others to be intemperate; also, do not become a cause for scandal to those to whom you wish to set an example by encouragement and by proof of a good life. THE TRAINING OF NUNS 13.[12]

ANGER RIGHTLY FELT. JOHN CASSIAN: And

certainly when we are disturbed at this very anger because it has stolen upon us against our brother, and we angrily cast out its deadly suggestions and do not permit it to maintain its noxious lair in the recesses of our heart. To be angry in this latter way is also taught us by that prophet who so eradicated this from his mind that he did not even want to take revenge on his own enemies, who had in fact been handed over to him by God, when he said, "Be angry and do not sin."[13] For when he wanted water from a well in Bethlehem and had been brought it by strong men from the midst of enemy troops, he at once poured it out on the ground and, angrily extinguishing his wanton and passionate desire in this way, he offered it as a libation to the Lord, rejecting his yearning and desire with the words "May the Lord be gracious to me, lest I do this. Shall I drink the blood of those men who went out and the danger of their souls?" INSTITUTES 8.8.[14]

---

[9]FC 65:120-21*. [10]Lk 21:34. [11]Dan 1:12, 16. [12]FC 62:208*. [13]Ps 4:4. [14]ACW 58:196-97.

24:1-9 DAVID NUMBERS THE PEOPLE

¹*Again the anger of the* Lord *was kindled against Israel, and he incited David against them, saying, "Go, number Israel and Judah." *²*So the king said to Joab and the commanders of the army,ʲ who were with him, "Go through all the tribes of Israel, from Dan to Beer-sheba, and number the people, that I may know the number of the people."*

j 1 Chron 21.2 Gk: Heb *to Joab the commander of the army*

Overview: As David's singular crime brought injury to all the people, so a few of the body of the church may block the light of its splendor by committing filthy acts (Salvian).

24:2 David Orders Joab to Number Israel

A Few Block the Church's Light. Salvian the Presbyter: You say these were the disgraceful acts of a few men and what was not done by all could not injure all. Indeed, I have said above quite often that the crime of one man was the destruction of many among the people of God, just as the people was ruined by Achan's theft,[1] just as pestilence arose from Saul's jealousy,[2] just as death came from the counting of the people by the holy David. The church of God is as the eye. As a speck of dirt, even though small, which falls into the eye blinds the sight completely, in the same way, if some, even though they are a few in the body of the church, commit filthy acts, they block almost all the light of the splendor of the church. The Governance of God 7.19.[3]

---

[1]Josh 7:1. [2]1 Sam 19. [3]FC 3:213*.

24:10-14 DAVID CONFESSES HIS SIN

¹⁰*But David's heart smote him after he had numbered the people. And David said to the* Lord, *"I have sinned greatly in what I have done. But now, O* Lord, *I pray thee, take away the iniquity of thy servant; for I have done very foolishly." *¹¹*And when David arose in the morning, the word of the* Lord *came to the prophet Gad, David's seer, saying, *¹²*"Go and say to David, 'Thus says the* Lord, *Three things I offerⁿ you; choose one of them, that I may do it to you.'" *¹³*So Gad came to David and told him, and said to him, "Shall threeᵒ years of famine come to you in your land? Or will you flee three months before your foes while they pursue you? Or shall there be three days' pestilence in your land? Now consider, and decide what answer I shall return to him who sent me." *¹⁴*Then David said to Gad, "I am in great distress; let us fall into the hand of the* Lord, *for his mercy is great; but let me not fall into the hand of man."*

n Or *hold over*   o 1 Chron 21.12 Gk: Heb *seven*

OVERVIEW: People are punished for the sins of their leaders because the hearts of rulers are disposed according to the merits of their people (GREGORY THE GREAT). David exemplifies the right response after sinning by humbly admitting his guilt before God: failing to do so would be worse than the sin itself (AMBROSE).

24:10 David Feels Remorse

GETTING THE LEADER THEY DESERVE. GREGORY THE GREAT: The characters, then, of rulers are so assigned according to the merits of their subjects, that frequently they who seem to be good are soon changed by the acceptance of power. As holy Scripture observed of the same Saul that he changed his heart with his dignity. Whence it is written, "When you were little in your own eyes, I made you the head of the tribes of Israel."[1] The conduct of rulers is so ordered with reference to the characters of their subjects that frequently the conduct of even a truly good shepherd becomes sinful as a result of the wickedness of his flock. For that prophet David, who had been praised by the witness of God himself, who had been made acquainted with heavenly mysteries, being puffed up by the swelling of sudden pride, sinned in numbering the people. And yet, though David sinned, the people endured the punishment. Why was this? Because in truth the hearts of rulers are disposed according to the merits of their people. But the righteous judge reproved the fault of the sinner by the punishment of those very persons on whose account he sinned. But because he was not exempt from guilt, as displaying pride of his own free will, he himself endured also the punishment of his sin. For that furious wrath which struck the people in their bodies prostrated the ruler of the people by the pain of his inmost heart. But it is certain that the merits of rulers and people are so mutually connected that frequently the conduct of the people is made worse from the fault of their pastors and the conduct of pastors is changed according to the merits of their people. MORALS ON THE

BOOK OF JOB 25.16.[2]

24:14 The Lord's Mercy Is Great

HUMBLED BEFORE GOD. AMBROSE: Again, when David had ordered the people to be numbered, he was deeply afflicted in heart and said to the Lord, "I have sinned greatly in the command I have made, and now, O Lord, take away the iniquity of your servant, because I have sinned exceedingly." And the prophet Nathan[3] was sent again to him to offer him the choice of three things, that he might select what he chose: a famine in the land for three years, flight from the face of his enemies for three months, or pestilence in the land for three days. And David answered, "These three things are a great distress to me, yet I shall fall into the hand of the Lord since his mercies are exceedingly great, and I shall not fall into the hands of men." David's fault was that he desired to know the number of all the people who were with him, and the knowledge of this he should have left to God alone.

And it is said that when the pestilence came upon the people on the first day at dinner time, when David saw the angel striking the people, he said, "I have sinned, I, the shepherd, have done evil and this flock, what has it done? Let your hand be upon me and upon my father's house." So the Lord repented, and he bade the angel to spare the people, but David to offer sacrifice, for sacrifices were then offered for sin, but now they are sacrifices of penance. Thus, by his humility he became more acceptable to God, for it is not strange that people sin, but it is reprehensible if they do not acknowledge that they have erred and humble themselves before God. LETTER 3.[4]

---

[1]See 1 Sam 15:17. [2]LF 23:126*. [3]It was not Nathan but Gad. [4]FC 26:22-23*. This letter was written about 390 to Emperor Theodosius to encourage his repentance for ordering a massacre in Thessolonica.

24:15-17 THE LORD SENDS A PESTILENCE UPON ISRAEL

[15]So the LORD sent a pestilence upon Israel from the morning until the appointed time; and there died of the people from Dan to Beer-sheba seventy thousand men. [16]And when the angel stretched forth his hand toward Jerusalem to destroy it, the LORD repented of the evil, and said to the angel who was working destruction among the people, "It is enough; now stay your hand." And the angel of the LORD was by the threshing floor of Araunah the Jebusite. [17]Then David spoke to the LORD when he saw the angel who was smiting the people, and said, "Lo, I have sinned, and I have done wickedly; but these sheep, what have they done? Let thy hand, I pray thee, be against me and against my father's house."

OVERVIEW: Deign to remain ignorant of why God has brought certain events to pass, such as why thousands died for David's sin: allow God to exercise his rightful power over his creation (JEROME). That David readily offered his life on behalf of his afflicted people demonstrates his knowledge that dying for Christ is more glorious than ruling in this world, since death frees the soul from the body (AMBROSE). Diligent pastors exhibit care for their flocks by offering themselves on behalf of their sheep when they are afflicted, as David did (APHRAHAT). Seen as an example of loving his enemies, David's willingness to suffer in place of his people while under the old covenant demands greater love and self-sacrifice of those under the new (CHRYSOSTOM).

24:15 Seventy Thousand Die from the Pestilence

CONDESCEND TO REMAIN IGNORANT. JEROME: Bring a yet graver charge against God and ask him why, when Esau and Jacob were still in the womb, he said, "Jacob I have loved, but Esau I have hated."[1] Accuse him of injustice because, when Achan the son of Carmi stole part of the spoil of Jericho, he butchered so many thousands for the fault of one.[2] Ask him why for the sin of the sons of Eli the people were well-nigh annihi-

lated and the ark captured.[3] And why, when David sinned by numbering the people, so many thousands lost their lives....Why should Christ's coming have been delayed to the last times? Why should he not have come before so vast a number had perished? Of this last question the blessed apostle in writing to the Romans most wisely disposes by admitting that he does not know and that only God does. Do you too, then, condescend to remain ignorant of that into which you inquire. Leave to God his power over what is his own; he does not need you to justify his actions. LETTER 133.9.[4]

24:17 Against Me and My Father's House

THE GOOD OF HUMILITY. AMBROSE: Good, therefore, is humility. It delivers those who are in danger and raises those who have fallen. This humility was known to him who said, "Behold, it is I that have sinned, and I the shepherd have acted wickedly; and these in this flock, what have they done? Let your hand be against me." Well does David say this who made his kingdom subject to God and did penance and, having confessed his sin, asked pardon. He attained salvation through humility. Christ humbled himself to

---

[1]Rom 9:13. [2]Josh 7. [3]1 Sam 4. [4]NPNF 2 6:278*.

raise up all, and whoever follows the humility of Christ attains the rest of Christ. On the Death of Theodosius 27.[5]

The Freedom of Death. Ambrose: Therefore since the apostle taught that a person who has passed out of this body will be with Christ, provided he deserves it, let us consider the nature of life and of death. We know from the teaching of Scripture that death is a freeing of the soul from the body, a kind of separation in man. For we are freed from this bond between soul and body, when we depart. . . . He [David] readily offered himself to death to atone for his offense against the Lord and presented himself, prepared to suffer God's vengeance for the well-being of his afflicted people. He knew that it was more glorious to die for Christ than to rule in this world, for what is more excellent than to become a victim for Christ? Death As a Good 3.8.[6]

The Penitent Leader. Aphrahat: He is a most diligent pastor who delivered over himself on behalf of his sheep. He is an excellent leader who gave himself in behalf of his sheep. . . . And when David numbered the flock of his sheep, wrath came upon them, and they began to be destroyed. Then David delivered himself over on behalf of his sheep, when he prayed, saying, "O Lord God, I have sinned in that I have numbered Israel. Let your hand be on me and on my father's house. These innocent sheep, how have they sinned?" So also [in this way] all the diligent pastors used to give themselves on behalf of their sheep.

But those pastors who did not care for the sheep, those were hirelings who used to feed themselves alone. Demonstration 10.2-3.[7]

Loving Neighbors and Enemies. Chrysos-

tom: And how is it possible (you say) that one should so love his neighbor as himself? If others had not done this, you might well think it impossible: but if they have done it, it is plain that from indolence it is not done by ourselves.

And besides, Christ enjoins nothing impossible, seeing that many have even gone beyond his commands. Who has done this? Paul, Peter, all the company of the saints. No, indeed if I say that they loved their neighbors, I say no great matter: they so loved their enemies as no one would love those who were likeminded with himself. For who would choose for the sake of those likeminded to go away into hell when he was about to depart into a kingdom? No one. But Paul chose this for the sake of his enemies, for those who stoned him, those who scourged him.[8] What pardon then will there be for us, what excuse, if we shall not show toward our friends even the very smallest portion of that love which Paul showed toward his enemies?

And before him too, the blessed Moses was willing to be blotted out of God's book for the sake of his enemies who had stoned him.[9] David also when he saw those who had stood up against him slain, said, "I, the shepherd, have sinned, but these, what have they done?" And when he had Saul in his hands, he would not slay him but saved him; and this when he himself would be in danger. But if these things were done under the old [covenant], what excuse shall we have who live under the new and do not attain even to the same measure with them? For . . . "unless our righteousness exceed that of the scribes and Pharisees, we shall not enter into the kingdom of heaven," how shall we enter in when we have even less than they? Homilies on Hebrews 19.4.[10]

---

[5]FC 22:319*. [6]FC 65:74-75*. [7]NPNF 2 13:383-84*. [8]See Rom 9:3. [9]Ex 32:32. [10]NPNF 1 14:456*.

24:18-25 DAVID ERECTS AN ALTAR TO THE LORD

[18]And Gad came that day to David, and said to him, "Go up, rear an altar to the LORD on the threshing floor of Araunah the Jebusite." [19]So David went up at Gad's word, as the LORD commanded. [20]And when Araunah looked down, he saw the king and his servants coming on toward him; and Araunah went forth, and did obeisance to the king with his face to the ground. [21]And Araunah said, "Why has my lord the king come to his servant?" David said, "To buy the threshing floor of you, in order to build an altar to the LORD, that the plague may be averted from the people." [22]Then Araunah said to David, "Let my lord the king take and offer up what seems good to him; here are the oxen for the burnt offering, and the threshing sledges and the yokes of the oxen for the wood. [23]All this, O king, Araunah gives to the king." And Araunah said to the king, "The LORD your God accept you." [24]But the king said to Araunah, "No, but I will buy it of you for a price; I will not offer burnt offerings to the LORD my God which cost me nothing." So David bought the threshing floor and the oxen for fifty shekels of silver. [25]And David built there an altar to the LORD, and offered burnt offerings and peace offerings. So the LORD heeded supplications for the land, and the plague was averted from Israel.

OVERVIEW: The selection and purchase of Jebusite land for the erection of an altar to the Lord prefigures Christ's rejection by the Jews and his coming to the Gentiles, with the promise of forgiveness having been purchased through his blood (CAESARIUS OF ARLES).

24:18-21 David Is Commanded to Build an Altar

WORTHY OF THE LORD'S ALTAR. CAESARIUS OF ARLES: Notice, brothers, that no place in the land of the Jews was found worthy for the altar of the Lord to be built; but in the land of the Gentiles a place is chosen where the angel is seen and the altar of the Lord is built, and thus the wrath of the almighty Lord is appeased. Then already was prefigured the fact that in the hearts of the Jews no worthy place could be found to offer spiritual victims; the land of the Gentiles, that is, the conscience of Christians, is chosen as the place for the Lord's temple. This the apostle clearly indicates when he rebukes the Jews and says, "It was necessary that the word of God should be spoken to you first, but since you have judged yourselves unworthy of eternal life, behold, we now turn to the Gentiles."[1] This means [that] because you have rejected Christ and have not prepared a worthy place on which to set the Lord's altar, we will put it in the land of the Gentiles, that is, in the hearts of all the people. For this reason the same apostle exclaims to us, "Holy is the temple of God, and you are this temple."[2] Now notice, dearly beloved, that the land of the Gentile king was chosen at the time when the Jewish people were struck by God's plague. This we see fulfilled in the Lord's passion; for when the Jewish people rejected the Lord and crucified him, then his altar was consecrated on the threshing floor of the Gentiles, that is, on every land. That is why the angel of the Lord stood on the threshing floor of the Gentile king; the true angel, Christ, visited the people of the Gentiles. SERMON 122.1.[3]

---

[1]Acts 13:46. [2]1 Cor 3:17. [3]FC 47:204-5*.

24:22-25 *David Purchases Araunah's Land and Oxen*

Purchased Through His Blood. Caesarius of Arles: Therefore, the king himself offered blessed David the threshing floor and oxen for a burnt offering, but King David refused to accept them without first paying a price. This, too, was fulfilled at the coming of our Lord and Savior, for he refused to take the hearts of the Gentiles for himself without first giving his precious blood for them. What, then, did he give? "Fifty shekels of silver," it says. In the number fifty the grace of the Holy Spirit is understood and the remission of sins is designated. Indeed, on the fiftieth day the Holy Spirit was sent to the apostles, and in the Old Testament the fiftieth year was dedicated to forgiveness and pardon. That David, to be sure, gave silver; our David, whose type the other prefigured, shed his precious blood. Thus, in order to buy the pagan king's threshing floor David offered fifty shekels; in order to build an altar to himself on the threshing floor of the Gentiles Christ, the true David, gave the grace of the Holy Spirit and forgiveness of sins on the fiftieth day. Therefore, brothers, since he has deigned to make a temple for himself in us and out of us, let him not suffer any insult in his home. If he does suffer injury because of our sins, he quickly withdraws, and woe to the unhappy soul from which he departs. Doubtless, if one is deserted by the light he will be seized by darkness. For this reason let us with his aid endeavor so to live that we may merit to have the good Lord not only as our guest but as a perpetual inhabitant: with the help of our same Lord Jesus Christ, to whom is honor and glory together with the Father and the Holy Spirit world without end. Amen. Sermon 122.2.[4]

---

[4]FC 47:205-6*.

APPENDIX

Ambrose

Cain and Abel *(De Cain et Abel)*	Cetedoc 0125
Concerning Widows *(De viduis)*	Cetedoc 0146
Consolation on the Death of Emperor Valentinian *(De obitu Valentiniani)*	Cetedoc 0158
Death as a Good *(De bono mortis)*	Cetedoc 0129
Duties of the Clergy *(De officiis ministrorum)*	Cetedoc 0144
Exposition of Psalm 118 *(Expositio psalmi cxviii)*	Cetedoc 0141
Exposition on the Gospel of Luke *(Expositio evangelii secundum Lucam)*	Cetedoc 0143
Flight from the World *(De fuga saeculi)*	Cetedoc 0133
Isaac, or the Soul *(De Isaac vel anima)*	Cetedoc 0128
Jacob and the Happy Life *(De Jacob et vita beata)*	Cetedoc 0130
Letters *(Epistulae)*	Cetedoc 0160
On His Brother Satyrus *(De excessu fratris Satyri)*	Cetedoc 0157
On Paradise *(De paradiso)*	Cetedoc 0124
On the Christian Faith *(De fide)*	Cetedoc 0150
On the Death of Theodosius *(De obitu Theodosii)*	Cetedoc 0159
On the Holy Spirit *(De Spiritu Sancto)*	Cetedoc 0151
The Prayer of Job and David *(De interpellatione Job et David)*	Cetedoc 0134

Aphrahat

Demonstrations *(Demonstrationes)*

Athanasius

Defense of His Flight *(Apologia de fuga sua)*	TLG 2035.012
Encyclical Letter *(Epistula encyclica)*	TLG 2035.006
Festal Letters *(Epistulae festalis)*	
Four Discourses Against the Arians *(Orationes tres contra Arianos)*	TLG 2035.042
History of the Arians *(Historia Arianum)*	TLG 2035.009
Letter to the Bishops of Egypt *(Epistula ad episcopos Aegypti et Libyae)*	TLG 2035.041
Life of St. Anthony *(Vita sancti Antonii)*	TLG 2035.047

Augustine

Admonition and Grace *(De correptione et gratia)*	Cetedoc 0353
Adulterous Marriages *(De adulterinis conjugiis)*	Cetedoc 0302
Against Faustus, a Manichean *(Contra Faustum)*	Cetedoc 0321
Against Julian *(Contra Julianum)*	Cetedoc 0351
Against Lying *(Contra mendacium)*	Cetedoc 0304

The Care to Be Taken for the Dead (*De cura pro mortuis gerenda*)   Cetedoc 0307

Christian Instruction (*De doctrina Christiana*)   Cetedoc 0263

City of God (*De civitate Dei*)   Cetedoc 0313

Confessions (*Confessionum libri tredecim*)   Cetedoc 0251

The Correction of the Donatists (*In Epistulae*)   Cetedoc 0262

Eight Questions of Dulcitius (*De octo Dulcitii quaestionibus*)   Cetedoc 0291

Explanations of the Psalms (*Enarrationes in Psalmos*)   Cetedoc 0283

Harmony of the Gospels (*De consensu evangelistarum libri iv*)   Cetedoc 0273

Homilies on 1 John (*In Johannis epistulam ad Parthos tractatus*)   Cetedoc 0279

Letters (*Epistulae*)   Cetedoc 0262

Letters of Petilian, the Donatist (*Contra litteras Petiliani*)   Cetedoc 0333

On Eighty-three Varied Questions
    (*De diversis quaestionibus octoginta tribus*)   Cetedoc 0289

On Grace and Free Will (*De gratia et libero arbitrio*)   Cetedoc 0352

On Patience (*De patientia*)   Cetedoc 0308

On the Soul and Its Origin (*De natura et origine animae*)   Cetedoc 0345

On the Spirit and the Letter (*De Spiritu et littera*)   Cetedoc 0343

On Various Questions to Simplician (*De diversis quaestionibus ad Simplicianum*)   Cetedoc 0290

Predestination of the Saints (*De praedestinatione sanctorum*)   Cetedoc 0354

Questions on the Heptateuch (*Quaestionum in heptateuchum libri septem*)   Cetedoc 0270

Sermons (*Sermones*)   Cetedoc 0284

Basil the Great

Homily Concerning Envy (*Homilia de invidia*)   TLG 2040.027

Homilies on the Psalms (*Homiliae super Psalmos*)   TLG 2040.018

Letters (*Epistulae*)   TLG 2040.004

The Long Rules (*Asceticon magnum sive Queaestiones [regulae fusius tractatae]*)   TLG 2040.048

On Humility (*De humilitate*)   TLG 2040.036

On the Spirit (*De Spiritu Sancto*)   TLG 2040.003

Preface on the Judgment of God (*Prologus 7 [De judicio Dei]*)   TLG 2040.043

Bede

Exposition of the Gospel of Luke (*In Lucae evangelium expositio*)   Cetedoc 1356

Four Books on 1 Samuel (*In primam partem Samuhelis libri iv*)   Cetedoc 1346

Homilies on the Gospels (*Homiliarum evangelii libri ii*)   Cetedoc 1367

On Genesis (*Libri quattuor in principium Genesis usque ad nativitatem
    Isaac et ejectionem Ismahelis adnotationum*)   Cetedoc 1344

On the Tabernacle (*De tabernaculo et vasis eius ac vestibus sacerdotum libri iii*)   Cetedoc 1345

Thirty Questions on the Book of Kings (*In Regum librum xxx quaestiones*)   Cetedoc 1347

Caesarius of Arles

Sermons (*Sermones*)   Cetedoc 1008

Cassian, John

Conferences (*Collationes*)   Cetedoc 0512

Institutes *(De institutis coenobiorum et de octo principalium vitiorum remediis)*   Cetedoc 0513

Cassiodorus
Expositions of the Psalms *(Expositio psalmorum)*   Cetedoc 0900

Clement of Alexandria
Christ the Educator *(Paedagogus)*   TLG 0555.002
Stromateis *(Stromata)*   TLG 0555.004

Clement of Rome
1 Clement *(Epistula i ad Corinthios)*   TLG 1271.001

Constitutions of the Holy Apostles *(Constitutiones apostolorum)*   TLG 2894.001

Cyprian
The Advantage of Patience *(De bono patientiae)*   Cetedoc 0048
Letters *(Epistulae)*   Cetedoc 0050
The Lord's Prayer *(De dominica oratione)*   Cetedoc 0043
To Quirinus: Testimonies Against the Jews *(Ad Quirinum)*   Cetedoc 0039

Cyril of Alexandria
Letters *(Epistulae in Concilium universale Ephesenum anno)*   TLG 5000.001

Cyril of Jerusalem
Catechetical Lectures *(Catecheses ad illuminandos)*   TLG 2110.003
Catechetical Lectures, Procatechesis *(Procatechesis)*   TLG 2110.001

Ennodius
Life of St. Epiphanius *(Vita Epiphanii)*   Cetedoc 1494

Ephrem the Syrian
Commentary on Genesis *(Commentarii in Genesim)*
Commentary on Tatian's Diatessaron *(In Tatiani Diatessaron)*
Homily on Our Lord *(Sermo de Domino nostro)*
Hymns on Paradise *(Hymni de paradiso)*
Hymns on the Nativity *(Hymni de nativitate)*

Eusebius of Caesaria
Ecclesiastical History *(Historia ecclesiastica)*   TLG 2018.002
Proof of the Gospel *(Demonstratio evangelica)*   TLG 2018.005

Evagrius of Pontus
Praktikos *(Practicus)*   TLG 4110.001

Fructuosus of Braga
General Rule for Monasteries (*Regula Monastica Communis*)

Gregory of Elvira
Origen's Tractates on the Books of Holy Scripture (*Tractatus
Origenis de libris Sanctarum Scripturarum*)   Cetedoc 0546

Gregory of Nazianzus
Against the Eunomians, Theological Oration 1(27) (*Adversus Eunomianos*)   TLG 2022.007
In Defense of His Flight to Pontus, Oration 2 (*Apologetica*)   TLG 2022.016
On Basil the Great, Oration 43 (*Funebris oratio in laudem Basilii Magni
Caesareae in Cappadocia episcopi*)   TLG 2022.006
On Holy Baptism, Oration 40 (*In sanctum baptisma*)   TLG 2022.048
On Theology, Theological Oration 2(28) (*De theologia*)   TLG 2022.008

Gregory of Nyssa
Against Eunomius (*Contra Eunomium*)   TLG 2017.030
Answer to Eunomius' Second Book (*Contra Eunomium*)   TLG 2017.030
The Life of Gregory the Wonderworker (*De vita Gregorii Thaumaturgi*)   TLG 2017.069
On Perfection (*De perfectione Christiana ad Olympium monachum*)   TLG 2017.026
On the Baptism of Christ (*In diem luminum [vulgo In baptismum
Christi oratio]*)   TLG 2017.014
On the Inscriptions of the Psalms (*In inscriptiones Psalmorum*)   TLG 2017.027

Gregory Thaumaturgus
Address of Thanksgiving to Origen (*In Originem oratio panegyrica*)   TLG 2063.001
Canonical Epistle (*Epistula canonica*)   TLG 2063.005

Gregory the Great
Dialogues (*Dialogorum libri iv libri duo*)   Cetedoc 1713
Forty Gospel Homilies (*Homiliarum xl in evangelica*)   Cetedoc 1711
Letters (*Registrum epistularum*)   Cetedoc 1714
Morals on the Book of Job (*Moralia in Job*)   Cetedoc 1708
Pastoral Care (*Regula pastoralis*)   Cetedoc 1712
Six Books on 1 Kings (*In librum primum Regum expositionum libri vi*)   Cetedoc 1719

Hilary of Poitiers
Homilies on the Psalms (*Tractatus super psalmos I-XCI*)   Cetedoc 0428

Hippolytus
On the Antichrist (*De antichristo*)   TLG 2115.003
The Refutation of All Heresies (*Refutatio omnium haeresium*)   TLG 2115.060

Horsiesi
Regulations (*Regulae*)

Incomplete Work on Matthew (*Opus imperfectum in Matthaeum*)

Irenaeus

Against Heresies (*Adversus haereses*)   TLG 1447.002

Isaac of Nineveh

Ascetical Homilies (*De perfectione religiosa*)

Isidore of Seville

On Ruth (*De Ruth*)

Jerome

Against Jovinianus (*Adversus Jovinianum*)   Cetedoc 0610
Against the Pelagians (*Dialogi contra Pelagianos libri iii*)   Cetedoc 0615
Commentary on the Minor Prophets (*Commentarii in prophetas minores*)   Cetedoc 0589
Homilies on Matthew (*Homilia in evangelium secundum Matthaeum*)   Cetedoc 0595
Homily on the Exodus (*De exodo, in vigilia Paschae*)   Cetedoc 0601
Homilies on the Psalms (*Tractatus lix in psalmos*)   Cetedoc 0592
Homilies on the Psalms, Alternate Series (*Tractatuum in psalmos series altera*) Cetedoc 0593
Letters (*Epistulae*)   Cetedoc 0620

John Chrysostom

Against the Anomoeans (*Contra Anomoeos [homilia 11]*)   TLG 2062.019
Commentary on Galatians (*In epistulam ad Galatas commentarius*)   TLG 2062.158
Discourses Against Judaizing Christians (*Adversus Judaeos [orationes 1-8]*)   TLG 2062.021
Discourse on Blessed Babylas (*De sancto hieromartyre Babyla*)   TLG 2062.041
Homilies Concerning the Statues (*Ad populam Antiochenum homiliae [de statuis]*) TLG 2062.024
Homilies on Colossians (*In epistulam ad Colossenses*)   TLG 2062.161
Homilies on 1 Corinthians (*In epistulam i ad Corinthios [homiliae 1-44]*)   TLG 2062.156
Homilies on 2 Corinthians (*In epistulam ii ad Corinthios [homiliae 1-30]*)   TLG 2062.157
Homilies on David and Saul (*De Davide et Saule*)   TLG 2062.115
Homilies on Ephesians (*In epistulam ad Ephesios*)   TLG 2062.159
Homilies on Genesis (*In Genesim [homiliae 1-67]*)   TLG 2062.112
Homilies on Hannah (*De Anna*)   TLG 2062.114
Homilies on Philippians (*In epistulam ad Philippenses*)   TLG 2062.160
Homilies on Repentance and Almsgiving
   (*De eleemosyna*)   TLG 2062.075
   (*De paenitentia [homiliae 1-9]*)   TLG 2062.027
Homilies on Romans (*In epistulam ad Romanos*)   TLG 2062.155
Homilies on the Gospel of John (*In Joannem [homiliae 1-88]*)   TLG 2062.153
Homilies on the Gospel of Matthew (*In Matthaeum [homiliae 1-90]*)   TLG 2062.152
Homilies on 1 Thessalonians (*In epistulam i ad Thessalonicenses*)   TLG 2062.162
Homilies on 2 Thessalonians (*In epistulam ii ad Thessalonicenses*)   TLG 2062.163
Homilies on 1 Timothy (*In epistulam i ad Timotheum*)   TLG 2062.164
Homilies on 2 Timothy (*In epistulam ii ad Timotheum*)   TLG 2062.165

Homilies on Titus (*In epistulam ad Titum*)   TLG 2062.166
Homily to Those Who Had Not Attended the Assembly
   (*In illud: Si esurierit inimicus*)   TLG 2062.068
On the Epistle to the Hebrews (*In epistulam ad Hebraeos*)   TLG 2062.168
On the Priesthood (*De sacerdotio*)   TLG 2062.085

John of Damascus
On Divine Images (*Orationes de imaginibus tres*)   TLG 2934.005
Orthodox Faith (*Expositio fidei*)   TLG 2934.004

Justin Martyr
Dialogue with Trypho (*Dialogus cum Tryphone*)   TLG 0645.003

Lactantius
Epitome of the Divine Institutes (*Epitome divinarum institutionum*)   Cetedoc 0086

Leander of Seville
The Training of Nuns (*Regula, sive liber de institutione virginum et contemptu mundi*)

Maximus of Turin
Sermons (*Collectio sermonum antiqua*)   Cetedoc 0219a

Methodius
Banquet of the Ten Virgins (*Convivium decem virginum*)   TLG 2959.001
On the Resurrection (*De resurrectione*)   TLG 2959.003

Nemesius of Emesa
On the Nature of Man (*De natura hominis*)   TLG 0743.001

Nicetas of Remesiana
Liturgical Singing (*De utilitate hymnorum*)
The Power of the Holy Spirit (*De Spiritus Sancti potentia*)

Novatian
On the Spectacles (*De spectaculis*)   Cetedoc 0070

Origen
Against Celsus (*Contra Celsum*)   TLG 2042.001
Commentary on Matthew (*Commentarium in evangelium Matthaei [lib.12-17]*)   TLG 2042.030
Commentary on the Gospel of John (*Commentarii in evangelium Joannis*)   TLG 2042.005
Commentary on the Song of Songs (*Commentarium in Canticum canticorum*)   Cetedoc 0198 2
Exhortation to Martyrdom (*Exhortatio ad martyrium*)   TLG 2042.007
Fragments on Jeremiah (*Fragmenta in Jeremiam [in catenis]*)   TLG 2042.010
Homilies on Exodus (*Homiliae in Exodum*)   TLG 2042.023
Homilies on Genesis (*Homiliae in Genesim*)   TLG 2042.022

Homilies on Jeremiah (*In Jeremiam [homiliae 1-11]*)   TLG 2042.009
   (*In Jeremiam [homiliae 12-20]*)   TLG 2042.021
Homilies on Joshua (*Homiliae in librum Jesu Nave*)
Homilies on 1 Kings (*Homiliae in librum Regum I*)   Cetedoc 0198 8
Homilies on Leviticus (*Homiliae in Leviticum*)   TLG 2042.024
Homilies on Numbers (*In Numeros homiliae*)   Cetedoc 0198 0
Homily on 1 Kings 28 (1 Samuel 28) (*De engastrimytho*)   TLG 2042.013
On Prayer (*De oratione*)   TLG 2042.008

Pachomius
Instructions (*Catecheses*)

Pacian of Barcelona
Letters (*Epistulae*)
On Penitents (*De paenitentibus*)

Paulinus of Milan
The Life of St. Ambrose (*Vita S. Ambrosii*)

Paulinus of Nola
Poems (*Carmina*)   Cetedoc 0203

Paulus Orosius
Defense Against the Pelagians (*Liber apologeticus contra Pelagianos*)   Cetedoc 0572

Peter Chrysologus
Sermons (*Collectio sermonum*)   Cetedoc 0227+

Prudentius
Hymns for Every Day (*Liber Cathemerinon*)   Cetedoc 1438
Scenes from Sacred History (*Tituli historiarum sive Dittochaeon*)   Cetedoc 1444
The Spiritual Combat (*Psychomachia*)   Cetedoc 1441

Pseudo-Clement of Rome
Recognitions (*Recognitiones*)   Cetedoc 0198 N (A)

Ignatius of Antioch
Letter to the Magnesians (*In Epistulae vii genuinae [recensio media]*)   TLG 1443.001

Salvian the Presbyter
The Governance of God (*De gubernatione Dei*)   Cetedoc 0485

Sulpicius Severus
Sacred History (*Chronicorum libri II*)   Cetedoc 0474

Symeon the New Theologian
Discourses *(Catecheses)*

Tertullian
Against Marcion *(Adversus Marcionem)*	Cetedoc 0014
An Answer to the Jews *(Adversus Judaeos)*	Cetedoc 0033
On Fasting *(De jejunio adversus psychicos)*	Cetedoc 0029
On Flight in Time of Persecution *(De fuga in persecutione)*	Cetedoc 0025
On Idolatry *(De idololatria)*	Cetedoc 0023
On the Resurrection of the Flesh *(De resurrectione mortuorum)*	Cetedoc 0019
On the Soul *(De anima)*	Cetedoc 0017
Prescriptions Against Heretics *(De praescriptione haereticorum)*	Cetedoc 0005
Scorpiace *(Scorpiace)*	Cetedoc 0022

Theodoret of Cyr
Ecclesiastical History *(Historia ecclesiastica)*	TLG 4089.003
Letters *(Ad eos qui in Euphratesia et Osrhoena regione, Syria, Phoeni)*	TLG 4089.034
On Divine Providence *(De providentia orationes decem)*	TLG 4089.032

Theophylact
Explanation of Matthew *(Ennarratio in evangelium s. Matthaei)*

Biographical Sketches &
Short Descriptions
of Select Anonymous Works

This listing is cumulative, including all the authors and works cited in this series to date.

Acacius of Beroea (c. 340-c. 436). Syrian monk known for his ascetic life. He became bishop of Beroea in 378, participated in the council of Constantinople in 381, and played an important role in mediating between Cyril of Alexandria and John of Antioch; however, he did not take part in the clash between Cyril and Nestorius.

Acacius of Caesarea (d. c. 365). Pro-Arian bishop of Caesarea in Palestine, disciple and biographer of Eusebius of Caesarea, the historian. He was a man of great learning and authored a treatise on Ecclesiastes.

Adamnan (c. 624-704). Abbot of Iona, Ireland, and author of the life of St. Columba. He was influential in the process of assimilating the Celtic church into Roman liturgy and church order. He also wrote *On the Holy Sites*, which influenced Bede.

Alexander of Alexandria (fl. 312-328). Bishop of Alexandria and predecessor of Athanasius, on whom he exerted considerable theological influence during the rise of Arianism. Alexander excommunicated Arius, whom he had appointed to the parish of Baucalis, in 319. His teaching regarding the eternal generation and divine substantial union of the Son with the Father was eventually confirmed at the Council of Nicaea (325).

Ambrose of Milan (c. 333-397; fl. 374-397). Bishop of Milan and teacher of Augustine who defended the divinity of the Holy Spirit and the perpetual virginity of Mary.

Ambrosiaster (fl. c. 366-384). Name given by Erasmus to the author of a work once thought to have been composed by Ambrose.

Ammonius (c. fifth century). An Aristotelian commentator and teacher in Alexandria, where he was born and of whose school he became head. Also an exegete of Plato, he enjoyed fame among his contemporaries and successors, although modern critics accuse him of pedantry and banality.

Amphilochius of Iconium (b. c. 340-345, d. c. 398-404). An orator at Constantinople before becoming bishop of Iconium in 373. He was a cousin of Gregory of Nazianzus and active in debates against the Macedonians and Messalians.

Andreas (c. seventh century). Monk who collected commentary from earlier writers to form a catena on various biblical books.

Antony (or Anthony) the Great (c. 251-c. 356). An anchorite of the Egyptian desert and founder of Egyptian monasticism. Athanasius regarded him as the ideal of monastic life, and he has become a model for Christian hagiography.

Aphrahat (c. 270-350; fl. 337-345). "The Persian

Sage" and first major Syriac writer whose work survives. He is also known by his Greek name Aphraates.

Apollinaris of Laodicea (310-c. 392). Bishop of Laodicea who was attacked by Gregory of Nazianzus, Gregory of Nyssa and Theodore for denying that Christ had a human mind.

Aponius/Apponius (fourth–fifth century). Author of a remarkable commentary on Song of Solomon (c. 405-415), an important work in the history of exegesis. The work, which was influenced by the commentaries of Origen and Pseudo-Hippolytus, is of theological significance, especially in the area of Christology.

Apostolic Constitutions (c. 381-394). Also known as *Constitutions of the Holy Apostles* and thought to be redacted by Julian of Neapolis. The work is divided into eight books, and is primarily a collection of and expansion on previous works such as the *Didache* (c. 140) and the *Apostolic Traditions*. Book 8 ends with eighty-five canons from various sources and is elsewhere known as the *Apostolic Canons*.

Arethas of Caesarea (c. 860-940) Byzantine scholar and disciple of Photius. He was a deacon in Constantinople, then archbishop of Caesarea from 901.

Arius (fl. c. 320). Heretic condemned at the Council of Nicaea (325) for refusing to accept that the Son was not a creature but was God by nature like the Father.

Arnobius the Younger (fifth century). A participant in christological controversies of the fifth century. He composed *Conflictus cum Serapione*, an account of a debate with a monophysite monk in which he attempts to demonstrate harmony between Roman and Alexandrian theology. Some scholars attribute to him a few more works, such as *Commentaries on Psalms*.

Athanasius of Alexandria (c. 295-373; fl. 325-373). Bishop of Alexandria from 328, though often in exile. He wrote his classic polemics against the Arians while most of the eastern bishops were against him.

Athenagoras (fl. 176-180). Early Christian philosopher and apologist from Athens, whose only authenticated writing, *A Plea Regarding Christians*, is addressed to the emperors Marcus Aurelius and Commodius, and defends Christians from the common accusations of atheism, incest and cannibalism.

Augustine of Hippo (354-430). Bishop of Hippo and a voluminous writer on philosophical, exegetical, theological and ecclesiological topics. He formulated the Western doctrines of predestination and original sin in his writings against the Pelagians.

Babai (c. early sixth century). Author of the Letter to Cyriacus. He should not be confused with either Babai of Nisibis (d. 484), or Babai the Great (d. 628).

Babai the Great (d. 628). Syriac monk who founded a monastery and school in his region of Beth Zabday and later served as third superior at the Great Convent of Mount Izla during a period of crisis in the Nestorian church.

Basil of Seleucia (fl. 444-468). Bishop of Seleucia in Isauria and ecclesiastical writer. He took part in the Synod of Constantinople in 448 for the condemnation of the Eutychian errors and the deposition of their great champion, Dioscurus of Alexandria.

Basil the Great (b. c. 330; fl. 357-379). One of the Cappadocian fathers, bishop of Caesarea and champion of the teaching on the Trinity propounded at Nicaea in 325. He was a great administrator and founded a monastic rule.

Basilides (fl. second century). Alexandrian heretic of the early second century who is said to have believed that souls migrate from body to body and that we do not sin if we lie to protect the body from martyrdom.

Bede the Venerable (c. 672/673-735). Born in Northumbria, at the age of seven, he was put under the care of the Benedictine monks of Saints Peter and Paul at Jarrow and given a broad classical education in the monastic tradition. Considered one of the most learned men of his age, he is the author of *An Ecclesiastical History of the English People*.

Benedict of Nursia (c. 480-547). Considered the most important figure in the history of Western monasticism. Benedict founded many monasteries, the most notable found at Montecassino, but his lasting influence lay in his famous Rule. The Rule outlines the theological and inspirational foundation of the monastic ideal while also legislating the shape and organization of the cenobitic life.

Besa the Copt (5th century). Coptic monk, disciple of Shenoute, whom he succeeded as head of the monastery. He wrote numerous letters, monastic catecheses and a biography of Shenoute.

Book of Steps (c. 400). Written by an anonymous Syriac author, this work consists of thirty homilies or discourses which specifically deal with the more advanced stages of growth in the spiritual life.

Braulio of Saragossa (c. 585-651). Bishop of Saragossa (631-651) and noted writer of the Visigothic renaissance. His *Life* of St. Aemilianus is his crowning literary achievement.

Caesarius of Arles (c. 470-543). Bishop of Arles renowned for his attention to his pastoral duties. Among his surviving works the most important is a collection of some 238 sermons that display an ability to preach Christian doctrine to a variety of audiences.

Callistus of Rome (d. 222). Pope (217-222) who excommunicated Sabellius for heresy. It is very probable that he suffered martyrdom.

Cassia (b. c. 805, d. between 848 and 867). Nun, poet and hymnographer who founded a convent in Constantinople.

Cassian, John (360-432). Author of the *Institutes* and the *Conferences,* works purporting to relay the teachings of the Egyptian monastic fathers on the nature of the spiritual life which were highly influential in the development of Western monasticism.

Cassiodorus (c. 485-c. 580). Founder of the monastery of Vivarium, Calabria, where monks transcribed classic sacred and profane texts, Greek and Latin, preserving them for the Western tradition.

Chromatius (fl. 400). Bishop of Aquileia, friend of Rufinus and Jerome and author of tracts and sermons.

Clement of Alexandria (c. 150-215). A highly educated Christian convert from paganism, head of the catechetical school in Alexandria and pioneer of Christian scholarship. His major works, *Protrepticus, Paedagogus* and the *Stromata,* bring Christian doctrine face to face with the ideas and achievements of his time.

Clement of Rome (fl. c. 92-101). Pope whose *Epistle to the Corinthians* is one of the most important documents of subapostolic times.

Commodian (probably third or possibly fifth century). Latin poet of unknown origin (possibly Syrian?) whose two surviving works suggest chiliast and patripassionist tendencies.

Constitutions of the Holy Apostles. See Apostolic Constitutions.

Cyprian of Carthage (fl. 248-258). Martyred bishop of Carthage who maintained that those baptized by schismatics and heretics had no share in the blessings of the church.

Cyril of Alexandria (375-444; fl. 412-444). Patriarch of Alexandria whose extensive exegesis, characterized especially by a strong espousal of the unity of Christ, led to the condemnation of Nestorius in 431.

Cyril of Jerusalem (c. 315-386; fl. c. 348). Bishop of Jerusalem after 350 and author of *Catechetical Homilies*.

Cyril of Scythopolis (b. c. 525; d. after 557). Palestinian monk and author of biographies of famous Palestinian monks. Because of him we have precise knowledge of monastic life in the fifth and sixth centuries and a description of the Origenist crisis and its suppression in the mid-sixth century.

Diadochus of Photice (c. 400-474). Antimonophysite bishop of Epirus Vetus whose work *Discourse on the Ascension of Our Lord Jesus Christ* exerted influence in both the East and West through its Chalcedonian Christology. He is also the subject of the mystical *Vision of St. Diadochus Bishop of Photice in Epirus.*

Didache (c. 140). Of unknown authorship, this text intertwines Jewish ethics with Christian liturgical practice to form a whole discourse on the "way of life." It exerted an enormous amount of influence in the patristic period and was especially used in the training of catechumen.

Didymus the Blind (c. 313-398). Alexandrian exegete who was much influenced by Origen and admired by Jerome.

Diodore of Tarsus (d. c. 394). Bishop of Tarsus and Antiochene theologian. He authored a great scope of exegetical, doctrinal and apologetic works, which come to us mostly in fragments because of his condemnation as the predecessor of Nestorianism. Diodore was a teacher of John Chrysostom and Theodore of Mopsuestia.

Dionysius of Alexandria (d. c. 264). Bishop of Alexandria and student of Origen. Dionysius actively engaged in the theological disputes of his day, opposed Sabellianism, defended himself against accusations of tritheism and wrote the earliest extant Christian refutation of Epicureanism. His writings have survived mainly in extracts preserved by other early Christian authors.

Dorotheus of Gaza (fl. c. 525-540). Member of Abbot Seridos's monastery and later leader of a monastery where he wrote *Spiritual Instructions*. He also wrote a work on traditions of Palestinian monasticism.

Ennodius (474-521). Bishop of Pavia, a prolific writer of various genre, including letters, poems and biographies. He sought reconciliation in the schism between Rome and Acacius of Constantinople, and also upheld papal autonomy in the face of challenges from secular authorities.

Ephrem the Syrian (b. c. 306; fl. 363-373). Syrian writer of commentaries and devotional hymns which are sometimes regarded as the greatest specimens of Christian poetry prior to Dante.

Epiphanius of Salamis (c. 315-403). Bishop of Salamis in Cyprus, author of a refutation of eighty heresies (the *Panarion*) and instrumental in the condemnation of Origen.

Epiphanius the Latin. Author of the late fifth-century or early sixth century Latin text *Interpretation of the Gospels*, with constant references to early patristic commentators. He was possibly a bishop of Benevento or Seville.

Epistle of Barnabas. See Letter of Barnabas.

Eucherius of Lyons (fl. 420-449). Bishop of Lyons c. 435-449. Born into an aristocratic family, he, along with his wife and sons, joined the monastery at Lérins soon after its founding. He explained difficult Scripture passages by means of a threefold reading of the text: literal, moral and spiritual.

Eugippius (b. 460). Disciple of Severinus and third abbot of the monastic community at Castrum Lucullanum, which was made up of those fleeing from Noricum during the barbarian invasions.

Eunomius (d. 393). Bishop of Cyzicyus who was attacked by Basil and Gregory of Nyssa for maintaining that the Father and the Son were of different natures, one ingenerate, one generate.

Eusebius of Caesarea (c. 260/263-340). Bishop of Caesarea, partisan of the Emperor Constantine and first historian of the Christian church. He argued that the truth of the gospel had been foreshadowed in pagan writings but had to defend his own doctrine against suspicion of Arian sympathies.

Eusebius of Emesa (c. 300-c. 359). Bishop of Emesa from c. 339. A biblical exegete and writer on doctrinal subjects, he displays some semi-Arian tendencies of his mentor Eusebius of Caesarea.

Eusebius of Gaul, or Eusebius Gallicanus (c. fifth century). A conventional name for a collection of seventy-six sermons produced in Gaul and revised in the seventh century. It contains material from different patristic authors and focuses on ethical teaching in the context of the liturgical cycle (days of saints and other feasts).

Eusebius of Vercelli (fl. c. 360). Bishop of Vercelli who supported the trinitarian teaching of Nicaea (325) when it was being undermined by compromise in the West.

Eustathius of Antioch (fl. 325). First bishop of Beroea, then of Antioch, one of the leaders of the anti-Arians at the council of Nicaea. Later, he was banished from his seat and exiled to Thrace for his support of Nicene theology.

Euthymius (377-473). A native of Melitene and

influential monk. He was educated by Bishop Otreius of Melitene, who ordained him priest and placed him in charge of all the monasteries in his diocese. When the Council of Chalcedon (451) condemned the errors of Eutyches, it was greatly due to the authority of Euthymius that most of the Eastern recluses accepted its decrees. The empress Eudoxia returned to Chalcedonian orthodoxy through his efforts.

Evagrius of Pontus (c. 345-399). Disciple and teacher of ascetic life who astutely absorbed and creatively transmitted the spirituality of Egyptian and Palestinian monasticism of the late fourth century. Although Origenist elements of his writings were formally condemned by the Fifth Ecumenical Council (Constantinople II, A.D. 553), his literary corpus continued to influence the tradition of the church.

Eznik of Kolb (early fifth century). A disciple of Mesrob who translated Greek Scriptures into Armenian, so as to become the model of the classical Armenian language. As bishop, he participated in the synod of Astisat (449).

Facundus of Hermiane (fl. 546-568). African bishop who opposed Emperor Justinian's *post mortem* condemnation of Theodore of Mopsuestia, Theodoret of Cyr and Ibas of Ebessa at the fifth ecumenical council. His written defense, known as "To Justinian" or "In Defense of the Three Chapters," avers that ancient theologians should not be blamed for errors that became obvious only upon later theological reflection. He continued in the tradition of Chalcedon, although his Christology was supplemented, according to Justinian's decisions, by the theopaschite formula *Unus ex Trinitate passus est* ("Only one of the three suffered").

Fastidius (c. fourth-fifth centuries). British author of *On the Christian Life*. He is believed to have written some works attributed to Pelagius.

Faustinus (fl. 380). A priest in Rome and supporter of Lucifer and author of a treatise on the Trinity.

Faustus of Riez (c. 400-490). A prestigious British monk at Lérins; abbot, then bishop of Riez

from 457 to his death. His works include *On the Holy Spirit*, in which he argued against the Macedonians for the divinity of the Holy Spirit, and *On Grace*, in which he argued for a position on salvation that lay between more categorical views of free-will and predestination. Various letters and (pseudonymous) sermons are extant.

The Festal Menaion. Orthodox liturgical text containing the variable parts of the service, including hymns, for fixed days of celebration of the life of Jesus and Mary.

Filastrius (fl. 380). Bishop of Brescia and author of a compilation against all heresies.

Firmicus Maternus (fourth century). An anti-Pagan apologist. Before his conversion to Christianity he wrote a work on astrology (334-337). After his conversion, however, he criticized paganism in *On the Errors of the Profane Religion*.

Fructuosus of Braga (d. c. 665). Son of a Gothic general and member of a noble military family. He became a monk at an early age, then abbot-bishop of Dumium before 650 and metropolitan of Braga in 656. He was influential in setting up monastic communities in Lusitania, Asturia, Galicia and the island of Gades.

Fulgentius of Ruspe (c. 467-532). Bishop of Ruspe and author of many orthodox sermons and tracts under the influence of Augustine.

Gaudentius of Brescia (fl. 395). Successor of Filastrius as bishop of Brescia and author of twenty-one Eucharistic sermons.

Gennadius of Constantinople (d. 471). Patriarch of Constantinople, author of numerous commentaries and an opponent of the Christology of Cyril of Alexandria.

Gerontius (c. 395-c.480). Palestinian monk, later archimandrite of the cenobites of Palestine. He led the resistance to the council of Chalcedon.

Gnostics. Name now given generally to followers of Basilides, Marcion, Valentinus, Mani and others. The characteristic belief is that matter is a prison made for the spirit by an evil or ignorant creator, and that redemption depends on fate, not on free will.

Gregory of Elvira (fl. 359-385). Bishop of Elvira

who wrote allegorical treatises in the style of Origen and defended the Nicene faith against the Arians.

Gregory of Nazianzus (b. 329/330; fl. 372-389). Cappadocian father, bishop of Constantinople, friend of Basil the Great and Gregory of Nyssa, and author of theological orations, sermons and poetry.

Gregory of Nyssa (c. 335-394). Bishop of Nyssa and brother of Basil the Great. A Cappadocian father and author of catechetical orations, he was a philosophical theologian of great originality.

Gregory Thaumaturgus (fl. c. 248-264). Bishop of Neocaesarea and a disciple of Origen. There are at least five legendary *Lives* that recount the events and miracles which led to his being called "the wonder worker." His most important work was the *Address of Thanks to Origen,* which is a rhetorically structured panegyric to Origen and an outline of his teaching.

Gregory the Great (c. 540-604). Pope from 590, the fourth and last of the Latin "Doctors of the Church." He was a prolific author and a powerful unifying force within the Latin Church, initiating the liturgical reform that brought about the Gregorian Sacramentary and Gregorian chant.

Hesychius of Jerusalem (fl. 412-450). Presbyter and exegete, thought to have commented on the whole of Scripture.

Hilary of Arles (c. 401-449). Archbishop of Arles and leader of the Semi-Pelagian party. Hilary incurred the wrath of Pope Leo I when he removed a bishop from his see and appointed a new bishop. Leo demoted Arles from a metropolitan see to a bishopric to assert papal power over the church in Gaul.

Hilary of Poitiers (c. 315-367). Bishop of Poitiers and called the "Athanasius of the West" because of his defense (against the Arians) of the common nature of Father and Son.

Hippolytus (fl. 222-245). Recent scholarship places Hippolytus in a Palestinian context, personally familiar with Origen. Though he is known chiefly for *The Refutation of All Heresies,* he was primarily a commentator on Scripture (especially the Old Testament) employing typological exegesis.

Horsiesi (c. 305-c. 390). Pachomius's second successor, after Petronius, as a leader of cenobitic monasticism in Southern Egypt.

Ignatius of Antioch (c. 35-107/112). Bishop of Antioch who wrote several letters to local churches while being taken from Antioch to Rome to be martyred. In the letters, which warn against heresy, he stresses orthodox Christology, the centrality of the Eucharist and unique role of the bishop in preserving the unity of the church.

Irenaeus of Lyons (c. 135-c. 202). Bishop of Lyons who published the most famous and influential refutation of Gnostic thought.

Isaac of Nineveh (d. c. 700). Also known as Isaac the Syrian or Isaac Syrus, this monastic writer served for a short while as bishop of Nineveh before retiring to live a secluded monastic life. His writings on ascetic subjects survive in the form of numerous homilies.

Isho'dad of Merv (fl. c. 850). Nestorian bishop of Hedatta. He wrote commentaries on parts of the Old Testament and all of the New Testament, frequently quoting Syriac fathers.

Isidore of Seville (c. 560-636). Youngest of a family of monks and clerics, including sister Florentina and brothers Leander and Fulgentius. He was an erudite author of comprehensive scale in matters both religious and sacred, including his encyclopedic *Etymologies.*

Jacob of Nisibis (d. 338). Bishop of Nisibis. He was present at the council of Nicaea in 325 and took an active part in the opposition to Arius.

Jacob of Sarug (c. 450-c. 520). Syriac ecclesiastical writer. Jacob received his education at Edessa. At the end of his life he was ordained bishop of Sarug. His principal writing was a long series of metrical homilies, earning him the title "The Flute of the Holy Spirit."

Jerome (c. 347-419). Gifted exegete and exponent of a classical Latin style, now best known as the translator of the Latin Vulgate. He defended the perpetual virginity of Mary, attacked Origen and Pelagius and supported extreme ascetic practices.

John Chrysostom (344/354-407; fl. 386-407).

Bishop of Constantinople who was noted for his orthodoxy, his eloquence and his attacks on Christian laxity in high places.

John of Antioch (d. 441/42). Bishop of Antioch, commencing in 428. He received his education together with Nestorius and Theodore of Mopsuestia in a monastery near Antioch. A supporter of Nestorius, he condemned Cyril of Alexandria, but later reached a compromise with him.

John of Apamea (fifth century). Syriac author of the early church who wrote on various aspects of the spiritual life, also known as John the Solitary. Some of his writings are in the form of dialogues. Other writings include letters, a treatise on baptism, and shorter works on prayer and silence.

John of Damascus (c. 650-750). Arab monastic and theologian whose writings enjoyed great influence in both the Eastern and Western Churches. His most influential writing was the *Orthodox Faith*.

John the Elder (c. eighth century). A Syriac author who belonged to monastic circles of the Church of the East and lived in the region of Mount Qardu (northern Iraq). His most important writings are twenty-two homilies and a collection of fifty-one short letters in which he describes the mystical life as an anticipatory experience of the resurrection life, the fruit of the sacraments of baptism and the Eucharist.

John the Monk. Traditional name found in *The Festal Menaion*, believed to refer to John of Damascus. *See* John of Damascus.

Josephus, Flavius (c. 37-c. 101). Jewish historian from a distinguished priestly family. Acquainted with the Essenes and Sadducees, he himself became a Pharisee. He joined the great Jewish revolt that broke out in 66 and was chosen by the Sanhedrin at Jerusalem to be commander-in-chief in Galilee. Showing great shrewdness to ingratiate himself with Vespasian by foretelling his elevation and that of his son Titus to the imperial dignity, Josephus was restored his liberty after 69 when Vespasian became emperor.

Julian of Eclanum (c. 385-450). Bishop of Eclanum in 416/417 who was removed from office and exiled in 419 for not officially opposing Pelagianism. In exile, he was accepted by Theodore of Mopsuestia, whose Antiochene exegetical style he followed. Although he was never able to regain his ecclesiastical position, Julian taught in Sicily until his death. His works include commentaries on Job and parts of the Minor Prophets, a translation of Theodore of Mopsuestia's commentary on the Psalms, and various letters. Sympathetic to Pelagius, Julian applied his intellectual acumen and rhetorical training to argue against Augustine on matters such as free will, desire and the locus of evil.

Justin Martyr (c. 100/110-165; fl. c. 148-161). Palestinian philosopher who was converted to Christianity, "the only sure and worthy philosophy." He traveled to Rome where he wrote several apologies against both pagans and Jews, combining Greek philosophy and Christian theology; he was eventually martyred.

Lactantius (c. 260-c. 330). Christian apologist removed from his post as teacher of rhetoric at Nicomedia upon his conversion to Christianity. He was tutor to the son of Constantine and author of *The Divine Institutes*.

Leander (c. 545-c. 600). Latin ecclesiastical writer, of whose works only two survive. He was instrumental in spreading Christianity among the Visigoths, gaining significant historical influence in Spain in his time.

Leo the Great (regn. 440-461). Bishop of Rome whose *Tome to Flavian* helped to strike a balance between Nestorian and Cyrilline positions at the Council of Chalcedon in 451.

Letter of Barnabas (c. 130). An allegorical and typological interpretation of the Old Testament with a decidedly anti-Jewish tone. It was included with other New Testament works as a "Catholic epistle" at least until Eusebius of Caesarea (c. 260/263-340) questioned its authenticity.

Letter to Diognetus (c. third century). A refutation of paganism and an exposition of the Christian life and faith. The author of this letter is unknown, and the exact identity of its recipient, Diognetus, continues to elude patristic scholars.

Lucifer (d. 370/371). Bishop of Cagliari and vigorous supporter of Athanasius and the Nicene Creed. In conflict with the emperor Constantius, he was banished to Palestine and later to Thebaid (Egypt).

Luculentius (fifth century). Unknown author of a group of short commentaries on the New Testament, especially Pauline passages. His exegesis is mainly literal and relies mostly on earlier authors such as Jerome and Augustine. The content of his writing may place it in the fifth century.

Macarius of Egypt (c. 300-c. 390). One of the Desert Fathers. Accused of supporting Athanasius, Macarius was exiled c. 374 to an island in the Nile by Lucius, the Arian successor of Athanasius. Macarius continued his teaching of monastic theology at Wadi Natrun.

Macrina the Younger (c. 327-379). The elder sister of Basil the Great and Gregory of Nyssa, she is known as "the Younger" to distinguish her from her paternal grandmother. She had a powerful influence on her younger brothers, especially on Gregory, who called her his teacher and relates her teaching in *On the Soul and the Resurrection*.

Manichaeans. A religious movement that originated circa 241 in Persia under the leadership of Mani but was apparently of complex Christian origin. It is said to have denied free will and the universal sovereignty of God, teaching that kingdoms of light and darkness are coeternal and that the redeemed are particles of a spiritual man of light held captive in the darkness of matter (*see* Gnostics).

Marcellus of Ancyra (d. c. 375). Wrote a refutation of Arianism. Later, he was accused of Sabellianism, especially by Eusebius of Caesarea. While the Western church declared him orthodox, the Eastern church excommunicated him. Some scholars have attributed to him certain works of Athanasius.

Marcion (fl. 144). Heretic of the mid-second century who rejected the Old Testament and much of the New Testament, claiming that the Father of Jesus Christ was other than the Old Testament God (*see* Gnostics).

Marius Victorinus (b. c. 280/285; fl. c. 355-363). Grammarian of African origin who taught rhetoric at Rome and translated works of Platonists. After his conversion (c. 355), he wrote against the Arians and commentaries on Paul's letters.

Mark the Hermit (c. sixth century). Monk who lived near Tarsus and produced works on ascetic practices as well as christological issues.

Martin of Braga (fl. c. 568-579). Anti-Arian metropolitan of Braga on the Iberian peninsula. He was highly educated and presided over the provincial council of Braga in 572.

Martyrius. *See* Sahdona.

Maximus of Turin (d. 408/423). Bishop of Turin. Over one hundred of his sermons survive on Christian festivals, saints and martyrs.

Maximus the Confessor (c. 580-662). Palestinian-born theologian and ascetic writer. Fleeing the Arab invasion of Jerusalem in 614, he took refuge in Constantinople and later Africa. He died near the Black Sea after imprisonment and severe suffering, having his tongue cut off and his right hand mutilated. He taught total preference for God and detachment from all things.

Methodius of Olympus (d. 311). Bishop of Olympus who celebrated virginity in a *Symposium* partly modeled on Plato's dialogue of that name.

Minucius Felix (second or third century). Christian apologist who was an advocate in Rome. His *Octavius* agrees at numerous points with the *Apologeticum* of Tertullian. His birthplace is believed to be in Africa.

Montanist Oracles. Montanism was an apocalyptic and strictly ascetic movement begun in the latter half of the second century by a certain Montanus in Phrygia, who, along with certain of his followers, uttered oracles they claimed were inspired by the Holy Spirit. Little of the authentic oracles remains and most of what is known of Montanism comes from the authors who wrote against the movement. Montanism was formally condemned as a heresy before by Asiatic synods.

Nemesius of Emesa (fl. late fourth century). Bishop of Emesa in Syria whose most important work, *Of the Nature of Man,* draws on several theological and philosophical sources and is the first exposition of a Christian anthropology.

Nestorius (c. 381-c. 451). Patriarch of Constantinople (428-431) who founded the heresy which says that there are two persons, divine and human, rather than one person truly united in the incarnate Christ. He resisted the teaching of *theotokos*, causing Nestorian churches to separate from Constantinople.

Nicetas of Remesiana (fl. second half of fourth century). Bishop of Remesiana in Serbia, whose works affirm the consubstantiality of the Son and the deity of the Holy Spirit.

Nilus of Ancyra (d. c. 430). Prolific ascetic writer and disciple of John Chrysostom. Sometimes erroneously known as Nilus of Sinai, he was a native of Ancyra and studied at Constantinople.

Novatian of Rome (fl. 235-258). Roman theologian, otherwise orthodox, who formed a schismatic church after failing to become pope. His treatise on the Trinity states the classic western doctrine.

Oecumenius (sixth century). Called the Rhetor or the Philosopher, Oecumenius wrote the earliest extant Greek commentary on Revelation. Scholia by Oecumenius on some of John Chrysostom's commentaries on the Pauline Epistles are still extant.

Olympiodorus (early sixth century). Exegete and deacon of Alexandria, known for his commentaries that come to us mostly in catenae.

Origen of Alexandria (b. 185; fl. c. 200-254). Influential exegete and systematic theologian. He was condemned (perhaps unfairly) for maintaining the preexistence of souls while purportedly denying the resurrection of the body. His extensive works of exegesis focus on the spiritual meaning of the text.

Pachomius (c. 292-347). Founder of cenobitic monasticism. A gifted group leader and author of a set of rules, he was defended after his death by Athanasius of Alexandria.

Pacian of Barcelona (c. fourth century). Bishop of Barcelona whose writings polemicize against popular pagan festivals as well as Novatian schismatics.

Palladius of Helenopolis (c. 363/364-c. 431). Bishop of Helenopolis in Bithynia (400-417) and then Aspuna in Galatia. A disciple of Evagrius of Pontus and admirer of Origen, Palladius became a zealous adherent of John Chrysostom and shared his troubles in 403. His *Lausaic History* is the leading source for the history of early monasticism, stressing the spiritual value of the life of the desert.

Paschasius of Dumium (c. 515-c. 580). Translator of sentences of the Desert Fathers from Greek into Latin while a monk in Dumium.

Paterius (c. sixth-seventh century). Disciple of Gregory the Great who is primarily responsible for the transmission of Gregory's works to many later medieval authors.

Paulinus of Milan (late 4th-early 5th century). Personal secretary and biographer of Ambrose of Milan. He took part in the Pelagian controversy.

Paulinus of Nola (355-431). Roman senator and distinguished Latin poet whose frequent encounters with Ambrose of Milan (c. 333-397) led to his eventual conversion and baptism in 389. He eventually renounced his wealth and influential position and took up his pen to write poetry in service of Christ. He also wrote many letters to, among others, Augustine, Jerome and Rufinus.

Paulus Orosius (b. c. 380). An outspoken critic of Pelagius, mentored by Augustine. His *Seven Books of History Against the Pagans* was perhaps the first history of Christianity.

Pelagius (c. 354-c. 420). Contemporary of Augustine whose followers were condemned in 418 and 431 for maintaining that even before Christ there were people who lived wholly without sin and that salvation depended on free will.

Peter Chrysologus (c. 380-450). Latin archbishop of Ravenna whose teachings included arguments for adherence in matters of faith to the Roman see, and the relationship between grace and Christian living.

Peter of Alexandria (d. c. 311). Bishop of Alexandria. He marked (and very probably initiated) the reaction at Alexandria against extreme doctrines of Origen. During the persecution of Christians in Alexandria, Peter was arrested and beheaded by Roman officials. Eusebius of Caesarea described him as "a model bishop, remarkable for his virtuous life and his ardent study of the Scriptures."

Philo of Alexandria (c. 20 B.C.-c. A.D. 50). Jewish-born exegete who greatly influenced Christian patristic interpretation of the Old Testament. Born to a rich family in Alexandria, Philo was a contemporary of Jesus and lived an ascetic and contemplative life that makes some believe he was a rabbi. His interpretation of Scripture based the spiritual sense on the literal. Although influenced by Hellenism, Philo's theology remains thoroughly Jewish.

Philoxenus of Mabbug (c. 440-523). Bishop of Mabbug (Hierapolis) and a leading thinker in the early Syrian Orthodox Church. His extensive writings in Syriac include a set of thirteen *Discourses on the Christian Life*, several works on the incarnation and a number of exegetical works.

Photius (c. 820-891). An important Byzantine churchman and university professor of philosophy, mathematics and theology. He was twice the patriarch of Constantinople. First he succeeded Ignatius in 858, but was deposed in 863 when Ignatius was reinstated. Again he followed Ignatius in 878 and remained the patriarch until 886, at which time he was removed by Leo VI. His most important theological work is Address on the Mystagogy of the Holy Spirit, in which he articulates his opposition to the Western filioque, i.e., the procession of the Holy Spirit from the Father and the Son. He is also known for his Amphilochia and Library (Bibliotheca).

Poemen (c. fifth century). One-seventh of the sayings in the *Sayings of the Desert Fathers* are attributed to Poemen, which is Greek for shepherd. Poemen was a common title among early Egyptian desert ascetics, and it is unknown whether all of the sayings come from one person.

Polycarp of Smyrna (c. 69-155). Bishop of Smyrna who vigorously fought heretics such as the Marcionites and Valentinians. He was the leading Christian figure in Roman Asia in the middle of the second century.

Potamius of Lisbon (fl. c. 350-360). Bishop of Lisbon who joined the Arian party in 357, but later returned to the Catholic faith (c. 359?). His works from both periods are concerned with the larger Trinitarian debates of his time.

Primasius (fl. 550-560). Bishop of Hadrumetum in North Africa (modern Tunisia) and one of the few Africans to support the condemnation of the Three Chapters. Drawing on Augustine and Tyconius, he wrote a commentary on the Apocalypse, which in allegorizing fashion views the work as referring to the history of the church.

Procopius of Gaza (c. 465-c. 530). A Christian exegete educated in Alexandria. He wrote numerous theological works and commentaries on Scripture (particularly the Hebrew Bible), the latter marked by the allegorical exegesis for which the Alexandrian school was known.

Prosper of Aquitaine (c. 390-c. 463). Probably a lay monk and supporter of the theology of Augustine on grace and predestination. He collaborated closely with Pope Leo I in his doctrinal statements.

Prudentius (c. 348-c. 410). Latin poet and hymn-writer who devoted his later life to Christian writing. He wrote didactic poems on the theology of the incarnation, against the heretic Marcion and against the resurgence of paganism.

Pseudo-Clementines (third-fourth century). A series of apocryphal writings pertaining to a conjured life of Clement of Rome. Written in a form of popular legend, the stories from Clement's life, including his opposition to Simon Magus, illustrate and promote articles of Christian teaching. It is likely that the corpus is a derivative of a number of Gnostic and Judeo-Christian writings. Dating the corpus is a complicated issue.

Pseudo-Dionysius the Areopagite (fl. c. 500). Author who assumed the name of Dionysius the Areopagite mentioned in Acts 17:34, and who composed the works known as the *Corpus Areopagiticum* (or *Dionysiacum*). These writings were the foundation of the apophatic school of mysticism in their denial that anything can be truly predicated of God.

Pseudo-Macarius (fl. c. 390). An anonymous writer and ascetic (from Mesopotamia?) active in Antioch whose badly edited works were attributed to Macarius of Egypt. He had keen insight into human nature, prayer and the inner life. His work includes some one hundred discourses and homilies.

Quodvultdeus (fl. 430). Carthaginian bishop and friend of Augustine who endeavored to show at length how the New Testament fulfilled the Old Testament.

Rufinus of Aquileia (c. 345-411). Orthodox Christian thinker and historian who nonetheless translated and preserved the works of Origen, and defended him against the strictures of Jerome and Epiphanius. He lived the ascetic life in Rome, Egypt and Jerusalem (the Mount of Olives).

Sabellius (fl. 200). Allegedly the author of the heresy which maintains that the Father and Son are a single person. The patripassian variant of this heresy states that the Father suffered on the cross.

Sahdona (fl. 635-640). Known in Greek as Martyrius, this Syriac author was bishop of Beth Garmai. He studied in Nisibis and was exiled for his christological ideas. His most important work is the deeply scriptural *Book of Perfection* which ranks as one of the masterpieces of Syriac monastic literature.

Salvian the Presbyter of Marseilles (c. 400-c. 480). An important author for the history of his own time. He saw the fall of Roman civilization to the barbarians as a consequence of the reprehensible conduct of Roman Christians. In *The Governance of God* he developed the theme of divine providence.

Second Letter of Clement (c. 150). The so-called *Second Letter of Clement* is an early Christian sermon probably written by a Corinthian author, though some scholars have assigned it to a Roman or Alexandrian author.

Severian of Gabala (fl. c. 400). A contemporary of John Chrysostom, he was a highly regarded preacher in Constantinople, particularly at the imperial court, and ultimately sided with Chry-

sostom's accusers. He wrote homilies on Genesis.

Severus of Antioch (fl. 488-538). A monophysite theologian, consecrated bishop of Antioch in 522. Born in Pisidia, he studied in Alexandria and Beirut, taught in Constantinople and was exiled to Egypt.

Shenoute (c. 350-466). Abbot of Athribis in Egypt. His large monastic community was known for very strict rules. He accompanied Cyril of Alexandria to the Council of Ephesus in 431, where he played an important role in deposing Nestorius. He knew Greek but wrote in Coptic, and his literary activity includes homilies, catecheses on monastic subjects, letters, and a couple of theological treatises.

Shepherd of Hermas (second century). Divided into five *Visions*, twelve *Mandates* and ten *Similitudes*, this Christian apocalypse was written by a former slave and named for the form of the second angel said to have granted him his visions. This work was highly esteemed for its moral value and was used as a textbook for catechumens in the early church.

Sulpicius Severus (c. 360-c. 420). An ecclesiastical writer from Bordeaux born of noble parents. Devoting himself to monastic retirement, he became a personal friend and enthusiastic disciple of St. Martin of Tours.

Symeon the New Theologian (c. 949-1022). Compassionate spiritual leader known for his strict rule. He believed that the divine light could be perceived and received through the practice of mental prayer.

Tertullian of Carthage (c. 155/160-225/250; fl. c. 197-222). Brilliant Carthaginian apologist and polemicist who laid the foundations of Christology and trinitarian orthodoxy in the West, though he himself was later estranged from the catholic tradition due to its laxity.

Theodore of Heraclea (d. c. 355). An anti-Nicene bishop of Thrace. He was part of a team seeking reconciliation between Eastern and Western Christianity. In 343 he was excommunicated at the council of Sardica. His writings focus on a literal interpretation of Scripture.

Theodore of Mopsuestia (c. 350-428). Bishop of Mopsuestia, founder of the Antiochene, or literalistic, school of exegesis. A great man in his day, he was later condemned as a precursor of Nestorius.

Theodore of Tabennesi (d. 368) Vice general of the Pachomian monasteries (c. 350-368) under Horsiesi. Several of his letters are known.

Theodoret of Cyr (c. 393-466). Bishop of Cyr (Cyrrhus), he was an opponent of Cyril who commented extensively on Old Testament texts as a lucid exponent of Antiochene exegesis.

Theodotus the Valentinian (second century). Likely a Montanist who may have been related to the Alexandrian school. Extracts of his work are known through writings of Clement of Alexandria.

Theophanes (775-845). Hymnographer and bishop of Nicaea (842-845). He was persecuted during the second iconoclastic period for his support of the Seventh Council (Second Council of Nicaea, 787). He wrote many hymns in the tradition of the monastery of Mar Sabbas that were used in the *Paraklitiki*.

Theophilus of Antioch (late second century). Bishop of Antioch. His only surviving work is *Ad Autholycum,* where we find the first Christian commentary on Genesis and the first use of the term *Trinity*. Theophilus's apologetic literary heritage had influence on Irenaeus and possibly Tertullian.

Theophylact of Ohrid (c. 1050-c. 1108). Byzantine archbishop of Ohrid (or Achrida) in what is now Bulgaria. Drawing on earlier works, he wrote commentaries on several Old Testament books and all of the New Testament except for Revelation.

Valentinus (fl. c. 140). Alexandrian heretic of the mid-second century who taught that the material world was created by the transgression of God's Wisdom, or Sophia (*see* Gnostics).

Valerian of Cimiez (fl. c. 422-439). Bishop of Cimiez. He participated in the councils of Riez (439) and Vaison (422) with a view to strengthening church discipline. He supported Hilary of Arles in quarrels with Pope Leo I.

Verecundus (d. 552). An African Christian writer, who took an active part in the christological controversies of the sixth century, especially in the debate on Three Chapters. He also wrote allegorical commentaries on the nine liturgical church canticles.

Victorinus of Petovium (d. c. 304). Latin biblical exegete. With multiple works attributed to him, his sole surviving work is the *Commentary on the Apocalypse* and perhaps some fragments from *Commentary on Matthew*. Victorinus expressed strong millenarianism in his writing, though his was less materialistic than the millenarianism of Papias or Irenaeus. In his allegorical approach he could be called a spiritual disciple of Origen. Victorinus died during the first year of Diocletian's persecution, probably in 304.

Vincent of Lérins (d. before 450). Monk who has exerted considerable influence through his writings on orthodox dogmatic theological method, as contrasted with the theological methodologies of the heresies.

Timeline of Writers of the Patristic Period

Location / Period	British Isles	Gaul	Spain, Portugal	Rome* and Italy	Carthage and Northern Africa
2nd century				Clement of Rome, fl. c. 92-101 (Greek)	
				Shepherd of Hermas, c. 140 (Greek)	
				Justin Martyr (Ephesus, Rome), c. 100/110-165 (Greek)	
		Irenaeus of Lyons, c. 135-c. 202 (Greek)		Valentinus the Gnostic (Rome), fl. c. 140 (Greek)	
				Marcion (Rome), fl. 144 (Greek)	
3rd century				Callistus of Rome, regn. 217-222 (Latin)	Tertullian of Carthage, c. 155/160-c. 225 (Latin)
				Minucius Felix of Rome, fl. 218-235 (Latin)	
				Hippolytus (Rome, Palestine?), fl. 222-235/245 (Greek)	Cyprian of Carthage, fl. 248-258 (Latin)
				Novatian of Rome, fl. 235-258 (Latin)	
				Victorinus of Petovium, 230-304 (Latin)	

*One of the five ancient patriarchates

Alexandria* and Egypt	Constantinople* and Asia Minor, Greece	Antioch* and Syria	Mesopotamia, Persia	Jerusalem* and Palestine	Location Unknown
Philo of Alexandria, c. 20 B.C. – c. A.D. 50 (Greek)				Flavius Josephus (Rome), c. 37-c. 101 (Greek)	
Basilides (Alexandria), 2nd cent. (Greek)	Polycarp of Smyrna, c. 69-155 (Greek)	*Didache* (Egypt?), c. 100 (Greek)			
Letter of Barnabas (Syria?), c. 130 (Greek)		Ignatius of Antioch, c. 35–107/112 (Greek)			
Theodotus the Valentinian, 2nd cent. (Greek)	Athenagoras (Greece), fl. 176-180 (Greek)	Theophilus of Antioch, c. late 2nd cent. (Greek)			*Second Letter of Clement* (spurious; Corinth, Rome, Alexandria?) (Greek), c. 150
Clement of Alexandria, c. 150-215 (Greek)	*Montanist Oracles*, late 2nd cent. (Greek)				
Sabellius (Egypt), 2nd–3rd cent. (Greek)					Pseudo-Clementines 3rd cent. (Greek)
			Mani (Manichaeans), c. 216-276		
Letter to Diognetus, 3rd cent. (Greek)	Gregory Thaumaturgus (Neo-caesarea), fl. c. 248-264 (Greek)				
Origen (Alexandria, Cae-sarea of Palestine), 185-254 (Greek)					
Dionysius of Alexandria, d. 264/5 (Greek)					
	Methodius of Olympus (Lycia), d. c. 311 (Greek)				

Timeline of Writers of the Patristic Period

Location	British Isles	Gaul	Spain, Portugal	Rome* and Italy	Carthage and Northern Africa
Period					
4th century				Firmicus Maternus (Sicily), fl. c. 335 (Latin)	
		Lactantius, c. 260- 330 (Latin)		Marius Victorinus (Rome), fl. 355-363 (Latin)	
				Eusebius of Vercelli, fl. c. 360 (Latin)	
			Hosius of Cordova, d. 357 (Latin)	Lucifer of Cagliari (Sardinia), d. 370/371 (Latin)	
		Hilary of Poitiers, c. 315-367 (Latin)	Potamius of Lisbon, fl. c. 350-360 (Latin)	Faustinus (Rome), fl. 380 (Latin)	
				Filastrius of Brescia, fl. 380 (Latin)	
			Gregory of Elvira, fl. 359-385 (Latin)	Ambrosiaster (Italy?), fl. c. 366-384 (Latin)	
			Prudentius, c. 348-c. 410 (Latin)	Faustus of Riez, fl. c. 380 (Latin)	
			Pacian of Barcelona, 4th cent. (Latin)	Gaudentius of Brescia, fl. 395 (Latin)	Paulus Orosius, b. c. 380 (Latin)
				Ambrose of Milan, c. 333-397; fl. 374-397 (Latin)	
				Paulinus of Milan, late 4th early 5th cent. (Latin)	
5th century				Rufinus (Aquileia, Rome), c. 345-411 (Latin)	
	Fastidius (Britain), c. 4th-5th cent. (Latin)	Sulpicius Severus (Bordeaux), c. 360-c. 420/425 (Latin)		Aponius, fl. 405-415 (Latin)	Quodvultdeus (Carthage), fl. 430 (Latin)
				Chromatius (Aquileia), fl. 400 (Latin)	
		John Cassian (Palestine, Egypt, Constantinople, Rome, Marseilles), 360-432 (Latin)		Pelagius (Britain, Rome), c. 354-c. 420 (Greek)	Augustine of Hippo, 354-430 (Latin)
				Maximus of Turin, d. 408/423 (Latin)	Luculentius, 5th cent. (Latin)
		Vincent of Lérins, d. 435 (Latin)		Paulinus of Nola, 355-431 (Latin)	
		Valerian of Cimiez, fl. c. 422-449 (Latin)		Peter Chrysologus (Ravenna), c. 380-450 (Latin)	
		Eucherius of Lyons, fl. 420-449 (Latin)		Julian of Eclanum, 386-454 (Latin)	

*One of the five ancient patriarchates

Alexandria* and Egypt	Constantinople* and Asia Minor, Greece	Antioch* and Syria	Mesopotamia, Persia	Jerusalem* and Palestine	Location Unknown
Antony, c. 251-355 (Coptic /Greek)	Theodore of Heraclea (Thrace), fl. c. 330-355 (Greek)	Eustathius of Antioch, fl. 325 (Greek)	Aphrahat (Persia) c. 270-350; fl. 337-345 (Syriac)	Eusebius of Caesarea (Palestine), c. 260/263-340 (Greek)	Commodius, c. 3rd or 5th cent. (Latin)
Peter of Alexandria, d. c. 311 (Greek)	Marcellus of Ancyra, d.c. 375 (Greek)	Eusebius of Emesa, c. 300-c. 359 (Greek)			
Arius (Alexandria), fl. c. 320 (Greek)	Epiphanius of Salamis (Cyprus), c. 315-403 (Greek)	Ephrem the Syrian, c. 306-373 (Syriac)	Jacob of Nisibis, fl. 308-325 (Syriac)		
Alexander of Alexandria, fl. 312-328 (Greek)	Basil (the Great) of Caesarea, b. c. 330; fl. 357-379 (Greek)				
Pachomius, c. 292-347 (Coptic/Greek?)	Macrina the Younger, c. 327-379 (Greek)				
Theodore of Tabennesi, d. 368 (Coptic/Greek)	Apollinaris of Laodicea, 310-c. 392 (Greek)				
Horsiesi, c. 305-390 (Coptic/Greek)	Gregory of Nazianzus, b. 329/330; fl. 372-389 (Greek)	Nemesius of Emesa (Syria), fl. late 4th cent. (Greek)		Acacius of Caesarea (Palestine), d. c. 365 (Greek)	
Athanasius of Alexandria, c. 295-373; fl. 325-373 (Greek)	Gregory of Nyssa, c. 335-394 (Greek)	Diodore of Tarsus, d. c. 394 (Greek)		Cyril of Jerusalem, c. 315-386 (Greek)	
Macarius of Egypt, c. 300-c. 390 (Greek)	Amphilochius of Iconium, c. 340/345- c. 398/404 (Greek)	John Chrysostom (Constantinople), 344/354-407 (Greek)			
Didymus (the Blind) of Alexandria, 313-398 (Greek)	Evagrius of Pontus, 345-399 (Greek)	Apostolic Constitutions, c. 375-400 (Greek)			
		Didascalia, 4th cent. (Syriac)			
	Eunomius of Cyzicus, fl. 360-394 (Greek)	Theodore of Mopsuestia, c. 350-428 (Greek)		Diodore of Tarsus, d. c. 394 (Greek)	
	Pseudo-Macarius (Mesopotamia?), late 4th cent. (Greek)	Acacius of Beroea, c. 340-c. 436 (Greek)		Jerome (Rome, Antioch, Bethlehem), c. 347-419 (Latin)	
	Nicetas of Remesiana, d. c. 414 (Latin)				
Palladius of Helenopolis (Egypt), c. 365-425 (Greek)	Nestorius (Constantinople), c. 381-c. 451 (Greek)	Book of Steps, c. 400 (Syriac)	Eznik of Kolb, fl. 430-450 (Armenian)		
		Severian of Gabala, fl. c. 400 (Greek)			
Cyril of Alexandria, 375-444 (Greek)	Basil of Seleucia, fl. 440-468 (Greek)				
		Nilus of Ancyra, d.c. 430 (Greek)		Hesychius of Jerusalem, fl. 412-450 (Greek)	
	Diadochus of Photice (Macedonia), 400-474 (Greek)				
				Euthymius (Palestine), 377-473 (Greek)	

Timeline of Writers of the Patristic Period

Location / Period	British Isles	Gaul	Spain, Portugal	Rome* and Italy	Carthage and Northern Africa
5th century (cont.)		Hilary of Arles, c. 401-449 (Latin)		Leo the Great (Rome), regn. 440-461 (Latin)	
		Eusebius of Gaul, 5th cent. (Latin)			
		Prosper of Aquitaine, c. 390-c. 463 (Latin)		Arnobius the Younger (Rome), fl. c. 450 (Latin)	
		Salvian the Presbyter of Marseilles, c. 400-c. 480 (Latin)		Ennodius (Arles, Milan, Pavia) c. 473-521 (Latin)	
		Gennadius of Marseilles, d. after 496 (Latin)			
6th century		Caesarius of Arles, c. 470-543 (Latin)	Paschasius of Dumium (Portugal), c. 515-c. 580 (Latin)	Epiphanius the Latin, late 5th–early 6th cent. (Latin)	Fulgentius of Ruspe, c. 467-532 (Latin)
			Leander of Seville, c. 545-c. 600 (Latin)	Eugippius, c. 460- c. 533 (Latin)	Verecundus, d. 552 (Latin)
			Martin of Braga, fl. 568-579 (Latin)	Benedict of Nursia, c. 480-547 (Latin)	Primasius, fl. 550-560 (Latin)
				Cassiodorus (Calabria), c. 485-c. 540 (Latin)	Facundus of Hermiane, fl. 546-568 (Latin)
7th century				Gregory the Great (Rome), c. 540-604 (Latin)	
				Gregory of Agrigentium, d. 592 (Greek)	
			Isidore of Seville, c. 560-636 (Latin)	Paterius, 6th/7th cent. (Latin)	
			Braulio of Saragossa, c. 585-651 (Latin)		
	Adamnan, c. 624-704 (Latin)		Fructuosus of Braga, d.c. 665 (Latin)		
8th-12th century	Bede the Venerable, c. 672/673-735 (Latin)				

*One of the five ancient patriarchates

Alexandria* and Egypt	Constantinople* and Asia Minor, Greece	Antioch* and Syria	Mesopotamia, Persia	Jerusalem* and Palestine	Location Unknown
Ammonius of Alexandria, c. 460 (Greek) Poemen, 5th cent. (Greek) Besa the Copt, 5th cent. Shenoute, c. 350-466 (Coptic)	Gennadius of Constantinople, d. 471 (Greek)	John of Antioch, d. 441/2 (Greek) Theodoret of Cyr, c. 393-466 (Greek) Pseudo-Victor of Antioch, 5th cent. (Greek) John of Apamea, 5th cent. (Syriac)		Gerontius of Petra c. 395-c.480 (Syriac)	
Olympiodorus, early 6th cent.	Oecumenius (Isauria), 6th cent. (Greek)	Philoxenus of Mabbug (Syria), c. 440-523 (Syriac) Severus of Antioch, c. 465-538 (Greek) Mark the Hermit (Tarsus), c. 6th cent. (4th cent.?) (Greek)	Jacob of Sarug, c. 450-520 (Syriac) Babai the Great, c. 550-628 (Syriac) Babai, early 6th cent. (Syriac)	Procopius of Gaza (Palestine), c. 465-530 (Greek) Dorotheus of Gaza, fl. 525-540 (Greek) Cyril of Scythopolis, b. c. 525; d. after 557 (Greek)	Pseudo-Dionysius the Areopagite, fl. c. 500 (Greek)
	Maximus the Confessor (Constantinople), c. 580-662 (Greek)	Sahdona/Martyrius, fl. 635-640 (Syriac)	Isaac of Nineveh, d. c. 700 (Syriac)		(Pseudo-) Constantius, before 7th cent.? (Greek) Andreas, c. 7th cent. (Greek)
		John of Damascus (John the Monk), c. 650-750 (Greek)			
	Theophanes (Nicaea), 775-845 (Greek) Cassia (Constantinople), c. 805-c. 848/867 (Greek) Arethas of Caesarea (Constantinople/Caesarea), c. 860-940 (Greek) Photius (Constantinople), c. 820-891 (Greek) Symeon the New Theologian (Constantinople), 949-1022 (Greek) Theophylact of Ohrid (Bulgaria), 1050-1126 (Greek)		John the Elder of Qardu (north Iraq), 8th cent. (Syriac) Isho'dad of Merv, d. after 852 (Syriac)		

Bibliography of Works
in Original Languages

This bibliography refers readers to original language sources and supplies thesaurus Linguae Graecae (=TLG) or Cetedoc Clavis (=Cl.) numbers where available. The edition listed in this bibliography may in some cases differ from the edition found in TLG or Cetedoc databases.

Ambrose. "De bono mortis." In *Sancti Ambrosii opera*. Edited by Karl Schenkl. CSEL 32, pt. 1, pp. 701-53. Vienna, Austria: F. Tempsky; Leipzig, Germany: G. Freytag, 1897. Cl. 0129.

———. "De Cain et Abel." In *Sancti Ambrosii opera*. Edited by Karl Schenkl. CSEL 32, pt. 1, pp. 337-409. Vienna, Austria: F. Tempsky; Leipzig, Germany: G. Freytag, 1897. Cl. 0125.

———. "De excessu fratris Satyri." In *Sancti Ambrosii opera*. Edited by Otto Faller. CSEL 73, pp. 207-325. Vienna, Austria: Hoelder-Pichler-Tempsky, 1895. Cl. 0157.

———. "De fide libri v." In *Sancti Ambrosii opera*. Edited by Otto Faller. CSEL 78. Vienna, Austria: Hoelder-Pichler-Tempsky, 1962. Cl. 0150.

———. "De fuga saeculi." In *Sancti Ambrosii opera*. Edited by Karl Schenkl. CSEL 32, pt. 2, pp. 163-207. Vienna, Austria: F. Tempsky; Leipzig, Germany: G. Freytag, 1897. Cl. 0133.

———. "De interpellatione Job et David." In *Sancti Ambrosii opera*. Edited by Karl Shenkl. CSEL 32, pt. 2, pp. 209-96. Vienna, Austria: F. Tempsky; Leipzig, Germany: G. Freytag, 1897. Cl. 0134.

———. "De Isaac vel anima." In *Sancti Ambrosii opera*. Edited by Karl Schenkl. CSEL 32, pt. 1, pp. 639-700. Vienna, Austria: F. Tempsky; Leipzig, Germany: G. Freytag, 1897. Cl. 0128.

———. "De Jacob et vita beata." In *Sancti Ambrosii opera*. Edited by Karl Schenkl. CSEL 32, pt. 2, pp. 1-70. Vienna, Austria: F. Tempsky; Leipzig, Germany: G. Freytag, 1897. Cl. 0130.

———. "De obitu Theodosii." In *Sancti Ambrosii opera*. Edited by Otto Faller. CSEL 73, pp. 371-401. Turnhout, Belgium: Brepols, 1955. Cl. 0159.

———. "De obitu Valentiniani." In *Sancti Ambrosii opera*. Edited by Otto Faller. CSEL 73, pp. 329-67. Vienna, Austria: Hoelder-Pichler-Tempsky, 1955. Cl. 0158.

———. *De Officiis*. In *Ambrosii mediolanensis opera*. Edited by Maurice Testard. Turnhout, Belgium: Brepols, 2000. Cl. 0144.

———. "De paradiso." In *Sancti Ambrosii opera*. Edited by Karl Schenkl. CSEL 32, pt. 1, pp. 263-336. Vienne, Austria: F. Tempsky; Leipzig, Germany: G. Freytag, 1897. Cl. 0124.

———. "De Spiritu Sancto." In *Sancti Ambrosii opera*. Edited by Otto Faller. CSEL 79, pp. 5-222. Vienna, Austria: Hoelder-Pichler-Tempsky, 1964. Cl. 0151.

———. "De viduis." In *De virginibus: De viduis*. Edited by Franco Gori. Sancti Ambrosii episcopi Mediolanensis Opera, vol. 14.1 pp. 243-319. Milan: Biblioteca Ambrosiana; Rome: Città nuova, 1989. Cl. 0146.

———. "Epistulae; Epistulae extra collectionem traditae." In *Sancti Ambrosii opera*. Edited by Otto Faller and M. Zelzer. CSEL 82. Vienna, Austria: F. Tempsky; Leipzig, Germany: G. Freytag, 1968-1990. Cl. 0160.

———. "Expositio Evangelii secundum Lucam." In *Sancti Ambrosii mediolanensis opera, Pars IV*. CCL 14, pp. 1-400. Turnhout, Belgium: Brepols, 1957. Cl. 0143.

———. "Expositio psalmi cxviii." In *Sancti Ambrosii opera*. Edited by Michael Petschenig. CSEL 62. Vienna, Austria: F. Tempsky; Leipzig, Germany: G. Freytag, 1913. Cl. 0141.

Aphrahat. "Demonstrationes (IV)." In *Opera omnia*. Edited by R. Graffin. Patrologia Syriaca 1, cols. 137-82. Paris: Firmin-Didot, 1910.

Athanasius. "Apologia de fuga sua." In *Athanase d'Alexandrie: Apologie à l'empereur Constance; Apologie pour sa fuite*. Edited by Jan M. Szymusiak. SC 56, pp. 133-67. Paris: Éditions du Cerf, 1958. TLG 2035.012.

———. "Epistula ad episcopos Aegypti et Libyae." In *Opera omnia*. PG 25, cols. 537-93. Edited by J.-P. Migne. Paris: Migne, 1857. TLG 2035.041.

———. "Epistula encyclica." In *Athanasius Werke*. Vol. 2.1, pp. 1-45. Edited by H. G. Opitz. Berlin: De Gruyter, 1940. TLG 2035.006.

———. "Epistulae festalis [Heortasticae]." In *Opera omnia*. PG 26, cols. 1351-444. Edited by J.-P. Migne. Paris: Migne, 1857.

———. "Historia Arianum." In *Athanasius Werke*. Vol. 2.1, pp. 183-230. Edited by H. G. Opitz. Berlin: De Gruyter, 1940. TLG 2035.009.

———. "Orationes tres contra Arianos." PG 26, cols. 11-526. Edited by J.-P. Migne. Paris: Migne, 1887. TLG 2035.042.

———. "Vita sancti Antonii." In *Opera omnia*. PG 26, cols. 835-976. Edited by J.-P. Migne. Paris: Migne, 1857. TLG 2035.047.

Augustine. *Confessionum libri tredecim*. Edited by L. Verheijen. CCL 27. Turnhout, Belgium: Brepols, 1981. Cl. 0251.

———. "Contra Faustum." In *Sancti Aurelii Augustini*. Edited by Joseph Zycha. CSEL 25, pp. 249-797. Vienna, Austria: F. Tempsky; Leipzig, Germany: G. Freytag, 1891. Cl. 0321.

———. "Contra Julianum." In *Opera omnia*. Edited by J.-P. Migne. PL 44, cols. 641-874. Paris: Migne, 1861. Cl. 0351.

———. "Contra litteras Petiliani." In *Sancti Aurelii Augustini*. Edited by Michael Petschenig. CSEL 52, pp. 3-227. Vienna, Austria: F. Tempsky; Leipzig, Germany: G. Freytag, 1909. Cl. 0333.

———. "Contra mendacium." In *Sancti Aureli Augustini opera*. Edited by J. Zycha. CSEL 41, pp. 469-528. Vienna, Austria: F. Tempsky, 1900. Cl. 0304.

———. "De adulterinis conjugiis." In *Sancti Aureli Augustini opera*. Edited by J. Zycha. CSEL 41, pp. 347-410. Vienna, Austria: F. Tempsky, 1900. Cl. 0302.

———. *De civitate Dei*. In *Aurelii Augustini opera*. Edited by Bernhard Dombart and Alphons Kalb. CCL 47-48. Turnhout, Belgium: Brepols, 1955. Cl. 0313.

———. *De consensu evangelistarum libri iv*. In *Sancti Aurelii Augustini*. Edited by Francis Weihrich. CSEL 43. Vienna, Austria: F. Tempsky; Leipzig, Germany: G. Freytag, 1904. Cl. 0273.

———. "De correptione et gratia." In *Opera omnia*. PL 44, cols. 915-46. Edited by J.-P. Migne. Paris: Migne, 1845. Cl. 0353.

———. "De cura pro moruis gerenda." In *Sancti Aureli Augustini opera*. Edited by J. Zycha. CSEL 41, pp. 621-59. Vienna, Austria: F. Tempsky, 1900. Cl. 0307.

———. *De diversis quaestionibus ad Simplicianum*. Edited by Almut Mutzenbecher. CCL 44. Turnhout, Belgium: Brepols, 1970. Cl. 0290.

———. "De diversis quaestionibus octoginta tribus." In *Aurelii Augustini opera*. Edited by Almut Mutzenbecher. CCL 44A, pp. 11-249. Turnhout, Belgium: Brepols, 1975. Cl. 0289.

———. "De doctrina christiana." In *Aurelii Augustini opera*. Edited by Joseph Martin. CCL 32, pp. 1-167. Turnhout, Belgium: Brepols, 1962. Cl. 0263.

———. "De gratia et libero arbitrio." In *Opera omnia*. PL 44, cols. 881-912. Edited by J.-P. Migne. Paris: Migne, 1861. Cl. 0352.

————. "De natura et origine animae." In *Sancti Aurelii Augustini De peccatorum meritis et remissione et de baptismo parvulorum ad Marcellinum libri tres, De spiritu et littera liber unus, De natura et gratia liber unus, De natura et origine animae libri quattuor.* Edited by Karl Franz Urba and Joseph Zycha. CSEL 60, pp. 303-419. Vienna, Austria: F. Tempsky; Leipzig, Germany: G. Freytag, 1913. Cl. 0345.

————. "De patientia." In *Sancti Aureli Augustini opera.* Edited by J. Zycha. CSEL 41, pp. 663-91. Vienna, Austria: F. Tempsky, 1900. Cl. 0308.

————. "De octo Dulcitii quaestionibus." In *Aurelii Augustini opera.* Edited by Almut Mutzenbecher. CCL 44A, pp. 253-97. Turnhout, Belgium: Brepols, 1975. Cl. 0291.

————. "De praedestinatione sanctorum." In *Opera omnia.* PL 44, cols. 959-92. Edited by J.-P. Migne. Paris: Migne, 1861. Cl. 0354.

————. "De spiritu et littera." In *Sancti Aurelii Augustini De peccatorum meritis et remissione et de baptismo parvulorum ad Marcellinum libri tres, De spiritu et littera liber unus, De natura et gratia liber unus, De natura et origine animae libri quattuor.* Edited by Karl Franz Urba and Joseph Zycha. CSEL 60, pp. 155-229. Vienna, Austria: F. Tempsky; Leipzig, Germany: G. Freytag, 1913. Cl. 0343.

————. "Enarrationes in Psalmos." 3 vols. In *Aurelii Augustini opera.* Edited by D. E. Dekkers and John Fraipont. CCL 38, 39 and 40. Turnhout, Belgium: Brepols, 1956. Cl. 0283.

————. "Epistulae." In *Sancti Aurelii Augustini opera.* Edited by A. Goldbacher. CCL 34, pts. 1, 2; 44; 57; 58. Turnhout, Belgium: Brepols, 1895-1898. Cl. 0262.

————. "In Johannis epistulam ad Parthos tractatus." In *Opera omnia.* PL 35, cols. 1379-2062. Edited by J.-P. Migne. Paris: Migne, 1841. Cl. 0279.

————. "Quaestionum in heptateuchum libri septem." In *Aurelii Augustini opera.* Edited by John Fraipont. CCL 33. Turnhout, Belgium: Brepols, 1958. Cl. 0270.

————. "Sermones." In *Augustini opera omnia.* PL 38 and 39. Edited by J.-P. Migne. Paris: Migne, 1844-1865. Cl. 0284.

Basil the Great. "Asceticon magnum sive Quaestiones [regulae fusius tractatae]." In *Opera omnia.* PG 31, cols. 905-1052. Edited by J.-P. Migne. Paris: Migne, 1857. TLG 2040.048.

————. "De humilitate." In *Opera Omnia.* PG 31, cols. 525-540. Edited by J.-P. Migne. Paris: Migne, 1885. TLG 2040.036.

————. *De Spiritu Sancto.* In *Basile de Césarée: Sur le Saint-Esprit.* Edited by Benoit Pruche. SC 17. Paris: Éditions du Cerf, 2002. TLG 2040.003.

————. "Epistulae." In *Saint Basil: Lettres.* Edited by Yves Courtonne. Vol. 2, pp. 101-218; vol. 3, pp. 1-229. Paris: Les Belles Lettres, 1961-1966. TLG 2040.004.

————. *Homilia de invidia.* In *Opera omnia.* PG 31, cols. 372-85. Edited by J.-P. Migne. Paris: Migne, 1885. TLG 2040.027.

————. "Homiliae super Psalmos." In *Opera omnia.* PG 29, cols. 209-494. Edited by J.-P. Migne. Paris: Migne, 1857. TLG 2040.018.

————. "Prologus 7 (De judicio Dei)." In *Opera omnia.* PG 31, cols. 653-76. Edited by J.-P. Migne. Paris: Migne, 1857. TLG 2040.043.

Bede. "De tabernaculo et vasis eius ac vestibus sacerdotum libri iii." In *Opera.* Edited by D. Hurst. CCL 119A, pp. 5-139. Cl. 1345.

————. *Homiliarum evangelii libri ii.* In *Opera.* Edited by D. Hurst. CCL 122. Turnhout, Belgium: Brepols, 1955. Cl. 1367.

————. "In Lucae evangelium expositio." In *Opera.* Edited by D. Hurst. CCL 120, pp. 1-425. Turnhout, Belgium: Brepols, 1960. Cl. 1356.

————. "In primam partem Samuhelis libri iv." In *Opera.* Edited by D. Hurst. CCL 119, pp. 1-287. Turnhout, Belgium: Brepols, 1962. Cl. 1346.

———. "In Regum librum xxx quaestiones." In *Opera*. Edited by D. Hurst. CCL 119, pp. 293-322. Turnhout, Belgium: Brepols, 1962. Cl. 1347.

———. "Libri quattuor in principium Genesis usque ad nativitatem Isaac et ejectionem Ismahelis adnotationum. In *Bedae Venerabilis opera*. Edited by Ch. W. Jones. CCL 118A. Turnhout, Belgium: Brepols, 1967. Cl. 1344.

[Caesarius of Arles]. *Sermones Caesarii Arelatensis*. 2 vols. Edited by D. Germani and G. Morin. CCL 103 and 104. Turnhout, Belgium: Brepols, 1953. Cl. 1008.

Cassian, John. *Collationes xxiv*. Edited by Michael Petschenig. CSEL 13. Vienna, Austria: F. Tempsky; Leipzig, Germany: G. Freytag, 1886. Cl. 0512.

———. "De institutis coenobiorum et de octo principalium vitiorum remediis." In *Johannis Cassiani*. Edited by Michael Petschenig. CSEL 17, pp. 1-231. Vienna, Austria: F. Tempsky; Leipzig, Germany: G. Freytag, 1888. Cl. 0513.

Cassiodorus. *Expositio Psalmorum*, 2 vols. Edited by M. Adriaen. CCL 97 and 98. Turnhout: Brepols, 1958. Cl. 0900.

Clement of Alexandria. "Paedagogus." In *Le pédagogue [par] Clement d'Alexandrie*. 3 vols. Translated by Mauguerite Harl, Chantel Matray and Claude Mondésert. Introduction and notes by Henri-Irénée Marrou. SC 70, 108, 158. Paris: Éditions du Cerf, 1960-1970. TLG 0555.002.

———. "Stromata." In *Clemens Alexandrinus*, vol. 2, 3rd ed., and vol. 3, 2nd ed. Edited by Otto Stählin, Ludwig Früchtel and U. Treu. GCS 15, 17, pp. 1-102. Berlin: Akademie-Verlag, 1960-1970. TLG 0555.004.

Clement of Rome. "Epistula i ad Corinthios." In *Clément de Rome: Épître aux Corinthiens*. Edited by Annie Jaubert. SC 167. Paris: Éditions du Cerf, 1971. TLG 1271.001.

Constitutiones apostolorum. In *Les constitutions apostoliques*, 3 vols. Edited by Marcel Metzger. SC 320, 329, 336. Paris: Éditions du Cerf, 1985-1987. TLG 2894.001.

Cyprian. "Ad Quirinum." In *Sancti Cypriani episcopi opera*. Edited by R. Weber. CCL 3, pp. 3-179. Turnhout, Belgium: Brepols, 1972. Cl. 0039.

———. "De bono patientiae." In *Sancti Cypriani episcopi opera*. Edited by C. Moreschini. CCL 3A, pp. 118-33. Turnhout, Belgium: Brepols, 1976. Cl. 0048.

———. "De dominica oratione." In *Sancti Cypriani episcopi opera*. Edited by C. Moreschini. CCL 3A, pp. 87-113. Turnhout, Belgium: Brepols, 1976. Cl. 0043.

———. *Epistulae*. Edited by G. F. Diercks. CCL 3B, 3C. Turnhout, Belgium: Brepols, 1994-1996. Cl. 0050.

Cyril of Alexandria. "Epistulae." In *Acta conciliorum oecumenicorum*. 7 vols. Edited by Eduard Schwartz. Berlin: Walter de Gruyter, 1927-29. TLG 5000.001.

Cyril of Jerusalem. "Catecheses ad illuminandos 1-18." In *Cyrilli Hierosolymorum archiepiscopi opera quae supersunt omnia*, 1:28-320; 2:2-342. 2 vols. Edited by W. C. Reischl and J. Rupp. Munich: Lentner, 1860 (repr. Hildesheim: Olms, 1967). TLG 2110.003.

———. "Procatechesis." In *Cyrilli Hierosolymorum archiepiscopi opera quae supersunt omnia*. Vol. 1, pp. 1-26. Edited by W. C. Reischl and J. Rupp. Munich: Lentner, 1848 (repr. Hildesheim: Olms, 1967. TLG 2110.001.

Ennodius. "Vita Epiphanii." In *Magni Felicis Ennodii Opera omnia*. Edited by Wilhelm Hartel. CSEL 6, pp. 331-83. Vienna: C. Geroldi, 1882. Cl. 1494.

Ephrem the Syrian. *Hymni de nativitate*. Edited by Edmund Beck, 2 vols. CSCO 186, 187 (Scriptores Syri 82, 83). Louvain: Secretariat du Corpus, 1959.

———. "Hymni de Paradiso." In *Des Heiligen Ephraem des Syrers Hymnen de Paradiso und Contra Julianum*. Edited by E. Beck. CSCO 174 (Scriptores Syri 78). Louvain: Imprimerie Orientaliste L. Durbecq, 1957.

————. "In Tatiani Diatessaron." In *Saint Éphrem: Commentaire de l'Evangile Concordant—Text Syriaque*, (Ms Chester-Beatty 709), Folios Additionnels. Edited by L. Leloir. Leuven and Paris, 1990.

————. "Sermo de Domino nostro." In *Des Heilig Ephraem Sermo de Domino Nostro*. Edited by E. Beck. CSCO 270 (Scriptores Syri 116). Louvain: Imprimerie Orientaliste L. Durbecq, 1966.

[Ephrem the Synian]. *Sancti Ephraem Syri in Genesim et in Exodum commentarii*. 2 vols. Edited by R. R. Tonneau. CSCS 152, 153 (Scriptores Syri 71, 72). Louvain: Imprimerie Orientaliste L. Durbecq, 1955.

Eusebius of Caesarea. "Demonstratio evangelica." In *Eusebius Werke, Band 6: Die Demonstratio evangelica*. GCS 23, pp. 1-492. Leipzig: Hinrichs, 1913. TLG 2018.005.

————. "Historia ecclesiastica." In *Eusèbe de Césarée. Histoire ecclésiastique*, 3 vols. Edited by G. Bardy. SC 31, 41, 55, pp. (1:)3-215, (2:)4-231, (3:)3-120. Paris: Éditions du Cerf, 1952, 1955, 1958. TLG 2018.002.

Evagrius of Pontus. "Practicus." In *Évagre le Pontique: Traité pratique ou le moine*. Vol. 2. Edited by Antoine Guillaumont and Claire Guillaumont. SC 171, pp. 482-712. Paris: Éditions du Cerf, 1971. TLG 4110.001.

Fructuosus of Braga. *Regulas Monastica Communis*. In *Scriptorum ecclesiasticorum, opera omnia*. PL 87, cols. 1109-30. Edited by J.-P. Migne. Paris: Migne, 1863.

Gregory of Elvira. "Tractatus Origenis de libris Sanctarum Scripturarum." In *Gregorii Iliberritani episcopi quae supersunt*. Edited by Vincentius Bulhart. CCL 69, pp. 1-146. Turnhout, Belgium: Brepols, 1967. Cl. 0546.

Gregory of Nazianzus. "Adversus Eunomianos (orat. 27)." In *Gregor von Nazianz: Die fünf theologischen Reden*, pp. 38-60. Edited by J. Barbel. Düsseldorf: Patmos-Verlag, 1963. TLG 2022.007.

————. "Apologetica (orat. 2)." In *Opera omnia*. PG 35, cols. 408-513. Edited by J.-P. Migne. Paris: Migne, 1857. TLG 2022.016.

————. "De theologia (orat. 28)." In *Gregor von Nazianz: Die fünf theologischen Reden*, pp. 62-126. Edited by J. Barbel. Düsseldorf: Patmos-Verlag, 1963. TLG 2022.008.

————. "Funebris oratio in laudem Basilii Magni Caesareae in Cappadocia episcopi (orat. 43)." In *Grégoire de Nazianze. Discours funèbres en l'honneur de son frère Césaire et de Basile de Césarée*, pp. 58-230. Edited by F. Boulenger. Paris: Picard, 1908. TLG 2022.006.

————. "In sanctum baptisma (orat. 40)." In *Opera omnia*. PG 36, cols. 360-425. Edited by J.-P. Migne. Paris: Migne, 1858. TLG 2022.048.

Gregory of Nyssa. "Contra Eunomium." In *Gregorii Nysseni opera*, 2 vols. Edited by W. Jaeger. Vol. 1.1, pp. 3-409; vol. 2.2, pp. 3-311. Leiden: Brill, 1960. TLG 2017.030.

————. "De perfectione Christiana ad Olympium monachum." In *Gregorii Nysseni opera*. Edited by W. Jaeger. Vol. 8.1, pp. 173-214. Leiden: Brill, 1963. TLG 2017.026.

————. "De vita Gregorii Thaumaturgi." In *Opera omnia*. PG 46, cols. 893-957. Edited by J.-P. Migne. Paris: Migne, 1863. TLG 2017.069.

————. "In diem luminum (*vulgo* In baptismum Christi oratio)." In *Gregorii Nysseni opera*. Edited by E. Gebhardt. Vol. 9.1, pp. 221-42. Leiden: Brill, 1967. TLG 2017.014.

————. "In inscriptiones Psalmorum." In *Gregorii Nysseni opera*. Edited by J. McDonough. Vol. 5, pp. 24-175. Leiden: Brill, 1962. TLG 2017.027.

Gregory Thaumaturgus. "Epistula canonica." In *Fonti. Fascicolo ix. Discipline générale antique (iie-ixe s.)*. Edited by Périclès-Pierre Joannou. Vol 2, pp. 19-30. Rome: Tipografia Italo-Orientale "S. Nilo," 1963. TLG 4092.005.

————. "In Originem oratio panegyrica." In *Grégorie le Thaumaturge: Remerciement à Origène suivi de la letter d'Origène à Grégoire*. Edited by Henri Crouzel. SC 148, pp. 94-182. Paris: Éditions du Cerf, 1969.

TLG 2063.001.

Gregory the Great. "Dialogorum libri iv." In *Dialogues*. 3 vols. Translated by Paul Antin. Introduction and notes by Adalbert de Vogüé. SC 251, 260, 265. Paris: Éditions du Cerf, 1978-1980. Cl. 1713.

———. "Homiliarum xl in evangelica." In *Opera omnia*. Edited by J.-P. Migne. PL 76, cols 1075-1312. Paris: Migne, 1857. Cl. 1711.

———. "In librum primum Regum expositionum libri vi (dub)." In *Opera*. Edited by Patrick Verbraken. CCL 144, pp. 47-614. Turnhout, Belgium: Brepols, 1963. Cl. 1719.

———. *Moralia in Job*. Edited by Mark Adriaen. CCL 143, 143A and 143B. Turnhout, Belgium: Brepols, 1979-85. Cl. 1708.

———. *Registrum epistularum*. 2 vols. Edited by Dag Norberg. CCL 140, 140A. Turnhout, Belgium: Brepols, 1982. Cl. 0714.

———. *Regula pastoralis*. Edited by Floribert Rommel and R.W. Clement. CCL 141. Turnhout, Belgium: Brepols, 1953. Cl. 1712.

Hilary of Poiter. *Tractatus super psalmos I-XCI*. Edited by Jean Doignon. CCL 61. Turnhout: Brepols, 1997. Cl. 0428.

Hippolytus. "De antichristo." In *Hippolyt's kleinere exegetische und homiletische Schriften*. Edited by Hans Achelis. GCS 1.2, pp. 1-47. Leipzig: Hinrichs, 1897. TLG 2115.003.

———. "Refutatio omnium haeresium." In *Hippolytus. Rufutatio omnium haeresium*. Edited by Miroslav Marcovich. PTS 25, pp. 53-417. Berlin: De Gruyter, 1986. TLG 2115.060.

Horsiesi. *Oeuvres de S. Pachôme et de ses disciples*. Edited by L. Th. Lefort. CSCO 159 (Scriptores Coptici 23). Louvain: Impremerie Orientaliste L. Durbecq, 1956.

Ignatius of Antioch. "Epistulae vii genuinae." In *Ignace d'Antioche: Polycarpe de Smyrne: Lettres: Martyre de Polycarpe*. 4th ed. Edited by P. T. Camelot. SC 10, pp. 56-154. Paris: Éditions du Cerf, 1969. TLG 1443.001.

Irenaeus. "Adversus haereses [liber 3]." In *Irénée de Lyon. Contre les heresies, livre 3*, vol. 2. Edited by Adelin. Rousseau and Louis Doutreleau. SC 211. Paris: Éditions du Cerf, 1974. TLG 1447.002.

Isaac of Nineveh. "De perfectione religiosa." In *Mar Isaacus Ninivita. De perfectione religiosa*, pp. 1-99. Edited by Paul Bedjan. Paris, 1966.

Isidore of Seville. "De Ruth." In the Oxford, Bodleian Library, MS Add. C. 16, fol. 98r-v, collated with London, BL, MS Royal 3 A.VII, fol. 65r-v. *See MEIT 8*.

Jerome. "Adversus Jovinianum." In *Opera omnia*. Edited by J.-P. Migne. PL 23, cols. 221-352. Paris: Migne, 1845. Cl. 0610.

———. *Commentarii in prophetas minores*. 2 vols. Edited by M. Adriaen. CCL 76 and 76A. Turnhout, Belgium: 1969-1970. Cl. 0589.

———. "De exodo, in vigilia Paschae." In *S. Hieronymi Presbyteri opera*. Edited by Germain Morin. CCL 78, pp. 536-41. Turnhout, Belgium: Brepols, 1958. Cl. 0601.

———. *Dialogus adversus Pelagianos libri iii*. Edited by C. Moreschini. CCL 80. Turnhout, Belgium: Brepols, 1990. Cl. 0615.

———. *Epistulae*. Edited by I. Hilberg. CSEL 54, 55 and 56. Vienna, Austria: F. Tempsky; Leipzig, Germany: G. F. Freytag, 1910-1918. Cl. 0620.

———. "Homilia in evangelium secundum Matthaeum." In *S. Hieronymi Presbyteri opera*. Edited by Germain Morin. CCL 78, pp. 503-6. Turnhout, Belgium: Brepols, 1958. Cl. 0595.

———. "Tractatus lix in psalmos." In *S. Hieronymi presbyteri opera*. Edited by G. Morin. CCL 78, pp. 3-352. Turnhout, Belgium: Brepols, 1958. Cl. 0592.

———. "Tractatus lix in psalmos, series altera." In *S. Hieronymi Presbyteri opera*. Edited by Germain Morin. CCL 78, pp. 355-447. Turnhout, Belgium: Brepols, 1958. Cl. 0593.

John Chrysostom. "Ad populam Antiochenum homiliae (de statuis)." In *Opera omnia*. Edited by J.-P. Migne. PG 49, cols. 15-222. Paris: Migne, 1862. TLG 2062.024.

———. "Adversus Judaeos (orationes 1-8)." In *Opera omnia*. Edited by J.-P. Migne. PG 48, cols. 843-942. Paris: Migne, 1862. TLG 2062.021.

———. "Contra Anomoeos (homilia 11)." In *Opera omnia*. Edited by J.-P. Migne. PG 48, cols. 795-802. Paris: Migne, 1862. TLG 2062.012.

———. "De Anna." In *Opera omnia*. Edited by J.-P. Migne. PG 54, cols. 631-76. Paris: Migne, 1862. TLG 2062.114.

———. "De Davide et Saule." In *Opera omnia*. Edited by J.-P. Migne. PG 54, cols. 675-708. Paris: Migne, 1862. TLG 2062.115.

———. "De eleemosyna." In *Opera omnia*. Edited by J.-P. Migne. PG 51, cols. 261-72. Paris: Migne, 1862. TLG 2062.075.

———. "De paenitentia (homiliae 1-9)." In *Opera omnia*. Edited by J.-P. Migne. PG 49, cols. 277-348. Paris: Migne, 1862. TLG 2062.027.

———. "De sacerdotio." In *Jean Chrysostome. Sur le sacerdoce*. Edited by A.-M. Malingrey. SC 272, pp. 60-372. Paris: Éditions du Cerf, 1980. TLG 2062.085.

———. "De sancto hieromartyre Babyla." In *Opera omnia*. Edited by J.-P. Migne. PG 50, cols. 527-34. Paris: Migne, 1862. TLG 2062.041.

———. "In epistulam ad Ephesios." In *Opera omnia*. Edited by J.-P. Migne. PG 62, cols. 9-176. Paris: Migne, 1862. TLG 2062.159.

———. "In epistulam ad Colossenses." In *Opera omnia*. Edited by J.-P. Migne. PG 62, cols. 299-392. Paris: Migne, 1862. TLG 2062.161.

———. "In epistulam i ad Corinthios (homiliae 1-44)." In *Opera omnia*. Edited by J.-P. Migne. PG 61, cols. 9-382. Paris: Migne, 1862. TLG 2062.156.

———. "In epistulam ii ad Corinthios (homiliae 1-30)." In *Opera omnia*. Edited by J.-P. Migne. PG 61, cols. 381-610. Paris: Migne, 1862. TLG 2062.157.

———. "In epistulam ad Galatas commentarius." In *Opera omnia*. Edited by J.-P. Migne. PG 61, cols. 611-82. Paris: Migne, 1859. TLG 2062.158.

———. "In epistulam ad Hebraeos (homiliae 1-34)." In *Opera omnia*. Edited by J.-P. Migne. PG 63, cols. 9-236. Paris: Migne, 1862. TLG 2062.168.

———. "In epistulam ad Philippenses." In *Opera omnia*. Edited by J.-P. Migne. PG 62, cols. 177-298. Paris: Migne, 1862. TLG 2062.160.

———. "In epistulam ad Romanos." In *Opera omnia*. Edited by J.-P. Migne. PG 60, cols. 391-682. Paris: Migne, 1862. TLG 2062.155.

———. "In epistulam ad Titum." In *Opera omnia*. Edited by J.-P. Migne. PG 62, cols. 663-700. Paris: Migne, 1862. TLG 2062.166.

———. "In epistulam i ad Thessalonicenses." In *Opera omnia*. Edited by J.-P. Migne. PG 62, cols. 391-468. Paris: Migne, 1862. TLG 2062.162.

———. "In epistulam ii ad Thessalonicenses." In *Opera omnia*. Edited by J.-P. Migne. PG 62, cols. 467-500. Paris: Migne, 1862. TLG 2062.163.

———. "In epistulam i ad Timotheum (homiliae 1-18)." In *Opera omnia*. Edited by J.-P. Migne. PG 62, cols. 501-600. Paris: Migne, 1862. TLG 2062.164.

———. "In epistulam i ad Timotheum (homiliae 1-10)." In *Opera omnia*. Edited by J.-P. Migne. PG 62, cols. 599-662. Paris: Migne, 1862. TLG 2062.165.

———. "In Genesim (homiliae 1-67)." In *Opera omnia*. Edited by J.-P. Migne. PG 53, 54, cols. 385-580. Paris: Migne, 1859-1862. TLG 2062.112.

————."In illud: Si esurierit inimicus." In *Opera omnia*. Edited by J.-P. Migne. PG 51, cols. 171-86. Paris: Migne, 1862. TLG 2062.068.

————."In Joannem (homiliae 1-88)." In *Opera omnia*. Edited by J.-P. Migne. PG 59, cols. 23-482. Paris: Migne, 1862. TLG 2062.153.

————."In Matthaeum (homiliae 1-90)." In *Opera omnia*. Edited by J.-P. Migne. PG 57-58. Paris: Migne, 1862. TLG 2062.152.

John of Damascus."Expositio fidei." In *Die Schriften des Johannes von Damaskos*, vol. 2, pp. 3-239. Edited by B. Kotter. PTS 12. Berlin: De Gruyter, 1973. TLG 2934.004.

————."Orationes de imaginibus tres." In *Die Schriften des Johannes von Damaskos*. Vol. 3. Edited by Bonifatius Kotter. PTS 17, pp. 65-200. Berlin: De Gruyter, 1975. TLG 2934.005.

Justin Martyr. "Dialogus cum Tryphone." In *Die ältesten Apologeten*, pp. 90-265. Edited by E. J. Goodspeed. Göttingen, Germany: Vandenhoeck & Ruprecht, 1915. TLG 0645.003.

Lactantius. "Epitome divinarum institutionum." In *L. Caeli Firmiani Lactanti Opera omnia*. Edited by Samuel Brandt. CSEL 19, pp. 673-761. Vienna, Austria: F. Tempsky; Leipzig, Germany: G. Freytag, 1890. Cl. 0086.

Leander of Seville."Regula, sive liber de institutione virginum et contemptu mundi." In *Pelagii II, Joannis III, Benedicti I summorum pontificum opera omnia*. Edited by J.-P. Migne. PL 72, cols. 873-94. Paris: Migne, 1849.

Maximus of Turin."Collectio sermonum antiqua." In *Maximi episcopi Taurinensis sermons*. Edited by Almut Mutzenbecher. CCL 23, pp. 1-364. Turnhout, Belgium: Brepols, 1962. Cl. 0219a.

Methodius."Convivium decem virginum." In *Opera omnia*. Edited by J.-P. Migne. PG 18, cols. 27-220. Paris: Migne, 1857. TLG 2959.001.

————."De Resurrectione." In *Methodius*. Edited by G. Nathanael Bonwetsch. GCS 27, pp. 226-420 *passim*. Leipzig: Hinrichs, 1917. TLG 2959.003.

[Nemesius of Emesa]. *Nemesii Emeseni De natura hominis*. Edited by Moreno Morani. Bibliotheca scriptorium Graecorum et Romanorum Teubneriana. Leipzig: Teubner, 1987. TLG 0743.001.

Nicetas of Remesiana."De spiritus sancti potentia." In *Sancti Petri Chrysologi Opera omnia, sanctorum Valeriani et Nicetae*. Edited by J.-P. Migne. PL 52, cols. 853-64. Paris: Migne, 1859.

————. "De utilitate hymnorum." Edited by C. H. Turner. *The Journal of Theological Studies*, vol. 24 (1923): 233-241.

Novatian."De spectaculis." In *Opera quae supersunt*. Edited by G. F. Diercks. CCL 4, pp. 167-79. Turnhout, Belgium: Brepols, 1972. Cl. 0070.

Opus imperfectum in Matthaeum. In *Opera omnia*. Edited by J.-P. Migne. PG 56, cols. 611-946. Paris: Migne, 1862.

Origen."Commentarium in Canticum Canticorum." In *Origenes Werke*. Vol. 8. Edited by W. A. Baehrens. GCS 33, pp. 61-241. Leipzig: Teubner, 1925. Cl. 0198 2/TLG 2042.026.

————."Commentarii in evangelium Joannis (lib. 1, 2, 4, 5, 6, 10, 13)." In *Origene. Commentaire sur saint Jean*, 3 vols. Edited by Cécil Blanc. SC 120, 157, 222. Paris: Éditions du Cerf, 1966-1975. TLG 2042.005.

————."Commentarium in evangelium Matthaei [lib.12-17]." In *Origenes Werke*, 2 vols. Vols 10.1 and 10.2. Edited by E. Klostermann. GCS 40.1, pp. 69-304; GCS 40.2, pp. 305-703. Leipzig: Teubner, 1935-1937. TLG 2042.030.

————."Contra Celsum." In *Origène Contre Celse*, 4 vols. Edited by M. Borret. SC 132, 136, 147 and 150. Paris: Éditions du Cerf, 1967-1969. TLG 2042.001.

————."De engastrimytho (Homilia in i Reg. [i Sam.] 28.3-25)." In *Origenes Werke*, vol. 3. Edited by E. Klostermann. GCS 6, pp. 283-294. Leipzig: Hinrichs, 1901. TLG 2042.013.

———. "De oratione." In *Origenes Werke*, vol. 2. Edited by P. Koestchau. GCS 3, pp. 297-403. Leipzig: Hinrichs, 1899. TLG 2042.008.

———. "Exhortatio ad martyrium." In *Origenes Werke*, vol. 1, pp. 3-47. Edited by P. Koetschau. GCS 2. Leipzig: Hinrichs, 1899. TLG 2042.007.

———. "Fragmenta in Jeremiam (in catenis)." In *Origenes Werke*. Vol. 3. Edited by Erich Klostermann. GCS 6, pp. 199-232. Leipzig: Hinrichs, 1901. TLG 2042.010.

———. "Homiliae in Exodum." In *Origenes Werke*, vol. 6. Edited by W. A. Baehrens. GCS 29, pp. 217-30. Leipzig: Teubner, 1920. Cl. 0198/TLG 2042.023.

———. "Homiliae in Genesim." In *Origenes Werke*. Vol. 6. Edited by W. A. Baehrens. GCS 29, pp. 23-30. Leipzig: Teubner, 1920. Cl. 0198/TLG 2042.022.

———. "Homiliae in Leviticum." In *Origenes Werke*, vol. 6. Edited by W. A. Baehrens. GCS 29, pp. 332-34, 395, 402-7, 409-16 Leipzig: Teubner, 1920. TLG 2042.024.

———. "In Jeremiam (homiliae 1-11)." In "Homiliae 2-3." *Origenes Werke*. Vol. 8. Edited by W. A. Baehrens. GCS 33, pp. 290-317. Leipzig: Teubner, 1925. TLG 2042.009.

———. "In Jeremiam [homiliae 12-20]." In *Origenes Werke*. Vol. 3. Edited by Erich Klostermann. GCS 6, pp. 85-194. Berlin: Akademie-Verlag, 1901. TLG 2042.021.

———. "Homiliae in Librum Jesu Nave." In *Opera Omnia*. Edited by J.-P. Migne. PG 12 cols. 825-948. Paris: Migne, 1862.

———. "Homiliae in Librum Regum I." In *Origenes Werke*. Vol. 8. Edited by W. A. Baehrens. GCS 33, pp. 1-25. Leipzig: Teubner, 1925. Cl. 0198 8.

———. "In Numeros homiliae." In *Origenes Werke*. Vol. 7. Edited by W. A. Baehrens. GCS 30, pp. 3-285. Leipzig: Teubner, 1921. Cl. 0198 0.

Pachomius. "Catecheses." In *Oeuvres de s. Pachôme et de ses disciples*. Edited L.T. Lefort. CSCO 159, pp. 1-26. Louvain: Imprimerie Orientaliste, 1956.

Pacian of Barcelona. "De paenitentibus." In *Opera omnia*. Edited by J.-P. Migne. PL 13, cols. 1081-90. Paris: Migne, 1845.

———. "Epistulae." In *San Paciano, Obras*. Edited Lisardo Rubio Fernandez. Barcelona: Universidad de Barcelona, 1958.

[Paulinus of Milan]. *Vita S. Ambrosii Mediolanensis Episcopi a Paulino Eius Notario ad Beatum Augustinum Conscripta: A Revised Text and Commentary with an Introduction and Translation*. By Sister Mary Simplicia Kaniecka. PSt 16. Washington, D.C.: Catholic University of America Press, 1928.

Paulinus of Nola. "Carmina." In *S. Pontii Meropii Paulini Nolani opera*. Edited by W. Hartel. CSEL 30, pp. 1-3, 7-329. Vienna: F. Tempsky, 1894. Cl. 0203.

Paulus Orosius. "Liber apologeticus contra Pelagianos." In *Sancti Paulus orosius. Opera*. Edited by C. Zangemeister. CSEL 5, pp. 603-64. Vienna: F. Tempsky, 1882. Cl. 0572.

Peter Chrysologus. *Collectio sermonum a Felice episcopo parata sermonibus extravagantibus adjectis*, 3 vols. In *Sancti Petri Chrysologi*. Edited by Alexander Olivar. CCL 24, 24A and 24B. Turnhout: Brepols, 1975-1982. Cl. 0227+.

Procopius of Gaza. *Commentarii in Josue*. Edited by J.-P. Migne. PG 87.1, cols. 992-1041. Paris: Migne, 1860.

———. *Commentarii in Judices*. Edited by J.-P. Migne. PG 87.1, cols. 1041-80. Paris: Migne, 1860.

Prudentius. "Liber cathemerinon." In *Opera*. Edited by M. P. Cunnigham. CCL 126, pp. 3-72. Turnhout, Belgium: Typographi Brepolis Editores Pontificii, 1966. Cl. 1438.

———. "Psychomachia." In *Aurelii Prudentii Clementis Carmina*. Edited by M. P. Cunningham. CCL 126, pp. 149-81. Turhout, Belgium: Brepols, 1966. Cl. 1441.

———. "Tituli historiarum sive Dittochaeon." In *Opera*. Edited by M. P. Cunningham. CCL 126, pp.

390-400. Turnhout, Belgium: Brepols, 1966. Cl. 1444.

[Pseudo-Clement of Rome]. "Recognitiones." In *Rekognitionen*. Edited by Franz Paschke and Bernhard Rehm. CGS 51. Berlin: Akademie-Verlag, 1965. Cl. 0198 N (A).

Salvian the Presbyter. "De gubernatione Dei." In *Ouvres*, vol. 2. Edited by Georges LaGarrigue. SC 220. Paris: Éditions du Cerf, 1975. Cl. 0485.

Sulpicius Severus. "Chronicorum libri II." In *Sulpicii Severi libri qui supersunt*. Edited by Karl Halm. CSEL 1, pp. 3-105. Vienna: C. Geroldi, 1866. Cl. 0474.

Symeon the New Theologian. *Catecheses*. Edited by B. Krivochéine and J. Paramelle. SC 96, 104. Paris: Éditions du Cerf, 1963-64.

Tertullian. "Adversus Judaeos." In *Opera*, vol. 2. Edited by E. Kroymann. CCL 2, pp. 1339-96. Turnhout, Belgium: Brepols, 1954. Cl. 0033.

———. "Adversus Marcionem." In *Opera*, vol. 1. Edited by E. Kroymann. CCL 1, pp. 437-726. Turnhout, Belgium: Brepols, 1954. Cl. 0014.

———. "De anima." In *Opera*. Edited by J. H. Waszink. CCL 2, pp. 781-869. Turnhout, Belgium: Brepols, 1954. Cl. 0017.

———. "De fuga in persecutione." In *Opera*. Edited by J. J. Thierry. CCL 2, pp. 1135-55. Turnhout, Belgium: Typographi Brepols Editores Pontificii, 1954. Cl. 0025.

———. "De idololatria." In *Opera*, vol. 2. Edited by A. Reifferscheid and G. Wissowa. CCL 2, pp. 1101-24. Turnhout, Belgium: Brepols, 1954. Cl. 0023.

———. "De praescriptione haereticorum." In *Tertulliani opera*. Edited by R. F. Refoulé. CCL 1, pp. 187-224. Turnhout, Belgium: Brepols, 1954. Cl. 0005.

———. "De resurrectione mortuorum." In *Opera*. Edited by J. G. Ph. Borleffs. CCL 2, pp. 919-1012. Turnhout, Belgium: Brepols, 1954. Cl. 0019.

———. "Scorpiace." In *Opera*. Edited by A. Reifferscheid and G. Wissowa. CCL 2, pp.1067-97. Turnhout, Belgium: Brepols, 1954. Cl. 0022.

Theodore of Mopsuestia. *Expositionis in Psalmos: Iuliano Aeclanensi interprete in latinum versae quae supersunt*. Edited by Lucas de Coninck. CCL 88A. turnhout, Belgium: Brepols, 1977.

Theodoret of Cyr. "De providentia orationes decem." Edited by J.-P. Migne. PG 83, cols. 556-773. Paris: Migne, 1859. TLG 4089.032.

———. "Ad eos qui in Euphratesia et Osrhoena regione, Syria, Phoeni." Edited by J.-P. Migne. PG 83, cols. 1416-33. Paris: Migne, 1859. TLG 4089.034.

———. "Historia ecclesiastica." Edited by L. Parmentier and F. Scheidweiler. *Theodoret. Kirchengeschichte*, 2nd ed. [GCS 44. Berlin: Akademie-Verlag, 1954]: 1-349. TLG 4089.003.

Theophylact. *Ennarratio in evangelium s. Matthaei*. Edited by J.-P. Migne. PG 123, cols. 143-488. Paris: Migne, 1859.

Bibliography of Works
in English Translation

Ambrose. "Exposition of the Gospel of Luke." In *MEIT, passim*. Translated by Lesley Smith. Kalamazoo, Mich.: Medieval Institute Publications, 1996.

———. *Funeral Orations by Saint Gregory Nazianzen and Saint Ambrose*. Translated by Leo McCauley, John Sullivan, Martin McGuire and Roy Deferrari. FC 22. Washington, D.C.: The Catholic University of America Press, 1953.

———. *Hexameron, Paradise, and Cain and Abel*. Translated by John J. Savage. FC 42. Washington, D.C.: The Catholic University of America Press, 1961.

———. *Letters*. Translated by Mary Melchior Beyenka. FC 26. Washington, D.C.: The Catholic University of America Press, 1954.

———. *Select Works and Letters*. Translated by H. De Romestin. NPNF 10. Series 2. Edited by Philip Schaff and Henry Wace. 14 vols. 1886-1900. Reprint, Peabody, Mass.: Hendrickson, 1994.

———. "Selections from Ambrose, Letters." In *Early Latin Theology*, pp. 175-278. Translated and edited by S. L. Greenslade. LCC 5. Philadelphia: Westminster Press, 1956.

———. *Seven Exegetical Works*. Translated by Michael P. McHugh. FC 65. Washington, D.C.: The Catholic University of America Press, 1972.

Aphrahat. "Select Demonstrations." In *Gregory the Great, Ephraim Syrus, Aphrahat*, pp. 345-412. Translated by James Barmby. NPNF 13. Series 2. Edited by Philip Schaff and Henry Wace. 14 vols. 1886-1900. Reprint, Peabody, Mass.: Hendrickson, 1994.

Athanasius. "Life of St. Anthony." In *Early Christian Biographies*, pp. 127-216. Translated by Sister Mary Emily Keenan. FC 15. Washington D.C.: The Catholic University of America, 1952.

———. *Selected Works and Letters*. Translated by Archibald Robertson. NPNF 4. Series 2. Edited by Philip Schaff and Henry Wace. 14 vols. 1886-1900. Reprint, Peabody, Mass.: Hendrickson, 1994.

Augustine. *Against Julian*. Translated by Matthew Schumacher. FC 35. Washington, D.C.: The Catholic University of America Press, 1957.

———. *Anti-Pelagian Writings*. Translated by Peter Holmes and Robert Ernest Wallis. NPNF 5. Series 1. Edited by Philip Schaff. 14 vols. 1886-1889. Reprint, Peabody, Mass.: Hendrickson, 1994

———. *Christian Instruction; Admonition and Grace; The Christian Combat; Faith, Hope and Charity*. Translated by Bernard M. Peebles. FC 2. Washington, D.C.: The Catholic University of America Press, 1947.

———. *City of God, Christian Doctrine*. Translated by Marcus Dods and J. F. Shaw. NPNF 2. Series 1. Edited by Philip Schaff. 14 vols. 1886-1889. Reprint, Peabody, Mass.: Hendrickson, 1994.

———. *Confessions*. Translated by Vernon Bourke. FC 21. Washington, D.C.: The Catholic University of America Press, 1953.

———. *Confessions and Enchiridion*. Translated by Albert Outler. LCC 7. Philadelphia: Westminster, 1955.

———. *Eighty-Three Different Questions*. Translated by David L. Mosher. FC 70. Washington, D.C.: The Catholic University of America Press, 1982.

———. *Exposition of the Psalms, 33-72*. Translated by Maria Boulding. WSA 16, 17. Part 3. Edited by

John E. Rotelle. New York: New City Press, 2000-2001.

———. *Expositions on the Book of Psalms*. Edited and annotated by A. Cleveland Coxe. NPNF 8. Series 1. Edited by Philip Schaff. 14 vols. 1886-1889. Reprint, Peabody, Mass.: Hendrickson, 1994.

———. *Four Anti-Pelagian Writings: On Nature and Grace, On the Proceedings of Pelagius, On the Predestination of the Saints, On the Gift of Perseverance.* Translated by John A. Mourant and William J. Collinge. FC 86. Washington, D.C.: The Catholic University of America Press, 1992.

———. *Homilies on the Gospel of John, Homilies on the First Epistle of John, Soliloquies.* Translated by John Gibb, et. al. NPNF 7. Series 1. Edited by Philip Schaff. 14 vols. 1886-1889. Reprint, Peabody, Mass.: Hendrickson, 1994.

———. *Letters.* Translated by Sister Wilfrid Parsons. FC 12, 18, 20, 30 and 32. Washington, D.C.: The Catholic University of America Press, 1951-1955.

———. "On the Spirit and the Letter." In *Augustine: Later Works*, pp. 182-250. Translated by John Burnaby. LCC 8. London: SCM Press, 1955.

———. *Sermon on the Mount, Harmony of the Gospels, Homilies on the Gospels.* Translated by William Findlay, S. D. F. Salmond and R. G. MacMullen. NPNF 6. Series 1. Edited by Philip Schaff. 14 vols. 1886-1889. Reprint, Peabody, Mass.: Hendrickson, 1994.

———. *Sermons.* Translated by Edmund Hill. WSA 5, 8 and 10. Part 3. Edited by John E. Rotelle. New York: New City Press, 1992-1995.

———. *The City of God.* Translated by Henry S. Bettenson with an introduction by David Knowles. 1972. Reprint, with an introduction by John O'Meara. Harmondsworth, Middlesex: Penguin Books, 1984.

———. *The City of God: Books VIII-XXII.* Translated by Gerald G. Walsh and Grace Monahan. FC 14, 24. Washington, D.C.: The Catholic University of America Press, 1952-1954.

———. "The Letters of St. Augustine." In *Prolegomena, Confessions, Letters*, pp. 219-593. Translated by J. G. Cunningham. NPNF 1. Series 1. Edited by Philip Schaff. 14 vols. 1886-1889. Reprint, Peabody, Mass.: Hendrickson, 1994.

———. *The Teacher, The Free Choice of the Will, Grace and Free Will.* Translated by Robert Russell. FC 59. Washington, D.C.: The Catholic University of America Press, 1968.

———. *The Writings Against the Manichaeans and Against the Donatists.* Translated by J. R. King. NPNF 4. Series 1. Edited by Philip Schaff. 14 vols. 1886-1889. Reprint, Peabody, Mass.: Hendrickson, 1994.

———. *Treatises on Marriage and Other Subjects.* Translated by Charles T. Wilcox, et al. FC 27. Washington, D.C.: The Catholic University of America Press, 1955.

———. *Treatises on Various Subjects.* Translated by Mary Sarah Muldowny et al. FC 16. Washington, D.C.: The Catholic University of America Press, 1952.

Basil the Great. *Ascetical Works.* Translated by M. Monica Wagner. FC 9. New York: Fathers of the Church, Inc., 1950.

———. *Exegetic Homilies.* Translated by Agnes C. Way. FC 46. Washington, D.C.: The Catholic University of America Press, 1963.

———. *Letters.* Translated by Agnes C. Way. FC 28. Washington, D.C.: The Catholic University of America Press, 1951, 1955.

———. *On the Holy Spirit.* Translated by D. Anderson, Crestwood, N.Y.: St. Vladimir's Press, 1980.

———. "The Letters." In *Letters and Select Works*, pp. 109-327. Translated by Blomfield Jackson. NPNF 8. Series 2. Edited by Philip Schaff. 14 vols. 1886-1889. Reprint, Peabody, Mass.: Hendrickson, 1994.

Bede. *Homilies on the Gospels.* 2 vols. Translated by Lawrence T. Martin and David Hurst. CS 110-11. Kalamazoo, Mich.: Cistercian Publications, 1991.

————. *On the Tabernacle*. Translated with notes and introduction by Arthur G. Holder. TTH 18. Liverpool: Liverpool University Press, 1994.

————. "Thirty Questions on the Book of Kings." In *Bede: A Biblical Miscellany*, pp. 81-143. Translated with notes and introduction by W. Trent Foley and Arthur G. Holder. TTH 28. Liverpool: Liverpool University Press, 1999.

Caesarius of Arles. *Sermons*. Translated by Mary Magdeleine Mueller. FC 31 and 47. Washington, D.C.: The Catholic University of America Press, 1956-1973.

Cassian, John. *Sulpicius Severus, Vincent of Lerins, John Cassian*. Translated by Edgar C. S. Gibson. NPNF 11. Series 2. Edited by Philip Schaff and Henry Wace. 14 vols. 1886-1900. Reprint, Peabody, Mass.: Hendrickson, 1994.

————. *The Conferences*. Translated and annotated by Boniface Ramsey. ACW 57. New York: Paulist Press, 1997.

————. *The Institutes*. Translated and annotated by Boniface Ramsey. ACW 58. New York: Paulist Press, 2000.

Cassiodorus. *Explanation of the Psalms*. Translated by P. G. Walsh. ACW 51, 52 and 53. New York: Paulist Press, 1990-1991.

Clement of Alexandria. *Christ the Educator*. Translated by Simon P. Wood. FC 23. Washington, D.C.: The Catholic University of America Press, 1954.

————. *Fathers of the Second Century: Hermas, Tatian, Athenagoras, Theophilus, and Clement of Alexandria*. Translated by F. Crombie, et al. ANF 2. Edited by Alexander Roberts and James Donaldson. 10 vols. 1885-1887. Reprint, Peabody, Mass.: Hendrickson, 1994.

————. *Stromateis: Books 1-3*. Translated by John Ferguson. FC 85. Washington, D.C.: The Catholic University of America Press, 1991.

Clement of Rome. "First Letter to the Corinthians." In *The Apostolic Fathers*, pp. 13-41. Translated by Francis X. Glimm, et al. FC 1. New York: Christian Heritage, Inc., 1947.

————. *The Apostolic Fathers*. Translated J. B. Lightfoot and J. R. Harmer. Edited by M. W. Holmes. 2nd ed. Grand Rapids, Mich.: Baker, 1989.

"Constitutions of the Holy Apostles." In *Lactantius, Venantius, Asterius, Victorinus, Dionysius, Apostolic Teaching and Constitutions, 2 Clement, Early Liturgies*, pp. 385-508. Edited by James Donaldson. ANF 7. Edited by Alexander Roberts and James Donaldson. 10 vols. 1885-1887. Reprint, Peabody, Mass.: Hendrickson, 1994.

Cyprian. *Letters 1-81*. Translated by Rose Bernard Donna. FC 51. Washington, D.C.: The Catholic University of America Press, 1964.

————. "Selections from Cyprian." In *Early Latin Theology*, pp. 113-172. Translated and edited by S. L. Greenslade. LCC 5. Philadelphia: Westminster Press, 1956.

————. "Three Books of Testimonies Against the Jews." In *Hippolytus, Cyprian, Caius, Novatian*, pp. 507-57. Translated by Ernest Wallis. ANF 5. Edited by Alexander Roberts and James Donaldson. 10 vols. 1885-1887. Reprint, Peabody, Mass.: Hendrickson, 1994.

————. *Treatises*. Translated and edited by Roy J. Deferrari. FC 36. Washington, D.C.: The Catholic University of America Press, 1958.

Cyril of Alexandria. *Letters 1-50*. Translated by John I. McEnerney. FC 76. Washington, D.C.: The Catholic University of America Press, 1985.

Cyril of Jerusalem. "Selections from the Catechetical Lectures." In *Cyril of Jerusalem and Nemesius of Emesa*, pp. 64-199. Edited by William Telfer. LCC 4. Philadelphia: Westminster Press, 1956.

————. *The Works of Saint Cyril of Jerusalem*. Translated by Leo P. McCauley and Anthony A. Stephenson. FC 61 and 64. Washington, D.C.: The Catholic University of America Press, 1969-1970.

Ennodius. "Life of St. Epiphanius." In *Early Christian Biographies*, pp. 301-351. Translated by Sister Genevieve Marie Cook. FC 15. Washington D.C.: The Catholic University of America, 1952.

Ephrem the Syrian. "Commentary on Genesis." In *St. Ephrem the Syrian: Selected Prose Works*, pp. 57-213. Translated by Edward G. Mathews and Joseph P. Amar. FC 91. Washington, D.C.: The Catholic University of America Press, 1994.

———. *Ephrem the Syrian: Hymns*. Translated by Kathleen E. McVey. The Classics of Western Spirituality. Mahwah, N.J.: Paulist Press, 1989.

———. *Hymns on Paradise*. Translated by Sebastian Brock. Crestwood, N.Y.: St. Vladimir's Seminary Press, 1990.

———. *Saint Ephrem's Commentary on Tatian's Diatessaron*. Translated by Carmel McCarthy. Journal of Semitic Studies Supplement 2. Oxford: Oxford University Press, 1993.

———. "Selections from Ephraim." In *Gregory the Great, Ephraim Syrus, Aphrahat*, pp. 167-341. Translated by J. B. Morris and A. Edward Johnston. NPNF 13. Series 2. Edited by Philip Schaff and Henry Wace. 14 vols. 1886-1900. Reprint, Peabody, Mass.: Hendrickson, 1994.

Eusebius of Caesarea. *Ecclesiastical History: Books 1-5*. Translated by Roy J. Deferrari. FC 19. Washington D.C.: The Catholic University of America Press, 1953.

———. *Proof of the Gospel*. 2 vols. Translated by W. J. Ferrar. London: SPCK, 1920. Reprint, Grand Rapids, Mich.: Baker, 1981.

Evagrius of Pontus. *The Praktikos and Chapters on Prayer*. Translated by John Eudes Bamberger. CS 4. Kalamazoo, Mich.: Cistercian Publications, 1981.

Fructuosus of Braga. "General Rule for Monasteries." In *Iberian Fathers*. Vol. 2, pp. 176-206. Translated by Claude Barlow. FC 63. Washington, D.C.: The Catholic University of America Press, 1969.

Gregory of Nazianzus. *Faith Gives Fullness to Reasoning: The Five Theological Orations of Gregory Nazianzen*. Translated by Lionel Wickham and Frederick Williams, with introduction and commentary by Frederick W. Norris. Leiden: E. J. Brill, 1991.

———. "Orations." In *Cyril of Jerusalem, Gregory of Nazianzen*. Translated by Charles Gordon Browne, et al. NPNF 7. Series 2. Edited by Philip Schaff and Henry Wace. 14 vols. 1886-1900. Reprint, Peabody, Mass.: Hendrickson, 1994.

Gregory of Nyssa. *Gregory of Nyssa's Treatise on the Inscriptions of the Psalms*. Translated by Ronald E. Heine. Oxford Early Christian Studies. Oxford: Clarendon Press, 1995.

———. "Life of Gregory the Wonderworker." In *St. Gregory Thaumaturgus: Life and Works*, pp. 41-87. Translated by Michael Slusser. FC 98. Washington D.C.: The Catholic University of America Press, 1998.

———. "On Perfection." In *Ascetical Works*, pp. 91-122. Translated by Virginia Woods Callahan. FC 58. Washington D.C.: The Catholic University of America Press, 1967

———. *Select Writings and Letters of Gregory, Bishop of Nyssa*. Translated by William Moore and Henry Austin Wilson. NPNF 5. Series 2. Edited by Philip Schaff and Henry Wace. 14 vols. 1886-1900. Reprint, Peabody, Mass.: Hendrickson, 1994.

Gregory Thaumaturgus. *Life and Works*. Translated by Michael Slusser. FC 98. Washington, D.C.: The Catholic University of America Press, 1998.

Gregory the Great. *Dialogues*. Translated by Odo John Zimmerman. FC 39. Washington, D.C.: The Catholic University of America Press, 1959.

———. *Forty Gospel Homilies*. Translated by David Hurst. CS 123. Kalamazoo, Mich.: Cistercian, 1990.

———. *Morals on the Book of Job*. Translated by Members of the English Church. 4 vols. LF 18, 21, 23 and 31. Oxford: John Henry Parker, 1844-1850.

———. *Pastoral Care*. Translated by Henry Davis. ACW 11. New York: Newman Press, 1950.

————. *Pastoral Rule and Selected Epistles*. Translated by James Barmby. NPNF 12. Series 2. Edited by Philip Schaff and Henry Wace. 14 vols. 1886-1900. Reprint, Peabody, Mass.: Hendrickson, 1994.

Hilary of Poitiers. "Select Works." In *Hilary of Poitiers, John of Damascus*. Translated by E.W. Watson, et. al. NPNF 9. Series 2. Edited by Philip Schaff and Henry Wace. 14 vols. 1886-1900. Reprint, Peabody, Mass.: Hendrickson, 1994.

Hipplytus. "Hippolytus." In *Fathers of the Third Century: Hippolytus, Cyprian, Caius, Novatian, Appendix*, pp. 9-266. Translated by J. H. MacMahon, et al. ANF 5. Edited by Alexander Roberts and James Donaldson. 10 vols. 1885-1887. Reprint, Peabody, Mass.: Hendrickson, 1994.

Horsiesi. "The Regulations of Horsiesios." In *Pahcomian Koinonia: Volume Two, Pachomian Chronicles and Rules*, 197-223. CS 46. Kalamazoo, Mich.: Cistercian, 1981.

Incomplete Work on Matthew. In *MEIT, passim*. Translated Lesley Smith. Kalamazoo, Mich.: Medieval Institute Publications, 1996.

Ignatius of Antioch. "Epistle to the Magnesians." In *The Apostolic Fathers with Justin Martyr and Irenaeus*, pp. 59-65. Translated by A. Cleveland Coxe. ANF 1. Edited by Alexander Roberts and James Donaldson. 10 vols. 1885-1887. Reprint, Peabody, Mass.: Hendrickson, 1994.

Irenaeus. "Against Heresies." In *The Apostolic Fathers with Justin Martyr and Irenaeus*, pp. 309-567. Translated by A. Cleveland Coxe. ANF 1. Edited by Alexander Roberts and James Donaldson. 10 vols. 1885-1887. Reprint, Peabody, Mass.: Hendrickson, 1994.

Isaac of Nineveh. *On Ascetical Life*. Translated by Mary Hansbury. Crestwood, N.Y.: St. Vladimir's Seminary Press, 1989.

————. *The Ascetical Homilies of Saint Isaac the Syrian*. Translated by the Holy Tranfiguration Monastery. Boston: Holy Transfiguration Monastery, 1984.

Isidore of Seville. "On Ruth." In *MEIT*, pp. 7-8. Translated by Lesley Smith. Kalamazoo, Mich.: Medieval Institute Publications, 1996.

Jerome. "Hebrew Questions on Chronicles." In *MEIT, passim*. Translated by Lesley Smith. Kalamazoo, Mich.: Medieval Institute Publications, 1996.

————. "Letters." In *Early Latin Theology: Selections from Tertullian, Cyprian, Ambrose and Jerome*, pp. 290-389. Translated by S.L. Greenslade. LCC 5. Philadelphia: Westminster Press, 1956.

————. "Letters." In *MEIT, passim*. Translated by Lesley Smith. Kalamazoo, Mich.: Medieval Institute Publications, 1996.

————. *Letters and Select Works*. Translated by W. H. Fremantle. NPNF 6. Series 2. Edited by Philip Schaff and Henry Wace. 14 vols. 1886-1900. Reprint, Peabody, Mass.: Hendrickson, 1994.

————. "The Dialogue Against the Pelagians." In *Dogmatic and Polemical Works*, pp. 221-378. Translated by John N. Hritzu. FC 53. Washington, D.C.: The Catholic University of America Press, 1965.

————. *The Homilies of Saint Jerome*. Translated by Marie Liguori Ewald. FC 48 and 57. Washington, D.C.: The Catholic University of America Press, 1964, 1966.

John Chrysostom. "Against the Anomoeans." In *On the Incomprehensible Nature of God*. Translated by Paul W. Harkins. FC 72. Washington, D.C.: The Catholic University of America Press, 1984.

————. *Commentary on Saint John the Apostle and Evangelist: Homilies 48-88*. Translated by Thomas Aquinas Goggin. FC 41. Washington, D.C.: The Catholic University of America Press, 1959.

————. "Discourse on Blessed Babylas and Against the Greeks." In *Apologist*, pp. 1-152. Translated by Paul W. Harkins. FC 73. Washington, D.C.: The Catholic University of America Press, 1985.

————. *Discourses against Judaizing Christians*. Translated by Paul W. Harkins. FC 68. Washington, D.C.: The Catholic University of America Press, 1979.

————. *Homilies on Galatians, Ephesians, Philippians, Colossians, Thessalonians, Timothy, Titus, and Philemon*. Translated by Gross Alexander, et al. NPNF 13. Series 1. Edited by Philip Schaff. 14 vols. 1886-

1889. Reprint, Peabody, Mass.: Hendrickson, 1994.

————. *Homilies on Genesis 46-67.* Translated by Robert Hill. FC 87. Washington, D.C.: The Catholic University of America Press, 1992.

————. *Homilies on Hannah, David and Saul.* Translated by Robert Charles Hill. COTH 1. Brookline, Mass.: Holy Cross Orthodox Press, 2003.

————. *(Homilies) On Repentance and Almsgiving.* Translated by Gus George Christo. FC 96. Washington, D.C.: The Catholic University of America Press, 1998.

————. *Homilies on the Acts of the Apostles and the Epistle to the Romans.* Translated by J. Walker, J. Sheppard and H. Browne. NPNF 11. Series 1. Edited by Philip Schaff. 14 vols. 1886-1889. Reprint, Peabody, Mass.: Hendrickson, 1994.

————. *Homilies on the Epistles of Paul to the Corinthians.* Translated by Talbot W. Chambers. NPNF 12. Series 1. Edited by Philip Schaff. 14 vols. 1886-1889. Reprint, Peabody, Mass.: Hendrickson, 1994.

————. "Homilies on the Epistle to the Hebrews." In *Homilies on the Gospel of St. John, Hebrews,* pp. 335-522. The Oxford Translation. NPNF 14. Series 1. Edited by Philip Schaff. 14 vols. 1886-1889. Reprint, Peabody, Mass.: Hendrickson, 1994.

————. "Homilies on the Gospel of Matthew." In *MEIT, passim.* Translated by Lesley Smith. Kalamazoo, Mich.: Medieval Institute Publications, 1996.

————. *Homilies on the Gospel of Saint Matthew.* The Oxford Translation. NPNF 10. Series 1. Edited by Philip Schaff. 14 vols. 1886-1889. Reprint, Peabody, Mass.: Hendrickson, 1994.

————. *On the Priesthood, Ascetic Treatises, Select Homilies and Letters, Homilies on the Statues.* Translated by W. R.W. Stephens, et al. NPNF 9. Series 1. Edited by Philip Schaff. 14 vols. 1886-1889. Reprint, Peabody, Mass.: Hendrickson, 1994.

John of Damascus. "An Exact Exposition of the Orthodox Faith." In *Writings,* pp. 165-406. Translated by Frederic H. Chase. FC 37. Washington, D.C.: The Catholic University of America Press, 1958.

————. *On the Divine Images: Three Apologies Against Those Who Attack the Divine Images.* Translated by David Anderson. Crestwood, N.Y.: St. Vladimir's Seminary Press, 1980.

Justin Martyr. "Dialogue with Trypho, A Jew." In *Apostolic Fathers, Justin Martyr, Irenaeus,* pp. 194-270. Translated by A. Cleveland Coxe. ANF 1. Edited by Alexander Roberts and James Donaldson. 10 vols. 1885-1887. Reprint, Peabody, Mass.: Hendrickson, 1994.

————. "The Dialogue with Trypho." In *Writings of Saint Justin Martyr,* pp. 137-366. Translated by Thomas B. Falls. FC 6. New York: Christian Heritage, Inc., 1948.

Lactantius. *The Divine Institutes: Books I-VII.* Translated by Mary Francis McDonald. FC 49. Washington, D.C.: The Catholic University of America Press, 1964.

————. "The Epitome of the Divine Institutes." In *Lactantius, Venantius, Asterius, Victorinus, Apostolic Teaching and Constitutions, 2 Clement, Early Liturgies,* pp. 224-255. Translated by William Fletcher. ANF 7. Edited by Alexander Roberts and James Donaldson. 10 vols. 1885-1887. Reprint, Peabody, Mass.: Hendrickson, 1994.

Leander of Seville. "The Training of Nuns and the Contempt of the World." In *Iberian Fathers,* vol. 1, pp. 183-228. Translated by Claude W. Barlow. FC 62. Washington, D.C.: The Catholic University of America Press, 1969.

Leo the Great. *Sermons.* Translated by Jane Freeland, et. al. FC 93. Washington, D.C.: The Catholic University of America Press, 1996.

Maximus of Turin. *The Sermons of St. Maximus of Turin.* Translated and annotated by Boniface Ramsey. ACW 50. New York: Newman, 1989.

Methodius. "Methodius." In *Gregory Thaumaturgus, Dionysius the Great, Julius Africanus, Anatolius and Minor Writers, Methodius, Arnobius,* pp. 309-412. Translated by William R. Clark. ANF 6. Edited by Alexander Roberts and James Donaldson. 10 vols. 1885-1887. Reprint, Peabody, Mass.: Hendrickson, 1994.

Nemesius of Emesa. "On the Nature of Man." In *Cyril of Jerusalem and Nemesius of Emesa*, pp. 224-453. Translated by William Telfer. LCC 4. Edited by John Baillie, John McNeill and Henry Van Dusen. Philadelphia: The Westminster Press, 1955.

Nicetas of Remesiana. "Niceta of Remesiana." In *Niceta of Remesiana, Sulpicius Severus, Vincent of Lerins, Prosper of Aquitaine*, pp. 3-78. Translated by Gerald G. Walsh. FC 7. Washington, D.C.: The Catholic University of America Press, 1949.

Novatian. *Novatian: The Trinity, the Spectacles, Jewish Foods, in Praise of Purity, Letters*. Translated by Russell J. DeSimone. FC 67. Washington, D.C.: The Catholic University of America Press, 1974.

Origen. *An Exhortation to Martyrdom, Prayer and Selected Works*. Translated by Rowan A. Greer. The Classics of Western Spirituality. New York: Paulist Press, 1979.

———. *Commentary on the Gospel According to John Books 1-32*. 2 vols. Translated by Ronald E. Heine. FC 80, 89. Washington, D.C.: The Catholic University of America Press, 1989-1993.

———. *Homilies on Genesis and Exodus*. Translated by Ronald E. Heine. FC 71. Washington, D.C.: The Catholic University of America Press, 1982.

———. *Homilies on Jeremiah, Homilies on 1 Kings 28*. Translated by John Clark Smith. FC 97. Washington, D.C.: The Catholic University of America Press, 1998.

———. *Homilies on Joshua*. Translated by Barbara Bruce. FC 105. Washington, D.C.: The Catholic University of America Press, 2002.

———. *Homilies on Leviticus: 1-16*. Translated by Gary Wayne Barkley. FC 83. Washington, D.C.: The Catholic University of America Press, 1990.

———. *Origen: Spirit and Fire*. Edited by Hans Urs von Balthasar. Washington, D.C.: Catholic University Press of America, 1984.

———. *Prayer, Exhortation to Martyrdom*. Translated by John O'Meara. ACW 19. Mahway, N.J.: Paulist Press, 1954.

———. *The Writings of Origen, Volume II: Origen Contra Celsum Books II—VIII*. Translated by Frederick Crombie. ANCL 23. Edinburgh: T&T Clark, 1894.

Pachomius. "Instructions." In *Pachomian Koinonia III*, pp. 13-49. Translated by Armand Veilleux. CS 47. Kalamazoo, Mich.: Cistercian Publications, 1982.

Pacian of Barcelona. "Pacian of Barcelona." In *Iberian Fathers*, vol 3, pp. 17-94. Translated by Craig L. Hanson. FC 99. Washington, D.C.: The Catholic University of America Press, 1999.

Paulinus of Milan. "Life of St. Ambrose." In *Early Christian Biographies*, pp. 25-66. Translated by John Lacy. FC 15. Washington, D.C.: The Catholic University of America Press, 1952.

Paulinus of Nola. *The Poems of St. Paulinus of Nola*. Translated by P. G. Walsh. ACW 40. Mahwah, N.J.: Paulist Press, 1975.

Paulus Oriosus. "Defense Against the Pelagians." In *Iberian Fathers (Volume 3): Pacian of Barcelona, Orosius of Braga*, pp. 95-167. Translated by Craig L. Hanson. FC 99. Washington, D.C.: The Catholic University of America Press, 1999.

Peter Chrysologus. *Saint Peter Chrysologus: Selected Sermons and Saint Valerian: Homilies*, pp. 1-282. Translated by George E. Ganss. FC 17. New York: Fathers of the Church, Inc., 1953.

Prudentius. *The Poems of Prudentius*, 2 vols. Translated by M. Clement Eagan. FC 43 and 52. Washington, D.C.: The Catholic University of America Press, 1962-1965.

Pseudo-Clement of Rome. "Recognitions of Clement." In *Twelve Patriarchs, Excerpts and Epistles, The Clementia, Apocryphal Gospels and Acts, Syriac Documents*, pp. 75-211. Translated by Thomas Smith. ANF 8. Edited by Alexander Roberts and James Donaldson. 10 vols. 1885-1887. Reprint, Peabody,

Mass.: Hendrickson, 1994.

Salvian the Presbyter. "The Governance of God." In *The Writings of Salvian the Presbyter*, 21-232. Translated by Jeremiah F. O'Sullivan. FC 3. Washington, D.C.: The Catholic University of America Press, 1962.

Sulpicius Severus. "The Sacred History." In *Sulpicius Severus, Vincent of Lerins, John Cassian*, pp. 71-122. Translated by Alexander Roberts. NPNF 11. Series 2. Edited by Philip Schaff and Henry Wace. 14 vols. 1886-1900. Reprint, Peabody, Mass.: Hendrickson, 1994.

Symeon the New Theologian. *Symeon the New Theologian: The Discourses*. Translated by C. J. de Catanzaro. The Classics of Western Spirituality. New York: Paulist, 1980.

Tertullian. "Anti-Marcion." In *Latin Christianity: Its Founder, Tertullian*. Translated by S. Thelwall, et al. ANF 3. Edited by Alexander Roberts and James Donaldson. 10 vols. 1885-1887. Reprint, Peabody, Mass.: Hendrickson, 1994.

———. "Flight in the Time of Persecution." In *Tertullian: Disciplinary, Moral and Ascetical Works*, pp. 271-307. Translated by Emily Joseph Daly. FC 40. Washington, D.C.: The Catholic University of America Press, 1959.

———. "On Fasting." In *Tertullian, Part Fourth; Minucius Felix; Commodian; Origen, Parts First and Second*, pp. 102-14. Translated by A. Cleveland Coxe. ANF 4. Edited by Alexander Roberts and James Donaldson. 10 vols. 1885-1887. Reprint, Peabody, Mass.: Hendrickson, 1994.

———. "On the Soul." In *Tertullian: Apologetical Works and Minucius Felix Octavius*, pp. 163-309. Translated by Rudolph Arbesmann. FC 10. Washington, D.C.: The Catholic University of America Press, 1950.

———. "Prescriptions Against Heretics." In *Early Latin Theology: Selections from Tertullian, Cyprian, Ambrose and Jerome*, pp. 25-64. Edited and translated by S. L. Greenslade. LCC 5. Philadelphia: Westminster, 1956.

Theodoret of Cyr. "Letters." In *Theodoret, Jerome, Gennadius, Rufinus: Historical Writings, etc.*, pp. 250-348. Translated by Blomfield Jackson. NPNF 3. Series 2. Edited by Philip Schaff and Henry Wace. 14 vols. 1886-1900. Reprint, Peabody, Mass.: Hendrickson, 1994.

———. *On Divine Providence*. Translated and annotated by Thomas Halton. ACW 49. New York: Newman Press, 1988.

———. "Questions on Ruth." In *MEIT, passim*. Translated by Lesley Smith. Kalamazoo, Mich.: Medieval Institute Publications, 1996.

———. "The Ecclesiastical History of Theodoret." In *Theodoret, Jerome, Gennadius, Rufinus: Historical Writings, etc.*, pp. 32-159. Translated by Blomfield Jackson. NPNF 3. Series 2. Edited by Philip Schaff and Henry Wace. 14 vols. 1886-1900. Reprint, Peabody, Mass.: Hendrickson, 1994.

Theophylact. *The Explanation by Blessed Theophylact of the Holy Gospel According to St. Matthew*. Introduction by Fr. Christopher Stade. House Springs, Mo.: Chysostom Press, 1992.

Authors/Writings Index